MEDIEVAL AND RENAISSANCE CLOTHING AND TEXTILES

MEDIEVAL DRESS AND TEXTILES IN BRITAIN

A MULTILINGUAL SOURCEBOOK

MEDIEVAL AND RENAISSANCE
CLOTHING AND TEXTILES

ISSN 2044–351X

Series Editors
Robin Netherton
Gale R. Owen-Crocker

This series focuses on the study and interpretation of dress and textiles throughout England and Europe, from the early medieval period to the sixteenth century. It seeks to bring together research from a wide variety of disciplines, including language, literature, art history, social history, economics, archaeology, and artifact studies. The editors welcome submissions that combine the expertise of academics working in this area with the more practically based experience of re-enactors and re-creators, offering fresh approaches to the subject.

The series is associated with the annual journal
Medieval Clothing and Textiles.

Proposals or queries should be sent in the first instance to the editors or to the publisher, at the addresses given below; all submissions will receive prompt and informed consideration.

Ms. Robin Netherton, robin@netherton.net

Professor Gale R. Owen-Crocker, gale.owencrocker@ntlworld.com

Boydell & Brewer Limited, PO Box 9, Woodbridge, Suffolk

Previous volumes in this series:

I
The Troyes Mémoire: The Making of a Medieval Tapestry
Translated by Tina Kane

MEDIEVAL DRESS AND TEXTILES IN BRITAIN

A MULTILINGUAL SOURCEBOOK

Edited by

LOUISE M. SYLVESTER
MARK C. CHAMBERS
GALE R. OWEN-CROCKER

THE BOYDELL PRESS

Editorial matter © Louise M. Sylvester, Mark C. Chambers
and Gale R. Owen-Crocker 2014

All Rights Reserved. Except as permitted under current legislation
no part of this work may be photocopied, stored in a retrieval system,
published, performed in public, adapted, broadcast,
transmitted, recorded or reproduced in any form or by any means,
without the prior permission of the copyright owner

The right of Louise M. Sylvester, Mark C. Chambers and Gale R. Owen-Crocker
to be identified as the authors of this work has been asserted in accordance with
sections 77 and 78 of the Copyright, Designs and Patents Act 1988

First published 2014
The Boydell Press, Woodbridge

ISBN 978-1-84383-932-3

The Boydell Press is an imprint of Boydell & Brewer Ltd
PO Box 9, Woodbridge, Suffolk IP12 3DF, UK
and of Boydell & Brewer Inc.
668 Mt Hope Avenue, Rochester, NY 14620, USA
website: www.boydellandbrewer.com

A CIP catalogue record for this book is available
from the British Library

The publisher has no responsibility for the continued existence or accuracy of URLs for external or third-party
internet websites referred to in this book, and does not guarantee that any content on such websites is, or will
remain, accurate or appropriate

This publication is printed on acid-free paper

Typeset by Word and Page, Chester, UK

Contents

List of Documents	vi
List of Plates	ix
Acknowledgements	x
Editorial Conventions	xi
Abbreviations	xii
Introduction	1
I. Wills	9
II. Accounts	56
III. Inventories and Rolls of Livery	89
IV. Moral and Satirical Works	127
V. Sumptuary Regulation, Statutes and the Rolls of Parliament	198
VI. Unpublished Petitions to King, Council and Parliament	237
VII. Epic and Romance	260
Glossary	357
Bibliography	401

List of Documents

I. Wills

1.	The will of Bishop Theodred	12
2.	The will of Wynflæd	12
3.	The will of Ælfgifu	14
4a.	The will of Æthelgifu	14
4b.	The Latin abstract of the will	16
5.	The will of the Ealdorman Æthelmær	18
6.	The will of Brihtric and Ælfswith	18
7.	The will of the Ætheling Æthelstan	18
8.	The will of Wulfwaru	20
9.	The will of Ælfric Modercope	22
10.	Ornamenta Willielmi episcopi primi	22
11.	Ornamenta Ranulphi episcopi	22
12.	Ornamenta Gaufridi episcopi	24
13.	Inspeximus and probate of the will of Martin of St Cross	24
14.	The will of Peter, of Aigueblanche	26
15.	The will of Hugh de Nevill	26
16.	The will of Margerie de Crioll	28
17.	The will of Elizabeth, wife of Sir Edmund Bacon	28
18.	Testamentum Thomæ Harpham	28
19.	Testamentum Elenæ de Bilburgh	30
20.	The will of John Pyncheon	30
21.	The will of Lady Alice West	32
22.	The will of Robert Aueray	32
23.	The will of Sir William Langeford, knight	34
24.	The will of John Chelmyswyk, esq.	34
25.	The will of Thomas Tvoky, esq.	36
26.	The will of Stephen Thomas	38
27.	The will of John Rogerysson	38
28.	The will of Thomas Bathe	40
29.	The will of John Olney	40
30.	The will of Lady Peryne Clanbowe	40
31.	The will of Sir Roger Salwayn, knight, of York	42

32.	The will of Roger Flore (or Flower), esq.	42
33.	The will of William Newland	44
34.	The will of John Credy, esq.	44
35.	The will of John Toker	46
36.	The will of Isabel Gregory	46
37.	The will of John Barnet	46
38.	The will of Walter Mangeard	48
39.	The will of Margarete Asshcombe (once Bloncit)	48
40.	The will of Roger Elmesley	48
41.	The will of Richard Bokeland, esq.	50
42.	The will of Richard Dixton, esq.	50
43.	The will of Nicholas Charleton	50
44.	The will of the Countess of Warwick	52
45.	The will of Sir Ralph Rochefort	52
46.	The will of Sir Thomas Brook, knight, of Cobham	52
47.	The will of Nicholas Sturgeon	54

II. Accounts

1a.	Extracts from the wardrobe accounts of Bogo de Clare	58
1b.	Wardrobe accounts of Bogo de Clare	58
2.	Expenses for the wedding of Elizabeth, countess of Holland	68
3.	Extracts from the roll of liveries of Elizabeth, countess of Holland	72
4.	Extracts from the roll of expenses of Thomas de Crosse	76
5.	Extracts from the London Mercers' accounts	82

III. Inventories and Rolls of Livery

1a.	St Paul's Cathedral inventory of 1245	90
1b.	St Paul's Cathedral inventory of 1295	100
1c.	St Paul's Cathedral inventory of 1402	110
2.	Extracts from a roll of liveries of Edward III, 1347–9	114

IV. Moral and Satirical Works

1.	Orderic Vitalis, *The Ecclesiastical History*	130
2.	William of Wadington, *Le Manuel des Pechiez*	132
3.	Robert Mannynge of Brunne, *Handlyng Synne*	142
4.	Thomas Gascoigne, *Loci e Libro Veritatum*	152
5.	John Bromyard, *Summa Predicantium*	154
6.	A late-medieval sermon	156
7.	'Song upon the Tailors'	156
8.	'Ne be þi winpil nevere so jelu ne so stroutende'	162
9.	'Against the Pride of Ladies'	162
10.	'A Dispitison bitwene a God Man and þe Devel'	164
11.	A satire on manners and costume	166
12.	Ballad against excess in apparel especially in the clergy	166
13.	Thomas Hoccleve, *The Regiment of Princes*	168
14.	John Lydgate, 'A Dyte of Womenhis Hornys'	176
15.	'The Good Wyfe Wold a Pylgremage'	178

16. 'The Thewis of Gud Women'	180
17. Peter Idley, *Instructions to his Son*	182

V. Sumptuary Regulation, Statutes and the Rolls of Parliament

1. 11 February 1188: 'Great Council at Geddington'	200
2. Act of October 1363	200
3. Parliamentary petition of April 1379	206
4. Parliamentary petition of September 1402	208
5. Act of December 1420	210
6. Act of the Scottish parliament, March 1429 [1430]	210
7. Ecclesiastical regulation	214
8. Act of April 1463	216
9. Statute of 1463–4	216
10. Parliamentary petition of January 1478	232

VI. Unpublished Petitions to King, Council and Parliament

1. Petition on behalf of children in the king's wardship, *c.* 1275–*c.* 1300?	240
2. Petition of Roger de Berners and William de Marny, *c.* 1322	240
3. Petition of Robert de Montfort, *c.* 1322	244
4. Petition of the weavers of York, 1342	246
5. Petition of the merchants of the Hanse, *c.* 1394?	248
6. Petition of Thomas and Margaret de Beauchamp, 1394–1349	250
7a. Petition on behalf of Agnes Balle, *c.* 1403	252
7b. Record of pardon issued to Agnes Balle, 16 August 1403	252
8. Schedule of bales of cloth attached to a petition, *c.* 1418–19?	254
9. Petition of the haberdashers and hatters of London, 1448	256

VII. Epic and Romance

1. *Beowulf*	264

The Constance Group

2. *The Lives of Two Offas*	284
3. Nicholas Trevet, *The Life of Constance*	286
4. Trevet's Story of Constance	288
5. The Tale of the Wife of Merelaus the Emperor	290
6. *Emaré*	292
7. John Gower's Tale of Constance	304
8. Geoffrey Chaucer, *The Man of Law's Tale*	304

The Launfal Group

9. Marie de France, *Lanval*	308
10. *Sir Landevale*	312
11. Thomas Chestre, *Sir Launfal*	316

The Freine Group

12. Marie de France, *Lai Le Fresne*	322
13. *Lay Le Freine*	328
14. *Sir Degrevant*	332
15. *Sir Gawain and the Green Knight*	342

Plates

Plates are found after page 196

1. Initial illumination showing William de Saint Calais (Karilepho, Carilef), bishop of Durham, from an eleventh-century manuscript containing Augustine's commentary on the Psalter
2. Opening of the Account of the Household of Bogo de Clare kept by Walter de Reyny for 25 December 1285 – 2 June 1286
3. Detail from an account book of William Loveney, Wardrobe Keeper, 1406–8
4. Detail from a list of expenses for the Wedding of Elizabeth, countess of Holland, 1297
5. Petition of the Merchants of the Hanse concerning excessive customs, *c.* 1394?
6. Petition of Thomas and Margaret de Beauchamp, 1394–49
7. Description of the two ladies of Hautdesert, *Sir Gawain and the Green Knight* (lines 952–60); late 14th century
8. Sir Gawain dresses for the Green Chapel, *Sir Gawain and the Green Knight* (lines 1926–34); late 14th century

Acknowledgements

We would like to express our gratitude to the Leverhulme Trust for the grant which made possible the research which went into this book.

We are also grateful to the staff of the British Library and the National Archives for their unfailing help.

Thanks also go to Ruth Briggs for help with Latin when we were puzzled, to Jane Roberts and Alex Rumble for assistance with difficulties in deciphering manuscripts, and to David Trotter and Natasha Romanova for advice on Anglo-French.

Finally, we are grateful to the anonymous readers for useful suggestions at an early stage, and for the final careful reading which saved us from many errors.

Editorial Conventions

The following editorial conventions have been used:

Editorial expansion: abbreviations and contractions in the texts have been expanded and are indicated by italics. In some instances – particularly in the material transcribed directly from manuscript sources – an inverted comma is placed at the end of a word to indicate where the specifics of language attribution (declension, conjugation, etc.) may have been deliberately obscured by use of abbreviation or suspension (discussed in Wright 2000).

Superscript characters have been left where appearing in sources (such as those following Roman numerals), except in certain cases of editorial expansion.

Roman numerals have been represented by Arabic numerals or words in the translations.

The **punctus elevatus** is represented by a semicolon in the extracts.

The letters **ash, eth, thorn** and **yogh** (Æ/æ, Ð/ð, Þ/þ, Ȝ/ȝ) and **crossed thorn** (ꝥ) have been maintained throughout as they appear in the sources.

The **Tironian note** for *et* in the Anglo-Saxon wills is represented as ⁊, following the source texts. Elsewhere, symbols for *et* are represented with an ampersand (&).

Crossed *h* and double crossed *l* have been represented with standard, uncrossed letter symbols.

u/v **and** *i/j*: in extracts from previously unpublished material, these letters have been regularised based on whether they are vocalic or consonantal. However, in material that derives from published texts, the original graphic representation has been maintained.

? Question marks are occasionally used in manuscript transcriptions and translations to indicate that the item or passage is presumed, illegible or unknown.

Abbreviations

Abbreviations for units of currency or measure have been left abbreviated in the extracts using the following conventions:

ob.	*obolus*, 'halfpenny(-ies)'
d.	*denarius/i*, 'pence'
s.	*solidus*, 'shilling(s)' (= apx 12 d.)
mar'	'mark(s)' (= apx 160 d.)
li.	'pound(s)' (= apx 240 d. or 20 s.)
uln'	*ulna, -e, æ*, etc., 'ell(s)' (or possibly 'yard(s)' – see glossary)

Other abbreviations

AF	Anglo-French or Anglo-Norman
AND	*Anglo-Norman Dictionary* (edition demarcated by *AND*1, *AND*2)
BL	British Library
CPR	*Calendar of Patent Rolls*
DMLBS	*Dictionary of Medieval Latin from British Sources*
DOST	*Dictionary of the Older Scottish Tongue*
EETS	Early English Text Society
EMDT	*Encyclopedia of Medieval Dress and Textiles of the British Isles c. 450–1450*
Godefroy	F. Godefroy, *Dictionnaire de l'ancienne Langue Française*
Latham	R. E. Latham, *Revised Medieval Latin Word-List from British and Irish Sources with Supplement*
LCCD	Lexis of Cloth and Clothing in Britain, *c.* 700–*c.* 1450 Project Database
ME	Middle English
MED	*Middle English Dictionary*
MS, MSS	manuscript(s)
OE	Old English
OED	*Oxford English Dictionary* (edition demarcated by *OED*2, *OED*3)
OF	Old French

Introduction

In the Middle Ages, very much more than today, dress was an identifier of occupation, status, wealth, gender and ethnicity. The textiles in circulation ranged from the opulence of gold *racamaz* of Lucca and cloth of gold *baldekyn d'outremer*, through to russet (a grey or brown woollen cloth) and the more utilitarian worsted (smooth wool cloth distinguished commercially from the more expensive woollens). Discussions of dress and textiles in the medieval period took place in a variety of spheres of activity, and it is therefore from a wide range of text types that information is to be obtained about the nature and sources of cloth, the desirability of particular garments and accessories and contemporary thinking about dress. Fashion is revealed by inference in the attempts to restrict the use of particular textiles, furs and ornaments to certain categories of people by means of sumptuary legislation. Fashion is also indicated, again by inference, and negatively, in the many diatribes inveighing against its various manifestations.

The discourses surrounding dress and textiles were constructed by the literate classes, clerical, aristocratic and mercantile, but were of concern across all the social scales. The seven chapters here contain extracts from wills; accounts of the Royal Wardrobe; inventories; moral and satirical works condemning contemporary fashions; sumptuary laws; petitions; an Old English epic; and insular romances. We have included wills dating back to the Anglo-Saxon period which are written in Old English, with the occasional Latin abstract. The Old English will of Æthelgifu (I.4*a*), a wealthy secular woman, makes several gifts of clothing: 'selle mon beornwynne minne blæwenan cyrtel is neaþene unrenod ⁊ hire betstan heafodgewædo ⁊ selle man lufetat ⁊ ælgifu godwife. hire .iii. godwebbenan cyrtlas. ⁊ wulfgife selle mon oðera hire dunnan cyrtla' (my blue gown which is untrimmed at the bottom and her best head-dresses are to be given to Beornwynn. And her three purple gowns are to be given to Lufetat and Ælgifu and Godwif, and Wulfgif is to be given some of her other, dun-coloured gowns). This will, in particular, offers us a unique insight into the dress of an eleventh-century woman and her ideas about what might be appropriate for other women to wear. Bequests of clothing from this time also include clerical garments such as chasubles: see, for example, the will of Bishop Theodred (I.1) in which the testator leaves, among others, 'mine to beste messehaclen þe ic habbe' (the two best chasubles that I have); 'min wite massehakele þe ic on Pauie bouhte' (my white chasuble which I bought in Pavia); and 'þe oþer gewele massehakele þat is ungerenad' (the other yellow chasuble which is unornamented). Such bequests are also found in later wills, for example the Latin will of Martin of St Cross dated 1259 (I.13) includes a 'vestimento bruddato integro' (a fully embroidered vestment); and Richard Dixton, in a will dated 1438 (I.42), leaves the chapel at Cirencester 'a cloth of Siluer, and a blak cloth of Damask sengill, & a gowne of Goldsmytheswerk, for to make vestimentes' (a cloth woven with silver thread and a cloth of black-coloured damask of single thickness and a gown of goldsmith's work to make vestments).

As well as clothes, we also find gifts of what sound like beautiful bed linen in wills from the Old English period onwards: Wynflæd (I.2) leaves 'an bedreaf' (a set of bedding). The Latin will of Thomas Harpham dated 1341 (I.18) includes the bequest to his son William of 'unum coverlit radiatum opera rosarum pulverisatum, unum chalon' et duo lynthiamina ac unum materas' (a striped bedspread scattered with roses, a bedcover and two sheets as well as one mattress). Lady Alice West's will of 1395 (I.21) is predominantly made up of bequests of bedding and soft furnishings, beginning with 'a bed of tapicerswerk, with alle the tapites of sute' (a bed of tapestry work, with all the tapestries of the set) and including best, second-best and third-best featherbeds.

The accounts offer a glimpse of the materials, the garments they were made into, and the costs of keeping an aristocratic household clothed. In the household accounts of the thirteenth-century aristocrat Bogo de Clare (II.1a, 1b), we see expensive orders such as '.iij. furruris de nigra boge pro dom. —— xxiiij. s"' (three linings of black lambskin for our lord —— 24 shillings); and 'vna furrura de alba Boge pro dom. —— x. s'. viiij. d"' (a lining of white lambskin for our lord —— 10 shillings, 9 pence). There are also items for servants, 'Item lib. Mag. Roberto Coco pro vno tabardo precepto dom. —— x. s"' (for Master Robert, cook, for a tabard, by order of our lord —— 10 shillings); even more expensively, the accounts for the first marriage of Elizabeth, countess of Holland (II.2), include the information for payments 'Pro xxxv op*erarariis per iiij dies & iiij noctes op*erant*ibus* ap*u*d London q*uorum* q*uo*libet eo*rum* cepit p*er* diem & noctem vj d.' (thirty-five tailors worked for four days and four nights in London for which each of them was paid sixpence per day and night).

The chapter on inventories contains lists of the property belonging to St Paul's Cathedral, London, compiled in 1245, 1295 and 1402 (III.1a, 1b, 1c). Items listed include vestments and soft furnishings in costly and highly ornamented textiles, such as the 'Capa fusca de panno serico breudata cum minutis gladeolis et minutis bisantiis et floribus minutis. Hanc breudare fecit Henricus Cancellarius, et postea Decanus' (dark cope of silk cloth embroidered with tiny fleurs-de-lis and tiny bezants and tiny flowers. Henry [de Cornhill] the chancellor [1217–41] and afterwards dean [1243–54] had this embroidery made). The inventories of St Paul's Cathedral include headings relating to types of vestment, such as 'De Tunicis et Dalmaticis' (Concerning Tunicles and Dalmatics) and also headings concerning specific fabrics belonging to the cathedral, such as 'De Baudekinis et Pannis Sericis' (Concerning Baudekins and Silk Cloths) including such gorgeous sounding cloths as 'Pannus alius magnus sericus rubeus, cum magnis rotis et binis leonibus cristatis in rotis purpureis, et flores inter rotas. Rex dedit H. Decano, et decanus postea dedit ecclesiae' (another large red silk cloth, with large wheels and pairs of maned lions in purple wheels and flowers between the wheels. The king gave it to Dean H[enry de Cornhill, probably]. And the dean afterwards gave it to the church). The inventory of 1295 includes a few different garments, such as those under the heading 'Sandalia' (ecclesiastical slippers) which include 'Sandalia de rubeo sameto cum caligis breudatis aquilis, leonibus, et rosis, et in summitate vinea breudata' (slippers of red samite with stockings embroidered with eagles, lions and roses, and at the top embroidered with a vine). Terms for vestments and individual ecclesiastical garments are familiar from the wills, and some of the same textiles appear in the final inventory: an alb, for example, is described as being of 'panno de Reynys' (a fine linen cloth probably made in, or associated with, Rheims in France).

We encounter a different sensibility in relation to cloth and clothing in the chapter devoted to moral and satirical works about contemporary fashion. Here we find complaints about the endless desire for novelty, which leads to the hacking about and altering of items of clothing: 'Ne dysgysen nat þy cloþyng' (Do not fashion your clothing in a new-fangled way) orders Robert Brunne in *Handlyng Synne* (IV.3); and similar advice, with a little more precision, is offered by Peter Idley when he says 'Leve cuttyng and Iaggyng of clothis' (Refrain from cutting and slashing your clothes) in *Instructions to his Son* (IV.17). The constant changing of outfits is cause for complaint: Idley comments that women 'must eche day haue chaunge newe' (have a new outfit every day). Another complaint concerns the fashion for women to wear their hair or head-dress shaped into two horns: a late-medieval sermon (IV.6) thunders about 'Women in þere degre withe theire gay heddys sett up on hey3te and ornyd, as it were an unresonabyll beeste' (women in their ranks with their pretty heads set up on high and horned as if they were senseless beasts). Immodestly cut garments for men are also cause for satire: 'Men mi3te, 3if he brech weore to-tore: Seon his genitras' (if he were to tear his underwear men could see his genitals; 'A Dispitison Bitwene a God Man and Þe Devel' (IV.10). So, too, are long trains and long wide sleeves, in 'The Regiment of Princes' (IV.13), Hoccleve expresses disgust 'To see oon walke in gownes of scarlet/ Twelve yerdes wyde, with pendaunt sleeves doun/ On the ground' (To see someone walk in a gown of scarlet twelve yards wide with sleeves hanging down to the ground). He says that this fashion would prevent a man being able to come to the rescue if anyone were to set upon his lord in the street. Extravagance in dress and fur trimming is also the subject of complaint, a theme held in common with the main thrust of the sumptuary legislation – that is, a concern that it is not possible to discern distinctions of rank because of the fashion for dressing above one's station: as Robert Brunne has it in *Handlyng Synne*, 'Noþeles euery man may/ Aftyr hys astate, make hym gay./ But whan he passyþ ouere mesure/ Þerof cumþ mysauenture' (any man can make himself attractive in accordance with his rank, but misfortune comes of going beyond what is reasonable).

Placing these texts within the context of medieval writing about clothes and fashion, as we have done here, shows up possible connections between the complaints about contemporary dress and the attempts to govern what people wore by legislative means. The earliest edict seeking to regulate dress that we have (V.1), dated 1188, includes a clause forbidding the slashing of garments: 'Et quod nullus habeat pannos decisos vellaceatos' (And none of the clothes are to be slashed [for ornamentation] or trimmed). Echoing the complaints in the moral and satirical works (or perhaps inspired by the same phenomena), we find that general requirements about the cut of clothing are also specified, for example that men's garments must be long enough to be decent. We find the descriptors for this in both Middle English and Anglo-French in the sumptuary legislation: 'as hit [...] shall covere his pryve membres and buttokes' in the Act of April 1463 (V.8) and 'comcell [...] covera sez privez membres & buttoks' in the Statute of 1463–4, the Anglo-French version drawn from the 1463 Act (V.9). This act of sumptuary legislation certainly indicates that there seem to have been overlapping concerns over the question of the semiotics of dress, that is, what people's clothing says about their social class. The Act of October 1363 (V.2) begins with a complaint that 'diverses gentz de diverses condicions usent diverse apparaill nient appertenant a lour estat' (various people of various conditions wear various apparel not appropriate to their estate). It includes prohibitions on the wearing of 'drape d'or, de soy ne d'argent, ne nul manere vesture embroidez' (cloth of gold, silk or silver, or any sort of embroidered clothing) by an esquire and anyone below the estate of knight; and a wide range of working country people are specifically included in the prohibitions and prescriptions:

> charetters, charuers, chaceours des charues, bovers, vachers, berchers, porchers, deyes et touz autres gardeins des bestes, batours des bledz et toutes maneres des gentz d'estat de garceon entendantz a husbonderie, et toutes autres gentz qe n'eient quarante solidees de biens, ne de chateux a la value de quarante soldz, ne preignent ne usent nul manere des draps sinoun blanket et russet l'aune de dousze deniers

> (carters, ploughmen, drivers of ploughs, oxherds, cowherds, shepherds, swineherds, dairy-maids and all other keepers of beasts, threshers of corn and all manner of people of the estate of groom attending to husbandry, and all other people who do not have forty shillings in goods, nor property to the value of forty shillings, may not have or wear any kind of cloth except blanket and russet of twelve pence for the ell).

There is also a restriction on the placing of 'eny bolsters nor stuffe of wolle, coton nor cadas, nor other stuffer in his doublet' (any padding or stuffing of wool, cotton or caddis, or any other material in his doublet) by yeomen and any men of lower rank preventing them from imitation of the fashionable body shape which the knightly class had assumed in the Act of April 1463.

From the thirteenth century onwards, we find petitions to the king and parliament that are concerned with cloth and clothing by individuals and groups. For example, a petition was made on behalf of a group of children in Edward II's wardship, probably in the final quarter of the thirteenth century (VI.1). The children are said to be in some distress, and they suggest that their lord has shamed them through denying them their allowance of clothing and basic provisions. Within their petition they note that 'par la ou eus soleyent prendre tabar e surcote de este; tut lour est sustret' (whereas they were accustomed to receive a tabard and summer surcoat, all of these have been withheld). Thomas and Mary de Beauchamp petitioned Richard II (VI.6) to fulfil the terms of a grant he had made to them concerning, among other things, 'deux litz un trussyngbed*es* sys peire de lyntheux · lintheux p*ur* les testes & pees & oraillers covenables ove tout l'apparaill & ceo q*ue* a ycell appent' (two beds, a travel/trundle bed, six pairs of linens, linens for the head and feet, and pillows suitable for their bed-linen as well as goods pertaining to the them). Many petitions were put forward on behalf of the guilds, such as the one by the weavers of York to Edward III and his council (VI.4) which illustrates concerns about competition from immigrant workers and the desire to establish a monopoly on specific cloths. The petitioners note that the king had granted by his charter and confirmed to the weavers that 'nul homme par tut le counteefreit ne freit faire draps rayes ne de colour · forque en la dite cite & en altres certeyns villes de les demeignes nostre dit seignour le Roy deinz mesme le counte sur forfaiture de .x. lj devers nostre seignour le Roy; et pur cele fraunchises avoir les ditz Tistours Deverwyk' graunterent rendre al Escheqer nostre seignour le Roy .x. li par an' (no one throughout the county shall make or cause to be made striped cloth nor coloured cloth, except in the said city and in certain other towns in the demesne of our said lord the king, in the same county, upon pain of forfeiture of ten pounds to our lord the king, and by that authority have the said Weavers of York consented to give to the Exchequer of our lord the king ten pounds per year). Their complaint is that foreign weavers from Brabant and elsewhere have been granted relief of taxes and other charges, and the York weavers cannot afford to pay their taxes and want a repeal of the privilege granted to foreigners.

Cloth and clothing also play telling parts in the one Old English epic and the romances that we have included here. Many of the stories are told again and again, with differing emphases on what the characters are wearing and varying glimpses of what seem to be the fashions of the day. In some cases, an earlier fashion moment is carried over in the translation of a text from Anglo-French to Middle English, as we see in the various versions of the Launfal story and the dress of his fairy mistress. As we might expect, the Anglo-Saxon epic poem *Beowulf* (VII.1) is principally concerned with armour, and our extracts begin with the question 'Hwæt syndonge searohæbbendra／ byrnum werede, þe þus brontne ceol／ ofer lagustræte lædan cwomon／ hider ofer holmas?' (What are you armour-bearing men, protected by mail coats, who in this way came bringing a steep ship over the sea-road, here over the waters?). Armour also makes an appearance in the romances, notably in the long scene of the arming of the hero in *Sir Gawain and the Green Knight* (VII.15): on a cold morning his chamberlain first 'clad hym in his cloþez þe colde for to were,／ And syþen his oþer harnays, þat holdely watz keped,／ Boþe his paunce and his platez, piked ful clene,／ Þe ryngez rokked of þe roust of his riche bruny' (dressed him in his clothes that would keep out the cold, and then his other gear that had been kept carefully, both his belly protection and his plate-armour, very brightly polished, the rings of his rich mail-coat burnished free of rust). Armour occasionally plays a part in the plot in romance: in *Sir Degrevant* (VII.14), we hear that 'The Eorlus doughder beheld／ That borlich and bolde.／ For he was armed so clen.／ [. . .] Was joy to behold' (The earl's daughter saw that stately and bold one for he was so splendidly armed [. . .] he was a joy to see). As in the wills, clothing and fabrics in romance signify wealth as seen in the gorgeous furnishings in Gawain's bedroom at the castle of Hautdesert: 'þer beddyng watz noble,／ Of cortynes of clene sylk with cler golde hemmez,／ And couertorez ful curious with comlych panez／ Of bryȝt blaunner aboue, enbrawded bi sydez,／ Rudelez rennande on ropez, red golde ryngez,／ Tapitez tyȝt to þe woȝe of tuly and tars,／ And vnder fete, on þeflet, of folȝande sute' (there the furnishings for the bed were magnificent: curtaining of elegant silk with bright gold borders and elaborate coverlets with beautiful panels of pure white ermine, embroidered at the edges. Curtains ran on cords through red-gold rings. Red Chinese silks hung on the walls, and underfoot on the floor were more of matching material). Melidor's bedroom in *Sir Degrevant* boasts similar décor:

> With testur and celure,
> With a bryght bordure
>   Compasyd ful clene.
>
> And all a storye as hyt was
> Of Ydoyne and Amadas,

> Perreye in ylke a plas,
>   And papageyes of grene.
>
> The scochenus of many knyght
> Of gold and cyprus was idyght,
> Brode besauntus and bryght,
>   And trewe lovus bytwene.
>
> Ther was at hur testere
> The kyngus owun banere;
> Was nevere beder ychere
>   Of empryce ne qwene.
>
> Fayr schetus of sylk,
> Chalk whyghth as the mylk,
> Quyltus poyned of that ylk,
>   Touseled they ware;
>
> Coddys of sendal,
> Knoppus of crystal
> That was mad in Westfal
>   With women of lare.
>
> Hyt was a mervelous thing
> To se the rydalus hyng
> With mony a rede gold ryng,
>   That home upbare.
>
> The cordes that thei on ran
> The Duk Betyse hom wan;
> Mayd Medyore hom span
>   Of meremaydenus hare.

(Her bed was blue, with a tester and canopy with a bright border neatly devised depicting the story of Ydoyne and Amadas. There were precious stones everywhere and green parrots and the coats of arms of many knights. It was adorned with gold and Cyprus gold, with bright bezants and true-love knots here and there. As a wall-hanging she had the king's own banner. There was never an empress nor a queen with a costlier bed. It had beautiful silk sheets, chalkwhite like milk; quilts embroidered in the same silk, that were tassled; pillows of fine silk; knobs of crystal that were made by skilled women in Westphalia. It was a wonderful thing to see the curtains hanging from the many gold rings that supported them. The duke of Betis brought back the cords that they ran on: the maid Melidor spun them from mermaids' hair.)

Dress and textiles in romance may also signify poverty. A detail which appears only in the later Middle English version of the Launfal story by Thomas Chestre (VII.11) concerns Launfal's inability to replace his nephews' worn-out clothing: 'They seyd, "Syr, our robes beth torent,/ And your tresourys all yspent,/ And we go the wyll ydyght"' (They said, 'Sir, our clothes are in tatters and your money is all spent and we are badly dressed').

Romances also tell us something about fashion and its relationship to the desired shape and presentation of the body, generally the female body, since the male body is so often cladin armour. Romance texts therefore function as one of the places where we learn to understand where our gaze is supposed to go: male and female readers are alike looking at the woman's body and the way that it is dressed. In the Anglo-French *Lanval* (VII.9), the eponymous hero sees two women coming through the forest towards him. Their clothes are costly and also reveal their figures: 'Vestues furent richement,/ Laciees mut estreitement' (they were richly dressed, laced very tightly). A similar example is provided by the glimpse we are offered of Tryamour towards the end of *Sir Launfal*: 'The lady was clad yn purpere palle,/ Wyth gentyll body and myddyll small,/ That semely was of syght;/ Her matyll was furryd with whyt ermyn,/ Yreversyd jolyf and fyn' (The lady was dressed in fine purple cloth. She had a graceful body and a slender waist that was lovely to look at. Her cloak was trimmed with white ermine with the edges turned back, prettily decorated). Clothing, or its lack, sometimes reveals the female body even more explicitly. Here we may turn to the early Middle English version of the poem, *Sir Landevale* (VII.10). Landevale sees a richly accoutred bed, 'Thereon lay that maydyn bright,/ Almost nakyd and vpright./ Al her clothes byside her lay;/ Syngly was she wrappyd, parfay,/ With a mauntell of hermyn,/ Coveride was with alexanderyn./ The mantell for hete downe she dede/ Right to hir gyrdill stede' (On it lay that bright maiden, almost naked and supine. All her clothes lay beside her; indeed, she was only wrapped in an ermine robe and covered with Alexandrian silk. Because of the heat, she had undone the robe as far as her waist).

No anthology can be encyclopaedic. Medieval drama has not been included in this *Sourcebook*, though its editors acknowledge that it frequently makes recourse to fashion, dress and display through costuming and dramatic sartorial licence. The jacket shortening scene in the play of *Mankind* (*c.* 1465; Eccles 1969: lines 671–721), for example, seems to echo some of the concerns of Edward IV's sumptuary legislation of 1463–4 (V.8 and 9) concerning the perceived shortness of men's dress in 1460s fashion. In fact, contemporary fashion abuses are frequently lampooned in the drama: in *The Castle of Perseverance* (*c.* 1425) the vice Pride (Superbia) tells Mankind to 'Loke þou blowe mekyl bost/ Wyth longe crakows on þi schos' (see that you make great boasts/ With long points on your shoes) (Eccles 1969: lines 1058–9); and a generation later in 'Passion Play I' from the so-called *N-Town Cycle*, the devil Lucifer recommends wearing 'A googly peyre of long pekyd schon/ hosyn enlosyd of þe most costyous cloth of Crenseyn' (a goodly pair of long, piked shoes,/ hose made with the most costly cloth of crimson), as well as other fashionable signs of vanity (Block 1922: 226, lines 69–70) – both drawing attention to anxieties and concerns expressed in many of the extracts collected in the present volume (including IV.12, 17, V.8 and 9, etc.). However, given the wide availability of the playtexts themselves and the continuing and thorough work of the Records of Early English Drama project and its publications (see http://www.reed.utoronto.ca/), it was decided that a separate chapter was unnecessary. References to individual playtexts are made in the introductions and notes accompanying the collected extracts.

Away from the medieval stage and aside from the fairy-tale world of romance and some of the more imaginative anti-fashion diatribes, the chapters in this volume frequently offer us the sense of having had a glimpse into the reality of life in the England of the Middle Ages, perhaps even of the materiality of the culture of the period. We know that truly recovering that culture through its material objects is almost impossible: the objects themselves cannot tell us what part they played in people's daily lives. We do, however, have access to the ways in which people wrote about those objects, in this case the clothes and fabrics that surrounded them in the wills that document the value of the garments and cloths to individuals; the laws that tried to preserve an idea of the social order visible in what people wore; and the fictions which record the desires which drive a fashion system, something which some historians have suggested first appears in the fourteenth century (Post 1955: 28–41; Blanc 2002: 157–72; although this has been widely disputed – see Heller 2007: 48–52). It is the texts which make the culture of the past available to us, and so we offer here previously neglected administrative documents alongside well-known poems of the medieval period in an attempt to capture something of the issues about dress and textiles that were important to medieval society. Each chapter consists of extracts from texts preceded by an introduction. These introductory sections are not standardised, but are tailored to the kinds of texts and the forms in which we have them in the information they offer so that some are more focused on content, some on questions of genre, and some on the manuscript contexts.

CHAPTER I

Wills

INTRODUCTION

The documents collected by Whitelock in *Anglo-Saxon Wills* (1930) give rise to a number of issues. Writing in the General Preface to her volume, Hazeltine suggests that the documents it contains are not wills but documents providing evidence of an oral contract (1930: vii–viii). In a discussion of the origins of property, however, Hudson observes that in the Anglo-Saxon period, provided specific and limited public dues were fulfilled, possession was secure. Land was transmissible, alienability and heritability had been established and were both subjected to and protected by royal authority (1994: 201). The writing in English of documents that we recognise as wills appears to have begun in Kent in the first half of the ninth century; there are no examples from other parts of England until the next century, though this knowledge is based on the chance survival of texts and cartularies from a few houses (including Canterbury, Rochester, Winchester and Westminster), and several of these supply only a single example (Whitelock *et al.* 1968: 19). The development of legal practices in the ecclesiastical houses involving the personal will shifted the nature of property and ownership in English law during and after the Conquest, and through the middle years of the thirteenth century the royal courts came to recognise the position of an executor as both the active and passive representative of the testator with acknowledged powers of arbitration (Sheehan 1988: 6). These developments all brought the medieval will closer to the modern model.

PERIOD AND LANGUAGE

More than fifty wills survive from the Anglo-Saxon period, although the majority of these are later copies by monastic scribes rather than survivals of contemporary forms (Whitelock 1930: xli). Besides the wills that are extant in the vernacular, Whitelock suggests that there are about a dozen Latin documents in medieval cartularies which are probably translations or abstracts of Old English wills. As an example, we include the Latin abstract of the will of Æthelgifu (4*b*) – although compared with the vernacular original, the Latin abstract is somewhat uninformative. Documentary evidence from the succeeding centuries is much rarer. A handful of thirteenth-century *ornamenta* or *mortuaries* may be found, although these are more properly inventories detailing the fabric and effects of particular bishops or ecclesiastical magnates, made at the time of death for the benefit of the successor. Several wills from the fourteenth century are in Latin – see, for example, those of Thomas Harpham and Elenæ de Bilburgh, while others, such as that of Sir William Langeford – have text in the vernacular following standard introductions in Latin probably derived from model wills which appear from about 1300. It has been suggested that wills of the first three centuries immediately following the Norman Conquest exist only in instances of extreme rarity (Guiseppi 1899: 351–2). For this reason we have included the will of the English knight, Hugh de Nevill, even though it was written in Acre where he had gone on crusade. De Nevill's will is written entirely in Anglo-French, but there are some fourteenth-century wills in a mixture of languages, illustrating the fairly common practice of codeswitching between Latin and a vernacular language (Anglo-French or Middle English) in this period. We find single-word switches such as the use of the Middle English *kyngle* (girdle or brooch) in the Latin will of Thomas Harpham; switched phrases, for example 'Vestments &c. to my chapel of Corby; also iiij towayls p' le autel des le une paire des armes de Leybourn' in the will of Margerie de Crioll which was recorded in Lincoln in 1319. A similar example is found in the will of John Pyncheon of London dated 1392 which begins in Anglo-French and then continues in Middle English: 'Ieo volle que la moneye soit despendu, cestassauoir, to þe pore Men þat han ben Men be-fore of god conuersacion'.

TYPES OF BEQUESTS OF CLOTH AND CLOTHING AND BENEFICIARIES

A number of Anglo-Saxon wills, such as those of Ealdorman Æthelmær, make gifts to the king. A gift to the king, or sometimes to a lord other than the king, is a common feature in tenth-century and later wills and may be called a *heriot* (Whitelock *et al.* 1968: 21). It is often paid in horses and weapons and money, though land is sometimes given and occasionally rings, as in the will of Brihtric and Ælfswith. We also find bequests to churches and other religious establishments alongside gifts to relatives and servants.

Bequests of clothing and textiles are rare in Anglo-Saxon wills; they become more common in the fourteenth century. In the will of Brihtric and Ælfswith 'healfne bænd gyldenne' is left. It is difficult to be sure what is meant by a *bænd* in this period, and Anglo-Saxon wills form an important element in the evidence. From the tenth and eleventh centuries the headband seems to have become a form of portable wealth (Dodwell 1982: 174; Owen-Crocker 2004: 225), and the will suggests that there was so much gold in them that their owners could arrange for them to be shared by several beneficiaries – as we see in Wulfwaru's will, which bequeathes 'anes bendes on twentigum mancussum goldes' to be shared among four servants.

In the later medieval period, although moveable goods, unlike land, were also subject to some customary limitations, they were more able to be disposed of as the testator desired. When textile items are mentioned, we may assume it is because the person making the will had some particular reason to name them, rather than because of simple custom or legal obligation (Burkholder 2005: 133). Testators sometimes leave clothing in sets, for example 'anes wifscrudes ealles' is left by Wulfwaru. Isabel Gregory leaves 'a blew goune and a grene kyrtyll' to one beneficiary and 'a cloke and a gounne of russet, furrit' to another. Other household textiles are frequently bequeathed in sets, for example the 'beste fetherbed, and a blu caneuas, and a materas, and twey blankettys, and a peyre schetes of Reynes, with the heued shete of the same, and sex of my best pilwes, [...] and a bleu couertour of menyuer, and a keuerlet of red sendel ypouthered with Cheuerons' as well as the two further sets of beds and bedding left by Lady Alice West, one of which she calls 'the stoffe of the bed'. We also see a full bed set, 'oone bed a peyre fustyans, and to þe oþer a peyre blankettis, and to ilk of þe too beddis too peyre schetys goode, and a matras and a canvas', enumerated in the will of Roger Flore. Sets of vestments appear as well: Wulfwaru's will includes 'anes mæssereafes mid eallum þam ðe ðærto gebyreð'; the *ornamenta* of Bishop Ranulph of Durham leaves 'unam casulam indici coloris cum largis orfrays; cum stola et manipula cum magnis Archangelis brudatis: et duas albas cum pavonibus'; and Lady Alice West bequeathes

> alle my vestymentz of my chapell, with the towailes longynge to the auter tapites whit and rede paled, and blu and red paled, with alle my grene tapites that longeth to my chapell forsayd, and with the frontels of the forsayd auter', and with alle the rydelles and trussynge cofres, and alle other apparaile that longeth to my chapelle forsayd

As Burkholder found in the corpus of wills that she examined, many testators provide little or no description of the fabrics left in their wills (2005: 140). Sometimes varieties are named: we see 'all my clothis of gold, and clothis of silke, with-oute ffurrereur' in the will of the countess of Warwick and 'quirtayns of worsted' and 'a gowne of gray russet furred wit Ionetis and wylde Catis' in the will of Thomas Tvoky. Colours are often specified and sometimes the means of production or decoration are mentioned as ways of distinguishing particular items: in the *ornamenta* of Bishop Galfrid of Durham there is mention of 'unam Albam nigram cum minutis lineis aureis' and in the will of Martin of St Cross, 'vestimento bruddato integro'. Lady Alice West describes one bed as 'of tapicers werk' with 'tapites [...] ypouthered with chapes and scochons'. Burkholder notes (2005: 152), textiles formed a substantial proportion of the movable goods bequeathed specifically in late-medieval England. The wills that we have from the Anglo-Saxon period and the later Middle Ages offer vital evidence about the garments and textiles that were in daily or occasional use and information about how these objects were valued by testators who chose to specify them as gifts or payments to those they were leaving behind.

EXTRACTS FROM WILLS

1. The will of Bishop Theodred

Date: between 942 and 951. Manuscript: Cambridge University Library, MS FF. 2. 33, fol. 48, the Sacrist's Register of the Abbey of Bury St Edmunds, written about the middle of the fourteenth century (Whitelock 1930: 99). The will is in Old English. The Prosopography of Anglo-Saxon England website notes that Theodred was bishop of London and of Elmham, that he lived in the time of King Æthelstan and went at his side to war against Olaf. The clothing referred to consists of three mass garments with colours and ornamentation specified. The will is mentioned by Dodwell in *Anglo-Saxon Art*; he comments that surface decoration is so much taken for granted that it is hardly ever alluded to. For the Anglo-Saxons, it was the undecorated that was exceptional. Bishop Theodred's remark in his will of 924–51 about an 'ungenerad' (unornamented) chasuble was to identify it as one without embroidery (1982: 37–8). Dodwell records that the Anglo-Saxons had associations with Pavia, northern Italy (cf. 'þe ic on Pauie bouhte' in the will). Its main importance was as a staging post on the journey from northern Europe to Rome and most Anglo-Saxon pilgrims journeying to Rome would break their journey there. Pavia was chiefly celebrated commercially for the sale of Byzantine fabrics. We can be fairly certain that Theodred's mass garments referred to are silk (Dodwell 1982: 131–2). There is, however, some ambiguity in the reference to '& al þat þe þerto bired' which might include matching vestments such as a stole and maniple, and an amice to protect the neck, or might refer to orphreys, seen as a separable ornament. The will is printed in Whitelock (1930), 2–5. The translation is Whitelock's.

And into sc̄e Paules kirke mine to beste messehaclen. þe hic habbe mid alle þe þinge þe þerto birið [...] and ic an Þeodred min wite massehakele þe ic on Pauie bouhte and `al´ þat þerto bireð. [...] And ic an Odgar þere gewele massehakele þe ic on Pauie bouhte. ⁊ þat þerto bireð. And ic an Gundwine þer oþer gewele massehakele þat is ungerenad. ⁊ þat þe þerto bireð. and ic spracacke þe red messehakele. ⁊ al þat þe þerto bired.

2. The will of Wynflæd

Probably composed in the middle of the tenth century and extant in a not very careful eleventh-century copy (BL, Cotton Charter, VIII, 38; Owen 1979: 195), the will is in Old English. According to the will, the testatrix's mother was called Byrhtwynne. Wynflæd also had a daughter named Æthelflæd, a son named Eadmær, a granddaughter (son's daughter) named Eadgifu, and a young grandson, Eadwold (son's son). The fact that she leaves furnishing and fabrics is significant, as is the fact that she is the first to go into detail about these. She tries to identify her garments with details but they are in fact ambiguous. We also see Wynflaed bequeathing people, slaves or bondwomen of some kind; cf. the full will of Æthelgifu in which she frees at least sixty individuals and bequeaths approximately the same number, including her goldsmith. The will is printed in Whitelock (1930), 10–15. The translation is adapted from Whitelock's. This will is discussed in Owen (1979) which quotes from Whitelock's (1930) edition.

Wynflæd cyð hu hio wile ymbe þæt hio hæfð ofer hyre dæg hio becwiþ into cyrcan hyre ofring ... u ⁊ hyre beteran ofr`i´ng-sceat [...] hio becwiþ Æðelflæde hyre dehter hyre agrafenan

And to St Paul's church I grant the two best chasubles that I have, with all the things which belong to them [...] and I grant to Theodred my white chasuble which I bought in Pavia, and all that belongs to it [...]. And I grant to Odgar the yellow chasuble which I bought in Pavia, and what belongs to it. And I grant to Gundwine the other yellow chasuble which is unornamented, and what belongs to it. And I . . . . . . the red chasuble and all that belongs to it.

Wynflæd declares how she wishes to dispose of what she possesses, after her death. She bequeathes to the church her offering . . . and the better of her offering-cloths [...]. And

beah ⁊ `hyre mentelpreon´ [...] ⁊ hio becwið Eadgyfe ane crencestran ⁊ ane sem[estra]n oþer hatte Edgyfu oþer hatte Æþelyfu [...] ⁊ Ælfwolde hyre twegen wesendhornas ⁊ an hors ⁊ hire re`a´de getelde. [...] ⁊ hio becwið him hyre goldfagan treowena*n* cuppan þæt he ice his beah mid þam golde [...] ⁊ hio becwiþ him twa mydrecan ⁊ þæranin*n*an an bedreaf eal þæt to anum bedde gebyreð [...] ⁊ hio becwið Æðelflæde Elhhelmmes dehter Ælfferes dohtor `þa geonran´ ⁊ hyre twilibrocenan cyrtel ⁊ oþerne linnenne oþþe linnenweb ⁊ Eadgyfe twa mydrecan ⁊ þæranin*n*an hyre be`t´sþe bedwahrift ⁊ linnenne ruwan ⁊ eal þæt bedrefþe þærto gebyreð ⁊ hyre betstan dunnan tunecan ⁊ hyre `beteran´ mentel [...] ⁊ hyre ealdan gewiredan preon is an .VI. mancussum ⁊ sylle man hyre .IIII. mancussas of hyre sa... bege ⁊ an lang healwahrift ⁊ oþer sceort ⁊ þrio sethrægel ⁊ hio an Ceoldryþe hyre blacena tunecena swa þer hyre leofre beo ⁊ hyre be`t´sð haliryft ⁊ hyre betsþan bindan ⁊ *Æþelflæde* þisse hwitan hyre cincdaðenan cyrtel ⁊ cuffian ⁊ bindan ⁊ finde Æðelflæd syþþan an hyre nun`s´crude loce hwæt hio betsð mæge Wulfflæde ⁊ Æþelgife ⁊ ice mid golde þæt hyra ægþer hyru hæbbe .LX. penenga *wyrþ* ⁊ Ceolwynne ⁊ Edburge þæt sy .XXX. penega wyrþ ⁊ þær synt twa micle myd`e´rcan ⁊ an hræglcysð ⁊ an lytulu towmyderce ⁊ eac twa ealde mydercan þenne an hio Æþelflæde on ælum þingum þe þær unbecweden bið on bocum ⁊ an swilcum lytlum ⁊ hio gelyfð *þæt* hio wille hyre saulle geþencan ⁊ þær synt eac wahriftu sum þe hyre wyrðe bið ⁊ þa lætan hio mæg syllan hyre wimmannon [...]

3. The will of Ælfgifu

Date: between 966 and 975, written in Old English. Manuscript: Codex Wintoniensis, written in the first half of the twelfth century, BL, Additional MS 15350, fol. 96. Printed in Whitelock (1930), 20–3. The translation has been adapted from Whitelock's.

And ic ánn mínæn cinæhlafordæ þæs landæs æt Weowungum and æt Hlincgelædæ. and æt Hæfæresham. and æt Hæðfælda. and æt Mæssanywyrðæ and æt Gyssic and twegea bæagas æigþær ýs ón hundtwælftigu*m*. mancussum [...] and þam æþelingæ þæs landæs æt Niwanhám. and anæs beages on þritegum mancussum. And þæra hlæfdigan anæs swyrbeages on hundtweltifigum mancussum and anæs beages on þritegum mancussum. [...] And Æþælfledæ mínæs broþur wífæ þæs bændes þæ ic hire alæneð hæfdæ.

4a. The will of Æthelgifu

Dated 980–90. Written in Old English. Whitelock observes that a record of the will exists in the form of a Latin abstract of it from the Cartulary of St Albans, BL, MS Cotton Nero D i, fols. 149–61, ed. Birch, *Cartularium Saxonicum* II, 1887 (cf. editions by Kemble [1840]; Thorpe, *Diplomatarium* [1865]; see also H. R. Luard, *Matthaei Parisiensis Chronica Majora VI: Additamenta*, pp. 12 ff. [1882], not mentioned by Birch). The testatrix was the sister of Ealdorman Byrhtnoth's widow. There is no certain trace of this Æthelgifu outside her will. The Æthelgifu who was mother of King Eadwig's wife Æthelgifu is probably too early, and the testatrix does not mention a daughter Æthelgifu or any connection with the royal family. Æthelgifu, the second wife of Ealdorman Ælfwine of East Anglia, is connected with Cambridgeshire and is a benefactress of Ramsey, whereas this testatrix

she bequeathes to her daughter Æthelflæd her engraved ring, and her brooch [...]. And she bequeathes to Eadgifu a woman crank-turner and a seamstress, the one called Eadgifu and the other called Æthelgifu. [...] And to Ælfwold her two buffalo-horns and a horse and her red tent. [...] and she bequeathes to him [Eadwold] her gold-adorned wooden cup in order that he may enlarge his ring with the gold [...]. And she bequeathes to him two chests and in them a set of bedding, all that belongs to one bed. [...] And she bequeathes to Æthelflæd, daughter of Ealhhelm, Ælfhere's younger daughter and her broken twill gown and another of linen or else some linen cloth. And to Eadgifu two chests and in them her best bed-curtain and a linen covering and all the bedding which goes with it, and . . . . . . her best dun tunic, and the better of her cloaks and [. . .] her old wired brooch which is worth 6 mancuses. And let there be given to her four mancuses from her . . . . . and a long hall-tapestry and a short one and three seat coverings. And she grants to Ceolthryth whichever she prefers of her black tunics and her best holy veil and her best headband; and to Æthelflæd the White her . . . gown and head-dress and headband, and afterwards Æthelflæd is to supply from her nun's vestments the best she can for Wulfflæd and Æthelgifu and supplement it with gold so that each of them shall have at least 60 pennyworth: and for Ceolwyn and Eadburg it shall be 30 pennyworth. And there are two large chests and a clothes' chest, and a little spinning box and two old chests. Then she makes a gift to Æthelflæd of everything which is unbequeathed, books and such small things, and she trusts that she will be mindful of her soul. And there are also tapestries, one which is suitable for her, and the smallest one she can give to her women.

And I grant to my royal lord the estates at Wing, Linslade, Haversham, Hatfield, Masworth and Gussage; and two rings each of a hundred and twenty mancuses [. . .]. And to the ætheling the estate at Newnham and a ring of 30 mancuses. And to the queen a neck ring of a hundred and twenty mancuses and a ring of thirty mancuses [. . .]. And to my brother's wife Æthelflæd the headband which I have lent her.

makes gifts only to local churches. The Æthelgifu who made a deathbed will in favour of Ely (*Liber Eliensis* II, c. 59) can be excluded for similar reasons, as also can two women of this name enrolled among the benefactors of New Minster, Winchester – namely the wife of Ealdorman Wulfsige and the wife of a priest Æthelric. She may be the woman who helped to support the oath of a certain Wynflæd at Cwicelmeshlæwe in 990–2, but this identification cannot be proved. Note the phrase 'of hire bende witsige v mancessas buton heo hit ær gedon hæfde' (five mancuses are to be cut from her band for Witsige, unless she should have done it before) suggesting that the band here is made of a precious metal, probably gold (though we cannot be sure). It could have been a textile band densely embroidered or brocaded with gold. It appears to be quite precious as five mancuses are cut from it for five separate beneficiaries. Whitelock *et al.* (1968) comment on the term 'godwebbenan' suggesting 'purple' and noting that Æthelgifu distinguishes her other kirtles by their colour. They also observe (1968: 83) that the kirtles could either have been woven from local fine white wool and dyed with indigenous vegetable dyes, or that the finest of Æthelgifu's kirtles may have been imported, or made locally from imported silk. See Crowfoot and Hawkes (1967); Rogers (2007: 212–13); Owen-Crocker (2004: 286; 2005: 41–52); Clegg Hyer (2012). Printed in Whitelock, Ker and Rennell (1968), 6–17. The translation has been adapted from Whitelock's.

[. . .] ⁊ wulfwunne mire mægan ane bledu ⁊ anne preon ⁊ an wahrift ⁊ an sethregl ⁊ eal betstow swylce heo þærto betst hæfð. ⁊ hire rotostan cyrtel ⁊ wulfmære hire mæge þa læssan seolfrenan cuppan ⁊ ceorfe man of hire bende witsige v mancessas buton heo hit ær gedon hæfde ⁊ v. leofwine wulfmæres suna ⁊ v. wulf mære mire swustur sunu ⁊ v. godwife ⁊ fv. ælfgife mire swustor dohtor. ⁊ selle mon beornwynne minne blæwenan cyrtel is neaþene unrenod ⁊ hire betstan heafodgewædo ⁊ selle man lufetate ⁊ ælfgifu ⁊ godwife. hire .iii. godwebbenan cyrtlas. ⁊ wulfgife selle mon oðera hire dunnan cyrtla. ⁊ syðþan dælen hiredwifmen þ oðer him betwinum ⁊ selle man leofsige .iii. wahrift swylce þær þonne bet sint. ⁊ ii. sethrægl ⁊ ii. Betstwo ⁊ dæle godwif ⁊ ælf gifu þa oðra him betwinum ⁊ hira æþer .ii. mydercan [. . .]

4*b*. The Latin abstract of the will

BL, MS Cotton Nero D i includes two thirteenth-century quires, fols. 149–61, which contain copies of Anglo-Saxon charters and papal privileges in favour of St Albans. A Latin abstract of the will of Æthelgifu appears on fol. 152. The Latin text is much shorter than the Old English and deals mainly with gifts of land. It does include two references to soft furnishing. Where the Old English reads 'for hio ⁊ for hire hlafordes' (for her and for her lord's soul), the translator puts 'concedo cum consensu domini mei regis'. This appears to be a deliberate alteration (rather than a mistranslation) intended to connect the bequest of lands to the witness list. The witness list, beginning with the king, is thought to have been added to the will as part of an attempt by the monks to recover one of the estates mentioned in the will which it lost after 1066 (Whitelock 1968: 40). The Latin abstract and the witness list attached to it printed in Whitelock, Ker and Rennell (1968), 38–9. The translation is by Louise Sylvester.

[. . .] ⁊ unam cortinam. ⁊ unum bancale concedo cum consensu domini mei regis.

And to Wulfwynn my relative a dish and a brooch and a wall-hanging and a seat-cover and all the best bedsteads that she has and her brightest gown, and to her relative Wulfmær the smaller silver cup. And 5 mancuses are to be cut from her band for Witsige, unless she should have done it before, and 5 for Leofwine, Wulfmær's son, and 5 for Wulfmær my sister's son, and 5 for Godwif and 5 for Ælfgifu, my sister's daughter. And my blue gown which is untrimmed at the bottom and her best head-dresses are to be given to Beornwynn. And her three purple gowns are to be given to Lufetat and Ælgifu and Godwif, and Wulfgifu is to be given some of her other, dun-coloured gowns. And afterwards her household women are to divide what is left between them. And three wall-hangings, the better of such as are then there, and two seat-covers and two bedsteads are to be given to Leofsige. And Godwif and Ælfgifu are to divide the others between them; and each of them is to have two chests.

[. . .] And one curtain and one seat cover left with the permission of my lord the king.

5. The will of the Ealdorman Æthelmær

Dated between 971 and 982 or 983. Written in Old English (manuscript: Liber Monasterii de Hyda, fol. 35b). The manuscript is said by Whitelock to be in the possession of the earl of Macclesfield, at Shirburn Castle, Watlington, Oxfordshire. It was compiled in the fourteenth century. Each Old English document is followed by translations into Latin and fourteenth-century English, which are full of errors and show that the scribe's knowledge of Old English was very slight. This will offers gifts to the king in the form of rings and indicates their value. There is an edition of the manuscript by Edward Edwards, 1866. Printed in Whitelock (1930) 24–6. The translation is adapted from Whitelock's.

And ic becweðe minum cynehlaforde to heregeatuwum iiii beagus on ðrym hund mancesum goldes and iiii sword and viii hors feower gerædode and iiii ungerædode and iiii helmas and iiii byrnan and viii speru and viii scyldas.

6. The will of Brihtric and Ælfswith

Date: between 973 and 987. Written in Old English: Manuscripts: (a) Textus Roffensis, fol. 144; (b) BL, Stowe 831, a late paper copy of (a). Whitelock's text is from (a). Relevant bequests concern a ring (type unspecified), neck ring and a band. Again, we perhaps see indications of comparative values of such items. Printed in Whitelock (1930), 27–9. Translation adapted from Whitelock's.

Ǽrest his kynehlaforde ænne beah. On hundeahtotigan mancysan goldes: ˥ an handsecs. On ealswa miclan. ˥ feower hors ˥ twa gerædede. ˥ twa sweord gefetelsode. ˥ twegan hafocas˙ ˥ ealle his heador hundas; ˥ ðære hlæfdian. Ænne beah on ðrittigan mancysan goldes˙ ˥ ænne stedan. to forespræce. þ se cwyde standan moste; [...] ˥ to Cristes circan .lx. mancys goldes .xxx. ðam biscope .xxx. ðam hirode˙ ˥ ænne sweorbeah. on .lxxx. mancys˙ ˥ twa cuppan solfrene. ˥ ðæt land æt Meapaham; ˥ to sče Augustine. ðrittig mancys goldes. ˥ twa cuppan seolfrene. ˥ healfne bænd gyldenne.

7. The will of the Ætheling Æthelstan

Written in Old English. 1014. There are four manuscripts of the will: (a) BL, Stowe Charter 37, a single sheet of vellum in an early-eleventh-century hand; (b) Christchurch, Canterbury, MS AA. H. 68; (c), and (d) BL, Additional MS 15350, fols. 43b, 50 (Codex Wintoniensis). Whitelock's text is taken from (a). The date of the endorsement to the Canterbury manuscript – 1015 – though in a late hand, is apparently correct (Whitelock 1930: 167). Ætheling (Prince) Æthelstan was King Ethelred II's son. He knew he was dying when he made these bequests. Unlike the other wills, which are in general speculative, this one gives us a picture of what he owned when he died. There is mention of a gold belt, probably associated with the sword and a ring. The Wulfric mentioned in the will appears to have been a metal-worker (he made the silver hilt), suggesting that this ring is made of metal. Printed in Whitelock (1930), 56–63. The translation is adapted from Whitelock's.

On godes ælmihtiges naman. Ic Æþelstan æþeling. geswutelige on þysum gewrite. hu ic mine áre. ˥ míne æhta. geunnen hæbbe. gode to lofe. ˥ minre saule to alysednysse. ˥ mines fæder Æþelredes cynges. þe ic hit æt geearnode. [...] ˥ ic geann in mid me. þær ic me reste. Criste. ˥ sče Petre. Þæs lands æt Eadburgebyrig. þe ic gebohte æt minum fæder.

And I bequeath to my royal lord as my heriot four rings of three hundred mancuses of gold, and four swords and eight horses, four with tack and four without and four helmets and four coats of mail and eight spears and eight shields.

First, to his royal lord a ring of eighty mancuses of gold and a short sword of the same value, and four horses, two with harness, and two swords with scabbards, and two hawks and all his staghounds. And to the queen a ring of thirty mancuses of gold, and a stallion, for her advocacy that the will might stand. [...] And to Christchurch 60 mancuses of gold, thirty for the bishop and thirty for the community, and a neck ring of 80 mancuses and two silver cups, and the estate at Meopham. And to St Augustine's thirty mancuses of gold and two silver cups and half a gold band.

In the name of Almighty God. I, Prince Æthelstan, declare in this document how I have granted my estates and my possessions to the glory of God and for the redemption of my soul and of my father's, King Ethelred's, from whom I acquired the property. [...] And to Christ and St Peter, at the place where I shall be buried, I grant along with my body the

mid twam hund mancosan goldes be gewihte. ⁊ mid .v. pundan seolfres. [. . .] ⁊ þ lánd at Mórdune. þ min fæder me to lét. Ic gean into þære stowe. for uncer begra saule. ⁊ ic hine þæs bidde for godes lufan. ⁊ for sc̄a Marían. ⁊ for sc̄e Petres. þ hit stándan mote. ⁊ þæs swúrdes mide þam sylfrenan hiltan. þe Wulfric worhte. ⁊ þone gyldenan fetels. ⁊ þæne beh þe Wulfric worhte [. . .]

8. The will of Wulfwaru

Dated between 984 and 1016. Written in Old English. The manuscript, Corpus Christi College, Cambridge, MS CI, fol. 88, is a twelfth-century Bath cartulary. This is one of the Anglo-Saxon wills which indicate that from the tenth and eleventh centuries the band became a form of portable wealth. Whitelock translates as 'headband' in the cases of Wynflæd's will (I. 2; two bequests) but as 'band' here. Wulfwaru's will gives one ring worth sixty mancuses of gold to St Peter's, another worth thirty mancuses of gold to her elder daughter, Gode, while a band worth twenty gold mancuses is to be shared among her four servants. Whitelock was not able to identify Wulfwaru or her children with people who appear elsewhere. We know from the will that Wulfwaru had daughters named Gode and Ælfwaru and sons named Wulfmær and Ælfwine. The Prosopography of Anglo-Saxon England website does not have any more information about her. Note 'anes mæssereafes mid eallum þam ðe ðærto gebyreð', implying the concept of a set of mass vestments; perhaps a stole, maniple etc. were included. This is a woman bequeathing mass vestments which would be worn by male ecclesiastics. They are not her own clothes and either must have been purpose-made already under her patronage, or she is bequeathing a sum of money to enable them to be made. In 'anes beddreafes mid wahryfte ⁊ mid hoppscytan ⁊ mid eallum þam þe þærto gebyreð', we see another set, this time of soft furnishings, seemingly also going to the church perhaps for the community to sell or convert into something else, or for use by a senior cleric or favoured guests. Printed in Whitelock (1930), 62–5. Translation adapted from Whitelock's.

Ic Wulfwaru bidde minne leofan hlaford Æþelred kyning him to ælmyssan. þ ic mote beon mines cwydes wyrðe. Ic kyðe þe leof her on ðisum gewrite hwæs ic geann into Baðum to Sc̄e Petres mynstre. for mine earman sawle. ⁊ for minra yldrena þe me min ar of com. ⁊ mine æhta. þ is þonne þ ic geann ðæder into ðære halgan stowe anes beages is on syxtigum mancussum goldes. ⁊ anre blede is on þriddan healfon punde. ⁊ twegea gyldenra roda. ⁊ anes mæssereafes mid eallum þam ðe ðærto gebyreð. ⁊ anes hricghrægles þæs selestan þe ic hæbbe. ⁊ anes beddreafes mid wahryfte ⁊ mid hoppscytan. ⁊ mid eallum þam þe þærto gebyreð. [. . .] And ic geann Godan minre yldran dehter þes landes æt Wunfrod. mid mete. ⁊ mid mannum. ⁊ mid eallre tilðe. ⁊ twegea cuppena on feower pundum. ⁊ anes bendes on ðritigum mancussum goldes. ⁊ twega preonas. ⁊ anes wifscrudes ealles. And Alfware minre gyngran dehter ic geann ealles þæs wifscrudes þe þer to lafe bið. [. . .] And ic geann Wulfmære minum suna anes heallwahriftes. ⁊ anes beddreafes. Ælfwine minum oðrum suna ic geann anes heallreafes. ⁊ anes burreafes. mid beodreafe. ⁊ mid eallum hræglum swa ðerto gebyreð. And ic geann minum feower cnihtum. Ælmære. ⁊ Ælfwerde. ⁊ Wulfrice. ⁊ Wulfstane. anes bendes on twentigum mancussum goldes. And ic geann eallum minum hiredwifmannum to gemanum anes godes casteneres wel gerenodes.

estate at Adderbury which I bought from my father for two hundred mancuses of gold, by weight, and for 5 pounds of silver [...] and the estate at Morden which my father allowed to me, I grant to that foundation for the souls of us both (and I beseech him, that for God's sake and for St Mary's and for St Peter's, my bequest may stand); and the sword with the silver hilt which Wulfric made and the gold belt and the ring which Wulfric made [...].

I, Wulfwaru, pray my dear lord King Ethelred, of his charity, that I may be entitled to make my will. I make known to you, Sire, here in this document, what I grant to St Peter's monastery at Bath for my poor soul and for the souls of my ancestors from whom my property and my possessions come to me; namely then, that I grant to that holy place there a ring which is worth sixty mancuses of gold, and a bowl of two and a half pounds, and two gold crosses, and a set of mass garments with everything that belongs to it, and the best back cloth that I have, and a set of bedding with wall-hanging and surrounding hanging and with everything that belongs to it. [...] And I grant to my elder daughter, Gode, the estate at Winford, with produce and men and all profits; and two cups of four pounds; and a band of thirty mancuses of gold and two brooches and one entire woman's outfit. And to my younger daughter Ælfwaru, I grant all of the woman's clothing which is left; and to my son Wulfmær a hall hanging and a set of bedding. To Ælfwine, my second son I grant a hall hanging and a hanging for a chamber, together with a tablecloth and with all the cloths that go with it. And I grant to my four servants Ælfmær and Ælfweard and Wulfric and Wulfstan, a band of twenty mancuses of gold. And I grant all my household women, in common, a good chest well decorated.

9. The will of Ælfric Modercope

Date: probably 1042 or 1043. Written in Old English. Manuscript: Cambridge University Library, MS FF. 2. 33, fol. 45. This is an interesting example of a man leaving textiles: a bed cover and also his tent (used for travelling). Printed in Whitelock (1930), 74–5. The translation is adapted from Whitelock's.

[…] And Alfric biscop I biquethe mine teld ⁊ min bedreaf þat ic best hauede vt on mi fare mid me. […]

10. Ornamenta Willielmi episcopi primi

Date: 4 January 1095 (1096). Written in Latin. William de Karilepho (Saint Carilef / Saint Calais; see Plate 1), abbot of St Vincent's in Normandy, was consecrated bishop of Durham (1081–96) at Gloucester during Christmastide, 1080, and was made Lord Chief Justice of England. He died at Windsor early in January 1096.

The notices of splendid robes which the monks of Durham obtained upon the death of each of its early bishops, are, strictly speaking, neither wills nor inventories, but mortuaries. King (1963: 13) mentions two fragments from the tomb of William of St Carilef, with 'silver-gilt thread in underside couching on silk, now discoloured to brown'. This seems to be the same person though the dates do not quite correlate. The textile fragments still survive: an embroidered chalice is still visible. Printed in Raine (1835), 1. The translation is by Louise Sylvester.

In primis, in exequiis Domini Willielmi Episcopi primi, qui obiit Anno Incarnationis Dominicæ M°LXXXXV^{to}, quarto nonas Januarii, habuit Ecclesia (Dunelm.) literam et equos deportantes corpus ejusdem Patris a Vindesorâ usque Dunelmum; et de ejusdem Capellâ habuit Ecclesia plurima ornamenta, videlicet v capas, quarum iij albæ et negræ; iij casulas, quarum ij albæ et una nigra, cum stolâ et manipulo magnis, in fine tantum brudatis; unum pannum album pro altari

11. Ornamenta Ranulphi episcopi

Date: quarto nonas January 1095. Written in Latin. Ranulph Flambard, justiciary and procurator-general under King William II (William Rufus), was consecrated bishop of Durham in 1099, having, as is reported, purchased the see for 1000 marks. He was the builder of Framwellgate Bridge, Norham Castle, and Kepier Hospital, and sites in the Durham area. He died in 1128. This is the first will which includes descriptions of embroidered motifs. Printed in Raine (1835), 2. The translation is by Louise Sylvester.

In exequiis Ranulphi Episcopi habuit Ecclesia [Dunelm.] ex Capellâ ejusdem, iiij capas, unam cum multis parvis perlis, aliam viridem cum magnis grifonibus, quæ dicitur capa Sancti Cuthberti, quia in eâ delatus fuit de parvâ Ecclesiâ usque in Chorum tempore istius Ranulphi Episcopi; alias duas cum magnis pavonibus; et unam casulam indici coloris cum largis orfrays; cum stolâ et manipulâ cum magnis Archangelis brudatis: et duas albas cum pavonibus; thuribulum unum argenteum: et, sicut habetur in gestis Episcoporum, addidit etiam ornamentis Ecclesiæ magna dorsalia quæ quondam pendebant ex ultrâque parte Chori, et etiam pallia, capas, casulas, tunicas quoque et dalmaticas.

[…] And I bequeath to Bishop Ælfric my tent and my bedding, the best that I had with me out on my journey. […]

First, concerning the funeral rites of lord William, first bishop, who died in the year of the incarnation of our Lord 1095 [by old reckoning], the fourth day before the nones of January, the church (Durham) had a litter and horses transport the body of this father from Windsor up to Durham, and the church had many ornaments/items from the chapel, namely five copes, of which three white and black; three chasubles, of which two white and one black, with a stole and great maniple, embroidered at the end; one white cloth for the altar […]

Concerning the funeral rites of Bishop Ranulph, held at the church (Durham), from the chapel of the same, four copes, one with many small pearls, another green with large griffons, which is called the cope of St Cuthbert, which was carried out of the small church into the choir in the time of this Bishop Ranulph; another two with large peacocks; and a chasuble of indigo colour with wide orphreys; with a stole and maniple with large embroidered archangels; and two albs with peacocks; a silver censer; and, as stated in the acts of bishops, he also added to the ornaments of the church a large dorsal which once hung from both sides of the choir and also palls, copes, chasubles, tunics and also dalmatics.

12. Ornamenta Gaufridi episcopi

Written in Latin. Galfrid or Geoffrey Rufus, chancellor of England, was consecrated bishop of Durham in early August 1133. He built the Chapter House of Durham, in which he was buried in 1141. Here we find a cope given a name, probably reflecting the iconography embroidered on it. The name seems unlikely for a donor but we have not been able to discover its significance. Printed in Raine (1835), 2–3. The translation is by Louise Sylvester.

In exequiis Galfridi Episcopi habuit Ecclesia [Dunelm.] funeralia ejusdem; et, de Capellâ, unam capam quæ dicebatur Zaphirus; et unam nigram casulam spissam; et unam Albam nigram cum minutis lineis aureis; stolam et manipulam nigras, eodem modo lineatas; et thuribulum unum argenteum; et cetera quæ pertinent ad Episcopi Capellam.

13. Inspeximus and probate of the will of Martin of St Cross

Date: November 1259 and recorded at the hospital of Sherburn. Written in Latin. The manuscript is Durham County Record Office, D/Sh/H/1030. Martin of St Cross was chaplain of the bishop of Durham, Nicholas Farnham; Phillipa Hoskin notes that he is little known but 'his will reveals that he was a remarkable person': wealthy and with wide-ranging interests in theology and links with academia despite his lack of academic training. His name discloses a link with Hampshire (his own family seems to come from this area). There were relations in south Devon, although he pursued an active career in the north.

Martin evidently had a good collection of silver and jewellery and it is possible that he traded in these (Hoskin 2005: xxxvii–xxxviii). His position as steward of Bishop Aymer of Valence indicates that if he acquired his great wealth during Farnham's episcopate (1241–9), he was a land agent at that time. Holding benefices outside the diocese was not uncommon, and by his death Martin had churches in more than one see. Other ecclesiastical rewards were also in the bishop's gift, and Martin was master of Sherburn Hospital, an episcopal foundation, by 1247 (Hoskin 2005: xli–xlii). The grant to Martin of the Cross of the custody of Sherburn Hospital is printed in Hoskin (2005), 32. He appears to have remained in the household of Farnham's successor, Walter Kirkham, and 'was also known as a deacon of the diocese of Exeter in 1255, dispensed for plurality on 9 August of that year, and was a canon of York by 1256' (Hoskin 2005: xlvi). In this case, we have newly transcribed the original manuscript and compared it against Raine's edition (1835: 6–11) and Hoskin's edition (2005: 97–101). The transcription is by Mark Chambers, and the translation by Louise Sylvester. Uncertain readings caused by recent damage to the manuscript are provided by Raine's edition. Abbreviations and contractions are expanded in italics.

Si sepultus fu*ero in* cimi*teri*o f*ratru*m minor*um*; lego ibide*m* centu*m* solid*os*; si apud Ebor', [capam meam] de rubeo samito cu*m* vestime*n*to bruddato integro & casula de samito rubeo q*ualite*r cu*n*q*ue* contingat de me; [si apud Schyreburn' ca]pam meam de panno ad auru*m* scil*icet* baudekin cu*m* vestime*n*to plenario de panno Yspa*n*nie ad auru*m* […] tertiam capam de serico ecclesi*e* b*eat*e Marie Karl', capelle s*an*c*t*i Edmu*n*di de Gatesheved tunicam & dalmatica*m* de cendallo viridi; & auriculare de serico ad textu*m* subportand*u*m. It*em* frontalle de serico radiato domui de Schyreburn' & unam tualliam nigr*a*m ad patenam. It*em* do*m*ino Ebor' anulu*m* meu*m* cu*m* rubeto maiori. It*em* do*m*ino Dunelm' anulu*m* cum saphyro maiori. […] It*em* anuli capia*n*t*ur* de meloribus existentibus Ebor' & dentur do*min*is Norwyc' & Karleol' ep*iscop*is. […] Item decano Ebor' & singulis can*on*icis residenciam facientibus unum anulu*m* aur*i* cu*m* saphiro pond*er*is circa .x. vel .xii. denar*iorum*. It*em* do*m*ino Roberto vicar*i*o de Aucland' unu*m* anulu*m* aur*i* & unam tualliam albam ad patenam. […] Item pannos

Concerning the funeral rites of Bishop Geoffrey, held at the church (Durham), for the funeral of the same and, of the chapel, one cope that is called Zaphirus; and one heavy black chasuble; and one black alb with minute gold thread; a stole and a maniple, both black, in the same style thread; and one silver censer; and the rest that belongs to the bishop's 'chapel'.

If I shall be buried in the cemetery of the brothers minor I leave the same 100 solidos; if at York, my red samite cope with the fully embroidered vestment and the red samite chasuble whatever happens to me. If at Sherburn my cope of cloth-of-gold, namely baudekyn, with the vestment entirely of Spanish cloth-of-gold. [. . .] The third cope, of silk, to the church of the Blessed Mary Karilioli (Carlisle). The tunic and dalmatic of green sendal to the chapel of St Edmund in Gateshead and the silk pillow on which the text was carried. Also the frontal of striped silk to the house of Sherburn and a black towel for the paten. Also to my lord the archbishop of York my ring with the large ruby. Also to my lord bishop of Durham a ring with a large sapphire. [. . .] Likewise the best of the existing rings of York, and they are to be given to my lords the bishops of Norwich and Carlisle. [. . .] Likewise the deacon of York and to each of the resident canons a gold ring with a sapphire of about 10 or 12 pence in weight. Likewise Lord Robert, vicar of Auckland, a gold ring and a white

meos de serico ecclesiis meis ubi fuerit necesse, & in quibus defectus fuerit. Item bursas de serico, laqueos & alia minuta jocalia [...] Item casulam de viridi lego ecclesie de Merton'. [...] Item Agathe sorori mee magnam zonam de nigro serico ad aurum cum apparatu argenti deaurati. [...] Item Waltero le Boen aliam zonam de serico ad aurum cum apparatu argenti deaurati, & cyphum argenteum planum cum cruce in fundo. [...] Item Agathe sorori mee magnum firmaculum meum de auro, & Ysabelle filie quondam sororis mee tertiam zonam de serico cum apparatu argenti deaurati. Item capellanis meis de Tydelfueshyde, Coleshulle, Felmingeham & vicariis meis Ebor' singulis unam de robis meis.

14. The will of Peter, of Aigueblanche

Dated at Sugwas (an episcopal manor house near Hereford) on 26 November 1268, which was the day immediately preceding that on which the bishop died. Written in Latin. Original probate copy of the will of Peter de Aqua-Blanca, bishop of Hereford from 1240 to 1268. Printed in Woodruff (1926), 1–9. The translation is by Louise Sylvester.

Item volumus et precipimus quod biblia nostra glossata vendatur et de precio panni emantur ad pauperes vestiendos. Item libros sermonum damus et legamus Johanni decano Herefordensi ita tamen quod pro illis solvat quinquaginta libras Viennenses de quibus panni emantur ..... et precium, ut dictum est, pauperibus erogetur. [...] Item legamus prenominate ecclesie nostre de Aqua bella omnes pannos ..... Item Hamoni de Aqua-Blanca frati nostro palfridum nostrum bellicensem, cum corpertorio nostro novo, et uno annulo aureo de melioribus. [...] Domine Ancille uxori domini Aymonis decem libras Viennenses .... . meliori annulo aureo cum saphiro; Domine Alicie uxori sue viginta libras Viennenses et unum annulum [...] Item legamus Iordano de Londia cappellano ..... robam nostram meliorem, scilicet tunicum et supertunicale de bloyeto sive de persico et mantellum eiusdem ..... ysoce filie sue supertunicale de camelino. [...] Item volumus quod vestes nostre, exceptis legatis ..... pauperibus capellanis et clericis erogentur, tam de panetria quam de garderoba.

15. The will of Hugh de Nevill

Date: 1267. Written in Anglo-French. This will was written in Acre whilst de Nevill was on crusade. Guiseppi (1899) notes that we have nothing but the testator's name and the arms on the seal to enable us to identify the testator's family connections. Not a single relative is mentioned. The instrument affects only personal property, and of the personal property mentioned, it is evident that it is only such as the testator had with him in the Holy Land or might have at the time of his death, should that event occur while he was in the same country (Guiseppi 1899: 355). We know from a letter written by Lady Hawisa de Nevill to her son Hugh and from a collection of the Nevill deeds that, because of the part he had played against his sovereign as an adherent of Simon de Montfort, Sir Hugh de Nevill's possessions were confiscated by the Crown in 1265 (Guiseppi 1899: 357–9). He was subsequently pardoned and his lands partially restored. Another document mentions his wife, Beatrice (Guiseppi 1899: 362). Hugh de Nevill must have died before 25 August 1269, because this is the date of the notarial instrument relating to the execution of his will (Guiseppi 1899: 363). Most of the bequests are in the form of money including bequests to the widows and orphans of Acre and money left to Estevene le Draper. Printed in Guiseppi (1899), 351–70. The translation is by Louise Sylvester.

towel for the paten. [...] Likewise my silk cloths to my churches where there is need and in which they are lacking. Likewise silk purses with drawstring and other small jewels. [...] Likewise I leave a green chasuble to the church of Merton. [...] Likewise to my sister Agatha my large girdle of black silk cloth-of-gold thread with gilded silver ornaments. [...] Likewise to Walter le Boen another girdle of silk cloth-of-gold with silver ornaments and the plain silver cup with a cross at the bottom. [...] Likewise to my sister Agatha my large gold buckle [...] and to Isabelle, daughter of my deceased sister, the third silk girdle with silver gilt ornaments. Likewise one of my robes to each of my chaplains of Tydelfueshyde [probably Tilshead/Tidulfhide, Wiltshire], Coleshill, Felmingham and my vicar of York.

[...] Likewise we wish and command that our glossed Bible be sold and some of the precious cloth sold to clothe the poor. Likewise we give and bequeath our books of sermons to John deacon of Hereford except for fifty pounds of Vienna cloth of which they may sell ..... and the price, as it is said to be dealt out to the poor. [...] Likewise we leave to our church of Aqua Bella mentioned above all the cloths ..... Likewise to our brother Hamon of Aqua-Blanca our war-horse, with our new horse-blanket, and one of the best gold rings . .... Lady Ancille wife of master Aymon ten pounds of Vienna [cloth] ... one of my better gold rings with sapphires; Lady Alice his wife twenty pounds of Vienna [cloth] and a ring ... Likewise I bequeath to Iordano de Londia, chaplain ... our best outfit, namely a tunic and surcoat of light-blue cloth or of dark-blue cloth and a matching cloak ..... To Ysoce his daughter a camelin surcoat. Likewise we wish that our clothes, except what is bequeathed ... chaplains and clerics may bestow on the poor, except for the cloths of the wardrobe.

Co est le testament sire Huue Nevile chivaler en le non del pere el fiz 't de le seint espirit. [...] Ä la maisun se⸠n Thomas de Cantirbiř en Acre mun palefrei feraunt e mes armures ke apendent a une personne. [...] Jo divis a sire Randouf de Munchensi ma petite espeie e vn fermeil oue ameraudes a sire Roƀ de Bridishale vn feremeil oue ameraudes a sire Rauf de Ekleshale vn anel de or. A Jakke mun vallet le paumer de chival Bai ke fu a Wiłł le fiz Symon ke jo li dunai oue tute les armures ke appendent a vn gentil home .e q⸠nze mars de sterling. [...] A p⸠ur de sein Gile vn fermeil de or A cest testament parfere e me dettes a q⸠ter jo voil e deuis ke me chiuaus e mes armures e tute mes autre choses seint venduz.

16. The will of Margerie de Crioll

Dated at Irencester [Cirencester], Saturday after the Annunciation 1319. This will is recorded in the episcopal registers of the diocese of Lincoln in Bishop Burhersh's Register of 1320–42. The will is in Middle English, although switching between Middle English and Anglo-French is very evident in it. This abstract of the will appears in Gibbons (1888), 4–5. The translation is by Louise Sylvester.

Vestments &c. to my chapel of Corby; also iiij towayls p' le autel des le une paire des armes de Leybourn. [...] To Lady Margery le Valence, whatever in my wardrobe was her mother's; [...] To Lady Margery de Say, a coffer at Irencester which belonged to Sir Robert Hereward, and a pyne de Euere which belonged to Saint Thomas of Canterbury. [...] To my nephew Sir Gilbert Petche, garments which Margaret de Wylughby gave me. [...] A Reynald mon keu mon chival lemonner a mon charre. To Elizabeth de Pavenham, a nun at Shaftesbyr, my pat' nost' of coral and white pearls, which the Countess of Penbrok gave me.

17. The will of Elizabeth, wife of Sir Edmund Bacon

Dated 1323 at Wakeley and proved at Caldewell, xviij Kal. Oct. (18 days before the Kalends of October – or 24 September) 1323. Written in Middle English. Printed in Gibbons (1888), 4. The translation is by Louise Sylvester.

To my husband, Sir Edmund, a cross and a pair of paternosters, &c. [...] Jewellery to my sisters Katherine de Breweus, & Margaret. To Rob. de Breweuse, a ruby ring. [...] Vestments to Dore Abbey.

18. Testamentum Thomæ Harpham

Date: 1341. The matrix language of this will is Latin with single-word switches in Middle English and Anglo-French. Many wills of this period contain interesting examples of codeswitching, examined by Herbert Schendl (2013). There is possible northern dialect indicated by the Norse loans. Printed in Raine (1836), 2–3. The translation is by Louise Sylvester.

et cum corpore meo ecclesiæ beati Johannis del Pike in Ebor. meliorem supertunicam meam cum capucio ejusdem sectæ fururatam, nomine mortuarii. [...] Item lego Katerinæ filiæ meæ unum coverlyt crocei coloris de operibus florum lilii, unum kyngle [...] collobium

This is the will of Sir Hugh Neville, knight, in the name of the Father, the Son and the Holy Spirit. [...] To the house of St Thomas of Canterbury in Acre my grey saddle-horse and my armour, which are appropriate for one person. [...] I bequeath to Sir Randolf of Munchen my small sword and a buckle with emeralds; to Sir Robert of Bridishale a buckle with emeralds; to Sir Ralf of Ekleshale a gold ring. To my valet Jack the ferrule of my bay horse which goes to Will, the son of Symon, to whom I hereby give all the armour which is appropriate to a gentleman, and 15 marks sterling [...] To the prior of St Giles a gold buckle. To this will to fulfil my debts which I wish to pay off I wish and bequeath that my horses and my armour and all my other possessions to be sold.

Vestments etc. to my chapel of Corby; also four towels for the altar [possibly towels for wiping church plate] depicting the coat of arms of Leybourn [Kent] [...] to Lady Margery le Valence, whatever in my wardrobe was her mother's; [...] To Lady Margery de Say, a coffer at Irencester which belonged to Sir Robert Hereward, and an ivory pin which belonged to St Thomas of Canterbury. [...] To my nephew Sir Gilbert Petche, garments which Margarte de Wylughby gave me. [...] To Reynauld my cook my cart horse with my cart. To Elizabeth de Pavenham, a nun at Shaftesbury, my coral and white pearl rosary, which the countess of Pembroke gave me.

To my husband, Sir Edmund, a crucifix and a rosary, etc. [...] Jewellery to my sisters Katherine de Breweus and Margaret. To Robert de Breweuse, a ruby ring. [...] Vestments to Dore Abbey.

and with my body to the church of the blessed John of the Pike in York my best surcoat with matching hood similarly furred, by way of a mortuary fee [...] Likewise I leave my daughter Katerina a yellow bedspread with lilies embroidered on it, a girdle [...] my long

meum longum coloris de appelblome cum tunicâ ejusdem coloris. Item lego Johanni filio meo robam meam de sendre cum omnibus garniamentis. Item lego Willielmo filio meo robam meam de albo kamelyn cum collobio ejusdem, unum coverlit radiatum opere rosarum pulverisatum, unum chalon' et duo lynthiamina ac unum materas. Item lego Agneti filiæ meæ tunicam meam de taune cum longo collobio et capucio fururatis ejusdem coloris. […] Item lego dictæ Agneti, filiæ meæ, unam archam, quæ fuit matris ejusdem Agnetis, unum coverlet diversorum operum cujus chaump est de viridi et coton, unum matras et duo linthiamina […]. Item lego Henrico Blome supertunicam meam de blueto cum capucio ejusdem coloris. […] Item lego domino Waltero de Harpham mantellum meum de Winchelsee.

19. Testamentum Elenæ de Bilburgh

Date: 1341. Written in Latin and Middle English. Printed in Raine (1836), 3–4. The translation is by Louise Sylvester.

In primis lego animam meam Deo, beatæ Mariæ et omnibus Sanctis, et corpus meum ad sepeliendum in cimiterio ecclesiæ Sancti Michaelis de Berefrido. Et pro mortuario meo unam supertunicam cum capucio. Item do et lego Agneti, filiæ Henrici de Coupmanthorp, unum annulum aureum cum lapide qui vocatur meraude. Item do et lego Margeriæ sorori meae unum courtby de blueto cum fururâ. Item do et lego Julianæ sorori meae unam tunicam de appelblome. Residuum vero omnium bonorum meorum post debita mea soluta do et lego Isabellæ sorori meæ. —— Executores meos, Thomam de Bilbrok patrem meum, et Isabellam sororem meam. In cujus —— Datum Ebor. die et anno predictis. Item do et lego ij^s. ad quatuor libras ceræ ad comburendum circa corpus meum. Item do et lego Marotae servienti meæ unum warniamente de melle.

20. The will of John Pyncheon

Dated the Vigil of St Matthew [20 September], 1392. Written in English, with a French insertion (mislabelled by Furnivall). Scholars are still undecided about the reasons for the codeswitching between vernaculars (rather than between Latin and a vernacular language) sometimes found in administrative documents of this period, in particular where equivalent terms exist in the matrix language. John Pyncheon was a citizen and jeweller of London. He is concerned to provide clothing and bedding for charitable purposes. Printed in Furnivall (1964), 3. The translation is by Louise Sylvester.

Ieo volle que la moneye soit despendu, cestassauoir, to þe pore Men þat han ben Men be-fore of god conuersacion, som man .xx.s, ant som ij Març, and som xl. s., aftyr þat here stat hat ben be-fore, and þat þey be of þe same Parche, and Of Petris and Cristoforys, or of oþere next þer by; & where me may wetyn eny powre lame, ore powre Blynde, in Ani plache in þe Towne, þat þey han Cloþys to hele hem fro colde, & Schetys to þam þat han nede.

apple-blossom coloured shirt with a tunic of the same colour. Likewise I leave my son John my silk outfit with all the trimmings. Likewise I leave my son William my white camelin robe with matching hood, a striped bedspread scattered with roses, a bedcover and two sheets as well as one mattress. Likewise I leave my daughter Agnet my orange-brown tunic with a long shirt and furred hood of the same colour. [. . .] Likewise I leave Agnet, my daughter mentioned above, a bed-frame which belonged to her mother, a bedspread of diverse work whose ground is of green and cotton, one mattress and two sheets [. . .]. Likewise I leave Henry Blome my surcoat of bluet with a hood of the same colour. [. . .] Likewise I leave Lord Walter of Harpham my cloak from Winchelsea.

First, I leave my soul to God, the blessed Mary and all the saints, and my body for burial in the cemetery of the church of St Michael of Le Belfrey [York]. And for my burial my one surcoat with a hood. Likewise I give and leave Agnet, daughter of Henry of Copmanthorpe, a gold ring with a gemstone called an emerald. Likewise I give and leave my sister Margery a jacket of blue cloth furred. Likewise I give and leave my sister Juliana a pink tunic. The rest of the goods that are truly mine after my debts have been paid, I give and leave to my sister Isabella. My executors are Thomas of Bilbrook, my father and Isabella my sister. At York on the aforesaid day and year. Also I give and leave 2 shillings towards four pounds of wax for the candles around my body. Also I give and leave to my servant Marot a garment of medley.

I wish the money to be spent, that is to say to the poor men who have previously been men of good conduct, 20 shillings to some men and 2 marks to some and 40 shillings to some according to the rank that they had before, and if they are of the same parish, of Peter and Christopher, or of another parish close by; and where I may know of any poor lame, or poor blind in any place in the town, so that they have clothes to protect them from the cold and sheets for those that are in need.

21. The will of Lady Alice West

Date: 1395. There is a Latin prologue as to the proof of the will on 1 September 1395 by Sir Thomas West and John Thurston, two of the executors named in it. Written in Middle English with Latin opening and closing section. We may note that the modern concept of a pair of sheets already existed, from the notion of 'a peyre schetes of Reynes'. We take 'alle the tapites of sute' to denote a set. Also, we note that 'towailes longynge to the auter' may be cloths with which to clean the vessels rather than cloths that hang on the altar, though this remains ambiguous when we compare the decorated and long towel in will I.25. Printed in Furnivall (1964), 4–10. The translation is by Louise Sylvester.

Also I deuyse to Thomas my sone, a bed of tapicers werk, with alle the tapites of sute, red of colour, ypouthered with chapes and scochôns, in the corners, of myn Auncestres armes. with that .I. bequethe to the same Thomas, the stoffe longyng' therto, that is to seye, my beste fetherbed, and a blu caneuas, and a materas, and twey blankettys, and a peyre schetes of Reynes, with the heued shete of the same, and sex of my best pilwes, wich that he wol chese, and a bleu couertour of menyuer, and a keuerlet of red sendel ypouthered with Cheuerons. Also .I. bequethe to the same Thomas my sone, an Halle, with docere, costers and bankers, of sute of that forseyde bed. Also y bequethe to the same Thomas my sone, a peyre Matyns bookis, and a peire bedes, and a rynge with which y was yspoused to god, which were my lordes his faderes. Also .I. deuyse to Iohane my doughter, my sone-is wyf, a bed paled blak and whit, with the tapites of sute, and the stoffe of the bed, that is to seye, my secunde best fetherbed, with caneuas materas, twey blanketes, a peyre shetis of Reynes, with the heued shete of the same, and a blu couertour of grys, and .iij. the beste pilwes after choys of the forseyde Thomas my sone. [. . .] Also I bequethe to the same Iohane alle my vestymentz of my chapell, with the towailes longynge to the auter', and my tapites whit and rede paled, and blu and red paled, with alle my grene tapites that longeth to my chapell forsayd, and with the frontels of the forsayd auter', and with alle the rydelles and trussynge cofres, and alle other apparaile that longeth to my chapelle forsayd. [. . .] Also .I. deuyse to [. . .] Alianore my doughter, a tawne bed of silk with hool celure and four curtyns of sute, and a keuerlit of selk ypoynet in that on side tawne, and in that other side blu; and the stoffe of the bed ther-wyth. that is to seye, my thridde beste fetherbed, with caneuas materas, twey blankettes, a payre shites of reynes, with an heuedshite of sute, and iij pilwes. [. . .] Also .I. bequethe xl. li to do make a vestiment, after deuys of my forsayd sone, to the cops of the hows of Crischerche wher' my body schal ligge, to bidde, and to rede and synge for my lordes soule forsayd, and myn, and for alle cristene soules while the world schal laste. and .I. wol that the same vestiment be mad and deliuered to the same hows of Crischerche withynne twelf moneth next after my deces.

22. The will of Robert Aueray

Date: 1410. Written in Middle English, with formal Latin opening and closing sections. Aueray was a member of the Cordwainers' Company, London. The Cordwainers' Company was the guild of shoemakers, one of the oldest livery companies in London. It took its name from cordwain, the finest goatskin leather, originating in Cordoba in Spain. The will includes gifts of two gowns and

Also I bestow on my son Thomas a bed of tapestry work, with all the tapestries of the set, red, scattered with metal mountings and coats of arms, in the corners, of my ancestor's arms. With that I bequeath to the same Thomas the furnishings that belong to it, that is to say my best featherbed, and a blue cloth sheet, and a mattress and two blankets, and a pair of Rheims linen sheets, with the head sheet of the same and six of my best pillows, whichever he chooses and a blue bedspread of miniver, and a coverlet of red silk scattered with chevrons. Also I bequeath to the same Thomas (my son), a hall hanging with dorsals, costers and seat covers to match the above-mentioned bed. Also I bequeath to the same Thomas (my son) a pair of matins books and a rosary, and a ring with which I was married to God, which belonged to my lord, his father. Also I bestow on Joan my daughter-in-law, a black and white striped bed, with the tapestries to match, and the furnishings of the bed, that is to say, my second-best featherbed, with canvas mattress, two blankets, a pair of Rheims linen sheets, with the matching head-sheet, and a blue bedspread of grey squirrel fur and the three best pillows remaining after my son Thomas's choice mentioned above. [. . .] Also I bequeath to the same Joan all the vestments of my chapel, with the cloths pertaining to the altar and my white and red striped and blue and red striped tapestries, with all my green tapestries that belong to my above-mentioned chapel, and with the frontals of the above-mentioned altar, and with all the curtains and packing chests and all the other equipment that belongs to my chapel mentioned above. [. . .] Also I bestow on [. . .] Alianore my daughter, a bed of tawny coloured silk, with full canopy and four matching curtains, and an embroidered silk coverlet with one side tawny and the other blue; and the furnishings of the bed with it, that is to say, my third best featherbed, with canvas mattress, two blankets, a pair of Rheims linen sheets with a matching headsheet and three pillows. [. . .] Also I bequeath 40 pounds to have a vestment made according to the design of my above-mentioned son for the copes of the house of Christchurch where my body shall lie, to pray and to read and sing for my above-mentioned lord's soul, and mine, and for all Christian souls while the world shall endure. And I wish the same vestment to be made and delivered to the same house of Christchurch within the year following my death.

hoods of the Cordwainers' livery. Bequests which are not related to cloth and clothing have been included here as they offer a context for the dress and textile bequests as well as a good indication of the legal language in which wills were frequently couched in this period. Printed in Furnivall (1964), 16–17. The translation is by Louise Sylvester.

Also y be-queþe to William Begelon a grene Gowne and a hoyd' percyd' wyth Ray, of the Cordywynerys leueray [. . .] Also y be-queþe to Johon Wyot a gowne and a hoyd of þe Cordewaneres leueray of .ij. Coloures, and also a postnet þat y lent hym / Also y be-queþe to herry Cole, a blewe gownne and peyr' of Rede hosyn / Also y be-queþe al þe Resydue of my godys to Ione my wyff, for to beyn myn' Executorice Cheff, and Iohn Robert oflondon' / for to ben Executour wyth her' / & y be-queþe to the same Iohn Robert/ iij. s. iiij d for hys trauayl, doyng for me as he wyll ansuere by-fore god / [. . .] Also I wele þat Herry cole, taylour, duellyng wyt-outen temple barre, be on of myne executours, & I be-queþe to hym, þe same herry cole, for hys trauayle .iij. s. iiij d.

23. The will of Sir William Langeford, knight

Date: 1411. Written in Middle English with Latin formal opening and closing sections. There are a number of (technical) terms for pieces of armour in Anglo-French, as we would expect in this period: 'paunce', 'rerebrace', 'vambrace', 'ventaile'. Here the testator also appears to be leaving his wife her own clothes. Printed in Furnivall (1964), 18–21. The translation is by Louise Sylvester.

[. . .] Also y be-qweythe to lucye my wyfe, [. . .] alle þe vtensyl of myn hows, þat ys to say, in halle, in Chambre, in Pantrie and Botrie, in larder and Kechyn, with alle hire apparure, þat ys to say, in cloþing', rynges, and alle oþer ornamentes, what so þey be, [. . .] Also y be-queythe to Robert, myn' heldest son, a reed bedde of worsteyd, with costers þat langyth þere-to, enbrawde with whyte fete, with a canvase, a materas, a pare of Blankettes .ij. pare of schetys; Also a basynet with a ventaile, a pare of vambrace and rerebrace, a Pare of legge herneys, an holle brest-plate, a paunce of stele, a pare glovis of plate white. Also to Elyzabeth, wyfe of þe forseyd Robert, a boorde cloþe with .ij. towelles of deuaunt of oo sute. Also y be-queyth to William my son, an aburioun of stele with a pallette Couerte with reede velwette, a pare of glovys of plate blacke. Also to Henre my son', an aburioun, a ketil Hatte. [. . .]

24. The will of John Chelmyswyk, esq.

Date: 1418. Shropshire. Written in Middle English with Latin title and closing formula, the latter relating to the probate. This testator does not have vestments to leave; what is of interest here is that he appears to be ordering them to be made, the expense at the discretion of the executors. Printed in Furnivall (1964), 30–5. The translation is by Louise Sylvester.

[. . .] Also I bequethe to the werkis of the body of the Parysshchirche of Seint Marie Magdaleyn' of Quatford in Shropeshire, & to ordeyne vestmentis & ornamentis in the same Chirche nedefull, after the discrecioun of my Executours, so that my soule be recommended in Goddys seruice there, C s'. [. . .] Item I bequethe to do ordeyne & bye ij vestmentis to serue to the forsaide ij Prestes that shull singe for me in the forsaide Chaunterie in the Chirche of seint Leonarde in Briggenorth, xl. s'. Also I wille that after the forsayde ij

Also I bequeath to William Begelond a green gown and a hood variegated with striped material, of the cordwainers' livery. [...] Also I bequeath to John Wyot a parti-coloured gown and a hood of the cordwainers' livery, and also a cooking pot that I lent him. Also I bequeath to Herry Cole a blue gown and a pair of red hose. Also I bequeath all the residue of my goods to Joan my wife, to be my chief executor, and John Robert of London to be executor with her. And I bequeath to the same John Robert 3 shillings and 4 pence for his work, doing for me as he will answer before God. [...] Also I wish Herry Cole, tailor, living outside Temple Bar to be one of my executors, and I bequeath to him, the same Herry Cole, 3 shillings and 4 pence for his work.

[...] Also, I bequeath to my wife Lucy [...] all the utensils of my house, that is to say, of the hall, the chamber, the pantry and the buttery, the larder and kitchen, with all their apparel, that is to say clothing, rings and all other accessories, whatever they are. [...] Also I bequeath to my eldest son Robert a red worsted bed, with side curtains embroidered with white ends, with a canvas cloth, a mattress, a pair of blankets and two pairs of sheets. Also a basinet with a ventaile, a pair of vambrace and rerebrace, a pair of leg harness, a complete breast-plate, a steel paunce, a pair of white iron gauntlets. Also to Elizabeth, wife of the above-mentioned Robert, a tablecloth with two matching frontals. Also I bequeath to my son William a steel harbergeon with a helmet covered with red velvet, a pair of black iron gauntlets. Also to my son Henry, a harbergeon and a round iron helmet.

Also I bequeath to the works of the body of the parish church of St Mary Magdalene of Quatford in Shropshire 100 shillings, and to supply the same church with vestments and accessories as needed at the discretion of my executors, so that my soul will be commended to God's service there. [...] Likewise I bequeath to commission and buy two vestments for the above-mentioned two priests who shall sing for me in the above-mentioned chantry in the church of St Leonard in Bridgenorth, 40 shillings. Also I wish that after the above-

Prestes haue fulfilled here vij ȝere seruice aforsaide, that than' the forsaide ij. vestmentes shull remayne & duelle still alwey in the forsaide Chaunterie to serue the prestes of the same Chaunterie, to the worshipe of God, as so longe as they may endure. [. . .] Item I bequethe to Ionet my wyfe, in the name of here Dowerye & of here parte belonging to here of al my godes mobles, xl. li of sterlinges, and all my beddynge & naperie, and alle myne arraye & necessaries in my chambre, and alle othere meuable Godes ther-in beyng', and alle manere apparaillement & necessaries longynge to the body of the same Ionet, Outake Golde & syluer, & myne owne werynge clothes, ij peire of my best shetes, & vj disshes & vj Sawcers of seluer. The wyche shetes .I. bequeth, that is to say, a peire to Sire William Lochard, And the tother peire to Maister Ion Marchall, Dene of Briggenorth. [. . .] Item I bequethe to the same Ionet, my ffurre of Calabre my best Cheyne of Gold, a doseyn spones of siluer, and a pece of siluer. Item I bequethe to Iohn' Yate, myn vncle, vp condicioun that he be one of myn' Executours, & take ministracioun of thys testament, vj dysshes of siluer, & my best Girdill of siluer. Item I bequethe, vp the same condicion, to Iohn' Page of Oxenbolde, x li of sterlinges. Item I bequethe, vp the same condicioun, to Iohn' Lemman', Citezein & Skynner of London', x li of sterlinges, & my worstede Goune with þe ffurre, & my Baselard harneysed with siluer. Item I be-quethe, vp the same condicioun, to Iohn' Baldok, Citezein & Waxchaundeler' of London', x març, & my furre of Fycheux. Item I be-quethe to the wyf of þe forsaide Iohn' Lemman, my litill Cheyne of Gold that serueth for myne arms. [. . .] Item I bequethe to the werkis of the body of the Parisshe Chirche of Tasseley in Shropeshire, & to ordeyne vestmentes & ornamentes in the same Chirche nedeful, after the discrecion of myne Executours, so that my soule be recommendid There in goddys seruice, C s. Item I wolle that sire Iohn' Hogenes, person' of Tasseley, & Richard Crowder, haue and reioise alle the hustilmentis of Beddyng', hallyng', pottys & pannes, & peauter vessell þat I left in kepyng' atte hay & Briggenorth, To haue & holde for here Rewarde that I am holde to hem.

25. The will of Thomas Tvoky, esq.

Date: 1418.written in Middle English with Latin title. The will is incomplete (Furnivall 1964: 36): what seems to be missing is any mention of who the beneficiary or beneficiaries were to be. Printed in Furnivall (1964), 36–7. The translation is by Louise Sylvester.

I. Thomas Tvoky, þorow godis grace esquier, make my testament in þis wyse. first I. be-queþe my sowle to almyghty god, and to his moder & mayden Marie, and to all þe Seyntes of Heuen / also my body to Holy erthe, wher that godys wil is, to be buried; also al myn Harneys, þat is to say, a bed of Lyn wit a hool silour' and Couerlet of þe same wroght wit mapil leues and fret of .iij. foill, & iij. nettes of Silk grene for quirtayns for the same bed / also a bed of red and grene Selour wit .iij. quirtayns of worsted; also þat on in warde of Anneys Elyngton', and a paire of schetes, .ij. paire of Blancketes, .ij. paire of schetes, .j. pylow of Doun, lengh of a yerd, .ij. Pylows of doun, lengh eueryche of half a ȝerd; also .vj. reof quisshens of worsted, .iiij. in ward of þe same Anneys; also a Materas for a bed; also a gowne of Sch[a]rlet wit brod sleues furred with gray; also a gowne of blew worsted furred wit þrotes and polles of Martrons; Also a gowne of gray russet furred wit Ionetis and wylde Catis; also a gowne of grene frese, in ward, &c, furryd with blak Lambe; also in ward &c, a furre of beuer and oter

mentioned two priests have fulfilled their seven years of service mentioned above, that then the above-mentioned two vestments shall remain and always be kept in the above-mentioned chantry to serve the priests of the same chantry for the worship of God, as long as they live. [...] Likewise I bequeath to my wife Jonet, in the name of her dowry and of the share belonging to her of all my movable goods, 40 pounds sterling, and all my bedding and household linen and all my attire and necessities in my chamber all other movable goods that are in there and all kinds of dress and necessities belonging to the body of the same Jonet, except for gold and silver, and the clothes that I wear, two pairs of my best sheets and six silver dishes and six silver saucers. The which sheets I leave, that is to say, a pair to Sir William Lochard, and the other pair to Master Jon Marshall, dean of Bridgenorth. . [...] Likewise I bequeath to the same Jonet my Calabre squirrel fur, my best gold chain, a dozen silver spoons, and a piece of silver. Likewise I bequeath to John Yate, my uncle, on condition that he act as one of my executors, and take on the administration of this testament, six silver dishes and my best silver-studded girdle. Likewise I bequeath, on the same condition, 10 pounds in sterling to John Page of Oxenbold. Likewise I bequeath, on the same condition, 10 pounds sterling and my worsted gown with the fur trimming, and my baselard decorated with silver to John Lemman, citizen and skinner of London. Likewise I bequeath, on the same condition, 10 marks and my polecat fur to John Baldok, citizen and waxchandler of London. Likewise I bequeath to the wife of the above-mentioned John Lemman, my little gold chain that serves as my coat of arms. [...] Likewise I bequeath to the works of the body of the parish church of Tasley in Shropshire 100 shillings to supply vestments and accessories in the same church as necessary at the discretion of my executors so that my soul be commended there to God's service. Likewise I wish that Sir John Hogenes, parson of Tasley, and Richard Crowder, have and rejoice in all the items of bedding, wall-hangings, pots and pans and pewter vessels that I left in safekeeping at Hay and Bridgenorth, to have and hold for their reward that I owe them.

I, Thomas Tvoky, esquire (through God's grace), make my will in this manner. First, I bequeath my soul to almighty God, and to Mary, his mother and a maiden, and to all the saints of heaven. Also my body to the holy earth, to be buried wherever it is God's will. Also my bedding, that is to say, a bed of linen with a whole canopy and a coverlet of the same embroidered with maple leaves and an ornamental design of three leaves and three nettes of green silk for curtains for the same bed. Also a red bed with a green canopy with three worsted curtains; also the one in the keeping of Anneys Elyngton, and a pair of sheets, two pairs of blankets, two pairs of sheets, one down pillow a yard in length, two down pillows each half a yard in length; also six coarsely woven worsted cushions, four in the keeping of the same Anneys; also a mattress for a bed; also a scarlet gown with broad sleeves furred with grey; also a blue worsted gown trimmed with fur from the throats and heads of martens. Also a grey russet gown furred with civets and wild cats; also a green frieze gown in the medled; also a Hewk of grene and other melly parted; also a Doubeled of defence couered with red Leþer; also ij. remenauntz of the Lynne bed; [al]so .xij. quysshons; also a Cloke of Blake russet; Also a Dobelet couered with Blak gote Leþer'; also a bordcloth the Lenghe of .v. ȝerdes of werk; also a towayl of werk, Lenghe .xj. ȝerdes.

26. The will of Stephen Thomas

Date: 1417–18. Of Lee, Essex. Written in Latin and Middle English with Latin closing formula. The will and codicil were made at Rouen. The testator was on a journey, and the gifts include gowns and hoods, and goods from a ship. Printed in Furnivall (1964), 37–41. The translation is by Louise Sylvester.

and also I do ȝow to wyt þat yt is my will þat Thomas Chesse schel haue me ȝyf þat y dey in hys bote with hym̄; and also þat he schel haue my best gowen̄ of þe kynges liuere þat is at home at my hous, and my golde rynge and my whystell. and also I do ȝow to wyt þat yt is my will þat Thomas Albwe schel haue þe best gowen' next þat is at home after þat, and a houd. and also y do ȝow wyt þat it is my will þat George Thomas my Cousyn' schel haue all þe gude and þe harnesse þat y haue att Hampton' in þe chippe, and be-syde; and þis þat is of þe see with me att Roon' he schel haue, all to-gedyr', saue þat Rychard Smytheot schel haue my Russet gowen' þat y wered, and my blac houd, and a noldd bassenet.

27. The will of John Rogerysson

Date: 1419–20. Of London. Written in Middle English with Latin opening and closing formulae. Printed in Furnivall (1964), 41–2. The translation is by Louise Sylvester.

Thes beth the godes that y, Iohn' Rogerysson', leve in a chyste in the hous of Roberd Leget dwellyng in the parysh of seynt Benet Fynk // And þis ys my wylle yf þat y dye, that Anneys Tukkys-worthe have þe beste bedbere, and Richard Gery þe nyxte, and Roberd Legat ij payre of schetis, and to þe same Roberd my Blewe gowne and my hode of Rede and Blak; And to Thomas Pykot my whit Ray gowne, and my rede Hode; and to Anneys Tukkysworth my best bordclothe, and the Towayle; and Rychard Gery the nexte bordclothe And Towayle; and Robard Legat iij quarters of white and Isabell hys wyf a bordcloth and a towayle; and to Wyllyam Pertnale, A payre schetis and a red doblet, and a keverlet of Blewe; And to Anneys Tukkysworth iiij noblis and the forseyd Cheste; And to Thomas Pertenall a peyre of shetis, and a dagger', and a Bowe wyth-owte pecis, and a payre hosen' of grene; and to Anneys Tukkys-worth the beste purse, and Thomas Pertnale the nyxte, and Isabell Leget the Thridde, and Alson' Okenden' the fourþe. And alle-so y bequethe to þe Church of seynt Benet a cope. [. . .] and my Sylvryn' Gyrdyll to Thomas Pertnale;

keeping, etc. trimmed with black lambskin; also in the keeping etc. a fur garment made from alternating beaver and otter fur; also a green hooded cloak in mi-parti, green and medley; also a padded doublet covered with red leather; also two remaining items belonging to the linen bed; also twelve cushions; also a black russet cloak; also a doublet covered with black goatskin leather; also an embroidered tablecloth 5 yards long; also an embroidered cloth, 11 yards long.

and also I want you to know that it is my wish that Thomas Chesse have my body if I die in his boat with him; and also that he have my best gown of the king's livery that is at home in my house, and my gold ring and my whistle. And also I want you to know that it is my wish that Thomas Albwe have the next best gown that is in my home, and a hood. And also I want you to know that it is my wish that George Thomas my cousin have all the goods and the clothing that I have at Hampton in the ship, and everything else; and that which is of the sea with me at Rouen he shall have, all together, except that Rychard Smytheot shall have my woollen gown that I wore, and my black hood, and an old helmet.

These are the goods that I, John Rogeryssone, leave in a trunk in the house of Robert Leget now living in the parish of St Benet Fink. And this is my will if I die, that Anneys Tukkysworthe have the best bedcover, and Richard Gery the next best, and Robert Legat two pairs of sheets, and I leave to the above-mentioned Robert my blue gown and my red and black hood. And to Thomas Pykot my white striped gown and my red hood; and to Anneys Tukkysworthe my best tablecloth, and the towel; and to Rychard Gery the next best tablecloth and towel; and to Robert Legat three quarters of white cloth and to Isabelle his wife a tablecloth and a towel; and to Wyllyam Pertnale, a pair of sheets and a red doublet, and blue coverlet; and to Anneys Tukkysworthe 4 nobles and the above-mentioned trunk; and to Thomas Pertenall a pair of sheets, and a dagger, and a bow made of one piece of wood, and a pair of green hose; and to Anneys Tukkysworthe the best purse, and to Thomas Pertnale the next best, and to Isabelle Leget the third and to Alison Okenden the fourth. And also I bequeath to the church of St Benet a cope [this may denote a request that a cope be made for the church] and my silver girdle to Thomas Pertnale.

28. The will of Thomas Bathe

Date: 1420. Of Bristol. Written in Middle English with Latin opening and closing formulae. Gifts in this will include shearings and wool. Bathe owns material in the process of being manufactured: fleeces and white (as yet undyed) cloth. These seem to be part of his stock in trade rather than personal possessions. Printed in Furnivall (1964), 45–7. The translation is by Louise Sylvester.

Also I ȝeue to þe forsayd Iohn Forster a gurdill of blake sylke y-linyde with rede lether, with a gode bokyll & a pendaunt, & in þe same pendaunt an ymage of seynt Christofre: in þe gurdill bey xlvj stodys of seluer. [...] Also I ȝeve to Kateryne Lewys my seruaunt [...] Also a gurdyll of þe old werke of seluer, & ouerguld, with a bocull and a pendaunt and xxxiij. stodys of syluer and ouerguld. Also I ȝeve to þe same Kateryne aneyuer gurdil of selke, of blake and grene and rede, with a bocull and a pendaunt, & a cheyne in þe pendant, with a cnapp; & in þe gurdill bey xxiij stodys, & all of seluer. [...] Also .iiij. gode golde rynges, [...] Also I ȝeve to the forsad Kateryne al my bankerus & my quyssonus, and a dosur of tamsery werke with an hert in þe myddyll. [...] Also I ȝeue to Kateryne Lewys my seruaunt iij. Curteynis of blew, þe best þat I haue to hang a-bout a bede; [...] Item dimidium þe zieren. and wolle that is in this house þe day of his dying, and all þe cloth . whyte&c þat is redy with-in þe hous att tyme of þe makyng of thys.

29. The will of John Olney

Date: 1420, proved, 1422. Of Weston. Written in Middle English with Latin title and closing formula. Printed in Furnivall (1964), 47–8. The translation is by Louise Sylvester.

and I bequeth to v poure men þat neden Beddyng. in the countrey nexst aboute, to euery off heme .I couerlete. I wytele, & I chete. & xij. d. off siluer, preyng for my soule, and for þe souleȝ be-forsaide.

30. The will of Lady Peryne Clanbowe

Date: 1422. Written in Middle English with Latin title and closing formula. Printed in Furnivall (1964), 49–51. The translation is by Louise Sylvester.

Also I bequeth, to cloth wyth ijc. poormen, xx. li. [...] Also I bequeth to þe same Robert a westment of rede cloth-of-gold with my massbooke and Chalys: The wych vessell, vestement, massbooke, and chalys aforseyd, to þe forsaide Roberd bequethen, I wole þat [he] haue hem vpon this condicion, þat he be good frend to my executours, and þat he lete hem note off ministracion off myn other goode on the Manere of Pychardisokell ne elles where. [...] Also I bequeth to sir Ion Skydmore, my newewe, a girdell of peerles. [...] Also I bequeeth to Iankyn Myles my seruaunt, xxli./, and myn eche daies gowne of marterount. Also I bequeth to sir Iohan Coyle, I pare bedes of corall. Also I bequeth to Elizabeth Ioye .x. li. and a booke of Englyssh, cleped pore caytife, and I gown furred with gret menyvere. Also I bequeth to Ionet Okbourn .x març and my sauter' helid with blake, and a gown furred with Cristy gray. [...] Also I bequeth to the wyffe of Iankyn' Miles a gown furred with Besshe. [...] Also I bequeth to þe chirch of ȝasore, fore my lord and his aunceteres, to serue in þe chirch, a peire vestimentis of blake, wherof þe same Chirch hath þe cope.

Also I give to the above-mentioned John Forster a black silk girdle lined with red leather, and with a good buckle and a pendant with an image of St Christopher in it: there are 46 silver studs in the girdle. [...] Also I give to my servant Katherine Lewys [...] also a silver and gilt girdle of the old fashion with a buckle and pendant and 33 silver and gilt studs. Also I give to the same Katherine another black, green and red silk girdle with a buckle and pendant, and a chain in the pendant with a tassel; and there are 23 studs, all silver, in the girdle. [...] Also four good gold rings [...], also I leave to the above-mentioned Katherine all my tapestry seat coverings and cushions and my embroidered dorser with a hart in the middle. [...] I also leave to my servant Katherine Lewys three blue curtains, the best that I have, to hang round a bed [...] Likewise half the shearings and wool that are in the house on the day of his dying and all the white cloth, etc. that is ready within the house at the time of the making of this will.

and I bequeath to five poor men who need bedding in the region close by, each of them to have one bedspread, one blanket, and one sheet and 12 pence of silver, praying for my soul and for the souls mentioned above.

Also I bequeath 20 pounds to clothe two hundred poor men. [...] Also I bequeath to the same Robert [Sir Robert of Whitney, testator's brother] a vestment of red cloth-of-gold with my mass book and chalice: the which vessel, vestment, mass book and chalice mentioned above bequeathed to the above-mentioned Robert, I wish him to have on this condition that he is a good friend to my executors, and that he does not prevent them administering my other goods on the manor estate of Ocle Pychard [Herefordshire], nor elsewhere. [...] Also I bequeath to Sir John Skydmore, my nephew, a girdle covered with pearls. [...] Also I bequeath to Jankyn Myles my servant 20 pounds and my everyday gown of marten fur. Also I bequeath to Sir John Coyle, one coral rosary. Also I bequeath to Elizabeth Joy 10 pounds and an English book called 'Poor Wretch', and one gown furred with squirrel. Also I bequeath to Jonet Okbourn 10 marks and my psalter covered with black cloth, and a gown furred with grey. [...] Also I bequeath to the wife of Jankyn Miles a gown furred with byse. [...] Also I bequeath to the church of Yazor, for the sake of my lord and his ancestors, a pair of black vestments, of which the same church has the cope, to serve in the church.

31. The will of Sir Roger Salwayn, knight, of York

Date: 1420. Written in Middle English with Latin title and closing formula. Printed in Furnivall (1964), 52–4. The translation is by Louise Sylvester.

Also I will þat þe forsaid freres [the grey friars of York] haue all my gownes off cloth off gold and off sylke, with-outyn þe ffurres. [. . .] Also I will .þat Pomfretth, skynner, of ʒorke, be paied of v. or vj. li, whedir þat hit be, for furres þat my lady my moder knowes off. Also I will þat William Tropmell, taillour, of London', and Hunt, brouderere, be paied of their billes for makyng off a liuerey of myn. Also I will þat Henry Lound haue a blake goun furred vi funes, and a habirgoun of Mylen, opyn be-for, þat Richard Stell haues in hys kepyng. [. . .] Also I will þat Gerard my brothir haue a newe fure of martirs, and I. habirgoun of millon'. Also I will þat Iohan my brothir haue I habirgoun of Gesseran. [. . .] Also I will þat all þe ffurrurs þat I haue, be sould and doon for my saule. Also I will þat Chace haue a habirion of myne.

32. The will of Roger Flore (or Flower), esq.

Date: 1424–5. Of London, and Oakham, Rutlandshire. Written in Latin with Middle English codicil (extracted here) and Latin closing formula. This will is interesting in that it lists full sets of household furnishings such as bedding, often naming each constituent, including a bed for the children made up of a 'couerlide' (coverlet or bedspread), 'tapite' (a piece of decorative fabric bearing a painted, embroidered, or woven pattern or figures and used as a coverlet or bed hanging), 'blankettis' (blankets or bed covers), two sets of sheets, a mattress and a 'canvas' (a sheet of fabric used for bedding). Note also the phrase 'my newe vestment þat I made last': the testator appears to have recently commissioned a vestment. Printed in Furnivall (1964), 55–64. The translation is by Louise Sylvester.

Also I wul he haue al myn other houshoold þat I haue atte Londen, except my bed of Tapistree, þe which I wull my welbeloved wife Cecile haue; þe which houshold is in myn In, in keping of my seruaunt Rolleston by bille endented, of which þe oone bille is in my trussing cofer'. I wol also my sayd sone Thomas haue my paled bed of wursted, white and rede, withþe costers þe which seruen for my chambre I lye Inne atte Okeham, and a rede bed of wursted with þe costers the which hengen in þe newe chamber' next my chamber'; and I wull he haue to þe oone bed a peyre fustyans, and to þe oþer a peyre blankettis, and to ilk of þe too beddis too peyre schetys goode, and a matras and a canvas; and I wull he haue oon fetherbed; and I wull he haue too seruauntes beddys for þe too said chambers. I wull also he haue too fyne bordeclothes, þe one of werk, þe oþer playn, with goode sanapes and wasshyngtowels, boþe for befor' mete and after'. [. . .] and too cors bordcloþes, and too peire cors sanapes, [. . .] and I wul þat ilk of my said childre haue a bed, þat is to say, couerlide, tapite, blankettis, too peyre schetes, matras, and canvas. And þan wul I þat my welbeloued wyfe Cecile haue alle þe remenaunt of my syluere vessell, pottes, peces, and spones, basyn and Ewer' of siluere, powderbox and salers of siluere, beddyng', napery and pewter vessell, brasse spytes, rakkes and branderne of erne; and all myn other howshold, saf suche as longeth to þe gamerye, I wul abyde to myn heyr'. [. . .] Also I wul þat my gownes for my body, þe which ben ffurred whith pelure, be dalt amongis my childre, to ilke after here degre and age, so þat Thomas and Anneys haue four' of þe best. And I wul þat þe

Also I wish the above-mentioned friars [the grey friars of York] to have all my gowns of cloth-of-gold and of silk, but not the furs. [...] Also I wish Pomfretth, skinner, of York to be paid the 5 or 6 pounds, whichever it be for furs that my mother knows about. Also I wish the bills of William Tropmell, tailor, of London and Hunt, embroiderer, for making a livery of mine to be paid. Also I wish Henry Lound to have a black gown furred with stone-marten and a habergeon from Milan, open at the front, which Richard Stell has in his keeping. [...] Also I wish my brother Gerard to have a new marten fur and one habergeon from Milan. Also I wish my brother Johan to have one coat of scale armour. [...] Also I wish all the furs I have to be sold for the sake of my soul. Also I wish Chace to have one of my habergeons.

Also I wish him [son Thomas] to have all the other household goods that I have in London except my tapestry bed which I wish my beloved wife Cecile to have; the which household is in my inn in the keeping of my servant Rollesten, indented by a bill, of which one copy is in my travelling box. I also wish my son Thomas, already mentioned, to have my bed of red and white striped worsted with the hangings from the room I sleep in at Oakham, and a bed of red worsted with the hangings which hang in the new room next to my room; and I wish him to have a pair of fustian blankets for one bed and a pair of blankets for the other bed, and two pairs of good sheets for each of the two beds and a mattress and a canvas and I wish him to have one featherbed; and I wish him to have two servant's beds for the two rooms mentioned. I also wish him to have two fine tablecloths, one embroidered, the other plain with good table runners and washing-towels, both before the meal and afterwards, [...] and two coarse tablecloths and two pairs of coarse table runners. [...] And I wish each of my above-mentioned children to have a bed: that is to say, bedspread, hanging, blankets, two pairs of sheets, mattress, and a canvas. And then I wish my beloved wife Cecile to have all the rest of my silver vessels, pots, pieces, and spoons, basins and jugs of silver, powderbox and silver saltcellars, bedding, linen, pewter vessels, brass roasting spits and their supports and iron trivets; and all the remainder of my household goods, except those that belong to the farm, I wish to be inherited by my heirs. [...] Also I wish my gowns that I wear which are furred to be shared among my children, to each according to their rank and age, so that

remenaunt of my cloþes for my body be dalt amonges my seruauntes,—of þe which I wul that Thomas Campion be þought on—to ilke after þeyr degrees. And .I. wul þat Robert my son haue oon of my swerdes, and one of my basilardes harneysed with siluere, and one of my siluere girdeles. And I wul þat Thomas my sone haue myn oþer siluere girdell, and myn oþer wepen and armerur'. [. . .] And I wul þat Anneys Samon, my wyfes moder, Margeret Spriggy, and Alys Rowele and Ionet Humberstone, Beatrice Swetenham, myn aunte, and my cosin Sithynge, half ilk of hem a gode goldringe, or a broche of gold, or a good peyr' of bedys, for a remembraunce of me. And I wil þe Maister' of Manton haf my pair' of bedys þat I vse my self, with þe x aues of siluere, and a pater noster ouer-gilt, preying him to haue mynde of me sumtime whan he seith oure lady sawter on hem.

First I wul and ordeyne that my ioint feffeȝ of my maners of Stenby and Braceby, with here appurtenaunces, in Lin[c]olne-shire, suffre my wyfe Cecile haue þe profiteȝ of þeim all þe while she lyveþ sool withoute husbond. And if she take þe mantel and þe rynge, and avowe chastite, than wul I þat forth-whith my said ioint feffes make her astate, for terme of hir' lif, of þe same too lordshipes, vp condicion þat she lyve sool, withoute husbond; [. . .] my wille is also þat my newe vestment þat I made last, be deliuered to myn Auter' in þe kyrke, þer to serue and abide in remembraunce of me while it wul endure, to þe wurshipe of god.

33. The will of William Newland

Date: 1425. Of London and Normandy. Written in Middle English with Latin opening and closing formulae. Newland was making his will before going on a journey. Printed in Furnivall (1964), 65–6. The translation is by Louise Sylvester.

and also it is my will þat Elianor of Coton' haue C març to her mariage, and a browded bed wiþ þe costures þerto

34. The will of John Credy, esq.

Date: 1426. Of London, Devonshire, etc. Written in Middle English with Latin title and closing formula. Printed in Furnivall (1964), 73–7. The translation is by Louise Sylvester.

Also I woll þat þe chirch of Newton haue my masseboke, my portus, my chaleys, my vestmentȝ, and my cruettis, [. . .] Of all my meuable godes which I haue, except my cloþing & harneys, I wol þat my wife haue half. [. . .] Also þat Richard Burdon, Skynner, haue x mark, a habergeon, a swerd harnesed, a wodeknyf harnesed, and a Dagger. Also I woll þat Alison Burdon his sister, haue a blewe bedde of Tapecery, a peir' blankettis, ij peir' shetys, & a selour with curteyns of carde. Also I woll þat Richard Burdon, skynner, haue a white bedde with roses, I peir' of shetis. [. . .] Also I woll þat Richard Quatremains haue my cheyne of gold, & my lesse swerd harneised.

Thomas and Anneys have four of the best. And I wish the remainder of the clothes that I wear to be shared among my servants, among whom I wish Thomas Campion to be included, to each according to their rank. And I wish my son Robert to have one of my swords and one of my daggers decorated with silver, and one of my girdles woven with silver thread. And I wish my son Thomas to have my other silver girdle and my other weapons and armour. [...] And I wish Anneys Samon, my wife's mother, Margeret Spriggy, Alys Rowele, Ionet Humberstone, Beatrice Swetenham, my aunt, and my cousin Sithynge each to have a good gold ring, or a gold brooch or a good rosary, as a memento of me. And I wish the Master of Manton to have the rosary that I myself use, with the ten silver rosary beads and a gilded rosary, praying that he think of me when he says the set of prayers on them.

First I wish and ordain that those jointly invested in trust with my manorial estates of Stainby and Braceby, with their rights, in Lincolnshire, allow my wife Cecile to have the profits from them as long as she lives alone without a husband. And if she takes the mantle and ring of ecclesiastical life and makes a vow of chastity then I wish my trustees to grant her a life interest in the two manors on condition that she lives alone without a husband. [...] My wish is also that the new vestment that I had made most recently be delivered to my altar in the church, to serve and remain there in remembrance of me, as long as it lasts, to honour God.

And also it is my wish that Elianor of Coton have 100 marks for her marriage and an embroidered bed with its side-curtains.

Also I wish the church of Newton to have my mass book, my portable breviary, my chalice, my vestments and my small ecclesiastical vessels. [...] I wish my wife to have half of all my movable goods except my clothing and bedding. [...] Also that Richard Burdon, skinner, have 10 marks, a habergeon, a sword with decorated hilt, a woodknife with decorated handle, and a dagger. Also I wish Alison Burdon, his sister, to have a blue bed with tapestry work, a pair of bedspreads, two pairs of sheets, and a canopy with linen curtains. [...] Also I wish Richard Burdon, skinner, to have a white bed with a pattern of roses, one pair of sheets. Also I wish Richard Quatremeains to have my gold chain and my smaller sword with decorated hilt.

35. The will of John Toker

Date: 1428. Of London. Vintner. Written in Middle English with opening and closing Latin formulae. The will specifies that Toker's clothing is to be sold and money divided among the bedridden. There was a lively trade in second-hand clothes in this period, especially in London; see Staples (2010). Printed in Furnivall (1964), 77–9. The translation is by Louise Sylvester.

Also I wil that the same Henry [Henry Thommissone, apprentice] haue in possession to his profite and easment duryng an hool ȝere next aftur myn obit day, Alle the encrece that is comyng of my wyne a-boue the stok, And more ouer all my peces and kuppes of siluer, peuder pottes, Naapri, and all the vtensilmentes longyng to my kechyn, as for that forsaid ȝer enduryng. [...] Also I wil that myn aray and clothyng to my body longyng, a-non' aftur my deces be sold, And the monei ther-of comyng & taken, I wil that hit be deuided and parted among pouere folk lieng bedred, and in other werkes of charite most plesyng to god and to the helthe of my soule.

36. The will of Isabel Gregory

Date: 1431–2. Of Hackney. Written in Middle English with Latin title and closing formula. The church of Isabel's burial and her executors are among the beneficiaries. Printed in Furnivall (1964), 91–2. The translation is by Louise Sylvester.

I, Isabel Gregory, I be-quethe my soule to god Almygthy, and to owre lady sent Mary, and all the company of heuen, & my body to be beryit in sent Austynyscherchhawe of Hakeney. I be-quethe the hey auter a bord-cloth is iij ȝerdys of lenthe or mor, (the tother is xj ȝerdys of lenthe). also I be-quethe the bed that I lyin in, to Aneys New-kole, saf the materas: that schall Idany Hale haue. I be-quethe to Iohn of the spetill, a schete, and a bras pot of a galon, and an old panne. al-so I be-quethe the [same] Idany a bofet; and to the same Idony, ij cosyonys. alsoI be-quethe to Ione my dowter, a blew goune and a grene kyrtyll, and a schete. al-so I be-quethe to I [so] Idany of the spetill, my wode and my Cole. also, I make and ordeyne that Will Seluester haue the gouernaunce. of all other godys that I have be-syde, I make a fre ȝefte to Will Seluester to selle, and to ȝeve for my soule and all Crystyne soulys, in the best maner that may ben' ordeynyt. al-so I be-quethe to Ionet Seluester a blake cote, furryd. allso I be-quethe to Thomas Formannis wyf a russet gounne lynyt with whythe blanket. also to Idany Hale a cloke and a gounne of russet, furrit.

37. The will of John Barnet

Date: 1433. Of London, Draper. Written in Middle English with Latin title and closing Latin formula. Again a testator is instructing that his clothing be sold for charitable purposes. Printed in Furnivall (1964), 93–4. The translation is by Louise Sylvester.

Also I beqwethe to my poore tenauntes, my govnys [to] be partyd after the devys of myn executours aboveseyd, everich of hem a govne. Also I will that my sangvyn govne be sold, & do for my sovle.

Also I wish that the same Henry [Henry Thommissone, apprentice] have in possession for his profit and comfort during the whole of the year following the day of my death all the earnings that arise from my labour above the basic stock. And moreover all my pieces and cups of silver, pewter pots, household linen and all the utensils belonging to my kitchen lasting for that above-mentioned year. And also I wish that all my clothing and the clothes belonging to my body be sold soon after my death and the money arising from that sale having been collected, I wish it to be divided and shared among poor people lying bed-ridden, and for other works of charity most pleasing to God for the health of my soul.

I, Isabel Gregory, bequeath my soul to God Almighty, and to Our Lady St Mary, and all the company of heaven and my body to be buried in St Augustine's church in the borough of Hackney. I bequeath a table-cloth that is 3 yards in length or more (the other is 11 yards in length) to the high altar. Also I bequeath to Aneys Newkole the bed that I sleep in, except for the mattress, that is for Idany Hale. I bequeath to John of the poorhouse a sheet and a brass gallon-pot and an old pan. Also I bequeath the same Idany a stool, and to the same Idany two cushions. Also I bequeath a blue gown and a green kirtle and a sheet to my daughter Joan. Also I bequeath my wood and my coal to Idany of the poorhouse. Also I ordain that Will Selvester have administrative control of all additional goods that I have. I make these a free gift to Will Selvester to sell and to give for my soul and for all Christian souls in the best way that may be ordained. Also I bequeath a black furred coat to Ionet Selvester. Also I bequeath a russet cloth gown lined with undyed wool cloth to Thomas Formann's wife. Also a cloak and a russet cloth furred gown to Idany Hale.

Also I bequeath my gowns to my poor tenants to be divided according to the plan made by my executors mentioned above, a gown to each of them. Also I wish my blood-red gown to be sold for the sake of my soul.

38. The will of Walter Mangeard

Date: 1433. Of London and Sussex, Cook. Written in Middle English with Latin title and closing Latin formula. This testator appears to be bequeathing a gown which he himself owned and wore to another man seemingly outside his family. Printed in Furnivall (1964), 94–5. The translation is by Louise Sylvester.

Item y foryeve & relese Walter Floode, Brewer, all the dette thet he oweht me. Item y bequethe to Iohn Floode his sone, oon' of my govnes longyng to my body, suche as myn' executours wyll deliuere.

39. The will of Margarete Asshcombe (once Bloncit)

Date: 1434. Of London, Widow. Written in Middle English with Latin title and closing formula. The testator bequeaths a sheet which is to be painted and used as two ecclesiastical hangings. Printed in Furnivall (1964), 96–7. The translation is by Louise Sylvester.

Also y bequethe to the Person of the churche of seynt Marie Stanyng in London, iij s' iiij d. Also y bequethe to the makyng or amendyng of the seyde churche, iij s' iiij d. Also y bequethe a shete to the seyde Chirche, to be peynted at the persons coste aforeseyde, forto hange to-fore ij auteres in the seyde Churche. [...] Also y bequethe to the wyf of William Oweyn' a ryng of golde with a ston, & a reson 'sans departir'. Also y bequethe to the wyf of William Hoton my cosyn', a ryng of golde with a crucifix abovne. also y be-quethe to Clemens, the woman that kepes me, a gowne of Musterdevylers, & a kyrtell of musterdevylers with grene sleues, & an hode of blak of lure, & an hod of blewe. [...] alsoo y bequethe to Aneys Copursmyth a combe of yverie, & to Aneys hir' mayden', a russet kyrtell furred with lambe.

40. The will of Roger Elmesley

Date: 1434. Of London, Waxchandler's Servant. Written in Middle English with Latin title and closing formula. Printed in Furnivall (1964), 100–2. The translation is by Louise Sylvester.

& to Iohn Woderof my beste goune & my beste hod, & the forre in the same goune, if so be that he leue that time; & elles, sell hit, & do hit for the loue of god, & yeue to pore housholders in coles. More-ouer y bequethe to Robert Sharp goddis-child, a litell fetherbed & ij peire smale shetes, & a peyre of large shetes goode, & a peire of blankettes, & ij goode pelewes, on large, & another lasse and feire ybored, & a whit couerlit & a red couerlit, & a good bordcloth with crosse werk, & another bordcloth with mylyngis at the ton' ende, in lenkethe ij ʒerdes; & on halfe large, & I towell of parys werk, viij yerdes of lenkethe; also too the beste sanapes, [...] & a bankar of blewe & blak, & iij quisshonus of the same colour vn-stopped; [...] also a peyre off bedes of siluer with a crucifix of siluer and y-gilt; also a payre bedes of blak gaudys of siluer & gilt, & a ryng' ther-on with clippyng' of ij handes, siluir & gilt.

Likewise I forgive and release Walter Flood, brewer, from all the debt that he owes me. Likewise I bequeath to John Flood his son one of the gowns which belongs to me, which my executors will deliver to him.

Also I bequeath to the clergyman of the church of St Mary Staining in London 3 shillings and 4 pence. Also I bequeath 3 shillings and 4 pence for the building or improvement of the said church. Also I bequeath a cloth to the said church to be painted at the aforesaid clergyman's cost, to hang before two altars [as altar frontal or as a banner in front of the chapel] in the said church [church of St Mary Staining] in London. [...] Also I bequeath a gold ring with a gemstone and the motto 'sans departir' to the wife of William Oweyn. Also I bequeath to the wife of William Hoton my cousin a gold ring with a crucifix above. Also I bequeath to Clemens, my housekeeper, a musterdevillers gown and a kirtle of musterdevillers with green sleeves and a hood of black cloth of Lierre, and a blue hood. [...] Also I bequeath to Aneys Copursmyth an ivory comb, and to Aneys her maid a russet gown trimmed with lambswool.

And to John Woodruff, if he is still alive at that time, my best gown and my best hood, and the fur in the gown, and if not, sell it and do so for the love of God, and give coal to poor householders. Moreover, I bequeath to my godchild, Robert Sharp, a little featherbed and two pairs of small sheets, and a pair of good large sheets, and a pair of bedcovers, and two good pillows, one large and another smaller, beautifully embroidered and a white coverlet, and a red coverlet, and a good tablecloth of patterned linen and another tablecloth 2 yards long with stripes on one end, and one half as large [in length], and one towel of Paris work, 8 yards in length; also two of the best table-runners [...] and a blue and black seat cover and three unstuffed cushions in the same colour [...] also a silver rosary with a silver and gilt crucifix; also a black rosary with large silver and gilt gauds, and a silver and gilt ring on it with clasping of two hands.

41. The will of Richard Bokeland, esq.

Date: 1436. Of All-Hallows the Greater, Thames Street, London. Written in Middle English with Latin title and closing formula. Printed in Furnivall (1964), 104–8. The translation is by Louise Sylvester.

All-so y wol that Thomas Rothewell haue myn Prymour & myn purple goune furred with martrons. All-so I wol that Iohn Melbourne haue my scarlet goune furred with martrouns.

42. The will of Richard Dixton, esq.

Date: 1438. Of Siscetre (Cirencester). Written in Middle English with Latin closing formula. The will includes a bequest of secular clothes to be turned into ecclesiastical vestments and the testator leaves cloth as well as clothing. Note the 'gowne furred with foynes': fur was used to line garments and it was deliberately exposed at the edges; sometimes better fur was stitched to the parts that showed. Also the 'slyt slyues y-furred': the sleeves have been slit to show the fur lining beneath, or the sleeves are slit for fashionable reasons and fur edges the slit (but does not necessarily line them). Printed in Furnivall (1964), 108–12. The translation is by Louise Sylvester.

Furst, I bequeth my sowle vnto god almyghty, vnto the Blessyd Virgine his moder sainte Marie & to all the compaigne of heuene, & my body to be buryed withyn the new Chapell of the Trinite at Siscetre. Item I bequeth to the saide chapell of Siscetre a cloth of Siluer, and a blak cloth of Damask sengill, & a gowne of Goldsmythes werk, for to make vestimentes & a C gertiers. [...] Item to Robert Greyndoor, squyer, my Serpe of siluer and my cheyne of goold. Item to Iane Greyndoor' his wyf, a couered cuppe of siluer, the wich I was wont to drynk of, and a Bracelet of Gold. [...] Item to sir Iohn' Trebell my confessour, xx markes, to synge for me ij yere in an honest place, where so euer he wooll, and iiij yerdes of blew cloth. [...] Item to William Reuell a gowne of Blake, furred with ficheux beyng' at the Fasterne, [...] Item to Iohn' Mody a gowne of grene Damaske lyned, & a nother gowne of Russet furred with blak, & xl s'. [...] Item to Edmond of Cornewayle an ersgerdyll of siluer. Item to Iohn Russell, squyer, a gowne of Rede Damaske furred with martrens, [...] Item to my seruant Iohn' Buelt, vj markes, & I gowne of Russet medley furred wit blak. Item to my wyf, all my stuff beyng' at the Fasterne, except a sangwen' gowne furred with martres, and the thyngys abouen' rehersed. [...] Item to Elizabeth Belliers a scarlet gowne furred with foynes. [...] Item to the saide Watkyn' Hardyng' a gowne of scarlet with slyt slyues y-furred, [...] Item to the saide William Estynton' a scarlet gowne [...] Item, all my clothynge & werynge harneys and beddynge at Vsk, I woll that the saide Watkyn' and William departe by-twene hem & here felawes, as they seme that goode ys, & that they delyuery to Hew Dausey an hoby & a gowne of grene damaske, and to euery of myn other men' an hors, whiles ther ben eny.

43. The will of Nicholas Charleton

Date: 1439. Of London, Skinner. Written in Middle English with Latin closing formula. Bequests include a gown of the livery of the London company of Skinners. Printed in Furnivall (1964), 112–15. The translation is by Louise Sylvester.

Also I wish Thomas Rothewell to have my devotional manual and my purple gown furred with marten. Also I wish John Melbourne to have my dark red gown furred with marten.

First, I bequeath my soul to God Almighty, to the Blessed Virgin his mother St Mary and to all the company of heaven, and my body to be buried in the new chapel of the Trinity at Cirencester. Likewise I bequeath to the said chapel of Cirencester a cloth woven with silver thread and a cloth of black-coloured damask of single thickness and a gown of goldsmith's work to make vestments and a hundred garters. [...] Likewise to Robert Greyndoor, squire, my ornamental silver chain and my gold chain. Likewise to Jane Greyndoor his wife the covered silver cup which I generally drank from and a gold bracelet. [...] Likewise to Sir John Trebell my confessor 20 marks to sing masses for my soul for two years in a suitable place of his choosing, and 4 yards of blue cloth. [...] Likewise to William Revell a black gown furred with polecat which is at the Fasterne. [...] Likewise to John Mody a lined green damask gown and another russet gown furred with black and 40 shillings. [...] Likewise to Edmond of Cornwall a silver belt. Likewise to John Russell, squire, a red damask gown furred with marten. [...] Likewise to my servant John Buelt, 6 marks and one gown of russet medley cloth furred with black. Likewise to my wife, all my goods which are at the Fastern, except a blood-red gown furred with marten and the things mentioned above. [...] Likewise to Elizabeth Belliers a scarlet gown furred with stone marten. [...] Likewise to the said Watkyn Hardyng a scarlet gown with slit sleeves edged with fur. [...] Likewise to the said William Estynton a scarlet gown. [...] Likewise I wish the said Watkyn and William to divide between them and their friends, in the way that seems best to them, all my clothes and accessories and bedding at Usk, and that they deliver a small horse and a green damask gown to Hew Dausey, and a horse, while any remain, to each of my other men.

All-so I be-que*th* to Thomas Dymmok, Skynner, of Glowcestre, my best gowne of the lyuere of Skynners craft, bot*h* furre and cloth, yif he be alyve; And to Watkyn' Ass*h*well my secunde best furre and gowne /

44. The will of the Countess of Warwick

Abstracted in Nicolas (1826), i. 239, which indicates that it was dated 1 December 1439, probate 4 February 1440. Written in Middle English with Latin opening and closing formulae. Nicolas notes that Isabel, countess of Warwick, was the daughter of Thomas le Despencer, earl of Gloucester, and second wife of Richard, fifth earl of Warwick. The will offers evidence of statues in church wearing crowns and of items being broken up for various purposes. Printed in Furnivall (1964), 116–19. The translation is by Louise Sylvester.

And that my grete temply with the Baleys be sold to the vtmest pryse, and delyueryd to the sayde Abbat and the howse of Tewkesbery, so they groche noʒt with my lyenge, and wit*h* suche thyng' as y woll haue done a-bowt my body. [. . .] All so I woll ther' be made of my grete sharpe, A Chaleys, and offryd to our' Lady In our' lady Chapell of the Howse of Tewkesbery. All-so I woll oure lady of Cauersham. haue a crowne of gold I-made of my cheyne that wey*th* xxv li, with-yn my panyer', and wit*h* other broken' gold that is ther In, and ij tabelettes, the tone of seynte Katryne, And the tother of seynt George; And the stonys that bene In hem, to be sett yn the saide Crowne. All so I woll the tabelet with the Image of oure lady with a glasse to-fore hit, be offred to our' lady of Walsyngham, and my gowne of grene Alyr' cloth-of-gold with wyde sleves, [. . .] and my weddynggown And all my clothis of gold, and clothis of silke, with-oute ffurrereur, eueryhon, I woll the howse of Tewkesbery haue hem, saue my Russet vellewet, I woll Seynt Wynfryde haue. All-so I woll that all my stonys and perles be sold to parforme my wyll, [. . .] And all-so I woll my sone Harry haue myn oyche with my grete diamond, and my Noyc*h* wit*h* my Baleys.

45. The will of Sir Ralph Rochefort

Date: 1439. First there is a Latin text described by Furnivall as 'Latin Testament of some Personalty' and then a Middle English text entitled by Furnivall 'Engish Will of the Real Estate and Residue of Personalty' with a Latin closing formula. Printed in Furnivall (1964), 120–8. The translation is by Louise Sylvester.

Item lego Reuerendo patri ac domino meo, domino Willelmo, dei gratia, Lincolnie episcopo, vnum anulum auri cum uno magno saphiro.

46. The will of Sir Thomas Brook, knight, of Cobham

Date: 1438–9. Of Cobham. Written in Middle English with Latin title and closing formula. The will calls for thirteen poor men clothed in white to hold a torch each at the burial mass. Here the charitable gesture of giving clothing to the poor (assuming they get to keep the white garments) is combined with using the poor to make a showy funeral. Printed in Furnivall (1964), 129–31. The translation is by Louise Sylvester.

Also I bequeath to Thomas Dymmok, skinner of Gloucester, my best gown of the livery of the company of Skinners, both fur and cloth, if he is yet alive; And my second best fur and gown to Watkin Asshwell.

And that my great head-dress with the rubies be sold for the highest price and delivered to the said abbot and the house of Tewkesbury so that they will not complain about my burial and the things that they will have done to lay out my body. [...] Also I wish a chalice to be made from my large baldric and offered to Our Lady in the chapel of the house of Tewkesbury. Also I wish our Lady of Caversham to have a gold crown made out of my chain that weighs 25 pounds inside my hamper and the other broken gold that is in it. And two panels, the one of St Katherine and the other of St George and the jewels that are in them are to be set in the said crown. Also I wish the panel with the image of Our Lady with the pane of glass in front of it to be offered to our Lady of Walsingham. And my gown of green cloth-of-gold of Lierre with wide sleeves. [...] And I wish the house of Tewkesbury to have my wedding dress and all my cloth-of-gold and silk clothes without fur trim, every one; except that I wish St Winifred to have my russet velvet. Also I wish all my jewels and pearls to be sold to fulfil the terms of my will, [...] Also I wish my son Harry to have my brooch with the large diamond and my brooch with the ruby.

Likewise I leave to my reverend father and lord, Master Wilhelm, by grace of God, in the parish of Lincoln, a gold ring with a large sapphire.

And all-so that þer be xiij pore men' clothid in white, holdyng' eche of hem a torghe brennyng' at the dirige & at the masse yn the day of my obyte.

47. The will of Nicholas Sturgeon

Date: 1454. Priest. Written in Middle English with Latin opening and closing sections. This will gives an indication of the iconography of hangings: the Nine Worthies in the hall, lions for the bedroom. Printed in Furnivall (1964), 131–4. The translation is by Louise Sylvester.

Item y bequeth to the parissh cherche of seynt Andrewe in Aysperton', a vestement of blak for prest, deacon', and subdeacon', of the prys of x. li, or within; [...] Furthermore, y bequethe to my cosyn Iohan Frowyk, my bed of grene sylke, wiþ the testour & Canape ther-to, palid tartyn' white and rede, And the gilde pece wiþ smale stones sett ther-on. [...] Item y bequethe to my cosyn Margrete Shipton' that other gripes eye, and bed of grene wurstede, with the costers longyng ther-to. Also y bequeth to my brother Iohn' Sturgeon' the hallyng with the ix wurthy, [...] Item y bequethe to Iohn Anglesey my seruaunt x li, And a blew bed with the lyoun Curteynes, Couerled, blankettis, a peyre of shetis and a gowne. Item y bequeth to Bartlet my seruaunt, xx s' and a gowne. [...] Item I bequethe to Iohn' Gardyner, xxvj s', viij d, and a Riding gowne with the hode. [...] Item y bequethe to Iohn' of the kechyn, vj s' viij d, And to be new arayd.

And also that there be thirteen poor men clothed in white, each holding a burning torch at the reading of the Office for the Dead and at the mass on the day of my commemorative mass.

Likewise I bequeath to the parish church of St Andrew in Ashburton black vestments for the priest, deacon and subdeacon costing 10 pounds or less; [...] Furthermore, I bequeath to my cousin John Frowyk my green silk bed, with its tester and canopy of white and red-striped tartarin, and the piece of gilded plate set with small stones. [...] Likewise I bequeath to my cousin Margaret Shipton that other griffon's egg vessel and the bed of green worsted with its side curtains. Also I bequeath to my brother John Sturgeon the wall-hanging with the [embroidered images of the] Nine Worthies, [...] Likewise I bequeath to John Anglesey my servant 10 pounds, and a blue bed with the lion curtains, coverlet, bedclothes, a pair of sheets and a gown. Likewise I bequeath to Bartlet my servant 20 shillings and a gown. [...] Likewise I bequeath to John Gardyner 26 shillings, 8 pence, and a riding gown with a hood. [...] Likewise I bequeath to John of the kitchen 6 shillings, 8 pence, and to have new clothing.

CHAPTER II

Accounts

INTRODUCTION

Wardrobe accounts represent an excellent source of information about the naming of medieval cloth, clothing and accoutrement, as well as providing detailed historical evidence of aspects of medieval economic and trade practices. Not only are a variety of textiles, garments, jewellery, footwear etc. specified by name, but frequently cuts and colours are detailed as well, giving a vivid, illustrative picture of medieval suits of garments (*robes* or *sectas*).

Most of the extracts below are drawn from accounts that are either long out of print (such as the accounts of Bogo de Clare in Extracts 1*a* and 1*b*) or which have been newly transcribed and translated from original manuscripts (such as the Royal Wardrobe accounts in Extracts 2–4). The two extracts from Bogo de Clare's accounts date from the end of the thirteenth century and demonstrate the range of kinds and costs of garments worn by a particularly flamboyant thirteenth-century bishop. The three subsequent extracts are all drawn from the accounts of the Royal Wardrobe (National Archives, MSS E 101), the first two demonstrating some of the purchases made on behalf of a royal princess, and the third showing a typical set of purchases made by Edward III's Royal Wardrobe in the mid-fourteenth century. Finally, the last extract (5) offers evidence of late Anglo-French account-keeping, showing cloth and clothing references from the fifteenth-century accounts of the London Mercers' Company.

Extracts 2–4 are all drawn from previously unpublished manuscripts, transcribed and translated by Mark Chambers, who takes full responsibility for any errors or misreadings. We are very grateful to Dr Alex Rumble from the University of Manchester for his assistance with the transcriptions.

EXTRACTS FROM THE WARDROBE AND
HOUSEHOLD ACCOUNTS OF BOGO DE CLARE, 1284–5

Bogo (Boeges, Bevis) de Clare was the third son of Richard de Clare, fifth earl of Hertford and seventh earl of Gloucester. He was the younger brother of Richard's successor, Gilbert de Clare (1243–95), who would side with Simon de Montfort during the Barons' Revolt and later switch sides to join the future Edward I (Guiseppi 1918; Altschul 1965).

Owing to his powerful family connections and their continuing patronage, Bogo de Clare's early life was one of indulgence and luxury, and his adulthood and career as a rising ecclesiastical magnate saw him develop quite a reputation for strategic promotion and the large-scale collection of benefices. By the end of his career, de Clare held stake in all but four dioceses in England. Spending most of his time in London, probably in houses near Aldgate, he seems to have proved the model absentee pluralist of his age (Summerson 2004; Guiseppi 1918).

The extracts below are taken from Bogo de Clare's wardrobe and household accounts for the years 1284–5, originally published in Guiseppi (1918). The accounts show substantial spending on household and retinue – not to mention clothing, furs and jewellery – of which the extracts are only a sampling. The accounts are contained in National Archives [PRO], MS E 101/91/1–3.

We have not had room here to include the additional account of 25 December 1285 – 2 June 1286, which was kept by Walter de Reyny. A much more substantial account, it is available in Guiseppi's edition and survives in duplicate with a counter-roll (National Archives [PRO], MS E 101/91/6 & 7 – see Plate 2). It demonstrates an expansion of bureaucratic record-keeping by de Clare's household that is probably 'in imitation of royal practice' and testifies further to the cleric's apparent avarice mixed with self-promotion (Guiseppi 1918: 7).

EXTRACTS FROM ACCOUNTS

1a. Extracts from the wardrobe accounts of Bogo de Clare, 14 June 1284 – 2 March 1285, kept by Abel de Horkeley

This short roll of accounts was compiled by de Clare's wardrobe keeper or clerk, Abel de Horkeley. Guiseppi (1918) suggests that it represents, 'not a true "compotus", but merely a list of receipts and expenditure of the office during this period without any attempt to add them up, […] a preliminary stage in the preparation of a final account' (Guiseppi 1918: 3). Extracts have been selected from the accounts printed in Guiseppi (1918: Appendix 1, 21–6). The translation is by Mark Chambers. The paragraph symbol ¶ in Guiseppi's text has been removed.

Item pro xx furruris ad opus armigerorum —— v. marce. precium furrure. iij. s'. iiij. d'.
Item pro xvj. furruris ad capucia eorundem —— xj. s'. xj. d'.
[…]
Item pro .iiij. vlnis panni pro dom. ad vnam supertunicam pro nemore [*wood, forest?*] —— xiij. s'. iiij. d'.
[…]
Item pro .iij. furruris de nigra boge pro dom. —— xxiiij. s'.
Item pro vna furrura de alba Boge pro dom. —— x. s'. viij. d'.
Item pro vna furrura ad caputium —— ij. s'. vj. d'.
[…]
Item lib. Mag. Roberto Coco pro vno tabardo precepto dom. —— x. s'.
[…]
Item pro .vj. peciis de cendallo liberatis Huchoni Cissori ad faciendas culcitras. —— .lxxij. s'. emptis de paulo lombard'.
[…]
In primis lib. Agneti Ancille domus pro supertunica sua combusta —— iij. s'. vj. d'.
Item Alano Carectario dom. pro supertunica sua —— xviij. d'.
Item Willelmo de Kenligworth' pro supertunica et capicio combustis —— xviij. d'.
[…]
[*Endorsement on 1st membrane:*]
Visus Compoti Abel de Horkel' de receptis et quibusdam expensis et liberacionibus factis [in hospicio] dom. Bogonis de Clara Anno domini Mº. ccº. Lxxxº. Quarto

1b. Wardrobe accounts of Bogo de Clare, 12 March 1284 – 11 October 1285, kept by Walter de Reyny, *garderobarius*

This account, made by the wardrobe keeper Walter de Reyny and drawn up by a clerk named William de Horton for 3 shillings, runs from St Gregory's Day 1284 to Michaelmas 1285. It is much more detailed than its predecessor and shows innovative accounting practices by the household.

Extracts have been selected from the accounts printed in Guiseppi (1918: Appendix 2, 28–36). The latter section of the account has not been included, as it simply totals many of the items above it. It includes totals for purchases of 'pers'' (perse), 'scarletus' (scarlet), 'mixtus' (mixed cloth), 'triple', 'worsted', 'bluetus' (bluet), 'radiatus' (striped cloth), 'jaunus' (yellow cloth) and 'burnettum' (burnet). It further includes payments made for cheaper fabrics of 'mappe', 'manutergia', 'canabus' (canvas), as well as 'tela' (fabric such as linen cloth, specifically 'tele de Leges', probably

Item, for twenty fur linings for the use of his squires —— 5 marks, price per lining, 3s. 4d.
Also, for sixteen fur linings for hoods for the same —— 11s. 11d.
...
Also, for 4 ells [yards? – cf. *uln'* in glossary] of cloth for our lord, for a surcoat 'for the forest' [?] —— 13s. 4d.
...
Also, for three fur linings of black budge for our lord —— 24s.
Also, for a fur lining of white budge for our lord —— 10s. 8d.
Also, for a fur lining for a hood —— 2s. 6d.
...
Also, delivered to Master Robert, cook, for a tabard, by order of our lord —— 10s.
...
Also, for six pieces of cendal, delivered to Huchon, tailor, to make cushions —— 72s., purchased from Paulo the Lombard.
...
Firstly, delivered to Agnes, servant of the household, for her burnt surcoat —— 3s. 6d.
Also, Alan, carter of the household, for his surcoat —— 18d.
Also, William of Kennilworth, for a burnt surcoat and hood —— 18d.
...
[*Endorsement on 1st membrane:*]
View of the accounts of Abel de Horkely of certain expenses and receipts and deliveries made [in the household] of our lord Bogo de Clare, in the year of our Lord 1284.

Liège in modern Belgium); as well as payments for silk cloths of 'scendallum' (cendal), 'samittum' (samite), 'scindon' (sindon), card, 'sargie' (sarge), 'paddus ad arum', as well as swords, spices, and certain liveries.

The extracts below and the excluded sections contain some individual items of interest to historians and to lexicographers, such as a seat of 'camoyseata nigra' (black chamois leather), bought from a merchant from Florence named Simon; a cloak of 'faldinga' (falding, an inexpensive cloth originally manufactured in or associated with Ireland) given to William Foljambe; and further totals for expenses of cloth and fur, including 'camelin' de Triple', 'cangium' (silk or cotton fabric – from an Arabic term), squirrel fur, 'strell' (strandling or strayling), 'boge' (budge), as well as further cheaper fabrics, swords and plate.

The translation is by Mark Chambers. The symbol ¶ in Guiseppi's text has been removed. Presumed readings in the translation are rendered in italics.

Expense:
Pro .x. vnciis et dimidia vncia et dimidio quarterono serici emptis ad consuendam vnam Culcitram de serenis factam ad opus domini .x. s'. vij. d'. o. precium vncie .xij.d'. Item pro .ij. vnciis et .j. quarterono serici emptis ad faciendos Crines in capitibus serenarum .ij. s'. iij. d'. quarteronum serici de colore Crinium .vj. d'. In veteri Cendallo empto ad cubitandum in Bordura pred. Culcitre .vj. s'. In Burrello empto ad cubitandum in pred. Bordura .xvj. d'. qua pred. culcitra consuebatur .xij. d'. Item de dono Custurariis consuentibus pred. Culcitram ad potandum .vj. d'. Item In stipendio Mag. ordinatis et facientis pred. Culcitram de conuencione dom. .xl. s'.

    Summa lxij. s'. vj. d'. o'.

Expense:
Item in lana empta ad cubitandum in vno Materacio de sindone rubeo dupplicato facto ad opus dom. per manus Hugonis de Oxonia .vj. s'. x. d'. Item pro Carpitura pred. lane .xij. d'. Item pro .iiij^{or}. vnciis serici emptis ad consuendum pred. Materacium .iij. s' viij. d'. precium vncie .xj. d'. In stipendiis operariorum consuencium pred. Materacium .v. s'. vj. d'. Item pro vna vncia serici empta et missa apud Tacheham precepto dom. .xij. d'. Item pro custura cuisdam Canabi de Card' facti ad lectum dom. .iiij. d'. o. Item pro vna libra lane empta ad cubitandum in quodam alio Materacio de sindone rubeo singulo cum Bordura interlaqueata facto ad opus dom. .ij. s'. Item pro .v. vnciis serici emptis ad consuendum pred. Materacium singulum .v. s'. precium vncie .xij. d'. Item pro factura et custura eisdem Materacii vna cum factura et custura .j. Bordure in supradicto Materacio duplo .xv. s'. vj. d'. Item pro dimidia pecia sidonis rubei debilis empta ad cubitandum in quodam Gardecors' viridi Facto ad opus dom. .iij. s'. iiij. d'. Item pro vna vncia et dimidia emptis ad consuendum pred. gardecors' et vnum alterum gardecors' de sindone rubeo factum ad opus dom. xviij. d'. precium vncie xij. d'. Item pro .ij. libris Coton' et .ij. libris Cadac' emptis ad cubitandum in pred. .ij. gardecors' .iiij. s'. vj. d'. Item pro factura et custura pred. duorum gardecorsatorum v. s'.

    Summa Lv. s'. ij. d'. o'.

Empcio pannorum:
De Waltero de Rokesleg' pro .x. vlnis et dimidia Pers' .xlvij. s'. iij. d'. precium vlne .iiij. s'. vj. d'. De Eodem pro vno panno mixto .vj. li'. vj. s'. viij. d'. De Anketino de Beca uilla pro .vij. vlnis Rad' .xv. s'. ij. d'. precium vlne .ij. s'. ij. d'.

Expenses:
For 10½ ounces and half a quarter of silk bought to sew [up] a cushion of Sirens made for our lord, 10s. 7d½d. [*obulus*, a halfpenny], price per ounce: 12d. Also, for 2 ounces and one quarter of silk bought to make hair on the head of the Sirens, 2s. 3d. per quarter of coloured silk hair, 6d. In old cendal, bought by the cubit, in the border of the aforesaid cushion, 6s. In burel-cloth, bought by the cubit, in the aforesaid border, 16d., *of which the aforsaid cushion was sewn*, 12d. Also, payment of drink for the seamsters for sewing the aforsaid cushion, 6d. Also, for workmen's wages for ordering and making the aforsaid cushion, as agreed by our lord, 40s.
    Total: 62s. 6½d.

Expenses:
Also, for wool bought by the cubit, for a mattress of lined, red sindon made for the use of our lord, by Hugh of Oxford, 6s. 10d. Also, for teasing the aforesaid wool, 12d. Also, for 4 ounces of silk bought for sewing the aforesaid mattress, 3s. 8d., price per ounce: 11d. In workmen's wages for sewing the aforesaid mattress, 5s. 6d. Also, for an ounce of silk bought and sent to Tacheham [Thatcham, Berkshire], by order of our lord, 12d. Also for stitching a certain canvas of carde, made for the bed of our lord, 4½d. Also, for a pound of wool bought by the cubit for another mattress of single red sindon with an interlaced border made for the use of our lord, 2s. Also, for 5 ounces of silk bought for sewing the aforesaid single mattress, 5s., price per ounce: 12d. Also, for making and stitching the same mattresses, together with making and stitching one border on the above-mentioned double mattress, 15s. 6d. Also, for half a piece of thin red sindon bought by the cubit for a certain green padded garment [gambeson?] made for the use of our lord, 3s. 4d. Also, for one ounce and a half bought for sewing the aforesaid padded garment, and another padded garment of red sindon made for the use of our lord 18d. price per ounce: 12d. Also, for 2 pounds of cotton and 2 pounds of caddice bought by the cubit [for] the aforesaid two padded garments 4s. 6d. Also for making and stitching the two aforesaid padded garments, 5s.
    Total: 55s. 2½d.

Purchases of cloth:
From Walter of Rokesley for ten and a half ells [yards?] of perse 47s. 3d, price per ell: 4s. 6d.
From the same for a mixed cloth, £6 6s. 8d.
From Anketin *de Beca ville* [Beville?] for 7 ells of striped cloth, 15s. 2d., price per ell: 2s. 2d.

De Eodem pro .iij. vlnis et dimidia de Burnet' et dimidia vlna Jaune .viij. s' precium vlne .ij. s'.
De Eodem pro dimidia Rad' empta ad opus Duncan' .xliij. s'. iij. d'.
De Eodem pro .iij. Rad' emptis ad opus Armigerorum .xij. li' precium panni .iiij. li'
De Eodem pro .iij. pannis de Burnet' ad opus eorundem .xij. li'. precium panni .iiij. li'
De Eodem pro vno panno de Scarlet' empto ad opus dom. .viij. li'. xiij. s'. iiij. d'
De Eodem pro vij. vlnis de Bluet' emptis pro Medico xxiij. s' iiij. d'. precium vlne .iij. s'. iiij. d'.
De Eodem pro .xxxix. vlnis tirreten' Mixte emptis pro dom. Bogone et .E. de Mortuo mari .vj. li'. xvj. s' vj. d'. precium vlne .iij. s'. vj. d'.
    Summa Lij. li'. xiij. s'. vij. d'.

Panni:
Pro .iij. peciis Worcested .Liiij. s' precium pecie xviij. s'
Item pro viij. vlnis de quodam panno Mixto .xxx. vj. s' precium vlne .iiij. s'. vj. d'.
Item pro .iiij. vlnis Burnett' emptis pro Caligis dom. .xviij. s' precium vlne .iiij. s'. vj. d'.
Item pro .iiij. vlnis Burnett' emptis ad perficiendam liberacionem armigerorum .xiij. s'. iiij. d'. precium vlne .iij. s'. iiij. d'.
Item pro .ij. Camelin' de Tripl' emptis pro dom. xxxiiij. s'. iiij. d'. precium Camelin' .xvij. s'. ij. d'.
    Summa vij. li'. xv. s'. viij. d'.

Banquaria:
Item pro vno Banquario empto per manus simonis Girard' .vj. s'.
Item pro vno Tapeto cum scuticis ad arma Regis Anglie .xx. s'
Item pro .iiij. tapetis seminatis cum Lucis albis .C. viij. s' precium pecie .xxvij. s'.
  —— Summa .vj. li'. xiiij. s'.

Retonsura pannorum:
[...]

Factura robarum dom. per Manus Hugonis de Oxonia a festo Pasche usque ad festum sancti Michaelis.
Pro factura et custura .j. Robe de pers' cum tabardo post Pa[s]cham .xviij. d'.
Pro factura et custura .viij. garminum de Pounac' contra Pentecostem .iij. s'.
Pro factura et custura .iiij. garminum de Worcested' lineatorum cum Cam' de Tripl' .ij. s'. vj. d'.
Pro factura et custura .j. Tunice de Cang' .viij. d'.
Pro factura et custura .ij. garminum de quodam panno Mixto .xij. d'.
Pro factura et custura .j. Coopertorii de veluett' .ij. s'.

Summa a festo Pasche vsque ad festum sancti Michaelis anno domini .M^{o}. cc^{o} lxxx^{o}. quinto x. s'. viij. d'.

Fururie:
Pro vna furura de Boga empta ad opus domini .x. s'.
Pro vna furura ad Capucia empta ad opus eisdem .ij. s'. vj. d'.

From the same for three and a half ells of burnet and half an ell of yellow cloth, 8s., price per ell: 2s.
From the same for half a striped cloth, bought for Duncan, 43s. 3d.
From the same for three striped cloths, bought for the squires, £12, price per cloth: £4
From the same for three cloths of burnet, bought for the same, £12, price per cloth: £4
From the same for a scarlet cloth, bought for our lord, £8 13s. 4d.
From the same for 7 ells of bluett, bought for the doctor, 23s. 4d., price per ell: 3s. 4d.
From the same for 39 ells of mixed tiretaine, bought for our lord Bogo and E. [Edmund] Mortimer [de Mortuo Mari], £6 16s. 6d., price per ell: 3s. 6d.
  Total: £52 13s. 7d.

Of cloth:
For three pieces of worsted, 54s., price per piece: 18s.
Also, for 8 ells of a certain mixed cloth, 36s., price per ell: 4s. 6d.
Also, for 4 ells of burnet bought for our lord's hose, 18s., price per ell: 4s. 6d.
Also, for 4 ells of burnet bought to complete the livery of the squires, 13s. 4d., price per ell: 3s. 4d.
Also, for two [pieces of] camelin of *Tripl'*, bought for our lord, 34s. 4d., price per camelin: 17s. 2d.
  Total: £7 15s. 8d.

Hangings/Coverings:
Also, for a banker bought by the hand of Simon Gerard, 6s.
Also, for a tapestry with escutcheons of the arms of the king of England, 20s.
Also, for four tapestries decorated [lit. 'seeded'] with white *Luke(s)*, 108s., price per piece: 27s.
—— Total: £6 14s.

Re-shearing cloth:
…

For making our lord's robes, by the hand of Hugh of Oxford, for the feast of Easter to the feast of St Michael:
For making and stitching one robe of perse with a tabard after Easter, 18d.
For making and stitching eight garments of *pounacium* for Pentecost, 3s.
For making and stitching three garments of linen worsted with a camelin of *Tripl'*, 2s. 6d.
For making and stitching one tunic of *cangium*, 8d.
For making and stitching two garments of a certain mixed cloth, 12d.
For making and stitching one cover of velvet, 2s.

Total for the feast of Easter to the feast of St Michael, the year of our lord 1285: 10s. 8d.

Fur:
For a fur (lining/trim) of budge, bought for our lord, 10s.
For a fur for a hood, bought for the same, 2s. 6d.

Pro vna furura et .j. Capucio de Boga emptis ad opus Duncan' .v. s'. vj. d'.
Pro .xxij. fururis et .xxij. Capuciis agni emptis pro Armigeris .iiij. li'. viij. s'. precium furure et Capucii .iiij. s'.
Pro .iij. fururis et .iij. Capuciis de Boga emptis pro eisdem .xij. s'. vj. d'. precium furure et Capucii .iiij. s'. ij. d'.
Pro vna furura de Squirello et .j. Capucio de strell emptis pro Medico .x. s'.
Pro .v. fururis et dimidia et .ij. Capuciis de Boga emptis pro robis dom. de scarl' .lx. s'. v. d'. precium furure .x.s'. j. d'. precium Capucii .ij. s'. vj. d'.
    Summa ix. li'. viij. s'. xj. d'

Tela:
Pro .lx vlnis tele de Leg' emptis ad opus dom. pro Linchiamentis .xlij. s'. vj. d'. precium vlne .viij. d'. o'.
Pro xlj. vlnis tele emptis emptis [*sic*] ad opus eiusdem pro lineis robarum .xxx. s'. ix. d'. precium vlne ix. d'.
    Summa lxxiij. s'. iij. d'.

Card' et Canabus:
Item pro .lxxij. vlnis Card' .xxj. s'. precium vlne .iij. d'. o'.
Item pro lxx. vlnis Canabi .xiij. s'. j. d'. o'. precium vlne .ij. d'. q^a.
    Summa xxxiiij. s'. j. d'. ob'.

Mappe:
Item pro .iiij.^{or} Manutergiis emptis pro garderoba .iiij. s'.
Item pro .iiij. Manutergiis emptis pro Pannetria .ij. s'. iiij. d'.
Item pro ij. Mappis Longis et .vj. Manutergiis pro supermappis .xxiiij. s'.
    Summa xxx. s'. iiij. d'.
[…]

Item pro vno Capello ferri […] ad opus eisdem empto .xij. s'. vj. d'. Item pro vna vlna tele empta ad cubitandum in vno Bracal' facto ad opus eiusdem per Manus .R. de Winton' .iij. d'. Item in Cotona empta ad cubitandum in pred. Bracal' per manus eisdem .j. d'. In laqueis sericis emptis ad pred. Bracal' .v. d'. per manus eisdem. Item pro factura et custura eisdem Bracal' .viij. d'. Item pro .vj. Duodenis Botonum [*sic*] emptis pro vna cloca domini videlicet de Curall' .iij. s'. precium Duodene .vj. d'. per Manus predicti .R. de Winton'. Item pro vna vlna Cindone empta ad ligandam pred. clocam .vj. d'.
    Summa .vij. li' xj. s'. iiij. d'.

[…]

Empciones facte de Simone Girard' et de sociis suis [et de *interl.*] Mercatoribus Luk' per Manus .W. de Reygny. […]

For a fur (lining/trim) and a hood of budge, bought for Duncan, 5s. 6d.
For 22 furs and 22 hoods of lambswool, bought for the squires, £4 8s., costing per fur and hood: <u>4s.</u>
For three furs and three hoods of budge, bought for the same, 12s. 6s., price per fur and hood: <u>4s. 2d.</u>
For a fur of squirrel and one hood of strayling/strandling [autumn squirrel fur], bought for the Doctor, 10s.
For five and a half furs and two hoods of budge, bought for robes for our lord of scarlet, 60s. 5d., price per fur: <u>10s. 1d.</u>, price for the hoods: <u>2s. 6d.</u>
    Total: £9 8s. 11d.

Linen cloth:
For 9 ells of cloth of *Liège* (?), bought for our lord, for sheets, 42s. 6d., price per ell: <u>8½d.</u>

For 41 ells of cloth bought for the same, for linen robes, 30s. 9d., price per ell: <u>9d.</u>

    Total: 73s. 3d.

Carde and Canvas:
Also, for 72 ells of carde, 21s., price per ell: <u>3½d.</u>
Also, for 70 ells of Canvas, 13s. 1½d., price per ell: <u>2¼ d.</u>
    Total: 34s. 1½d.

Napery:
Also, for four handtowels, bought for the wardrobe, 4s.
Also, for four handtowels, bought for the pantry, 2s. 4d.
Also, for two long cloths and six handtowels for table linens, 24s.
    Total: 30s. 4d.
[…]

Also, for an iron helmet…, bought for the use of the same, 12s. 6d. Also, for an ell of linen, bought by the cubit, in one padded garment (probably a breech girdle), made for the use of the same, by the hand of R. de Winton, 3d. Also, in cotton, bought by the cubit, for the aforesaid padded garment, by the hand of the same, 1d. In silk laces, bought for the said padded garment, 5d., by the hand of the same. Also, for making and sewing the same padded garment, 8d. Also for six dozen buttons, bought for the lord's cloak, namely *de Curall'* (of coral?), 3s., price per dozen: <u>6d.</u>, by the hand of the aforesaid R. de Winton. Also, for an ell of sindon, bought to bind the aforesaid cloak, 6d.
    Total: £7 11s. 4d.

…
Purchases made of Simon Girard and of his companions, of Merchants of Lucca, by the hand of W. de Reygny. . . .

sindon:

De Simone Girard' [...] vj. pecie sindonis rubei fortis ponderis lx vnciarum lxx. s'. precium vncie xiiij. d'.

De Eodem pro .iij. peciis sindonis de cursu rubei .xx. s'. precium pecie .vj. s'. viij. d'.

De Eodem pro vna pecia samuti rubei fortis .viij. li'. xiij. s'. iiij. d'.

De Eodem .ij. pecie sindonis viridis fortis .xxviij. s'. viij. d'. precium pecie xiiij. s'. iiij. d'.

De Eodem ij. pecie sindonis rubei fortis xxvj. s'. viij. d'. precium pecie .xiij. s'. iiij. d'.

De Eodem .vj. pecie sindonis rubei de cursu .xl. s' precium pecie vj. s'. viij. d'.

De Eodem pro vno panno auri .xvj. s'.

De Eodem .j. pannus de kenchia .xvj. s'

De Eodem .j. pecia sindonis Ind' fortis.

De Eodem .v. vlne pannorum mixtorum empte ad opus dom. .xxv. s'. precium vlne .v. s'.

ACCOUNTS OF THE ROYAL WARDROBE AND RELATED DOCUMENTS

There were hundreds, if not thousands, of accounts produced by the medieval department of the Royal Wardrobe. The exchequer Pipe Rolls for Henry I's reign (1100–35) record a division of the royal household into the 'camera' (chamber) and the 'garderoba' (wardrobe). Before this, these institutions are mentioned in the Domesday Book. Later they are detailed in King Stephen's *Constitutio Domus Regis* but appear only occasionally in other preserved documents. It is clear that under the reign of Henry II, the chamber took on a much more prominent role than previously, independent from but audited by the state treasury now formally called the Exchequer. The chamber collected and dispersed moneys used daily by the king and his household *in lieu* of the Exchequer. As the king's immediate source of day-to-day finance, it was variously located or else had officers and resources which travelled with the king, unlike its Westminster-based counterpart (Lyon *et al.* 1983: xi–xxii).

Several changes occurred to the household offices during John's reign (1199–1216), including the rise of the royal wardrobe as a distinct and important household office, arguably more prominent than the chamber. As in earlier periods, it continued to be a moveable collection or storehouse of royal valuables, but it gained a number of new officers with increasingly important and varied responsibilities. This increasing prominence continued through Henry III's reign (Lyon *et al.* 1983: xxv–xxvi).

The first identifiable account of the royal wardrobe submitted to the Exchequer is found amongst the Pipe Rolls of Henry III (printed in Tout 1920: I, 233–8). It records a list of receipts and expenses of the household from 5 January to 10 April 1227, submitted by the clerks Walter of Brackley and Walter of Kirkham. In the years that follow, we find the development of the office of the controller of the wardrobe, whose duty it was to keep a counter-roll of the official roll tendered to the Exchequer twice annually for audit (Lyon *et al.* 1983: xxvii–xxix).

By the 1230s, there is evidence of separate wardrobes being kept for the king's household, the queen's household, and, later, of the households of other royals, each distinguished from the Great Wardrobe and each submitting rolls for audit to the Exchequer. Moreover, the king's wardrobe during this period seems to have been made more and more responsible for carrying out a wider variety of orders and obligations, usually sealed under the small (privy) seal. By Edward I's reign (1272–1307) the operation of the Great Wardrobe had become the preeminent office of the royal household, involving itself in many activities of state, only declining in favour of the chamber late

Sindon:

Of Simon Girard..., six pieces of heavyweight red sindon, 60 ounces, 70s., price per ounce: 14d.

Of the same, for three pieces of sindon of red *cursu* [striped cloth?], 20s., price per piece: 6s. 8d.

Of the same, for a piece of heavy red samite, £8 13s. 4d.

Of the same, for two pieces of heavy green sindon, 28s. 8d., price per piece: 14s. 4d.

Of the same, for two pieces of heavy red sindon, 26s. 8d., price per piece: 13s. 4d.

Of the same, for six pieces of red sindon of *cursu*, 40s., price per piece: 6s. 8d.

Of the same, for a cloth-of-gold, 16s.

Of the same, for one cloth of *kenchia*, 16s.

Of the same, for one piece of heavy sindon *Ind'*

Of the same, for 5 ells of mixed cloth bought for our lord, 25s., price per ell: 5s.

in Edward's reign (Lyon *et al.* 1983: xxix–xxxi). This includes making purchases and issuing credit and receipts for men and material relating to military campaigns, for castle building and repairs, alongside more everyday activities such as overseeing purchases of clothing, tack, spices, wax, victuals and so forth. During Edward's reign, the Wardrobe was headed by a keeper (variously called the 'thesaurarius', 'custos garderobe', 'gardeyn', 'tresorer', etc.) who conducted a daily audit of household expenses and rendered accounts to the exchequer, and was assisted by the controller ('contrarotularius') who kept the counter-roll (Lyon *et al.* 1983: xxxiii).

Under Edward I, the operations and supplies controlled by the Wardrobe grew so multifarious that a permanent store-house was required in the Tower of London. More than this, it consistently overspent through the latter years of the fourteenth century, so much so that it took twenty-five years after Edward's death fully to audit the Wardrobe accounts. Under Edward II's tumultuous reign, its independent spending powers were severely limited by the barons. Many of these former powers were revived again during Edward III's various campaigns in Scotland. Lyon *et al.* includes a detailed discussion of the complicated financial arrangements that grew up around Edward I and Edward IIs' Great Wardrobe, as well as a comprehensive discussion of the office under Edward III (1983: xxxiv+).

2. Expenses for the wedding of Elizabeth, countess of Holland, 1297 (National Archives [PRO], MS E 101/354/21)

This tiny, single membrane account is one of a number of manuscripts recording expenses and accounts surrounding preparations for the marriage of Elizabeth of Rhuddlan (a.k.a. Elizabeth Plantagenet) to the count of Holland (see Plate 4).

Elizabeth – also called 'Isabel' – was the youngest daughter of Edward I and Elizabeth of Castile, elder sister to Edward II, and she was apparently the first 'Elizabeth' in the English royal family. In 1285, at the age of two, she was engaged to the infant John (*Jan*), eldest son of the count of Holland. John was raised in England, where he lived until news of his father's murder in 1295. At a stroke, John became John I, count of Holland, Zeeland, and lord of Friesland. Just over a year later, on 7 January 1297, Elizabeth and John were married at Ipswich.

The document records some of the out-of-pocket expenses encountered by one of Elizabeth's tailors, Thomas, and his staff. It notes that the young princess's bridal dress took thirty-five tailors working four days and nights to finish, and that it was embroidered with silk and adorned with buttons of silver and gold. Other evidence records that Elizabeth wore a gold coronet set with rubies, emeralds and pearls (Green 1857: 14).

As a matter of fact, a fairly accurate picture can be drawn of the preparations and execution of Elizabeth's marriage to the count, based on a number of relevant surviving documents held in the National Archives and in the British Library. The information below was, of course, later enrolled in the annual *Wardrobe Book* kept by the Wardrobe Keeper for 25 Edward I (BL, Additional MS 7965). National Archives, MS C 47/3/48/21, filed amongst the Chancery documents, contains an additional account of dresses made for the ceremony by Elizabeth's tailor, Henry (who is mentioned in the account below). MS E 101/354/16 contains a memorandum of gold and silver articles given to Elizabeth by her father.

The account below is interesting for a number of reasons. Not only does it appear to be an on-the-job, running account kept by those in charge of making and transporting Elizabeth's wedding dress and accoutrements, it also contains details of how and when such items were transported. Transcription and translation are by Mark Chambers. Customary Latin abbreviations and suspensions have been extended in italics. There is a great deal of damage to the manuscript; presumed or suggested readings are offered in italics and illegible passages are indicated.

Expensis facte per Thomas Cissore' pro operibus Countesse Holland
contra sponsal' eiusdem [... *damage to the MS*] anno regni regis Edwardi XXV°

Pro xxxv operarariis per iiij dies & ⁱⁱⁱʲ noctes operantibus apud London . quorum quolibet
eorum cepit per diem & noctem vj d.
    Summᵃ —— lxx s.

¶ Item pro filo empto dimidia Mᵃrca Summᵃ   —— vj. s'. viij. d.
¶ Item pro factura Linthiaminum   —— vj. s'. viij. d.
¶ Item pro serico empto   —— iiij. s'
¶ Item pro botonibus argent' & deaurat'   —— vij. s'. vj. d.
¶ Item pro candel' empt'   —— ij. s'. vj. d.
¶ Item pro anulis ad cortin' emptis   —— ij. s'. iij. d.
¶ Item pro j. Braello ad cortin'   —— vij. d.
¶ Item pro locatione domus   —— iiij. s'.
¶ Item pro portagio   —— vj. d.
¶ Item pro factura canabeorum   —— xj. d.
¶ Item in expens' dicti Henr' comorant' apud London' circa predicta opera per viij dies
capientis per die iij d.
    Summᵃ —— ij s'.
¶ In expnsis dicti Henr' & ij garcionum comrant' apud Gype
Wis custodient' totum harnesium per viij dies capientis per die vj d.
    Summᵃ —— iiij s'.
¶ Item in passag' perdicta harnois' de Gypewis usque Cat
tesWade   x[?]iii. d.

¶ Item cariag' eiusdem harn' de CattesWade usque Cole
cester' cum ij carrtis & viij equis   —— iij s'.
¶ Item pro cariag' de Colecestre usque London' cum ij car
rtis & viij equis per [???]ˣⁱⁱⁱʲ[?] [*the word on the line here is illegible, with what looks like xiiij (9)
written above it*] dictas capient' per diem iij s'[?]
    Summᵃ —— xv s'[?] xij s'.
¶ In expesis Henr' cissor ᵃⁿᵈ ʲ ᵍarcione de Cattes Wade cum pred'
harn' versus London per vj??? dictas [*sic*]. capientis per diem iij d.
ob.   —— ij s' iij d. xv??
    Summᵃ [???] [???] li. [????] [????, *mostly illegible*]

Expenses made by Thomas, tailor, for work for the countess of Holland for the wedding of the same, in the 25th year of the reign of King Edward

For thirty-five tailors [workers], for four days and four nights work in London, for which each of them took 6d. per day and night
       Total —— 70s.

¶ Item, for thread purchased at half a mark, Total: —— 6s. 8d.
¶ Also, for making sheets/linings —— 6s. 8d.
¶ Also, for silk purchased —— 4s.
¶ Also, for silver and gilt buttons —— 7s. 6d.
¶ Also, for candles purchased —— 2s. 6d.
¶ Also, for curtain rings purchased —— 2s. 3d.
¶ Also, for one cord/tie for the curtain[s] —— 7d.
¶ Also, for letting a house —— 4s.
¶ Also, for portage —— 6d.
¶ Also, for making canvases —— 11d.
¶ Also, in expenses of the said Henry, dwelling in London for the duration of the aforesaid work, for eight days, 3d. taken per day
       Total —— 2s.
¶ In expenses of the aforesaid Henry and two grooms [servants] dwelling in Ipswich and keeping all of the equipment for eight days, 6d. taken per day
       Total —— 4s.
¶ ~~Also, in passage for the aforesaid equipment from Ipswich to Cattawade~~ [Cattawade, in Suffolk, about 10 miles north-east of Colchester and about 10 miles south-west of Ipswich]
       ???d.
¶ Also, in carriage for the same equipment from Cattawade to Colechester, with two carts and eight horses —— 3s.
¶ Also, for carriage from Colchester to London, with two carts and eight horses for ? the said, 3s.? taken per day
       Total —— ~~15s.?~~ 12s.

¶ In expenses of Henry, tailor and one servant come from Cattawade with the aforesaid harness to London, for ???, 3½d., taken per day
       —— ~~2s. 3d.~~ ?
       Total: ???

3. Extracts from the roll of liveries of Elizabeth, countess of Holland (31 Edward I: 20 November 1302 – 19 November 1303; National Archives, MS E 101/364/29, memb. 1)

The two-membrane document (National Archives [PRO], MS E 101/364/29) containing the roll of liveries of Elizabeth of Ruddlan, countess of Holland, is an excellent example of a document of its type. It is written in a clear, rounded Anglicana script which is relatively easy to transcribe, and the full and undamaged survival of the roll is remarkable for a document of its type and era. Moreover, it has previously remained untranscribed, untranslated and unexamined.

Elizabeth was widowed suddenly in 1299, when her husband the count of Holland died – probably of dysentery. The eligible princess was not a single widow for long. On 14 November 1302 – just six days before the roll begins its record – Elizabeth was married to Humphrey de Bohun, earl of Hereford and Essex and Constable of England. The roll records the livery given by Elizabeth's household for the thirty-first to thirty-third years of Edward I's reign.

The roll therefore contains a record of the livery given to members of Elizabeth's household during the early years of her second marriage. It records types of garments and gifts, materials, amounts and prices, as well as the names of recipients. In this way it sheds invaluable light on the garments, colours and textures of an early-fourteenth-century princess's household livery.

The transcription and translation are by Mark Chambers. Only items listed for the first year (31 Edward I) are shown, without the repeated tallies of individual items listed below the annual total. The *punctus elevatus* is represented by a semicolon. Common abbreviations and suspensions are extended in italics. Presumed or uncertain readings are offered in italics, and illegible items are represented with question marks.

[*Written in the left margin in a heavier hand:* **Anno .xxxj.**]

D*o*m*i*ne Elizab*et* Countisse Holland in p*re*cio uni*us* panni mixti in grana sibi lib*erat'* p*er* Thom*as* de Virson ad roba*m* suam de natali anni ; tricesimi ; primi ; p*re*cii vij. li. | iiij*or*. | fur*uris* m*iniver* [*menevera, meneverus, etc.*] d*i*midia p*ro* supertunicas p*re*cii cui*us*libet xxx s. uni*us* capuc' m*iniver*. ad capam p*re*cii xvj. s. | et uni*us* capuc' m*iniver*. pr*e*cij x. s. sibi liber' p*ro* roba p*re*dicta —— xv. li. xij. d. [*written in right margin:*] **probatum**

Eidem in p*re*cio .iij. pann*orum* .dimidia. de blueto azureto ad robas d*omi*ne Johanne de Mereworth Alic' Bretoun Johanne de Westone Elizab*et* de Waterynge Elizab*et* filie d*omi*ne Egid*ie* | d*omi*norum Stephan' de Brawode & Mich*ael* de Clare capellan*i*. p*re*cii panni ; c. s. | quatuor fur*uris* m*iniver* p*ro* supertunica p*re*cii cui*us*libet .xxx. s. uni*us* furure de gr*o*sso vario p*re*cii. xxx. s. | iij fur*uris* de popre. v. fur*uris* destrallyng p*re*cii cui*us*libet xij. s. iiij*or*. capuc*ii* m*iniver*. p*re*cii cui*us*libet .dj. m*a*rcas*unius* pane ad mantell ad robas p*re*dic*te* Countisse p*re*cii Lxvj s. viij d. —— xxxiiij. li. ix. s. iiij. d. **probatum**

Eidem in p*re*cio | uni*us* panni | et .v. uln'. radiati afforc'. sibi lib*erat'* ad robas Johanne Malemeyns *Huardi* de Holl*andie* William de Rollestone | & Henr*ici* ciss*oris* p*re*cii panni ; v. m*a*rcas. | iiij*or*. fur*uris* agni. pr*e*cii cui*us*libet [*sic*] p*ro* supertunica p*re*cii cui*us*libet iij. s. iiij*or*. capuc*ii* de Boge | p*re*cii cui*us*libet .ij. s. vi. d. eisdem lib' ad d*i*ctas robas —— cij. s. v. d. **probatum**

To the Lady Elizabeth, countess of Holland, the purchase [or 'value'?] of one mixed cloth, dyed 'in-grain', delivered to her [or 'for livery'?] by Thomas de *Virson*, for her robe of the Nativity, for the thirty-first regnal year, costing £7, 4½ fur linings of miniver for a surcoat each costing 30s., one hood of miniver with a cape or cope, costing 16s., and one hood of miniver costing 10s., delivered to herself for the aforesaid *robe* —— £15 12d.   *approved*

To the same, the purchase of 3½ cloths of azure bluett, for robes of the lady Johanna de Merewyth ['one of the faithful ladies who had been her companions in Holland, and who had remained with her ever since' (Green 1857: 39)], Alicia Bretun, Johanna Weston, Elizabeth Watering [the countess's maids of honour], and Elizabeth Fitz Giles, of the lords Stephen de Brawode and Michael de Clare, chaplains, costing per cloth 100s. Four fur linings of miniver for supertunic[s], each costing 30s. One fur lining of *grover* costing 30s. three fur linings of *pople* [summer squirrel fur], five fur linings of *strandling* [autumn squirrel fur] each costing 12s., four hoods of miniver each costing ½ mark, one pane for a mantle for robes for the aforesaid countess costing 66s. 8d. —— £34 9s. 4d.   *approved*

To the same, the purchase of one cloth and 5 ells of lined ray delivered to her [or 'for livery'] for the robes of John Malmains, Howard de Holland, William de Rolleston, and Henry, tailor [he appears in the previous extract], costing per cloth 5 marks, four fur linings of lambswool, each costing [*sic*] for surcoats each costing 3s., four hoods of budge, each costing 2s. 6d., delivered to the same for the aforesaid robes —— 102s. 5d.   *approved*

Eidem in precio | vij. uln' de perso | sibi liberat' | ad robas Willi*am* clerici capelle ei*us*dem precii ulne iiij. s. iiij. d. un*ius* furure agn*i* | precii .iiij. s. et unius capuc*ii* de Boge precij .ij. s. vj. d. p*ro* roba sua p*re*dic*ta* ⸺ xxviij. s. x. d **probatum**

Eidem in precio | duo*rum* panno*rum* | viij. uln' rad*iati* stanford sibi liberat' ad robas vallett*orum* suo*rum* | de offic' | vid*e*licet Petri cissoris | Robinetti de butell' un*ius* nunc*ii* sui ___andi | de cam*er* Reginaldi CokeWald | ~~Henrici de camera~~ [*written above:* William Coci] Hermanni de Holland | Baldewyn de camera | cuis*ibet* eo*rum* .vij. uln' prec*ii* panni L. s. viij furu*ris* agn*i* albar*um* p*ro* supertunic*as* | prec*ii* cuius*libet* .ij. s. vj. d. sibi liberat' ad d*i*ctas robas furrand' ⸺ vj . li . xvj. s. viij. d. **probatum**

Eidem in precio | unius panni de scarleto sanguineo sibi liber*at'* ad robam suam de festo Pasch anno xxxj. xiiij. [*written above the preceding number:* li] xiij. s. iiij. d. | iiij^{or}. furu*ris* dim*i*dia. de m*i*niver p*ro* supertunic*as* prec*ii* cui*us*l*ibet* .xxx. s. un*ius* capuc*ii* m*i*niver. puratis p*ro* cap*a* prec*ii* .xvj s. un*ius* capuc*ii* m*i*niver. de iiij. tir'. prec*ii* .x. s. un*ius* pane ad mantell prec*ii* .v. m^ar*cas* ⸺ xxvj. li. xij. d. **probatum**

Eidem in prec*io* unius panni de Brusceles | sibi liberat' ad robam suam de ascencione p*er* Thom*as'* de Virzon precij x. li. | iiij^{or}. pec*iis* cindonis afforc' | eidem lib*erat'* pro roba predic*ta* prec*ii* pec*ia* .xiij. s. iiij. d. ⸺ xij. li. xiij. s. iiij. d. **probatum**

Eidem in prec*io* | trium panno*rum* . dim*i*dia rub' mixti in grana liber*at'* pro robis estivalibus familie sue p*re*dic*te* prec*ii* panni c. s. | v. pec*iis* cindon' afforc' | prec*ii* pec*ia*. j. m^ar*cam* | & un*ius* p*e*c*ia* di*mi*dia cindon' de *cursu* prec*ii* pecia. vij. s. ⸺ xxj. li. vij. s. ij. d. **probatum**

Eidem in precio .xiiij. uln' de blueto | albo | prec*ii* ulne .iij. s. iiij. d. xiij. uln' rad*iati* afforc'. prec*ii*. ulne ij. s. ix. d. pro rob*is* estivalibus scutiferor*um* suor*um* predictor*um* pro?[*text obscured*] | & in precio .iiij^{or}. furu*ris* agn*i* [*written above the previous:* prec*ii* furure iij s.] | eis*dem* pro robis suis p*re*d*i*ctas lib*er*at' iiij. li. xvij s. ij. d. **probatum**

Eidem in precio un*ius* panni de colore sibi liberat' pro roba sua de festo s*an*cti Edwardi precii .viij. li. | iiij^{or}. fu*ruris* de m*i*niver . precii cui*us*l*ibet* .xxx. s. un*ius* capuc*ii* m*i*niver . prec*ii* .xvij. s. un*ius* capuc*ii* m*i*niver . de .iiij. tir'. prec*ii* x. s. ⸺ xv. li. vij. s. **probatum**

Eidem in precio un*ius* panni | mixti in grana | sibi liber*at'* ad festum omn*ium* s*an*ctorum | prec*ii* .jx. li. iiij^{or}. furu*ris* m*i*niver pro supertunic*as* prec*ii* cuius*libet* .xxx. s. un*ius* capuc*ii* ad capam prec*ii* .xvi. s. j. capuc*ii* purat*i* prec*ii* .x. s. j. pane | prec*ii* .v. m^ar*cas* xix. li. xij. s. viij. d. **probatum**

Eidem in precio | un*ius* pelic' de Grisi*s* | sibi liberat' p*ro* sesona hiemali anni presentis ⸺ L. s. **probatum**

Eidem pro retonsura .xviij. panno*rum* | vid*e*licet pro quo*libet* | de ~~.xij.~~ [*crossed out; written above the previous in darker ink:* **.xj.**] ij. s. & pro quo*libet* de residuo xvj. d ⸺ ~~xxxij . s.~~ [*crossed out; written after in darker ink:* xxx. s.] **probatum**

To the same, the purchase of 7 ells of *perse*, delivered to her [or 'for livery'] for the robes of William, clerk of the chapel, the same costing per ell, 3s. 4d., one fur lining of lambswool costing 3s., and one hood of budge costing 2s. 6d., for his aforesaid robes —— 28s. 10d.   **approved**

To the same, the purchase of two cloths and 8 ells of striped stanford, delivered to her [or 'for livery'] for the robes of her valets 'of office': namely Peter her tailor, Robinet of the buttery, one of her grooms, ? of the chamber, Reginald Cokewald, ~~Henry of the chamber~~ William (the) Cook, Herman of Holland, Baldwyn of the chamber: to each of them 7 ells, costing per cloth 50s. Eight fur linings of white lambswool for surcoats, each costing 2s. 6d., to be delivered for lining the aforesaid robes —— £6 16s. 8d.   **approved**

To the same, the purchase of a cloth of sanguine scarlet delivered to her for her robe for the Feast of Easter of the 31st regnal year, £14 13s. 4d. 4½ fur linings of miniver for surcoats, each costing 30s. A hood of trimmed miniver for a cape, costing 16s. A hood of miniver of four tiers, costing 10s. A pane for a mantel costing 5 marks —— £26 12d.   **approved**

To the same, the purchase of a cloth of Brussels delivered to her for her robe of the Ascension, by Thomas de Virzon, costing £10. four pieces of lined sindon [cendal?], delivered to the same for the aforesaid robe, costing per piece 13s. 4d. —— £12 13s. 4d.   **approved**

To the same, the purchase of three and a half mixed red cloths dyed 'in grain', delivered for summer robes for her aforesaid household, costing per cloth 100s. five pieces of lined sindon [cendal?], costing per piece 1 mark, and 1½ pieces of sindon [cendal?] *de cursu*, costing per piece 7s. —— £21 7s. 2d.   **approved**

To the same, the purchase of 14 ells of white bluet, costing per ell 3s. 4d. 14 ells of lined ray, costing per ell 2s. 9d., for summer robes of squires of the aforementioned ?, and the purchase of four fur linings of lambswool [above the previous: 'costing per fur 3s.'] for her robes delivered to the aforesaid, £4 17s. 2d.   **approved**

To the same, the purchase of one cloth of colour delivered to her for her robe for the feast of St Edward, costing £8. four fur linings of miniver, each costing 30s. One hood of miniver, costing 17s. One hood of miniver of four tiers, costing 10s. —— £15 7s.   **approved**

To the same, the purchase of a mixed cloth dyed 'in grain', delivered to her for the feast of All Saints costing £9. four fur linings of miniver for surcoats, each costing 30s. A hood for a cape costing 16s. one trimmed hood costing 10s. one pane costing 5 marks. £19 12s. 8d.   **approved**

To the same, the purchase of a pelisse of *gris* delivered to her for the winter season of the present year —— 50s.   **approved**

To the same, for finishing/re-shearing eighteen cloths, for each of twelve ['11' written above], 2s., and for each of the remaining, 16d. —— ~~32 s.~~ 30s.   **approved**

Eid*em* in p*re*cio .vj. pec' karde | sibi lib*erat*' p*er* Thomam de Querle | p*re*c*ii* cuius*libet* pec' .vj. s. —— xxxvj. s.

Eid*em* in p*re*cio .xx^ti. uln' canabi' | lib*erat*' p*er* vices p*ro* d*i*c*t*is pan' | & fur' mitrissand & saluo custodiend' p*er* vices | p*re*c*ii* ulne .iij. d. [*inserted above the line:* <u>v. s'.</u>] diversis portag' | cartag' & discar*atag*' facis p*ro* eisd*em* anno p*re*dicto, v. s. ? x. s.

Eid*em* in p*re*cio .xxx. uln' tele de Leges | p*re*c*ii* ulne .xij. d. xxvij. uln' canabi . p*re*c*ii* ulne .iij. d. Lx. uln' mappa . p*re*c*ii* ulne xij. d. xxx. uln' tuall' . p*re*c*ii* ulne vj. d. vend' eid*em* p*er* vices anno p*re*dicto. p*er* Querle —— cxj .s. ix. d.   **probatum**

      Summa —— **clxxiiij li** ~~xvj. s.~~ ^xiiij. s.^ **iiij. d.**

4. Extracts from the roll of expenses of Thomas de Crosse, Clerk of the Great Wardrobe, 1342–3 (National Archives, MS E 101/389/14, memb. 1)

This wardrobe account has been studied by clothing historians (particularly Newton 1980), because it seems to contain a number of new cuts and styles used by Edward III and his court for tournaments at Dunstable and other places, around the time of his son Lionel's betrothal to Elizabeth de Burgh, fourth countess of Ulster. Lionel ('of Antwerp'), later duke of Clarence, would have been about five years old at the time; the countess was ten.

    The account was drawn up under the supervision of Thomas de Crosse, Clerk of the Royal Wardrobe, and the opening membrane deals with purchases for the king and his retinue for festivals and celebrations during the year, as well as gifts of clothing given to the king (from the duke of Cornwall, the future 'Black Prince'; from Thomas de Hatfield, Lord Privy Seal and future bishop of Durham, etc.). There are many interesting items of cloth, clothing, accoutrement, furnishings and production methods in the Latin account, many of which have been borrowed or else recently derived from vernacular usage ('frounciat' & butonat'': frounced and buttoned), or are wholesale borrowings ('kaynett': kennet, a type of cloth; 'couerchiefs'; 'tartaryn': tartarin, a silk, tabby-woven textile).

    In her otherwise excellent study on *Fashion in the Age of the Black Prince*, Stella Mary Newton makes a great deal of the reference to 'Paddebury', suggesting that it might be a kind of garment, perhaps associated with a place of manufacture (1980: 134). However, it is clear that this is a misreading of the entry 'Unius tunice [...] domino regis datis [*sic*] per J. Paddebury' (of a tunic... given to the king by J. [John] Paddebury). John Paddebury is mentioned in the *Calendar of Patent Rolls* for Edward III in 1349 (vol. 8, p. 268), and before 1370, a 'John de Paddebury' was apparently granted £10 annually by the king's letters patent, 'to be received at the Exchequer during his life, for the good services rendered by him to the same Lord the King' (Devon 1835: 30).

    The account also includes entries 'pro perfornacione unius furur' de' (for preparing a fur of) 'Benre' or 'Bevre', in order to line a cloak and a pair of gloves for the king. Under its entry for 'perfornire, ~iare', the *DMLBS* reads 'Benre' here ('of Bern', possibly?). Whilst the minims are very difficult to distinguish in this document, it is possible that the word should read instead 'Bevre' (beaver, beaver fur).

    The extract represents a transcription of the first membrane of this eight-membrane Wardrobe account. The script is small, neat, regular and heavily abbreviated, and appears to be by the same hand throughout. The transcription and translation are both by Mark Chambers. Common abbreviations and suspensions have been expanded in italics. Uncertain or illegible readings are offered in italics and in square brackets.

To the same, the purchase of six pieces of card delivered to her by Thomas de Querle, each piece costing 6s. —— 36s.

To the same, the purchase of 20 ells of canvas, delivered on occasion, to ship and store the aforesaid cloths and furs, costing 3d. per ell, 5s. for various portage, cartage and discartage of the same, for the aforesaid year, 5s. [??] 10s.

To the same, the purchase of 30 ells of Liège linen, costing 12d. per ell. 27 ells of canvas, costing 3d. per ell. 60 ells of *mappa*, costing 12d. per ell. 30 ells of towel, costing 6d. per ell. Bought on occasion for the aforesaid year, by Querle —— 111s. 9d. *approved*

Total —— £174 16s. [14s.], **4d.**

Expense minute & nec*cessar*ie magne garderobe d*om*ini regis E' *ter*cii post conquestum facte tam *per* Thomam de Crosse clericum eiusdem garderobe q*uam* p*er* diversos officiarios eiusdem garderobe in anno regii predicti d*om*ini regis: sextodecimo:

[*written in left margin*:] Joh*ann*es Marreys cissor d*om*ini Regis

John Marreys, cissori d*om*ini regis p*r*o diversis custub*is* & expens*is* p*er* ips*um* factis & appositis circa f*act*ur' talliatur' consutur' fururac' & p*ur*filac' & operaciones d*ive*rsas rob' tunic' sup*er*tunic' & al*iis* diversis rerum & garniament*is* tam p*r*o corp*or*e ipsius regis q*uam* p*r*o diversis magnatib*us* & al*iis* de p*re*cepto ipsius regis p*er* diversas vices infra tempus huius compoti . VIDELICET iiij^or robarum long' & iiij^or robarum curt' qualibet rob' long' & curt' de .vj. garmiament*is* faciend' fururand' p*u*rfiland' & capuc' rob' curt' liniand' & sup*er*tunic' curt' frounciat' & butonat' ante pectus p*r*o corpore ipsius d*om*ini regis con-*tra* festa O*mn*ium s*an*ctor*u*m purificaci*oni*s & pasche sciliet p*ro* qualibet roba long*a* & curta .xij. s'. xlviij. s'. Unius robe long*e* de iiij^or garniament' de pann' rub' mixt' de brucell faciend' & liniand' con*tra* fes*tum* pentecostes . p*ro* d*omi*no rege sup*er*tunic' curt' frounciat' p*r*o rege & botonat' ante . anno p*re*senti .viij. s'. Unius robe long*e* de .iij. garniament' de panno marbryn' faciend' & liniand' p*r*o d*om*ino rege con*tra* idem fes*tum* .vj. s'. Unius robe long*e* de iiij^or garniam*ent*' sup*er*tunic' c*ur*t' frounciat' & botonat' ante facte de pann' d*om*ino regi dat' p*er* d*om*ino Ducem Cornub' [. . .] cum fur' ad eandem faciend' fururand' & p*ur*filiand' .viij. s'. Unius tunice frounciate & botonate & unius capucio de pann' porr' de brucell faciend' furur' & capuc' liniand' p*r*o rege .ij. s'. Triu*m* tunicar*um* frounciat*arum* & botonat*arum* de pann' viridi de brucell p*r*o rege & duobus militibus suis contra Tor-niamentu*m* de Dunstaple faciend' fururand' .v. s'. iiij. d. scili*cet* p*r*o tunica regis .ij. s'. & utriusque militibus .xx. d. xxxij. tunicarum de pann' radiati faciend' fururand' & frounciand' cum tot capuciis albis. pro scutiferis regis pro eodem tornamento .xxxij. s'. Trium manticar*um* de panno scarlett' & brucell faciend' & liniand' p*r*o secret' d*om*ini regis infra portand' & cariand' .vj. s'. ij. d. Unius mantice magne de corio faciend' & liniand' p*r*o gen-taculo regis infra cariand' .ij. s'. Unius capucio d*om*ini regis faciend' & liniand' de panno de brucell .ij. d. ij. par*i*a braccar*um* de pann' lane faciend' p*r*o rege & liniand' cum tela de reyns p*r*o yeme .xij. d. ix tunicarum frounciatarum & botonatarum de pann' kaynett' cum tot capuciis de pann' viridi faciend' p*r*o d*om*ino rege & viij. militibus suis p*r*o hastilud apud North*a*mpton de p*re*cepto ipsius regis sciliet pro tunica regis cum capucio .ij. s'. & qualibet alia tunica cum capucio xx. d. xv. s'. iiij. d. xxv. tunicar*um* cum tot capuciis de secta p*re*dicta pro xxij. armiger*is* regis & regine & iij. ministrall suis faciend' contra hastiliud p*re*dicta de p*re*cepto regis .xxv. s'. scili*cet* p*r*o qualibet tunic' cum capucio .xij. d. duar*um* tunicar*um* frounciatarum & botonatar*um* cum capuciis & ij. magnis clochis de pann' viridi mixt' & brun' mixt' de brucell pro rege facined' & liniand' x. s'. scili*cet* p*r*o utraque tunic' cloch' & capuc' .v. s'. Duar*um* sup*er*tunicar*um* estivali frounciatar*um* & botonatar*um* ante pectus cum capucio de panno scarletto & viridi de brucell p*r*o d*om*ino rege .vj. s'. scili*cet* p*r*o utraque .iij. s'. Unius robe long*e* de iiij^or garniament' de panno mixto de Brucell p*r*o d*om*ino Duce faciend' & liniand' de p*re*cepto ipsius d*om*ini regis vj. s'. iij. corsettorum faciend' & unius tunice liniande pro rege iiij. s'. iij. tunic' iiij. courtepet' & ij. mantell cum iij. capuciis pro rege faciend' p*r*o tempore estivali de pann' viridi de brucell ix. s'. viij. d. cccclij. tunicarum cum tot capuciis faciend' & garnissand' p*r*o tot marinariis d*om*ini reg^is contra passagium suum ultra mare xj. li'. vj. s'. scili*cet* pro qualibet tunic' cum capucio .vj.d.

Detailed and necessary expenses of the Great Wardrobe of the Lord King Edward the Third, made by Thomas de Crosse, clerk of the same Wardrobe, and by various officials of the same wardrobe, in the sixteenth regnal year of the aforesaid king.

[*written in left margin*:] John Marreys, tailor of the lord king

John Marreys, tailor of the lord king, for various costs and expenses made by the same, concerning the making, tallying, cutting, lining with fur, trimming with fur and embroidering of divers suits, tunics, surcoats and other various things and garments, not only for the body of the king himself but also for various nobles and others, by order of the king, at various times during the period of this account; NAMELY, of four long suits and four short suits, each long suit and short suit of six garments, for making, for lining with fur and for trimming, and for lining the hood of the short suit, and the short surcoat, 'frounced' and provided with buttons on the front of the chest, for the body of the same the lord king, for the feast of All Saints, the Purification and Easter, namely for each long and short suit, 12s.: 48s. For making and lining one long suit of four garments of red mixed-cloth of Brussels, for the feast of Pentecost. For the lord king, a short surcoat, 'frounced', for the king and provided with buttons on the front, *for the current year*: 8s. For making and lining a long suit of three garments of marbrin [cloth] for our lord king, for the same feast: 6s. For making, lining and trimming one long suit of four garments, the short surcoat 'frounced' and provided with cloth buttons on the front, given to the lord king by our the lord duke of Cornwall [the future Edward, Black Prince of Wales] [...] with fur for the same: 8s. For making and trimming one tunic, 'frounced' and provided with buttons, and for lining one hood of leek-green [*porrey*] cloth of Brussels, for the king: 2s. For making and lining three tunics, 'frounced' and provided with buttons, of green cloth of Brussels, for the king and two of his knights for the Tournament at Dunstable: 5s. 4d.; namely, for the king's tunic(s), 2s., and for [those for] the two knights 20d. For making, lining and 'frouncing' 32 tunics of striped cloth, with white hoods, for the king's esquire(s) for the same tournament: 32s. For making and lining three travel bags [*portmanteau*] of cloth of scarlet and of Brussels, to store and to carry the lord the king's seal: 6s. 2d. For making and lining one large travel bag [*portmanteau*] of leather to carry the king's breakfast: 2s. For making and lining a hood for the lord king, of Brussels cloth: 2d. For making two pairs of breeches of woollen cloth for the king and for lining with linen of Rheims for winter: 12d. For making nine tunics, 'frounced' and provided with buttons, of cloth of kennet with hoods of green cloth, for the lord king and eight of his knights, for the tournament at Northampton, on the king's orders; namely for the king's tunic with a hood, 2s., and each of the other tunics with hoods 20d.: 15s. 4d. For making 25 tunics with hoods, of the aforesaid suit, for 22 squires of the king and queen and three of their minstrals, for the aforesaid tournament, by order of the king: 25s.; namely, for each tunic with a hood, 12d. For making and lining two tunics, 'frounced' and provided with buttons, with hoods, and two great cloaks of mixed green and mixed brown cloth of Brussels for the king: 10s.; namely, for each tunic, cloak and hood, 5s. Two summer surcoats, 'frounced' and provided with buttons on front of the chest, with a hood of scarlet and green cloth of Brussels, for the lord king: 6s.; namely, for each 3s. For making and lining one long robe of four garments, of mixed cloth of Brussels, for the lord duke by order of the same lord king: 6s. For making three corsets and lining one tunic for the king: 4s. For making three tunics, three *courtepeis* [short jackets] and two mantles with three hoods for the king, for summer time, of green cloth of Brussels: 9s. 8d. For making and ornamenting/embroidering 452 tunics, with hoods, for as

Unius tunice cum capucio pro haketon' regis & ij. braccis faciend' & liniand' pro domino rege .ij. s'. ij. d. Unius tunice botonate & frounciate de pann' frys' regi datis per J. Marreys faciend' & fururand' .ij. s'. Unius tunice cum capucio & j magne cloch' de eodem secta frounciata & botonata ante pectus pro domino rege faciend' fururand' & capuc' liniand' .iiij. s'. Lxij. par' rob' lin' pro rege de tela lin' faciend' xlj. s'. iiij. d'. scilicet pro quolibet pari .viij. d'. iiij voluper' & ij. couerchiefs radiat' de serico de tela lin' [sic] de reyns faciend' & garnissand' pro capite domini regis .ij. s'. iiij. couerchiefs .xij. voluper' & ij capdehustes de tela de reyns pro domino rege .vj. s'. iij. foteclothes pro lecto regis de tela parys' ix. d. [this number is presumed, as there appears to be an additional (erroneous?) minim before the x] et pro chausons facend' per pedibus regis per vices infra tempus huius compoti xij d. Et [beginning of this line is quite faded] pro .ij. capuciis regis liniand' videlicet q. domino regi dat' per dominum Ducem . & j de panno suo proprio iiij. d'. iiij [written above the previous: xx]vij paria caligarum de panno de Brucell | in grano | & scarlettis pro rege faciend' pro vices infra tempus huius compoti scilicet pro qualibet pari j. d'. ob. x. s'. x. d'. ob. v canevac' de canab' faciend' pro trussag' diversis garniamentis regis x d. Unius robe longe pro domino rege faciend' fururand' & purfiliand' de panni serici de iiij^or garniamentis contra solempnitates nupciarum domini Lionelli filii sui una tunica botonata & supertunic' curt' frounciat' ante cum lanternis aurifabr' xij s'. ^Et trium tunicarum trium magnorum cloch' domini regis faciend' & fururand' pro yeme contra passagum suum versus Brytanum pro qualibet tunic' & cloch' .iiij. s'. xij. s'. et pro fururat' alia vj. garniamentis cum furur' de Grys pro rege contra idem passagum fururand' .vj. s'. pro fururac' iij. pari cirotecarum cum dere pro rege contra idem passagium scilicet pro quolibet pari .ij. s'. vj. s'. pro performacione unius furur' de Benre [Bevre?] pro quada' cloch' regis ij. s'. Unius tunice frounciate & botonate domino regis datis per J. Paddebury faciend' & fururand' .ij. s'. pro ij. laqueis de serico. cum agulettorum argenti pro quadam mantica regis .xviij. d. iiij. butons serici ad eandem .viij. d'. ij. s'. ij. d. pro urinalibus [written above: & cass' pro eisdem de corio ferro ligat'] empt' per vices isto anno pro lecto regis per Gillot' de Oldecare vj. s'. viij. d. Et pro ij cathedris pro camera domini plicabilis precii utriusque .x. s'. & pro ij. cathedris plicabilis pro garderoba regis privata. precii .xxj. s'. xlj. s'. Unius tunice & unius mantell de pann' tartaryn' faciend' & liniand' cum taffata de pann' & taffata domino regi dat' per Phillipam de Weston' ij. s'. iiij. d. Unius robe de iij. garniament' supertunic' frounciat' & botonat' faciend' & liniand' de pann' regi datis per Thomam de Hatfeld' .iiij. s'. Unius tunice cum capucio frounciate & botonate pro domino rege de dono H. Dengaingum contra passagium suum versus partes Brytanum .ij. s'. pro —— vj. plusculis & xij. anul' arg' pouder' [or ponder'?] .xxj. s'. x. d. pro bractalibus regis [written above: empt' per dictum Johannem Marreys] una cum [?] viij. s'. [written above the previous: scilicet pro factura eorum de pluscul' & anul'] xxix. s'. x. d. pro dearacione h'nes [?] cuiusdam gladij regis .xvj. d. pro iij pari cirotecarum magn' de cervo & fururat' de Benre [Bevre?] pro domino rege prec'cuiuslibet par' v. s'. xv. s'. pro xxxiiij. lb. candel parys' .prec' lb. j d. ob'. quae emptis & expenditis noctanter super predictis operacionibus pro festinacione pro vices infra tempus huius compoti iiij. s'. xj. d. ob. Et pro quodam hospicio per ipsium cissorem conducto per totum tempus huius compoti in quo opera domini regis predicta perficiebantur c. s'.

—— **SUMMA XXXVIJ li. XV s.**

many mariners of the lord king for his passage over the sea: £11 6s.; namely, for each tunic with a hood, 6d. A tunic with a hood for [sic] an aketon for the lord king, and for making and lining two breeches for the lord king: 2s. 2d. For making and lining with fur a tunic, provided with buttons and 'frounced', of frieze cloth, given to the king by John Marreys [Newton suggests that this tunic was given to Marreys by the king (Newton 1980: 16), although the wording here recommends the opposite]: 2s. For making and lining with fur a tunic with a hood, one great cloak of the same suit, 'frounced' and provided with buttons on the front of the chest, for the lord king and for lining the hood: 4s. For making 62 pairs of linen [?] robes for the king of linen cloth: 41s. 4d.; namely, for each pair, 8d. For making and ornamenting/embroidering four scarves and two striped coverchiefs of silk of linen cloth of Rheims for the head of the lord king: 2s. four coverchiefs, twelve scarves and two *capadoses* of cloth of Rheims for the lord king: 6s. three 'foot cloths' for the king's bed of Paris cloth: 9d. [?]. And for making shoes for the feet of the king from time to time during the period of this account: 12d. *And* for lining two of the king's hoods, namely those given to the lord king by the duke, and one of his own cloth: 4d. For making 87 pairs of hose of cloth of Brussels, dyed in grain and of scarlet, for the king, from time to time during the period of this account, namely for each pair, 1½d [*obulos* = halfpenny]: 10s. 10½d. For making five sheets of canvas for carrying various garments of the king: 10d. For making, lining and trimming a long robe of silk cloth, for the lord king, of four garments, for the betrothal ceremonies of his son Lionel: a tunic, provided with buttons, and a short surcoat, 'frounced' in front, with golden lanterns [?]: 12s. And to make and to line three tunics and three great cloaks for the lord king for winter, for his passage to Brittany, for each tunic and cloak 4s.: 12s. And for lining another six garments with fur of *grys* for the king for the same passage: 6s., for the lining with fur of three pairs of gloves with [deerskin?] for the king, for the same passage: that is, for each pair, 2s.: 6s. For preparing a *furrura* [group of furs] of beaver [?] for a certain cloak of the king, 2s. For making and lining a tunic, 'frounced' and provided with buttons, given to the king by J[ohn] Paddebury, 2s., For two laces of silk with aglets of silver for a travelling bag of the king, 18d. four buttons of silk for the same, 8d.: 2s. 2d. For the purchase of chamber pots [?] [*written above*: and a case for the same of leather (?) fastened with iron] during the course of the year for the king's bed, by Gillot' de Oldecare: 6s. 8d. And for two folding chairs for the lord's chamber, each costing 10s., and for two folding chairs for the king's private wardrobe costing 21s.: 41s. For making and lining a tunic and a mantle of tartarin cloth with taffeta, from cloth and taffeta given to the lord our king by Phillip de Weston: 2s. 4d. For making and lining a robe of three garments: a surcoat, 'frounced' and provided with buttons, of cloth given to the king by Thomas de Hatfield [Thomas de Hatfield was Keeper/Lord of the Privy Seal 1344–5 and subsequently bishop of Durham]: 4s. A tunice with a hood, 'frounced' and provided with buttons, for the lord king as a gift of H. Degayn for his passage to Brittany: 2s. For —— six buckles and twelve rings of [*or* 'powdered with' / 'heavy'?] silver, 21s. 10d., for *bractalibus* of the king [bought by the said John Marreys], one *with* 8s. [that is, for the making of their buckles and rings]: 29s. 10d. For gilding [the harnesses of] certain swords of the king: 16d., For three pairs of large gloves of deerskin and furred with beaver [?], for the lord king, each pair costing 5s.: 15s. For 34lbs. of Paris candles, price per pound, 1½d., which were bought and expended by night during the aforesaid work for expediency during the course of this account: 4s. 11½d. And for lodging the tailors for the entire time of this account in which the aforesaid work for the lord king was completed: 100s.

—— **TOTAL : £37 15s.**

5. Extracts from the London Mercers' accounts, fifteenth century

Lisa Jefferson's edition (2009) of the accounts of the London Mercers' Company is interesting for many reasons – for demonstrating the development of a major civic mercantile guild, for its evidence for mixed-language account keeping, for its contribution to our understanding of medieval London's economic history, etc. – but, of course, it provides us with valuable information about the way in which particular cuts, colours, cloths and accoutrements were named in fourteenth- and fifteenth-century documents. As Jefferson relates, the accounts were drawn from the so-called *Wardens Accounts* which ran from *c.* 1390 to *c.* 1464 and were originally analysed by H. J. Creation in a University of London M.Phil. thesis in 1976, from the Mercers' *Book of Ordinances* of the 1430s, analysed by J. M. Parker, also in a University of London M.Phil. thesis (in 1980); and from the *Renter Wardens' Account Book*, running from 1442 to 1500 (Jefferson 2009: 1–18).

The extracts provided below give a snapshot of clothing references in the accounts during the first three decades of the fifteenth century. Despite occasional use of Latin, (Anglo-)French was the primary, or 'matrix', language used in the accounts until 1458–9, when English took over. Jefferson notes that the 'accuracy' of the French arguably declines in the accounts from about the 1420s and points out that English lexical items frequently appear within the French matrix (Jefferson 2009: 24–5). For example, in the entry of 1413–14 below for 'Aournementz des auters' (accoutrements for the altars), we find payment for linen and for workmanship on 'les auter-clothes' (the altar cloths). For 1420–1, we find receipt of payment from one 'Alice Corsmaker' (a corse-maker?) for admission to the 'Sylkwommannes craft' (guild or company of silk producers), and in 1423–4, we find 12 pence paid to William Rippingale for 'waschyng' (washing) some albs.

A detailed history of the London Mercers' Company may be found in Anne Sutton's study *The Mercery of London: Trade, Goods and People, 1130–1578* (2005), which makes extensive reference to the accounts. All of the extracts below are taken from Jefferson 2009, pp. 208–388. The translation is adapted from this edition, and we have included notes to the extracts where relevant.

1407–8 [p. 208]:
Item, paié a Sire William Hedyngdoun pur lez orfreys de une chesible de velvet en grayn embroydez, q'il ad donee ovesqe une missale aprés son decesse, ambedeux al oeps del mercerye – xxxiii s. iii d.

1409–10 [p. 232]:
Veilles parementz appertenantz al mistere:
Item, ils ont delyvree a les avantditz gardeyns par eux esluz les veilles parementz pur lour auter, queux Sire William Hedyngdoun, le chapelein de la mercerye, lour delyvrera, c'est assavoir une chalice d'argent ové le patene [MS: 'patene enorrez', the latter word firmly scored out] poisent xvi ounces iii quarterons, pris xlii s. Item, une veille chesible ové les parures de tartaryn raié, une aube et une amyte et une towaille pur estre desuis l'autre, pris tout – viii s. Item, veille huch lié de ferre, pris – x s.

Doune de Sire William Hedyngtoun, chapeleyn del mercerye:
Item, ils ount delivrez as ditz novelles gardeyns par eux esluz les choses desoutz escriptz queux le dit Sire William Hedyngdoun lour delyvra auxy, et queux mesme Sire William ad dounee de sa bone volentee a la comunealtee de la mistere del mercerye, c'est assavoir une novelle lyvre appellee missale, pris x marcz. Item, une chesible de velvet rouge champ soie embraudé de esteilles d'or ové les parures, aube et amytes, pris – liii s. iii d.

1407–8 [p. 209]:
Also, paid to Sir William Hedyngton for the embroidered orphreys of a velvet chasuble dyed in grain, which he has bequeathed after his death with a missal, both of them for the use of the mercers' mystery – 33 s. 4.

1409–10 [p. 233]:
Old ornaments belonging to the mistery:
Also, they handed over to the aforesaid wardens elected by them the old ornaments for their altar which Sir William Hedyngton, chaplain of the mercers' mistery, handed over to them, i.e. a silver chalice and paten, weighing 16¾ oz., value 42s. Item, an old chasuble of striped tartarin with its accoutrements, an alb and an amice and a cloth to go over the top of the altar, value of the whole – 8s. Item, an old chest bound with iron, value – 10s.

Gift of Sir William Hedyngton, chaplain of the mercers' mystery:
Also, they handed over to the said new wardens elected by them the things written below which the said Sir William Hedyngton had also handed over to them, and which the same Sir William had of his goodwill given to the commonalty of the mercers' mistery, i.e. a new book called a missal, value 10 marks. Item, a chasuble of red velvet with a silk ground, embroidered with golden stars, with the accoutrements, alb and amice, value – 53s. 4d.

1413–14 [p. 266]:
Fyn d'assent:
Item, receu de Johan Middeltoun pur ceo q'il ne port poynt de ray – iiii s. viii d. [...]

Aournementz des auters:
Item, paié pur teille et overaigne de les auterclothes depeyntez contrefaitz une drap d'or ynde et blanke, vidz. front, reredos, deux cortynes, depeyntez d'ambes partz touz costes – iii li. ii s. ii d.

1413–14 [p. 268]:
Item, paié pur teille et overaigne de les auterclothes et une chesible contrefaitz une drap d'or ynde et blanke, vidz. front, reredos, deux cortines, depeyntez d'ambes partz, une chesible del suite ové l'albe, et un ymage remuable pur quaresme appellé Pité – en tout – liii s. ii d.

1414 [p. 270]:
Biens del mistere:
Item, ils ont delyveré auxy une chesible de drap d'or attaby large, ové l'albe, q'ils avoient des executours Robert Guphey qe vaut pluis qe – v marcz.
Item, ils ont delyvree canvas pur coverer l'auter pur poudre – vaut – xiiii d.

1415–16 [p. 286]:
Item, paié a Isabelle Bally pur frenge de soy – ii s. vi d.
Item, paié a Maude Dentoun pur frenge de soy – ii s. viii d.
Item, paié a Piers Dyker pur amender auterclothes – ii s. iiii d.

1420–1 [p. 328]:
Fyn pur l'entré d'une femme:
Memorandum, receu de Alyce Corsmaker [n257: 'It is just possible that this should read "Alyce, corsmaker", i.e. that it is not a surname but a definition of her trade as one who makes "corses" = "A ribbon or band of silk (or other material), serving as a ground for ornamentation with metalwork or embroidery, and used as a girdle, garter, etc." (OED)'] pur un fyn pur entrer en Sylkwommannes craft vi s. viii d.

1421–2 [p. 336]:
Foreins costes:
Item, paié a Johan Carpenter pur iii lettres envoiez a Gant, Brugge, et Ipre – xxxiii s. iiii d.
Item, a Richard Lyndesay pur une supplicacioun a lez Maire et Aldermanz pur Johan van Neweden, ducheman, webbe – vi d.
Item, a Rauf, Sergeant del Chambre, pur somoner lez maistres dez Webbes et le dit Johan Neweden pur comparoire devant le Maire – xii d.
Item, a Johan Carpenter pur l'entré del descharge du dit Johan Neweden de sa franchise – ii s.
Item, a Richard Lyndesay pur l'escrire d'une lettre mys par William Waldern a la companye del Estaple a Caleys – viii d.

1413–14 [p. 267]:
Fine by agreement:
Also, received from John Middleton because he does not wear 'ray' [striped cloth] – 4s. 8d. [n121: 'Presumably this year's livery had been of striped cloth'] …

Accoutrements for the altars:
Also, paid for linen and the workmanship of the altar-cloths, painted to imitate cloth-of-gold, in blue and white, i.e. frontal, reredos, two curtains, painted on both sides, costs in all – £3 2s. 2d.

1413–14 [p. 269]:
Also, paid for linen and the workmanship of the altarcloths and of a chasuble imitating cloth-of-gold, in white, i.e. frontal, reredos, two curtains, painted on both sides, a matching chasuble with alb, and a movable image for Lent called a Pity – in all – 53s. 2d.

1414 [p. 271]:
Goods belonging to the mistery:
Also, they handed over also a chasuble of cloth-of-gold, of wide tabby silk, with the alb, which they obtained from Robert Guppey's executors and which is worth more than 5 marks. Item they handed over a canvas cloth to cover the altar [and protect it from] dust – worth – 14d.

1415–16 [p. 287]:
Also, paid to Isabelle Bally for silk fringe – 2s. 6d.
Also, paid to Maud Denton for silk fringe – 2s. 8d.
Also, paid to Piers Dyker for mending the altar cloths – 2s. 4d.

1420–1 [p. 329]:
Fee for the admission of a woman:
Memorandum, received from Alice Corsmaker for a fee for admission to the Silkwomen's craft – 6s. 8d.

1420–1 [p. 337]:
Foreign costs:
Also, paid to John Carpenter [the Common Clerk of London] for three letters sent to Ghent, Bruges, Ypres – 33s. 4d.
Also, to Richard Lyndesey [a scrivener] for a petition to the Mayor and aldermen concerning John Van Uden, 'Dutchman', linenweaver – 6d.
Also, to Ralph, serjeant of the [Gildhall] Chamber, for summoning the wardens of the Linenweavers and the said John Van Uden to appear before the Mayor – 12d.
Also, to John Carpenter for entering up the expulsion of the said John Van Uden from his freedom – 2s.
Also, to Richard Lyndesey for the writing of a letter sent by William Walderne to the company of the Staple at Calais – 8d.

1423–4 [p. 354]:
Item, paié pur repayryng de ii vestementes, stoles et fanonis – v s.
Item, paié pur ii newe aubis – vi s. viii d.
Item, paié a Sire William Ripyngale pur waschyng de abbis – xii d.

1425–6 [p. 368]:
Item, pur laver lynges del chapel et fasoun de i obligacioun et i paire endentures entre le rayman et nous – xvi d.

1427–8 [p. 388]:
John Pydmylle faut i chaperon al dirige de Richard Whityngton – iiii d.

1423–4 [p. 355]:
Also, paid for the repair of two sets of vestments, stoles and fanons – 5s.
Also, paid for two new albs – 6s. 8d.
Item, paid to Sir William Rippingale for the washing of the albs – 12d.

1425–6 [p. 369]:
Also, for the washing of the chapel linen and the drawing up of a bond obligatory and a pair of indentures between ourselves and the raymerchant – 16d.

1427–8 [p. 389]:
John Pidmylle lacked a hood at Richard Whittington's obit [commemoration, rather than funeral, for 'Dick Wittington'].

CHAPTER III

Inventories and Rolls of Livery

INTRODUCTION

As with the accounts extracted in the previous chapter, rolls of inventories, livery and other forms of medieval business writing provide an excellent source for the detailed naming of medieval clothing and textiles. Often the intent in such record-keeping is not just to keep an accurate record of who possessed or who received what, but to provide a precise description of the item or garment in question.

The three extracts which open the chapter are all drawn from the very detailed inventories of the medieval cathedral of St Paul in London, dating from the middle and later part of the thirteenth century and from the beginning of the fifteenth. The descriptive detail they provide of vestments, altar cloths, cathedral plate and so forth is exceptionally descriptive for the text type, and gives us a very vivid account of the cloth and clothing in the cathedral's possession at the times of the inventories.

These are followed by a collection of extracts taken from the middle of a roll of liveries of Edward III for 1347–9. The extracts are noteworthy because they contain various items of dress and accoutrements for royal tournaments and celebrations, including some of the first references to the uniforms of the Order of the Garter, as well as costumes for *ludi* (pageants, entertainments) celebrated at Christmas.

EXTRACTS FROM THE INVENTORIES

THREE INVENTORIES OF ST PAUL'S CATHEDRAL

Inventories compiled in 1245, 1295 and 1402 list the treasures, including metalwork, books, vestments and soft furnishings, belonging to St Paul's Cathedral, London. They testify to the vast quantities, the richness of fabric and the gold and jewelled ornament of the textiles owned by the cathedral. The first two inventories coincide with a period of expansion of the Norman cathedral ('old St Paul's'), the fourth to be built on the site, which was, by its completion in 1314, one of the largest in Europe, with a 400-foot spire and a magnificent rose window. In the 1530s King Henry VIII would begin confiscating church wealth and dissolving monasteries. About the same time more austere approaches to worship were advocated as a result of the Protestant Reformation, rendering outdated the medieval Church's relics in their magnificent shrines, opulent furnishings and sumptuous vestments. Most gold-encrusted textiles were probably destroyed, often burnt, in the sixteenth and seventeenth centuries to recover the precious metal. The old St Paul's building itself, already in a state of disrepair, was further damaged in the Fire of London and was demolished in 1667 to be replaced by the domed cathedral which stands on the site today.

The selections below reflect the range of textiles, their colours and the ornament on them, showing changes in descriptive vocabulary and cataloguing principles between the three inventories. The texts are taken from W. Sparrow Simpson, 'Two Inventories of the Cathedral Church of St Paul, London, dated respectively 1245 and 1402', *Archaeologia* 50, 1887, part II, 439–519 (1245 at pp. 464–500; 1402 at pp. 500–18); and the inventory from 1295 is from William Dugdale, *The History of St Paul's Cathedral in London . . .* with continuations by Henry Ellis, 3rd edn, London, 1818, pp. 311–35, incorporating Simpson's corrections to Dugdale/Ellis, which do not affect the passages selected below, but do affect the count of vestments. The text of the latter was originally printed in William Dugdale's 1716 edition of *The History of St. Paul's Cathedral in London*. The texts are translated by Gale R. Owen-Crocker and Mark Chambers. Bracketed information on persons is partly taken from Simpson's notes with some editorial additions; duplicated text noted by Simpson is omitted.

1a. St Paul's Cathedral inventory of 1245

The inventory largely lists individual vestments, apart from a few sets, cataloguing the cathedral's holdings in terms of vestment-types, beginning with the more precious examples. It shows awareness of former owners and includes some items already very old, going back to Anglo-Saxon times in some cases. The predominant fabric is samite, a heavy lustrous silk cloth in a twill weave. The compiler gives considerable detail of the design of decoration on textiles, but is vague on technicalities, relying heavily on the word *aurifrigium* but once mentioning that a cloth is 'pulverizatur' (powdered) with bezants. The inventory lists episcopal regalia including 4 mitres; 3 sets of 'sandalia' or ecclesiastical slippers with accompanying under-socks/stockings; 4 pairs of gloves; 17 cushions; 108 copes, divided into those with precious ornaments and those without; 12 morses, fasteners for copes, here listed separately; 34 chasubles; twenty-nine tunicles, of which 14 are listed together with dalmatics, and one single dalmatic; 29 vestment sets, mostly consisting of apparels, stole, maniple and amice, plus 10 other amices and two stole and maniple sets; precious silk cloths, including 33 baudekins (rich silk textiles often woven with silver or gold thread, and embroidered), 19 cloths of 'aresta' (a silk cloth with a herringbone ground weave, richly patterned with various motifs such as birds and flowers) and one black samite; furnishings for the choir including 5 cushions and 16 hangings, two of the latter silks of 'aresta'; and two carpets (or possibly

hangings) and 11 curtains, either the smaller 'cortina' or the larger 'vela'. Items which belonged to, or were given by, the same person are usually listed together in each category (though the same person may occur in more than one category). Old and less valuable items are usually placed at the end of a list.

De Baculis et Ornamenta Episcopalibus
[. . .] Mitra de alba purpura breudata stellis et lunulis ante et retro. In stellis utrinque sunt topatii et almandine. In circulo inferiori sunt quasi bisantii triphuriati cum lapidibus peridotis, et similiter thau cum lapidibus. [. . .]
Mitra alba cum aurifrigio vineato et floribus lapparum. [. . .]
Sandalia et caligae de rubeo samito satis bono et novo, cujus caligae sunt breudatae circulis interius continentes aquilas et dracones interius forratae croceali viridi sendato. Sandalia sunt breudata aliis floribus furrata indico sendato cum semellis de coreo.
Sandalia alia de indico samito, cujus caligae sunt breudatae scalopis Sancti Jacobi et leonibus, furratae rubeo sendato, et ornatae aurifrigio. Sotulares breudatae floribus sine semellis.
Quatuor paria cyrotecarum antiquarum addubbata circulis deauratis.

De Cathedris et Pulvinaribus
Pulvinar ad textum portandum de opere sartacinito [*sic*] aliquantulum vetus in quo scribuntur Willelmus et Albreda.
Pulvinar novum, totum consutum nodis de serico, quod fuit Mauricii de Herlawe. [. . .]

De Capis sericis magis preciosis
Capa, quae dicitur Alardi Decani, est de purpureo samito, breudata rosis, stellis, et gladeolis, et lunulis, cum tassellis, in quibus breudantur Sanctus Petrus et Sanctus Paulus. Ad hanc capam pertinet morsus auri, ut dicetur inferius. [. . .]
Capa, quae dicitur Ricardi Episcopi, est de purpureo samito, satis nova, leopardis et floribus internodatis breudata. Haec habet morsum argenteum cum ymaginibus Petri et Pauli massitiis, cum quatuor angelis ad quatuor angulos.
Capa Magistri Ricardi de Storteford est de nigro samito, breudata vineis, griffonibus, et volucribus, cum tassellis breudatis floribus auri puri.
Capa ejusdem altera de rubeo samito plana, addubbata de aurifrigio de auro puro.
Capa Willelmi Episcopi de viridi samito peroptimo, breudata ymaginibus Beatae Virginis anterius, et angelis cum thuribulis, et sagittariis. Habet morsum, ut dicetur inferius. [. . .]
Capa quae dicitur magistri Rogeri capellani est de albo samito in anterioribus limbis angelis breudatis cum thuribulis. Pulverizatur tota bisantiis breudatis. Habet morsum connexum de plano sine gradibus, in cujus medio est presme contrafacta.
Capa magistri Ricardi Ruffi est de rubeo samito, breudata sagittariis, cum tassellis, in quorum uno martirizatur Stephanus, in alio Thomas. Haec habet morsum argenteum oblongum, cum duobus gradibus; in cujus crista sunt tres cornelinae sculptae cum Onichinis.
Capa, quae fuit Radulphi Decani, est de purpureo samito, cum bono aurifrigio, breudata gladeolis duplicibus foliis anteriis. [. . .]
Capa fusca de panno serico breudata cum minutis gladeolis et minutis bisantiis et floribus

Concerning staves and episcopal ornaments
A mitre of white *purpura* embroidered with stars and crescent moons front and back. In the stars on both sides are topazes and garnets. In the circle below are golden plates pierced with trefoils with peridot stones and likewise tau crosses with gemstones.
A white mitre with lappets decorated in gold with vines and flowers.
Ecclesiastical slippers and stockings of red samite, new and of good quality, of which the stockings are embroidered with circles containing eagles and dragons, the interior lined with yellowish-green sendal. The slippers are embroidered with other flowers, the interior lined with indigo sendal with soles of leather.
Another pair of slippers of indigo samite, of which the stockings are embroidered with scallop shells of St James and lions, lined with red sendal and ornamented with goldwork. Slippers without soles embroidered with flowers.
Four pairs of gloves of the old fashion, adorned with gilded circles.

Concerning chairs and cushions
A cushion for carrying the text, made of Saracen work, rather old, on which is inscribed William and Albreda.
A new cushion, stitched all over with silk knots, which belonged to Maurice of Herlaw [prebendary of Twyford in 1218].

Concerning silk copes of greater value
A cope, said to have belonged to Dean Alard [Alard de Burnham, 1200–16], of purple samite, embroidered with roses, stars, and fleurs-de-lis and crescent moons, with tassels, on which are embroidered St Peter and St Paul. To this cope belongs a gold morse, described below.
A cope which is said to have belonged to Bishop Richard [probably Richard de Ely or Fitzneale, bishop 1189–98], of purple samite, relatively new, embroidered with interlaced leopards and flowers. This has a silver morse with massive images of Peter and Paul with four angels at the four corners.
A cope of Master Richard of Stortford [prebendary and chancellor, died *c.* 1215], of black samite, embroidered with vines, griffons and birds of prey, with tassels embroidered with flowers of pure gold.
A cope, another of the same, of plain red samite adorned with gold work of pure gold.
A cope of Bishop William, of green samite of the best quality, embroidered with images of the Blessed Virgin on the front, and angels with thuribles, and archers. It has a morse, as described below.
A cope said to belong to Master Roger the chaplain, of white samite embroidered on the front edges with angels with thuribles. It is powdered all over with embroidered bezants. It has a plain morse without notches (?), in the middle of which is an artificial presm [an inferior kind of emerald].
A cope of Master Richard Ruff is of red samite, embroidered with archers, with tassels,

minutis. Hanc breudare fecit Henricus Cancellarius, et postea Decanus. [...]
Capa Rogeri de Wigornia est de albo diaspero, breudata aquilis expansis, cum lunis et stellis, et habet morsum oblongum; in cujus cristae medio est perla, adjectis duobus topaziis ad duo capita. [...]

De Capis minus preciosis
Capa, quae dicitur archidiaconi Nicholai, est de albo sameto plano, cum tassello pectorali quadrato contexto margaritis albis et viridibus contrafactis et filo auri in orbicularibus puro et tracto contexto.
Capa alia ejusdem vetus est de panno serico ut dicitur imperiali cum pavonibus et arboribus contexto. [...]
Capa quae dicitur Magistri Nicholai est nigra tota plana cum tassellis parvis juxta aperturam sub mento gladeolata magnis gladeolis.
Capae tres quae fuerunt Osberti de Camera, quarum duae sunt de croceo sameto et sine tassellis planae. Tercia de rubeo sameto cum tassellis de purpura breudatis cum angelis. [...]
Capa vetus de albo baldekino vineata et arboreta purpura gracili cum ymaginibus malefactis: fuit R. Archidiaconi Midlesex'. [...]
Item capa de Waleden' de panno de Arista rubeo cum aviculis albis.
Item duae capae de panno de Arista, quarum una facta fuit de panno, quam dedit Eustachius episcopus; alia de panno episcope Rogeri, cum trifoliis. Novae sunt: tenent inde choristae.

Morus caparum, qui non attachiantur continue ad Capas
Morsus Alardi Decani de auro puro habet amatistam in medio cristae, saphyrum in sinistro latere, cornelinum in dextro sculptum, praetor alios minutos lapides et grossos.
Morsus Willelmi Episcopi de auro puro cum saphiro in medio cristae et duobus cornelinis sculptis sibi collateralibus, cum saphiris et aliis lapidibus preciosis. [...]

De Casulis
[...] Casula Godivae de Coventria est de quo panno nigro minutissime ginillato, cum gemellis purpureis et rubeis cum aurifrigio, fino interhumerali breudatur arbor auro sine lapidibus.
Casula Hugonis de Orivall est de diaspero albo plano orbiculariter operata avibus et arboribus in orbicularibus, contextum cum optimo aurifrigio cum tassellis, anteriori facto de filo aureo tracto de eodem breudato ymagine majestatis limbis aurifrigia dorsalis consutis stricta linea margaritarum.

on one of which is a martyrdom of St Stephen, on the other St Thomas [St Thomas of Canterbury, Thomas à Becket, martyred 1170]. This has a silver, oblong morse, with two notches; on the crest of which are three engraved cornelians with onyxes.
A cope, which belonged to Dean Ralph [Ralph de Diceto, chronicler, who became dean in 1181, died c. 1200], of purple samite, with good quality goldwork, embroidered with double fleurs-de-lis on the front.
A dark cope of silk cloth embroidered with tiny fleurs-de-lis and tiny bezants and tiny flowers. Henry [de Cornhill], the chancellor [1217–41] and afterwards dean [1243–54], had this embroidery made.
A cope of Roger of Wygornia [prebendary 1192], of white diasper, embroidered with open-winged eagles, with moons and stars, with an oblong morse, in the middle of the crest of which is a pearl, in addition to two topazes on the two extremities.

Copes of lesser value
A cope, which is said to have belonged to archdeacon Nicholas, of plain white samite with square pectoral tassels woven with white pearls and artificial green ones and pure, drawn gold thread woven in circular patterns.
Another cope [belonging to] the same is old, of the silk cloth which is called 'imperial' woven with peacocks and trees.
A cope which is said to have belonged to Master Nicholas, all plain black with small tassels near the opening under the chin decorated with large fleurs-de lis.
Three copes which belonged to Osbert de Camera, of which two are of yellow samite and plain without tassels. The third of red samite with tassels of *purpura*, embroidered with angels.
An old cope of white baudekin decorated with vines and trees of light purple with poorly executed (?) images; it belonged to R. archdeacon of Middlesex.
Also a cope of Walden [Essex] of red cloth of *arista* with little white birds.
Also two copes of cloth of *arista* of which one was made of cloth which Bishop Eustace gave; the other of cloth from Bishop Roger, with trefoils. They are new; held by the choir.

Morses of copes which are no longer attached to the copes
A morse of Dean Alard of pure gold, having an amethyst in the middle of the crest, a sapphire in the left side, a carved cornelian in the right besides other small and large gemstones.
A morse of Bishop William of pure gold with a sapphire in the middle of the crest and two carved cornelians on both sides, with sapphires and other precious stones.

Concerning chasubles
A chasuble of Godiva of Coventry [wife of the eleventh-century earl of Mercia],[1] of black cloth finely striped with purple and red stripes with gold work, finely embroidered between the shoulders with a gold tree, without gemstones.
A chasuble of [Bishop] Hugh de Orivalle [died 1084–5], of plain white diaper with embroidery in roundels of birds and trees in roundels woven with the best goldwork with tassels, the front made of the same drawn gold thread embroidered in the same way, with an image

---

[1] In 1295, this chasuble of 'Godithae de Coventre' is described as 'suspensa et fracta, reservatur ad faciendum alias' (suspended and broken, reserved to make others). Not included here.

Casula de rubea purpura cum nobili tassello in interhumerali breudato Agno Dei cum duobus esmallis magnis et rotundis et cristallis cum literis interpositis.

Casula de purpura quasi marmorea plana ornata aurifrigio fino anterius aurifrigiato et in dorso consuitur margarita interhumeriale consimiliter; in cujus fine est tassellus brevis, a quo egrediuntur iiij^{or} gladeoli, et circumdatur illud per tassellos perlis, in cujus medio est lapis vitreus rubeus.

Casula quae dicitur Sancti Aelphegi est de sameto croceo viridenti plana, ornata aurifrigio bono interhumerali lato, breudato cum lapidibus vitreis, aurifrigiata posteriori subhumerali texto leonibus et avibus tassellis anteriori parvo de filo auri tracto cum perlis. [...]

Casula ejusdem de nigra purpura quasi marmorea plana cum aurifrigio bono interhumerali breudato quadam arbore frondibus quasi vinealibus circumflexis.

Casula ejusdem de albo diaspero orbiculari opera quasi ex leonibus vetus est et addubbata aurifrigiis mediocribus. [Reservatur ad aliud.] [...]

Casula R. de Clifford' est de viridi sameto croceali aliquantulum spisso aurifrigiata stricto et bono aurifrigio.

Casula Petri Blesensis est de sameto sanguineo sive epatico plano aurifrigio lato. In tassello anteriori scribitur litteris Archidiaconus London'.

De Tunicis et Dalmaticis

Tunica et dalmatica de rubeo sameto peroptimo, quas dedit Magister Laurentius Romanus, aurifrigio competenti in limbis cum borduris de eodem sameto aureis.

Tunica de croceo sameto, quam dedit P. Wintoniensis Episcopus nova et aurifrigiata bene cum bordura ejusdem panni aurea cum avibus expansis et Grifonibus et manicis factis in bordura.

Tunica de viridi sameto, quam dedit Martinus de Pateshull, cum bordura bene aurifrigiata, et cum borduris strictis inferioribus de eodem panno, et borduris in humeris cum leonibus et sagittariis et manicis de eadem bordura. [...]

Tunica de imperiali cum arboribus rubeis et leonibus cum avibus aureis sine bordura inferiori cum humerali ex auro contexto. [...]

Tunica de panno quodam marmoreo spisso cum rotis et giffones infra rotas de serico purpureo cum humeris undatis albo et oculis croceis. [...]

Tunica de dyaspero marmoreo spisso quasi purpura sine aurifrigio.

Tunica et dalmatica de imperiali croceo et indico contexto arboribus sine aurifrigio, quae fuerunt Prioris de Achon. [...]

Tunica et dalmatica de panno serico de arest' cum avibus et pomulis croceis pinalibus, quae factae fuerunt de duobus pannis quos rex dedit. [...]

Dalmatica de opera saracenico inveterata et perforata undique, nullius precii.

of the divine majesty with gold fringe, the back sewn with a narrow line of pearls.
A chasuble of red *purpura* with a splendid tassel between the shoulders, embroidered with the *Agnus Dei* [Lamb of God] with two large, round enamel plaques, and crystals, with letters in between.
A chasuble of *purpura* resembling plain marble, finished with fine goldwork on the front, and on the back similarly stitched with pearls between the shoulders, on the end of which is a short tassel on which run four fleurs-de-lis, and circled with pearl tassels, in the middle of which is a red glass stone.
A chasuble which is said to have belonged to St Alphege [archbishop of Canterbury, died at the hands of Vikings, 1012], of plain yellow-green samite, ornamented with good-quality, extensive goldwork between the shoulders, embroidered with glass stones, worked with gold on the back, woven beneath the shoulders with lions and birds, with small tassels of gold thread on the front in lines with pearls.
A chasuble of the same [Master H. of Norhampton] of black *purpura*, resembling marble, with good quality goldwork between the shoulders, embroidered with certain tree fronds as if wound round with vines.
A chasuble of the same of white diasper with circular embroidery work resembling lions; it is old and adorned with middle-quality goldwork. [*Written in another hand:* It is reserved for another]
A chasuble of R. de Clifford, of yellowish-green, rather heavy samite, worked with narrow and good quality goldwork.
A chasuble of Peter of Blois of plain blood-red or liver-coloured samite, with broad goldwork. On a tassel on the front [Simpson's commentary says 'tassels', plural, p. 449] is inscribed in letters 'Archdiaconus London'.

Concerning tunicles and dalmatics
A tunicle and dalmatic of the very best red samite, which Master Laurentius Romanus [prebendary] gave, with suitable goldwork in the hems [or fringes] with borders of the same samite, of gold.
A tunicle of yellow samite, which was given by P., bishop of Winchester, new and finely worked in gold with a border of the same cloth, gold with open-winged birds and griffons and sleeves [?] made in the borders.
A tunicle of green samite, given by Martin of Pateshull, with a border finely worked in gold and with narrow, lower borders of the same cloth, and with edging on the shoulders with lions and archers, and sleeves of the same edging.
A tunicle of imperial with red trees and lions, with gold birds, without a border at the bottom, with a humeral/shoulders woven of gold.
A tunicle of the same [imperial] cloth, marbled, thick, with wheels and griffons below the wheels of purple silk with undulating shoulders of white and with yellow eyes.
A tunicle of marbled diasper, quite thick as if it were *purpura*, without goldwork.
A tunicle and dalmatic of yellow and indigo imperial, woven with trees, without goldwork, which belonged to the prior of Achon.
A tunicle and dalmatic of silk cloth of Arista with birds and small yellow pine cones which were made from two cloths given by the king.
A dalmatic of Saracen work, old and full of holes, of no value.

De Vestimentis et eorum pertinentiis
Vestimentum Gilberti Episcopi habet paruras de purpura fusca; breudantur cum stellis et lunulis; stola et manipulus de eodem panno et amictus. In fine stola breudatur Abraham et Melchisedech. In manipulo Jacob. In amicto xij. Apostoli. Deputatur ad officium mortuorum. [Totus deputatur apud Berling.]
Vestimentum Ricardi Episcopi habet paruras de rubeo sameto breudato cum leonibus incedentibus caudis erectis et floribus interlaqueatis. Stola et manipulus de eodem panno, in quorum extremitatibus breudatur arbor cum duabus avibus et leonibus. Amictus est de aurifrigio puro cum barris de margaritis. [...]
Vestimentum aliud ejusdem habet paruras indici sameti breudatas leonibus, aquilis, arboribus sibimet superpositis. Stola et manipulus ejusdem sameti breudantur ymaginibus. In eorum extremitatibus breudatur Thomas et Paulus; Erkenwaldus et Ricardus episcopus. Medium amicti de filo auri tracto florigeratum margaritis. Urlatur aurifrigio stricto in extremitatibus adaucto. [...]
Vestimentum aliud ejusdem cum paruris nigri sameti breudatis cum majestate et apostolis cum albis faciebus sine superscriptione. Stola et manipulus de indico sameto breudati ymaginibus apostolorum et prophetarum, nominibus designatis. In quorum extremitatibus breudantur Sanctus Thomas et Oswaldus, Nicholaus, et Edmundus. Amictus est de aurifrigio plano puri auri. Limbatur veteribus aurifrigiis strictis. [...]

De Baudekinis et Pannis Sericis
Baudekinum de rubeo sameto cum grifonibus de auro, quorum alae contingunt se; in cujus contiguitate est flos; [de dono Regis.] [...]
Item duo alii baudekini purpurei coloris cum griffonibus erectis sese post tergum respicientibus, quorum alae contigue erigunt flosculum gladeoli aurei, in cujus medio est flos rubeus; et omnes de dono Regis.
Item duo baudekini consimiles de dono reginae, bordati rubeo et purpurea rotati, infra quas sunt volucres biscipites cum alis expansis, in quorum umbilico sunt stellae rubeae et purpureae. [...]
Pannus de aresta magnus et longus cum campo indico et minutis avibus et floribus inter virgulas.
Pannus alius magnus sericus rubeus, cum magnis rotis et binis leonibus cristatis in rotis purpureis, et flores inter rotas. Rex dedit H. Decano, et decanus postea dedit ecclesiae.
Pannus alius de aresta bordatus ex transverso cum avibus et pomis pineorum interjectis.

De culcitris et Pannis pendentibus in choro
Culcitra Willelmi Episcopi de rubeo sameto, cum panno rotato.
Culcitra de croceo sendato, cum sameto rotato, cum leonibus post tergum se respicientibus, quam legavit Johannes Tholosanus. [...]

Concerning vestments and things belonging to them

The vestment set of Bishop Gilbert [perhaps Gilbert Foliot, bishop 1163–87] has trimmings of dark *purpura*; they are embroidered with stars and crescent moons; a stole and maniple of the same cloth and an amice. Abraham and Melchisedech are embroidered at the end of the stole; on the maniple, Jacob; on the amice, the twelve Apostles. This is assigned to the office of the dead. [All is assigned *at (apud)* Burling (an Essex manor belonging to St Paul's; in a different hand)]

The vestment set of Bishop Richard has apparels of red samite, embroidered with lions *passant* [*incedentibus*; cf. *DMLBS*, s.v. 'incedere'] with erect tails and with interlaced flowers. A stole and maniple of the same cloth, the ends of which are embroidered a tree with two birds and lions. The amice is of pure goldwork with bands of pearls.

Another vestment set of the same [Master H. of Norhampton], having trimmings of indigo samite embroidered with lions, eagles, with trees placed above them. A stole and maniple of the same samite embroidered with images. On their ends are embroidered St Thomas and St Paul; St Erkenwald and Bishop Richard [there had been three former bishops of this name. The bishop depicted may have been the first of them, Richard de Belmeis, 1108–27]. In the middle of the amice drawn gold thread, ornamented with pearls. Edged with narrow goldwork which increases at the ends.

Another vestment set of the same [Roger the chaplain] with trimmings of black samite embroidered with [Christ in] majesty and Apostles with white appearance without superscriptions. A stole and maniple of indigo samite embroidered with images of apostles and prophets, designated by name. On the ends are embroidered St Thomas and St Oswald, St Nicholas and St Edmund. The amice is of plain goldwork, of pure gold. It is fringed with old, narrow goldwork.

Concerning baudekins and silk cloths

A baudekin of red samite with griffons of gold whose wings touch each other; on which is attached a flower; [given by the king (in another hand)].

Also two other baudekins of purple colour with erect griffons back-to-back to each other, whose adjoining wings lift blossoms of golden fleurs-de-lis, in the middle of which is a red flower; and all given by the king.

Also two similar baudekins given by the queen, embroidered with red and purple wheels, below which are two-headed birds of prey with wings extended, in the middle of which are red and purple stars.

A large and long cloth of Arista with an indigo field and tiny birds and flowers between rods [or streaks].

Another large red silk cloth, with large wheels and pairs of maned lions in purple wheels and flowers between the wheels. The king gave it to Dean H[enry de Cornhill, probably]. And the dean afterwards gave it to the church.

Another cloth of Arista embroidered across with birds and pinecones interposed.

Concerning cushions and cloths hanging in the choir

A cushion of Bishop William of red samite, with rolled cloth.

A cushion of yellow sendal, with rolled samite, with lions looking over their backs, which John de Tholosan [sheriff of London in 1237] commissioned.

Duo panni serici de aresta veteres nigri cum griffonibus, quos dedit G. Foliot, episcopus. […]

Quatuor panni de serico veteres, limbati croceo indico sameto, cum griffonibus et leonibus, quos Robertus de Clifforð dedit. […]

De tapetiis et Velis
Quatuor thalones (probably for *chalones*) cum kanabo lato cortine in choro.
Veteres ymagines cortinarum sine kanabo. […]
Velum quod est ante magnam crucem.
Duo vela quae sunt ad duas cruces in duabus alis ecclesiae.

1b. St Paul's Cathedral inventory of 1295

The inventory includes items mentioned in the earlier one and recent acquisitions. It retains the association of vestments with previous owners. This writer is more concerned than the last to assign values to metal items, evidently according to weight; the morses and other items are valued in shillings and pence. The writer records when articles have lost gemstones and pearls, and when cloth is damaged, mentioning the recycling of some items. Much of the metalwork is now described as silver gilt, rather than gold. The cathedral's holy relics now include the burial garments attributed to 'S. Edmundus Confessor' a conflation of St Edmund and St Edward the Confessor, both English kings. Among the textiles ciclaton and velvet are now mentioned. The writer shows awareness of different embroidery techniques and once uses the word *pulverizata* ('powdered') to describe scattered embroidery. Heraldic devices begin to appear as ornament.

The list catalogues 28 morses; 9 mitres, among which are listed 5 pairs of gloves, one pair accompanied by an episcopal ring; 8 pairs of slippers with buskins and 1 pair of slippers alone; 23 cushions; 133 copes; 18 separate amices, along with one set of apparels for an amice; 48 vestment sets, 44 of which are referred to as 'vestimenta' and 4 as albs variously accompanied by apparels; 3 stole and maniple sets, with 2 separate maniples; 25 tunicle and dalmatic sets along with 10 separate tunicles and 1 separate dalmatic; 51 chasubles; corporals (linen cloths placed on the altar, on which the host and chalice are laid) which are itemised according to their containers, 8 boxes and one; 10 offertory cloths; 2 'abstersoria' (cloths used by the celebrant for wiping his fingers after handling the host); and 2 altar frontals. 144 items appear under the heading 'Baudekyni' though only the first 118 are inventoried specifically as 'baudekynus' and the rest may be other precious cloths; 6 hanging pillows ('cuclitrae pendules') and 20 other cloths grouped with them; and 27 items under the heading cloths of Arista, though again only the first group described (12 of them) are specifically called by the name of the cloth. The inventory then enumerates individually the treasures of each chapel and altar of St Paul's and of the church of St Faith located in the crypt, which include some vestments and altar cloths.

Morsus
Morsus Alardi Decani triforiatus, de auro puro cum kamahutis et aliis lapidibus multis, et perlis sine defectu, ponderans xxxii^s. vi^p. […]
Morsus Ricardi Archidiaconi Colecestriæ argenteus deauratus cum ymaginibus majestatis Petri et Pauli, et supra unius Angeli, et inferius collatoris Morsus, cum lapidibus in circulis triphoriatus, ponderans xxix^s. vii^p. […]

Feretria
Item Vasculum cristallinum ornatum pede et turriculo argenteo, in quo continentur de

Two old black silk cloths of Arista, with griffons, which Bishop G[ilbert] Foliot (1162/3–1187/8) gave.
Four old silk cloths, fringed, of yellow-indigo samite, with griffons and lions which Robert de Clifford gave.

Concerning carpets [or hangings] and curtains
Four chalons with a wide canopy, curtains in the choir.
Old [embroidered?] images from curtains, without a canopy.
The curtain before the great cross.
Two curtains at the two crosses in two other churches.

Morses
The morse of Dean Alard, trefoil, of pure gold with cameos and many other gemstones and flawless pearls, worth 32 shillings and 6 pence.
The morse of Archdeacon Richard of Colchester: gilded silver with great images of St Peter and St Paul, and above of an angel, and below of the donor of the morse, ornamented with gemstones in circles, worth 29 shillings and 7 pence.

Shrines
Also a crystal vessel with ornamented foot and small silver tower, containing part of the

Alba et de Casula, et Dalmatica, in quibus S. Edmundus Confessor fuit tumulatus, de dono Roberti de Binetre. [...]

Mitrae
Una Mitra breudata cum stellis anterius et posterius, insertis lapidibus in laminis argenteis deauratis, et deficit unus lapis in altero pendulorum, et in parte anteriori septem lapides et multae perlae, et in parte posteriori quatuor lapides et multæ perlæ. [...]
Item una Mitra breudata cum stellis, et anterius est Cornelinus, continens caput hominis gravatum, et ornatur laminis argenteis deauratis, et lapidibus insertis: et deficit lapis unus in parte posteriori, et in altero pendulorum deficiunt tres cathenulæ, cum karolis argenteis appensis; et dedit hanc mitram Fulco Basset. [...]
Item ciroteæ simul apparatus, et annulus pontificalis aureus triphoriatus, cum topacio magno, et aliis multis lapidibus ornatus.
Item Mitra Henrici de Sandwyco Episcopi, breudata duabus stellis anterius, et duabus stellis posterius, et ornata rotellis argenteis deauratis, insertis lapidibus et perlis multis; et deficiunt in anteriori parte unus lapis, et duo in pendulis. Ciroteæ similis sunt apparatus. [...]

Sandalia
Item Sandalia de rubeo sameto cum caligis breudatis aquilis, leonibus, et rosis, et in summitate vinea breudata, sotulares sunt breudatæ ad modum Crucis.
Item Sandalia bona et nova breudata cum aquilis et grifonibus, et illa cum caligis proximis suprascriptis habet Ricardus Episcopus, et una caliga tantum ejusdem operis est inventa. [...]
Item Sandalia cum caligis de rubeo sameto diasperato, breudata cum ymaginibus Regum in rotellis simplicibus.

Pulvinaria
Pulvinar S. Edithæ de panno de Ciglatun. [...]
Item duo pulvinaria antiqua breudata. Item septem alia consuta de serico, et duo de panno inciso, et unum opertum de Ciglatoun, et unam opertum de albo filo nodato, de quibus omnibus fiant Pulvinaria convenientia ad cathedras ministrantium in Choro: et de quinque istorum facta fuerunt duo pulvinaria magna ad Cathedras.

Capae
Capa Alardi decani de nigro sameto, cum Petro et Paulo in pectorali, breudata cum stellis. [...]
Item Capa Galfridy de Lucy Decani, de sameto purpureo, breudata cum lucellis et radice Jessæ. [...]
Item Capa de purpurea sameto, cum stellis et leopardis breudata, de dono Willielmi Blondell. [...]
Item Capa fasca de panno serico, quae fuit Martini de Patshulle, cum flosculis. [...]
Item Capa Godefridi de Weseham, de rubeo sameto, breudata cum ymaginibus Regum et Episcoporum. [...]

alb, chasuble and dalmatic in which St Edmund Confessor was buried, given by Robert de Binestre.

Mitres

A mitre embroidered with stars in front and behind, inset with gemstones in plates of gilded silver, and lacking one gemstone in one of the lappets [or *pendulae*] and in the front part seven gemstones and many pearls, and in the back four gemstones and many pearls.

Also a mitre embroidered with stars, and at the front is a cornelian containing the engraved head of a man, and ornamented with silver-gilt plates, and inlaid with stones; and it is lacking one gemstone in the back part, and in the one of the lappets is lacking three ornamental chains, weighted with silver rings/circlets; Fulco Basset [probably the bishop of London of this name, who died in 1259] gave this mitre.

Also gloves decorated similarly, and an episcopal ring of gold, trefoiled, with a large topaz, and ornamented with many other gemstones.

Also the mitre of Bishop Henry of Sandwich [died 1273], embroidered with two stars on the front, and two stars on the back, and ornamented with small silver-gilt wheels, inlaid with gemstones and many pearls; and there are lacking one gemstone in the front part and two in the lappets. Matching gloves are supplied.

Ecclesiastical slippers

Also slippers of red samite with stockings [or buskins] embroidered with eagles, lions and roses, and at the top embroidered with a vine, the shoes/soles embroidered in the form of a cross.

Also good, new slippers embroidered with eagles and griffons, which, like those aforementioned with stockings, were owned by Bishop Richard, and one [set of] stockings much of the same work is found.

Also slippers with stockings of red, diapered samite, embroidered with images of a king in simple wheels.

Cushions

The cushion of St Edith [of Wilton? Died 984] of ciclaton cloth.

Also two ancient embroidered cushons. Also seven such sewn of silk, and two of 'cut' cloth (perforated?), and one with a cover of ciclaton, and one with a cover of white knotted thread, all of which were cushions used on [or perhaps adapted for] the chairs of the ministers in the choir; and from five of these were made two large cushions for the chairs.

Copes

The cope of Dean Alard in black samite with St Peter and St Paul on the chest, embroidered with stars.

Also the cope of Dean Galfred de Lucy, of purple samite, embroidered with crescents and the Tree of Jesse.

Also a cope of purple samite, embroidered with stars and leopards, which William Blondell gave.

Also a dark cope of silk cloth, which belonged to Martin of Patshull, with little flowers.

Also the cope of Godfrid de Weseham, of red samite, embroidered with images of kings and bishops.

Item Capa Magistri Thomae Essewy de rubeo baudekino, cum equis armatis. [...]
Item Capa de albo sameto, breudata cum rotellis et citacis, quam dedit Will. Passemere.
Item duæ Capæ de albo diaspro, cum capitibus et leopardis coronatis, quam dedit Petrus de Newport.
Item Capa Roberti le Moyne de cendato afforciato albo, cum margaritis ante, loco morsus. [...]
Item Capa Willielmi Episcopi de viridi sameto, breudata cum angelis, et sagittariis, preciosa. [...]
Item Capa de sameto croceo, quam dedit Petrus Epise. Winton. [...]
Item Capa de panno Jaunensi, cum circulis et avibus croceis, et leopardis. [...]
Item Capa Gileberti de Stratton, de panno aureo, lineato cum sendato rubeo afforciato. [...]
Item Capa purpureæ coloris cum rotellis et duobus leopardis infra rotas se invicem continentes. [...]
Item Capa Johannis Maunsel, de panno aureo qui vocatur ciclatoun. [...]
Item Capa Fulconis Episcopi consuta de serico, opera pulvinario, arboribus croceis et albis. [...]
Item Capa Roberti de Clifford de spisso panno fracta. Assignatur ad tunicas puerorum. [...]
Item Capa ejusdem de quodam panno Antiocheno, cujus campus niger, cum ereminis de aurifilo contextis.
Item Capa Magistri Johannis de S. Claro, de quodam panno Tarsico, viridis coloris, cum pluribus piscibus et rosis de aurifilo contextis. [...]
Item Capa de dono domini Raduphi de Staneford de Indico velvetto, cum aurifrigio de rubeo velvetto, cum platis et perlis desuper positis.

Amicti per se
[...] Item Amictus breudatus de auro puro, cum rotellis, et amatistis, et perlis, et deficiunt ix. lapides et perlæ. [...]
Item Amictus de rubeo sameto breudato de aurifilo cum leonibus, et floribus in rotellis et lapidibus insertis et deficiunt xi. lapides. [...]
Item duo Amicti veteres, quorum unus de opere Saracenis, et alius de sameto viridi, breudato cum avibus in circulis. [...]
Item Amictus cum parva contexta de nodulis de filo aureo, viridi et rubeo serico, cum nodulis serico compositus de magnis perlis albis, de dono Ricardi de Gravesende Londinensis Episcopi. [...]

Vestimenta
Vestimentum Ricardi Episcopi habet paruram de rubeo sameto, breudato cum Leonibus incedentibus, caudis erectis, et floribus interlaqueatis, stola et manipulis de eodem panno, in quorum extremitatibus breudatur arbor cum duabus avibus et leonibus. Amictus est de aurifrigeo puro cum barris de perlis, et deficiunt multæ perlæ. [...]
Item Vestimentum Ricardi Episcopi habet paruram Indici sameti, breudatam cum Apostolis, nominibus singulorum suprascriptis: stola et manipuli ejusdem panni, et breudati Apostolis cum albis faciebus. In estremitate stolae breudatur S. Nicholaus et Oswaldus, et in manipulis Erkenewaldus et Edmundus. Amictus de aurifrigio, cum perlis et granis aureis, ubi deficiunt plures perlæ et grani, urlatur aurifrigio puro et stricto. [...]

Also the cope of Master Thomas Essewy, of red baudekin, with armoured horses.
Also a cope of white samite, embroidered with small wheels and parrots, given by William Passemere.
Also two copes of white diaper, with crowned heads and leopards, given by Peter of Newport.
Also the cope of Robert le Moyne of reinforced white sendal, with pearls on the front, in place of a morse.
Also the cope of Bishop William of green samite, embroidered with angels and archers, of high quality.
Also a cope of yellow samite which Bishop Peter of Winchester gave.
Also a cope of yellow cloth with circles and yellow birds and with leopards.
Also the cope of Gilbert of Stratton, of cloth of gold, lined with reinforced red sendal.
Also a cope of purple colour with wheels and two leopards below the wheels in an alternate succession.
Also the cope of John Maunsel, of cloth of gold which is called ciclaton.
Also the cope of Bishop Fulco sewn of silk, in 'cushion work', with yellow and white trees.
Also the cope of Robert de Clifford of thick, frayed cloth; designated for the boys' tunicles.
Also a cope of the same [Lord Edmund, count of Cornwall] of Antioch cloth, with a black ground with *ereminis* [ermine(s)?] woven in gold.
Also the cope of Master John of St Clare, of cloth of Tars, of green colour, with many fishes and roses woven in gold thread.
Also the cope given by Master Ranulf de Stanford of indigo velvet, with goldwork [or orphrey work] of red velvet, with plates and pearls set thereon.

Individual amices
Also an amice embroidered in pure gold, with little wheels, and amthysts and pearls; and lacking nine gemstones and pearls.
Also an amice of red samite, embroidered in gold thread with lions, and with flowers roundels, and set with gemstones; and lacking eleven gemstones.
Also two old amices, of which one is of 'Saracen work' and the other of green samite, embroidered with birds in circles.
Also an amice with a small woven pattern of knots of gold thread, of green and red silk, with silk knots made up of large white pearls, given by Bishop Richard of Gravesend, London [who became bishop in 1280 but did not die until 1303, after this inventory was made].

Vestments
A vestment set of Bishop Richard, of red samite embroidered with walking lions, with tails erect, and interlaced flowers, a stole and maniple of the same cloth, in the ends of which are embroidered a tree with two birds and lions. The amice is of pure goldwork with bands of pearls, and is lacking many pearls.
Also a vestment set of Bishop Richard, having trimming of indigo samite, embroidered with Apostles, named up above individually; a stole and maniple in the same cloth, and embroidered with apostles with white faces. On the ends of the stole are embroidered St Nicholas and St Oswald, and on the maniple St Erkenwald and St Edmund. The amice is of goldwork, with pearls and gold seeds, where many pearls and seeds are lacking; bordered with pure and narrow goldwork.

Item aliud Vestamentum ejusdem habet paruram de opere plumario, diversi coloris. Amictus de opere plumario consutus cum nodis auri et argenti, habens Crucem in medio, sine stola et manipulo. [...]

Item duo paria Vestimentorum unius sectæ de opere pectineo, facta fuerunt de quadam casula quæ fuit Fulconis Basset, cum duobus amictibus. Duo manipuli, et duæ stolæ ejusdem operis. [...]

Stolae et Manipuli, per se
Stola et Manipulus in medio de Ciglatoun, limbati in circuitu aurifrigio, et in extremitate breudati cum nodulis de perlis et lapillis insertis; et deficiunt in manipulo ix lapides, in stola tres. [...]

Item Manipulus de opera pectineo, cum nodis contextis argenti filo, et in extremitatibus de aurifrigio, cum floribus et listis de perlis albis parvulis. Stola de serico viridi contexta cum nodulis de aurifilo, cum extremitatibus similibus manipulo præcedenti. [...]

Tunicae et Dalmaticae
[...] Item Tunica et Dalmatica de rubeo sameto, cum stricto aurifrigio, cum borduris in posteriori parte, et floris cum capitibus draconum de auro. [...]

Item Tunica et Dalmatica de Indico baudekino veteri, cum avibus deauratis in stricto aurifrigio.

Item Tunica de croceo sameto, quam dedit Wintoniensis Episcopus Petrus.

Item Tunica de viridi sameto, quam dedit Martinus de Pateshulle. [...]

Item Tunica et Dalmatica de serico albo diasperato de arest.

Item tria paria Tunicarum et Dalmaticarum de albo diaspro, quas dedit Magister Andreas de London. [...]

Casulae
Casula Nicholai Archidiaconi de rubeo sameto preciosa, cum vineis de perlis in modum amplae Crucis in dorso. [...]

Item Casula de rubeo sameto vetus, cum aurifrigio nodato. [...]

Item Casula Wulfrani de Indico sameto, bona et preciosa, cum pectorali et imaginibus Petri et Pauli de fino auro, et humerali vineato de fino auro breudato, et lapidibus insertis, et extremitate talari consimili. [...]

Item Casula de sindone purpurea linita cendata viridi, bene ornate aurifrigio, de dono H. de Sandwyco.

Item Casula quae fuit Magistri Henrici de Norhampton, de nigro purpuro, bona cum dorsali de aurifrigio optimo. [...]

Item Casula viridis scutulata variis Armis, et bono aurifrigio, data pro anima Reginæ Alianoræ junioris.

Item Casula quæ fuit S. Elphegi de sameto croceo, cum dorsali pulcro de aurifrigio, lapidibus insertis. [...]

Item casula de quodam panno Tarsico, cum rubeo panno diasperato auro, cum arboribus et cervis de aurifilo contextis, cum aurifrigio de Armis Regum Franciæ et Aragoniæ, de dono Willielmi Cissoris Alianoræ Reginæ junioris; et assignatur per ipsam ad Missam beatæ Virginis, pro anima dictæ Reginæ.

Also another vestment set of the same [Fulco Basset] with ornament of 'feather work' [embroidery] of different colours. An amice of 'feather work', sewn with gold and silver knots, having a cross in the middle, without stole or maniple.
Also two pairs of vestment sets, one of a suit of 'comb work', consisting of a chasuble which was Fulco Basset's, with two amices. Two maniples and two stoles of the same work.

Individual stoles and maniples
A stole and maniple of ciclaton in the middle, edged round about with goldwork, and at the ends embroidered with knots of pearls and set with gemstones; and the maniple is lacking nine gemstones, the stole three.
Also a maniple of 'comb work' with knots of silver thread woven in, and on the ends of goldwork with flowers and edges of tiny white pearls. The stole of green silk, woven with knots of gold thread, with edges similar to the aforementioned maniple.

Tunicles and dalmatics
Also a tunicle and dalmatic of red samite, with narrow goldwork, with borders/embroidery on the back part, and flowers with heads of dragons in gold.
Also a tunicle and dalmatic of old indigo baudekin, with golden birds in narrow goldwork.
Also a tunicle of yellow samite, which Peter, bishop of Winchester gave.
Also a tunicle of green samite, which Martin of Pateshulle gave.
Also a tunicle and dalamatic of white silk diasper of Arista.
Also three pairs of tunicles and dalmatics of white diasper, which Master Andrew of London gave.

Chasubles
The chasuble of Archdeacon Nicholas of precious red samite, with vines of pearls in the shape of a large cross on the back.
Also a chasuble of old red samite, with goldwork knots.
Also the chasuble of Wulfran, of indigo samite, good and precious, with a pectoral and with images of St Peter and St Paul in fine gold, and a humeral decorated with vines embroidered in fine gold, and set with gemstones, and similarly on the end of the *talaris* [ankle-length garment].
Also a chasuble of purple sindon lined with green cendal, well ornamented with goldwork, which H. de Sandwich gave.
Also a chasuble which belonged to Master Henry of Northampton, of black *purpura*, good, with a dorsal of the best goldwork.
Also a green chasuble decorated with shields of various coats of arms, and good quality goldwork, given for the soul of Queen Eleanor the younger [wife of Henry III, died 1291].
Also a chasuble which was St Alphege's of yellow samite, with a beautiful dorsal of goldwork, set with gemstones.
Also a chasuble of the aforementioned cloth of Tars, with red cloth of gold diasper, woven with trees and deer of gold thread, with goldwork of the coats of arms of the kings of France and Aragon, given by William Cissor for Queen Eleanor the younger; and designated by him for the Mass of the Blessed Virgin, for the soul of the said queen.

Corporalia
Una Capsa magna breudata ex scutis ad corporalia, cum cruce ex literis.
Item alia Capsa breudata cum Majestate ex parte una, et *undata* cum floribus ex alia cum *corporalibus*. [...]
Item una Bursa breudata de armis variis, de dono Walteri de Essex. [...]

Offertoria
Unem Offertorium stragulatum, de rubeo et viridi. [...]
Item duo Offertoria bendata, de opere Saraceno, de dono ejusdem Roberti. [...]

Abstersorium
Duo Abstersoria de panno lineo, cum extremitatibus bordatis de serico, ad extergendum digitos post perfusionem in majori Altari.

Frontalia
Unum Frontale de nigro sameto, cum burris et vineis de aurifrigio bono ad majus Altare.
Item aliud Frontale strictum breudatum cum pluribus diversis scutis; et in medio breudantur ymagines Crucifixi. Mariæ et Johannis, et in extremitatibus ymagines Petri et Pauli Apostolorum, de dono Magistri Johannis de S. Claro ad idem Altare. [...]

Baudekyni
Quadraginta autem inventi fuerunt Baudekyni vetustissimi.
Item xxxi mediocres. Item vi. *alutill* meliores, de quibus II de dono J. de Chishulle, et unus de dono Almæ de Bathonia, et unus de dono Dominæ A. Reginæ junioris, et unus de funere J. Fraunceys, et unus de dono Domini Henrici Regis. [...]
Item Baudekynus purpureus cum magnis rotellis, et griffonibus, de dono Domini E. Regis, Willielinus Decanus habuit, et nondum restituit. [...]
Item Baudekynus murretus, cum nodis et floribus, de dono Reginæ. [...]
Item Baudekynus rubeus, cum Sampsone constringente ora leonum, de dono Almarici de Lucy, pro anima G. de Lucy. [...]

Culcitræ
Sex Culcitræ pendules, debiles, quarum una de panno de Arest, parvi valoris.
Item xx. panni, de serico, penduli, quarum quidam cum borduris, et quidam parvi valoris; et de uno istorum factæ sunt duæ Capæ, et duo tradebantur ad armaturam faciendam, præcepto Decani.

Panni de Arest
Item tres magni panni penduli consuti, in quorum quolibet continentur sex panni de Arest, parvi valoris; quorum duo tradebantur ad armaturam faciendam, præcepto Decani. Item unus pannus de Arest. [...]

Corporals
A large corporal cover [or case] embroidered with scutcheons on the material, with a cross of letters (?).
Also another cover [or case] embroidered with [Christ in] Majesty on one side, and covered with flowers, on the other with *corporalibus* (?).
Also a burse embroidered with various coats of arms, which was given by Walter of Essex.

Offertory cloths
A striped [or panelled] offertory cloth of red and green.
Also two bordered/embroidered offertory cloths, of Saracen work, given by Robert [de Binestre].

Abstersoria
Two *abstersoria* of linen cloth, with ends bordered/embroidered in silk for the wiping of fingers after affusion at the High Altar.

Altar frontals
One frontal of black samite with *burris* (l. *barris*; strips or bands) and vines of good quality goldwork at the High altar.
Also another frontal narrowly embroidered with many different shields; and in the middle are embroidered images of the crucifixion: St Mary and St John, and in the ends images of the apostles St Peter and St Paul, given by Master John of St Clare to the same altar.

Baudekins
Moreover 40 extremely old baudekins were inventoried.
Also 31 mediocre. Also six *patched* (?), better, of which two were given by J. De Chishulle and one was given by Alma of Bathonia and one given by Lady Queen A. the younger [Eleanor?] and one for the funeral of J. Fraunceys, and one was given by lord King Henry [probably Henry III, died 1272].
Also a purple baudekin with large wheels and griffons, which was given by lord King Edward (Edward I succeeded in 1272)]. Dean William [probably William de Montfort who held the office from 1285 to 1294] had it and has not yet given it back.
One murrey baudekin, with knots and flowers, given by the queen.
One red baudekin, with Samson binding the lion's mouth, given by Almaric de Lucy, for the soul of G. De Lucy.

Cushions
Six hanging cushions, worn [out], of which one is of cloth of Arista, of little value.
Also twenty cloths of silk, hanging, of which some are with embroidery and some of little value; and from one of these two copes were made, and two were handed over at the making of the wardrobe, by order of the dean.

Cloths of Arista
Also three large sewn hanging cloths, each made of six cloths of Arista, of little value, of which two were handed over at the making of the wardrobe, by order of the dean. Also one cloth of Arista.

Item unus pannus, cujus campus aureus, cum Leonibus et aquilis bicapitibus de aurifilo contextis in philetris rubeis, datus pro anima Domini W. de Valencia militis, anno Domini supradicto. [...]

1c. St Paul's Cathedral inventory of 1402

The author of the third inventory approaches the task more economically, initially listing groups of vestments (copes, chasubles and tunicles) in terms of their location on rods within four wardrobes in the Treasury, which were evidently arranged by colour. Others for everyday use were kept in the Treasury but not in wardrobes. Some albs, amices, stoles and fanons were kept in canvas wraps and a number of precious cloths are described as being in chests. Among the items which are not described as being in containers, the order sometimes becomes random, with sandals appearing among furnishings and curtains and frontals among amice groups. Among silk textiles the new textile name *Rakemaske* appears, velvet is more frequent and more than once embroidery is said to be 'pulverizato' (powdered). The linen cloth of Rheims is also documented several times. Most of the associations of vestments with former bishops and deans of London have been lost, though some donor names are still remembered and some very old textiles survive, including the cushion associated with St Edith and the chasuble said to have been St Alphege's. In the main collection are listed 179 copes; 51 chasubles; 92 tunicles; and 124 groups, mostly consisting of albs, amices, apparels, fanons and stoles, usually three or four of each though some groups are short of a stole and stoles are not included among vestments for boy choristers; maniples are no longer mentioned; 3 morses, 23 sudaria, 8 mitres and 5 pairs of gloves are listed with other episcopal regalia, including 3 episcopal rings. There are 4 pairs of sandals, which now lack the 'caligas' (stockings or buskins) which regularly accompanied them before. Among furnishings there is considerable focus on cushions (now called 'quissini' rather than 'culcitra'), of which there are 18; and pillows, numbering 15. There are also 16 curtains, now called 'ridelli'; 3 altar frontals and an Easter banner, and 201 precious textiles, many kept in chests.

In primis, in primo Armariolo existente in angulo in parte occidentali ex parte dextra sunt xxiiij^{or} perticae in quibus pendent hujusmodi vestimenta, videlicet:
In prima pertica tres Capae preciosae de panno aureo albi coloris auripictae cum floribus et coronis aureis de dono Domini Johannis Ducis Lancastriae.

[Copes, tunicles, chasubles]
[...] In iiij. pertica iij Capae de panno aureo albi coloris pulverisatae cum literis aureis videlicet M. et Angelis et certis circumferenciis. [...]
In xj^a pertica j Capa j Casula ij Tuniculae de rubeo veluto de dono Domini Walteri Aldebery pulverisato cum coronis aureis.
In xij pertica j Capa cum Casula et ij Tuniculis de panno aureo rubei coloris de dono Domini W. Courtenay cum aurifrigiis pulverisatis cum cignis argenteis. [...]
In xvij. pertica j Casula de rubeo pulverizata cum gladiis et floribus et una Capa auripicta preciose cum multis historiis bibliae in ymaginibus aureis. [...]
In xix. pertica ij Capae de panno aureo rubei coloris pulverizato cum diversis ymaginibus aureis. [...]
In secundo Armariolo proxime sequenti sunt xxvj perticae, quarum quatuor sunt vacuae et nullatenus occupatae, unde de xxij perticis occupatis est nunc loquendum.

Also one cloth of which the field is gold, with lions and two-headed eagles woven in gold thread in red receptacles, given for the soul of lord W. De Valencia, soldier, in the year stated above [1296].

Firstly, in the first wardrobe standing in the corner in the western part on the right side, there are 24 rods, on which hang certain vestments, as follows:
On the first rod, three precious copes of white-coloured cloth-of-gold, painted in gold with flowers and gold crowns, given by Lord John, duke of Lancaster [John of Gaunt, son of Edward III].

[Copes, tunicles, chasubles]
On the 4th rod, three copes of white-coloured cloth-of-gold powdered with gold letters, namely M. and Angels and a particular border.
On the 11th rod, one cope, one chasuble, two tunicles of red velvet given by Lord Walter Aldebery, powdered with gold crowns.
On the 12th rod, one cope with chasuble and two tunicles of red-coloured cloth-of-gold given by Lord W. Courtenay with goldwork powdered with silver swans.
On the 17th rod, one chasuble of red powdered with swords and flowers and one valuable gold-painted cope with many biblical stories in gold images.
On the 19th rod, two copes of red-coloured cloth-of-gold powdered with various gold images.
In the second wardrobe situated nearby are 26 rods, four of which are empty and not occupied; the 22 occupied rods will now be discussed:

In prima pertica ij Capae de panno aureo rubei coloris, quarum una de velveto rubeo cum leonibus aureis et aurifrigiis de coleriis Domini Ducis Lancastriae et servo [cervo] in medio cujuslibet colerii jacente ex dono domini Roberti Whiteby, et alia de rubeo veluto cum magnis Rosis aureis et aurifrigiis cum ymaginibus aureis, ex dono M. J. Appelby, quondam Decani.

In secunda j Casula ij Tuniculae et ij Capae de panno aureo rubei coloris ejusdem sectae cum aurifrigiis blaviis pulverizato cum leopardis aureis. [...]

In vj. pertica iiij^{or} Capae de panno serico novo et satis vilis precii viridis coloris pulverizato cum coronis aureis et leonibus. [...]

In xj. pertica j Casula ij Tuniculae de panno aureo nigri coloris pulverizato cum feris bestiis aureis. [...]

In xix. j Capa j Casula et ij Tuniculae de panno aureo blavii coloris pulverizato cum coronis aureis, quibus singulis sunt infixae ij pennae de Ostrich. [...]

In xxij. una Casula crocei coloris, quae quondam fuit Sancti Alphegi, et j Capa ejusdem coloris pulverizata cum angelis. [...]

In tertio Armariolo ...

In iij. pertica tres Capae albi coloris de Rakemaske videlicet de debili panno auro.

Albae, Amictae, stolae et fanones

In primis in domo Thesauraria una alba cum una amicta de panno de Reynys cum paruris aureis de historia sancti Thomae Cantuariensis in ymaginibus cum j stola et j fanone rubei coloris.

Item una alia alba de panno de Reynys cum j amicta ejusdem panni et paruris ac j stola et j fanon rubei coloris auripictae diversimode cum margaritis. [...]

Et omnia praedicta sunt involuta in uno panno de Canevas.

§ Item in uno alio panno de Canevas j alba j amicta de panno de Reynys cum j stola et j fanone et paruris auripictis cum diversis ymaginibus in colore rubeo et albo. [...]

Item tres aliae albae iij amictae de bono panno lineo cum ij stolis iij fanonibus et paruris de serico blaveo enbroudato cum coronis aureis de pennies de Ostrich. [...]

Item ij Ridelli pro summo altari de panno serico stragulato tendente quodammodo ad sectam supradictam. [...]

Item unus pannus aureus blavii coloris operatus cum cignis et leopardis aureis et rotulis argenteis, et una longa parura pro dicto altari ejusdem coloris, cum lepardis aureis. [...]

Item vj paria pallarum benedictarum de panno lineo, quarum duo paria sunt de opere Parisiensi pro summo altari in uno canevas. [...]

Item iij albae iij amictae de panno de Reynys cum paruris de serico purpurei et rubei coloris operatis cum antiquis ymaginibus et leopardis aureis cum ij stolis et iij fanonibus ejusdem sectae, ex dono domini Rogeri Waltham, involutis in uno panno de Canevas. [...]

Item vj albae vj amictae cum paruris antiquis de serico albo pulverizato cum stellis rubeis, ordinatae pro pueris choristis. [...]

Item iij Morsus argentei deaurati ornate cum diversis lapidibus et margaritis impressi et diversis ymaginibus impositis.

Item ij sudaria de panno lineo ornata cum serico et filis sericis.

Item vj sudaria bona antique de serico stragulata et operata cum auro et serico diversi coloris. [...]

On the first rod, two copes of red-coloured cloth-of-gold, of which one of red velvet with gold lions and with orphreys [depicting] the collar of the lord duke of Lancaster and a hart lying in the middle of each collar; given by Lord Robert Whiteby, and another of red velvet with large gold roses and orphreys with gold images, given by M. J. Appleby, former dean.
On the second (rod), one chasuble, two tunicles and two copes of red-coloured cloth-of-gold of the same suit, with blue (?) orphreys powdered with gold leopards.
On the 6th rod, four copes of silk cloth, new and relatively cheap, green-coloured, powdered with gold crowns and lions.
On the 11th rod, one chasuble, two tunicles of black-coloured cloth-of-gold powdered with gold wild beasts.
On the 19th [rod], one cope, one chasuble and two tunicles of blue- (dark-?) coloured cloth-of-gold, powdered with gold crowns on one of which are attached two ostrich feathers.
On the 22nd, a chasuble of yellow colour, which was once St Alphege's and one cope of the same colour, powdered with angels.
In the third wardrobe [. . .] on the third rod, three copes of racamaz, of poor [?thin] cloth-of-gold.

Albs, amices, stoles and fanons
Firstly, in the Treasury, an alb with one amice of cloth of Rheims with gold apparels (showing) the story of St Thomas of Canterbury in images with one stole and one fanon of red colour.
Also another alb of cloth of Rheims with one amice of the same cloth and ornamental apparels, but one stole and one fanon of red colour, embroidered in gold in various ways with pearls.
And all the aforesaid are wrapped in a canvas cloth.
Also in another canvas cloth, one alb, one amice of cloth of Rheims with one stole and one fanon and gold-painted apparels with various images in red and white colour.
Also three other albs, three amices of good quality linen cloth with two stoles, three fanons and ornamentation of blue silk embroidered with gold, ostrich-feather crowns.
Also two curtains for the top of the altar of striped silk cloth of the same suit as the aforesaid.
Also one blue-coloured cloth-of-gold worked with gold swans and leopards and silver roundels, and a long decorative band for the aforesaid altar of the same colour, with gold leopards.
Also six pairs of holy palls of linen cloth, of which two pairs are of Paris work for the top of the altar, in a canvas (wrapper).
Also three albs, three amices of cloth of Rheims with apparels of purple and red-coloured silk worked with old images and gold leopards, with two stoles and three fanons of the same suit, given by Lord Roger of Waltham, wrapped in a cloth of canvas.
Also six albs, six amices with old apparels of white silk powdered with red stars, designated for the boy choristers.
Also three gilded silver morses ornamented with various gemstones and inlaid pearls and with various images attached.
Also two *sudaria* of linen cloth ornamented with silk and silk threads.
Also six old *sudaria* of good quality, of striped silk and worked with gold and silk in various colours.

Item j Mitra bona et preciosa de dono bonae memoriae domini Simonis de Sudberya impressa cum margaritis et lapidibus preciosis, et cum duobus labellis ejusdem sectae.
Item j Mitra antique de panno albo serico enbroudato cum ij stellis magnis aureis ex utraque parte et impressa in diversis locis cum margaritis et aliquibus lapidibus preciosis cum ij labellis. [...]
Item iiij^{or} magni Quissini de panno aureo antiquo frisiati cum viridi serico. [...]
Item ij° magni Quissini de panno serico blavii coloris, cum Cruce alba magna per totum, et in quolibet quarterio Crucis est operatum capud unius leonis aureum.
Item ij° Quissini, unus major et alter minor, de rubeo velveto et viridi. [...]
Item vij pulvinaria unius sectae de serico viridi pulverizata cum draconibus rubeis.
Item j pulvinar antiquum de serico nigro acupicta cum diversis bestiis, quod vocatur pulvinar Sanctae Edithae. [...]
Item iiij^{or} paria sandalia bona de panno aureo operata diversi coloris.
Item unum aliud par sandalium de rubeo serico antiquo operato cum ymaginibus aureis. [...]
Item unum vexillum de serico viridis coloris pro magna Cruce tempore pascali cum ymaginibus Petri et Pauli auripictis in eodem. [...]
Item in prima Cista sunt xxxviij° panni aurei novi de Rakemaske coloris rubei. [...]
Item in eadem Cista sunt duae magnae peciae de panno aureo antiquo consuti et facti de ij pannis integris de opere antiquo, tendentes in majori parte ad colorem rubeum. [...]
Item in secunda Cista sunt xxxviij° panni aurei de Rakemask', quorum xviij° sunt rubei coloris, et xviij sunt blavii coloris. [...]

[*From a short inventory of the contents of the Lady Chapel, 7 July 1445, written on the blank leaves of the inventory of 1402*]

<u>In capella beatae Mariae</u>
Item iiij tapeta antiqua rubii coloris quorum tria sunt cum scutis et armis et tertium cum circumferencia viridi et rosis albis.
Item tria alia tapeta blavii coloris cum popyniayes et rosis rubiis.
Item ij quissini de veluto rubeo enbroudato cum cerenis et meremad*is*, arma tenentibus ex una parte et scutis in tribus dentricibus ex altera parte. [...]
Item iiij pannae lineae depictae de albo et nigro quorum tres pendunt circa pulpitum exterius. [...]
Item unum frontale de panno Damasceno aureo cum marginibus de cerico rubeo lionibus argenteis contextis cum quinque paginibus de rubeo Damasceno diversis ymaginibus et leonibus argenteis desuper contextis cum uno frontello sibi annexo cum popynjayes et draconibus de viridi cerico. [...]
Item unus pannus cilicinus pro magno altari beatae Mariae Virginis. [...]

2. Extracts from a roll of liveries of Edward III, 1347–9 (National Archives, MS E 101/391/15, membs 7–11)

In a now antiquated volume of *Archaeologia* (31: 1846), the scholar N. H. Nicolas printed a reasonably faithful transcription of the manuscript now housed in the National Archives and numbered E 101/391/15. Nicolas' transcription does not attempt to expand the abbreviations and suspensions, nor is a translation offered.

Also one good quality and valuable mitre given of good remembrance by Lord Simon of Sudbury, inlaid with pearls and precious gemstones, and with two lappets of the same design.
Also one antique mitre of white silk cloth embroidered with two large gold stars on both sides and inlaid in various places with pearls and other precious gemstones with two lappets.
Also four large cushions of old cloth-of-gold fringed with green silk.
Also two large cushions of blue-coloured silk cloth, with a large white cross throughout, and in each quarter of the cross is worked the head of a lion in gold.
Also two cushions, one large and the other small, of red velvet and green.
Also seven cushions of one suit, of green silk powdered with red dragons.
Also one antique cushion of black silk embroidered with various animals, which is said to be the cushion of St Edith.
Also four good pairs of sandals of cloth-of-gold, worked with different colours.
Also another pair of sandals old red silk worked with gold images.
Also a banner of green-coloured silk for the great cross at Easter time with images of St Peter and St Paul depicted in gold on them.
Also in the first chest are 38 new cloths-of-gold of *racamaz*, red-coloured.
Also in the same chest are two large pieces of old cloth-of-gold, sewn and made from two complete cloths of antique workmanship, holding in the most part to the colour red.
Also in the second chest are 38 cloths of *racamaz*, of which eighteen are of red colour, and eighteen are of blue colour.

In the chapel of the Blessed Mary
Also four old hangings of red colour of which three have shields and coats of arms and the third with a green border and white roses.
Also three other blue hangings with parrots and red roses.
Also two cushions of red velvet embroidered with sirens and mermaids, holding coats of arms in one side and triple-toothed shields on the other side.
Also four linen cloths painted with white and black, of which three hang round the outside of the pulpit.
Also a frontal of gold damascene cloth with edges of red silk with silver lions woven in with five panes of red Damascene with various images and silver lions woven above with a frontal associated with it, with parrots and dragons in green silk.
Also one hair cloth for the large altar of the Blessed Virgin Mary.

The manuscript was produced by the Royal Wardrobe and is a twenty-six-membrane long roll of liveries running from the twenty-first to the twenty-third years of Edward III's reign. In August of 1347 Edward's armies had succeeded in taking Calais after a protracted siege, and entries for the roll reflect some of the celebrations that followed Edward's victory. Amongst entries for regular deliveries of cloth, furs, other mercery and furnishings, there are passages detailing clothing and costumes provided for tournaments and entertainments ('ludos') in celebration of the victory. The various 'crests' and 'heads' and visors described for celebrations at Guildford (Surrey) and Otford (Kent) at the end of the extract are discussed by Twycross and Carpenter (2002: 136–7, 313). The extracts listed below have been selected as they represent items of cloth, clothing and costumes for occasional or celebratory use rather than clothing or livery of everyday wear.

The extracts also give us an early representation of the motto of the newly founded Order of the Garter, on Membrane 8, Item 9: 'Hony soit qui mal y pense' ('Shame on him who thinks this evil'). Regarding the garter decoration adorning the king's mantle and hood (Item 10), Stella Mary Newton suggests that 'although powdered all over [these garments] … it was a three-dimensional object in that it was equipped with a silver buckle, silver pendants and silver bars' (Newton 1980: 43).

We have compared Nicolas's transcription with the original manuscript and have extended major abbreviations and expansions in italics (cf. Nicolas 1846: 29–38) but have left superscript characters *in situ* where not obscuring the meaning. For manuscript reference and navigation, we have provided item numbers in square brackets for Membranes 8 and 11. The translation is by Mark Chambers.

Et ad fac*iendum* una*m* tunica*m* & .j. courteby *pro* R*e*ge de pa*n*no vir*i*di long*o pro* venacione & .j. tunica*m* & .j. courteby *pro* d*o*m*i*no Joh*ann*e de Grey de eodem pa*n*no de dono R*e*gis
    —— viij. uln*e* pa*n*ni vir*i*di mixt'   p*ann*' long'

Et ad fac*iendum* .j. tunica*m* & capuc*i*o duplex de pa*n*no bleu longo *pro* R*e*ge ad hastilud*um* suu*m* Cantuar*iam* & ad eandem tunicam fururand'
    —— iiij. uln*e*   p*ann*' bleu long'
    —— j. fur' de .ccxl. ventr'   m*i*niver pur'

Et comp*utat*' ad .j. capuciu*m* duplex & ad .ij. p*ar*ia calig*arum pro* R*e*gis fac' de p*a*nno bleu longo
    —— iij. uln*e* .j. quarterium   p*ann*' bleu long'

Ed ad fac*iendum* .xliiij. visers fac*i*t *pro* hastilud*um* Cantuar*iam pro* R*e*gis Comit*is* Baro*n*ibus milit*i*b*us* & d*o*minab*us* & *pro* coop*or*tura selle R*eg*is ad hastilud*um* & ad alia n*e*c*e*ssar*i*a p*er* hastilud*um* inde fac'
    —— dj. pec' sindon'   afforc'
    —— v. uln*e* tel' de   Reyns
    —— v. pell' de   baseyne
    —— xvij. uln*e* de   Worstede

[… *Membrane 8:*]

And for making a tunic and one courtepy for the king, of green long cloth, for hunting, and one tunic and one courtepy for John de Grey of the same cloth, given by the king
    —— 8 ells[2] of mixed green cloth   long cloth

And for making one tunic and a double hood of blue long cloth for the king for his tournament at Canterbury, and furring the same tunic
    —— 4 ells   blue long cloth
    —— one lining of 249 bellies   'pured' miniver

And reckoning for one double hood and for two pairs of hose for the king, made of blue long cloth
    —— 3 ells and 1 quarter   blue long cloth

And for making 44 visors, made for the tournament at Canterbury, for the king, counts, barons, knights and ladies, and for a seat cover for the king for the tournament, and for other necessaries made for the tournament thereafter
    —— ½ piece of sindon   reinforced
    —— 5 ells of linen   of Rheims
    —— 5 pelts of   sheepskin
    —— 17 ells of   worsted

[... *Membrane 8 (items numbered here 1–10)*:]

---

[2]   Whilst we have followed tradition by translating Latin *ulna* as 'ell', R. D. Connor argues that *ulna* usually referred to, in fact, a yard of approximately 36 inches (Connor 1987: 83).

[1] JOHANI DE COLONIA Armatori domini nostri Reg^{is} ad faciendum .c. garniamentis de fustien' alba ad opus & de precepto ipsius domini nostri Reg^{is} punctat' & stuffat' cum cotoun
 —— Dccccxx. ulne de   fustien' alba
 —— cclx. lb de   cotoun
 —— xxx. lb   fili albi lini

[Item 2: for a worsted bed for the king ...]

[3] Et ad faciendum .lxxij. standardos de armis Reg^{is} qu^{a}rtellatis consuend' purfiliand' & depingend'
 —— xxix. pec' de Worsted'   Worsted'
 —— vj. pec' de   Card'
 —— xviij. lb   fili lini
 —— xij. lb   fili lane

[4] Et pro factura .ccxliiij. standardos de Worsted' & tela Anglia cum leopardo integro in capite & subtus arma sancti Georgij
 —— xxxiij. pec' de   Worsted'
 —— ccccxx. ulne curt'   tele Anglie
 —— xvij. pec' de   Card'
 —— xxix. lb   fili lyni
 —— xvij. lb   fili lane

[Item 5: for making pennons for the king's ships ...]

[6] Et ad faciendum .Dccc. penuncell pro lanceis armigerorum & aliorum hominum ad arma Reg^{is} de armis Sancti Georgij
 —— xvj. pec' de   Worsted'
 —— cccxxiiij. ulne curt'   tele Anglie
 —— xij. lb   fili lini

[7] Et ad faciendum .ij. stremar' de Worsted' uno uterque (?) de armis qu^{a}rtellatis & altero de armis qu^{a}rtellatis cum ymagine sancti Laurencij in capite operato de .j. pala alba pouderat' cum garteriis bluet' Et ad faciendum .ij. stremar' curt' de armis Reg^{is} qu^{a}rtellatis. Et ad faciendum .ij. Guydones de eisdem armis Reg^{is}
 —— xviij. pec' de Worsted'   Worsted'
 —— j. pec' & dj. de   carde
 —— xviij. lb   fili lini
 —— xij. lb   fili lane
 —— vij. lb   candelarum cere
 —— xxiiij. lb   cord' rubant de filo

[8] Et ad faciendum .xvj. pauillion' pro pisanibus Reg^{is} unde .iiij. de syndon' & tela de Reyns & .xij. de tela de Wilton'
 —— iiij. ulne sindon'   afforc'
 —— vij. ulne curt' tele de   Reyns

[1] To John of Colchester, armourer of our lord the king, for making 100 garments of white fustian, for the use and by order of our lord the king, quilted and stuffed with cotton
- —— 920 ells of   white fustian
- —— 260 pounds of   cotton
- —— 30 pounds   of white linen thread

[... for a worsted bed for the king ...]

[3] And for making 72 standards of the king's arms quartered, to have sewn, trimmed and painted
- —— 29 pieces of worsted   worsted
- —— 6 pieces of   card
- —— 18 pounds   of linen thread
- —— 12 pounds   of wool thread

[4] And for making 244 standards of worsted and English linen with a whole leopard on the top and beneath the arms of St George
- —— 33 pieces of   worsted
- —— 420 short ells   of English linen
- —— 17 pieces of   card
- —— 29 pounds   of linen thread
- —— 17 pounds   of wool thread

[... (to make pennons for the king's ships) ...]

[6] And for making 800 pennons for the lances of the king's squires and other men-at-arms, with the arms of St George
- —— 16 pieces of   worsted
- —— 324 short ells   of English linen
- —— 12 pounds   of linen thread

[7] And for making two streamers of worsted, one with arms quartered and the other with arms quartered with an image of St Laurence on the top, worked with one white stripe, powdered with blue garters. And for making two short streamers with the king's arms quartered. And for making two pennons of the same arms of the king.
- —— 18 pieces of worsted   worsted
- —— 1½ pieces of   card
- —— 18 pounds   of linen thread
- —— 12 pounds   of wool thread
- —— 7 pounds   of candle wax
- —— 24 pounds   of cord ornamented (?) with thread

[8] And for making sixteen coverings for the king's pisanes [piece of armour protecting chest and neck], four of sindon and linen of Rheims and twelve of linen of Wilton
- —— 4 ells of sindon   reinforced
- —— 7 short ells of linen of   Rheims

—— xv. uln*e* curt' tele de	Wilton' [Wilton, in Wiltshire, near Salisbury]
—— ij. lb de	Cotoun
—— iij. lb	fili lini

[9] Et ad facien*dum* un*um* lect*um* de Taffata bluet' *pro* Rege poudr' c*um* garteriis continentib*us* istud dictatem (*sic, dictamen*) Hony soit q*ui* mal y pense

—— clvj. uln*e* curt' de	Taffata
—— ij. pec' de	Carde
—— iij. pec' sindon' de	Triple
—— ij. lb dj auri	Cipre
—— iij. lb dj. serici	sericum
—— xvj. lb	corda*rum* & rubant fili

[10] Et *pro* factura uni*us* clamidis super*tunice* tunice & capucij *pro* corp*ore* Reg*is* de panno long' bluet' poudr' c*um* garteriis parat' c*um* boucles & pendent*is* de argent' deaur*atum*

—— x. uln*e* panni long' bluett'	pann' long'
—— iiij. uln*e* cendall	afforc'
—— dj. pec' de	carde
—— dj. lb auri in plate	aur' in plate
—— j. lb de serico	Sericum
—— clxviij. bouclis *pro* garteriis de ar*gent*' de aur'	boucles ar*gent*'
—— clxviij. pendant*is pro* eisd*em* garteriis de argent'	pendaunt ar*gent*'

[... *Membrane 9 (Nicholas 1846: 34–5), including the manufacture of garments for the king: a jupon of blue taffeta, 'powdered' with garters, with buckles and pendants of silver gilt; a doublet of satin, a garment of white fustian stuffed with sindon, silk and other 'stuff'; a jupon of 'stuff' with the king's arms quartered, of red and indigo velvet; a jupon of blue satin 'powdered' with blue garters prepared with buckles and pendants of silver gilt; 4 scutcheons (shields) with the king's arms quartered;* ...]

Et ad facien*dum* .xl. nubes *pro* diversis garn*i*amentis Reg*is* broudat' de auro argento & serico c*um* un*um* E in medio de auro garnit' c*um* stell*is* p*er* totam campedine*m*

—— j. lb auri de	cipre
—— j. lb argent' de	cipre
—— dj. p*e*c' sindon'	afforc'
—— dj. lb serici	se*r*icum

[... *for making items for the Feast of the Nativity, including: 6 pennons of sindon for trumpets and clarions; a velvet bed of divers colours for the king and bedding belonging therto; a closet for the king's chapel of sindon de triple;* ...]

—— 15 short ells of linen of   Wilton

—— 2 pounds of   cotton
—— 3 pounds of   linen thread

[9] And for making a bed of blue taffeta cloth for the king, powdered with garters stating this motto: *honi soit qui mal y pense*.

    —— 156 short ells of   taffeta
    —— 2 pieces of   card
    —— 3 pieces of sindon of Triple
    —— 2½ pounds of gold (thread)   of Cyprus
    —— 3½ pounds of silk   silk
    —— 16 pounds   of cord & *ribbon thread*

[10] And for making a mantle, surcoat, cloak and hoods for the body of the king, of blue long cloth, powdered with garters decorated with buckles and pendants of silver gilt

    —— 10 ells of blue long cloth   long cloth
    —— 4 ells of cendal   heavy/lined
    —— ½ piece of   card
    —— ½ pound of gold plate   gold plate
    —— 1 pound of silk   silk
    —— 168 buckles for the silver
         gilded garters   silver buckles
    —— 168 pendants for the same
         silver garters   silver pendants

[... Membrane 9 (Nicholas 1846: 34–5) ...]

And to make 40 covers (*nubes?*) for divers garments for the king, embroidered with gold, silver and silk, with a gold 'E' in the middle, garnished with stars all over the (back)ground

    —— 1 pound of gold (thread) of   Cyprus
    —— 1 pound of silver (thread) of   Cyprus
    —— ½ piece of sindon   heavy/lined
    —— ½ pound of silk   silk

Et ad faciendum .xiiij. tunicas & totidem capuc' de panno curto blueto contra hastiludium de Bury

   —— ij. pann' coloris curt'   color' curt'
   —— dj. lb fili lini   filum lini
   —— j. qu^{a}r' serici   sericum
   —— iiij. ulne syndon'   afforc'

[…*for making 5 pennons for trumpets and clarions; for making 4 cushions of green velvet; etc.…*]

Et ad faciendum unum doublett' de velvetto glauco & azure pro domino Lionell filius Regis contra hastiludium de Wyndesores. Et ad cooperiendum .j. par' platarum .j. par de quisseux cooperat cum velvett' viridi. Et ad cooperiendum .ij. par' platarum pro dominis Johanne de Gaunt & Edmundo de Langele de velvett purpre

   —— j. pec' .j. ulne   velvetto
   —— iiij. ulne tele Anglie   tela Anglia
   —— dj. lb serici   sericum
   —— ij. lb de   cotoun

[… *to make 2 beds of worsted cloth, etc., for the king's trip to Normandy* …]

Et ad faciendum ludos domini Regis ad festum Natale domini celebratur apud Guldeford' anno Regis .xxj°. in quo expendebantur .iiij. (xx *written above the previous*) .iiij. tunice de bokeram diversorum colorum .xlij. viseres diversorum similitudinum .xxviij. crestes .xiiij. cloc' depicte .xiiij. capita draconum .xiiij. tunice alb' .xiiij. capit' pavonum cum alis .xiiij. tunice depicte cum ocul' pavonum .xiiij. capit' cygnorum cum suis alis .xiiij. tunice de tela linea depicte .xiiij. tunice depicte cum stellis de auro & argento vapulat'

   —— xlvj. pec' de   Bokeram
   —— lxvi. ulne curt'   Tele Angl'
   —— viij. pelles de   Roan
   —— vj. lb   fili de lyno
   —— xiiij. similitudines fac' mulierum viseres:
   —— xiiij. similitudines facierum hominum
     cum barba
   —— xiiij. similitudines capit' angelorum de
     argent'
   —— xiiij. crestes cum tibiis reuersat' & crestes:
     calciat'
   —— xiiij. crestes cum montibus & cuniculis
   —— xiiij. cloch' depicte   cloch' depicte
   —— xiiij. capita draconum   capita draconum
   —— xiiij. tunice alb' depicte   tunice de Bokeram
   —— xiiij. capita pauonum   capita pauonum
   —— xiiij. paria alarum pro eisdem ale pauonum
     capita
   —— xiiij. tunice depicte cum ocul' tunice depicte cum
     pauonum   ocul' pauonum

And for making fourteen tunics and whole hoods of short blue cloth for the tournament at Bury

  —— two short coloured short cloths coloured (uniform) short
  —— ½ pound of linen thread linen thread
  —— 1 quarter of silk silk
  —— 4 ells of sindon lined

[…*for making five pennons for trumpets and clarions; for making four cushions of green velvet;*…]

And for making a doublet of grey velvet and azure for the lord Lionel, son of the king, for the tournament at Windsor. And for making one pair of plates, one pair of cuisses [thigh armour] fashioned with green velvet. And for making two pairs of plates for the lord John of Gaunt and Edmund of Langley, of purple velvet

  —— 1 piece & 1 ell of velvet
  —— 4 ells of English linen English linen
  —— ½ pound of silk silk
  —— 2 pounds of cotton

[… *to make two beds of worsted cloth, etc., for the king's trip to Normandy* …]

And for making entertainments (*ludos*, plays? masques?) for the lord king for Christmas, celebrated at Guildford (Surrey) in the 21st regnal year, for which was purchased 28 tunics of buckram of various colours, 42 visors of various likenesses, 28 crests, 14 painted cloaks, 14 dragon heads, 14 white tunics, 14 peacock heads with wings, 14 painted tunics with eyes of peacocks, 14 swans' heads with their wings, 14 tunics of painted linen cloth, 14 painted tunics stamped with gold and silver stars

  —— 46 pieces of buckram
  —— 66 short ells of English linen
  —— 8 skins of roan [goatskin]
  —— 6 pounds linen thread
  —— 14 likenesses made of women visors:
  —— 14 likenesses made of men with beards
  —— 14 likenesses of angels' heads of silver
  —— 14 crests with pipes (? *tibiis*) trimmed and 'shoed' (? *calciat'*) crests:
  —— 14 crests with 'hills' (? *montibus*) and 'troughs' (? *cuniculis*)
  —— 14 painted cloaks painted cloaks
  —— 14 dragon heads dragon heads
  —— 14 painted white tunics tunics of buckram
  —— 14 peacock heads peacock heads
  —— 14 pairs of wings for the same heads peacock wings
  —— 14 tunics painted with peacock eyes tunics painted with peacock eyes

—— xiiij. capita cygno*rum*	capita cygno*rum*
—— xiiij. paria ala*rum pro* eisdem capiti*bus*	ale cygno*rum*
—— xiiij. t*u*nice de tela lin*ea* depicte	t*u*nice linie depicte
—— xiiij. t*u*nice depicte c*um* stell*is*	t*u*nice depicte c*um* stell*is*

[*Membrane 10; Membrane 11...*]

[6] Et ad fac*iendum* ludos Reg*is* ad f*estu*m Natal*e d*omini a*n*no Reg*is* .xxij^do. celebrat*um* apud Otteford' (Otford, Kent) ubi expendeba*ntur* vis*er*es vid*elicet* xij. capita ho*m*inu*m* & desup*er* tot capita leonu*m* .xij. capita ho*minum* & tot capita elephantu*m* .xij. capita ho*minum* c*um* alis vesp*er*tilionu*m* .xij. capita de wodewose .xvij. capita virgunu*m* xiiij. sup*er*tunice de worsted' rub' guttate c*um* auro & lineate & rev*er*sate & totide*m* tunice de worsted' virid*i*

—— xij. capit*a* lionum & ho*m*inum	—— vis*er*es:
—— xij. capit*a* ho*m*inum & elephantu*m*	
—— xij. capit*a* ho*m*inum cum al*ia* vesp*er*tilionu*m*	
—— xij. capit*a* de wodewoses	
—— xvij. capit*a* virginu*m*	
—— xv. pec' de	—— bokeram'
—— xlviij. uln' curt'	—— tele Angl'
—— M^l. folia auri	—— folia auri
—— iij. lb. de	—— filo lyni
—— iiij. pell' de	—— roan

[7] Et ad fac*iendum* unu*m* hernes' de bokeram' albo *pro* Reg^e extencellato c*um* argento v*idelicet* tunica & scut' operat' c*um* dictamine Regis hay hay. the wythe swan. by godes soule .j. am thy man. & cropar' pectorale testar' & arcenar' extencell*ato* c*um* argento

—— iij. pec' & dj. de	—— bokeram
—— ccc. folia arg*enti*	—— folia arg*enti*
—— xij. uln' de	—— taffata
—— dj. pec' de	—— carde

[8] Et ad fac*iendum* ludos Reg*is* in festo E*p*iphianie *d*omini celebrato apud Merton', ubi expendebant*ur* .xiij. vis*er*es cum capitibus draconum & .xiij. vis*er*es cum captitibus ho*m*inum h*a*bentib*us* dyademata .x. cou^tepies de bokeram nigro & tela linea Angl'

—— xxvj.	—— viseres
—— ij. pec' de	—— bokeram
—— xij. uln' c*ur*t'	—— tele Angl'

— 14 swan heads	swan heads
— 14 pairs of wings for the same heads	swans' wings
— 14 tunics of linen cloth painted	tunics of painted linen
— 14 tunics painted with stars	tunics painted with stars

[*Membrane 10; Membrane 11. . .*]

[6] And for making entertainments for the lord king for Christmas of the 22nd regnal year, celebrated at Otford (Kent), for which was purchased visors: namely twelve heads of men and above each head a lion, twelve heads of men and on each head an elephant, twelve heads of men with the wings of bats (or wasps), twelve heads of wodewoses [wild men of the woods], twelve heads of virgins, fourteen surcoats of red worsted spotted with gold and lined and trimmed, and as many tunics of green worsted

— 12 heads of lions and men	visors:
— 12 heads of men and elephants	
— 12 heads of men with bat's (or wasps) wings	
— 12 heads of wodewoses	
— 17 heads of virgins	
— 15 pieces of	buckram
— 48 short ells	English linen
— a thousand (pieces?) of gold leaf	gold leaf
— 3 lbs. of	gold thread
— 4 skins of	roan (goatskin)

[7] And for making harness of white buckram for the king, spangled with silver, namely a tunic and shield embroidered with the king's motto: 'Hay, hay, the white swan; by God's soul, I am thy man', and a crupper, pectoral, tester and saddle bow spangled with silver

— 3½ pieces of	— buckram
— 300 leaves of silver	— silver leaf
— 12 ells of	— taffeta
— half a piece of	— card

[8] And for making entertainments for the lord king on the Feast of the Epiphany celebrated at Merton (Surrey), for which was purchased thirteen visors with the heads of dragons and thirteen visors with the heads of men with crowns, ten courtepies of black buckram and English linen cloth

— 26	— visors
— 2 pieces of	— buckram
— 12 short ells	— English linen

CHAPTER IV

Moral and Satirical Works

INTRODUCTION

Exhortations against contemporary and novel fashions are found in a variety of genres and forms: this chapter includes extracts from an ecclesiastical history, sermons, manuals of general advice, instructions ostensibly written specifically for sons (*Peter Idley's Instructions to his Son*) or daughters (the 'God Wyf Wold a Pylgremage'), and satirical writing. They are written variously in prose and verse including rhyming ditties and ballads, one with the jingling rhyme scheme aaaa. The form of a text does not appear to be a guide to its seriousness: Lydgate's 'Horns Away' is described by his biographer as a poem which resists the obvious possibilities for satire seen in, for example, Hoccleve's *Regiment of Princes*, instead offering a serious and philosophical disquisition (see Pearsall 1970).

The main complaints concern the constant desire for novelty, a desire which leads to such unnecessary activities as the hacking about and altering of existing garments, and the changing of outfits several times a day. Different texts have different emphases: the earliest text we print here is almost solely concerned with men's fashion; in some later texts the opprobrium is directed solely towards women's styles of dress: G. R. Owst remarks that it is woman as 'lover of finery, the mirror of fashion [. . .] that calls down the full fury of the English preachers in satire and complaint' (1961: 390). Sometimes the concern is only with one particular aspect of modish styling, such as the fashion for women to wear their hair in two horns.

A survey of the texts included here shows that the trends which attract the greatest ire are those relating to men's shoes, in particular long pointed shoes, sometimes with the points so long that they were thought to be joined to the wearer's ankle by a chain, and tight shoes which conceal the shape of the feet: fashions in men's shoes are mentioned in three texts. Two texts mention, with disgust, the fashion for long hair on men, making them look effeminate. This is linked to sin as it was thought to license or even encourage sodomitic behaviour; goatee beards on fashion-conscious gallants also pose a problem. Two texts comment on the fashions in men's upper body garments: these are deemed to be too tight or to be creating a new silhouette through being padded, and a further three writers pour scorn on the inadequate and immodest covering provided by short gowns (this may apply to men or women). Long wide sleeves are pointed to in two texts, while long trains are mentioned in no fewer than five.

Complaining about effeminacy, Orderic Vitalis states that men's long wide sleeves cover their hands, preventing them from doing anything, and that they are almost incapable of walking quickly or doing any kind of useful work because of their long trains. In a similar moment in the *Regiment of Princes*, Hoccleve observes:

> I putte cas that his foos him assaille
> Sodeynly in the street: what help shal he
> Whos sleeves encombrous so syde traille
> Do to his lord? He may him nat availle;
> In swich a cas he nis but a womman;
> He may nat stande him in stide of a man.

(I put the case to you that his enemies suddenly attack him in the street: what help would he – whose unwieldy sleeves hang down so as to be swept elegantly along – be to his lord? He cannot assist him. In such a case he is nothing but a woman; he cannot stand in the place of a man.)

The complaints about women's fashions are most vociferous on the subject of the decoration of their heads and hair. No fewer than seven texts complain about decorated heads with the women's hair being arranged in the horned style, or with buns on each side, with a further writer complaining about hair that is curled with hot irons and covered with a cap; in two of the texts the addition of rich crowns or garlands to women's heads is a source of dismay. One text comments unfavourably on women's use of cosmetics to make their faces paler while a further three are disgusted by the dying of wimples yellow and/or the use of fake frontels to deceive men. Two texts deplore low necklines, and one each open-sided clothes and sleeveless kirtles. It should also be noted that many of the adverse comments about wide sleeves and long trains are aimed at women's dress.

The texts differ, too, with regard to whether it is the fashion or fashionable item itself that is the focus of complaint (as in the examples above), or if the main thrust is the sin occasioned by adherence to fashion. Pride is a theme which runs through much of the writing presented here: women's hair crops up again as an explicit source of pride, particularly in her roll of hair that she should tend at home rather than in church. Women are also accused of taking pride in, and showing off in, borrowed finery. Three texts refer to pride in ornamented cloaks and furred hoods, while a further two mention extravagance in dress and fur trimming, with the implication that the wearer is not troubled by how these were acquired. Three texts refer to the remodelling of clothes, for example by cutting or slashing them. Here the sins encompass wasting time and looking for praise. Forming part of the taxonomy of the seven deadly sins which underlies many of these texts, the issue of immodest dress seems to have provided writers and preachers with a way to interpret this form of wickedness. The sin most commonly referred to is the related one of wishing to be admired. Here women come in for particular opprobrium, being accused of going from street to street to show off their clothes, with the implication of a particular kind of admiration, made explicit in the accusation that there are married women who dress to attract the sexual attention of other men (though one text concedes that men who fall for this are also culpable).

A related issue is the type of immodesty in dress which makes the wearer appear to be of a higher rank than is in fact the case: no fewer than five texts mention this phenomenon.

This theme runs through the sumptuary laws of the period (cf. Chapter V), though it is difficult to tell whether the impetus for both the complaints and the legislation is the same or if one set of discussions gave rise to the other. The sharp comments on dress seem to reflect anxiety about the clarity of the status of the high-born and the fear of mistaking a middle- or lower-class person for someone of rank and distinction. The problem is also, as in the sumptuary laws, sometimes couched as one of extravagance: people dressing above their station is said to be causing impoverishment throughout the country as people waste their money on acquiring the latest fashions, those fashions including garments made with excessive amounts of fabric (see, for example, Hoccleve's *Regiment of Princes*).

Many of the texts reproduced here have been buried from sight for some time. They are taken from printed editions rather than manuscripts, but in many cases these editions date from nineteenth- and early-twentieth-century scholarship.

EXTRACTS FROM MORAL AND SATIRICAL WORKS

1. Orderic Vitalis, *The Ecclesiastical History*

Orderic Vitalis was an Anglo-Norman historian, whose *Ecclesiastical History*, written in Latin in the 1120s and 1130s, combines powers of acute observation with deep disapproval of contemporary social mores. His work describes how what Orderic calls *effeminati* at the court of William II of England (1087–1100) were among those who set the new fashions (Harris 1998: 89). Many new fashions of the early twelfth century demanded close-fitting garments and an exaggerated emphasis on length and slenderness. Books VII and VIII contain Orderic's plan to write a general history of the Normans (Chibnall 1973: xiii). There is no internal evidence of the date of Book VII but a reasonable hypothesis is that it was written between 1130 or 1131 and 1133, and Book VIII between 1133 and 1135, possibly with additions a year or two later (Chibnall 1973: xix). The text is printed in Chibnall (1973), 186–92. The translation has been adapted from Chibnall. The *punctus elevatus* is represented with a semicolon.

Hic [Count Fulk] in multis reprehensibili et infamis erat; multisque uitiorum pestibus obsecundabat. Ipse nimirum quia pedes habebat deformes, instituit sibi fieri longos et in summitate acutissimos subtolares; ita ut operiret pedes, et eorum celaret tubera quæ vulgo vocantur uniones. Insolitus inde mos in occiduum orbem processit; levibusque et novitatum amatoribus vehementer placuit. Unde sutores in calciamentis quasi caudas scorpionum quas vulgo pigacias appellant faciunt; idque genus calciamenti pene cuncti diuites et egeni nimium expetunt. Nam antea omni tempore rotundi subtolares ad formam pedum agebantur; eisque summi et mediocres clerici et laici competenter utebantur. At modo seculares peruersis moribus competens scema superbe arripiunt, et quod olim honorabiles uiri turpissimum iudicauerunt, et omnio quasi stercus refutauerunt, hoc moderni dulce quasi mel estimant, et ueluti speciale decus amplectentes gestant.

Robertus quidam nebulo in curia Rufi regis prolixas pigacias primus cepit implere stuppis; et hinc inde contorquere instar [188] cornu arietis. Ob hoc ipse cornadus cognominatus est; cuius frivolam adinventionem magna pars nobilium ceu quoddam insine probitatis et virtutis opus mox secuta est. Tunc effeminati passim in orbe dominabantur indiscipline debachabantur sodomiticisque spurciciis fœdi catamitæ flammis urendi turpiter abutebantur. Ritus heroum abiciebant, hortamenta sacerdotum deridebant; barbaricumque morem in habitu et vita tenebant. Nam capillos a vertice in frontem discriminabant, longos crines veluti mulieres nutriebant, et summopere comebant, prolixisque nimiumque strictis camisiis indui tunicisque gaudebant. [. . .] Illi enim modestis vestiebantur indumentis, optimeque coaptatis ad sui mensuram corporis [. . .] Ast in diebus istis veterum ritus pene totus novis adinventionibus commutatus est. Femineam mollitiem petulans juventis amplectitur; feminisque viri curiales in omni lascivia summopere adulantur. Pedem articulis ubi finis est corporis colubrinarum similitudinem caudarum imponunt; quas velut scorpiones præ oculis suis prospiciunt. Humum quoque pulverulentam interularum et palliorum superfluo sirmate verrunt; longis latisque manicis ad omnia facienda manus operiunt, et his superfluitatibus onusit celeriter ambulare uel aliquid utiliter operari uix possunt. Sincipite scalciati sunt, ut fures; occipitio autem

Count Fulk was a man with many reprehensible, even scandalous, habits, and gave way to many pestilential vices. Being a man with deformed feet he had shoes made with very long and pointed toes, to hide the shape of his feet and conceal the growths that are commonly called bunions. This encouraged a new fashion in the western regions, which delighted frivolous men in search of novelties. To meet it cobblers fashioned shoes like scorpions' tails, which are commonly called 'pulley-shoes', and almost all, rich and poor alike, now demand shoes of this kind. Before then shoes always used to be made round, fitting the foot, and these were adequate to the needs of high and low, both clergy and laity. But now laymen in their pride seize upon a fashion typical of their corrupt morals that once honourable men judged shameful and all rejected as rubbish [literally 'dung'], that modern people think sweet as honey and wear as a special distinction.

Robert, a certain worthless fellow at King Rufus's court, first began to stuff the long 'pulley-toes' and in this way bend them into the shape of a ram's horn. As a result he was nicknamed Cornard. The frivolous fashion he had set was soon imitated by a great part of the nobility as if it had been an achievement of great worth and importance. At that time effeminates set the fashion in many parts of the world: foul catamites, doomed to eternal fire, unrestrainedly pursued their revels and shamelessly gave themselves up to the filth of sodomy. They rejected the traditions of honest men, ridiculed the counsel of priests, and persisted in their barbarous way of life and style of dress. They parted their hair from the crown of the head to the forehead, grew long and luxurious locks like women, and loved to deck themselves in long, over-tight shirts and tunics. [...] Our ancestors used to wear decent clothes, well-adapted to the shape of their bodies [...] But in these days the old customs have almost wholly given way to new fads. Our wanton youth is sunk in effeminacy, and courtiers, fawning, seek the favours of women with every kind of lewdness. They add excrescences like serpents' tails to the tips of their toes where the body ends, and gaze with admiration on these scorpion-like shapes. They sweep the dusty ground with the unnecessary trains of their robes and mantles; their long, wide sleeves cover their hands whatever they do; impeded by these frivolities they are almost incapable of walking quickly or doing any kind of useful

prolixas nutriunt comas ut meretrices. Olim penitentes et capti ac peregrini usualiter intonis erant, longasque barbas gestabant; indicioque tali penitentiam seu captionem vel peregrinationem spectantibus pretendebant. Nunc vero pene universi populares cerriti sunt et barbatuli; palam manifestantes specimine tali quod sordibus libidinis gaudeant ut fœtentes hirci. Crispant crines calamistro, caput uelant vitta sive pilleo. Vix aliquis militarium procedit in publicum capite discooperto; legitimeque secundum apostoli preceptum [190] tonso. Exterius itaque habitu gestuque monstrant; quales interius conscientias habeant et qualiter per artum callum ad Deum percurrent. [...]

Alii quoque plures litterati sophistæ magnos questus protulerunt de flagitiis et erumnis huius seculi, quos secutus in presenti opusculo breviter memini; quo tempore cisalpes cepit [192] ineptia pigatiarum, et superflua prolixitas capillorum atque vestium terræ sordes frustra scopantium.

2. William of Wadington, *Le Manuel des Pechiez*

This Anglo-French treatise dated *c.* 1220 – *c.* 1240 is the basis for the Middle English *Handlyng Synne* (see extract 3 below). The text of *Le Manuel des Pechiez* was originally edited by Frederick Furnivall (1862) from two manuscripts, BL, MSS Harl. 273 and 4657. A brief discussion of the work, along with an image of one manuscript leaf, may be found on the University of Nottingham's Manuscripts and Special Collections website at http://www.nottingham.ac.uk/ManuscriptsandSpecialCollections//learning/medievalwomen/theme8/AdviceonBehaviourandDress.aspx (Summerwill 2010; accessed 18 July 2014). The extracts below are adapted from Furnivall (1901), Parts 1 & 2, EETS, os 119 and 123. The italicised tale at lines 166–82 is not included by Robert of Brunne in *Handlyng Synne*. It appears as a footnote in Furnivall's edition (1901: I.119). The translation is by Louise Sylvester.

Des set pechiez mortels; le premier si est orgoyl
[...]
Ki de ces cheuols est trop geluʒ,
Cum sunt suuent les orgoilluʒ;
Ou de autre manere de atiffement
Qu a la teste ou al cors apent,
Ceo ne deueʒ vblier,
Si dreit vous voleʒ confesser
Trop est geluʒ de sun croket
Qe a la messe souent la main met;
Plus i gist, ceo crey, sun qeor,
Que ne fet pur ces pechiéʒ plurer.
Assez se purra hom atiffer
En autre lu qe al muster.
Ki ad sa face coluré
Autrement qe Deu l'ad furme,
De blanket ou de rouencel;
Ceo est orgoil, per seint Michel;
Outrage est, a demesure,

work. They shave the front part of their head, like thieves, and let their hair grow very long at the back, like harlots. Up to now penitents and prisoners and pilgrims have normally been unshaven, with long beards, and in this way have publicly proclaimed their condition of penance or captivity or pilgrimage. But now almost all of our fellow countrymen are crazy and wear little beards, openly proclaiming by such a token that they revel in filthy lusts like stinking goats. They curl their hair with hot irons and cover their heads with a fillet or a cap. Scarcely any knight appears in public with his head uncovered and decently shorn according to the Apostle's precept. So in their outward dress and bearing they reveal their character and show in what fashion they follow the narrow path of God. [...]

Also many other learned writers have composed long laments about the sins and sorrows of this age. Following their example, I have given a brief account in this modest work of the time when men in northern parts adopted the foolish fashions of pulley-toes and long and flowing hair and garments that sweep up all the filth on the ground for no useful purpose.

<u>Of the Deadly Sins: the First of which is Pride</u>
[...]
One who is too proud of his hair as proud people often are, or of other kinds of ornamentation of the head or body should never forget that it is right that to confess. One who is excessively proud of her hairstyle and is always putting her hand to it during mass will not cry for her sins. Such a person can adorn her hair at another place than a church. One who colours her face differently from the way God made her with powder or rouge, by St Michael this is pride, it is an immeasurable outrage not to be satisfied with what God made. Of decorated heads the less said the better for each man well knows these come from pride, and those

Quant ne est payé de la deu feture.
De testes fardés poy dirrum,
Car ceo siet ben chescun hom,
Qe de orgoil vient; et perdue sunt
Tieles qe per vanite le funt.
Dames cornueʒ, passer voley   (3331–53)

[Furnivall's subtitle: *The Tale of the Proud Lady, who was burnt to ashes again and again in Hell by a Burning Wheel*]

De une dame de grant renun,
Qe femme esteit de vn riche hom,
Cointe fu mult durement,
De sa teste nomement;
Quant meus viure desira,
Hors de ceste siecle passa.
Tost apres qe morte esteit,
Vn bacheler malade giseit,
Qe sun seignur aueit mult chier,
Sun seruise li feseit amer.
Vn iur, al malade resembleit
Qe a li sa dame veneit;
Qe le suisit, li comanda,
Car merueille grant li mustrera.   (3361–74)

Qatre deables tost veneient,
E vne reo ardante porteient;
Sur la teste la dame la mistrent,
Eiesques a cendre le arcistrent.
Autre feyʒe est viue releué –
Sa dame ci li ad semblé –
Mes les deables la reo ardant
Sur luy mettent meintenant,
Qe en pudre le art autre fée.   (3387–95)

Treis feiʒ l'arcistrent, cum li sembla;
Allas la peyne qe ele mena!
Mes ele tuʒ iurs releueit,
Car en peynes morir ne poeit.
La resun apres ad cunté
A l'home qe la fu mené,
Pur quei ele esteit ensi pené
De la reo ardente enflaminé.
'Ceste peine', dist, 'que vous veeʒ,
Pur ceo, seofre ieo, sacheʒ,
Pur orgoilluse atiffement

whose pride is such, they are lost. Let pass women who go about with horns.
[…]

There was a woman of great renown who was married to a rich man. She was highly adorned and particularly her head. She wanted to be the most desired beyond all those of her society. Soon after she died, a squire who had been very dear to her lord and whose service made him beloved fell ill. One day, his illness made it seem as if his lady came to him and commanded him to follow her so that she could show him a great wonder.
[…]

Four devils soon came carrying a burning wheel. They put it on the lady's head, until it had burned to cinders. Afterwards the woman who had appeared to him got up again alive, but the devils put the burning wheel on to her head again until it had turned to ashes again.
[…]

Three times they burnt it, as it seemed to him: alas, the pain that she was dealt but she always got up again for she could not die of the pain. After, she told the man she had led there the reason why she was in such pain from being set on fire by the burning wheel. 'This pain that you see,' she said 'know that I suffer it because of prideful ornamentation namely of my head in order to be looked at and more praised for beauty when I went among

De ma teste nomement.
Car pur este regardé,
E de bealte plus preisé
Quant ieo veneie entre gent,
Me atiffai trop cointement.
Ore seofre ceste peine dure
Pur ma orgoillous atiffur.
Mun seignur, pur deu garnieʒ,
Qe pur sun boban ne seit peneʒ;
Car a tiel iur pur ueir murra;
Si il ne s'amende, perdu serra'.
'E vus', dit eole, 'al hostel aleʒ,
Car, solun ceo qe me est mustreʒ,
Sans faille a tiel iur murrez;
De vos pechiéʒ vus confesseʒ'.
Ensi lur est auenu;
Car, seignur et seriant ambedou
Morirent al iur terminé;
Par tant est le cunt verifié.
Mult fet dunques a duter,
Par orgoil sei atiffer.   (3399–430)

Ou de trop riche robe vous cointeʒ,
Pur estre de la gent plus preiseʒ, —
Tut vient de orgoil, ceo sacheʒ;
Pur le amur deu, le lesseʒ.
Nepurquant, chescun, solun ceo qe il est,
Cointer li purra, ci li plest.
Mes, quant passe sun afferant,
Bien veeʒ qe li peche en tant.
E femme bele se peot cointer,
Pur plus sun barun pleiser;
Mes garde qe ne passe mesure;
Bone entente, de peché ne eyt cure.
Trop pechent en lur cointises
Ki estudient en noueleries,
E, pur estre plus regardé,
Vnt lur cointises souent changé;
Apertement mustrent en verité
Qe lur vie est tut en vanité.
Ki bien souent fu purpensé
Od quele robe ert en tere cuché,
Poy freit force de tiel orgoil
Cum menent les vns, et ceo est doyl.
Pur ceo, vn ensample vous cunterai,
Qe cuntre euʒ en liure troué ay.   (3433–56)

people I adorned myself too elegantly. Now I suffer this grievous pain because of my prideful ornamentation. My lord, I warn you for the sake of God, one who is not punished for his pride, on this day will truly die, he will be lost if he does not mend his ways.' 'And you,' said she, 'go to communion, for one thing has been shown to me: without fail till the day of your death, make sure you confess your sins.' For this way, when it comes to you, for lord and servant will both die on their appointed day, because this story is so true, many then should fear to adorn themselves out of pride.

[…]

Or if you adorn yourself with too costly a dress in order to be the most praised of all people, all this comes of pride, know this and for the love of God leave it. Nevertheless, anyone, no matter who he is, may adorn himself as it pleases him, but when he goes beyond his rank, you can well see that such behaviour is sinful. And a beautiful woman may adorn herself the more to please her husband but she should take care not to go beyond what is reasonable. Good intention is not a remedy for sin. Those who make a study of novelty and are constantly changing their adornment in order to be looked at more sin too much in their decoration for their lives are filled with emptiness for they are often thinking about how their robe will lie on the ground. Then the power of this pride which leads them in this example that I have given you, will always imprison them.

[…]

[Furnivall's subtitle: *The Tale of the Knight and Monk who loved new fashions*]

> Vn chiualer, par sa folur
> Trop cointes estoit, cum sunt plusur,
> Cest se aueit aturné
> En la sesun de esté
> Vne cote perecé;
> Mes esteit apres mustré
> Qe deu ne fu mie bien paié
> Del cointise qe il ad vsé.
> Vn iur est alé praer
> Pur sun gain anoiter;
> Ces enimis l'unt encuntré
> Od la preye qe il ad mené.
> La force fu lur plus grant;
> Pur ceo, l'unt oscis meintenant.
> Les amis al chiualer oscis,
> Qe si cointes fu, ieo vous dis,
> Sun cors vnt al muster porté,
> E, cum est custume, enterré.
> Ces chatels unt pus parti,
> Pur poures fere prier pur li.
> Quant vindrent a sa cote duner,
> Tuʒ le comencent a refuser;
> Mes vn clerc les ad prié
> Qe cele cote li fust duné.
>   Ore oyeʒ la vengance dée.
> Quant la cote out fublé,—
> Vn fu surd de ly trop ardant,
> E sun cors ard meintenant;
> Le feu de arder n'adnient cessé
> Tant cum de sun cors fu rien troué.
> Par tant vous ad deu ben mustré
> Qe la cote esteit escomengé;
> Pur ceo, nul poure home dé
> Receiure ne la volt de grée,
> Pur le orgoil qe il ad mené
> Ki la cote aueit aturné.
> Certes, bien dust estre blamé,
> E ceo ad la veniance ben mustré.
> Clerk cointe ordené,
> Baneour est al maufé.
> Mes ore, par lur ribaudries
> Estudient entur noueleries
> Les clers, cum fussent lay gent;
> Deus i mette amendment ! (3457–500)

A knight, in his madness, was very fashionable, as many are. In the summer he had made for him a slashed coat, but it was afterwards shown that God was not at all pleased by the ornamentation that he had used. One day when he had gone to plunder to increase his spoils, his enemies met him together with the booty that he had got. Their power was too great for him and they killed him forthwith. The friends of the killed knight who was so adorned, I tell you, they took his body to the monastery and buried it according to custom. They then divided up his property to provide for the poor, to make them pray for him. When they came to giving the coat, everyone began to refuse it, but one clerk asked them if the coat could be given to him.

Now see God's vengeance. When the coat was put on a burning fire came from it and his body was immediately destroyed by fire. The flames of the fire did not stop burning until nothing could be found of his body. In this way God clearly showed that the coat was cursed and because of that, from then on no poor man wanted to receive the item because of the pride which had led the knight to have the coat made. Certainly he was condemned and vengeance was demonstrated. A clerk who is fashionable beyond his rank is a standard-bearer for the devil. But now through their debauchery they concern themselves entirely with novelty. May God correct clerks who behave like noblemen!
[...]

Pur estre de plus grant bobant;
Ou en lit richement aturné,
E noble chiuals et herneis dorré,—
Tut est orgoil et vanité,
De tuȝ cels serreȝ a-copé.   (3510–14)

Des dames, dium nous auant,
Qe trop longes robes uunt trainant;
Meuȝ vaudreit en almoine duné,
Quant qe traine desuȝ le pée.   (3521–4)

[*How the Devil has power over Women's Trains*]

Par .i. example coe confirmerai
K'en 'la somme de vices' trouai;
Ke .ii. moines ensemble alerent,
Vne femme lung treinant encunterent;
L'un de eus l'ad mut regardé,
Pus fist vn grant risé;
L'autre ly demande pur koy il rist.
'Volunters' fet il, e pus ly dist,—
'La femme ke ilokes alait,
Vn deble sur sa coue seait;
E kuant sa coue saka vers ly,
Le deble en vn wassel chai;
En la boue ueuttra mut vilement,
E a coe rys ioe veraiement'.
Par tant poez vous tuz beu sauer
Ke le deble del coue lung ad poer.

Les gympeus ausi safroneȝ,
Plus malement les auient d'asseȝ ;
Meins sunt beles, ceo me est auis,
Lessent ceo dunc tutdis.
Ki en les rues vet iuant,
Home ou femme sei demustrant,
Si ceo fet pur estre desiré,
En sun qeor ad ia peché.   (3525–32)

Le setime pecche mortel ke est dit leccherie
[…]
Bien se deit chescun garder
Pur mal entente sey urner [var. *aurner*]
Pur estre plus tost desiré,
Cum funt, allas, les vns de gré;

In order to show off more by means of a richly prepared bed, and noble horses and golden harness, all is pride and emptiness, of all this you are condemned.
[…]

Of women, of whom we have spoken before, who wear very long trailing robes it would be better if the train under her foot were given away for charity

[*How the Devil has power over Women's Trains*]

By one example it is confirmed that in 'the Book of Vices' we find that two monks walking together met a women with a long train. One of them looked at her then produced a great laugh, the other asked why he was laughing. 'Willingly', he said, and then said to him – 'The woman who is walking in that place has a devil on her train and it is pulling her by the train towards him. The devil is in a bog, he will completely overcome her in the mud, and truly, it is at this that I am laughing'. And through that you can know that a long train gives the devil power. If their wimples are also dyed with saffron, their torments will be much worse. They are less beautiful, in my opinion than if they left them as always. Those who go thus in the streets, men or women show that they do this in order to be desired and their trains lead them to sin.
[…]

The seventh deadly sin is said to be lechery
Everyone should guard against ornamenting themselves with evil intention to be more desired, as some do, alas, for their pleasure. For both are great sins. When you are desired and desire another

> Car ambe-dous sunt grant peché,
> Quant vout estre desiré,
> E desire autre pur mesfere;
> Le seint le dit, le poeʒ crere.
>
> Consentir deit nul hom
> A nul fornicaciun.   (6041–50)

3. Robert Mannynge of Brunne, *Handlyng Synne*

Robert of Brunne's Middle English *Handlyng Synne* was written in 1303 (Furnivall 1901). Internal evidence suggests that Robert Mannyng was born at Brunne, but was never a canon in any monastery of that place, since he calls himself of Brunne soon after the year 1303 and in 1338. It appears also that he was a canon of the Gilbertine Order in the priory of Sempringham (Lincolnshire) for fifteen years (1288–1303). Between the years 1327 and 1338, he tells us, he completed his translation of Langtoft's *Chronicle* and for a brief time during that period was in the House of Sixhille, another Gilbertine priory in the same county (Furnivall 1862: v). Robert disclaims all invention and styles himself as a compiler and narrator of other people's stories (Furnivall 1862: xiii–xiv). The text contains the stories of the proud man with the coat who is set upon and the woman who was burnt (cf. extract from Peter Idley's *Instructions to his son* II.B.176–280). The text below has been adapted from Idelle Sullens's scholarly edition of 1983. A version of the text (based on BL, MS Harley 1701 and Oxford Bodleian 415) was originally edited and published by Furnivall in 1862, and re-edited for the Early English Text Society in 1901. This edition is available electronically through the Corpus of Middle English Prose and Verse (at http://name.umdl.umich.edu/AHA2735.0001.001, accessed 18 July 2014). The translation is by Louise Sylvester.

> *The Seven Sins;— and first of Pride*
> […]
> ʒyf þou art prout of þyn her,
> As proud men beyn eurywher,
> Or ʒyf þou tyffyst þe ouer proudly,
> Ouer mesure on þy body,
> Swych synne ys nat þe leste.
> Y rede þe: telle hyt to þy prest.
>
> Be nat proud of þy croket,
> Yn þe cherche to tyffe and set.
> At home mayst þou þy croket werche
> And nat at þy messe yn þe cherche.
> And of þese berdede bukkes also,
> Wyþ hemself þy moche mysdo,
> Þat leue crystenmennys acyse,
> And haunte al þe newe gyse.
> Þerwhyles þey hadde þat gyse on hand
> Was neure grace yn þys land.
> Of proud wymmen wlde y telle,

to do evil, the saint says, the less you are believed. No man should consent to any fornication.

The Seven Sins;— and first of Pride
[…]
If you are proud of your hair, as proud men are everywhere, or if you ornament your body over much and too proudly, this will not be the least of your sins. I advise you: tell your priest about it.

Do not be proud of your ornamental roll of hair and sit and adorn it in church. You can do your hair at home and not at mass in church. And these bearded gallants who have too much to do to themselves, who leave the ways of Christian men and practise the new fashions. All the while they have fashion in hand, God's favour will never be present in the land. I would like to speak of proud women, but they are quickly angry and violent. As for

But þey are sone wroth & felle.
Of þese þat are so foule & fade
Þat make hem feyrer þan god hem made,
Wyþ oblaunchre or wyþ ouþer flour
To make hem whytter of koloure,
Gret pryde hyt ys and vyle outrage,
Þat she ys nat payd of goddys ymage.
Heuedys tyffed wyþ gret pryde
Wyþ her & wyþ hornys syde,
Men mowe wete hyt ys gret synne
To haue moche pryde þer ynne.
Men seye & haue seyd here before,
For swych pryde are wymmen forlore.
Ryche ladyys of gret renouns
Þey do make hem ryche corouns.
Þey may make to here auenaunt
But ouer mesure ys nat couenaunt.   (3201–34)

The Tale of the Proud Lady, who was burnt to ashes again and again in Hell by a Burning Wheel

Þer was a lady, a lordys wyff,
Here feyrhede was yn renoun ryff.
Moche she louede feyr tyffyng
On here hed ouer al þyng,
For to be holde þe feyrest lady
Of alle þo þat wonede here by.
[…]
Whan she was ded, sone aftyrward,
Here squyer toke a syknes hard,
Þat here lorde held of gret prys
For he was aman yn seruyse wys.
As he lay yn hys bed anyght,
Hym þoghte hys lady com to hym ryght
And seyde þus: 'rys & go wyþ me.
A merueyle shal y shewe to þe.'
[…]
Þys wheyl þat was set on here heued
Brende here al þat noght was leued.
Eft she ros whan she was brent
And hadde þe same turment,
And brende ryght as she dede before.
[…]
Þan askede he here why þat hyt was
Þat she suffred swych pyne. 'Alas, alas,'
She seyde, 'y suffre þys mysauenture

those who are so disgusting and hostile who make themselves more attractive than God made them using cosmetic powder or else flour to make themselves look paler, it is great pride and a disgusting outrage that they are not satisfied with God's image. Men must know that it is a great sin to have great pride in heads decorated with great pride with hair and wide horns at the side: men say, and have said here before, that women are damned because of such pride. Rich ladies of great renown make fine crowns for themselves. They may make them for their pleasure but beyond moderation it is not appropriate.
[…]

The Tale of the Proud Lady, who was burnt to ashes again and again in Hell by a Burning Wheel

There was a lady, a lord's wife. Her forehead was of widespread renown. Above anything, she greatly loved beautiful dressing on her head, in order to be judged the most attractive woman of all those who lived nearby.
[…]
Soon after she had died, her squire, on whom her lord placed a high value, because he was a man wise in service, became very ill. As he lay in his bed one night, it seemed to him his lady came and said as follows: 'Rise and go with me. I will show you a wonder.'
[…]
This wheel that was placed on her head burned there until nothing was left. She rose again after she had been burnt and had the same torment again, and burned just as she had done before.
[…]
Then he asked her why it was that she suffered so much pain. 'Alas, alas,' she said, 'I suffer this misfortune because of the excessively beautiful decoration I had

For on myn hed ouer feyr tyffure,
For whan y shulde agher go or ryde,
Y dyghte myn hed ful moche wyþ pryde,
For to be preysed ouer alle ladys;
And of pryde to bere þe prys,
And among knyghtes yn halle,
Y wlde be holde feyrest of alle.
[...]
Ryght at þat terme þat she seyde,
Þe knyght and þat squyer deyde.
Be þat tokenyng weyl men knewe
Þat þe tale was ryght and trewe.
Þarfore hyt ys gret doute,
Wymmen to tyffe here hedes aboute.   (3243–312)

Ne dysgyse nat þy cloþyng
Ouer mesure for þy preysyng.
Alas, hyt shulde so betyde,
Manyone are lost for here pryde.
Shal grace neuer come yn þat land
Þere men haue swych gyse yn hand.
God and grace are wyþ hem wroth
Þat haue for pryde dysgysede here cloth.
Noþeles euery man may
Aftyr hys astate make hym gay.
But whan he þassyþ ouer mesure
Þer of cumþ mysauenture.
Gentyl men ofte for swych desert
Falle at þe laste yn grete pouert.
A weddyde wyff may atyre here
Þat here husbunde loue noun but here;
For hys loue she may hyt do,
But for noun ouþer mannys so.
Ȝyt swyche y rede þat þey so fare
Þat here pryde make hem nat bare.
Gretlych þey synne yn here queyntyse
Þat nouelrye al day areyse,
For to be preysyd & of gret syght,
Al day dysgyse hem at here might.
For soþe hyt semyþ weyl to be
Al here lyff yn vanyte.
But wlde þey þenke þat make swych strut
Yn what robe þey shul yn erþe be put,
Þey shulde nat make hyt so amys
Ȝyf þey þoghte ofte on þys.

on my head, for when I was supposed to walk or ride, I did my hair with so much pride, in order to be praised above all other women; and, out of pride, to carry the prize, and so that I would be judged the most beautiful of all by the knights in hall.'
[...]
Just at the time that she said, the knight and the squire died. Men knew well by that sign that the story was accurate and true. Therefore it is very dangerous for women to place decorations about their heads.
[...]

Do not fashion your clothing in a new-fangled way immoderately in order to be praised. Alas that it should happen but many a person is damned for their pride. God's grace will never come into a land where men hold this fashion so dear. God and providence are angry with those who have changed their clothing out of pride. Nevertheless, every man may make himself attractive in accordance with his rank, but misfortune comes of going beyond what is reasonable. Frequently noble men end up in poverty because of this desert. A married woman may dress herself so that her husband will love none but her: she may do this to earn his love but not to gain that of any other man, yet I believe that they do behave like this, that their pride does not allow them to forbear this. Those that rush towards novelty all day greatly sin in their ingenuity. In order to be praised and to have a great appearance, they alter their appearance as much as they can all the time. For truly it seems a good thing to them to spend their whole lives on frivolity. But would they think that they would make such a proud display in the robe in which they will be buried. They would not go so wrong if they often thought about that.

Y shal ȝow telle a lytyl wyght
How hyt befel onys of a knyght.

The Tale of the Knight and Monk who loved new Fashions

Þer was a knyght þat louede nouelrye,
As manyone haunte now þat folye.
He dede do make hym yn þe somers tyde,
A kote perced queyntly wyþ pryde.
And god was nat þer of payd,
For yn hys pryde he was betrayd.
Þys knyght ȝede vppon a day
Aboute robbory to gete hys pray.
Homward as he hys pray ledde,
Wyþ hys enmys he was bestedde.
Wyþ fors þey gunne wyþ hym to fyght
And slogh þere þys yche knyght.
Þe knyghtys frendys herde seye
How he was slayn be þe weye;
Ful feyre for hym þan gunne þey werche:
Þey byryed þe body feyre at þe cherche.
Hys frendys departede hys kateyl
Among þe pore men, and þat was weyl.
Whan þey come at þe kote gysyng
To dele hyt among hys ouþer þyng,
Before þe pore men hyt was broght.
Þe pore men seyde þey wlde hyt noght.
A clerk stode þo þere besyde
And preyde for þe kote of pryde;
To werne hyt hym, þey þught loth.
Þey toke and ȝaue þys clerk þe cloth.
Þys clerk was glad whan he hyt hadde:
Þys kote on hym asswyþe he cladde.
Se now here a grete myschaunce
Com ryght as for veniaunce.
Ryght as he was yn þe kote al dyght,
A fere brennyng on hym gan lyght,
And brende hys body down to þe grounde,
Whyles oght of hym myghte be founde.
Þere shewede god weyl be þat cas
Þat þe kote acursed was,
And tokenede weyl sorowe & wrake
Þat no pore man wlde hyt take
For pryde of þe newe gyse
Aȝens crystenmennys wyse.

In a little while I shall tell you about what happened once to a knight.

The Tale of the Knight and Monk who loved new Fashions

There was a knight who loved novelties as many now follow that foolish course. In the summer time he proudly had made for himself an intricately slashed coat and God was not pleased by this, for in his pride he was betrayed. This knight set out one day upon a robbery to get his prey. As he was bringing his prey home, he was set upon by his enemies who began to fight violently with him and they killed the same knight. The knight's friends heard about how he was killed on the road and they set to work on his behalf. They buried his body decently in the church. His friends divided his goods among the poor and that was fine. When they came to disposing of the coat to share it out with his other property, it was put before the poor but they said they did not want it. One clerk who was standing at the side asked for the coat of pride. They were reluctant to refuse him: they took the garment and gave it to the clerk. This clerk was glad when he had it and he immediately dressed himself in the coat. See here now, a great misfortune came just as if for vengeance. Just as he was arrayed in the coat, a burning fire alighted on him and razed his body to the ground. Soon nothing of him could be seen. By this example God demonstrated that the coat was cursed and that it betokened sorrow and misfortune, so that no poor men would take it because pride in new fashions goes against the ways of Christian men. But the clerk was, in any case, mad to wear a coat beyond his rank. Here you may see that God is angry with those who alter their clothing and a clerk who brings notoriety upon himself is much to blame.

But þe clerk was wode algate
To were a cloth aȝens hys state.
Here mowe ȝe se þat god ys wroth
Wyþ hem þat dysgyse here cloth.
And a clerk ys moche for to blame
Þat brynth hemself yn foul fame.
Clerk ordeyned yn dygnyte
Þat haunteþ swyche iolyte,
Noþeles of þe newe gyse,
Þe deuyl haþ made hym chef iustyse.
And ȝyf he yn folye begynne to stoute,
Þan beryþ he þe deuyls baner aboute.
Moche folk ys þarwyþ blent:
God do þer of amendement.   (3353–408)

Y seye for þo þat haue gret pryde
Yn hygh hallys and yn wyde,
Ȝyf þou delyte þe yn ryche beddyng,
Yn hors, yn harneys, or yn feyr rydyng,
Al ys pryde and vanyte.
Of al shalt þou acouped be.   (3429–34)

What seye ȝe men of ladys pryde
Þat goun traylyng ouer syde?
Ȝyf a lady were ryghtly shreue,
Better hyt were yn almes ȝeue.
To saule help hyt myghte do bote
Þat traylyþ lowe vndyr here fote.
Wymples, kerchyues, saffrund betyde,
Ȝelugh vndyr ȝelugh þey hyde.
Þan wete men neuer wheþer ys wheþer,
þe ȝelugh wymple or þe leþer.
Wymmen þat go fro stret to stret
One or ouþer for to mete,
Of pryde cumþ swych desyre,
For þey haue on here feyre atyre.
But she wyle to þe prest þat telle,
She may þar fore go to helle.
For yn as moche as she douþ men synne,
Yn so moche shal she haue plyght ynne.
And wymmen haue y seye of þo
Þat borwe cloþes yn to karol go,
Þat pore pryde god hyt loþes,
Þat make hem proud of ouþer mens cloþes.   (3441–62)

The devil has made himself chief justice of new fashions, and if a clerk ordained in dignity nevertheless pursues such frivolity and in his folly begins to be rebellious, he waves the devil's banner about. Many people are blinded by this; may God heal them.

[…]

I say for those who have great pride in high and wide hangings, if you delight in fine bedding, in horses, gear, or in fair riding, it is all pride and vanity: you will stand accused of all of it.

[…]

What do you men say about the pride of women whose gowns hang down the side. If a woman confessed properly, it would be better given to charity. That which trails under her foot might help the soul to do penance. Wimples and kerchieves dyed with saffron: they hide yellow under yellow. Then men do not know which is which, the yellow wimple or the leathery skin. Women go from street to street to meet one another: that desire comes from pride because they have on their best clothes. Unless she tells that to the priest, she might go to hell because of it. For inasmuch as she is causing men to sin, so much will she be in danger from it. And women, have I spoken of them, who borrow clothes to go dancing in, God hates that poor pride that makes them show off in other people's clothes.

[…]

Of Lechery

[…]
Lecherye ys also gret ȝernyng
To be desyred þurgh feyr cloþyng.
What wymmen hem tyffe wyþ owne wyl,
To foly loue ouþre men to tyll.
Ȝyf men, þurgh here feyr atyre
Wyþ hem to do foly haue desyre,
Þey shul answere for here synne,
For þey are rote & fyrst begynne.
Noþeles þe consentour
Shal be holde for a lechour.
Euen peyne shul þey bere,
Þe toon þe touþer shal answere.   (7613–24)

4. Thomas Gascoigne, *Loci e Libro Veritatum*

Thomas Gascoigne (1403–58), writing in the mid-fifteenth century, comments on what he sees as the vices of the age: Owst points out that Gascoigne is under the impression that the fashion for long trains began during the reign of Richard II and Anne of Bohemia although we find it condemned in English sermons in the thirteenth century (Owst 1961: 338–9). Specific offences of dress are singled out for attack, in particular low-necked dresses, which Gascoigne suggests became generally popular in the early years of Henry VI's reign (Owst 1961: 396). The extract below has been adapted from the edition of Rogers (1881), 11–12 and 144–5. The translation is by Ruth Briggs and Mark Chambers.

<u>Contra caudas dominarum</u> [note: Ista cauda quæ Anglice 'trayn' vocatur quia trahitur, et ad malum trahit]
Item tales caudas relinquerent dominæ, ut priores sanctas dominas et Deo acceptas imitarentur, qui talibus usæ non fuerunt. Nam secundum relacionem antiquorum, in tempore Annæ reginæ Angliæ et uxoris regis Ricardi nec ante tempus illud vestes dominarum ad terram descenderunt cum caudis.

Ornatus
Iste enim ornatus preciosus et superfluus, et apertus, nudans pectora mulieris, et ostendens colorem fuco, i.e. unguento, false adquisitam, et ornatus virorum, jam nuper inductus, citra annum 1429, plura mala causavit, in superbiendo, et in fornicando, et in adulterando, et in Sodomia, ut notum et pluribus. Homines enim femorum formam ostendunt et genitalium per aperturam togæ, et braccis jam non utuntur, sed caligis, in quibus forma magnitudinis membrorum turpiter ostenditur. Talis ornatus primo movet ad magna peccata, et retrahit mentes, quando de Deo cogitarent, ad pessima desideria et ad actus malos.

Item, ad turpia verba, quæ sunt dampnabilia, et ad tactus impudicos, qui in ardore libidinis alligant animam, et mentem captivant a sua libertate.

Of Lechery

[...]
Lechery is also a great longing to be desired because of beautiful clothing. Those women who ornament themselves to their own pleasure love to lure other men to foolish desire. If men, because of their beautiful attire desire to make love to them, they should answer for their sin, for they are the root cause and first beginning. Nevertheless, he who consents should be held to be a lecher and should suffer equal pain, the two of them shall answer for it together.

Against the trains of mistresses: [That train which in English is called 'trayn' because it is drawn along (*trahitur*) and draws (*trahit*) one towards evil]
Also, mistresses should abandon such trains, in order to imitate earlier holy mistresses and those acceptable to God, who did not use such things. For, according to the information of the ancients, in the time of Anne, queen of England and wife of King Richard (and not before that time), the clothes of mistresses descended as far as the ground with trains.

Adornment
For that finery is expensive and unnecessary and revealing, baring a woman's bosoms and flaunting a colouring falsely acquired by rouge, i.e. by an unguent; and the finery of men, as just recently introduced since the year 1429, has caused too many evils, in arrogance, in fornication, in adultery, in sodomy, as is known in all too many ways. For men show off the shape of their thighs and their genitals through the slit in their gown, and do not now use breeches, but stockings, in which the shape of the size of their members is displayed in a shameful fashion. Such finery firstly leads to many sins and distracts minds, when they should be thinking about the Lord, to the worst desires and to evil acts.

Also, [such finery leads] to shameful speech, which deserves condemnation, and to immodest touching, which binds the soul in the ardour of lust and takes the mind from its freedom into captivity.

Item, expensas magnas causant, et sic consequenter retrahunt homines, et impediunt, quod nec possunt nec volunt expendere bona circa sancta opera, et circa salutem animarum, et circa libros scribendos, et multiplicandos, et corrigendos, et circa pueros ad scholam, et prædicatores verbi Dei in patria exhibendos; quia jam cura destruitur per indignam promotionem, et per pluralitates, et per perpetuum malum in appropriatione ecclesiarum parochialium. Ornatus et vestes institutæ erant ad servandum naturam a nocivis et malis, et ut per talia signa cognoscatur unum officium ab alio, et eciam ut per illa ornamenta visa, reducat memoriæ onera suæ curæ, officii, seu gradus. Nudatio autem pectorum mulieris, quæ jam inolevit in juventute Henrici Sexti, regis Angliæ, circa annum Domini 1429, non est propter necessitatem naturæ, nec officii, nec gradus, sed magnum allectamentum est peccati videntibus, et venenum obtulit, quamvis ex gratia Dei nemo ex illo biberet, et ideo in quantum in ipsa est animas videncium interficit.

5. John Bromyard, *Summa Predicantium*

Owst suggests that John Bromyard's *Summa Predicantium* is a collection of sermon material from fourteenth-century England and that its contents may reach back even further (Owst 1961: 224). Material concerned with the sins associated with fashionable dress is extracted below. The text is printed in Bromyard (1586). The translations have been adapted from those in Owst (1961), 313; 396–7; 395; 397.

Cap. II: *Bellum*
[p. 94a: 10] Sic in bello spirituali, quia serui diaboli potenter contra dominum suum, in quadreagesima surrexerunt, suumque dominum negaverunt. Isto tempore diabolus parat fortissimè exercitum suum contra eum in choreis, & spectaculis. Adduces milites, & militissas suas, in quolibet peccato armatos, habentes pro galea cornua, & capitegia, & frontalia. [...]

Cap. I: *Labor*
[p. 438a: 12] Ubi terum inueniuntur, qui ita pectus nudarent, & pedes in strictissimis caleis [*calceis*] arctarent, & corpus, ita diligenter ornarent pro amore Dei, sicut faciunt superbi ut, suas & aliorum perdat animas
[...]

Cap. VII: *Luxuria*
[p. 461a: 20] in muliere namque impudice ornata ad capiendas animas sertum in capite est: quasi unus carbo vel titio inferni pro igne illo accedendo sic cornua alterius, sic collum nudatum sic firmaculum in pectore, sic de omnibus curiositatibus totius corporis
[...]

Also, they cause great expense and thus consequently drag men backwards and hinder them, because neither are they able nor do they want to spend their wealth on holy works, or on the salvation of souls, or on the writing and copying and correcting of books, or on [sending] boys to school, or on presenting preachers of the word of God in our land; for already this care of souls is being destroyed through unworthy advancement and through the plurality of ecclesiastical benefices and through perpetual wrongdoing in the appropriation of parish churches. Finery and clothing was instituted in order to protect human nature from harm and evils and in order that, through such symbols, one office might be discerned from another, and also so that through the visible nature of those adornments it should bring to mind the duties of one's care of souls, of one's office, or of one's status. However, the baring of a woman's bosoms, which had already become fashionable in the youth of Henry VI, king of England, around the year 1429, serves not the needs of nature, nor of one's office, nor of one's status, but is a great enticement to sin for those who look at them, and has introduced poison, although by the grace of God no-one drinks from it, and for this reason, inasmuch as there is poison in this very act of baring the bosoms, it destroys the souls of those who look at them.

Cap. II: *War*
Because the servants of the Devil have rebelled stoutly against his dominion and have denied his rule, at that season [spring after Lent] he makes ready his army against them in mightiest array in the dances and pageants, leading forth his knights and amazons armed with every sin, having, for their helmet, horns and head-dresses and frontlets.
[…]
Cap. I: *Work*
Where, again, shall be found those who would lay bare their breast and compress their feet in the tightest shoes and thus diligently adorn their body for love of God, as do the proud, to destroy their own souls and those of others?
[…]
Cap. VII: *Pride*
In the woman wantonly adorned to capture souls, the garland upon her head is as a single coal or firebrand of Hell to kindle men with that fire; so too the horns of another, so the bare neck, so the brooch upon the breast, so with all the curious finery of the whole of their body.

6. A late-medieval sermon

This fifteenth-century sermon is edited from Oxford Bodleian Library, MS e Museo 180, fols. 69v–75 by A. J. Fletcher. While discussing the sin of pride, the preacher criticises women's 'horned' head-dress and ostentatious jewellery. The text is printed in Fletcher (1998), 89–108. The translation is by Louise Sylvester.

The first and the eldeste of þese same vij dowȝters of þe fowle fende of helle Sathanas, sche was cald P*ride*, þe whiche was a fowle name to hevenly pepill. And for encheson þat þe fende wold mary hyr [to þe] pepill [of þe worlde,] he hathe sett on hyr a gay name, and sche is called Honestye, so þat a prowde man or a prowde woma*n* is called an honest man or an honest woman. [. . .] Women in þer*e* degre withe their*e* gay heddys sett up on heyȝte *and* ornyd, as it were an unresonabyll beeste, and þ*er* gay bedis withe litill devocion and thereon ryng*is* full gay; hyr kyrtell sleveles to make hem to seme prayti to syn*n*e, and many oþer tokens. What, is þat pride? Nay syr, it is clenlynes and honeste.

7. 'Song upon the Tailors'

The foreign and extravagant fashions in dress which were prevalent provided a constant subject for popular outcry against the upper classes. Wright suggests that contemporary manuscript illustrations indicate that such complaints were responding to the fashions of the day (Wright 1839: 51). The original is in BL, MS Harley 978 fol. 99 and is a production of the reign of Henry III (1216–72), a time when luxury in dress was much satirised and not infrequently commented upon by the clergy (Fairholt 1849: 1). The poem is in Latin and Anglo-French. The text is printed in Fairholt (1849), 1–6, which is a reprint of Wright (1839), 51–6. The translation is by Ruth Briggs and Louise Sylvester.

> *In nova fert animus mutatas dicere formas*
> *Corpora, Dii cœptis, nam vos mutastis et illas,*
> *Aspirate meis*
>
> Ego dixi, dii estis;
> Quæ dicenda sunt in festis
>   Quare prætermitterem?
> Dii, revera, qui potestis
> In figuram novæ vestis
>   Transmutare veterem.
>
> Pannus recens et novellus
> Fit vel capa vel mantellus,
>   Sed secundum tempora
> Primum capa, post pusillum
> Transmutatur hæc in illum;
>   Sic mutatis corpora.
>
> Antiquata decollatur
> Decollata mantellatur,
>   Sic in modum Proteos

The first and eldest of these same seven daughters of the foul fiend of hell Satan was called Pride, which was a disgusting name to the heavenly people. And on the pretext that the fiend wanted to marry her to the people of the world, he gave her a pretty name, and she is called Honesty, so that a proud man or a proud woman is called an honest man or an honest woman. [...] women in their ranks with their pretty heads set up on high and horned, as if they were senseless beasts, and their pretty beads with little devotion and with very pretty rings on them. Their kirtle is sleeveless to make them seem attractive to sin, and many other signs. What, is that pride? No, sir, it is cleanness and honesty.

> My mind prompts me to speak of transformations into new bodies. You gods, look favourably on my undertakings, for you are the ones who transformed those forms.
>
> I have said: you are gods – why should I not use the required liturgy of festival days? You are in truth gods, you who are able to transform an old garment into the shape of a new one.
>
> The cloth, fresh and new, becomes either a cape or a cloak; but if we are talking about the timing, first it becomes a cape, then after little time this former garment is transformed into the latter. In this way you change 'bodies'.
>
> Now out of fashion it has its collar cut off; once the collar has been removed

Demutantur vestimenta;
Nec recenter est inventa
    Lex metamorphoseos.

Cum figura sexum mutant;
Prius ruptam clam reclutant
    Primates ecclesiæ;
Nec donatur, res est certa,
Nisi prius sit experta
    Fortunatum Tiresiæ.

Bruma tandem revertente,
Tost unt sur la chape enté
    Plerique capucium;
Alioquin dequadratur,
De quadrato retundatur,
    Transit in almucium.

Si quid restat de morsellis
Cæsi panni sive pellis,
    Non vacat officio;
Ex hiis fiunt manuthecæ
Manutheca quidem Græcè
    Manuum positio.

Sic ex veste vestem formant,
Engleis, Tyeis, Franceis, Normant,
    Omnes generaliter;
Ut vix nullus excludatur.
Ita capa declinatur,
    Sed mantellus aliter.

Adhuc primo recens anno,
Nova pelle, novo panno,
    In arca reconditur;
Recedente tandem pilo,
Juncturarum rupto filo,
    Pellis circumciditur.

Sic mantellus fit apella;
Ci git li drap, e la pel là,
    Post primum divortium;
A priore separata
Cum secundo reparata
    Transit in consortium.

it is converted into a cloak. In this way garments change their shape in the same way as Proteus; nor is the law of metamorphosis a recent invention.

With their shape they change their sex; the church primates surreptitiously close back up what before was split; nor is it given as a gift, the issue is clear-cut, unless it has first experienced the fate of Tiresias.

When the winter at last returns, most people immediately attach a hood to their cloak; as for the remainder of the garment, it is squared up, then the edges of the square are rounded and it becomes an amice.

If anything remains of the trimmings from the cutting of the cloth or hide, it does not lack a function; gloves are made from these; a glove, indeed, is called *manutheca*, from the Greek words for 'placing of the hands'.

Thus from one item of clothing they fashion another – Englishmen, Germans, French and Normans, all of a kind – to the extent that scarsely anyone is an exception. In this way a cape is rejected, but a mantle not so.

Still brand new in its first year, with the hide still fresh, the cloth still new, it is stored away in a chest. At length when the fur starts to wear off the skin, when the thread of the seams breaks, the skin is 'circumcised'.

In this way the cloak becomes a Jew; here lies the cloth, there lies the skin after this first divorce; separated from their earlier union, restored with their second, passing into a cohabitation.

Quod delictum dices majus?
Istud palam est contra jus:
    Nam si nupsit alteri,
Conjugium est violatum,
Dum fit novo copulatum
    Reclamante veteri.

N'est de concille, ne de sene,
Deus dras espuser à une pene,
    E si nus le juggium;
Permittunt hoc decreta? non:
Sed reclamat omnis canon
    Non esse conjugium.

Pannus primum circumcisus,
Viduatus et divisus
    A sua pellicula,
Jam expertus Judaismum,
Emundatur per baptismum
    A quacumque macula.

Circumcisus mundatusque,
Est adeptus utriusque
    Legis testimonium;
Quem baptismus emundavit,
Cum secunda secundavit,
    Pelle matrimonium.

Pilis expers, usu fractus,
Ex Esaü Jacob factus,
    Quant li peil en est chaü,
Inversatur vice versa,
Rursus idem ex conversa
    Ex Jacob fit Esaü.

Pars pilosa foris paret,
Sed introrsus pilis caret
    Vetustas abscondita;
Datur tamen, k'il n'i eit perte,
Servienti, pur deserte,
    Mantellus hypocrita.

What will you say is a greater crime? This is clearly against the law: for if it has married another, the marriage has been violated; the old partner cries out in protest while the conjoining takes place with the new.

It is not advisable, nor sensible, to marry two cloths to one fur, and so we judge it. Do the decrees permit this? No! Every religious statute cries out in protest that this is no marriage.

The cloth having first been 'circumcised', widowed and separated from its skin, having now experienced 'Judaism', it is cleansed through baptism from any stain of sin [i.e. it is re-dyed].

Once circumcised and washed clean, and having secured the witness of both covenants, he whom baptism has washed clean has entered into a second marriage with a second skin.

Devoid of hair, worn out by use, from an Esau it becomes a Jacob; when the hair has fallen out from it, in turn the process is inverted: from a Jacob it becomes again conversely an Esau.

The hairy part is visible on the outside, but on the inside the aged part of the garment, hidden away, is hairless. However, so that it isn't wasted, this hypocritical cloak is given to a servant for his reward.

8. 'Ne be þi winpil nevere so jelu ne so stroutende'

These two couplets on the vanity of fashion (as designated by Robbins 1975) were written in the margin of BL, MS Cotton Cleopatra C iv, fol. 22r in a thirteenth-century hand (Wright and Halliwell 1843: 14). This verse is printed in Wright and Halliwell (1843), 15. The translation is by Louise Sylvester.

> Ne be þi winpil nevere so jelu ne so stroutende,
> Ne þi faire tail so long ne so trailende,
> That tu ne schalt at evin al kuttid bilevin,
> And tou schalt to bedde gon so nakid as tou were [borin].

9. 'Against the Pride of Ladies'

Written in a south-west Midland dialect in the late thirteenth or early fourteenth century, this poem is an intense outburst against the vanity of women of the lower and middle classes who assume the elaborate mode of dress that was fashionable around 1300 (Robbins 1975). It appears to be directed against the fashions in women's clothing, which had become so prevalent as to be aped by the middle and lower classes (Fairholt 1849: 40). Fairholt notes that Wright considers this poem to be a production of the reign of Edward I (1272–1307), though the headnote in Wright (1839: 153) says 'reign of Edw. II' (1307–27). The work is driven by intense moral feeling and disgust: the author attacks the offenders with bitter, passionate invective, expressive of the attitude of the clergy toward the excesses of fashion (Robbins 1975). It appears in BL, Harley MS 2253, fol. 61v. The text was reprinted in Fairholt (1849), 40–2, from Wright's edition (1839), 153–5. The translation is by Louise Sylvester.

> Nou hath prude the pris in everuche plawe;
> By mony wymmon un-wis y sugge mi sawe,
> For ȝef a ledy lyne is leid after lawe,
> Uch a strumpet that ther is such drahtes wil drawe;
>   in prude
>   Uch a screwe wol hire shrude
>   Thah he nabbe nout a smoke hire foule ers to hude.
>
> Furmest in boure were boses y-broht,
> Levedis to honoure ichot he were wroht;
> Uch gigelot wol loure, bote he hem habbe soht;
> Such shrewe fol soure ant duere hit hath a-boht;
>   in helle
>   With develes he shule duelle,
>   For the clogges that cleveth by here chelle.
>
> Nou ne lacketh hem no lyn boses in to beren;
> He sitteth ase a slat swyn that hongeth is eren.
> Such a joustynde gyn uch wrecche wol weren,
> Al hit cometh in declyn this gigelotes geren;
>   upo lofte

Even if your wimple is ever so yellow and so extended, and your beautiful train so long and so trailing that in the evening you cut what is left over, you will still go to bed as naked as you were born.

Now pride takes the prize in every game. In respect of many unwise women I utter this speech, for if a lady's linen is put on according to the usual practice, each loose woman that there is will use such tricks. In pride each shrew will have her outfit though she has not a smock to hide her disgusting arse.

First buns of hair were brought to the bower, I think they were done to honour ladies. Each tart will frown, unless she has sought them out. Dearly has such a sour and unpleasant thing been bought. She will live in hell with devils because of the lumps that are attached to her jowls.

Now they do not lack linen to carry their buns in, they sit like a slit pig whose ears hang down. Each wretch wants to wear such a jutting out device, these harlots'

> The devel may sitte softe,
> Ant holden his halymotes ofte.
>
> ȝef ther lyth a loket by er outher eȝe,
> That mot with worse be wet for lat of other leȝe;
> The bout and the barbet wyth frountel shule feȝe;
> Habbe he a fauce filet, he halt hire hed heȝe,
>   to shewe
>   That heo be kud ant knewe
>   For strompet in rybaudes rewe.

10. 'A Dispitison bitwene a God Man and þe Devel'

This fourteenth-century poem appears in the Vernon Manuscript (Oxford, Bodleian Library, MS Eng. poet.a.1), and it relates an argument between a man walking back from church alone and the devil, who accosts him and asks him what he heard in the sermon. The sermon was on the seven deadly sins and this extract concerns pride. The text is printed in Horstmann (1892), 329–54; an electronic edition of which is available in the Corpus of Middle English Prose and Verse at http://quod.lib.umich.edu/c/cme/APE7335.0001.001/1:2.37?rgn=div2;view=fulltext (accessed 18 July 2014). The translation is by Louise Sylvester.

>   Viterede hodes and Clokes also,
> Al þat vile pride schal don hem ful wo;
> Þei struye godes good þer-wiþ: And torne hit to fen,
> Þat muche mihte helpe: Sely pore men.
> Now is non worþ a fart,
> But he bere a baselart
> I-honget bi his syde,
> And a swynes Mawe, & al is for pride.
> Godus grame, stirap on his cappe is knit,
> Þat an vnche haþ he not on for to sit;
> Muche meschef and gret colde: On his hers he has,
> Men miȝte, ȝif he brech weore to-tore: Seon his genitras.
>   And also þis wymmen: Þat muchel haunteþ pride,
> Wiþ hornes on heore hed: Pinned on vch a syde,
> Maad of an old hat: And of a luytel tre,
> Wiþ selk scleyres I-set aboue: Apparisaunt to be;
> Heore Reuersede gydes: On hem are streyt drawe –
> But al be of þe newe aget: Hit is not worþ an hawe.
> Þei wenen a ben ful feire: And wonder foul þei be;
> And a wolden be-þenken hem: Of heore priuete
> And hou foule þei are: In soule and in bodi,
> Þei ouȝte wiþ heore wepyng: Make heore chekes rodi.   (265–86)

gear is all going downhill. The devil may sit comfortably up on high and hold his court often.

If a curl lies by ear or eye it must be wet with pus for lack of other soap. The back and chin parts of the head-dress and the frontel will be stained. If she has a fake headband she holds her head high. To show that she is famous and known as a harlot in the ranks of the debauched.

Ornamented hoods and also cloaks, all that disgusting pride will bring them to grief. They strive for God's goodness with it: and turn to filth that which might help them greatly – wretched poor men. Now none of them is worth a fart unless he carries a basilard hanging by his side, and a swine's belly, and it is all for pride. God's rage, a stirrup is knitted on his cap but he has not got an inch to sit on. He has much suffering and great cold on his arse: men could see his genitals, if he were to tear his underwear.

And also these women who practice so much pride with horns on their heads, pinned on each side, made of an old hat, and of a little tree, they wear their turned-back and trimmed gites tight, with silk veils worn above: to be on display – everything is of the new fashion. It is of little value. They think they are very beautiful, but they are incredibly ugly. And they should think of their modesty and how disgusting they are, in soul and in body, they should make their cheeks red with their weeping.

11. A satire on manners and costume

This late-fourteenth-century poem, which appears in BL, Harley MSS 536 and 941, is entitled by Robbins (1975: 1439) 'On the Times of Richard II'. Fairholt suggests that the allusion to the long pointed toes which he believes came into fashion in the reign of Richard II is sufficient to fix the date of composition, but see Chambers (2009) for a more recent view about the dating of this fashion in footwear. Owst observes that the poem is a typical macaronic complaint, in Latin and English, upon the evil times of the reign of Richard II, which speaks explicitly of efforts of the pulpit and in this case their palpable failure (Owst 1961: 403). Printed in Fairholt (1849), 44–8, the extract (lines 67–85) appears on pp. 46–7. This poem has recently been re-edited by Dean (1996). The translation is by Gale Owen-Crocker (the Middle English) and Ruth Briggs (the Latin).

> Brodder then ever God made *humeris sunt arte tumentes;*
> Narugh thei be, though thei seme brod, *nova sunt factio gentis.*
> [Dean: Narow thay bene, thay seme brod, *nova sunt haec respice gentes*]
> Thei bere a new faccion, *humeris in pectore tergo;*
> Goddes plasmacion *non illis complacet ergo.*
> Wyde colers and hygh, *gladio sunt colla parata;*
> Ware the prophecy *contra tales recitata.*
> Long sporres on her heles, *et rostra fovent ocriarum;*
> Thei thinke it doith welle, *non sicut regula Sarum.*
> A strecte [Dean: 'strayt'] bende hath the hose, *laqueantur a corpore crura;*
> Thei may not, I soppose, *curvare genu sine cura;*
> Whan other kneelis, *pro Christo vota ferentes,*
> Thei stonde on here helis, *sed non curvare valentes.*
> For hurtyng of here hose, *non inclinare laborant;*
> I trow, for her longe toes, *dum stant ferialiter orant.*
> Many men thei lette *et turbant ad sacra stando;*
> Cristes curse thei gete, *nisi Deus instat aliquando.*
> Wantounly brestes *procedunt arte prophana;*
> Prechour ne prestes *possunt hæc pellere vana.*
> With poyntes full stronge *caligas de more sigillant,*
> Now shorte and now longe, *ut venter ecce vacillant.*
> Now knokelyd elbowes *manace laqueant lacerale;*
> In frost and snowes, *ut aves spectant laqueatæ.*

12. Ballad against excess in apparel especially in the clergy

Robbins entitles this poem, which appears in BL, MS Harley 372 and was composed in the mid-fifteenth century, 'Against Proud Galaunts', observing that it consists of two parts: two stanzas blaming these men of fashion with their high caps, short gowns, long piked shoes, and long hair for having 'brought this lond to gret pyne', and four stanzas giving the gallants' reply to these charges, namely that priests also follow the fashions in dress for short stuffed doublets and pleated gowns and are as lewd as the gallants they condemn (Robbins 1975: 1470). It is printed in Fairholt (1849: 56–7). The translation is by Louise Sylvester.

Broader than ever God made, they puff out their shoulders artificially;
They are narrow, though they seem broad, these gents have the 'new look'
They wear a new fashion, with the shoulder sat at the back of the chest;
God's creation, therefore, does not please these people.
Wide and high collars, their necks are prepared for the sword;
Be mindful of the prophecy proclaimed against such people.
Long spurs on their heels, they adore the points of their boots;
They think it suits well, but not according to the rule of Salisbury.
The hose have a strict band, the legs are caught in a noose by the body;
They may not, I suppose, bend the knee without difficulty;
When others kneel offering up prayers to Christ,
They stand on their heels unable to bend.
For fear of damaging their hose they go to great lengths not to bend;
I believe for the sake of their long toes they pray while standing even on holy days.
They impede many men and they cause much trouble at the altars by their standing;
They get Christ's curse except when God sometimes pursues them.
Wantonly, their breasts they protrude in an unholy fashion;
Neither preacher nor priests can deter these vanities.
With large points [laces] they fasten their shoes, as fashion dictates,
Now short now long, behold, they vary like the wind
Their slit sleeves expose their knobby elbows
They look like snared birds in frost and snow.

>Ye prowd galantts hertlesse,
>With your hygh cappis witlesse,
>And your schort gownys thriftlesse,
>Have brought this lond in gret hevynesse.
>
>With your long peked shone,
>Therfore your thrifte is almost don;
>And your longe here in to your eyen,
>Have brought this lond to gret pyne.
>
>Ye poope holy prestis full of presomcion,
>With your wyde fueryd hodes, voyd of discrecion;
>Un to your owyn prechyng of contrary condition,
>Whech causeth the people to have lesse devocion.
>
>Avauncid by symony in cetees and townys,
>Make shorter your taylis and broder your crownys,
>Leve your short stuffede dowblettes and your pleytid gownys,
>And kepe your owyn howsyng, and passe not your boundis.
>
>Repreve not other men, I shall tell you whye,
>Ye be so lewyd your selfe there setteth no many you bye.
>Yt is not but a schame ye wold be called holly,
>For worse dysposyd people levyth not under the skye.
>
>Ffirst make fre yourselfe, that now to syne be bounde,
>Leve syne and drede, than may ye take on hande
>Other to repreve, and that I understonde,
>Ye may amende all other and bryng pese to londe.

13. Thomas Hoccleve, *The Regiment of Princes*

The Middle English poem is extant in 45 manuscripts. It includes an envoy addressed to Henry, Prince of Wales, who became king in 1413, and allusions in the poem suggest that it must have been composed in 1411–12 (Matthews 1972: 748). This extract, deploring current extravagance in dress among all classes, includes themes familiar from the sumptuary legislation from as early as 1336 and 1363 and from petitions to parliament on the subject (cf. Chapter V), namely that people were continuing to dress above their estate and that this was causing impoverishment throughout the country. Details of the particular male fashions being described by Hoccleve differ substantially from the 'short stuffede dowblettes' and tight male garments of the two previous extracts. What is probably being described here is the 'houppelande', a voluminous, flowing, usually belted garment with full, wide sleeves, worn by both men and women in the late fourteenth and early fifteenth centuries (see *EMDT*, s.v. 'houppelande'). The extract comes from Blyth's edition (1999: 51–5), which is based on BL, Arundel MS 38. The translation is by Louise Sylvester.

>But this me thynkith an abusioun,
>To see oon walke in gownes of scarlet

You proud and heartless men of fashion with your silly high caps and your worthless short gowns, you have brought this land to grief.

With your long piked shoes your wealth is almost gone, along with your long hair in your eyes, you have brought this land to great pain.

You hypocritical priests full of presumption, with your wide furred hoods, without any prudence, of an opposite condition to your own preaching, which causes people to have less devotion.

Advanced by simony in cities and towns, you make your trains shorter and your crowns broader. Leave your short, stuffed doublets and your pleated gowns, and keep to your own houses and do not overstep your bounds.

Do not reprove other men. I will tell you why: you are so ignorant yourselves that no retinue follows you. It is nothing but a shame that you want to be called holy, for no worse-intentioned people live under the heavens.

First free yourself, who now are tied to sin. Leave sin and fear, then you can take others in hand to reprove them, and, as I understand, you may amend all others and bring peace to the land.

But this I consider a violation of propriety to see someone walk in gowns of scarlet twelve

Twelve yerdes wyde, with pendaunt sleeves doun
On the ground, and the furrour therin set,
Amountyng unto twenti pound or bet.
And if he for it paied have, he no good
Hath left him wherwith for to bye an hood.

For thogh he gette foorth among the prees
And overlooke every poore wight,
His cofre and eek his purs been penylees;
He hath no more than he gooth in right.
For land, rente, or catel he may go light;
The weighte of hem shal nat so moche peise
As dooth his gowne. Is swich array to preise?

Nay, soothly, sone, it is al mis, me thynkith,
So poore a wight his lord to countrefete
In his array; in my conceit it stynkith.
Certes to blame been the lordes grete,
If that I durste seyn, that hir men lete
Usurpe swich a lordly apparaille;
It is nat worth, my chyld, withouten faille.

Sumtyme afer men mighten lordes knowe
By hir array from othir folk, but now
A man shal studie and musen a long throwe
Which is which. O lordes, it sit to yow
Amende this, for it is for your prow;
If twixt yow and your men no difference
Be in array, lesse is your reverence.

Also ther is anothir neewe get:
A foul waast of clooth and an excessyf
Ther gooth, no lesse in a mannes typet
Than of brood clooth a yerde, by my lyf;
Me thynkith this a verray inductyf
Unto stelthe. Waar hem of hempen lane,
For stelthe is medid with a chekelewe bane.

Let every lord his owne men deffende
Swich greet array, and thanne, on my peril,
This land withynne a whyle shal amende.
In Goddes name, putte it in exyl;
It is a synne outrageous and vyl;
Lordes, if yee your estat and honour
Loven, fleemeth this vicious errour.

yards wide with sleeves hanging down to the ground, and the fur trimming set within it amounting to twenty pounds or more. And if he has paid for it, he has no wealth left to him with which to buy a hood.

For though he goes about among the crowds and overlooks every poor man, his money box and also his purse are penniless; he has no more than what he stands up in. He is light on land, rent or cattle: they do not weigh as much as his gown does. Is such array to be praised?

No, truly, son, it is all wickedness, I think, so poor a man to impersonate his lord in his clothing; in my opinion it stinks. Certainly, great lords are to blame, if I dare say, who let their men usurp such aristocratic dress; it is not worthy, my child, without doubt.

Some time ago men could tell lords from other people by their clothes, but now a man might study and ponder for a long time which is which. O lords it is up to you to amend this, for it is for your benefit; if there is no difference in dress between you and your men, your honour is less.

Also there is another new fashion: a disgusting and excessive waste of cloth. There goes, no less than a yard of broadcloth into a man's tippet, by my life. I think this is a true inducement to stealing. They should beware of the gallows, for theft is rewarded with an edict that is apt to choke.

Let every lord prohibit his own men from wearing such fine clothing, and then, on my oath, within a short time this land will improve. In God's name, banish it. It is an outrageous and vile sin. Lords, if you love your rank and honour, drive out this vicious error.

What is a lord withouten his meynee?
I putte cas that his foos him assaille
Sodeynly in the street: what help shal he
Whos sleeves encombrous so syde traille
Do to his lord? He may him nat availle;
In swich a cas he nis but a womman;
He may nat stande him in stide of a man.

His armes two han right ynow to doone,
And sumwhat more, his sleeves up to holde.
The taillours, trowe I, moot heeraftir soone
Shape in the feeld; they shul nat sprede and folde
On hir bord, thogh they nevere so fayn wolde,
The clooth that shal been in a gowne wroght;
Take an hool clooth is best, for lesse is noght.

The skynner unto the feeld moot also --
His hous in Londoun is to streit and scars
To doon his craft; sumtyme it was nat so.
O lordes, geve unto your men hir pars
That so doon, and aqweynte hem bet with Mars,
God of bataille; he loveth noon array
That hurtith manhode at preef or assay.

Who now moost may bere on his bak at ones
Of clooth and furrour hath a fressh renoun;
He is a lusty man clept, for the nones.
But drapers and eek skynners in the toun
For swich folk han a special orisoun,
That droppid is with curses heer and there,
And ay shal til they paied be for hir gere.

In dayes olde, whan smal apparaille
Souffysid unto hy estat or mene,
Was greet houshold wel stuffid of vitaille;
But now housholdes been ful sclendre and lene,
For al the good that men may repe or glene
Waastid is in outrageous array,
So that housholdes men nat holde may.

Pryde hath wel lever bere an hungry mawe
To bedde than lak of array outrage.
He no prys settith by mesures lawe,
Ne takith of him clooth, mete, ne wage;
Mesure is out of land on pilgrimage;
But I suppose he shal resorte as blyve,
For verray neede wole us therto dryve.

What is a lord without his retinue? I put the case to you that his enemies suddenly attack him in the street: what help would he be whose unwieldy sleeves hang down so as to be swept elegantly along give to his lord? He cannot assist him. In such a case he is nothing but a woman; he cannot stand in the place of a man.

His two arms have more than enough to do to hold up his sleeves. The tailors, I believe, cut in the field: they cannot spread and fold the cloth that will be made into a gown on their tables, however much they want to. It is best to take a whole cloth, for less than that is nothing.

The furrier must also go into the field – his house in London is too narrow and cramped to ply his craft; once it was not so. Oh lords, give your men who do this their shares and make them better acquainted with Mars, god of war. He does not like any clothes that damage manliness at trials or tests.

He who must now bear both cloth and fur on his back at once has a new fame: he is called a vigorous man for the time being. But drapers and also furriers in the town have a special prayer for such people, scattered here and there with curses, and always will be till they are paid for their gear.

In the old days, when a small amount of clothing was enough for a high rank or household, great houses were well filled with food; but now households are slender and lean, for all the good that men may reap or glean is wasted on outrageous outfits, so that men cannot keep their households.

Pride would much rather carry a hungry mouth to bed than be outraged by lack of fine clothing. He sets no price by the law of measures, nor takes cloth, food or wages. Moderation is out of the country on a pilgrimage; but I suppose he will return before long, for need will drive us to it.

Ther may no lord take up no neewe gyse
But that a knave shal the same up take.
If lordes wolden wirken in this wyse
For to do swiche gownes to hem make
As men dide in old tyme, I undirtake,
The same get sholde up be take and usid,
And al this costlewe outrage refusid.

Of Lancastre Duk John, whos soule in hevene
I fully deeme and truste sit ful hye --
A noble prince, I may allegge and nevene --
Othir may no man of him testifie;
I nevere sy a lord that cowde him gye
Bet lyk his estat; al knyghtly prowesse
Was to him girt - o God, his soule blesse!

His garnementes weren nat ful wyde,
And yit they him becam wondirly wel.
Now wolde God the waast of clooth and pryde
Yput were in exyl perpetuel
For the good and profyt universel;
And lordes mighte helpe al this, if they wolde
The old get take, and it foorth use and holde.

Than mighte silver walke more thikke
Among the peple than that it dooth now.
Ther wolde I fayn that were yset the prikke --
Nat for myself, I shal do wel ynow --
But, sone, for that swiche men as thow,
That with the world wrastlen, mighte han plentee
Of coyn, whereas yee han now scarsetee.

Now hath this land but litil neede of bromes
To sweepe away the filthe out of the street,
Syn syde sleeves of penylees gromes
Wole it up likke, be it drie or weet.
O Engeland, stande upright on thy feet!
So foul a waast in so symple degree
Banisshe, or sore it shal repente thee.

If a wight vertuous but narwe clothid
To lordes courtes now adayes go,
His conpaignie is unto folkes lothid;
Men passen by him bothe to and fro,
And scorne him for he is arraied so.
To hir conceit is no wight vertuous
But he that of array is outrageous.

No lord can take up a new fashion without a knave taking up the same one. If lords would want to behave in this way, to have such gowns made for them as men had in olden times, I undertake that the same custom would be taken up and used, and all this costly outrage renounced.

Duke John of Lancaster, whose soul sits high up in heaven I wholly judge and trust – a noble prince, I may declare and claim or no man would testify differently about him; I never saw a lord who could conduct himself more appropriately to his rank; all knightly prowess was given to him – O God bless his soul!

His garments were not very wide, and yet they suited him wonderfully well. Now the waste of cloth and pride should be perpetually banished, God willing, for the sake of universal good and benefit: and lords could help all this, if they would take the old custom and use and keep it from now on.

Then silver might walk more widely among the people than it does now. There I greatly wish that the goal was set – not for myself, I shall do well enough – but, son, so that men like you, who struggle with the world, might have plenty of money, whereas now you have a scarcity.

Now this land has little need of brooms to sweep away the filth from the street, since the wide sleeves of penniless men will lick it up, whether it is dry or wet. Oh England, stand upright on your feet, so disgusting a waste in such a simple degree! Banish it or you will bitterly regret it.

If a virtuous but poorly dressed man goes to a lord's court nowadays, his company is hateful to people: men pass him by both coming and going, and snub him because of the way he is dressed. To their minds no one is virtuous except one whose outfit is outrageous.

> But he that flatere can or be a baude,
> And by tho tweyne fressh array him gete,
> It holden is to him honour and laude.
> Trouthe and clennesse musten men forgete
> In lordes courtes, for they hertes frete;
> They hyndren folk. Fy upon tonges treewe!
> They displesance in lordes courtes breewe. (421–553)

14. John Lydgate, 'A Dyte of Womenhis Hornys'

The extravagant horned head-dresses worn by women in the early fifteenth century are an obvious target for satire, but Lydgate 'offers a serious and considered explanation, with analogies from nature and history, of how horns are philosophically unacceptable within the docrine of natural beauty' (Pearsall 1970: 218). The Middle English poem, from the early fifteenth century and entitled 'Horns Away' in the various Early English Text Society editions, appears in twelve manuscripts. The text is printed in McCracken (1961), 662, with u/v distinctions normalised as in Halliwell's earlier edition (1840), 46–9. The translation is by Louise Sylvester.

> *Here gynneth a dyte of womenhis hornys*
> Off God and kynde procedith al bewte;
> Crafft may shewe a foreyn apparence,
> But nature ay must have the sovereynte.
> Thyng countirfeet hath noon existence.
> Tween gold and gossomer is greet dyfference;
> Trewe metall requeryth noon allay;
> Unto purpos by cleer experyence,
> Beute wol shewe, thogh hornys wer away.
>
> Ryche attyres of stonys and perre,[1]
> Charbonclys, rubyes of moost excellence,
> Shewe in dirknesse lyght where so they be,
> By their natural hevenly influence.
> Doublettys of glass yeve a gret evydence,
> Thyng counterfeet wol faylen at assay;
> On this mater concludyng in sentence,
> Beute wol shewe, thogh hornes were away.
>
> Aleyn remembreth – his compleynt who lyst see,
> In his book of ffamous elloquence –
> Clad al in flours and blosmes of a tre
> He sauh nature in hir moost excellence,
> Upon hir hed a kerche of Valence,
> Noon other richesse of counterfet array:
> Texemplyfie by kyndely provydence,
> Beute wol shewe, thogh hornes wer away.

---

[1] This line appears as 'Riche attyrs of gold and perry' in Furnivall (1866).

Except one who can flatter or be a pimp, and by those two means get fresh outfits, he is obliged to worship and praise. Men must forget truth and purity in lords' courts, for they trouble their hearts; they hinder people. Down with honest tongues! They brew resentment in lords' courts.

Here begins a poem about women's horns.
All beauty comes from God and nature. Skill may produce a different appearance but nature must always reign. Counterfeit things have no real existence. There is a great difference between gold and something worthless. True metal does not need any alloy. To the point at issue, by plain experience, beauty will be evident, even without horns.

Fine ornaments of jewels and precious stones, carbuncles, rubies of the highest excellence, shine in darkness wherever they are, by their natural heavenly influence. Imitation jewels of glass offer great evidence, a counterfeit thing will fail when you test it. On this matter, a concluding sentence, beauty will be evident, even without horns.

Remember Alanus, his complaint if you want to look, said in his book of famous eloquence that he saw nature clothed all in flowers and blossoms and on her head a headcloth of Valence, no other finery of counterfeit dress, to show through natural providence: beauty will be evident, even without horns.

Famous poetis of antyquyte,
In Grece and Troye renomed of prudence,
Wrot of Queen Heleyne and Penolope,
Of Pollycene, with hir chast innocence;
For wyves trewe calle Lucrece to pr*e*sence;
That they wer faire ther can no ma*n* sey nay;
Kynde wrouht hem *with* so gret dyllygence,
Ther beute kouth, hornys wer cast away.

Clerkys recorde, by gret auctoryte,
Hornes wer yove to bestys ffor dyffence —
A thyng contrarye to ffemynyte,
To be maad sturdy of resystence.
But arche wives, egre in ther vyolence,
Fers as tygres for to make affray,
They have despit, and ageyn concyence,
Lyst nat of pryde, then hornes cast away.

  Lenvoye.
Noble pryncessis, this litel schort dyte,
Rudely compyled, lat it be noon offence
To your womanly mercifull pyte,
Though it be rad in your audyence;
Peysed every thyng in your iust adv*e*rtence,
So it be noon dysplesaunce to your pay,
Under support of your pacyence,
Yeveth example hornes to cast away.

Grettest of vertues ys humylyte,
As Salamon seith, sonne of sapyence,
Most was accepted onto the Deyte,
Taketh heed herof, yeveth to his wordis credence,
How Maria, whiche hadde a premynence
Above alle women, in Bedlem whan she lay,
At Crystys birthe no cloth of gret dispence,
She wered a kovercheef, hornes wer cast away.

15. 'The Good Wyfe Wold a Pylgremage'

This Middle English poem is preserved in one manuscript only: National Library of Wales, Brogyntyn MS ii.1 (formerly known as Porkington MS 10), a manuscript recently made available in a digitised format by the National Library of Wales (at http://www.llgc.org.uk/index.php?id=amiddleenglishmiscellanybro, accessed 18 July 2014). The handwriting points to the latter half of the fifteenth century (Mustanoja 1948: 131). The unknown author appears to have had intimate contact with the life and views of common people to judge from the choice of similes, proverbs and other phrases (Mustanoja 1948: 134). The poem was printed in an edition by Mustanoja (1948), 173–5. The translation is by Louise Sylvester.

Famous poets of antiquity renowned in Greece and Troy for their wisdom, wrote of Queen Helen and Penelope, of Polyxena, with her chaste innocence. For faithful wives, call Lucretia to mind. No man can say that they were not beautiful. Nature made them with such diligence, their beauty may be known, even without horns.

Scholars record, with great authority, that horns were given to animals to defend themselves. They are a thing that is contrary to femininity, to make strong in resistence. But dominating women, keen in their violence, fierce as tigers to make fights, they have contempt, and against their consciences. Do not wish to be proud, throw away your horns.

    Envoy
Noble princesses, let this short little rhyme, rudely compiled, cause no offence to your womanly, merciful pity, though it may be read in your hearing. Weigh everything up with just attention, so that it will be no detraction to your pleasure, with the support of your patience, give a good example of throwing away horns.

The greatest of virtues is humility, as Solomon, son of wisdom, says, and it is most acceptable to God. Take heed of it then, and believe his words, how Mary, who had pre-eminence above all women when she lay in Bethlehem at Christ's birth, had no rich clothing, she wore a headcloth, horns were thrown away.

Schowe not thyselfe to proude, passynge thyn astat,
To make men loke aftor þe and aske, 'Who ys that?'
A genttyll woman, or a callot, men wyll deme thow arte.
Wer non odor aray this weke þen thow meyst wer allgatt.
    Witt an O and a I, men wyll sey þis,
    'Be wyne hope men mey se wher þe tavern ys.'

Doȝttor, in all company vppon þe hallyday,
Wheþor þou wylt daunce or synge, or witt thy fellowys pley,
Honge thy gordoll nott to low, but take þe knot away,
Wher no bedys about þe but hit fall for thyn araye.
    Witt an O and a I, thus men wyll tell,
    'The corsser hathe his palfrey dyȝt all redy for to sell.'

Doȝttor, seyd þe good wyfe, hyde thy legys whyte,
And schew not forth thy stret hossyn, to make men have delytt;
Thow hit plese hem for a tym, hit schall be thy despytt,
And men wyll sey of þi body þou carst it but lytt.
    Witt an O and an I, seyd hit ys full ryve,
    'The bocher schewyth feyr his flesche, for he wold sell hit full
    blythe.' (13–30)

16. 'The Thewis of Gud Women'

This Middle Scots poem is extant in two manuscripts of the late fifteenth century, one dated 1487. It is not actually a mother's address to her daughter, although its contents are very much the same as other instructions in that genre. Here 'the Gud Wyf' points out several qualities (Old Scots 'thewis' denotes 'qualities' or 'behaviour') of good and bad women. The poem does not seem to exclude women of higher social standing (Mustanoja 1948: 136). The version of the poem in Cambridge University Library, MS Kk. 1.5 is excerpted here. It is edited and printed in a facing page edition with the version in St John's College, Cambridge, MS G.23, in Mustanoja (1948), 177–96. The translation is by Louise Sylvester.

    Nocht outragous in hire cleithinge,
    Bot plane maner and gudly thing;
    Nocht our-costlyk na sumptewous,
    To mak vthir at hire inwyous,
    Na couet nocht cleithing mar deir
    Na be resone suld hir effeir;
    And þocht scho be cled honestly,
    Desyr nocht to be sen forthi. (29–36)

Do not display yourself too proudly in a manner above your rank to make men look after you and ask 'Who is that?' Men will think you are a gentlewoman or a foolish woman. Do not wear any other clothing during the week than you could wear any time. *With an O and an I, men will say this, with joyful hope men may see where the tavern is.*

Daughter, in all company during the festival, whether you want to dance or sing or amuse yourself with your friends, do not hang your belt too low, but take the knot away. Do not wear any beads about you, except what is necessary to your outfit. *With an O and an I, thus men will tell it, the rider has dressed up his horse all ready to sell it.*

Daughter, said the good wife, hide your white legs and do not show your tight hose, to please men. You will please them for a time, but then they will despise you and will say that you give away your body freely. *With an O and an I, it is quite openly said, the butcher shows off his meat so that he can happily sell it.*

[A good woman should be] Not outrageous in her clothing, but have a plain manner and honourable things; not overexpensive or sumptuous to make others envious; and [she should] not covet dearer clothing nor, by reason, should it be proper for her. And though she is dressed honestly, she should not wish to be noticed for it.

17. Peter Idley, *Instructions to his Son*

Peter Idley served as gentleman falconer and under-keeper of the royal mews and falcons and subsequently as Controller of the King's Works throughout the kingdom. Both offices included robes of office evidenced by payments recorded by the Clerk of the Wardrobe of the Royal Household and mandates given to the Keeper of the Great Wardrobe (d'Evelyn 1935: 12–13). Two records are extant of the livery of robes to Idley, which demonstrate his rank. In 1457, the livery robes recorded by Stratton (as Clerk) for the winter season were nine yards of long-cloth of colour ('colo*ris* long*i*'), one hood made of thirty-two bellies of pured miniver, and a fur of bys consisting of eight timber, or bundles of forty skins each; and for the summer livery, nine yards of scarlet cloth and one of tartarin. Idley's grant (as Controller) consists only of four yards of cloth 'colo*ris* long*i*' for his winter vesture (d'Evelyn 1935: 18, referencing PRO Exchequer Accounts, Wardrobe and Houshold, Bundle 410/14, fol. 9a, col. I).

Idley's *Instructions to his Son*, composed c. 1450, fits into a framework already established in English in the Old English period, the 'Fæder larcwidas'. The contemporary and personal elements are only a small proportion of the work but they give a sense of the period as well as the character of the father. Some of the ideas behind the sumptuary laws, notably the notion that rank should be reflected in dress or it will not be legible, are strong themes in the poem's sections on dress. Idley's *Instructions* are extant in eight manuscripts, six from the fifteenth century (d'Evelyn says seven manuscripts but she seems not to have known of one of them, according to Mustanoja 1948: 35). The work does not draw on a very wide range of sources: Book I is based on two Latin treatises of Albertanus of Brescia, *Liber Consolationis et Consilii* and *Liber de Amore et Dilectione Dei et Proximi*; Book II on Robert Mannyng's *Handlyng Synne* (see extracts above for material on dress) and Lydgate's *The Fall of Princes* (d'Evelyn 1935: 36). The standard edition is that of d'Evelyn (1935), whose text is from Cambridge University Library, MS. Ee.4.37. The translation is by Louise Sylvester.

> Looke such clothynge as þou shalt weere,
> Keepe hem as clenly as þou can,
> And all the Remen*au*nt of thy geere:
> Ffor clothyng ofte maketh man.
> Be as pure as flour*e* taken fro the brann
> In all thy clothyng and al þyn arraye,
> But goo not *euer* to nyce *and* gay.
>
> Leve cuttyng and Iaggyng of clothis,
> ffelawship of women and tauernes alsoo   (I. 99–107)
>
> Be not straunge of hatte, hoode, ne hure
> Of thy tonge be free in gentill speche   (I. 120–1)
>
> By vitaille and vesture mannes lyffe is ladde;
> Who wanteth this, his lyffe may not laste   (I. 673–4)
>
> De malis guerre
> Iff a man of hye degree and grete astate,
> Mighty of possession and riche of goode,
> If he p*er*seuer in weer, striff, and debate,
> It woll make hym weere a threedbare hoode   (I. 736–9)

Be careful about what kinds of garments you wear and keep your clothes and all the rest of your gear as clean as you can for often clothes make the man. Be as pure as the flour that is sifted from the bran in all your clothing and all your attire, but never go about dressed too well and brightly.

Refrain from cutting and slashing your clothes and avoid the companionship of women and also taverns. [...]

Do not wear an elaborate hat, hood or cap and do not hold back in noble conversation. [...]

Man's life depends on food and clothing and the life of one who lacks these will not last long. [...]

On the evils of war
If a man of noble birth and high estate, great in possessions and rich in goods, if he should persevere in war, strife and argument, he will end up wearing a threadbare hood. [...]

Now I-wys it were well doon to knowe
The difference betwene a damysell and a mayde,
ffor al be ylike when they stonde on a rowe.
But y woll telle you what exp*er*iens said,
And in what wyse they be *entired* and arraied:
Maidens were calles of silk and of threde
And dameselles *kercheiffes* aboue pynned *on þeir heide*.

Wyfes may not to churche till they be entired,
Ibrideled and peytrelled to shewe hir arraye,
And feeted abowte as a hakeney to be hired;
She*y*s double so *wrothe* if ony be so gay;
And oo thyng I loue that is most to my pay;
Ther hangeth a kercheiff so lowe that a man can not espye
To loke vndrenethe to beshrewe hir Iye.   (II.A. 1035–48)

How the goodis be goten, therof no force,
Be it *be* right or wronge, so it be hadde.
They be trapped in furres to glorefie the cors;
The wyffe and the children must goodly be cladde   (II.A. 1119–22)

In suche foule lust *is* hir most delite
And to make hir freisshe *with* newe atires;
She spareth for no cost to geve men appetite,
To sett vp hir hornes *with* longe wires;
And to be made moche of she gretly desires.
She will be redy *with* the twynkelyng of an eye
W*ith* hir croked instrument *to* encrees and multeplye.

Of oon straunge thyng she holt hir not apaied –
She must eche day haue chaunge newe;
And if ony be bet*ter* than she arraied
Or haue clothyng of a *fressher* hewe,
Than to haue therof she woll *fast* pursue,
And w*ith* all hir laboure hir wittes to applie
W*ith* hir croked instrument *to* encrees and multeplie.   (II.A.1791–1804)

Bet*ter* it were to goo ragged in an olde cote
Than to leese that precious Iuell, his name   (II.A.2232–3)

I reporte me yf now vsed be pride inordinate;
Neu*er* more I trowe sith God was born,
And that in eu*er*y degree and eche astate.
ffirst to begynne at the heede, the heere is not shorn
But hangeth downe to the browe beforn
Like to an hors toppe of the Irisshe facion:
We be called the verri aapes of eu*er*y nacion.

Now I know that it is good to know the difference between a damsel and a maid, since they all look alike when they stand in a row. But I will tell you what experience says, and in what manner each is coiffed and dressed: maids wear head-dresses of silk and of thread and damsels wear kerchiefs pinned up on their heads.

Wives will not go to church until they are dressed, trussed up in harness to show off their outfits, and showing themselves about like a cab for hire. She is doubly angry if anyone else is as well dressed. And one thing I love that pleases me most; when a headcloth hangs so low that a man cannot see to look underneath to berate her eyes. [. . .]

It does not matter how their goods were got, rightly or wrongly, as long as they have got them. They are elaborately dressed in furs to glorify their bodies, their wives and children must be well dressed. [...]

Her greatest pleasure is in such disgusting desire and to make herself pretty with new outfits. She spares no cost to give men an appetite, she sets up her horned hairstyle with long wires; she greatly wishes for a fuss to be made of her. She will be ready in the twinkling of an eye to increase and multiply with her bent instrument.

She does not gain pleasure from one outlandish thing – every day she must have a new outfit. And if anyone is better dressed than she, or has more brightly coloured clothes, she rushes to have the same as quickly as possible, and she applies her mind and all her work to increase and multiply with her bent instrument. [. . .]

It is better to go about in rags wearing an old coat than to lose that precious jewel, his good name. [...]

I will tell you again if inordinate pride is now in practice. Never more, I think, since God was born, and in every degree and each estate. First to begin with the head, the hair is not cut but hangs down to the forehead like the top of an Irish horse: we are called true 'apes' by every nation.

Go firther, than, to the shap of hir clothis:
They be cutted on the buttok even aboue the rompe.
Eu*er*y good man *truly* suche shappe lothes;
It maketh hym a body short as a stompe,
And if they shull croke, knele, othir crompe,
To the middes of the backe the gowne woll *not* reche:
Wolde Ih*es*u they were than wi*th*out hoose or breche!

A man shall not now kenne a knave from a knyght,
ffor al be like in clothyng and array,
In fresshe doublett*es* of silk strecchyng vp right,
And few pens in her purs, y trowe, to pay;
No force of the getyng, so the *garment* be gay;
This maketh hem to *ken* the craft of a theif
And to blot the paupers of London in eu*er*y leif.

Now an ordre wold be hadde w*ith* vertu and grace
In eu*er*y creature aboue all thyng
In eu*er*y contree and in eu*er*y place,
And specially to begynne about the kyng,
Not oonly to speke of arraie as in clothyng
Called inordynat, whiche is a grete offence,
But also of norture and curtesie and due reu*er*ence.

Eche man to kenne hymsilf and his bet*t*er
A page, a grome, and *a grome*, a yoman by right,
As the A. B. C. is made *in* ordre *by lettyr*,
A yoman, a squyer, and a squyer, a knyght,
And so to the highest and grettest of might;
And as they be in ordre set of degree,
Right so shall her clothyng and *arraie* bee. (II.B.22–70)

Narracio [*The Tale of the Clerk and the gay Coat*]
Ther was a knyght that loued nyce array;
New shappis his fantasie was to devise.
He wolde that non were so galaunt *and* gay
As he, and that in all man*er* of wyse:
Twoo or thre shappes might not suffise,
Suche was his appetite and his hertis desire,
To be arraied giselie and of a straunge atire.

Amonge all othir he hadde a ffresshe cote
Was all to-Iagged w*ith* poisies on eu*er*y side,
And botoned w*ith* silu*er*e to the harde throte.
His mynde was sette so highlie on pride;

Then go further, to the shape of their clothes: they are cut on the buttocks even above the rump. Every good man truly hates this shape; it makes the body as short as a stump, and if they should bend, kneel, or crouch, the gown will not reach to the middle of the back: would to God that they were then without hose or breeches.

A man will now not know a knave from a knight, for they are both alike in dress and apparel, in new silk doublets stretching right up, and few pennies in their purses, I think, to pay. No matter how it is got, as long as the garment is bright. This makes them learn the craft of a thief and to blot every page of the paupers of London.

Now an order should be made with goodness and grace regarding every creature above all in every country and in every place and especially to begin with the king not only discussing array as in clothes which are called immodest, which is a great offence, but also of upbringing, manners and due respect.

Each man is to know himself and his better: a page from a groom, and a groom from yeoman as is right. As the A. B. C. is made in order by letter, a yeoman from a squire, and a squire from a knight. And so to the highest and mightiest. And as they are arranged in order of rank, so shall their clothing and ornament be. [. . .]

Tale: [*The Tale of the Clerk and the Gay Coat*]
There was a knight who loved fine clothing. His imagination was always devising new shapes. He wished that no one would be so handsome and fair as he, and that in all different sorts of ways: two or three shapes were not enough, such was his appetite and his heart's desire, to be foppishly dressed and in unusual clothes.

Amongst everything else he had a new coat, all slashed with heraldic emblems on every side and furnished with silver buttons up to the throat. His mind was set so much on his pride. But

But Dame Fortune *with* an vnware clappe
Bokeled hym in a clothyng of anothir shappe.

It felle so that this galaunt was at debate
With diu*er*se gentiles of his contree;
Eche of hem hadde othir gretely in hate,
To drawe to accorde he wolde not aggre.
It fortuned this galaunt so that he
App*ar*eilled hym to ride in his fresshe arraye
And toke his hors and rode his way.

And at vnset steven this gentilmen met
W*ith* this galaunt vndir a forest side;
They felle in hande and hym al to-bet,
And shortly sloughe hym for all his pride
[…]
Amonge poore men the contree aboute;
Eu*ery* garment, bothe gowne and hoode
They delte it freely to all the route;
But to take the gay cote men were in dowte.
Ther was no poore man wolde it resceyue,
But eu*ery* man fro hym ganne it weyve,

Excepte a clerke was in that prees;
He desired they wolde yeve hym that clothe;
He cried vppon hem and wolde not cease,
And to praye for the soule he made an othe.
To denye hym his cote they were lothe,
But toke this clerk the garment gay
He cast it vppon hym and went his way.

So what vengeaunce fille of this werke
ffor this inordinate pride and highe presumpcioun;
A sodeyn wildefeire fille vppon this clerke
And al to asshis made a finall consumpcion;
Thus Godde shewed in his soden caas
That this gisie garment acursed was.

ffor ther was no poore man wolde haue that clothe,
It was so disgysed, Iagged, and torn.
God was displeased therw*ith* and wrothe,
ffor it wold not serue, it was split and lorn;
In *vnhappy* season he was geten and born
To put his soule in payne and distresse
ffor suche inordinate pride and Newfangilnesse.

Dame Fortune with a surprise stroke of fortune buckled him into clothing of a different shape.

It came about that this gallant was in dispute with various gentlemen of his country. Each of them greatly hated the others, they could not agree to come to a settlement. It happened that this gallant dressed himself to go riding in his new clothes and took his horse and went on his way.

These gentlemen unexpectedly met with this gallant under the edge of the forest. They came to blows and beat him thoroughly, and soon killed him for all his pride.
[…]
They gave away every garment, gown and hood, to poor men all over the country they gave them out freely to the whole crowd. But men were dubious about taking the bright coat. There was no poor man who would accept it, every man waved it away from himself.

Except a clerk who was in that crowd. He wished that they would give him that garment. He begged them and would not stop, and he made an oath to pray for the [gallant's] soul. They were reluctant to deny him his coat, so the clerk took the bright garment, put it on and went on his way.

So what vengeance came of this work for this inordinate pride and high presumption? A sudden wildfire came upon this clerk and consumed him finally all to ash. Thus God showed in his unexpected way that this elegant garment was cursed.

For there was no poor man who would take that garment, it was so altered, cut and torn. God was displeased by it and angry, for it would not do, it was split and lost. He was conceived and born in an unlucky time to put his soul in pain and distress for such inordinate pride and novelty.

A clerk that in ordre hath take ony degree
Shuld forsake novelries of this newe guyse,
And kepe hym like a clerke and leeve suche Iolite;
All man*er* of vnclennesse he shold dispise;
Than shall he to worshi*ppe* encrees and arise
And honour*e* the place that *he* cometh froo:
This of verri *dutee* he oweth to doo.

What sey ye now of ladies, gentilwomen, and othir,
Vse they ony pride in this daies as ye suppose?
Yees! and she bee as oolde as Abrah*aum*s modir
She woll be lothe in arraie onythyng to loose;
She woll depeynte hirsilf as fresshe as ony rose,
With wymples and tires wrapped in pride:
Yelow vndre yelow they cou*er*e and hide.

Ffor if the beawte begynne to amminysshe and fade,
Then can they werke w*ith* a certen floure
To pullisshe hem othir wyse then eu*er* God made,
And set vppon hem a more fresshe coloure,
And *couer yt with* goolde the skynne to socoure,
That man wote not whethir is whethir –
The yelow goolde or the tawny *lethyr*.
[…]
It is now harde to discerne and knowe
A tapester, a Cookesse, or an hostellers wyffe
ffro a gentilwoman, if they stonde in a rowe;
ffor whoo shal be *fresshest* they ymagyne and stryve.
They that suffree so hir wyffes, God lete hem neu*er* thryve!
It maketh hem lay to wedde bothe bokill and targe:
Dame Beelecheese hath fredom to renne at hir large.

Narracio [*The Tale of the Lady burnt for her Pride*]
Now of a ladie that gretlie pride vsed
I wolle telle you a tale shortlie as I can.
How she might be *fresshest* she gretly mused,
And specially on hir heed *above* any woman;
And for she wold seeme feirest of all othir than
She made her tires – ther were noon suche,
Neither in valowe that were half so riche.   (II.B.176–280)

All to asshes this lady was brent,
And aft*er* roose ageyn alive as she was;
And efte she had the same torment;
They brent *hyr* ageyn this was the caas   (II.B.323–6)

A clerk who has taken any rank in holy orders should leave behind novelties of this new fashion, and keep himself like a clerk and leave such merriment. He should despise all kinds of impurity: then he should increase his prayers and arise and honour the place that he comes from. He is obliged to do this out of clear duty.

Now what do you say about ladies, gentlewomen and others, do they have any pride these days as you suppose? Yes, even if she were as old as Abraham's mother she woud hate to cede any part of her dress. She will depict herself as fresh as any rose, with wimples and head-dresses wrapped in pride: yellow under yellow they cover and hide.

For when the beauty begins to diminish and fade, they can work with a certain flour to adorn themselves in ways other than God ever made, and put a fresher colour on themselves, and cover it with gold to help the skin, so that no one knows which is which – yellow gold or tawny leather. [...]

Now it is hard to distinguish and know a barmaid, a cook, or an innkeeper's wife from a gentlewoman if they stand in a row. For they wonder and strive to know who shall be most attractive. Those who allow their wives to do likewise, may God never allow them to prosper! It makes them risk both buckler and shield: Dame 'Beautiful Thing' is free to run at large.

Tale: [*The Tale of the Lady burnt for her Pride*]
Now I will tell you a tale as briefly as I can about a woman who was very proud. She constantly wondered how she could be most attractive, and especially more than any woman about her head. And because she wanted to seem the most beautiful of all she made her head-dresses such that there were none so valuable as them nor half so fine. [...]

This lady was burnt all to ashes and then she got up, just as alive as she had been; and then she received the same torment, they burnt her again, this was how it was. [...]

The knight axed for what cause and whye
She suffred this payne all this woo.
She said, 'for *in* pride y bare me so hye
I nyst not in therthe how I might goo   (II.B.330–3)

I wolde haue be holde the feirest of all,
Ffreisshist hede and most richest entired;
Me hadde bet*ter* have goon in a symple call
Than *with* this whele thus paynfullie be fired'   (II.B.337–40)

But ther is a feende that is called Trieslincellis,
And biddeth a man lie still and take his reste;
And thoughe the preist and the clerkis ryngge the bellis,
He seith, 'Cou*ere* the cloislie and kepe thy neste;
[…]
And dresseth a *softe* pelowe closed in his arme;
Thus Treslencellis kepith hym warme,
And at ix of the clok or x he woll hym dresse
To com *to þe sacryng scantly* of the *messe*.
[…]
And *biddeth* hym to abide, he maketh grete haste,
Till *he* haue doon vppon hosen and piked shon,
Sit vppon his gowne and gurde in the waste   (II.B.904–27)

The knight asked what the cause was of all her pain and why she suffered all this sorrow. She said 'because I carried myself so high with pride I didn't know what would befall me on this earth. [...]

I wanted to be held the most beautiful of all, with the most attractive head and the most richly attired; I had better have gone about in a simple head-dress than be so painfully burnt with this wheel. [...]

But there is a devil that is called Trieslincellis who tells men to lie still and rest; and though the priests and the clerks ring the bells, he says, 'Cover yourself up and stay in bed'.
[...]
And arranges a soft pillow under his arm. Thus Treslencellis keeps him warm, and at nine o' clock or ten he will dress himself so that he is just in time to make the consecration of the mass.
[...]
And tells him to wait, he hurries and rushes till he has put on hose and pointed shoes, is wearing his gown and has belted it around his waist.

Plates

1. Initial illumination showing William de Saint Calais (Karilepho, Carilef), bishop of Durham, from an eleventh-century manuscript containing Augustine's commentary on the Psalter. © The Chapter of Durham Cathedral, ref. MS B.II.13, fol. 102r.

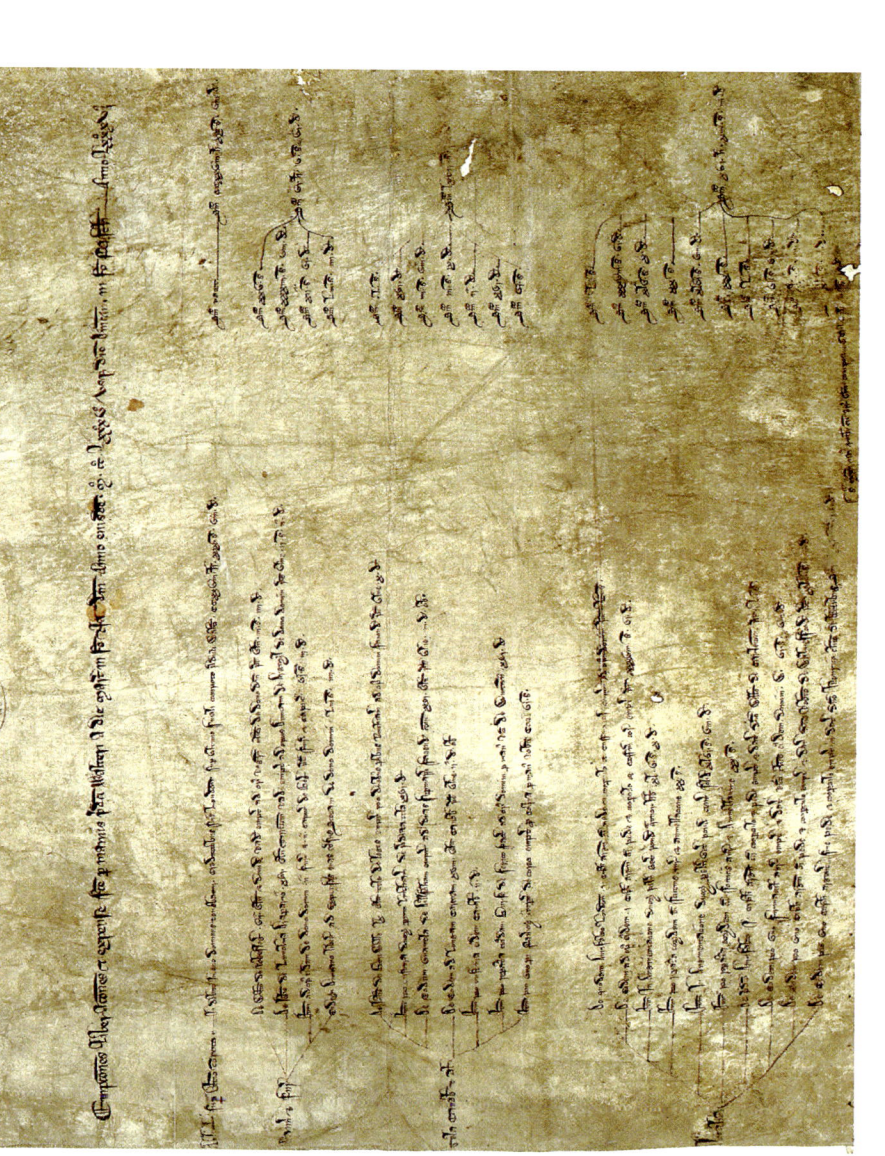

2. Opening of the Account of the Household of Bogo de Clare kept by Walter de Reyny for 25 December 1285 – 2 June 1286. © The National Archives, ref. MS E 101/91/6, membrane 1.

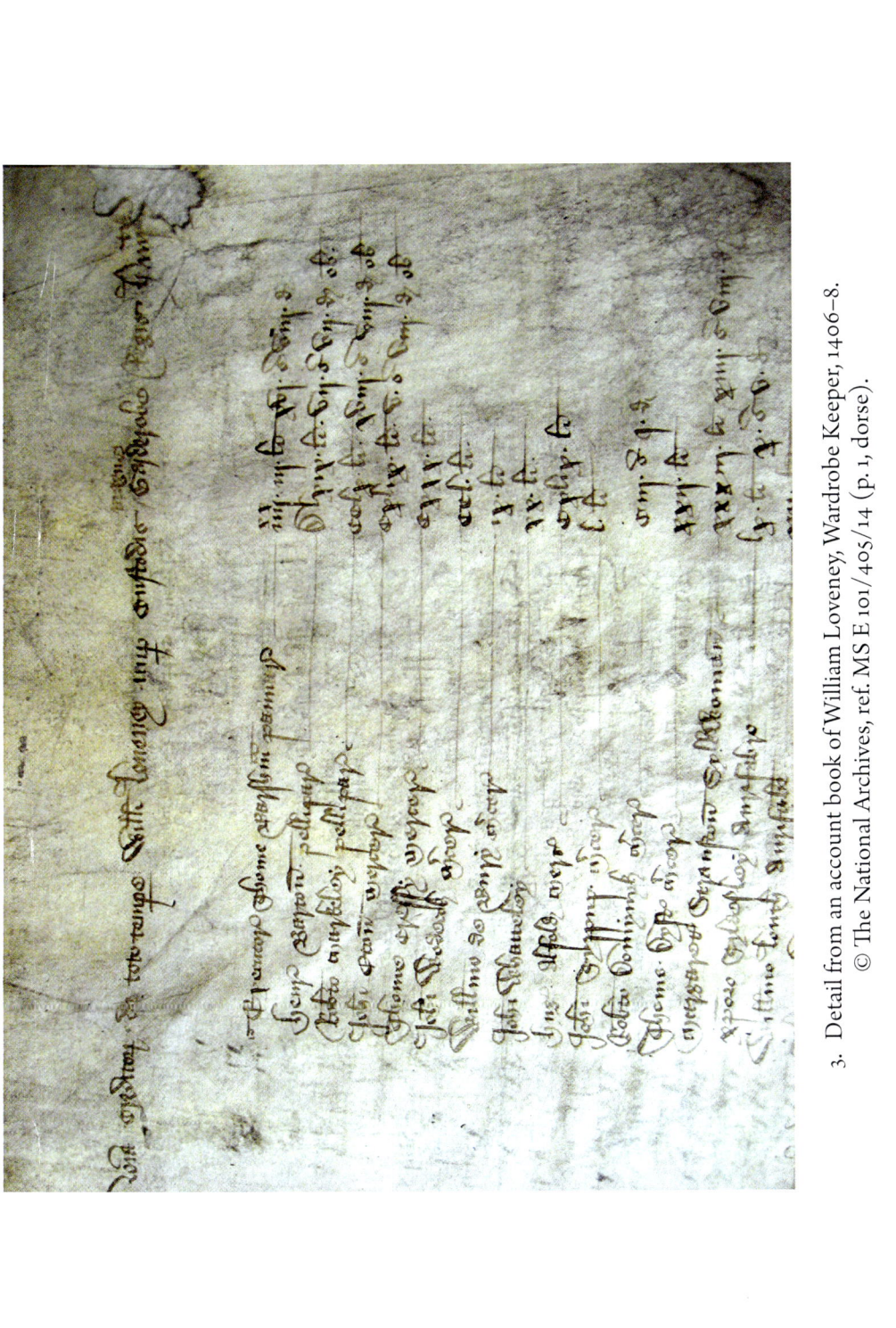

3. Detail from an account book of William Loveney, Wardrobe Keeper, 1406–8. © The National Archives, ref. MS E 101/405/14 (p. 1, dorse).

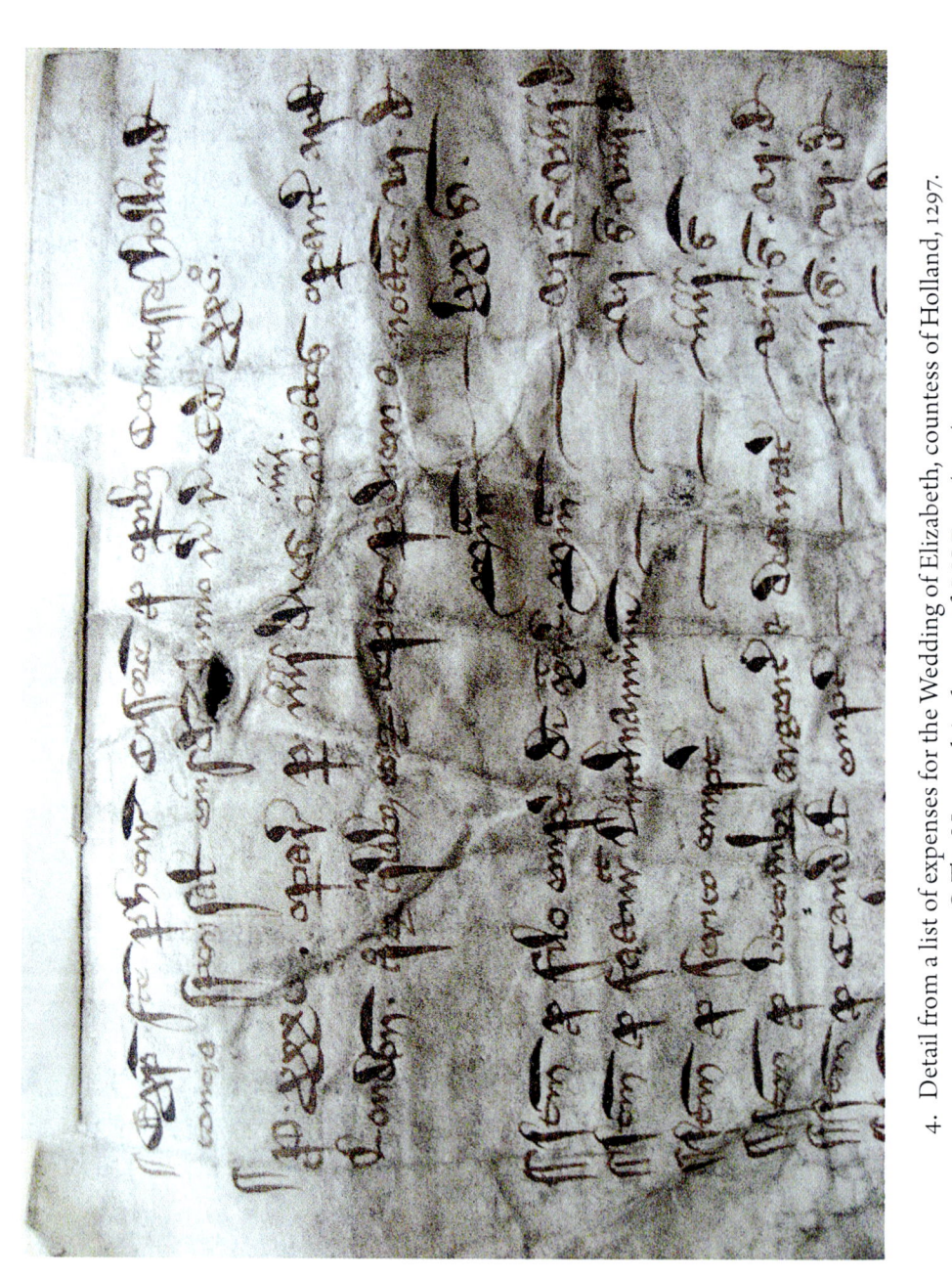

4. Detail from a list of expenses for the Wedding of Elizabeth, countess of Holland, 1297. © The National Archives, ref. MS E 101/354/21.

5. Petition of the Merchants of the Hanse concerning excessive customs, c. 1394?. © The National Archives, ref. MS SC 8/125/6225.

6. Petition of Thomas and Margaret de Beauchamp, 1394–49.
© The National Archives, ref. MS SC 8/221/11037.

7. Description of the two ladies of Hautdesert, *Sir Gawain and the Green Knight* (lines 952–60); late 14th century. © The British Library Board, ref. MS Cotton Nero A.x. (art. 3) fol. 103/107v (detail).

8. Sir Gawain dresses for the Green Chapel, *Sir Gawain and the Green Knight* (lines 1926–34); late 14th century. © The British Library Board, ref. MS Cotton Nero A x. (art. 3) fol. 116/120v (detail).

CHAPTER V

Sumptuary Regulation, Statutes and the Rolls of Parliament

INTRODUCTION

Little first-hand evidence of sumptuary legislation in England survives from before the preserved enrollments of parliamentary proceedings, which were kept from the end of the thirteenth century. Following a brief proscription of items of dress worn by the crusaders and pilgrims to the Holy Land in 1188 (part of the introduction of the so-called 'Saladin Tithe' of 1188; extracted as no. 1 below), there is little recorded evidence of centralised attempts to regulate dress in Britain. Localised sumptuary laws appear early in southern European towns and cities (in Italy dating back to ancient Rome), and precedent for many of the individual details of the English sumptuary laws may be found in earlier laws from Italy, France and other continental sources (Newton 1980: 131–2).

France has records of socially categorised restrictions on dress dating from as early as 1279 and 1294. The French laws are intimately concerned to regulate the display of the ranks of the secular and clerical elite. Sarah-Grace Heller has observed how these thirteenth-century laws differ from those that follow in England and France in the later centuries, in that they do not dictate particular fashions, and 'are more concerned with stabilizing how much a person could consume and display relative to his or her income rather than with prohibiting dubious attire' (Heller 2004: 313–25). In England, this differs markedly from the sumptuary legislation of the later-medieval and Tudor periods.

In England in 1313, Edward II's government passed a law forbidding the wearing of arms or armour in parliament (Luders *et al.* 1810: I.10 – 1313, 7th Edw. II). This obviously had more to do with fear of violence or rebellion in the chamber than any broad, social or economic anxieties informing traditional sumptuary law. Then in 1337, Edward III's government passed a law forbidding the importation of cloth or clothing from lands outside England, Ireland, Scotland or Wales, or the exportation of domestic wool (Luders *et al.* 1810: I.280–1). It has been suggested that this statute, and the sumptuary restrictions accompanying it, were protectionist measures for the domestic wool trade (Bell and Ruse 1972: 23). The restriction on imports was repealed in 1362 following pressure from the merchants (Luders *et al.* 1810: I.374), but various trade restrictions on cloth and clothing appear frequently in legislation from later parliaments (Hunt 1996: 299–302).

The 1337 statute contains a further clause stating that no one under the rank of knight or lady shall 'use peleure en ses draps' (use fur in their clothing). This is generally considered the earliest sumptuary law of the English parliament, and it was echoed locally: within a few decades, the city of London ruled that prostitutes were not allowed to wear fur such as budge (low-quality wool) or lambswool (Hunt 1996: 302). Hunt points out that laws restricting the use of fur would have been rather repressive given Britain's cold climate. Their substance was relaxed by the subsequent act of 1363. This major piece of clothing legislation (extracted below) was the first detailed and systematic set of sumptuary laws passed by the English parliament.

The primary English and Scottish acts and statutes governing dress and apparel – as well as occasional parliamentary petitions which request sumptuary legislation – are extracted in the examples listed below. Running through the fourteenth and fifteenth centuries, they conclude with the detailed 'ordinances of array' passed during Edward IV's early reign and subsequently enrolled as statutes. Edward IV's government passed further major statutes in 1483. Elizabeth I's government would carry on this tradition; compared to their predecessors the Tudors passed a great deal of English sumptuary legislation. Then in 1604, James I repealed all previous sumptuary statutes (Luders *et al.* 1819: IV, pt. 2, 1050–2), and in the centuries that followed British sumptuary legislation remained limited, if not non-existent (Hunt 1996: 321).

THE SOURCE TEXTS

The 'Rolls of Parliament' refer to the recorded meetings of parliament enrolled from the reign of Edward I (1272–1307) to the reign of Henry VII (1485–1509), when the Rolls were superseded by other means of official record-keeping. The Rolls are written in Latin, Anglo-French and (later) Middle English, and represent a chief source of evidence of the primary languages of law and administration in later-medieval England. In general they record the business of parliament for its bi-annual sitting – at Easter and Michaelmas – with occasional gaps, adjustments and other exceptions. Not only do the surviving Rolls contain items of legal and political administration (afterwards known as 'statutes'), but they also include many of the petitions to king and parliament or summaries of these, along with subsequent rulings. Many of the Rolls from Edward I's reign are made up almost entirely of 'petitions', many of which were translated from the Anglo-French used whilst in session, into Latin for enrollment (Given-Wilson 2005; Sayles 1975: 71 and 75–84). Many individual petitions were never enrolled in the official records and have never been published. Selections from these un-enrolled petitions have been transcribed and edited in the following chapter.

'Statues' refer to the official, enrolled legislation of the land, frequently the same as or the products of the Rolls of Parliament (see Given-Wilson 2005; and Richardson and Sayles 1981: xxv, 9–17). During certain parliaments, rolls of statutes were presented in translation, as we see in the example of the Anglo-French statute of 1463–4 which translates statutory details of the Middle English Roll of Parliament for that year (extracts 8 and 9 below).

EXTRACTS FROM SUMPTUARY REGULATION, STATUTES, THE ROLLS OF
PARLIAMENT AND OTHER SOURCES

1. 11 February 1188: 'Great Council at Geddington'

Written in Latin. In February 1188, King Henry II convened a council at Geddington (in modern Northamptonshire) in order to discuss terms and raise money to shore up Christian losses in the Holy Land. The proceedings of this council survive in a British text: the not wholly reliable *Chronicle* of Gervase of Canterbury (*c.* 1141–*c.* 1210) printed in William Stubbs's 1879 edition.

It is clear that the council oversaw the introduction of the so-called 'Saladin Tithe', along with other royal directives, including proscribed items of clothing for knights travelling to the Holy Land. These laws were pronounced simultaneously in England by Henry and in France by his counterpart King Philippe-August, in preparation for the Third Crusade (Lloyd 2002: 57; Heller 2004: 313–14). The pronouncement concludes with a clause protecting the washerwomen accompanying the camp from undue suspicion. The extract is printed in Stubbs 1879: 409. The translation is by Mark Chambers.

[Article] V. Statutum est quod nullus enormiter juret, et quod nullus ludat ad aleas vel ad decios, et quod nullus post proximum Pascha utatur vario vel grisio vel sabelo vel scarlato et quod omnes contenti sint duobus ferculis ex empto. Et quod nullus ducat secum aliquam mulierem in peregrinatione, nisi forte aliquam lotricem peditem, de qua nulla habeatur suspicio. Et quod nullus habeat pannos decisos vel laceatos.

2. Act of October 1363 (37 Edward III)

Written in Anglo-French; October 1363. The Rolls of Parliament which survive from the late-medieval period were collected, transcribed, edited and published in the six-volume *Rotuli Parliamentorum* (Strachey 1783). This was the primary edition of the Rolls used in scholarship until 2005, when a fully re-edited and expanded edition was made available online and subsequently in print: Given-Wilson *et al.* (2005): http://www.sd-editions.com/PROME; and Brand *et al.* (2012).

The earliest recognisable piece of sumptuary legislation in the Rolls appeared in October 1363, when Edward III's government put forward an act containing a hierarchy of clothing restrictions based on social rank. The text quoted below represents a petition put forward by the 'communes' (knights and burgesses) for the king's approval (Ormrod 2005: 'Edward III, Parliament of October 1363', items 25–32; also Strachey 1783: I.278–9). This portion of the roll has the following subtitle: 'Ces sont les Petitions des Com'unes, & les Respons sur elles faites' (These are the petitions of the commons, and the response[s] concerning them; Strachey 1783: I.276, our translation).

The petition was approved, and was repeated (verbatim following the 'Responsio') as the 'Statut' de Victu & Vestitu' An° xxxvij' (Statute of diet and apparel of the 37th [regnal] year; Luders *et al.* 1810: I.378). It was recorded in the Rolls of Parliament and also – with occasional variant spellings – on a roll of 'ordinanciones' for the 37th year of Edward's reign (ibid.). Despite its approval, the statute must have proved unpopular. After complaints from the commons and the merchants, it was repealed just over a year later (Ormrod 2005: 'Edward III, Parliament of January 1365', item 11; also Strachey 1783: I.286).

Regarding the legal status of the act/ordinance, W. Mark Ormrod (2005: Introduction) notes that 'the commons petitioned only in general terms, and that the very detailed arrangements made to graduate society according to patterns of consumption was evidently left to the council [...]'. He continues,

It has been ordained that no-one swears immoderately, and that no one plays games of chance or dice, and that no-one, after next Easter, wears vair, grey fur, sable or scarlet, and that all shall be content with the two meals provided. And that no one takes any woman on pilgrimage, except perhaps certain washerwomen of the infantry, of which there is to be no suspicion. And that no one has clothes slashed (for ornamentation) or decoratively trimmed.

In the closing plenary session of the parliament of 1363, the chancellor informed the lords and commons that the measures taken in the new laws on trade and apparel 'were new and never before witnessed' (item 38), and seemingly asked that, given uncertainty about their impact, they be registered as an ordinance (that is, temporary legislation) rather than as a statute (that is, a permanent measure)

The 1363 act or ordinance begins with a usual formula common to most subsequent sumptuary legislation, suggesting that it causes national impoverishment ('le tresor de la terre destruit'; the treasure of the land is destroyed). This formula was repeated and reworded in various acts and statutes by future parliaments (cf. below), and has been discussed in critical assessments (see Jaster 2006).

The act/ordinance is also useful for demonstrating some of the general names for various ranks of society at the time from across the social spectrum, not specified and limited to the elite as in later sumptuary laws (Hunt 1996: 305–6). It also details popular items of dress as well as the names of various furs available in the 1360s ('budge', 'ermine', 'lettice', 'miniver', etc.). It specifies prohibitions on items of women's dress, including the use of ermine-fur, weasel-fur or 'perre' (gemstones) for the wives and children of knights or esquires whose income was less than £200 per year (item 27). In addition, it makes an exception for items of head-dress, and it nearly echoes a 1294 French sumptuary law banning the use of expensive furs on clerical garments except 'chapperons' (hoods or floppy hats; trans. by Heller 2004: 333).

The text is taken from Ormrod 2005: 'Edward III, Parliament of October 1363', items 25–32, and the translation has been adapted from this edition.

[Item] 25. Item, monstrent les communes: qe come diverses vitailles dedeinz le roialme sont grandement encherrez, par cause qe diverses gentz de diverses condicions usent diverse apparaill nient appertenant a lour estat; c'estassaver, garceons usent apparaill des gentz de mestire, et gentz de mestire apparaile des valletz, et valletz apparaile des esquiers, et esquiers apparaill de chivalers, l'un et l'autre pellure qe seulment de reson appertienent as seignurs et chivalers, femmes povres et autres apparaile des dames, povres clercs pellure come le roi et autres seignurs. Issint sont les marchandises susdites a plus grant pris qe ne soleient estre, et le tresor de la terre destruit, a grant damage des seignurs et communes. Dont ils priont remede, si ce soit avys as seignurs du conseil.

Responsio.
Quant a la peticion mise avant par les communes d'exces d'apparaill des gentz outre lour estat, en tresgrande destruccion et empovrissement de la terre, par quele cause toute la richesse du roialme est a poi consumpte et anientiz, est ordeine par manere qe s'ensuit:

Premerement, quant as garceons, […] q'ils eient draps pur lour vesture ou chauceure, dont le drap entier ne passe deux mars; et q'ils ne usent drape de plus haute pris de lour acat, n'autrement, ne nul chose d'or, d'argent, n'embroidez, aymelez ne de soye, ne rien appendant des dites choses. Et soient lour femmes, files et enfantz de mesme la condicion en lour vesture et apparaill; et ne usent nuls voiles passant la voile dousze deniers.

25. Also, the commons declare: that whereas the prices of various victuals within the realm are greatly increased because various people of various conditions wear various apparel not appropriate to their estate; that is to say, grooms wear the apparel of craftsman, and craftsmen wear the apparel of gentlemen, and gentlemen wear the apparel of esquires, and esquires wear the apparel of knights, the one and the other wear fur which only properly belongs to lords and knights, poor and other women wear the dress of ladies, and poor clerks wear fur/clothing like those of the king and other lords. Thus the aforesaid merchandises are at a much greater price than they should be, and the treasure of the land is destroyed, to the great damage of the lords and the commonalty. Wherefore they pray remedy, if it is the opinion of the lords of the council.

Answer.
As regards the petition put forward by the commons concerning the excess of dress of people beyond their estate, to the very great destruction and impoverishment of the land, for which reason all the wealth of the realm is on the point of being consumed and destroyed, it is ordained in the manner that follows:

'First, as regards grooms, [...] they shall have cloths for their clothing or shoes, of which the whole cloth shall not exceed 2 marks; and they shall not wear clothes of a higher price of their purchase or otherwise, or anything of gold or silver, or embroidered, enamelled or of silk, or anything belonging to the said things. And their wives, daughters and children shall be of the same condition in clothing and apparel; and they shall not wear any veil worth more than 12d.

26. Item, qe gentz de mestere d'artifice et d'office appellez yomen ne preignent ne usent drape de plus haute pris pur lour vesture ou chauceure qe deinz quarante soldz le drape entier, par voie d'acat, n'autrement; ne perre, drape de soy, ne d'argent, ne ceynture, cotel, fermaill, anel, garter, n'ouches, rubans, cheisnes, bendes, sealx n'autre chose d'or ne d'argent, ne nul manere d'apparaill embroidez, aymelez ne de soy, par nul voie. Et qe lour femmes, files et enfantz soient de mesme la condicion en lour vesture et apparaill; et qe eles ne usent nul voile de soy, mes soulement de fil fait deinz le roialme, ne nul manere de pellure ou de bugee mes soulment d'aignel, conil, chat et gopil.

27. Item, qe esquiers et toutes maneres de gentils gentz desouz l'estat de chivaler qe n'ont terre ou rente a la value de cent livres par an ne preignent ne usent drape pur lour vesture ou chauceure de plus haut pris qe deinz le pris de quatre mars et demy le drape entier, par voie d'acat n'autrement; ne q'ils ne usent drape d'or, de soy ne d'argent, ne nul manere vesture embroidez, anel, fermaill n'ouche d'or, ruban, ceynture, ne nul autre apparaile ne hernies d'or ne d'argent, ne riens de perre, ne nul manere de pellure. Et qe lour femmes, filese et enfantz soient de mesme la condicion quant a lour vesture et apparaill, saunz ascun revers ou purfil; et qe eles ne usent esclaires, crimiles ne troefles, ne nul manere d'apparaill d'or, d'argent ne de perre. Mes qe esquiers eantz terre ou rente a la value de deux centz livres par an et outre peussent prendre et user drape du pris de cynk mars le drape entier, et drape de soy et d'argent, ruban, ceynture et autre apparaill resonablement garniz d'argent. Et qe lour femmes, files et enfantz peussent user pellure revers de menevoir, saunz ermyns ou letuses ou ascun manere d'apparaill de perre, sinoun pur lour testes.

28. Item, qe marchantz, citeins et burgeis, artificers, gentz de mestere, sibien deinz la citee de Loundres come aillours, qe ont clerement biens et chateux a la value de cynk centz livres, et lour femmes et enfantz, peussent prendre et user en manere come les esquiers et gentils gentz qe ont terre et rente a la value de cent livres par an. Et qe les marchantz, citeins et burgeis q'ont clerement biens et chateux outre la value de mill livres, et lour femmes et enfantz, puissent prendre et user en manere come les esquiers et gentils gentz q'ont terre et rente a la value de deux centz livres par an. Et qe nul garceon, yoman ne servant des marchantz, marchandie artificer ou gentz de mestere ne use autrement en apparaile qe n'est ordeine des garceons et yomen des seignurs paramont.

29. Item, qe chivalers qe ont terre ou rente deinz la value de deux centz mars par an preignent et usent drape de sis marcs le drape entier pur lour vesture, et nounpas de plus haute pris. Et q'ils ne usent drape d'or, ne cloche, mantel ne goune fururez de menevoir purez, manches d'ermyns, ne nul apparaill broidez de perre n'autrement. Et qe lour femmes, files et enfantz soient de mesme la condicion, et qe eles ne usent revers d'ermyns, ne de letuses esclaires, ne nul manere d'apparaill de perre sinoun pur lour testes. Mes qe touz chivalers et dames qe ont terre ou rente outre la value de quatre centz mars par an tanqe a la somme de mille livres par an usent a lour volente, forspris ermyns, letuses et apparaille de perre sinoun pur lour testes.

26. Also, that craftsmen and people called yeomen shall not take or wear cloth for their clothing or shoes of a higher price than 40s. for the whole cloth, by way of purchase or otherwise; nor precious stones, cloth of silk, nor of silver, no belt, knife, brooch, ring, garter, or clasps, ribbons, chains, bracelets [or similar; *bendes*], seals or other things of gold or silver, or any manner of apparel embroidered, enamelled or of silk, in any way. And that their wives, daughters and children shall be of the same condition in their clothing and apparel; and that they shall not wear any veil of silk, but only of yarn made within the realm, nor any manner of fur or budge except only that of lamb, rabbit, cat and fox.

27. Also, that esquires and all manner of gentlemen below the estate of knight who do not have land or rent to the amount of £100 a year shall not take or wear cloth for their clothing or shoes of a higher price than within the price of 4½ marks for the whole cloth, by way of purchase or otherwise; and they shall not wear cloth-of-gold, silk or silver, or any manner of embroidered clothing, ring, brooch, clasp of gold, ribbon, belt or any other apparel or attire of gold or silver, or any precious stones, or any manner of fur. And their wives, daughters and children shall be of the same condition as regards their clothing and apparel, without any turning back or fur trimming; and that they shall not wear adornments, open work ['crimpings' in Ormrod 2005] or knick-knacks, or any manner of apparel of gold, silver or precious stones. But esquires having land or rent to the value of £200 a year and more may take and wear cloth of the price of 5 marks for the whole cloth, and cloth of silk, of silver, ribbon, belts and other apparel reasonably decorated with silver. And their wives, daughters and children may wear fur reveres of miniver, without ermine or weasel-fur or any manner of apparel of precious stones, except for their heads.

28. Also, that merchants, citizens and burgesses, artisans and craftsmen, within the city of London as well as elsewhere, who clearly have goods and chattels to the value of £500, and their wives and children, may take and wear in the same manner as the esquires and gentlemen who have land and rent to the value of £100 a year. And that the merchants, citizens and burgesses who clearly have goods and chattels above the value of £1000, and their wives and children, may take and wear in the same manner as the esquires and gentlemen who have land and rent to the value of £200 a year. And that no groom, yeoman or servant of merchants, artisans or craftsmen may wear in apparel otherwise than is ordained above for the grooms and yeomen of lords.

29. Also, that knights who have land or rent within the value of 200 marks a year may take and wear cloth of 6 marks for the whole cloth for their clothing, and nothing of a higher price. And they may not wear cloth-of-gold, or a cloak, mantle or gown lined with pured miniver, sleeves of ermine or any apparel embroidered with precious stones or otherwise. And that their wives, daughters and children shall be of the same condition, and that they shall not wear reveres of ermine, or adornments of weasel-fur, or any manner of apparel of precious stones, except for their heads. But that all knights and ladies who have land or rent above the value of 400 marks a year up to the sum of £1000 a year shall dress at their will, with the exception of ermine, weasel-fur and apparel of precious stones, and these only on their heads.

30. Item, qe les clercs qe ont degre en eglise cathedrale, collegiale ou es escoles, et clercs du roi q'ont tiel estat qe demande pellure, facent et usent solonc la constitucion d'ycelles. Et touz autres clercs q'ont outre deux centz marchees de rente par an usent et facent come les chivalers de mesme la rente. Et les autres clercs deinz mesme la rente usent come les esquiers de cent livres de rente. Et qe touz ceux, sibien chivalers come clercs, qi par ceste ordinance puissent user pellure en yverne, par mesme la manere usent en este linure.

31. Item, qe charetters, charuers, chaceours des charues, bovers, vachers, berchers, porchers, deyes et touz autres gardeins des bestes, batours des bledz et toutes maneres des gentz d'estat de garceon entendantz a husbonderie, et toutes autres gentz qe n'eient quarante solidees de biens, ne de chateux a la value de quarante soldz, ne preignent ne usent nul manere des draps sinoun blanket et russet l'aune de dousze deniers; et usent lour ceyntures et lienge tele accordant a lour estat. Et q'ils vivent de manger ou de boire par manere come a eux affiert, et nounpas excessivement. Et est ordeine qe si nul use ou face au contraire des nuls des pointz susdites, q'il forface devers le roi toute l'apparaill q'il avera issint use contre la fourme de ceste ordinance.

32. Item, au fin qe ceste ordinance quant a la pris et usage de draps soit maintenuz et gardez en touz pointz saunz emblemure, soit ordeinez et establiz qe touz les fesours de draps deinz le roialme d'Engleterre, sibien hommes come femmes, se conforment de faire lour draps solonc les pris limitez par ceste ordinance. Et qe touz les drapers achatent et purvoient lour sortes acordantz a mesme le pris; parensi qe si grande plente de tieux draps soit faite et mis a vendre en chescun citee, burgh et ville marchande et aillours deinz le dit roialme, qe pur defaute de tieux draps la dit ordinance ne soit enfraint en nul point, sur peine de forfaire au roi toute l'apparaile q'ils usent contre ceste ordinance. Et a ce soient les fesours des draps et drapers constreintz par qeconqe voie qe meltz semblera au roi et son conseil. Et commencera ceste ordinance a la chandelure preschein avenir.

3. Parliamentary petition of April 1379 (Richard II), requesting sumptuary legislation

Written in Anglo-French. In the parliament of April 1379, amongst a number of items regulating trade and importation duty (items 54 and following), the commons petitioned the king for some aspects of sumptuary legislation to be reinstated. The petition enrolled as Item 55 requests that knights or ladies who 'cannot spend £40 a year' should be proscribed from wearing jewellery, fur, cloth-of-gold, ribbon of gold or silk cloth. The king agrees to consider the issue before the next parliament but no subsequent action seems to have been taken. The extract is taken from Martin 2005: 'Richard II, Parliament of April 1379', item 55 (and is also recorded in Strachey 1783: III.66). The translation is Martin's.

55. Item, qe nul homme ne femme deinz le dit roialme, forspris chivalers et dames, ne use nul manere de perree, pelleure, draps d'or, ne ribane d'ore, ne drap de soye, s'il ne poet dispendre .xl.li. par an, sur paine de forfaiture de quanqe il use a contraire d'ycestes.

Responsio.
Le roi s'advisera tanqe a proschein parlement.

30. Also, that clerks who hold positions in cathedral churches, collegiate churches or in schools, and clerks of the king who have such estate as requires fur, shall act and dress according to the constitution of the same. And all other clerks who have above £200 marks of rent a year shall dress and act as knights of the same rent. And the other clerks within the same rent shall dress as the esquires of £100 rent. And that all those, knights as well as clerks, who by this ordinance may wear fur in winter, in the same manner shall wear lawn in summer.

31. Also, that carters, ploughmen, drivers of ploughs, oxherds, cowherds, shepherds, swineherds, dairymaids and all other keepers of beasts, threshers of corn and all manner of people of the estate of groom attending to husbandry, and all other people who do not have 40s. in goods, nor chattels to the value of 40s., shall take or wear no manner of cloths except blanket and russet of 12d. for the ell; and they shall wear their girdles of linen according to their estate. And they shall support themselves with food and drink in the manner which belongs to them, and not excessively. And it is ordained that if anyone shall wear or act to the contrary of any of the aforesaid points, he shall forfeit to the king all the apparel which he will have thus worn contrary to the form of this ordinance.

32. Also, to the end that this ordinance, as regards the price and wearing of clothes, be maintained and observed in all points without impairment, it is ordained and established that all makers of cloth within the realm of England, men as well as women, shall agree to make their cloths according to the price limited by this ordinance. And that all the drapers shall buy and provide their lengths of cloth in accordance with the same price; so that so great an abundance of such cloths shall be made and put up for sale in each city, borough and market town and elsewhere in the said realm, that the said ordinance shall not be broken in any point for default of such cloths, on penalty of forfeiting to the king all the apparel that they wear contrary to this said ordinance. And the makers of cloths and drapers shall be bound to this by any way that seems best to the king and his council. And this ordinance will begin at upcoming [feast of] Candlemas.

55. Item, that no man or woman within the said kingdom, except knights and ladies, shall wear any kind of gemstones, fur, cloth-of-gold, or ribbon of gold, or cloth of silk, if they cannot spend £40 a year, on pain of forfeiting whatever they wear if they contravene this.

Answer:
The king will consider it further before the next parliament.

4. Parliamentary petition of September 1402 (Henry IV), requesting sumptuary legislation

Written in Anglo-French. The commons petitioned for sumptuary legislation again in September of 1402 – this time to Henry IV's government – for a reinstatement or reintroduction of aspects of sumptuary law. The king's 'Responsio' contains no specific statutory action, but it does give authority to his council to pass ordinances restricting attire as it sees fit. It further directs that his subjects 'se governent en leurs arraies chescun selonc soun degre, en lessant les superfluitees' (should maintain themselves in their attire each according to his degree, abandoning excesses).

This petition was repeated almost verbatim a few years later in the rolls for March 1406 (item 110), asking for greater clarity and enforcement. On that occasion, the king again agreed to consider the issue but again no subsequent legislative action seems to have taken place. Hunt suggests that the petitions and the king's responses are the result of constitutional disputes between Crown and parliament regarding the proper jurisdiction of sumptuary legislation (Hunt 1996: 425, note 24).

The 1402 petition contains several important terms for fur, cloth and clothing, including burgeoning fashions such as the 'grosses maunches' (large sleeves) that were becoming increasingly popular in aristocratic men's fashion towards the end of the fourteenth century. It is noteworthy for its detailed treatment of clerical dress, requesting, for example, the prohibition of furred 'chaperons' (hoods, cowls or similar headgear), of a length passing the shoulder blades, for all but the highest ranks of cleric. It also specifically treats women's clothing, restricting the use of several kinds of fur to the wives and daughters of knights, their ladies-in-waiting, and wives of certain officials (such as wives of the mayors of London, York and Bristol). The extract is taken from Given-Wilson 2005: 'Henry IV, Parliament of September 1402', item 76 (also cf. Strachey 1783: III.506). The translation has been adapted from Given-Wilson.

76. Item, priount les communes: qe ordeigne soit en cest present parlement qe nulle homme, si ne soit banret ou de pluis haute estate, use draps d'or, de velwet, draps de cremosyn, draps de velwetmotley, grosses maunches pendantz overtez ne closez, ne nulle longe goune qe touche la terre, ne furre d'ermyn, letuce, ne de martir; savez toutdis as gentz d'armes, quant ils sont armez, q'ils purront user vesture ce qe lour plerra. Et qe nulle clerc use grosses chaparons furrez ne linez qe passent les poyntz de l'espaules, si ne soit ercevesqe, evesqe, archedekyn, ou dean en l'esglise cathedralle ou collegialle, ou chanons en ycell, ou maistres de la chancele nostre seignur le roy, et chaunceller et barons de l'escheqer, et autres grauntz officers des courtz le roy, maistres de divinitee, doctours en l'un ley ou en l'autre, ou regentz deinz les universitees: ne qe nulle clerc use furre de menyvere, ne de puree de gray ne de byce, ne nulle manere de hernois endorrez, s'il ne soit d'estat ou degrees avauntditz: ne qe null clerc use purfile de ermyn ne de letuce, s'il ne soit ercevesqe ou evesqe: ne qe nulle esquier use furre de gray, cristigray, menyvere, ne bice, forspris les mairs qe sount, ount estez, ou pur le temps serrount, en les citees de Loundres, Everwyk, ou en la ville de Bristuyt. Et qe vadlet ne use nulle furre, forsqe d'angnelle, gupille, conyng, et oterre. Et qe nulle homme use baselardes, seintures, daggers, cornues, herneises d'argent, ne nulls autres hernoises d'argent, s'il n'ad terres, tenementz, ou rentz, a la value de xxli. par an, ou biens et chateux a la valuz de ccli. les enfantz des gentz eiantz terres ou tenementz en enheritance a la value de l marcz par an, ou biens et chateux a la valuz de ccli. exceptz. Et qe les femmes de nulle esquier, si ne soit dame, ne usent nulle furre d'ermyne, letuce, menyvere, pured de gray, forspris les femmes des ditz mairs, et les gentils femmes du roygne, et la chief damoiselle de chescune princesse, ducesse, ou countesse. [. . .]

76. Also, the commons pray that it might be ordained in this present parliament that no man of lesser rank than a banneret should use cloth-of-gold, of velvet, cloth of crimson, cloth of motley-velvet, large sleeves hanging open or closed, nor any long gown which touches the ground, nor fur of ermine, weasel, or marten; saving always that men of arms, when they are armed, may use such clothing as they wish. And that no clerk shall use large fur-trimmed or lined hoods which extend beyond the base of the shoulders, unless he is an archbishop, bishop, archdeacon, or dean in a cathedral or collegiate church, or a canon of those or a master of our lord the king's chancery, or the chancellor or a baron of the exchequer, or one of the other great officers of the king's courts, a master of divinity, a doctor in the one law or the other, or a regent within the universities: nor that any clerk should use fur of miniver, nor of trimmed grey or brown [s.v. *byce*], or any kind of gilded attire, unless he is of the aforesaid estate or degree: nor that any clerk should use furring of ermine or of weasel unless he is an archbishop or bishop; nor that any esquire should use fur of grey, cristigray, miniver, or brown, except those who are, or have been, or shall be, mayors in the cities of London, York, or the town of Bristol. And that a valet should not use any fur except for lamb, fox, rabbit and otter. And that no man should use baselards [a kind of dagger or short sword], girdles, daggers, horns, silver harnesses, nor any other silver attire, unless he has lands, tenements, or rents to the value of twenty pounds a year, or goods and chattels to the value of two hundred pounds, except the children of people who have lands or tenements by inheritance to the value of 50 marks a year or goods and chattels to the value of £200. And that no wife of any esquire, unless she is a lady, should use any fur of ermine, weasel, miniver, of pured grey, except the wives of the said mayors, gentlewomen of the realm, and the chief lady-in-waiting to any princess, duchess, or countess. [...]

Et si ascun persone soit ent duement atteint, forface a roy les draps, furres, et hernoys ensy usez, et paiera a roy c s. de quele somme eit le roy l'une moite, et celui qe suy l'autre moite. Et qe cest estatut comence de tenir lieu de jour de chare emparnant proschein avenir.

Responsio.
Le roy voet comander a toutz estatez de soun roialme q'ils se governent en leurs arraies chescun selonc soun degre, en lessant les superfluitees. Et en outre, voet nostre dit seignur le roy qe ceux de soun conseil aient poair par auctoritee de parlement de faire ordinances sur les dites arraies par bone deliberacioun.

5. Act of December 1420 (Henry V): regarding gilding and silver-plating

Written in Anglo-French. Henry V's government seems not to have been very concerned with sumptuary legislation, with the exception of this short 'quasi-sumptuary statute' of December 1420, regarding the use of silver and gilded metal. The Crown rules that silver plating is reserved for items such as the spurs of knights and the apparel of barons and the higher estates. It further dictates that any offending 'enorrour' (metalsmith) is to be fined up to ten times the value of the decorated object and jailed for a year – a designation that is less particular in the resulting statute (Luders *et al.* 1816: II.203, c. iii). Exception is made for holy ornaments and church goods. The extract is found in Given-Wilson 2005 'Henry V, Parliament of December 1420', item 18 (also cf. Strachey 1783: IV.126). The translation is Given-Wilson's.

18. Item, priont les ditz communes, qe nulle persone enorre en temps avenir ascunes des geynes appellez shethes, ne metaille, sinoun argent; ne argente nulle metaille, forsprisez les esperons dez chivalers, et tout l'apparaille qe appartient al baroun, et desuis celle estate; sur peyne de forfaiture de vie, et de membre, et sez terres et tenementz, de fee simple, biens et chateux, de le enorrour ou argenter desuisditz, come en cas de felonie; et qe ceste ordinance se comence a tenir lieu, al fest de Pasch proschein avenir.

Responsio.
Soit il come est desiree par la peticione, forspris les peines contenuz en mesme; et qant a les peines [a ordeinerz] en ceo cas, encourge l'enorrour la peine de forfaire au roy dys foitz a taunt come la chose issint enorree soit de value, et auxi l'emprisonement d'un an. Et qe les justices de la paix eient poair d'ent enquerrer et ceo pleinement terminer. Et eit la persone qe ferra la suite vers cely q'ent serra atteint, la tierce partie du la dite peine pecuniere: purveu toutz foitz, qe les ornaments de seinte esglise purront estre enorrez, ceste ordinance nient obstant.

6. Act of the Scottish parliament, March 1429 [1430] (James I)

Written in Old Scots. Under James I of Scotland, the Scottish parliament passed one of its earliest recorded acts of sumptuary legislation during its regular session in Perth on 6 April 1429 (1430 in modern reckoning). The text preserves items of medieval terminology of cloth and clothing in the Old Scots legal dialect. An earlier, brief act had been passed in 1424–5 (Hunt 1996: 35), but this subsequent act is useful in that it details the arms and armaments which each of the king's

And if any person should be duly convicted of this, he should forfeit to the king the cloth, fur, and harness which he is using and pay 100 shillings to the king, of which sum the king should have one half and he that sues the other half. And let this statute take effect from the feast of Carniprivium [Shrove Tuesday] next.

Answer.
The king wishes to command all the estates of his realm that they should maintain themselves in their attire each according to his status, abandoning excesses. And moreover, our said lord the king wills that those of his council should have power by authority of parliament to make ordinances concerning the said attire by their good deliberation.

18. Also, the said commons pray that in future no person shall coat any scabbards called sheaths, or any metal, except with silver; nor silver-plate any metal except the spurs of knights, and all the apparel that pertains to a baron or man of higher estate; on pain of forfeiting life and limb, and all his lands and tenements in fee-simple, and goods and chattels, by the aforesaid metalsmith or silver-plater, as in a case of felony; and that this ordinance shall begin to hold force next Easter.

Answer.
Be it as requested in the petition, excepting the penalties suggested in the same; with regard to the penalties to be ordained in this matter, let the metalsmith incur the penalty of forfeiting to the king ten times the value of the object thus gilded, and also imprisonment for a year. And that the justices of the peace shall have the power to enquire into this and fully settle it. And let the person who brings the suit against the person who is accused have a third of the said pecuniary penalty: provided at all times that ornaments of holy church may be decorated, notwithstanding this ordinance.

masculine subjects were required to possess and to wear. It further commands that they are to be 'enarmyt as a gentill man aucht to be' (armed as a gentleman ought to be). It begins by limiting silk cloths, certain furs, and other items of clothing to ranks of knights, lords, burgesses, their wives and to other social and economic categories.

The extract is adapted from Thomson *et al.* (1814–75: II, 18–19) in comparison with the *Records of the Parliaments of Scotland* recently published online by the Scottish Parliament Project (MacIntosh *et al.* 2007–13). Common abbreviations and suspensions in Thomson's edition have been extended in italics. The Tironian *et* symbol is represented by ampersand (&), and vowel *v* has been replaced with *u*, but other archaisms from Thomson's edition have been maintained in order to preserve some of the look of the manuscript text. The translation has been substantially adapted from MacIntosh *et al.* (2007–13: 1430/12–18).

(Item 8 is listed as item 12 in MacIntosh et al. 2007-13 [online]; 9 as 13, and so forth).

8 [12]. ITEM the king w*ith* þe avys of þe hail p*ar*liame*n*t has statute and ordanit þat na man sall weir clathis of silk na furring*is* of m*er*trik*is* fun3eis puray na grece na nane oþ*er* riche furring bot allan*er*ly knycht*is* and lord*is* of ij*c* m*ar*k*is* at þe lest of 3erly rent ande þar eldest son*n*is & þar air*is* but speciale leif of þe king asskit & obtenit Ande at nane uthir weir broudry na perle na bul3eone bot array þai at þar awin list in all uthir honest aray as serp*is* belt*is* uches & chen3eis & þ*at* und*er* þe payn of eschet of þe aray to þe king to be takyn & raisyt to quha*m* he com*m*itt*is* power

9. ITEM it is statut þ*at* na burgess w*ith*in burgh duelland wer ony furring as befor is saide outan ald*er*ma*n* bal3eis & þe consal of þe toun þe wif*is* to be arayit ef*ter* þe estat of þar husband*is* und*er* þe samyne payn forsaid to be raisyt be ald*er*ma*n* & bal3eis

10. ITEM it is statut þ*at* na 3ema*n* na common to landart*is* wer hewyt clathes siddar na þe kne na 3it ragyt clathes bot allan*er*ly centynal 3emen in lord*is* housis at rid*is* w*ith* gentill me*n* þar mast*er*is þe quhilk*is* sal haf narow slew*is* & litil pok*is* & rych*t* sa þ*at* þe com*m*onis wif*is* [. . .] wer nouþ*er* lang tail na syde nekit hud*is* na pok*is* on þar slef*is* na costly curches as lawn or ryns & all gentill me*n*is wif*is* be not arayit excedand þe estate of þar husband*is*

11. ITEM Be þe awys of þe haill p*ar*liame*n*t it is statute and ordanit þat ilk man þat may dispende 3erly xx li3 or at has j*c* li3 in movabil gud*is* þat he be wele horsit & haill enarmyt as a gentill ma*n* aucht to be And uþ*er* sympillar of x li3 of rent or L li3 in gud*is* haif hat gorgeat or pesane with rerebrasar*is* vambrasar*is* & gluff*is* of plate brest plat pans & legsplent*is* at þe lest or bet*ter* gif him lik*is*

12. ITEM þ*at* ilk 3eman þ*at* is of xx li3 in gud*is* haif a gude doublat of fence or ane habergeon ane yrn hat with bow and schefe suerde buklar & knyfe And all uþ*er* 3emen of x li3 in gud*is* hif bow and schefe suerde and buklar and knyff And þe 3ema*n* þat is nane archer na can not deyll with a bow sall haif a gude sou*er* hat for his hede & a doublat of fence with suerde & buklar & a gude ax or ell*is* a brogit staff

8 [12]. Also, the king, with all the advice of the whole parliament, has made statute and ordained that no man shall wear clothes of silk, nor furs of pine martens, beech martens, trimmed fur nor untrimmed, nor any other rich fur, except only knights and lords of 200 marks at least of yearly rent, and their eldest sons and their heirs, without special leave of the king asked and obtained. And that no other person wear embroidery nor pearl nor bullion, but array themselves at their own pleasure in all other honest array such as sarpes (ornamental chains), belts, ouches (buckles/clasps) and chains, etc. And this under the pain of escheat (forfeiture) of the array to the king, to be taken and raised (to the person) to whom he commits power.

9. Also, it is decreed that no burgess dwelling within a borough wear any fur, as is said before, except aldermen and bailiffs and the council of the town. And the wives are to be arrayed after the estate of their husbands under the same foresaid penalty, to be raised by the alderman and bailiffs.

10. Also, it is decreed that no yeoman nor commoner to landward wear coloured clothes longer than the knee, nor yet any ragged clothes, but only sentinel yeomen in lords' houses that ride with gentlemen, their masters; which (clothes) shall have narrow sleeves and little pokes. And likewise neither that commoners' wives . . . wear either long tail, nor side necked hoods, nor pokes on their sleeves, nor costly caps such as lawn or Rheims. And all gentlemen's wives are not to be arrayed exceeding the estate of their husbands.

11. Also, by the advice of the whole parliament, it is made statute and ordained that each man that may spend £20 yearly, or has £100 in moveable goods, that he be well horsed and fully harnessed as a gentleman ought to be. And other more simple people of £10 of rent or £50 in goods have hat, gorget and pisane with rerebraces, vambraces and gloves of plate, breast plate, pauncers and leg splints at least, or better if he likes.

12. Also, each yeoman that is of £20 in goods shall have a good defensive doublet or a habergeon, an iron hat with a bow, quiver, sword, buckler and knife. And all other yeomen of £10 in goods (shall) have a bow, quiver, sword and buckler and knife. And the yeoman that is no archer, and cannot draw a bow, shall have a good sure hat for his head and a defensive doublet with sword and buckler, and a good axe, or else a pointed staff.

13. ITEM it is statute and ordanit þat ilk baron within hym self sall se & ordane his men to be bodyn as is befor writtyn [...]

14. ITEM it is statute þat ilk burges hafand L liӡ in gud*is* salbe hail enarmyt as a gentil man aucht to be And at þe ӡema*n* of lawer degre ande burges of xx liӡ be bodyn with sou*er* hate & doublat habergeone suerd buklar bow schefe & knyfe Ande at he þat is na bowman haf a gude ax or wapy*n*is of fens as is forsaide Ande þe balӡeis sal rays þe payn in þe burgh gif it be not kepit as is forsaide þat is to say of ilk harnest man iiij s at þe first warnyng at þe secund warnyng viij s ande at þe thrid tym a mark and sa furth quhil he be wele enarmyt Ande of ilk ӡema*n* at þe first tym ij s at þe next tym iiij s & at þe thrid tym viij s ande sa furth quhil he be wele enarmyt

7. Ecclesiastical regulation: injunctions from the bishop's visitation to Ankerwyke Priory, 1441

Written in Middle English; 10 October 1441. Whilst this chapter is primarily concerned with attempts by the *secular* authorities to regulate dress in medieval Britain, the Church, of course, made regular attempts to stipulate the dress of Christians, especially that of its own clergy. Arguably the first conspicuous ecclesiastical legislation to affect British clergy in the High Middle Ages resulted from the Fourth Lateran Council held in Rome in 1215, called by Pope Innocent III: Canon 16 issued from the Council regulated the length of clerical dress (that it be not too long or too short) and that 'superfluous ornamentation' in dress should be avoided (Tanner 1990: 243; cf. Smith 2012: 63–7).

With regard to home-grown attempts by ecclesiastical authorities to regulate the dress of clergy, the single example provided here is from a brief set of injunctions imposed by the bishop of Lincoln in 1441. It was originally transcribed and published in Thompson's edition of *Visitations of Religious Houses in the Diocese of Lincoln* (Thompson 1918).

William Alnwick was elevated to the bishopric of Lincoln in 1436. Several of his injunctions recorded during the course of his official visitations to religious houses in his diocese show evidence of attempts to limit and to stipulate the dress of clergy – particularly the female religious. In the instance below, the sisters of Ankerwyke Priory (in modern Buckinghamshire) are given injunctions by the bishop for their 'grete and notable defautes... dewe reformacyone requirying', including limits on their dress and personal adornment. This injunction is in response to accusations made against Clemence Medforde, the (evidently) opulently dressed prioress of Ankerwyke at the time. In her earlier examination by the bishop she had confessed to wearing all except the cloth of Rheims ('Reynes' in Thompson's translation), and she claimed that she only wore the fur cap 'of estate' (status) on medical grounds. The text is from Thompson (1919: 3–4); translation adapted by Mark Chambers.

14. Item priorissa vtitur anulis aureis quamplurimum sumptuosis cum diuersis gemmis et eciam zonis argentatis et deauratis et cericis veils, et nimium eleuat velum supra frontem, quod frons patens totaliter ab omnibus potest videri, et fururis vtitur de vario. Fatetur vsum plurium anulorum et zonarum et velorum cericorum et eleuacionem velorum ; fatetur eciam vsum furrarum de vario [...]

15. Item vtitur camisiis de panno Reinensi, cuius vlna valet xvj*d*. Negat articulum.

13. Also, it is made statute and decreed that each baron within himself shall see and ordain his men to be armed as is written before. [...]

14. Also, it is decreed that each burgess having £50 in goods shall be fully armed as a gentleman ought to be, and that the yeoman of lower degree and the burgess of £20 be armed with sure hat and doublet, habergeon, sword, buckler, bow, quiver and knife. And that he that is no bowman have a good axe and weapons of defence, as is foresaid. And the bailiffs shall raise the penalty in the borough, and if it is not kept as is foresaid, that is to say of each armed man 4 shillings at the first warning, 8 shillings at the next warning, a mark at the third, and so forth until he is well armed. And of each yeoman 2 shillings at the first, 4 shillings at the next and 8 shillings at the third time, and so forth until he is well armed.

14. Also the prioress wears very costly gold rings with divers precious stones, and also girdles silvered and gilded over and silken veils, and she wears her veil too high above her forehead, so that her forehead, being entirely uncovered, can be seen by all, and she wears furs of vair. She confesses the use of several rings and girdles and silken veils and a high carriage for her veils; she confesses also the use of furs of vair. [...]

15. Also she wears shifts of cloth of Rheims, which costs sixteen pence per ell. She denies the article.

16. Item vtitur tunicis laqueatis *cum* cerico *et acubus argenteis et deauratis* et sic fecit omnes moniales vti. Fatetur articulum quo ad vsum suum proprium [...]

17. Item vtitur pileo status furrarato cum bugeo supra vela. Fatetur, propter tamen infirmitates varias in capite [...]

The possible sartorial licentiousness signalled by veils worn on high on the forehead had, of course, been a complaint since the time of Chaucer's Prioress (cf. Power 1922: 76; see the description of the Prioress in Chaucer's 'General Prologue' in Benson 1987: GP, 118–62).

The Middle English extract provided below is from Bishop Alnwick's injunctions dated 10 October 1441. It is printed in Thompson (1919: 8a–b). The translation is by Mark Chambers.

Also we enioyne yowe [...] that none of yow, the prioresse ne none of the couente, were no vayles of sylke ne no syluere pynnes ne no gyrdles herneysed wyth syluere or golde, ne no mo rynges on your fyngres then onne, ye that be professed by a bysshope, ne that none of yow use no lased kyrtels, but butonede or hole be fore, *ne* that ye use no lases a bowte your nekkes wyth crucyfixes or rynges hangyng by thayme, ne cappes of astate obowe your vayles (Thompson attempts a reading of a marginal note here, noting that the margin is badly damaged: '[...] *nekkes of* [...] *othere then* [*your r*]*ule askes*'; 1919: 8b, note 7), and that ye so atyre your hedes that your vayles come downe nyghe to your yene.

8. Act of April 1463 (Edward IV) *and*

9. Statute of 1463–4 (Edward IV) – the Anglo-French version drawn from the 1463 Act

Written in Middle English, Edward IV's major 'ordenaunce of aray' or sumptuary laws of April 1463 represent a detailed attempt to apply social and economic control over his subjects' dress and expenditure. Since the last substantial English sumptuary laws (no. 2 above), there had been various attempts by Crown and parliament to control the expense and affects of household liveries, including 1 Rich. II (1377), 13 Rich. II (1389), 16 Rich. II (1392), 20 Rich. II (1396–7), 1 Hen. IV (1399), 2 Hen. VI (1400), 7 Hen. IV (1405), 8 Hen. VI (1429), and continuing after with 8 Edw. IV (1468), 12 Edw. IV (1472), 3 Hen. VII (1487), 19 Hen. VII (1503; identified in Hunt 1996: 425, note 27). But there had been no major sumptuary legislation. This act seems, again, to have been part of a protectionist strategy, and it is flanked by acts dealing with the cloth trade and the textile industry (Hunt 1996: 306).

This act is also intimately concerned with placing limits on male fashions, especially those which alter or amplify the traditional silhouette. Doublet padding and stuffing is restricted to those above the rank of yeoman, and several technical lexical items are listed ('bolsters', 'stuffe', 'wolle', 'coton', 'cadas', 'stuffer'). The fashion of wearing very short jackets or tunics is forbidden to knights and others under the estate of lord, esquire or gentleman. The act requires that a man's garment should be tailored to a length long enough to 'covere his pryve membres and buttokes' (8*i* below; also compare the extract from Peter Idley's *Instructions to his Son* (IV.17) and the jacket-shortening episode in the play of *Mankind* (Eccles 1969: 671–721); as early as the late fourteenth century, of course, Chaucer's Parson had decried the 'horrible disordinat scantnesse of clothynge' he perceived, 'that thurgh hire shortnesse ne covere nat the shameful membres of man, to wikked entente' (Benson 1987: PT, l. 421–2)).

Moreover, the contemporary practice of wearing long pointed or 'piked' footwear is also restricted to men of higher rank; two inches in length is specified. Cordwainers are forbidden

16. Also she wears kirtles laced with silk and pins of silver and gilt, and has made all the nuns wear similar. She confesses the article so far as regards her own wearing [...]

17. Also she wears above her veil a cap of estate furred with budge. She confesses thereto; it is, however, because of divers infirmities [she claims] in her head [...]

Also we enjoin you [...] that none of you – not the prioress nor any of the convent – wear veils of silk, nor silver pins, nor girdles decorated with silver or gold, nor any more rings on your fingers than one (you that are professed by a bishop), nor that any of you use any laced kirtles, but buttoned or closed at the front, nor that you use any laces about your necks with crucifixes or rings hanging on them, nor caps of estate above your veils, and that you attire your heads so that your veils come down near to your eyes.

from making such footwear; this particular prohibition is echoed later on in the Roll in a common petition (item 55; also cf. Luders *et al.* 1816: II.414–15, c. 7). Such silhouette-altering male fashions were railed upon by polemicists in the period and were here limited by statute.

Interestingly as well, the act forbids the wearing of purple silk for those who were not lords. 'Royal' purple – originally associated with the very expensive Tyrian purple dye but by this period referring to various colours ranging from crimson and dark red to purple and royal blue – was greatly prized in antiquity and had been restricted in the Roman and Byzantine Empires. This seems to be the first time it was limited by parliamentary action in England. A subsequent act of January 1483 limited the use of purple silk to the royal family alone (item 25).

During the reign of Henry VI it had become common practice to record such parliamentary proceedings in the Middle English of the chamber, then to translate the statutes arising into Anglo-French for separate enrolment. For comparison, the corresponding Anglo-French statute arising from this 1463 sumptuary legislation is extracted beside the Middle English below. The two texts mirror each other very closely: many cloth and clothing terms are simply borrowed or transferred from one language to the other, while a few are translated ('girdell overgilt' → 'ceinctures suisorrez', 'shoen' → 'solers', etc.). Both versions share lexical items of a technical vocabulary, unascribable to any single language community. This phenomenon is apparent throughout the other texts in this volume and in later-medieval writing in general.

In January 1478, a petition was offered to parliament, requesting enforcement of the previous act as well as a series of clarifications and alterations (extract no. 10 below). This was followed in January 1483 by the 'Act of Apparel' of 22 Edward IV, which restates, amplifies or else alters many of the proscriptions and allowances detailed in the 1463 act. Its preamble virtually repeats the earlier act, recalling the

> dyvers statutes touchyng the restreynte of the excessive apparell of the people of this realme within the same by longe tyme used, to the utterist inpoverysshyng therof, as well in the tyme of youre gratious reigne, as in the tyme of youre noble progenitours, hath ben made and ordeyned; for noun due execution of which statutes, thys youre seid realme is brought into over grete mysery and povertie, and like to renne to gretter, on lesse then remedy therfore be soner provided. (Horrox 2005: 'Edward IV, Parliament of January 1483', item 25; cf. Luders *et al.* 1816: II.468–70)

The text is extracted from Horrox 2005: 'Edward IV, Parliament of April 1463', item 20 (also cf. Strachley 1783: V.504–6). The translation is adapted from Horrox's.

The Anglo-French statute below would have been drawn up from the wording of the Middle English parliamentary proceedings. The two versions translate each other fairly closely, with exceptions and items of interest discussed in the notes following. Notice that certain titles of offices ('Aldermen') retain an English form, while others ('Maires', 'Viscountz', etc.) appear to be borrowings from Anglo-French. This extract is from Luders *et al.*1817: III.399–405 (c. 5). Standard contractions and suspensions have been expanded in italics. The letters *a–p* assigned to the paragraphs are editorial and are not from the source text.

[20.] Prayen the commyns in this present parlement assembled, to calle to youre blessed remembraunce, [...] dyvers ordenauncez and statutez made in this youre reame for the apparell and aray of the commyns of the same, aswell of men as of women, soo that noon of theym shuld use nor were noon inordynat aray, but oonly accordyng to their degreez. Which statutez and ordenauncez notwithstondyng, for lak of punysshment and puttyng theym in due execucion, the commyns of this youre seid reame, aswell men as women, have used, and daily usen, excessive and inordynat arayes, to the grete displeasure of God, enpoverysshing of this youre seid reame, and enriching of straunge reames and cuntrees, and fynall distroiyng of the husbondrie of this youre seid reame.

a. Wherfore it may please youre highnes, [...] to ordeyn and stablissh that noo knyght under the astate of a lord, other than lordes children, nor noo wyf of eny such knyght, fro the fest of Purificacion of Oure Lady next comming, were eny manere cloth-of-gold, or eny manere corses wrought with gold, or eny furre of sables. And yf any such knyght doo the contrarie, or suffre his wyfe or childe, the same childe beyng under his rule or governaunce, to doo the contrarie, that then he forfeit, at every defaute, .xx.li. to youre highnes.

b. And also to ordeyn and stablissh that noo bacheler knyght, nor his wyfe, fro the seid fest, were eny cloth of velewet uppon velewet, but such knyghtes as been of the ordre of the garter, and their wyfes, uppon peyn to forfeit to your highnes at every defaute, .xx. marc.

c. And also to ordeyn and stablissh that noo persone under thastate of a lorde, fro the seid fest, were eny manere cloth of silke

Item prierent les Commones en le dit parlement assemblez au nostre dit soverain seignur le Roy, de reducer a sa remembrance, [...] diverses ordenances & estatutz en cest Roialme, pur lapparell & araie des Commonez dicell sibien des hommes come des femmes, Issint que null deux duisset user ne were null enordiat araie, forsque soulement accordant a lour degrees ; quelx estatutz & ordenances nient constristeantz, pur defaute de puncion & mettre diceux en due execucion, les Commonez du dit Roialme auxibien hommes com femmes ount usez & journement usent excessivez & enordinatz araies, a graund dispeasire Dieu, enpoverissement de cest dit Roialme, & enricher des Roialmes & pais estraunges, a finall destruccion del husbondrie de cest dit Roialme :

a. Si nostre dit seignur le Roy [...] ad ordeigne & establie, que null Chivalier desoubz lestate de seignur autre que enfantz des seignurs, ne nulle femme d'ascune tiel Chivalier, a le fest de Purificacion de nostre Dame que serra en lan de nostre seignur Mille CCCC lxv. were ascun manere draps dor, ou ascune maners corses overez oveque or, ou ascun furre de Sables ; et si ascun tiel Chivalier face le contrarie ou suffre sa femme ou enfant, mesme lenfant esteant desoubz sa rule ou governement, a fere le contrarie, que lors ils forface a chescun defaute xx li. au Roy :

b. et auxi ad ordeigne & establie que null Bachelier Chevalier ne sa femme a le dit fest were ascun drap de velewet sur velewet, forsque tielx Chivaliers qi sont del ordre del Jartier & leur femmes ; sur peine de forfeire au Roy a chescun defaute xx Marcs.

c. Et auxint ad ordeigne & establie que nulle persone, desoubz lestate de seignur, a le dit fest were ascun manere drap de soie

The commons assembled in this present parliament pray you to call to mind [...] various ordinances and statutes made in this your realm concerning the apparel and clothing of the commons of the same, both men and women, so that none of them should use or wear inappropriate clothing, but only that according with their degree. Notwithstanding these statutes and ordinances, for want of punishment and their enforcement, the commons of this your said realm, both men and women, have worn and daily wear extravagant and inappropriate clothing, to the great displeasure of God, the impoverishment of this your said realm, and the enrichment of foreign realms and countries, and the complete destruction of the husbandry of this your said realm.

a. Wherefore may it please your highness, [...] to ordain and decree that no knight below the status of lord, other than the children of lords, or the wife of any such knight, from the feast of the Purification of Our Lady next shall wear any kind of cloth-of-gold, or any kind of girdles made with gold, or any fur of sable. And if any such knight does the contrary, or allows his wife or child, the same child being under his rule or governance, to do the contrary, that he shall then forfeit £20 for every offence to your highness.

b. And also to ordain and decree that no knight bachelor or his wife, from the said feast, shall wear any cloth of velvet on velvet, except knights of the order of the garter and their wives, on pain of forfeiting 20 marks to your highness for every offence.

c. And also to ordain and decree that no one below the status of lord, from the said feast, shall wear any kind of purple silk cloth, beyng of the colour of purpull, uppon the peyn to forfeit to youre highnes at every defaute, .x.li.

d.   And also to ordeyn and stablissh that noo squier nor gentilman, nor noon other under the degree of a knyght, nor noon of their wyfes, except lordes sonnes, their wyfes, lordes doughters, squiers for youre body and their wyfes, use or were, fro the seid fest, eny velewet, sateyn fugery, or eny counterfett cloth of silke lyke unto the same, or eny corses wrought like to velewet or to sateyn fugery, or eny furre of ermyn, uppon the peyn to forfeit, at every defaute, .x. marc unto youre seid highnes.

e.   And ferthermore to ordeyn and stablissh that noo squier nor gentilman, nor noon other man nor woman under the degreez above rehersed, use or were, fro the seid fest, eny damaske or sateyn, except squiers menialx, sergeauntez, officers of your honorable houshold, yomen of the croune, yomen of youre chambre, and squiers and gentilmen havyng possessions to the yerely value of .xl. li., and their wyfes and wydowes havyng lyke possessions, and the doughters unmaried of persones havyng possessions to the yerely value of an .c.li.; uppon the peyn to forfeit to youre highnes at every defaute, .c. s. Provided alwey that the steward, chamberleyn, tresorer and countroller of youre honorable houshold, and youre kervers and knyghtes for youre body, and their wyfes, may use and were furres of sables and ermyns. And that the mayers of the cite of London, that be or have been, or hereafter for the tyme shalbe, and their wyfes, may use and were such aray as is afore lymyted unto bacheler knyghtes and to their wyfes. And that such as bee or have been, or for the tyme shalbe, aldermen or recorders of the same cite; and also that all maires and shirrefs of citees, tounes and

esteant de colour du purpull, sur peine de forfeire au Roy a chescun defaute x li.

d.   Et auxint ad ordeigne & establie que nulle Esquier ne gentil homme, ne null autre desoubz le degree de Chevalier, ne null de leur femmes, forsprisez fitz des seignurs, leurs femmes filles as seignurs esquiers pur le corps du Roy, & leurs femmes, use ou were a le dit fest ascun Velewet, satain fugeree, ou ascun coutrefet drap le soie resemblant a le mesme, ou ascuns Corses overez resemblantz a velewet ou a satain fugeree, ou ascun pellure dermyne ; sur peine de forfeire au chescun defaute x marcs au nostre dit seignur le Roy :

e.   et enoustre ad ordeigne & establie que null Esquier ne gentil homme, ne null autre homme ne femme desoubz les degrees desuis rehersez, use ou were a le dit fest ascun damaske ou satain ; forsprisez esquiers menialx sergeantz officers del hostell du Roy, Vadlettes del corone, Vadlettes del chambre du Roy, & Esquiers & gentilz hommes aiantz possessions al annuell value de xl li. & leur femmes & vieus eiantz semblez possessions, & les files demariez de persones eiantz possessions al value de C li. per an ; sur peine de forfeire au Roy a chescun defaute Cent sous. Purveu toutz foitz que le Seneschall Chamberlein Tresorer Countrollour del hostell du dit Roy, & ses Trencheours & Chevaliers pur son corps & leurs femmes, puissent user & were furres de Sables & ermyns : et que les Maires del Citee de Loundres, qi sont ou ount estez ou enapres pur le temps serront, & leurs femmes, puissent user & were tiel araie com devaunt est limite as Bacheler Chevaliers & leurs femmes : et que tiux queux sont ou ount estez ou pur le temps serront Aldermen ou Recorders de mesme la Citee, et auxi que toutz Maires & Viscountz des Citees Villes & Burghs dicest roialme,

on pain of forfeiting £10 to your highness for every offence.

d. And also to ordain and decree that no esquire or gentleman, or anyone else below the degree of knight, or their wives, except the sons of lords and their wives, the daughters of lords, esquires for your body and their wives, shall use or wear, from the said feast, any velvet, satin brocade, or any cloth of silk simulating them, or any girdles made to imitate velvet or satin brocade, or any fur of ermine, on pain of forfeiting 10 marks to your said highness for every offence.

e. And furthermore to ordain and decree that no esquire or gentleman, or any other man or woman below the degrees cited above, shall use or wear, from the said feast, any damask or satin, except household esquires, serjeants, officers of your honourable household, yeoman of the Crown, yeomen of your chamber, and esquires and gentlemen with possessions to the yearly value of £40, and their wives and widows with similar possessions, and the unmarried daughters of persons with possessions to the yearly value of £100; on pain of forfeiting 100s. to your highness for every offence. Provided always that the steward, chamberlain, treasurer and controller of your honourable household, and the carvers and knights for your body, and their wives, may use and wear furs of sable and ermine. And that the mayors of the city of London, who are or have been or shall be in office, and their wives, may use and wear the clothing restricted above to knights bachelor and their wives. And that those who are or have been or shall be aldermen or recorders of the same city, and also all mayors and sheriffs of the cities, towns and boroughs of this

boroughs of this reame, such as be [shires] corporat, and all maires and baillifs of all other citees, and of every of the tounes of the .v. portes, and the barons of the same portes, such as hath be chosen and assigned, or in tyme to come shalbe chosen and assigned to doo their service in the coronacion of the kyng or of the quene; and maires and baillifs of boroughs corporat, beyng shire tounes, and the maires and baillifs of Colchestre and Lynne; and the recorders of the seid citees, boroughs and tounes, beyng shires corporat, and of all other citees, nowe beyng recorders, or that have been, or hereafter shalbe, and the aldermen of the same, and their wyfes in lyke wise; may use and were such aray as is afore lymyted unto squires and gentilmen afore specified havyng possessions of the yerely value of .xl.li.

f. And also to ordeyn and stablissh that noo man, but such as have possessions to the yerely value of .xl.li. or above, use or were, fro the seid fest, eny furres of martirons, funes, letyce, pured grey, menyver, nor noo wyf, sonne, doughter or servaunt of eny such man, the same sonne and doughter beyng in his rule and governaunce, nor noo woman wydowe, but such as have possessions of the seid yerely value of .xl.li., use or were eny of the seid furres, or eny girdell harneysed with gold or with silver in eny part therof overgilt, or eny corse of silke made oute of this reame, or eny kerchef wherof the price of a [plyght] shall excede the somme of .iij. s. .iiij. d. uppon peyn to forfeit to your highnes, for every defaute therof, .v. marc. Provided alwey that the forseid squiers menialx, sergeauntez, officers of youre seid houshold, yomen of the coroune, yomen of youre chambre and squiers and gentilmen havyng possessions of the seid yerely value of .xl.li.; and the forseid maires, recorders, aldermen, shirrefs and baillyfs of every of

tieux queux sont Countreez corporez, & toutz Maires & Baillifs de toutz autres Citees, & de chescun de les ['de les' repeated (Luders et al. 1817: 400b, note 1)] Cynque Portes & les Barons des mesmes les Portes, tieux queux ount estez esluz & assignez, ou en temps avenir serront esluz & assignez, a fere lour service en la Coronacion du Roy ou de Roigne, et Maires & Baillifs des Burghs corporez esteantz Shiretownes, & les Maires & Baillifs de Colchestre & Lynne, & les Recorders de les ditz Citees Burghs & Villes esteantz Countees corporeez, & de toutz autres Citees, ore esteantz Recorders ou queux ount estez ou enapres serront, & les Aldermen diceux, & leurs femmes, en semblable maner puissent user & were tiel araie come devaunt est limitez as Esquiers & gentilz hommes devaunt especifiez eiantz possessions del annuell value de xl li.

f. Et auxint ad ordeigne & establie que null homme, forsque tiel qi ad possessions al annuell value de xl li. ou a desuis, use ou were a le dit fest ascuns furres de Martrons letuse pure Grey ou pure Meniver, ne nulle femme fitz file ou servaunt dascun tiel homme, mesmes les fitz & file esteantz en sa rule & governement, Ne nulle femme Vieu, forsque tiel qe ad possessions du dil annuell value de xl li, use ou were ascuns de les ditz furres, ou ascune ceincture garnisse oveque or ou oveque argent en ascun part dicell suisorre ou ascune corse de soie fait hors de cest Roialme, ou ascun coverchief dont le price dun plite passera le some de iij s. iiij d. ; sur peine de forfeire au Roy pur chescun defaute ent cynque marcs. Purveu toutz foitz que les ditz Esquiers menialx sergeantz Officers del hostell du roy, Vadlettes del corone, Vadlettes du chambre du Roy & Esquiers & gentilx hommes eiantz possessions du dit annuell value de xl li. & les avant ditz Mairs Recorders Aldermen Viscountz & Baillifs de chescun de les ditz Citeez Villes & Burghs,

realm which are counties, and all mayors and bailiffs of all other cities, and of each of the towns of the Cinque Ports, and the barons of the same ports who have been chosen and assigned, or shall be chosen and assigned in future, to perform their service in the coronation of the king or queen, and mayors and bailiffs of boroughs corporate which are county towns, and the mayors and bailiffs of Colchester and Lynn, and the recorders of the said cities, boroughs and towns which are counties, and of all other cities, now being recorders, or who have been or hereafter shall be, and the aldermen of the same, and their wives likewise, may use and wear the clothing restricted above to esquires and gentlemen with possessions to the yearly value of £40.

f. And also to ordain and decree that no one without possessions to the yearly value of £40 or more shall use or wear, from the said feast, any furs of martens, beech martens, weasels [lettice], trimmed grey, miniver, and no wife, son, daughter or servant of such a man, the same son and daughter being under his rule and governance, or any widow, except those who have possessions to the yearly value of £40, shall use or wear any of the said furs, or any girdle trimmed with gold or silver gilt anywhere, or any silk girdle made outside this realm, or any headcloth of which the price per length exceeds 3s. 4d. on pain of forfeiting 5 marks to your highness for every offence. Provided always that the aforesaid household esquires, serjeants, officers of your said household, yeomen of the Crown, yeomen of your chamber and esquires and gentlemen with possessions to the yearly value of £40; and the aforesaid mayors, recorders, aldermen, sheriffs and bailiffs of each of the said cities, towns and boroughs, and the said barons of the Cinque

the seid citees, tounes and boroughs, and the seid barons of the .v. portes, and their wyfes, may use and were the forseid furres of mattrones, funes, letyce, pured grey or pured menyver; and also that [their seid wyfes may] use and were gilt gyrdils and kerchiefs of the price of a plyte of .v. s.

g. And ferthermore to ordeyn and stablissh that noo man, but such as hath possessions of the yerely value of .xl. s., use nor were in aray for his body, fro the seid fest, eny fustian, bustian nor fustian of napuls, scarlet cloth engreyned; nor noo pellure but blak lambe or white lambe; all maiers, aldermen, shirrefs, barons of the .v. portes, baillifs of citees and boroughs, and other afore provided, and their wyfes, and the meniall servauntez of yomens degree of lordes, knyghtes, squiers and other gentilmen, havyng possessions of the seid yerely value of .xl.li., except; uppon peyn to forfeit to youre highnes, at every defaute, .xl. s.

h. And also to ordeyn and stablissh that noo yoman, nor noon other persone under that degree, fro the fest of Seint Peter called thadvincle next commyng, use nor were in the aray for his body, eny bolsters nor stuffe of wolle, coton nor cadas, nor other stuffer in his doublet, save lynyng accordyng to the same; uppon the peyn to forfeit to youre highnes, at every defaute, .vi. s. .viij. d.

i. And ferther to ordeyn and stablissh that noo knyght under thastate of a lorde, squier, gentilman nor other persone, use or were, from the fest of All Halowen next commyng, eny gowne, jaket or cloke, but it be of such lengh, as hit, he beyng upright, shall covere his pryve membres and buttokkes, uppon the peyn to forfeit to youre highnes, at every defaute, .xx. s.

j. And also to ordeyn and stablissh that noo taillour make, after the same fest, to eny

& les ditz Barons de les Cynque Portes, & leur femmes, puissent user & were les ditz furres de martrons funes letuse pure Grey ou pure menyver, & auxi qe leur ditz femmes puissent user & were ceinctures suisorrez & coverchiefs, del price dun plite, de cynque souldz.

g. Et enoultre ad ordeigne & establie, que null homme, forsque tiel qi ad possessions dannuell value de xl s, use ne were en araie pur son corps a le dit fest ascun fustian bustian ne fustian de Napuls, scarlet drap en graine, ne nulle pellure forsque dagnell noire ou dagnell blanc ; toutz Maires Aldermen Viscountz Barons de les Cynque Portz Baillifs de Citees & Burghs & autres pardevaunt purveuez, & leur femmes, & les menialx servauntz de yomens degree des seignurs, Chevaliers Equiers & autres gentilx hommes eiantz possessions du dit annuell value de xl li., exceptz ; sur peine de forfeire au Roy a chescun defaute xl s.

h. Et auxi ad ordeigne & establie, que null vadlet ne null autre persone desoubz cell degre, a le fest de Seint Père appelles ladvincle que serra en lan de nostre seignur Mille CCCClxv. use ne were en araie pur son corps ascuns bolsters ne stuffe de laine, Coton ne cadas, nautre stuffure en son perpoint sauf linure accordant al mesme ; sur peine de forfeire au Roy al chescun defaute vj s. viiij d.

i. Et oultre ad ordeigne & estaplie, que null Chevalier desoubz lestate de seignur esquier gentilhomme ne nautre persone use ou were a le fest de toutz seintz qi serra en lan nostre Mille CCCClxv. ascun govne Jaket ou cloche, sil ne soit de tiel longeure com cell, celuy esteant toutdroit, covera sez privez membres & buttoks ; sur peine de forfeire au Roy a chescun defaut xx s :

j. et auxi ad ordeigne & establie que null Taillour face apres mesme le fest au ascun

Ports, and their wives, may use and wear the aforesaid furs of martens, beech martens, weasels [lettice], trimmed grey or trimmed miniver; and also that their said wives may use and wear gilt girdles and headclothes priced at 5s a length.

g. And furthermore to ordain and decree that no one without possessions to the yearly value of £40 shall use or wear as bodily clothing, from the said feast, any fustian, bustian or fustian of Naples, scarlet cloth dyed in grain; or any skin but that of black or white lamb; excepting all mayors, aldermen, sheriffs, barons of the Cinque Ports, bailiffs of cities and boroughs, and others previously listed, and their wives, and the household servants of the degree of yeomen of lords, knights, esquires and other gentlemen with possessions to the said yearly value of £40; on pain of forfeiting 40s to your highness for every offence.

h. And also to ordain and decree that no yeoman, or any other person below that degree, from the feast of St Peter ad Vincula next, shall use or wear as bodily clothing any padding or stuffing of wool, cotton or caddis, or any other material in his doublet, except its lining, on pain of forfeiting 6s. 8d to your highness for every offence.

i. And further to ordain and decree that no knight below the status of lord, esquire, gentleman or any other person shall use or wear, from the feast of All Saints next [1465], any gown, jacket or cloak which is of such a length that when he stands upright it does not cover his private parts and buttocks, on pain of forfeiting 20s. to your highness for every offence.

j. And also to ordain and decree that no tailor, after the same feast, shall make for

persone, eny gowne, jaket or cloke of lesse lengh, or doublet stuffed contrarie to the premissez, uppon the same peyne at every defaute.

k.   And also to ordeyn and stablissh that noo knyght under thastate of a lorde, squier, gentilman or other persone, use nor were, from the seid fest of Seint Peter, eny shoes or boteux, havyng pykes passyng the lengh of .ij. ynches; uppon the peyn to forfeit to youre highnes, at every defaute, .xl. d.

l.   And also to ordeyn and stablissh that yf eny corvyser make eny pykes of shoen or boteux, after the seid fest of Seint Peter, to eny of the seid persones, contrarie to this acte, forfeit also to youre highnes, at every defaute, .xl. d.

m.   And also to ordeyn and stablissh by the seid auctorite that noo servaunte to husbondrie, nor commen laborer, nor servaunt to eny artificer, inhabitaunt oute of citee or borough, after the forseid fest of All Halowes, use nor were in their clothyng, eny cloth wherof the brode yerde shall excede in price .ij. s.; nor that eny of the same servauntez or laborers suffer eny of their wyfes to were or use, from the same fest, eny clothyng of hyer price then is afore lymyted to their husbondes; nor that they suffre eny of their seid wyfes, after the same fest, to use or were eny kerchiefs wherof the price of the plight shall excede .xij. d.; nor that eny of the same servauntez nor laborers, after the same fest, use or were eny close hoses, nor eny hoses wherof the peyre shall excede in price .xiiij. d.; nor that the same servauntez or laborers, nor noon of their wyfes, fro the same fest, were eny girdell harneysed with silver; uppon peyne to forfeit, for every defaute, to your highnes .xl. d.

n.   And forasmoch as the kerchiefs daily brought into this reame, enducen grete

persone ascune govne Jaket ou cloche de meindre longeur, ou perpoint stuffe, contrarie a les premesses, sur mesme la peine, a chescun defaute :

k.   et auxi ad ordeigne & establie que null Chevalier, desoubz lestate de seignur, esquier gentil homme ou autre persone, use ne were a le dit fest de Seint Peere ascuns solers ou boteaux eiantz pikes passantz la longeur de deux pountz, sur peine de forfeire au Roy al chescun defaute quarant deniers ;

l.   et auxi ad ordeigne & establie que si ascun Corueser ascuns pikes de solers ou boteaux apres le dit fest de Seint Peere au ascun des ditz persones contrarie a cest ordenaunce, forface ensement au Roy a chescun defaut qarant deniers.

m.   Et auxint ad ordeigne & establie par la dit actorite que null servaunt de husbondrie, ne commone laborer ne servaunt au ascun artificer enhabitant hors del Citee ou Burgh, apres le dit fest de toutz seintz use ne were en leur vesture ascun drap, dount le brodeyerde passera en price ij s. Ne que ascun mesmes les servaunts ou laborers suffre ascune de leurs femmes duser ou were a mesme le fest ascun vesture de pluis hault price que est devaunt limite a lour Barons, Ne que ceux suffrent ascune de leurs ditz femmes apres mesme le fest duser ou were ascuns couverchiefs dont le price del plite passera dousze deniers ; Ne que ascun de les mesmes servauntes ne laborers puis mesme le fest use ou were ascuns chausez closez, ne ascuns chauses dont le paire passera en price xiiij d ; Ne que les mesmes servaunts ne laborers ne null de leurs femmes a mesme le fest were ascun ceincture garnisse dargent, su peine de forfeire por chescun defaute au Roy xl. deniers :

n.   et pur ceo que les coverchiefs journement apportez en cest Roialme enducent graund

anyone any gown, jacket or cloak of a shorter length, or a padded doublet contrary to the aforesaid, on pain of the same penalty for every offence.

k. And also to ordain and decree that no knight below the status of lord, esquire, gentleman or other person shall use or wear, from the said feast of St Peter, any shoes or boots with points longer than two inches, on pain of forfeiting 40d to your highness for every offence.

l. And also to ordain and decree that if any shoemaker makes any points for shoes or boots, after the said feast of St Peter, for any of the said persons, contrary to this act, he shall also forfeit 40d to your highness for every offence.

m. And also to ordain and decree by the said authority that no agricultural worker, or common labourer, or servant of any craftsman living outside a city or borough, after the aforesaid feast of All Saints, shall use or wear in their clothing any cloth which costs more than 2s. the broad yard; and that none of the same servants or labourers shall allow their wives to wear or use, from the same feast, any clothing of higher price than specified above for their husbands; or that they allow their said wives, after the same feast, to use or wear any headcloths of which the price per length exceeds 12d.; or that any of the same servants or labourers, after the same feast, use or wear any joined hose, or any hose costing more than 14d. the pair; or that the same servants or labourers, or their wives, from the same feast, wear any girdle trimmed with silver; on pain of forfeiting 40d to your highness for every offence.

n. And inasmuch as the headcloths (*kerchiefs/coverchiefs*) daily brought into this realm

charge and cost in the same, and in effect in waste, that it may like youre seid highnes by the seid auctorite to ordeyn and stablissh that noo persone, after the fest of Seint Michell tharchangell next commyng, selle in any parte within this reame, eny lawne, nyfels, umple or eny other manere of kerchiefs wherof the price of a plight shall excede .x. s.; uppon the peyn to forfeit to youre highnes, for every plight sold at hyer price, .xiij. s. .iiij. d.

o [...]

p. Provided alwey that this ordenaunce of aray in noo wise prejudice nor hurt eny persone of or for usyng or weryng eny honourement, vesture or apparaill in doyng dyvyne service and attendyng therto; nor that this ordenaunce [extende] to the justicez of eny of your benches, maister or keper of youre rolles, maisters of your chauncery, barons of youre eschequer, nor chaunceller of the same, which nowe been or hereafter shalbe, nor to eny of theym. Provided also that the scolers of the unyversiteez of this reame, and scolers of eny unyversite oute of this reame, may use and were such aray, as they may use and were after the rule of the seid unyversiteez; this acte notwithstondyng. Provided also that henshmen, herawdes, purcyvauntes, swerdeberers to mayers, messyngers and mynstrelles, nor eny of hem, nor pleyers in their enterludes, be not comprised in this acte; nor eny persone as for weryng eny purces, pawteners, or crounes of cappes for children, be in eny wise comprised in the same. Provided also that this acte in noo wise extend to eny manere of aray to be necessariely used in werre, or in fetes of the same.

charge & cost en le mesme, & en effect en gast, Nostre dit seignur le Roy par lactorite suisdit ad ordeigne & establie, que nulle persone aps le fest de Seint Michell larchangel que serra en lan de seignur Mille CCC lxv vende en ascune part dedeinz cest Roialme ascune lavne Nifels umple ou ascun autre manere dez couverchiefs dount le price dun plite passera x s. sur peine de forfeire au Roy pur chescun plite venduz a pluis haulte price xiij s. iiij d.

o. [...]

p. Purveu toutz foitz que cest ordenaunce darraie en null manere prejudice nendamage ascun persone, de ou pur user ou weryng dascun ornament vesture ou apparaille en faisant divine service & a icell entendant ; Ne que cest ordenaunce extende as Justices dascun des Bancs du Roy, Maister ou Gardein de rolles, maistres del Chauncellarie du Roy, Barons deschequer du Roy, ne Chaunceller dicell, qui ore sont ou enapres serront, ne as ascuns deux. Puveu ensement que les Scolers des Universitees cesty roialme, & Scolers dascune Universite hors de cest roialme, puissent user & were tiel araie com ceux puissent user & were solonc la rule de les ditz Universiteez, cest ordenaunce nient contristeant. Purveu auxi que Hensmen, Heroldes, Purcyvauntez, Swerdeberers as Maires, Messagers & Ministrelles, nascun deux ne Jouers en lour entreludes ne soient comprisez en cest ordenaunce ; Ne ascun persone come pur weryng dascuns burses pauteners ou corounes pur cappes des enfaunts soit en ascun maner comprise en icell. Purveu auxi que cest ordenaunce en null maner extende au ascun manere darraie destre necessarement usez, en guerre ou en feetes del mesme.

Responsio.
Le roy ad graunte cest petition et toutz les articles comprises en ycell; et voet qe l'ordenaunce sur ceo a faire, ne comence d'apprendre sa force et effect, devant les festes nommes en ycell, qi serront en l'an de nostre seignour .mccclxv.

encourage great expenditure and cost and in effect are wasteful, may it please your highness by the said authority to ordain and decree that no one, after Michaelmas next [1465], shall sell in any part of this realm any lawn, nifles [see glossary], umple [a kind of fine cloth; see glossary] or any other kind of headcloth which costs more than 10s. per length; on pain of forfeiting 13s. 4d to your highness for every length sold at a higher price.

o. [...]

p. Provided always that this ordinance of array shall in no way prejudice or harm anyone with regard to using or wearing any adornment, vesture or apparel in celebrating and serving at divine service; nor shall this ordinance extend to the justices of any of your benches, the master or keeper of your rolls, masters of your chancery, barons of your exchequer, or the present or future chancellor of the same, or to any of them. Provided also that the scholars of the universities of this realm, and the scholars of any university outside this realm, may use and wear such array as they are allowed to use and wear by the rules of the said universities; notwithstanding this act. Provided also that no henchmen, heralds, pursuivants, swordbearers to mayors, messengers and minstrels, or any of them, or players in their interludes, shall be included in this act; or that anyone shall be in any way included in the same because of wearing any purses and pouches, or the crowns of children's caps. Provided also that this act shall not extend in any way to any kind of array necessary in war, or in feats of arms.

Answer.
The king has granted this petition and all the articles contained in the same; and he wills that the ordinance to be made on this shall not take effect before the feasts named in the same, which will be in the year of our lord 1465.

10. Parliamentary petition of January 1478 (Edward IV), requesting alterations to the previous statute

The text of this Middle English petition is extracted from Horrox 2005, 'Edward IV, Parliament of January 1478', item 30 (also cf. Strachey 1783: VI.188–9). The translation is adapted from Horrox's.

30. To the kyng oure liege lord; prayen the comons in this present parlement assembled, that where in your parlement begon and holden at Westm', the .xxix. day of Aprill, in the third yere of youre noble reigne, amonges other, an ordenaunce and statute conteynyng certeyn articles for thapparall and aray of the comons of this reame, aswell men as women, was made; and for lak of due execution of the same statute and ordenaunce, more inordynate, excessive and outeragious aray hath be sithen used then before, to the grettest ympoverysshyng in that that ever grewe in this reame, and more gretter is like to growe, if it be not refourmed, by puttyng in due execution the ordenaunce and statute aforesaid. [...] that it may be ordeyned by the auctorite of this present parlement, that the said statute begynne and take effecte fro the fest of Seynt Michell thArchangell next comyng, and not before; and that noon of your lieges be hurt or endamaged for eny thyng doon or used, or tobe doon or used ayenst the same statute, from the makyng therof unto the same fest of Seynt Michell, but that they and every of theym, ayenst your highnes, by the auctorite of this present parlement, in that partie for ever be quyte and discharged.

[...] be it therfore ordeyned [and] declared by the auctorite of this present parlement, that every persone that is, hath bee, or hereafte[r] [   ][   ][   ] shalbe maier, alderman, shiref, baillif or other chief governour of eny citee, burgh, or eny [of the .v. po]rtes, and the barons of the same, that hath doo their service in the tyme of your coronation, or of the quene, or hereafter shall doo, and the governours of every other toune beyng in any wyse corporat within this reame, by whatsoever name or names they or eny of theym be named or called, and their wyfes, may use and were such and like aray as is assigned and lymyted in the said statute and ordenaunce, the said .iij.^{d} yere made, to persones and their wyfes havyng possessions to the yerely value of .xl.li. And also that it be ordeyned by the said auctorite, that no persone other then is afore specified, not havyng possessions to the yerely value of .xx.li. or above, after the forseid fest of Seynt Michell, use or were in their apparaill any cloth of sylk, chamelet, [   ][   ][   ] or wollen cloth made oute of this reame, uppon peyn to forfeit at every defaute .xl. s.

And ferther it be ordeyned by the said auctorite that the wyfe and doughters unmaried of every persone havyng possession to the yerely value of .x.li. and above, may use and were frontlettes of blak velvet, or of any other cloth of silk of the colour of blak. And over, that it shalbe leefull to the wyfe and doughters unmaried of every persone havyng possessions to the yerely value of .xx.li. or above, to use and were in their colers, ventes and slefes of their gownes and hukes, sateyn, chamelet, sarcenet or tarteron.

And also that it be leeful to the wyfe and doughters unmaried of every person havyng possessions to the yerely value of .xl.li. and above, to use and were in their colers, ventes and slefes of their gounes and hukes, sarcenet or tarteron: the forseid statute the said .iij.^{de} yere made, or any matier in any [article] theryn comprised, notwithstondyng.

30. To the king our liege lord; the commons assembled in this present parliament pray, that where in your parliament begun and held at Westminster on 29 April in the third year of your noble reign [1463], among other things an ordinance and statute was made containing certain articles concerning the apparel and attire of the commons of this realm, men as well as women; and for want of proper execution of the same statute and ordinance more inordinate, excessive and outrageous attire has since been used than before, to the greatest impoverishment that ever occurred in this realm, and it is likely to become even greater if it is not reformed by properly executing the aforesaid ordinance and statute. [...] that it be ordained by authority of this present parliament that the said statute commence and take effect from Michaelmas next, and not before; and that none of your lieges shall be harmed or damaged for anything done or used, or to be done or used, against the same statute since it was made up to the same Michaelmas, but that they and each of them shall be quit and discharged forever towards your highness, by the authority of this present parliament, in that respect.

[...] be it therefore ordained and announced by authority of this present parliament that every person who is, has been, or shall subsequenly be a mayor, alderman, sheriff, bailiff or other chief officer of any city, borough or any of the Cinque Ports, and the barons of the same who performed their service at the time of your coronation or that of the queen, or shall do so in future, and the officers of every other town which is incorporated in any way within this realm, by whatever name or names they or any of them are named or called, and their wives, may use and wear such and like attire as assigned and restricted in the said statute and ordinance made in the said third year to persons and their wives who have possessions to the annual value of £40. And also that it be ordained by the said authority that any person, other than those specified above, who does not have possessions to the annual value of £20 or more shall not use or wear after Michaelmas aforesaid in their apparel any silk cloth, camlet or woollen cloth made outside this realm, upon pain of forfeiting 40s. for every offence.

And further be it ordained by the said authority that the wife and unmarried daughters of every person who has possessions to the annual value of £10 and more may use and wear frontlets of black velvet or of any other black silk cloth. And moreover, that it shall be lawful for the wife and unmarried daughters of every person who has possessions to the annual value of £20 or more to use and wear in their collars, vents and sleeves of their gowns and hukes, satin, camlet, sarsenet or tarterin.

And also that it shall be lawful for the wife and unmarried daughters of every person who has possessions to the annual value of £40 and more to use and wear in their collars, vents and sleeves of their gowns and hukes, sarsenet or tarterin: notwithstanding the aforesaid statute made in the said third year, or any matter included in any article in it.

[…]

And ferthermore, that it be ordeyned by the said auctorite, that every lady and gentilwoman, after the deth of her husbond, have her libertie to were and use all such and like aray, as she did or myght have doon in the life of her husbond, any tyme sithen the makyng of the said statute and ordenaunce made the forseid third yere; the same statute and ordenaunce notwithstondyng.

Responsio.
Le roi le voet.

[…]

And furthermore, that it be ordained by the said authority that every lady and gentlewoman, after the death of her husband, shall have freedom to wear and use all such and like attire as she did or might have done in the lifetime of her husband at any time since the making of the said statute and ordinance made in the aforesaid third year; notwithstanding the same statute and ordinance.

Answer.
The king wills it.

CHAPTER VI

Unpublished Petitions to King, Council and Parliament

INTRODUCTION

The collection of Public Records Office (National Archives) documents classified as 'SC 8' include 347 manuscript bundles (or 'files'), containing in total 17,621 petitions addressed variously to king, council and parliament. Collectively known as 'Ancient Petitions', they represent the medieval legal process of petitioning for grace, favour and restitution that became a primary feature of English royal and parliamentary legal processes from the thirteenth to sixteenth centuries.

The earliest petitions survive from Henry III's reign. It was during the reign of Edward I, however, when the practice of petitioning really came into prominence, initiated by an apparent shift in government policy in the 1270s which allowed the king more involvement in local affairs whilst giving the king's subjects greater access to royal favour or judgement (Dodd 2007: 19). The policy allowed aggrieved parties to hire a properly trained clerk to produce a petition, addressed directly to the king, to his parliament or his advisors, in order to have restitution for a grievance or have inquiry made into a particular case. English monarchs carried on the practice to greater and lesser extents through the whole of the late-medieval period.

PRIVATE VS. 'PUBLIC' PETITIONS

So-called 'private' petitions from individuals, local groups, communities and religious houses were often used when the courts of the county, hundred, borough or vill were thought to be insufficient for achieving satisfaction. Most of the petitions extracted here are 'private' in nature. Almost all were also 'un-enrolled', in that they were not recorded in any systematic way on the records of the rolls of parliament.

During the early years of Edward I's reign, such so-called 'private' petitions began to be left off the parliamentary rolls, whilst enrolment was reserved solely for petitions concerning 'public' business. The distinction between them is often far from clear. In general, 'private' petitions resulted in a ruling that only affected the petitioner or petitioners, rather than resulting in general legislation (Dodd 2007: 2, 127, 157). The petitions transcribed and edited here may be considered 'private'.

During Edward II's reign one begins to see petitions addressed directly to the commons rather than the king or council. By the fifteenth century, many private petitions – often addressed to the commons – were again being enrolled directly in parliamentary records, and many of these were subsequently printed in the *Rotuli Parliamentorum* (Strachey *et al.* 1783).

SURVIVAL OF THE PETITIONS

Private petitions such as the majority of those below were normally written on a small, rectangular piece of parchment with or without an endorsement. A number of these would later be gathered and threaded together into a 'bundle' inside a rough outer cover (Dodd 2007: 330). Recently the Ancient Petitions project has made digitised versions of the 347 files of 'SC 8' petition manuscripts available online through the National Archives' documents online service (http://www.nationalarchives.gov.uk/documentsonline/default).

As mentioned above, all of the earlier petitions were originally enrolled in the records of parliament. Up until the 1330s they could either be enrolled *verbatim* or as brief Latin abstracts. At first the rolls were kept by the Exchequer but from the 1320s were transferred to the Chancery, which probably resulted in the decline of recording all petitions – including 'private' – on the rolls (Dodd 2007: 326–7).

Only a small portion of the thousands of existing petitions have been transcribed or published. The eighteenth-century *Rotuli Parliamentorum* contain edited versions of several hundred, mostly enrolled petitions, but the volumes are now quite antiquated and dating and transcription occasionally unreliable. The recent, substantial project Parliamentary Records of Medieval England – or PROME – re-transcribed and edited a number of these enrolled petitions, but many were not included because they could not be dated accurately to a particular parliament (see Given-Wilson 2005: 'General Introduction'). In particular, the *Rotuli* contain readings of a great tranche of petitions associated with Edward II's reign which were not subsequently included in PROME (Phillips 2005: 'Edward II: 1307–1327, Introduction').

One finds a large number of petitions resulting from the baronial revolt of 1321–2, Edward's subsequent quelling of that revolt and his reinvesting of the Despensers (Ormrod 2008: 77). There are only fragmentary parliamentary rolls surviving from these years (none for 1322). The editors of the *Rotuli* seem to have included a number of transcripts of these imprecisely dated petitions in order to fill out the parliamentary business for the period. These were subsequently dropped from PROME. The petition shown in Extract 3 is an example: it was edited in the original *Rotuli* but has been newly transcribed and edited here as it contains significant lexical items for cloth and clothing of interest to the present study.

Individual petitions were often copied or recorded elsewhere, and there are cases of multiple survivals. For example, an unpublished petition of 1463–5 (SC 8/29/1410) was submitted by the silkwomen and 'throwsters' of London, asking for legislation to limit foreign merchants from importing various articles of worked and unworked silk ('of the worst quality'). The petition is essentially an attempt to protect the London craftwomen's monopoly on the silk trade, and it contains a number of lexical items of interest ('silkewomen', 'throwesters', 'silkework', 'wrought silke', 'thrown rybans', 'laces', 'corses', 'silke wolle'). However, the petition exists in a near-identical version – SC 8/29/1411 – which *was* enrolled on the roll of the parliament of 3–4 Edward IV (Horrox 2005: 'Edward IV, Parliament of April 1463', item 21; also Strachey et al. 1783: 4.506a–b). As this very similar version is available in many libraries, SC 8/29/1410 has not been transcribed here.

Many petitions referred to other departments of government were subsequently copied or else summarised in other places: such as on the plea rolls of the court of King's Bench (Public Records Office class KB 27) or the two series of Exchequer Memoranda Rolls (E 159 and E 368). Some of the petitions that were not included in the *Rotuli* have since been dated based on evidence from other documents: Extract 2 below, for example, is a previously unedited petition resulting from the baronial revolt of 1321–2 that is datable by references in the Patent Rolls.

LANGUAGE

As with many late-medieval administrative and legal documents, Anglo-French was the customary language for medieval petitions. Anglo-French was the spoken language of law and administration in England until the Statute of Pleadings of 1362 which required the use of English in legal proceedings. Because the earliest petitions were in essence 'written substitutes [...] for oral proceedings' (Ormrod 2009: 36), their customary language was quickly established as Anglo-French (a few early petitions were written in Latin – primarily those from the clergy).

Middle English first appears in a petition of 1344: SC 8/192/9580 (Ormrod 2009: 36; transcribed in Chambers and Daunt 1931). It is rare for this period. Only from around 1423 do enrolled petitions began to appear regularly in Middle English as well as the customary Anglo-French. From the 1430s Middle English became the standard language for all petitions (Dodd 2007: 189, 290–1).

It is clear that petitions were normally 'heard' or presented orally in parliament or to an appropriate arbitrator (a receiver in the Exchequer, Chancery, etc.). Dodd supposes that increasingly petitions would have been translated into English for quick oral presentation, despite almost always being recorded in standard Anglo-French (292–3):

> [Petitions were] written in a very controlled environment in which administrative and legal convention was actually more important in determining the form taken by the petition that any consideration to have the petition 'speak the language'. (294)

Language use in the petitions which survive should therefore be seen within the mixed-language environment of later-medieval English law and administration, rather than as necessarily a record of the spoken language. Mark Ormrod notes, for example, that 'for a while under Henry VI the common petitions become a hybrid of French and English' (2007: 40, note 37). As with other documents in this volume, many Anglo-French petitions transcribed below contain frequent intrusions of Middle English or Latin lexical items.

EXTRACTS FROM THE PETITIONS

1. Petition on behalf of children in the king's wardship, *c.* 1275–*c.* 1300? (National Archives, MS SC 8/196/9797)

This petition, probably dating from the final quarter of the thirteenth century, was made on behalf of a group of children in Edward II's wardship. Apparently the children are in some distress at having been denied substantial portions of their regular livery and request that these allowances be returned to their original levels. The petition contains many interesting lexical items referring to details of children's livery. It records that the livery included measures of bread from the 'panetrye' (pantry), wine and beer from the 'botelerye' (butlery or buttery), meat from the 'quysine' (kitchen), firewood in the winter, items of bedding and named garments: including a 'tabar' (tabard, tunic) and a 'surcote de este' (a 'summer' surcoat).

Transcription and translation are by Mark Chambers. The text is in a clear Anglicana hand typical of the late thirteenth century, crowded onto the parchment in twelve lines. The matrix (or 'base') language is Anglo-French. There is no endorsement (the customary reply or response normally recorded on the reverse of the petition). There is clear evidence of moisture damage but nothing significantly obscuring the text. There are only a few abbreviations and suspensions; these have been expanded in italics in the extract. *Punctus elevatus* is indicated by semicolon. Suggested or uncertain readings – primarily due to fading or damage – are placed in italics. Lacunae are indicated by ellipses in square brackets.

A Lour lyg[*e seg*]nur le Rey monstrent les enfants de garde ke ho*ni* lour ad sustret de lour lyve*rees* ceo est a saver par la ou eus soleyent prendre de la panetrye quatre darres de payn les deus darres les sount soustret E par la ou eus soleyent prendre de la botelerye deus galons de vyn e deus de cervayse eus ne p*r*enent mes ke un pycher de vyn e un autre de cervayse E p*ar* la ou eus soleyent prendre de la quysine quatre yes de grose chare ; les deus yes les sount sustret · E ausy p*ar* la ou eus soleyent prendre pur rost deus gelynes ou quatre deners ; eus ne p*r*enent for une gely ne ou deus deners E par la au eus soleyent aver buche en la seson e lytere ; a une p*ar*tie des enfaunz est sustret · E par la ou eus soleyent prendre tabar e surcote de este ; tut lour est sustret E une partye de la chaundelrye ; lour est sustret · De ces poynz avant no mees prient eus nostre seynur le Reys ke il les face redrescer si ly plest issy ke eus [. . .]yent sustenaunce *cum* aver soleyant Desi*cum* eus ne unt autre sustenur ne *m*eyntenur fors ke ly.

2. Petition of Roger de Berners and William de Marny, *c.* 1322 (National Archives, MS SC 8/33/1604)

One of a number of petitions dating to sessions of parliament *c.* 1322, this petition relates how Roger de Berners and William de Marny fulfilled the king's commission to raise 700 foot soldiers, providing them with armament and clothing and leading them to Newcastle. Berners and Marny claim that they bought the soldiers cloth for garments ('cotes'), bought them armour and also paid their wages, but that the counties from which these men were recruited have only reimbursed the petitioners for the garments. Berners and Marny request the king to rectify the oversight and recompense them for their good deed.

The children of the wardship show their liege lord the king that he shames them by depriving them of their liveries, that is to say that whereas they were accustomed to take from the pantry four measures of bread, two measures have been withheld, and whereas they were accustomed to take from the buttery two gallons of wine and two of beer they now only receive a pitcher of wine and another of beer, and whereas they were accustomed to take from the kitchen four measures of red meat, two measures have been withheld. And also whereas they were accustomed to take for dinner two hens or four *deners* [Anglo-French *deniers* = pence?], they no longer receive one hen nor two *deners*. And where they were accustomed to have firewood in season, and bedding, this has been withheld from a number of the children. And whereas they were accustomed to receive a tabard and summer surcoat, all of these have been withheld. And provision of candles have been withheld from them. Of the above points they have no (*portion?, messuage?*), they pray our lord the king should cause them to be redressed if he pleases, so that they [...] sustenance to which they have become accustomed, as they have no other sustainer or maintainer but him.

The National Archives catalogue notes that the document must date to *c.* 1322, the date scribbled in a later hand on the guard (the backing strip to which the petition has been sewn), because the *Calendar of Patent Rolls* records that Berners and Marny were commissioned to raise the troops and lead them to Newcastle on 25 March 1322 (*CPR Ed.. II* 1904: 4.96). There seems to be an early reference to 'Candlewick Street' in line 11, that district of London which during Edward III's reign would become associated with the manufacture of inexpensive cloth (cf. Newton 1980: 137). This would be a very early reference, and – although the passage is damaged – the line appears to read: 'each cloth of 36 ells in length, wholly fulled and finished, which comes from Candlewick Street'.

The transcription and translation are by Mark Chambers. The manuscript contains seventeen lines of text with some abbreviation and suspension, and there is no endorsement. There is substantial fading with moisture damage in the upper right-hand corner, narrowing and running all the way down the right edge. This fading obscures portions of the text, and there is the occasional fold. Often minims can be difficult to distinguish. The frequently illegible text in the extract is indicated by parentheses in square brackets. Primary abbreviations and suspensions have been expanded and uncertain readings are suggested in italics. The Tironian symbol for *et* is represented with an ampersand. Presumed or uncertain readings are offered in italics in the translation.

A notre seignur le Roy monstrent Rogger de Berners & William de Marny q' come notre seignur le Roy les [. . .]ission de ellire · v[. . .] homes a peedes plus vaillauntz & puissauns en les countez de Essex & de Hereford aussi bien dedeinz fraunchises come de [. . .]s les villes de Colechester Seint Auban · E q' les ditz vij^c · homes a pee fuissent armez des aketouns bacynetz & gauntz de plates au meyns & garni[. . .] des [. . .] des q' [. . .] [. . .] ussient meutz eider & vestutz de une sute & amener a notre seignur le Roy les dites gentz a pee issint armez & vestuz & issint qil y feissent a d[. . .] ville de [. . .] Chastel sur Tyne as utaves de la Trynyte a plus tart ; E q' les ditz · vij^c homes fuissent mys en vynteynes centeynes & conestables [. . .] vous nous sire comaundaunt & engoygnaunt totes autres choses entrelessez ; les ditz homes eslire des armes garnyr & vestez feissoms & a [. . .] si come est avandist ; & ceo sicome vous & votre honur amassoms & votre indignacion eschure ; & nous & les noz sauver sauncz damage volioms [. . .] feissoms; issint q' de ascune necligence en ascune manere ne puissoms estre reprove ; treshonurable seignur voz comaundementz avons [. . .] homes en les countez avauntditz les plus puissauns & vaillaunts des ditz countez ensemblement ove les centeners [. . .] quele part q' vous nous voudriez oveques eux avoir comaundee d'estre alez ; Treshonurable seignur endroit de lour vestures avan[. . .]e · draps chescun drap contenaunt en longure xxxvj. aunes moillez & tounduz ove la laoure q' apent de CandelWekstrete ; issint q' chescune cote & [. . .] pur lour vesture est du pris de v. soutz · treshonurable seignur ceo q' vous nous chargastes si ferniclement q' come nous vous [?] & votre honour & [. . .] dedeigne eschure ; achata[. . .]es . j^c. armures cest a savoir aketouns . bacinetz / & gauntz de plate cheskun herneys ; pris de .xx. soutz ; issint q' les gentz ne puissent dire q' pur notre necligence ne pur breftee de temps ; fuissent despurunz · e a totes cestes voz comaundementz parfaire ; nene avoms resceu de dites countez mesqe .iiij^{xx}. iiij. li. & x. s'. & ceo pur vesture pur lour cotes & nule riens pur lour armures ne pur lour despenses ne pur centeners ; & a[. . .] paiez graundement de noz deners pur voz comaundementz parfaire ; par quei nous vous prioms treshonurable seignur q' vous ne voillez suffrer q' nous soioms desperdauntz pur notre bien fet

To our lord the king Roger de Berners and William de Marny show that, as our lord the king [...]ission to select [700] foot soldiers, from the bravest and mighty in the counties of Essex and Hereford, both within and without the authority (*franchises*) and (from) the towns of Colchester (Essex) and St Albans (Hertfordshire), and that the said 700 foot soldiers were armed with aketons, helmets and gauntlets for the hands, and garments (?) [...] better to aid (?), and similarly attired, and to bring to our lord the king the said foot soldiers so armed and clothed, and that they should have (?) [...] to the town of (New)castle-upon-Tyne by the octaves of the Trinity [1 June] at the latest, and that the said 700 men were to be ordered in scores [groups of 20], hundreds and constables [?... *illegible*] you our lord (they) command and enjoin, all the other things omitted ; the said men we have led, equipped with arms and vested, and [...] such as said before, and so that you and your honour we might increase, and your indignation eschew, and us and ours to remain protected/immune, [...] so that of any negligence we may in no way be accused, right honourable lord your commandments we have [... *illegible*] men in the aforesaid counties, together with the most able and worthy of the said county within the *hundreds*, [...] together wherever you would wish with them to be commanded to go; very honourable lord, with regard to their clothing afore(*said*), [...] cloth, each cloth containing 36 ells in length, fulled and finished the entire breadth, which come from (?) Candlewick Street, and that each coat and [...] for their clothing, costing 5 shillings, most honourable lord, as you have charged us so ardently that as we [...] your contempt to avoid, purchased 100 (pieces of) armour: namely aketons, helmets, and gauntlets, each of them equipped, costing 20 shillings, so that the men cannot say that by our negligence nor for shortness of time *they should be deprived*. And fulfilling all these your commandments, we have received nothing from the said counties except 84 pounds and 10 shillings, and this for cloth for their coats, and nothing for their armour nor for their expenses nor for *centeners*, and (*we have*) expended a great deal of our money to fulfil your commandments. Therefore we pray you, most honourable lord, that you will not stand for us to be misfortuned/ruined by our good deed.

3. Petition of Robert de Montfort, *c.* 1322 (National Archives, MS SC 8/4/193)

National Archives, MS SC 8/4/193 is one of a number of petitions resulting from the unsuccessful baronial revolt against Edward II in 1321–2; an edited version of this petition was included in the original *Rotuli Parliamentorum* (Strachey *et al.* 1783: I.388). It is addressed to the king and his council and goes on to list a number of incidental items of cloth and clothing in a manner that is typical of the petitions. In this case we are given the names for several items of annual livery formerly belonging to a clerk named Robert de Mountfort (possibly *de Mundford*; see Phillips 2005: note p. 388).

The petition relates that Robert had been granted the livery for life by Lord Bartholomew de Badlesmere. When Lord Badlesmere and other conspirators rebelled against Edward II, his estate became forfeit, and Robert's annual livery apparently went with it. Lord Badlesmere was executed on 14 April 1322, presumably just prior to the petition. With his livery in arrears, Robert petitioned for its reinstatement.

From the middle of the fourteenth century the term *livery* began to be used specifically to refer to a garment or uniform granted by a king or lord to a servant or retainer, and it clearly holds these connotations here. The petition names a number of items of clothing formerly granted to Robert each year, recording specifics such as 'pelure' (fur lining or trimming) for an 'open' and a 'closed' surcoat as well as miniver fur for a 'chaperon' (hood). It also requests the regular allowance of 'demy drap de colur covenable pur clerk d'estat' (half-cloth of colour suitable for the rank of clerk), also part of Robert's livery.

Later in the fourteenth century there were a number of parliamentary statutes passed in an effort to control the giving of livery and to stipulate materials and articles of dress (from Richard II's reign in 1377 up to Henry VII's in 1503; see Hunt 1996: 425, note 27). In this earlier petition one can get a sense of the legal and domestic ramifications of this late-medieval social practice.

The petition is written on a single membrane of rectangular parchment, here with twelve lines of text plus three lines of description in the lower right-hand corner, very well preserved in a clear Anglicana script. The petition's matrix language is Anglo-French. The first line contains the address 'To our lord the king, if it pleases him, and to his council', and a four-line endorsement is written vertically on the reverse in the same hand. The common inscription 'Coram rege' (before the king) is written below it.

Transcription and translation are by Mark Chambers. Most conventional suspensions have been expanded in italics; abbreviations are indicated by an inverted comma. As in many Anglo-French documents from this period, instances of 'seignour' (lord) are represented by 'seign' or similar, with the superscript symbol for *-ur/-eur/-our* above the *n*. The Tironian symbol for *et* is represented with an ampersand. Presumed or uncertain readings are offered in italics in the translation.

A no*stre* seign*eur* le Roi si le plet & a son conseil prie Robert de Mountfort clerk' qe de ceo qe sire Beralmeu de Badlesmere qe ad forfez ceo qe en li est dever no*stre* seign*eur* le roi le estote tenu par bone obligacion ensele de son sele en demy drap de colur covenable pur clerk' destat oveqes la pelure pur surcot clos & pur surcot overt oveqes un chap*er*on de menuveyr a rescevire chescun an a Castelcombe en Wiltes' a la feste de touz seinz a tote sa vie pur leritage memes celi Robert qi a ly aferreit apres la mort sire Willem de Mountfort son frere dount le dit sire Beralmeu par poer de sa seignorie li fesoit fere a ly un escrit de son dreit, relesser a ly & par taunt li g*r*aunta & dona la dite liveree a te*r*me de sa vie et obligea a ceo le dit maner de Castelcombe qi est chief man*er* de son dit heritage a la destr' le dit Robert en qi mayn q*i* le man*er* deveigne a quel temps qe la dite lyverree ly seit arere; quel

Robert de Mountfort, clerk, prays our lord the king, if it pleases him, and his council, that whereas Lord Bartholomew de Badlesmere, who had forfeited that which our lord the king gave him through good obligation sealed with his seal – one half-cloth of colour suitable for a clerk's estate, with the fur for a 'closed' surcoat and for an 'open' surcoat, and with a hood of miniver – to be received each year at Castle Combe in Wiltshire, at the feast of All Saints, for the rest of his life in inheritance for the same Robert, which was due to him after the death of his brother William de Mountfort, the said Sir Bartholomew, by power of his lordship, made a writ releasing him from his rights, and thereby granted and gave him [Robert] the said livery, for the rest of his life, and pledged *by this* the said manner of Castle Combe, the chief manor of his heritage, to the [legal] destress of the said Robert, in whose possession

maner est ore devenu en la mayn nostre seigneur le Roi par la forfeture le dit Beralmeu & la dite lyveree est arere au dit Robert du terme de la feste de touz seinz dreyn passe ; voille nostre seigneur le Roi grauntier & comandier si li plet qe gre seit fet au dit Robert de sa dite lyveree qest arere du terme avantdit & pur le temps avenir ; ou q'il le voille fere rebailler son escrit q'il fist de ceo au dit Bertilmeu par poer de sa seignorie issint q'il ne seit tiele manere desheritee s'il ne eit le dit petit profit a ly du & graunte.

 Petitio par Roberto de Monte forti clerico
 de iure exaudienda ad instant' Williami de Chestrefeld
[*Response on the dorse*]:
Ostendat id quot habet de pensione, & assignent' justicias ad inquirend' veritatem faci, & super continuacione seisine suie &ct., et returnata inquisiatio fiat justicia

4. Petition of the weavers of York, 1342 (National Archives, MS SC 8/238/11890A)

The National Archives manuscript SC 8/238/11890A is a petition to Edward III and his council, submitted on behalf of the weavers' guild of York in 1342. The weavers point out that the charter granted to them by Henry II, the king's great-grandfather, states that no weaver in the county of Yorkshire should make striped or coloured cloth, except in the city of York and certain other places of the king's demesne (and for this they must pay a certain sum). The manuscript numbered SC 8/238/11890B is a copy of that charter. The weavers of York complain that King Edward has allowed weavers from the Low Countries freedom from taxes and tallages, along with other aliens living in York and in other places, with the result that the local guild is now too poor to pay its lease ('ferme').

 Only the first eight lines of the petition are extracted below. The remaining lines (9–11) request that the franchise granted to the aliens might be repealed. The petition further requests that a writ of *fieri facias* (a writ of execution after judgement obtained in a legal action for debt) be issued to all weavers in Yorkshire, by a new charter, whenever the York weavers' lease is in arrears – or else that they might be discharged of their lease. There is no endorsement.

 While the document does not contain a significant amount of new cloth and clothing terminology, it does offer a glimpse of the legal manoeuvring of fourteenth-century guilds in the cloth trade. The document also specifies charges for making cloth 'rayes' or 'de colour' without special licence in Henry II's Yorkshire – charges the York weavers apparently wish updated and applied by the current king as well.

 The transcription and translation are by Mark Chambers. There is some minor damage on the edges of the manuscript but nothing significantly obscuring the text, except a thumbnail-size mark on the lower left-hand corner (indicated below with ellipses in square brackets). The matrix language is Anglo-French. Conventional abbreviations and suspensions have been expanded and uncertain readings suggested in italics. The Tironian symbol for *et* is represented with and ampersand; the *punctus elevatus* is represented with a semicolon.

A nostre seignour le Roy & a son consail monstrent les Tistours de la cite Deverwyk' · que com le Roi Henr' besaiel nostre seignour le Roy qorest graunta par sa chartre & conferma a les Tistours de la dite cite que nul homme par tut le countee freit ne freit faire draps rayes ne de colour · forque en la dite cite & en altres certeyns villes de les demeignes nostre dit seignour le Roy deinz mesme le counte sur forfaiture de .x. lj devers nostre seignour le Roy ; et pur cele ffraunchises avoir les ditz Tistours Deverwyk' graunterent rendre al Escheqer nostre seignour le Roy .x. lj par an ; sicom en la dite chartre plus pleynement est contenu Et

the manor *came when the said livery went into arrears.* This manor is now come into the possession of our lord the king, by forfeiture of the said Bartholomew, and the said livery is in arrears to the said Robert from the term of the feast of All Saints passed. Wishing our lord the king to grant and to command, if it pleases him, that satisfaction should be made to the said Robert for the said livery that is in arrears, for the term aforesaid and for the future, or that *he should wish to reissue his writ that he made* concerning the said Bartholomew, by the power of his lordship, so that he is in no way disinherited should he not give and grant the said small income to him.

    Petition for Robert de Mountfort, clerk,
      by right of hearing, at the instance of William de Chesterfield
[*Response on the dorse*]:
He should show that which he has of the pension, and justices should be assigned to enquire into the truth of the matter and upon the continuation of his seisin etc., and the inquisition is to be returned, and let justice be done.

The weavers of the city of York show our lord the king and his council that as King Henry, great-grandfather of our lord the king, did grant by his charter and confirmed to the weavers of the said city, that no-one throughout the county shall make or cause to be made striped cloth or coloured cloth, except in the said city and in certain other towns in the demesne of our said lord the king, in the same county, upon pain of forfeiture of 10 pounds to our lord the king, and by that authority have the said weavers of York consented to give to the Exchequer of our lord the king 10 pounds per year, as specified in more detail in the said

puis n*os*t*r*e dit seign*our* le Roy qorest graunta as gens de mesme la faculte de Brabant' & as altres aliens de*mur*rauntz en la dite cite & en di*ver*s lieus deynz le dit counte qils s*er*rou*nt* quites de taxes & taillages & de totes alt*r*es charges deve*r*s n*os*t*r*e *dit* seign*our* le Roy et auxint aut*r*es tistours dynzens oeverunt en le counte avaunt dit hors des ditz cite & villes encontre la tenure de la ch*ar*t*r*e avauntdit issint q*ue* les dit Tistours Deverwyc' sount si enpoverys qils ne pount lour ferme paier Parquei prient les ditz Tistours Deverwik' a n*os*t*r*e seign*our* le Roy & son consail q*ue* liu pleise la frauncl*ise* a les aliens issint grauntez repeller & brefes *de* fieri fac*is* s*ur* toutz les Tistours denz le dit counte p*ar* novele ch*ar*t*r*e qaunt la dite ferme est arrere g*r*auntir ou eux de la dite ferme de [. . .] de tut descharger de puis qils ne poent lour frauncl*ise* enioier

5. Petition of the merchants of the Hanse concerning excessive customs, *c*. 1394? (National Archives, MS SC 8/125/6225)

The merchants of the Hanse (later described collectively as the 'Hanseatic league') were an association of traders based originally in German-speaking Saxony and Westphalia. Their presence dominated the fur trade and trade in other merchandise in much of northern Europe from at least the thirteenth century, and the late-medieval English clothing trade was no exception. In England the association's main 'kontor' (a Hanse merchant's hall) was established in London by at least the fourteenth century; it was also known as the Steelyard (cf. Veale 1966: 68, 75).

This petition, written around 1394 on behalf of the Hanse resident in England, accuses the customs collectors of Southampton of collecting 'unwarranted and excessive' new customs on cloth imported by the merchants. It further relates that the merchants held privileges and charters protecting their merchandise from such unwarranted customs, but that the collectors in Southampton have not followed orders to cease collection and to return the excess amounts. The petition asks that certain lords ('seignours') be appointed to examine the case in order to find a resolution.

The transcription and translation are by Mark Chambers. The manuscript is in good condition and the text is written in fourteen neat, tightly spaced lines and is in an Anglo-French matrix language (see Plate 5). Abbreviations and expansions have been extended in italics and the Tironian *et* symbol represented with an ampersand. Presumed or uncertain readings are offered in italics in the translation.

> A n*os*t*r*e tresexcellent & tresredoubtee seign*our* le Roy & de ses
> treessages seign*our*s de cest p*r*esent p*ar*lement

Monstrent toutz les m*er*chantz del Hans d'alemagne repairantz al Royalme d'engleterre q*ue* les baillifs & custume*r*s desouthampton constreignent les m*er*chantz av*au*ntditz de paier novels imposicions & custumes pur diverses m*er*chandises encountre lour previleges & liberteez de lour · chartre & ancien usage dount les ditz merchantz ount pursuez du parlement a parlem*en*t de conseill a conseill pur avoir remedie ou vous tresredubtee seign*our* par avis de vos tressages seign*our*s nadgairs en v*os*t*r*e parlement grauntastes brief sur peyne de C. li. le quelle est forfaite a vous hors de v*os*t*r*e Chaunc' direct as ditz baillifs & custumers de surseir de tiels novels imposicions & d'avoir l'argent ent pris en la dit Chaunc' a un certein jour de quel rien est fait · Et q'ils sount tenuz de paier certeins custumes comprises deins lour chartres pur draps d'assise & iij. d. al livre de touz autres draps estraites pieces de draps & kerseys queux ne sont d'assise come piert p*ar* diverses evidences del Escheqer exemplefiez en la Chaunc' de n*os*t*r*e tresnoble aiel l'an de son regne xxx.v p*ar* queux custumes

charter, and since our said lord the present king has granted to those of the same trade of Brabant, and to other foreigners resident in the said city and in various places within the said county, that they shall be quit of taxes and tallages and of all other charges towards our lord the king, and also other resident weavers working in the aforesaid county outside the said city and towns, contrary to the tenor of the charter aforesaid, so that the said weavers of York are so impoverished that they cannot pay their 'farm' [the lease on their holdings]. Therefore the said weavers of York pray our lord the king and his council that he might be pleased to repeal the privilege granted to the foreigners, and briefs of *fieri facias* given to all the weavers of the said county by a new charter, when the said lease is in arrears, or that they may be wholly discharged of the said lease as they are unable to enjoy their privileges.

To our most excellent and most mighty lord the king and his
most wise lords of this present parliament

All the merchants of the Hanse of Germany residing in the realm of England show how the bailiffs and customs officers of Southampton compelled the aforesaid merchants to pay new impositions and customs for divers merchandise contrary to their privileges and liberties of their charter and former usage, therefore the said merchants have sued *from parliament to parliament and from council to council*, to have remedy, whereby your most mighty lord, by the advice of your most wise lords, recently granted a brief in your parliament, under pain of 100 pounds, the which to be forfeit to you, from your Chancery, directed to the said bailiffs and customs officers, to desist from such new impositions and to have the money taken into said Chancery by a certain day, of which nothing has been done, and that they are bound to pay certain customs contained in their charters for cloth of assize, and 3d. per pound for all other narrow cloths, piece of cloth and kerseys not of the assize, as is apparent in various evidences of the Exchequer, duplicated in the Chancery, of your most noble

les ditz merchantz ount amensnez hors lour draps du Royalme saunz impediment tanqz une novel ordinance fuist fait de draps estreites & kerseys par voz officers encountre lour anciens usages & en arerissement de les ditz merchantz & de vostre custume Et q'ils sont grevez en plusours autres pointz comprises en lour chartre en touz voz portz deins vostre Roialme encontre les previleges & liberteez par voz nobles progenitours grauntez et par vous ratifiez & confermiez. Que plese a vostre treshaut & tresredoubtee seignourie par avis de voz tressages seignours en ceste present parlement de charger vostre Chaunceller d'envoier pur les ditz baillifs & custumers a eux charger de deliverer l'argent en lour garde & de surseir de lour maneys prises & d'ordeigner que les ditz merchantz paront amesner hors du Royalme draps estroites pieces & kerseys solonk lours anciens usages & custumes & de assigner en ceste present parlement certeins seignours de examiner lour pointz & privleges comprises en lour chartre es queux les ditz merchantz ount estee grevez & a grauntier ab ditz seignours plein poair de fair remedie en ycelles pur dieux & en ouvre de charitee

6. Petition of Thomas and Margaret de Beauchamp, 1397–99 (National Archives, MS SC 8/221/11037)

In the second half of the 1390s, Thomas and Margaret Beauchamp petitioned Richard II, asking the king to make good on a grant he had apparently made the couple at Windsor. The petition notes that grant included items of bedding and clothing, as well as silverware and kitchen utensils, clothing and equipment for a resident chaplain, and goods ('beins') for Margaret's chamber. This petition relates to the aftermath of the forfeiture on 28 September 1397 of Thomas, formerly the earl of Warwick, who had apparently seized the goods, and thus pre-dates Thomas's restoration in November 1399 (three weeks after Richard II's deposition). The petition further requests carriages, trappings and horses for Margaret. There is no endorsement (see Plate 6).

The transcription and translation are by Mark Chambers. This Anglo-French document contains a number of apparent Middle English compounds of interest ('trussyngbedes', 'paxbrede', 'clothsekkes', 'barhides'). Abbreviations and suspensions have been expanded in square brackets; suggested or uncertain readings are in italics. The Tironian et symbol is represented by an ampersand.

A nostre tresexcellent & tresredoute seignour nostre seignour le Roi

Plese graunt a voz poveres oratours Thomas de Beauchaump & Margarete sa femme deux litz un trussyngbed sys peire de lyntheux · lintheux pur les testes & pees & oraillers covenables ove tout l'apparaill & ceo que a ycell appent & vessell d'argent cest assavioir deux duzein d'esquilles & un duzein de saucers un basyn & un ewer a vostre graciouse ordinance naperie un vestment entier pur un chapellein ovec l'entier apparaill del autere ovesque missale chalice cruetis & paxbrede vessell & autres necessaries pur la quisine ove clothsekkes & barhides et autre de vostre graciouse seignourie graunt al dit Margarete sa vesture pellure & tout l'aparaill & biens pur son corps & sa chambre horspris setz perre & juellis come tresredoute seignour de vostre habundant grace grantastes a Wyndesore devant la parlement et en outre luy graunter au dit dame un chare ovesque un couple de chivalx & un chariot ovesque un autre couple des chivalx ove tout l'apparaill pur les ditz chare chariot & chivalx d'apprest d'aler al meer & revener au roi as costages del dit dames trovant suffissance surete as comisioners q' liu ferrent livere des ditz chare chariot chivalx & apparaill rendre arier au roy et que le eit necessaries el cousyn d'achate

grandfather, in the thirty-fifth year of his reign, by which customs the said merchants have brought their cloths out of the realm without impediment, until a new ordinance was made by your officers, concerning narrow cloths and kerseys, contrary to their ancient usages and to the detriment of the said merchants and of your custom, and they are aggrieved in many other respects set out in their charter, in all your ports within your realm, contrary to the privileges and liberties granted by your noble progenitors and ratified and confirmed by yourself. Might it please your most high and most mighty lordship, by the advice of your most wise lords in this present parliament, to charge your chancellor to send for the said bailiffs and customs officers and command them to deliver the money in their possession and to (stay?) their surities, and to ordain that the said merchants may export from your realm pieces of narrow cloth and kerseys, according to their ancient usage and customs, and to assign in this present parliament certain lords to examine their provisions and privileges set out in their charter, in which the said merchants have been aggrieved, and to grant to the said lords full power to remedy the same, for God and by way of charity.

To our most excellent and most mighty lord, our lord the king

Please give to your poor petitioners Thomas de Beauchamp and Margaret his wife two beds, a travel/trundle bed, six pairs of linens, linens for the head and feet, and pillows suitable for their bed linen as well as goods pertaining to them, and silver vessels, that is two dozen spoons and a dozen saucers, a basin and a pitcher, by your most gracious ordinance, napery, a complete set of vestments for a chaplain with a complete set of furnishings for the altar, as well as a missal, chalice, cruets, and a pax-board, vessels and other necessaries for the kitchen, with cloth sacks, rawhide bags/trunks, and also by your gracious lordship grant the said Margaret her clothing, fur and all that belongs to them and goods for her person and her chamber, excepting *a set* of gems and jewels, as, most mighty lord, by your abundant grace, you granted at Windsor before parliament. And further to grant to them for the said lady a cart together with a pair of horses and a carriage, with another pair of horses with all the trappings for the said cart, carriage and horses on loan [as a prest], to go to sea and return to the king, at the expense of the said lady, offering sufficient guarantee to the commissioners which have delivered the said cart, carriage, horses and trappings, to be returned/repaid to the king, and that which was otherwise necessary to buy for his cousin.

7a. Petition on behalf of Agnes Balle, *c.* 1403 (National Archives, MS SC 8/255/12724)

On 16 August 1403, Henry IV issued a pardon to Agnes Balle, wife of William, after she had been accused of stealing several items of clothing, jewellery, accessories and money from one Alice, wife of the carpenter Richard Belly. The petition extracted here clearly precipitated the king's pardon, which is recorded in the Patent Rolls (see extract 7b below). The petition is written on behalf of Agnes and her husband, and it notes that at the time of its composition, Agnes was being held in the gaol in the parish of All Hallows-the-Less in the ward of Dowgate in London. The petition obviously predates the pardon of 16 August 1403, but by how many weeks or months it is impossible to deduce with any certainty.

The text is written in Anglo-French with a Latin endorsement. The same hand is used throughout. Written to the right of the opening address is an endorsement: 'this petition was granted at Kennington by the king'.

The transcription and translation are by Mark Chambers. There is visible damage to the manuscript, including a vertical tear down the right-hand side, obscuring the entire right-hand side of the text. In the transcription, ellipses in square brackets at the end of each line indicate lacunae caused by the tear. Abbreviated forms for 'price' (Anglo-French *pris/price*; Latin *precium, pretium, precii*) are indicated with standard abbreviation and inverted commas (the *de* following indicates the sense 'priced at', 'valued at', 'worth'). The abbreviation *d.* indicates Anglo-French *deners* / Latin *denarii* (pence) while the abbreviation *s.* indicates 'shillings'. Presumed or uncertain readings are offered in italics in the translation.

ista billa concessa fuit apud Kenyngton' pro dominum Regen[…]
A n*ost*re tresexcellent & tressoverein s*eig*nour le Roy

Supplie humblement v*ost*re povere oratrice Annes la feme a William Balle q*ue* come ele est enditz de ceole gele en l[…] quart en la p*ar*ishe de toutz seintz le petit en la garde de dowegate de londres une toge de colo*ur* de blue furrez […] kertill de russet pric' de xij d. un smok pric' de vj. d. un broche d'argent dorez pric' de xij d. vne burse pric'[…] pric' ij d. deux kercheves pric' xij d. vn chaperon pric' xij d. & iij s. iiij d. en monoie nombrez d'une A[…] illoeqes esteantz felonement embla pleise a v*ost*re hautesse & t*re*s graciouse seigour de v*ost*re grace esp*ec*iale grantier a d[…] avaunditz & ceo p*our* dieu & en oevre de charite

7b. Record of pardon issued to Agnes Balle by the king on the Patent Rolls, 16 August 1403 (National Archives, MS C 66/369, memb. 6)

This previously unpublished document containing Agnes Balle's royal pardon is part of the voluminous record of the Patent Rolls. These were previously held in the Chancery and are now in the National Archives. The document is written in heavily abbreviated Latin; it is obviously the official response to the petition above. It allows us not only to compare the Latin items of vocabulary used here with their Anglo-French counterparts in the petition, but also to reconstruct some of those missing or damaged parts of the petition with the details recorded in the Patent Rolls. A summary is given in *CPR Hen. IV*: 4 Henry IV, 2.265.

The membrane contains fifteen separate items of business, the record of Alice and William's pardon coming ninth. The identifying summary 'De predonacione Balle' (concerning the pardon of [Agnes] Balle) is written in the left margin next to the item.

[*This petition was granted at Kennington by the king*]
To our most excellent and most sovereign lord the king

The poor petitioner Agnes, wife of William Balle, humbly requests, that as she is held (indicted) in the gaol in . . . quarter in the parish of All Hallows-the-Less in the ward of Dowgate of London, an overgarment of blue cloth, a furred (lined or trimmed) . . . kirtle of russet worth 12d. a smock worth 6d. a brooch of gilded silver with silver worth 12d., a purse worth . . . worth 2d., two kerchiefs worth 12d. a hood worth 12d., and 3s. 4d. in money from a certain *Alice* . . . these things being feloniously stolen, please your highness and most gracious lord, of your special grace to grant to (*the said* . . .) aforesaid, and this for God and by way of charity.

The transcription and translation are by Mark Chambers. There is a fold down the middle of the text obscuring individual words in each line. Latin abbreviations and suspensions and suggested or uncertain readings in the transcription are indicated in italics. The Tironian *et* symbol is represented by an ampersand.

R*ex* Om*nibus* Ballivis & fidelibus suis ad quos &c. sal*ute*m. Sciatis q*uo*d cum Agnes ux*or* William Balle ind*icata*ta existat de eo q*uo*d ipsa in vigilia Om*nium* S*anctorum* anno regni n*o*stri quarto in parochia Om*nium* S*anctorum* in Warda de Dowegate London' unam togam blodij coloris furratam cum cuniculis p*re*cii [...]x solidor*um* & octo denarior*um* unu*m* kyrtyll de russeto p*re*cii duodecim denarior*um* unam camisiam p*re*cii sex denarior*um* unu*m* monile argenti de aurat' p*re*cii duodecim denarior*um* unam bursam p*re*cii qua*t*uor denarior*um* septem anulos auri p*re*cii vigniti solidor*um* unu*m* cordon' p*re*cii duor*um* denarior*um* duo velamina p*re*cii duodecim denarior*um* unu*m* capucinum p*re*cii duodecim denarior*um* & tres solidos & qu*a*tuor denarios in pecunia nu*m*erata cuiusdam Alicie ux*or*is Ric*ar*di Belly carpenter ibide*m* existencia felonice furata fuit Nos de g*ra*tia n*o*stra speciali p*er*donavim*u*s eidem Agneti sectam pacis n*o*stre que ad[...]s v*er*sus ipsam p*er*tinet p*ro* feloniis sup*ra*dictis unde ind*icta*ta rettata vel appellata existit aceciam waviar' si qua in ipsam hiis occ*asion*ibus fuerit p*ro*mulgata & firmam pacem n*o*stram ei inde concedim*u*s, ita tamen q*uo*d stet recto in curia n*o*stra, si quis v*er*sus eam loqui volu*er*it de p*er*missis seu alique p*er*missor*um* in cuius & c' T*este* R*e*ge apud Westm' xvj die augusti

8. Schedule of bales of cloth attached to a petition, *c.* 1418–19? (National Archives, MS SC 8/302/15059)

The petition to which this schedule is attached (National Archives, MS SC 8/302/15058) is similar in theme to the petition at Extract 5 above (on the merchants of the Hanse) and proves an interesting indictment of the London customs officials in the late 1410s. It relates how a group of Venetian merchants residing in London were apparently taxed twice on the same shipment of cloth. One of the merchants, named as Robert Cunteryn, had arranged for six bales on a ship to Sandwich to be loaded onto a Venetian galley at the port. These bales were ultimately unable to be accommodated on the galley and were returned to London, resulting in customs on the bales being demanded a second time. The petitioners requested that the customs officials desist charging this second round of customs duty.

The schedule attached to the petition is transcribed below (SC 8/302/15059). The schedule records several interesting types of material, including pieces of 'Gildeford', a type of cloth originally produced or sold in the town of Guildford in Surrey from the fourteenth century and popular with the Italian merchants residing in England in the fifteenth century (Bradley 1994: pp. 61–2 and note 53, p. 75). Its quality was prescribed by statute by Richard II in 1391 (Given-Wilson 2005: 'Richard II: Parliament of November 1391', item 16). The schedule remains a brief but vivid snapshot of some lexical items from the early-fifteenth-century London cloth trade and a fascinating artefact of medieval technical language.

The transcription and translation are by Mark Chambers. The small rectangular manuscript contains eight lines of highly abbreviated, quickly written text, listing the contents of the bales of cloth mentioned in the petition in a Latin matrix language. Some individual characters are difficult to distinguish. Lines 7–8 were scribbled some time later and are only partially legible. Standard abbreviation and suspension symbols have been expanded in italics (the 9-shaped symbol representing *-us*, the backwards hook representing *-er* and the 4-shaped symbol representing

The king to all his bailiffs and his lieges, etc. greetings. Know that whereas Agnes, wife of William Balle, *stands accused*, on the eve of All Saints in the fourth year of our reign, in the parish of All Saints in the ward of Dowgate, London, of feloniously stealing a blue coloured tunic (*toga*) furred with rabbits, worth 10 [?, *CPR* says 6] shillings and 8 pence, a kirtle of russet worth 12 pence, a chemise worth 6 pence, a gilded silver necklace worth 12 pence, a purse worth 4 pence, seven gold rings worth 20 shillings, a 'cordon' worth 2 pence, two veils worth 12 pence, a hood worth 12 pence, and 3 shillings, 4 pence in money of a certain Alice, wife of Richard Belly, carpenter, we, of our special grace, pardon the same Alice the liability to prosecution for breach of peace which pertains to us against her on account of the aforesaid felonies for which she stands indicted, adjudged or accused, or of any female outlawry, if such were proclaimed against her on those grounds, we grant her our lasting peace on this matter, provided, however, that she will stand to right in our court if anyone wishes to implead them on that matter or in any other matter. In testimony of which, etc. Witnessed by the king at Westminster, 16th day of August.

-rum). Other terminal abbreviation symbols are indicated by inverted comma. Uncertain readings are in italics, while illegible text is represented by ellipses in square brackets.

numerus ij	lx dusseyns panni del' [...]iest l pec' de Gildeford cont' xxxviij virg'
numerus v	xxvj pec' de Gildeford cont' ix^c xx viij virg'
numerus xij	xxx pec' del [...]iest cont' lx duoden'
numerus xxij	xvi pec' de Gildeford cont' v^c xl virg'
numerus xxv	xxiij pec' de Gildeford cont' vij^c lxxx virg'
numerus xxvj	ciij pec' strict' pann' d'essex cont' cx duod

collect' Subsidy tri' solid*orum* de *dolio* & [...] de libra
[...] per[...] cust [...]

9. Petition of the haberdashers and hatters of London, 1448 (National Archives, MS SC 8/307/15336)

This petition on behalf of the haberdashers and hatters of London asks the king to annul letters patent he had granted to the guild of 'hurers', otherwise known as the 'cappers'. Apparently the letters, which were being kept unsealed in the Chancery, guaranteed the cappers the right of search of all those who made or sold headwear within the city ('hures bonetz and cappes withinne þe said citee') and within a four-mile radius. The petition suggests that this right of search gave the cappers a powerful monopoly, to their benefit alone, driving up prices and hurting the livelihood of the 3000 poor people who made their living around the city in the same trade ('pore peple ... þat have ben dayly living therby'). The haberdashers and hatters state that the cappers obtained these letters by deceit and false evidence which was 'colourably' conveyed, and they ask the king to instruct his chancellor to return the letters to the king so that they may be annulled.

The petition is written in Middle English rather than Anglo-French. Middle English petitions began to appear by the 1430s, and by the middle of the century Middle English had replaced Anglo-French as standard (Dodd 2007: 291). Of course words of Anglo-French derivation – particularly legal terms – continued to appear in such documents (*suppliantz* in line 7 for example). There are several late-medieval cloth and clothing lexical items, especially occupational titles (*haberdasshers, hatters, hurers*). While the occupation title *hurer* (derived from Anglo-French and Old French *hure*, cap) was not necessarily obsolete by this period, it is qualified in the text here as referring to a 'capper' ('hurers other wise clepud cappers').

The transcription and translation are by Mark Chambers. The text of the manuscript is written in twenty even lines with a large margin to the top, left and bottom. There is no endorsement. The manuscript has a large lacuna in the upper-left section, obscuring much of the first five lines of text including the opening address. Missing or illegible text is indicated here with ellipses in square brackets. The few abbreviations and suspensions have been expanded and suggested or uncertain readings are given in italics.

S[...] [...] in youre citee of London of haberdasshers and hatters that where þe hurers other wise cle*pu*d cappers enfran*ch*ised in the sa[...] [...]*ers* to have þe serche of alle them that selle or make hures bonetz and cappes withinne þe said citee and iiii mile aboute þe s[...] [*di*]sceytes used in the werking and sale of suche hures bonetz and cappes with many other suggestions conteyned in thair said [...] [...] *is* youre noble Reame assembled in your said two parliementz by experience and naturell reason considering wel that þeir said

no. 2   60 dozen cloths *del'...iest*, one piece of Guildford containing 38 yards
no. 5   26 pieces of Guildford containing 928 yards
no. 12   30 pieces *del'...iest* containing 60 dozens
no. 22   16 pieces of Guildford containing 540 yards
no. 25   23 pieces of Guildford containing 780 yards
no. 26   103 pieces of straight cloth of Essex containing 105 dozens

collect' subsidy ... shillings *per tun* and ... *in the pound*
... p(er...) cust...

S[...] [...] in your city of London, of haberdasshers and hatters, that where the 'hurers', otherwise called cappers, enfranchised in the sa[...] [...]ers to have the search of all of those that sell or make hats, bonnets and caps within the said city and for 4 miles around the s[...] *d*iceits used in the manufacture and sale of such hats, bonnets and caps, with many other suggestions contained in their said [...] [...] *is* youre noble realm assembled in your said two parliaments by experience and natural reason, considering well that their said [...] [...]

[…] […] owne singuler availle and to grete hurt of the *comm*one people of this youre said Reame lete *c*rosse the said bille and wold not graunte to þer p*r*edices[…] and also þe mair and ald*er*men of your said citee have called the said hurers and other persones expert and connyng in the same craft by fore *h*em and […] and alle thair said suggestions hard and examined so that they have clevery conceyved and understande as youre said suppliantz trust that þe said sute of the said hurers is only for their owne singuler ava*i*lle and to grete hurt of your people and also þat þeir suggestions are but feyned and coloured knowing well amonge all other charges þat þer ben iij m^c of pore peple within þe said citee and iiij mile aboute it þat ben called werkers of the said hures bonetz and cappes þat have ben dayly living therby the which if the said hurerz had the serche o*ver* hem shuld goo abegging and p*er*issh for defaute and no*n* shulde werke þe said hures bonetz and cappes but such as þei wold assigne þe whiche were ful like to be ful fewe in nombre not able to serve the x^{the} part of þe people so þat by reson it shuld cause grete derthe of hures bonetz and cappes for every hure bonette and cappe wherof is now grete plente and easy price shuld be þanne st*o*rd and of double price or more than þei be of now neverthelasse the said hurers assayeng alle þe wayes and menes þat þei cowde to have þeir entent singulerly to their owne availl and to þe grete hurt of your peple as above have sued now late by billes unto your highnesse to have þe said serch shewing you colourably the disceytes and suggestions aforesaid and nought enfourmyng you of the trouthe wherupon at þat time it liked your said highnesse to graunte þerin youre free patent*es* to have þe said serche according to thier said bill the which free patent*es* are writen heng yet in your chauncl*er*ye nowt seled wherefore please it to youre roiall maieste of youre speciall grace tenderly to considre þe p*r*omisses and ther upon in *e*ase and availl of your people to comande your chanceller of England and keper of youre prive seel by your gracious l*et*t*r*es under your signet to sende unto youre noble presence all such evidences aswel the said l*et*t*r*es patentz and billes subscribed with youre gracious hand*es* as other writing*es* and there to be cancelled and anulled at þe Reverence of God and in weye of charite

own singular avail and to great hurt of the common people of this your said realm, *repeal?* the said bill, and would not graunt to their *predecessors* [...] and also the mayor and aldermen of your said city, have summoned the said hurers and other people expert and skilled in the same craft before them, and [...] and all their said suggestions heard and examined so that they have cleverly conceived and understand, as your said suppliants believe, that the said suit of the said hurers is only for their own singular avail and to great hurt of your people, and also that their suggestions are feigned and coloured, knowing well among all other charges that there are 3000 poor people within the said city and for 4 miles around, that are called workers of the said hats, bonnets and caps and that make their daily living therby, the which, if the said hurers had the search of them, should be forced into begging and perish for default, and none of them should manufacture the said hats, bonnets and caps but only those they would licence, the which are likely to be very few in number not able to serve a tenth part of the people, so that by reason it shuld cause a great shortage of hats, bonnets and caps, for every hat, bonet and cap which is now in great supply and of a reasonable price would then be stored and of double the price or more than they are now. Nevertheless, the said hurers, attempting all the ways and means that they can to have their entent singularly to their own avail, and to the great hurt of your people as above, have lately sued, by bills unto your highness, to have the said search, showing you colourfully the deceits and suggestions aforesaid and not informing you of the truth, whereupon at that time it pleased your said highness to grant therein your free patents, so that they may have the said search according to their said bill, the same free patents which are written and still hanging in your Chancery, unsealed. Thus may it please your royal majesty, of your special grace, to consider diligently the promises, and thereupon for the ease and help of your people, to command your Chancellor of England and Keeper of your Privy Seal, by your gracious letters, under your signet, to send to your noble presence all such evidences including the said letters patent and bills subscribed with your gracious handwriting as well as other writings, and to have them cancelled and annulled, for reverence of God and by way of charity.

CHAPTER VII

Epic and Romance

INTRODUCTION

Clothing in epic is, as one might expect, mainly concerned with armour, though details about that are found in romances as well. Clothing in romance fulfils a number of functions, some conventional, some less so. One of its purposes is to define expectations associated with class and gender: we may note the costly garments offered to Gawain at Bertilak's castle in *Sir Gawain and the Green Knight*:

> And þenne a meré mantyle watz on þat mon cast
> Of a broun bleeaunt, enbrauded ful ryche
> And fayre furred wythinne with fellez of þe best,
> Alle of ermyn in erde, his hode of þe same (878–81)

In *Lay le Freine*, before Le Freine's mother leaves her by a convent, she takes

> a riche baudekine
> That hir lord brought from Costentine
> And lapped the litel maiden therin (137–9)

and fastens a gold ring to her arm by a silk thread in order that those who find the baby will see that she comes from a noble family ('nee de bone gent', 121–34, as Marie de France has it). Clothes often feature in lists of gifts signifying the wealth and generosity of the giver: Degrevant, for example,

> lovede well almosdede,
> Powr men to cloth and fede (81–2)

Launfal, too,

> gaf gyftys largelyche,
> Gold and sylver and clothes ryche' (28–9)

When poverty descends on Launfal, Arthur's nephews abandon him, saying

> 'Syr, our robes beth torent,
> And your tresour ys all yspent' (145–6)

The importance of dress and textiles varies widely even within narratives telling all or parts of the same stories. Unlike the versions of the Constance story in the *Vita Duorum Offarum*, Trivet's *Anglo-Norman Chronicle*, the English version of the *Gesta Romanorum*, Chaucer's *Man of Law's Tale*, and Gower's *Confessio Amantis*, the narrative in *Emaré* is propelled by an object, an elaborately worked cloth, the gift of the king of Sicily to the emperor, Emaré's father, and subsequently, in the form of a robe, a gift from the emperor to his daughter. Particular objects such as these appear in so many Breton lays that they are considered a defining element of the genre (Hopkins 2000: 71): when Le Freine gives up her embroidered cloth, she unknowingly prepares the way for her mother to reclaim her.

Items of clothing also function symbolically with occasional overtones of the supernatural in romance narratives. In *Sir Launfal*, after Tryamour's supernatural powers have brought him wealth, Launfal holds feasts for the poor and distressed and buys horses and clothing. When he betrays Tryamour by boasting about her, he loses everything and

> Hys armur, that was whyt as flour,
> Hyt becom of blak colour (776–7)

In connection with this, we may note that the moral status of characters in medieval drama is sometimes signalled by the black or white costumes described in scripts and account books (Twycross 1983: 32). In *Sir Gawain and the Green Knight*, Gawain refuses the ring he is offered by Lady Bertilak but cannot resist the gift of her girdle when she tells him of its magical properties:

> For quat gome so is gorde with þis grene lace,
> While he hit hade hemely halched aboute,
> Þer is no haþel vnder heuen tohewe hym þat myȝt
> For he myȝt not be slayn for slyȝt vpon erþe (1851–4).

TEXTS

The corpus of romance texts of the medieval period includes a number of poems in which textiles and garments are treated with a perhaps unexpected level of detail and precision. Several of these texts formed the starting point for this chapter, chiefly *Emaré*, *Sir Launfal*, *Sir Degrevant* and *Sir Gawain and the Green Knight*. The former two may be seen to exist within families of romances, which we have labelled the 'Constance Group' and the 'Launfal Group', and each family includes versions written in Latin and Anglo-French found in British manuscripts. *Sir Degrevant*, as has been noted, is an orphan, a composite romance which does not fit into the families of subject matter found in courtly romances (Davenport 2000: 111). It does, however, include detailed descriptions of furnishings and accoutrements of the bedroom of the earl's daughter, Melidor, which mean that it is particularly interesting for the study of the vocabulary of textiles in Britain in this period. We have also included two texts which were chosen partly for period (in order to include something from the corpus of Old English), partly for genre (in order to include an epic) and partly because of the vivid depictions of the arming of the hero. As may be seen, the lexicon of cloth and clothing they contain in addition to the descriptions of armour turned out to be unexpectedly rich and so they seem worthy bookends to this chapter.

THE LEXIS OF CLOTH AND CLOTHING

We have noted the precision in the terminology for cloth and clothing in many of these romances amounting almost to the appropriation of a technolect for poetic purposes. In *Lanval*, the women encountered by the hero wear garments which are 'laciees estreitement' (tightly laced). This detail indicates the way in which shifts in fashion in the twelfth century find their way into the fictions of the time. We know that belts and laces tightened loose fabrics closely around the upper body (Harris 1998: 89; Smith 2008: 96) and this period saw an increase in the importance attached to the proper fit of garments: 'estroit vestu' (in a close-fitting robe) or 'menu cosu' (stitched up tightly) are among the prime epithets describing the dress of heroines in the romances, lays and *chansons de geste* of the period (Harris 1998: 90).

Sir Degrevant includes a number of what appear to be technical terms from the fields of architecture and food as well as clothing, which are otherwise recorded only in documents like wills, inventories and accounts of building works; for example, the word 'nevyn', probably meaning 'ornamental clasp'. The poem also includes a number of vocabulary items which are found in poetry only in *Sir Degrevant* and one or two alliterative texts: for example 'bagges' (badges), 'jesseraund' (a piece of armour of mail and padded cloths), and 'pallwork' (work in costly/purple cloth) (see Davenport 2000: 117). This kind of technolect approach is also found in *Sir Gawain and the Green Knight*, in which a number of the vocabulary items in the semantic field of cloth and clothing appear to be attested in English only in this text; for example, 'tolouse' (some kind of high quality fabric from Toulouse, France); and two terms signifying the wrapping of cloth round some part of the body, 'enfoubled' (covered or veiled) and 'chymbled' (wrapped up), for which the poem supplies the only citations in the *Middle English Dictionary*. Similarly 'toreted' (edged, ornamented; perhaps veiled) and 'treleted' (latticed, interlaced, meshed) are only attested in *Sir Gawain and the Green Knight*.

Some of the romance texts mingle realistic, even technical, detail with the stuff of fantasy, as W. A. Davenport comments in connection with the description of Melidor's bed in *Sir Degrevant*. The bed is an object of art: highly coloured in azure, with a bright border, green parrots, escutcheons, gold discs and fleurs-de-lis, and adorned with the love-story of Ydoyne and Amadas, silken sheets, an embroidered quilt with tassels, silken pillows with Wesphalian crystal ornaments, and curtains with cords of mermaid hair (Davenport 2000: 124). Similarly, in *Emaré*, the heroine's robe has been described by several scholars as having magical powers: Laskaya and Salisbury (1995), for example, call it 'the enchanted robe' and point to the emperor's reaction to it as

> 'Sertes, thys ys a fayry,
> Or ellys a vanyté!' (104–5)

This response is swiftly explained by the narrator, however, as being due to the glittering of the jewels, which cover the cloth so thickly that the emperor cannot see the material (97–101) (Hopkins 2000: 73). *Emaré* can be seen as being rooted in the everyday matters of court life in its inclusion of the detail of the needlework Emaré is taught to do in childhood, 'Golde and sylke forto sewe' (58–9); it comes in useful when, in exile, she teaches others: 'She tawghte hem to sewe and marke' (376), and when she finds herself in Rome, we learn that she 'sewed syke werk in bour' (730). Hopkins suggests that the poem 'repeatedly underlines the correlation between Emaré's gracious manners and her ability to sew, each characterised as an acquired accomplishment befitting her birth' (2000: 74). It is not just the sewing, but the sewing of gold and silk, both befitting to high birth. This commingling of precise, technical vocabulary for the details of dress and textiles and symbolic, occasionally magical properties, is one of the elements that accounts for the particular atmosphere created in the fictions of the medieval period.

EXTRACTS FROM EPIC AND ROMANCE TEXTS

1. *Beowulf*

Beowulf is a heroic poem written in Old English, which survives in a single manuscript, dated between *c.* 950 and *c.* 1050. Its subject matter largely concerns aristocratic warfare and fights between the hero and monsters, so the garments that are mentioned are almost exclusively battle-gear – mail coats and helmets. The boar-ornamented helmets and mail coats of interlinked rings belong to a seventh-century tradition, as demonstrated by archaeological evidence. Only one apparently non-metal garment is mentioned in the poem; that is the *hrægl* given to Beowulf by Queen Wealhtheow. Unfortunately *hrægl* is the most non-specific of Old English garment terms, so although the word in this context is sometimes translated 'cloak' it could be another garment, or merely a length of cloth; most likely the poet deliberately leaves it to the audience's imagination to conjure up something rich and desirable as is often the case in this text. The poet mentions personal jewellery, arm-rings, neck-rings and clasps, emphasising their opulence and value, but again without descriptive detail. Other textiles mentioned are woven wall-hangings, and a standard, both evidently decorated with gold; and the sail of Beowulf's ship. The text is taken from E. V. K. Dobbie (ed.), *Beowulf and Judith*, The Anglo-Saxon Poetic Records, 4 (London and New York, Columbia University Press, 1953). The translation is by Gale R. Owen-Crocker.

Beowulf has travelled from Geatland to Denmark to defeat the monster Grendel, which has been ravaging the Danish court for twelve years. The Danish coastguard challenges Beowulf and his men but is impressed by their appearance. He particularly notices their armour, but recognises that Beowulf has a personal magnificence that is not simply created by splendid equipment.

'Hwæt syndon ge   searohæbbendra,
byrnum werede,   þe þus brontne ceol
ofer lagustræte   lædan cwomon,
hider ofer holmas?   * * * le wæs
endesæta,   ægwearde heold,
þe on land Dena   laðra nænig
mid scipherge   sceðþan ne meahte.
No her cuðlicor   cuman ongunnon
lindhæbbende;   ne ge leafnesword
guðfremmendra   gearwe ne wisson,
maga gemedu.   Næfre ic maran geseah
eorla ofer eorþan   ðonne is eower sum,
secg on searwum;   nis þæt seldguma,
wæpnum geweorðad,   næfne him his wlite leoge,
ænlic ansyn.   Nu ic eower sceal
frumcyn witan,   ær ge fyr heonan,
leasceaweras,   on land Dena
furþur feran.   Nu ge feorbuend,
mereliðende,   minne gehyraþ
anfealdne geþoht: Ofost is selest
to gecyðanne   hwanan eowre cyme syndon'.   (237–57)

'What are you armour-bearing men, protected by mail coats, who in this way came bringing a steep ship over the sea-road, here over the waters. [For a long time] I have been coastguard, kept watch over the sea, so that no hostile people might raid the land of the Danes with a naval force. Never have shield-bearing warriors come here more openly; nor do you know clearly [that you have] permission of the warriors, the consent of the kinsmen. I have never seen a greater nobleman over the earth than one of you is, warrior in armour; that is not a retainer, made splendid by weapons, unless his appearance, his beautiful form, is deceptive. Now I must know your origin, before you go far from here, journey further into the land of the Danes as spies. Now you foreigners, sea-voyagers, hear my plain thought: it is best to make known speedily from where you are come.' [...]

As they proceed to the king's hall the poet describes their battle-garments, boar images over the cheekpieces of the helmets and shining mail coats, which chink as they walk along. They place their shields and spears down peacefully, giving the poet the opportunity to describe them, conventionally. The shields are round, of lime wood. The spears are of ash wood.

      Eorforlic scionon
ofer hleorberan gehroden golde,
fah ond fyrheard . . . (303–5a)

      Guðbyrne scan
heard hondlocen, hringiren scir
song in searwum, þa hie to sele furðum
in hyra gryregeatwum gangan cwomon.
Setton sæmeþe side scyldas,
rondas regnhearde, wið þæs recedes weal,
bugon þa to bence. Byrnan hringdon,
guðsearo gumena; garas stodon,
sæmanna searo, samod ætgædere,
æscholt ufan græg; wæs se irenþreat
wæpnum gewurþad. (321b–331a)

Beowulf assures the king of Denmark that he has come to kill the monster that is attacking his hall. However, if he should die in the attempt, he asks that his mail coat, an heirloom from his grandfather Hrethel, be returned to his own king, Hygelac. The mail coat is of such exceptional workmanship that it is attributed to the legendary Germanic smith, Weland.

'. . . Onsend Higelace, gif mec hild nime,
beaduscruda betst, þæt mine breost wereð
hrægla selest; þæt is Hrædlan laf,
Welandes geweorc . . .' (452–5)

Beowulf tells how his mail coat protected him in a previous encounter against sea monsters.

'. . . Wæs merefixa mod onhrered;
þær me wið laðum licsyrce min,
heard, hondlocen, helpe gefremede,
beadohrægl broden on breostum læg
golde gegyrwed. Me to grunde teah
fah feondscaða, fæste hæfde
grim on grape; hwæþre me gyfeþe wearð
þæt ic aglæcan orde geræhte,
hildebille; heaþoræs fornam
mihtig meredeor þurh mine hand . . .' (549–58)

In the Danish royal hall, Beowulf takes off his armour and dispenses with his sword in preparation for his encounter with the monster Grendel, since the monster does not fight with weapons. He lies down to wait on the bedding which is supplied in the hall.

Boar images, decorated with gold, shone over their cheek-guards, shining and hardened by fire [. . .]. The battle garment shone, hard, hand-locked, the bright ring-iron sang in their armour when they came advancing towards the hall in their terrible gear. The men, weary of the sea, placed their wide shields, round, wondrously strong, against the wall of the building. Then they moved to the bench. Their mail coats rang, the battle armour of the men. Their spears, weapons of the seamen, stood all together, ash-wood, grey above; the iron-equipped troop was distinguished by its weapons.

'. . . If battle takes me, send Hygelac the best of battle clothes, the greatest of garments, which protects my breast; it is an heirloom of Hrethel, the work of Weland . . .'

'. . . The minds of the sea fishes became aroused; my body shirt, hard, hand-linked, gave me help there against the hateful creatures. The woven battle-garment, adorned with gold, lay on my breast. A fierce enemy-ravager dragged me to the bottom, the grim creature had me fast in its grip; nevertheless, it was granted to me that I should reach the monster with my point, with my battle-sword; the rush of battle carried off the mighty sea-beast through my hand. [. . .]'

Ða he him of dyde isernbyrnan,
helm of hafelan, sealde his hyrsted sweord,
irena cyst, ombihtþegne,
ond gehealdan het hildegeatwe. (671–4)

Hylde hine þa heaþodeor, hleorbolster onfeng
eorles andwlitan, ond hine ymb monig
snellic særinc selereste gebeah. (688–90)

Beowulf defeats the monster Grendel. After his victory the hall, which is called 'Heorot' (Hart), is decorated with golden hangings, and Beowulf is rewarded by the king of Denmark.

Ða wæs haten hreþe Heort innanweard
folmum gefrætwod. Fela þæra wæs,
wera ond wifa, þe þæt winreced,
gestsele gyredon. Goldfag scinon
web æfter wagum, wundorsiona fela
segca gehwylcum þara þe on swylc starað. (991–6)
[...]
Forgeaf þa Beowulfe bearn Healfdenes
segen gyldenne sigores to leane;
hroden hildecumbor, helm ond byrnan,
mære maðþumsweord manige gesawon
beforan beorn beran. Beowulf geþah
ful on flette; no he þære feohgyfte
for sceotendum scamigan ðorfte.
Ne gefrægn ic freondlicor feower madmas
golde gegyrede gummana fela
in ealobence oðrum gesellan.
Ymb þæs helmes hrof heafodbeorge
wirum bewunden walu utan heold,
þæt him fela laf frecne ne meahton
scurheard sceþðan, þonne scyldfreca
ongean gramum gangan scolde.
Heht ða eorla hleo eahta mearas
fætedhleore on flet teon,
in under eoderas. Þara anum stod
sadol searwum fah, since gewurþad;
þæt wæs hildesetl heahcyninges,
ðonne sweorda gelac sunu Healfdenes
efnan wolde. Næfre on ore læg
widcuþes wig, ðonne walu feollon.
Ond ða Beowulfe bega gehwæþres
eodor Ingwina onweald geteah,
wigca ond wæpna, het hine wel brucan. (1020–45)

Then he took off his iron mail coat, [and] the helmet from his head, gave his ornamented sword, the choicest of iron weapons, to an attendant, and commanded him to look after the battle-gear. [...] Then the warrior brave in battle lay down; a cheek-pillow received the nobleman's face; and around him many a bold sea-warrior sank on to his bed in the hall. [...]

Then it was quickly commanded that Heorot should be decorated inside with hands. There were many of them, men and women, who adorned the wine-hall, the guest-hall. Gold-decorated textiles shone along the walls, many wonderful sights for each of the men who stare on such things. [...] Then the son of Halfdane gave Beowulf a golden standard as a reward for victory. Many saw the decorated battle-banner, helmet and mail coat, a famous treasure-sword carried before the man. Beowulf drank from a cup on the floor; he had no need to be ashamed in front of the [arrow]-shooters because of the gift-giving [i.e. he had reason to be proud of the rewards he received]. I have never learned of many men more generously giving to others at the ale-bench four [such] treasures, decorated with gold. Around the top of the helmet, as a protection for the head, outside, clung a crest, wound with wires so that the many perilous leavings of the battlestorm might not harm him, when the shield-warrior has to advance against the enemy. Then the protector of warriors commanded eight horses with [gold]-plated bridles to be led onto the floor, into the enclosures. On one of them stood a saddle, decorated with skill, adorned with treasure. It was the battle seat of the high king, when the son of Halfdane wished to perform the play of swords. Never did the very famous warrior fail at the [battle-]front, when slaughtered men fell. And then the protector of the Ingwine granted control of both, steeds and weapons, to Beowulf, commanded him to use them well. [...]

The minstrel sings of the Fight at Finnsburg, when armour failed to protect warriors and was burned on the funeral pyre with their corpses.

>Ad wæs geæfned   ond icge gold
>ahæfen of horde.   Herescyldinga
>betst beadorinca   wæs on bæl gearu.
>Æt þæm ade wæs   eþgesyne
>swatfah syrce,   swyn ealgylden,
>eofer irenheard,   æþeling manig
>wundum awyrded;   sume on wæle crungon.   (1107–13)

Queen Wealhtheow rewards Beowulf and hopes her gifts will inspire him to be loyal to her young sons; though the poet predicts that the king of the Geats will be killed wearing the neck ring she gives.

>Him wæs ful boren   ond freondlaþu
>wordum bewægned,   ond wunden gold
>estum geeawed,   earmreade twa,
>hrægl ond hringas,   healsbeaga mæst
>þara þe ic on foldan   gefrægen hæbbe.   (1192–6)

>Þone hring hæfde   Higelac Geata,
>nefa Swertinges,   nyhstan siðe,
>siðþan he under segne   sinc ealgode,
>wælreaf werede;   hyne wyrd fornam,
>syþðan he for wlenco   wean ahsode,
>fæhðe to Frysum.   He þa frætwe wæg,
>eorclanstanas   ofer yða ful,
>rice þeoden;   he under rande gecranc.
>Gehwearf þa in Francna fæþm   feorh cyninges,
>breostgewædu   ond se beah somod;
>wyrsan wigfrecan   wæl reafedon
>æfter guðsceare,   Geata leode,
>hreawic heoldon.   Heal swege onfeng.
>Wealhðeo maþelode,   heo fore þæm werede spræc:
>'Bruc ðisses beages,   Beowulf leofa,
>hyse, mid hæle,   ond þisses hrægles neot,
>þeodgestreona,   ond geþeoh tela,
>cen þec mid cræfte   ond þyssum cnyhtum wes
>lara liðe . . .'   (1202–20)

The warriors rest after their triumph.

>Eode þa to setle.   Þær wæs symbla cyst;
>druncon win weras.   Wyrd ne cuþon,
>geosceaft grimme,   swa hit agangen wearð

The pyre was prepared and [?] gold brought up from the hoard. The best battle warrior of the war-Scyldings was ready on the pyre. On the pyre was easily seen the blood-stained shirt, the swine all-golden, iron-hard boar, many a nobleman destroyed by wounds; certain ones perished in the slaughter. [. . .]

The cup was borne to him and friendship offered with words, and twisted gold presented willingly: two arm ornaments, a garment and rings [including] the greatest of neck rings which I have ever learned of on earth. [. . .] Hygelac of the Geats, Swerting's nephew, had that ring on his last expedition after he defended treasure, protected the booty of slaughter, under [his] banner. Fate took him after he looked for trouble, out of arrogance, a feud against the Frisians. Then he, powerful prince, wore that ornament, the precious stones, over the cup of waves [i.e. overseas]. He perished under his shield. Then the life of the king, his breast-garment and the ring together passed into the power of the Franks; inferior warriors plundered the slain after the carnage, the people of the Geats occupied the place of corpses. The hall became noisy. Wealhtheow made a speech, she spoke in front of the company: 'Take this ring, dear Beowulf, enjoy it with good luck, young man, and make use of this garment, treasures of the [Danish] people, and thrive well, brave in your skill; and be kind in your advice to these boys. [. . .]'

Then she went to her seat. That was the choicest of feasts; men drank wine. They did not know fate, grim destiny, as it came to many of

eorla manegum,   syþðan æfen cwom
ond him Hroþgar gewat   to hofe sinum,
rice to ræste.   Reced weardode
unrim eorla,   swa hie oft ær dydon.
Bencþelu beredon;   hit geondbræded wearð
beddum ond bolstrum.   Beorscealca sum
fus ond fæge   fletræste gebeag.
Setton him to heafdon   hilderandas,
bordwudu beorhtan;   þær on bence wæs
ofer æþelinge   yþgesene
heaþosteapa helm,   hringed byrne,
þrecwudu þrymlic.   (1232–46a)

A second monster, mother of Grendel, has taken them all by surprise and killed a man. Beowulf prepares to fight the monster in her underwater lair.

                Gyrede hine Beowulf
eorlgewædum,   nalles for ealdre mearn.
Scolde herebyrne   hondum gebroden,
sid ond searofah,   sund cunnian,
seo ðe bancofan   beorgan cuþe,
þæt him hildegrap   hreþre ne mihte,
eorres inwitfeng,   aldre gesceþðan;
ac se hwita helm   hafelan werede,
se þe meregrundas   mengan scolde,
secan sundgebland   since geweorðad,
befongen freawrasnum,   swa hine fyrndagum
worhte wæpna smið,   wundrum teode,
besette swinlicum,   þæt hine syðþan no
brond ne beadomecas   bitan ne meahton.
Næs þæt þonne mætost   mægenfultuma
þæt him on ðearfe lah   ðyle Hroðgares;
wæs þæm hæftmece   Hrunting nama.
þæt wæs an foran   ealdgestreona;
ecg wæs iren,   atertanum fah,
ahyrded heaþoswate;   næfre hit æt hilde ne swac
manna ængum   þara þe hit mid mundum bewand,
se ðe gryresiðas   gegan dorste,
folcstede fara;   næs þæt forma sið
þæt hit ellenweorc   æfnan scolde.   (1441–64)

Beowulf dives into the water and his mail coat does indeed save him from water monsters, but the borrowed sword fails. His mail coat saves him again.

Æfter þæm wordum   Wedergeata leod
efste mid elne,   nalas ondsware

the noblemen after evening came and Hrothgar went to his apartment, the powerful man to rest. Countless noblemen guarded the building as they had often done before. They moved the bench-planks; bedding and pillows were spread over. A certain one of the beer-drinkers sank on to his hall-bed ready and doomed. They placed their round battle-shields, the bright wooden boards, at their heads; there on the bench, over [each] nobleman was easily seen the tall battle-helmet, the ringed mail coat, a mighty wooden spear. [...]

Beowulf dressed himself in noble clothing, not at all did he fear for his life. The battle mail coat, woven with hands, wide and cunningly decorated, would have to seek out the deep, it knew how to protect the body, so that the battle grip, malicious grasp of anger, would not reach his breast, harm his life; but the shining helmet protected his head, he who was to stir up the bottom of the lake, seek the surging water. It [the helmet] was encircled with splendid bands, just as the smith of weapons made it in days of old, wondrously created [it], set it round with swine-figures, so that afterwards no sword or battle blade might bite into it. It was not the least of powerful aids that Hrothgar's spokesman [Unferth] loaned him in his need. The hilted blade was called Hrunting. It was one of the foremost of ancient weapons; the edge was iron, decorated with poison twigs [probably a branching pattern made prominent by etching with acid] hardened in the blood of battle; it had never failed in battle any of the men who grasped it with their hands, he who dared to go on perilous expeditions to the meeting place of the hostile. That was not the first time it had to carry out a courageous deed. [...]

After these words the prince of the Weder-Geats advanced with courage, was not willing to wait

   bidan wolde; brimwylm onfeng
   hilderince. Ða wæs hwil dæges
   ær he þone grundwong ongytan mehte.
   Sona þæt onfunde se ðe floda begong
   heorogifre beheold hund missera,
   grim ond grædig, þæt þær gumena sum
   ælwihta eard ufan cunnode.
   Grap þa togeanes, guðrinc gefeng
   atolan clommum. No þy ær in gescod
   halan lice; hring utan ymbbearh,
   þæt heo þone fyrdhom ðurhfon ne mihte,
   locene leoðosyrcan laþan fingrum.
   Bær þa seo brimwylf, þa heo to botme com,
   hringa þengel to hofe sinum,
   swa he ne mihte, no he þæs modig wæs,
   wæpna gewealdan, ac hine wundra þæs fela
   swencte on sunde, sædeor monig
   hildetuxum heresyrcan bræc,
   ehton aglæcan. (1492–1512a)

   Ofsæt þa þone selegyst ond hyre seax geteah,
   brad ond brunecg, wolde hire bearn wrecan,
   angan eaferan. Him on eaxle læg
   breostnet broden; þæt gebearh feore,
   wið ord ond wið ecge ingang forstod.
   Hæfde ða forsiðod sunu Ecgþeowes
   under gynne grund, Geata cempa,
   nemne him heaðobyrne helpe gefremede,
   herenet hearde . . . . (1545–53a)

Beowulf has killed the second monster. He and his men leave Denmark and return to Geatland.

        Gewat him on naca
   drefan deop wæter, Dena land ofgeaf.
   Þa wæs be mæste merehrægla sum,
   segl sale fæst; sundwudu þunede.
   No þær wegflotan wind ofer yðum
   siðes getwæfde; sægenga for,
   fleat famigheals forð ofer yðe,
   bundenstefna ofer brimstreamas,
   þæt hie Geata clifu ongitan meahton,
   cuþe næssas. Ceol up geþrang
   lyftgeswenced, on lande stod. (1903b–1913)

Beowulf shares the treasures he has won with his own king, Hygelac, and queen, Hygd.

for any answer. The surge of water received the battle warrior. Then it was a long part of the day before he was able to perceive the bottom. At once, the creature who watched over the expanse of flood, fiercely ravenous, for fifty years, grim and greedy, discovered that one of the race of men from above was exploring the territory of monsters. Then she gripped at him, seized the battle warrior in a terrible clasp. Nevertheless she did not penetrate his uninjured body. Ring [-mail] surrounded him outside, so that she was not able to penetrate the interlocked mail shirt with her hateful fingers. Then when she came to the bottom, the sea wolf carried the prince of rings to her dwelling so that he could not, however brave he was, wield weapons; but many wondrous creatures harassed him in the water, many sea-beasts attacked his battle shirt with hostile tusks. Monsters pursued [him]. [. . .] Then she sat on her hall guest and drew her knife, broad and shiny-edged. She intended to avenge her child, her only offspring. The woven breast-net lay on his shoulder. It saved his life, withstood entry from point and from edge. The son of Ecgtheow, the Geat warrior, would have perished then underground, had not the battle-garment, hard war-net, given him help. [. . .]

He went onto the ship to stir the deep water, it left the land of the Danes. Then there was by the mast a certain sea-cloth, a sail held fast with rope. The sea-wood thundered. The wind over the waves did not hinder the journey of the ship there [i.e. the wind was in their favour]. The sea-voyager advanced; it floated, foamy-necked, forth over the wave, the bound ship over the ocean-streams, so that they were able to perceive the Geat cliffs, familiar promontories. The vessel pressed forward, driven by the wind, [until] it grounded on land. [. . .]

Het ða in beran   eaforheafodsegn,
heaðosteapne helm,   hare byrnan,
guðsweord geatolic,   gyd æfter wræc:
'Me ðis hildesceorp   Hroðgar sealde,
snotra fengel,   sume worde het
þæt ic his ærest ðe   est gesægde;
cwæð þæt hyt hæfde   Hiorogar cyning,
leod Scyldunga   lange hwile;
no ðy ær suna sinum   syllan wolde,
hwatum Heorowearde,   þeah he him hold wære,
breostgewædu.   Bruc ealles well!'
Hyrde ic þæt þam frætwum   feower mearas
lungre, gelice,   last weardode,
æppelfealuwe;   he him est geteah
meara ond maðma.   Swa sceal mæg don,
nealles inwitnet   oðrum bregdon
dyrnum cræfte,   deað ren[ian]
hondgesteallan.   Hygelace wæs,
niða heardum,   nefa swyðe hold,
ond gehwæðer oðrum   hroþra gemyndig.
Hyrde ic þæt he ðone healsbeah   Hygde gesealde,
wrætlicne wundurmaððum,   ðone þe him Wealhðeo geaf,
ðeod[nes] dohtor,   þrio wicg somod
swancor ond sadolbeorht;   hyre syððan wæs
æfter beahðege   breost geweorðod.   (2152–76)

Long ago, the last survivor of a great race buried his ancestral treasure in a mound.

'Heald þu nu, hruse,   nu hæleð ne moston,
eorla æhte!   Hwæt, hyt ær on ðe
gode begeaton.   Guðdeað fornam,
feorhbealo frecne,   fyra gehwylcne
leoda minra,   þara ðe þis lif ofgeaf,
gesawon seledream.   [Ic] nah hwa sweord wege
oððe fe[ormie]   fæted wæge,
dryncfæt deore;   dug[uð] ellor sceoc.
Sceal se hearda helm   [hyr]sted golde
fætum befeallen;   feormynd swefað,
þa ðe beadogriman   bywan sceoldon,
ge swylce seo herepad,   sio æt hilde gebad
ofer borda gebræc   bite irena,
brosnað æfter beorne.   Ne mæg byrnan hring
æfter wigfruman   wide feran,
hæleðum be healfe.   Næs hearpan wyn,
gomen gleobeames,   ne god hafoc

Then he [Beowulf] commanded to be brought in the boar's-head standard, the helmet that towered in battle, the grey mail coat, the splendid battle sword, and afterwards related their story: 'Hrothgar, wise king, gave me this battle dress; he commanded me in a certain speech that I should tell you about his superlative gift. He said that King Hiorogar, prince of the Scyldings, had it for a long time. Nevertheless he was unwilling to give it, the breast garment [mail coat], to his [Hiorogar's] son, the bold Heoroweard, although he was well-disposed to him. Enjoy it all well!'. Then I heard that four swift horses, alike, apple-yellow, followed in the track of the treasures. He [Beowulf] gave him [King Hygelac] horses and treasures as a gift. So ought a kinsman to do, not to weave a web of hostility against the other with secret cunning, plot the death of a comrade. His nephew was very dear to Hygelac, hard in battle, and each was mindful of benefits towards the other. I heard that he gave to Hygd, daughter of a prince, the neck-ring, splendid with wondrous treasures, which Wealhtheow gave to him, together with three horses, supple and bright-of-saddle. After the receiving of the ring her breast was adorned. [...]

'Hold thou now, earth, now men are not able to, the possession of noblemen! Lo, good men previously obtained it from you [i.e. the precious metals were mined out of the earth in the first place]. Death in battle, perilous life-destruction, has taken the life of each of my people, who gave up this life, had experienced joys in the hall. I do not have anyone who wears the sword or polishes the plated cup, the precious drinking vessel. The band of warriors has departed elsewhere. The hard helmet, decorated with gold, must be deprived of its plates. The polisher sleeps, who should burnish the battle-mask. Likewise the battle garment, which endured in battle the bite of iron weapons over the breaking of shields, decays along with the warrior. Nor may the mail coat journey wide along with the war-chief, by the side of heroes. There is no joy

>   geond sæl swingeð,   ne se swifta mearh
>   burhstede beateð.   Bealocwealm hafað
>   fela feorhcynna   forð onsended!'   (2247–66)

A dragon occupies the mound. Meanwhile Hygelac is killed in Frisia. Beowulf escapes with thirty mail coats.

>   [. . .]   Þonan Biowulf com
>   sylfes cræfte,   sundnytte dreah;
>   hæfde him on earme   [ana] XXX
>   hildegeatwa,   þa he to holme [be]ag.   (2359b–2362)

The fire-breathing dragon has emerged and destroyed the Geats' royal hall. Now king of the Geats, in his old age, Beowulf has to fight it.

>   Gegrette ða   gumena gehwylcne,
>   hwate helmberend,   hindeman siðe,
>   swæse gesiðas: 'Nolde ic sweord beran,
>   wæpen to wyrme,   gif ic wiste hu
>   wið ðam aglæcean   elles meahte
>   gylpe wiðgripan,   swa ic gio wið Grendle dyde.
>   Ac ic ðær heaðufyres   hates wene,
>   oreðes ond attres;   forðon ic me on hafu
>   bord ond byrnan.   Nelle ic beorges weard
>   forfleon fotes trem,   ac unc furður sceal
>   weorðan æt wealle,   swa unc wyrd geteoð,
>   metod manna gehwæs.   Ic eom on mode from
>   þæt ic wið þone guðflogan   gylp ofersitte.
>   Gebide ge on beorge   byrnum werede,
>   secgas on searwum,   hwæðer sel mæge
>   æfter wælræse   wunde gedygan
>   uncer twega.   Nis þæt eower sið
>   ne gemet mannes,   nefne min anes,
>   þæt he wið aglæcean   eofoðo dæle,
>   eorlscype efne.   Ic mid elne sceall
>   gold gegangan,   oððe guð nimeð,
>   feorhbealu frecne,   frean eowerne!'   (2516–37)

Young Wiglaf comes to help him, carrying his father's sword.

>   . . . gomel swyrd geteah,
>   þæt wæs mid eldum   Eanmundes laf,
>   suna Ohteres.   Þam æt sæcce wearð,
>   wrœcca[n] wineleasum,   Weohstan bana
>   meces ecgum,   ond his magum ætbær
>   brunfagne helm,   hringde byrnan,

of the harp, entertainment with the music-wood, nor does a good hawk swing through the hall, nor does the swift horse beat the courtyard. The evil surge [death] has sent forth many of the race of men!' [...]

... from there Beowulf came by his own skill, swimming. He [alone] had on his arm 30 battle garments, when he took to the water.

Then he greeted each of the men, bold helmet-bearers, dear companions, for the last time: 'I would not wish to carry a sword, a weapon, against the worm, if I knew how else I might fight against the monster, to grapple with it boastingly as I did formerly with Grendel. But I expect there hot battle-fire, breath and poison; therefore I have on me shield and mail coat. I do not wish to flee the space of a step from the guardian of the barrow, but for us two it will happen for us both at the ramparts as fate, the lord of each of men, allots. I am brave at heart, so that I refrain from boasting against the battle-flier. You await on the barrow, protected in mail coats, warriors in armour, which of the two of us can endure wounds better after the slaughterous rush. It is not your undertaking, nor fit for any man except mine alone, that he should deal out might against the monster, perform heroic deeds. I shall gain the gold with courage, or war, life-peril, shall take your lord! [...]

He [Wiglaf] drew an old sword; it was [called] among men the heirloom of Eanmund, Ohtere's son, to whom Weohstan [Wiglaf's father], a friendless exile, became the slayer with sword edge in conflict, and carried away to his kinsmen the bright helmet, ringed mail coat, ancient

>   eald sweord etonisc;   þæt him Onela forgeaf,
>   his gædelinges   guðgewædu,
>   fyrdsearo fuslic . . . (2610b–2618a)

Beowulf's sword snaps and he is fatally injured; Wiglaf is burned wounding the monster. Beowulf kills it with his seax.

>   Þa gen sylf cyning
>   geweold his gewitte,   wællseaxe gebræd
>   biter ond beaduscearp,   þæt he on byrnan wæg;
>   forwrat Wedra helm   wyrm on middan.   (2702b–2705)

Wiglaf plunders the dragon's hoard.

>   Ða ic snude gefrægn   sunu Wihstanes
>   æfter wordcwydum   wundum dryhtne
>   hyran heaðosiocum,   hringnet beran,
>   brogdne beadusercean   under beorges hrof.
>   Geseah ða sigehreðig,   þa he bi sesse geong,
>   magoþegn modig   maððumsigla fealo,
>   gold glitinian   grunde getenge,
>   wundur on wealle,   ond þæs wyrmes denn,
>   ealdes uhtflogan,   orcas stondan,
>   fyrnmanna fatu   feormendlease,
>   hyrstum behrorene;   þær wæs helm monig
>   eald ond omig,   earmbeaga fela
>   searwum gesæled.   Sinc eaðe mæg,
>   gold on grund[e],   gumcynnes gehwone
>   oferhigian,   hyde se ðe wylle.
>   Swylce he siomian geseah   segn eallgylden
>   heah ofer horde,   hondwundra mæst,
>   gelocen leoðocræftum;   of ðam leoma stod,
>   þæt he þone grundwong   ongitan meahte,
>   wræte giondwlitan.   (2752–71a)

The infamous history of the Geats includes the killing of the Swedish king Ongentheow by brothers Eofor and Wulf.

>   Þær wearð Ongenðiow   ecgum sweorda,
>   blondenfexa,   on bid wrecen,
>   þæt se þeodcyning   ðafian sceolde
>   Eafores anne dom.   Hyne yrringa
>   Wulf Wonreding   wæpne geræhte,
>   þæt him for swenge   swat ædrum sprong
>   forð under fexe.   Næs he forht swa ðeh,
>   gomela Scilfing,   ac forgeald hraðe

giant-made sword. That Onela gave him, his kinsman's battle-garments, ready armour. [...]

Then yet, the king himself kept his head, drew a battle-knife, bitter and battle-sharp, that he carried on his mail coat; the protector of the Weder-Geats cut through the worm in the middle. [...]

Then, I heard, after the speech the son of Weohstan quickly obeyed his wounded lord, battle-sick, carried his ring-mail, woven battle-shirt, under the roof of the barrow [i.e. Wiglaf, still in his armour, entered the barrow]. Then, rejoicing in victory, the proud young retainer saw there as he passed by the seat, a quantity of precious jewels, gold glinting, lying on the ground, wonders on the wall, and the den of the worm, the ancient flier-by-night, cups standing, vessels of men of old, without a polisher, deprived of ornaments. There was many a helmet, old and rusty, quantities of arm-rings, skilfully twisted. Treasure easily may, gold in the ground, overpower each of the race of men, hide it who will! Likewise he saw hanging high over the hoard a standard all of gold, the greatest of wonders made with hands, woven with the skill of hands. From it shone a light so that he was able to see the ground surface, look over the works of art. [...]

There was the grey-haired Ongentheow brought to bay with the edges of swords, so that the people's king had to submit to a decree of Eofor. Wulf, son of Wonred, struck him angrily with his weapon so that, because of the blow, blood sprang forth from the veins under his hair. The old Swede was not afraid, however, but he quickly repaid the slaughterous blow with a worse exchange, after

  wyrsan wrixle wælhlem þone,
  syððan ðeodcyning þyder oncirde.
  Ne meahte se snella sunu Wonredes
  ealdum ceorle ondslyht giofan,
  ac he him on heafde helm ær gescer,
  þæt he blode fah bugan sceolde,
  feoll on foldan; næs he fæge þa git,
  ac he hyne gewyrpte, þeah ðe him wund hrine.
  Let se hearda Higelaces þegn
  bradne mece, þa his broðor læg,
  eald sweord eotonisc, entiscne helm
  brecan ofer bordweal; ða gebeah cyning,
  folces hyrde, wæs in feorh dropen.
  Ða wæron monige þe his mæg wriðon,
  ricone arærdon, ða him gerymed wearð
  þæt hie wælstowe wealdan moston.
  Þenden reafode rinc oðerne,
  nam on Ongenðio irenbyrnan,
  heard swyrd hilted ond his helm somod,
  hares hyrste Higelace bær. (2961–3188)

Weapons and armour are piled on Beowulf's funeral pyre to burn with him; a great funeral mound is built over his ashes and metalwork taken from the dragon's lair is buried there with him. It is still there, as useless to men as it was before.

  Him ða gegiredan Geata leode
  ad on eorðan unwaclicne,
  helmum behongen, hildebordum,
  beorhtum byrnum, swa he bena wæs;
  alegdon ða tomiddes mærne þeoden
  hæleð hiofende, hlaford leofne. (3137–42)

  Hi on beorg dydon beg ond siglu,
  eall swylce hyrsta, swylce on horde ær
  niðhedige men genumen hæfdon,
  forleton eorla gestreon eorðan healdan,
  gold on greote, þær hit nu gen lifað
  eldum swa unnyt swa h[it ær]or wæs. (3163–8)

the people's king turned in that direction. The bold son of Wonred was not able to give the old man a counter blow, but he [Ongentheow] had previously sheared the helmet on his head, so that he had to sink down, stained with blood, fell on the earth. He was not yet doomed, but he recovered, although the wound injured him. The hard retainer of Hygelac [i.e. Eofor] when his brother lay [wounded], let the broad blade, the ancient, giant-made sword, break the giant helmet over the shield-wall. Then the king, the people's guardian, sank down, he was mortally wounded. Then there were many who bound up his kinsman [i.e. Eofor's kinsman, Wulf] raised him up quickly, when it was revealed to them that they could control the place of slaughter. Meanwhile one warrior plundered another, took from Ongentheow his iron mail coat, hard hilted sword and his helmet together, carried the armour of the grey-haired man to Hygelac. [...]

Then the people of the Geats prepared for him a splendid pyre on the earth, hung with helmets, battle-shields, bright mail coats, as he had requested. Then lamenting warriors laid the famous prince, their dear lord, in the middle. [...] They placed in the barrow rings and clasps, all such ornaments which, earlier, hostile men had removed from the hoard. They let the earth hold the wealth of noblemen, gold in the ground, where it now yet remains, as useless to men as it was before.

THE CONSTANCE GROUP

Emaré is one of the romance texts in which an item of clothing is pivotal. Its narrative falls into the category known as the Constance-saga. This story was quite popular in late-medieval literature and British versions are found in the *Vita Duorum Offarum*, Trivet's *Anglo-Norman Chronicle*, the English version of the *Gesta Romanorum*, Chaucer's *Man of Law's Tale*, and Gower's *Confessio Amantis*. Its basic plot concerns a Christian woman who is banished by or flees her incestuous father, becoming the object of the attention and love of a heathen king who converts to Christianity and marries her. Her incensed mother-in-law propagates the idea that Constance has given birth to a monster and she is put to sea with her infant child. Miracles and ultimately recognition reunite her with her husband (and sometimes father) before their deaths. Here extracts that include references to cloth and clothing are provided with an attempt to offer comparisons across the different versions.

2. *The Lives of Two Offas*

The Constance story is found in the *Vitae Offarum Duorum*, a text which appears to have been compiled by a cleric attached to the Benedictine abbey at St Albans, Hertfordshire. It is extant in three major St Albans manuscripts, BL, MS Additional 62777; Cotton Claudius E iv; and Cotton Nero D i, each of which presents the same text with no significant discrepancies. A separate version of the *Life of Offa I* exists in a manuscript from the St Albans cell at Tynemouth, Northumberland, BL, MS Cotton Vitellius A xx (Swanton 2010: xxi). The Latin narrative once believed to have been the work of Matthew Paris is the oldest in time, generally being dated to the later twelfth or early thirteenth century, and therefore has a claim to be the first version of the Constance-saga, even though it is one of the least faithful to the general plot (see Schlauch 1927: 65). In this version Constance is not put to sea but is taken to a remote wilderness where her life is spared on account of her beauty, but not the lives of her children who are torn limb from limb (though they cry even after this and are restored by a devout hermit). The story is found in *Matthaei Paris Historia Major et Duorum Offarum Merciorum Regum*, ed. Wil. Wats, London, 1684. Extracts providing an analogue to Chaucer's *Man of Law's Tale* are printed in Furnivall, Brock and Clouston (1872), pp. 73–84. The entire work is edited and translated by Swanton (2010) from Cotton Nero D i; the Constance selection appears on pp. 21–36 with the text on the odd-numbered pages and facing page translation and is the version reproduced here.

Cuius sonitum secutus, inter densos frutices uirginem singularis forme et regii apparatus, set decore uenustissimam [*V* uestitam], ex insperato reperit. [...]
[The returning king hears that his wife and children have been killed in accordance with a forged letter purportedly from him.] Hiis auditis, risus in luctum, gaudium in lamenta, iubilus in singultus flebiter conuertuntur. Totaque regia ululatibus personuit et meroribus. Lugensque rex diu tam immane infortunium, induit se sacca cilicino, aspersum cinere, ac multipliciter deformatum. [...]

Having followed this sound [of sobbing and lamenting], he [Offa, now king] unexpectedly found among dense fruit trees a maiden of matchless looks and regal bearing, and extremely beautifully adorned [*V* beautifully clothed].

[The returning king hears that his wife and children have been killed in accordance with a forged letter purportedly from him] When he heard these things, laughter turned to grief, delight to laments, joyfulness to doleful sobs. The whole kingdom resounded with wailing and grief. And mourning such a dreadful tragedy for a long time, the king put on sackcloth, sprinkled himself with ashes, and disfigured himself in many other ways.

3. Nicholas Trevet, *The Life of Constance*

Les Chronicles of Nicholas Trevet survives in eleven Anglo-Norman manuscripts and an early-fifteenth-century Middle English translation (Correale 2005: 288–9). In Trivet's version Constance is instructed not in the textile arts but, because she is an only child, her father has her taught Christianity, the seven sciences (logic, physics, morals, astronomy, geometry, music, perspective) and various languages. Throughout the narrative, the descriptions of the court and the reception of Constance are not grounded in physical detail but rather make use of general terms such as 'la nobleie de la court & la gentil signurie Tyberie' (the splendour of the court, and the great lordship of Tiberius); 'Puis fu la pucele & les cristiens resceu del souldan & de sa mere, a grant honour & a grant nobleie' (Then were the maiden and the Christians received by the Sultan and his mother with great honour, and with great splendour). When Constance is put to sea, the food with which the ship is stocked is mentioned, but only 'la richesse & le tresour' that the Emperor Tiberius had sent with her are added. The text is printed in Brock (1872, vol. 1), 2–53, text on odd-numbered pages with facing page translation, which makes use of BL, MS Arundel 56 collated with Stockholm Kungliga Bibl. D.1311a (III). The Constance story from MS Oxford Magdalen 45, an earlier manuscript not known to Brock, is printed in Schlauch (1941), 165–81. The Constance story is printed in Correale (2005) from Paris, Bibliothèque Nationale, MS franç. 9687, 296–329 as Correale believes that this manuscript comes closest to resembling Chaucer's copy. The text here is that of Brock; his translation is slightly adapted.

e en cele neef fist la soudane mettre la pucele saunz sigle, & sauntz neuiroun [...]. E quant les Mariners que estoient pres de la riuail en lour neefs virent ceste merueile, ceo est assauoir vne pucele de bele e genti afeiture, mes descoloure, en estraunge atir e estoffe de graunt tresour, alerent al gardeyn del chastel [...]. Qar en la-iournaunte de la uyt a quele Elda deuoit entrer le chastel en le turnant del Roy, Puis que hermyngilde e constaunce estoient forment endormies apres longes veiletz e orisouns, cist, que tut estoit pris en la mayn al diable, trencha la goule hermingilde, sa dame, e coste constaunce, que fu forment endormie en mesme le lyt. E quant il auoit parfait la felonie, musca le coteil senglaunt en constaunt lorier la pucele. [...] Et pur ceo comaunda a Elda en forfesture de vie & de sez ter & qua ut qil auoit & deshe[r]itement de tout son linage qe deynz quatre iours apres lez lettres luez, feit apparailer vne neef & vitaile pur cync aunz de manger & boire pur constaunce, e en la neef mettre mesme le tresor que fu en sa primer neef troue, & que en mesme la manier en cele neef, sauntz sigle & sauntz nauiroun ou saunz nul autre engyn, fut oue soun enfaunt Moris de la terre exile [...] Et Thelous, de la garde trop lee e ioyous, en la nuyt parfounde descendi soul, portaunt graunt tresour dor e dargent & peres preciousez [...]. Et com ly rois erra soun chemin par cites e viles, de iour, en Engleterre, luy vindrent encountrauns hommes e femmes, enfauntz e veilars, e le reuilerent de crie e ledengge, gettauntz sur lui et les seuns tay e ordure & grosses peres, e femmes e enfauntz deuestuz par despyt luy moustrerent lour derere [...]. 'Qar de moy, ne de ma femme, ne de mon enfaunt vous nen auie pite, ne ieo de vous ia pite naueray.' Et a ceo ly coupa la teste e le corps tut apecees, com ele iut nue en soun lit.

... and in this ship, the Sultana [Constance's mother-in-law. She has just discovered that Constance is one of three survivors of the massacre of Christians she arranged] caused the maiden to be put, without sail or oar [...] And when the mariners, who were near the shore in their ships, saw this marvel, that is to wit, a maiden of fair and graceful form, but pale, in strange attire, and furnished with great treasure, they went to the warden of the castle [Elda, the castle is in Northumberland] [...] For in the dawn after the night in which Elda was to enter the castle on his return from the king, when Hermingild [Elda's wife who loves and looks after Constance] and Constance were soundly asleep after long watchings and prayers, this man [a Saxon knight of Elda's household, left in charge, who has been trying to seduce Constance], who as wholly taken in the devil's hand, cut the throat of Hermingild, his lady, beside Constance who was sleeping soundly in the same bed. And when he had accomplished the crime, he hid the bloody knife behind the maid Constance's pillow. [...] [Constance is vindicated and marries the king, Alla].

[...] [Donegild, Constance's second mother-in-law, intercepts the letters proclaiming the birth of Constance's child, sending word that he is a monster]. Therefore he [the king] commanded Elda [in a letter forged by his mother in his name stating that if Constance remained in the land war and destruction would follow], on pain of forfeiting his life and his lands and whatever he had, and of disinheritance of all his lineage, that within four days after reading the letters, he should cause a ship to be prepared and provisioned for five years with food and drink for Constance, and have put in the ship the same treasure which was found in her former ship, and that she, with her child Maurice, should be exiled in the same manner in this ship without sail, or oar or any other mechanism [...]

[Constance arrives at the castle of an emir who orders his seneschal, Thelous, to look after Constance, who insists on sleeping aboard her boat]. And Thelous, very glad and joyous of the charge, went down alone at dead of night, bearing great treasure of gold and silver and precious stones [he tries to seduce Constance who pushes him overboard].

[...] [Having triumphed in Scotland King Alla searches for Constance in England] And as the king went his way through cities and towns by day, in England, there came against him men and women, children and old men, and reviled him with crying and reproaches, throwing upon him and his men mud and filth and great stones; and women and naked children, in mockery, showed him their hindquarters [...].

[Alla discovers his mother's treachery and confronts her] 'For you had no pity on me, nor on my wife, nor on my child, neither will I ever have pity on you.' And with that he cut off her head and hewed her body all to pieces, as she lay naked in her bed.

4. Trevet's Story of Constance

Trevet's chronicle also occurs in a later Middle English translation probably made early in the fifteenth century and preserved in a unique manuscript dating from the mid- to late fifteenth century at Harvard's Houghton Library, fMS Eng 938 (Rose 1992–3). Although this version is very close to the Anglo-French, we may notice subtle differences relating to cloth and clothing: while in the Anglo-French the sultan's mother sends Constance away in a boat 'saunz sigle, & sauntz neuiroun' (without sail and oar), here she is 'withoute pooles or orys' (without masts or oars). The Constance section is printed in Furnivall, Brock and Clouston (1876, vol. 3), 223–50 and in Whitehead (1960), 224–53. The translation is by Louise Sylvester.

And than in that shyp that vngoodly morderes, the sowdans moder, put that mayde Constaunce withoute pooles or orys [...]. And whan the marineres, the whyche were nere the brynke of the londe in her shyppes, sawe thys meruayle, that ys to say, a mayden full fayr', and of a full ientell feture, but grely discolored with a straunge atyre, And wele stored with full grete tresoure [...]. And when hermigilde and Constaunce were strong a sleepe after theyre grete wachyng and grete prayeres, that same traytoure the whyche gafe hymself all [t]o geder in to the deuell handes, cutte a to the throte of hermigil hys lady, besyde Constaunce, whan she was strong a sleepe in the same bed. And whan he had full done his felony, he hyd hys knyfe, all blody, under the pylowe of the mayden Constaunce. [...]

Wherefore he commanded to Olda, in peyne of forfayteure of hys lyfe, And of hys londes and goodes, and of all that he had, And also under peyne of disheritament of all hys linage, that withyn iiij dayes after that he had resceyuyd hys letters, that he shulde ordeyne a Shyp for to be arrayed, and vytayle therein for .v. yere, of mete and drynke, for Constaunce and her chulde; And in the same shyp to be putthe same tresoure the whyche was found in her furst shyp; And in the same manerwyse, withoute poole or Oore, orells any other maner engine or habiliment for a shyp, And her chylde Morys to be put withyn the shyp with her, And soo she to be exiled oute of the londe as she com in.[...]

And thys Thelous, the Stewarde foresede, was full glad and ioyfull hereof. and in the derke nyght he wente doun to here alone, and bore to her grete tresoure of golde and syluer and of precious stones. [...] And as the kyng wente and come by day by the hygh weyes by Cytees and by tounes in ynglonde, there come men wemen and Chyldren and oolde folke crying and reuylyng the kyng and caste foule harlatrye opon hym with grete stones ayenst hys breste. And men wemen and chylderen despoyled hemselfe naked for despyte, and shewed to hym her pryuytees behynde [...] 'ffor thow, of me, neythere of my wyfe, neyther opon my chylde, thow haddest no pite, ne I shall neuer haue pyte opon the.' And with that worde he smote of her' hede, and hacked her' body all to peces as she laye naked in her bedde. [...] And than the Senatoure wente doune in hys paleys, and commaunded hys wyfe to come doune with Constaunce in her moste goodly atyre and aray to see the kyng.

And then that ungodly murderess, the sultan's mother [Constance's mother-in-law. She has just discovered that Constance is one of three survivors of the massacre of Christians she arranged], put that young woman Constance in that ship without poles or oars [...]

[The boat arrives at the Northumbrian shore] And when the sailors who were in their ships near the shore saw this wonder; that is to say, a very beautiful young woman with graceful features but very pale and strangely dressed. And provisioned with a very great amount of treasure [...].

And when Hermengild [the wife of Olda, the keeper of the castle near where Constance's boat landed] and Constance were fast asleep, exhausted from their long vigil and prayers, that same traitor [a Saxon knight and Olda's steward who has been trying to seduce Constance] who had given himself entirely into the devil's hands, cut the throat of his lady Hermengild beside Constance when she was fast asleep in the same bed. And when he had committed his crime, he hid his knife, all covered in blood, under the pillow of the young woman Constance. [...] [Constance is vindicated and marries the king, Alle].

[Domild, Constance's second mother-in-law, intercepts the letters proclaiming the birth of Constance's child, sending word that he is a monster]. Therefore he [the king] ordered Olda [in a letter forged by his mother Domild saying that if Constance remained in his land there would be war and invasion by strangers], on pain of forfeiture of his life, his lands, his goods, and all he had, and also on pain of disinheritance of all his lineage, that within four days of receiving his letters, he should order a ship to be prepared with provisions in it for five years' worth of food and drink for Constance and her child. And in the same ship should be placed the treasure that was found in her first ship. And in the same way, without pole or oar or any other kind of mechanism or equipment for a ship. And her child Maurice was to be put in the ship with her and thus she was to be exiled from the land in the same way that she had arrived in it. [...]

And this steward Thelous, mentioned above [steward of the admiral by whose castle Constance's ship comes to shore, and who is charged with Constance's care], was very glad and joyful about it. And in the dark night he went down to her alone and took a great treasure of gold, silver and jewels to her. [...]

[Having triumphed in Scotland, Alle serches for Constance in England] And as the king came and went during the day along the highways of the cities and towns of England, men, women, children and old people cried out against the king and reviled him and threw great rubbish on him with rocks against his breast. And men, women and children exposed themselves for spite and showed him their backsides [...].

[Alle discovers his mother's treachery and confronts her] 'Because you had no pity on either me, my wife or my child, I shall never have pity on you'. And with those words he cut off her head and hacked her body to pieces as she lay naked in bed [...].

And then the senator went down to his palace and ordered his wife to come down with Constance dressed her best in her finest clothes.

5. The Tale of the Wife of Merelaus the Emperor

This text appears in the English version of the *Gesta Romanorum* in BL, MS Harley 7333, one of the manuscripts in which texts apparently derived from John Shirley's manuscript collection were copied. In this narrative, the empress having been left in charge when the emperor goes to the holy land, his brother the steward makes repeated attempts to seduce her and is imprisoned. She frees him before her husband can return and have him put to death. He makes a second attempt and, when rebuffed, leaves her stripped and hanging from a tree. An earl out hunting frees her in order to have her teach his young daughter. His steward, too, wishes to seduce the empress and, in revenge at being rebuffed, frames her for his murder of the earl's daughter. She is banished, ransoms a man from the gallows, and then sends the man to a ship to buy clothes for her. The shipmaster agrees to sell her some of his clothes but having bribed her servant to bring her to the ship, he sails away with her, threatening seduction or drowning. Her prayers are answered by a storm but, unknown to each other, both the empress and the shipmaster are saved. She lives with nuns and heals the sick following their confessions and all is revealed, including her identity, so she is reunited with the emperor. The text is printed in Furnivall, Brock and Clouston (1872), 57–70. The translation is by Louise Sylvester.

Then she brouȝt him out of the prison', and gert bathe him, and clyppe him, and shave him; and thenne she araide him in precious clothing' [...] Thenne he nakid hire evene to þe smok, and honge hire by þe heeris vp on an Oke; Whenne þe Erle sawe þat, he merveilide hiely, and smot þe horse with sporis [...] Þe Erle took hire downe, and brouȝt hire to his castelle, and took his douȝter in to hire kepinge; and therefore she lay in þe same chambir þat þe contesse lay in. [...] And whenne [the steward] fond alle on slepe, he lokid aboute by liȝt of þe lampe, and sawe þe bed of þe Emperesse; And whenne he sawe þe Emperesse liggynge with the Erlis douȝter, he drowe out a knyfe, and cutte the throte of the childe; And thenne putte priuyliche þe knyfe in the hond of þe Emperesse Thus Emperesse was full of sorowe, and dude on hire clothis, and took hire palfray and rood toward þe eest; [...] Happid soone aftir, þat þer come a shippe, I-chargid with many maner of marchaundise; and whenne þe lady hurde speke þerof, she sade to hire seruaunt, 'Go to þe shippe, and loke if þou see ony goode clothis for me.' The seruaunt entrid the shippe, and fonde þer many diuerse precious clothis; [...] So þe maister come to hire, and worshipfully salusyd hire; And þe lady spake to him for cloth for hire weryng', and he grauntid hir'. [...] Thenne saide he, 'þou shalt go to hire, & say to hire, þat I woll not late out my clothe by no way to no creature, and so make hire come to me to shippe; [...] When the traitour hadde receivid his meede, he went to his lady, and tolde hire howe þe maister wolde not sende his cloth out of his shippe, – 'But he prayed you, þat ye woll come down' to þe watir, and þer ȝe shull see and haue clothis at your owne will [...]. And then þe maister, seynge a gret wynde to rise vp, he sette vp the sayle, and faste rowyde; [...] And she drowe a curtyne, when she was in, betweyne hir and him; [...] And thei maade hire come forth, and speke with þe Emperour. The emperesse hydde hire face with a wympill, for she wolde not ben y-knowe.

Then she brought him out of prison and had him bathed, his hair cut and had him shaved and then she dressed him in fine clothing [...].

Then he stripped her down to the smock and hung her by the hair from an oak tree. When the earl saw that, he was very astonished and he kicked his horse with his spurs. [...] The earl took her down and brought her to his palace and gave his daughter into her keeping and so she slept in the same room as the countess [...]. And when the steward found that everyone was asleep, he looked around by the light of his lamp and saw the empress's bed. And when he saw the empress lying with the earl's daughter, he drew a knife and cut the child's throat and then secretly put the knife into the empress's hand. The empress was full of sorrow. She put on her clothes, took her horse and rode eastwards [...].

It happened that soon after a ship arrived filled with different kinds of merchandise; and when the lady heard it spoken of, she said to her servant, 'Go to the ship and look and see if there are any good clothes for me'. The servant went onto the ship, and found a lot of different fine clothes there [...].

So the master came to her and greeted her respectfully; and the lady spoke to him about clothes for her to wear, and he offered some to her [...].

Then he said, 'you will go to her and say to her that I will not let my clothes out by no means to anyone, and so make her come to me on the ship [...].

When the traitor had received his reward, he went to his lady, and told her how the master would not send his clothes out of the ship – but he asked you to come down to the water and there you will see and have whatever clothes you wish [...].

And then the master, seeing a big wind rising up, set up the sail and rowed fast [...].

And she drew a curtain, when she was in, between her and him; [...].

And they made her come forward and speak to the emperor. The empress hid her face with a wimple, for she did not want to be recognised.

6. *Emaré*

The Middle English *Emaré* is extant in only one manuscript, BL, MS Cotton Caligula A ii. Although the manuscript dates from the early fifteenth century, the dialect features in *Emaré* indicate a late-fourteenth-century North-East Midlands or East Anglian dialect (Laskaya and Salisbury 1995). In this version of the Constance narrative the heroine is exiled because of her refusal to marry her father. Rescued from the sea, she marries the king of Galys, but is exiled a second time with her infant son, as a result of her mother-in-law's machinations. The narrative concludes with a reunion uniting the three generations of males in the protagonist's family: father, husband and son. Unlike the analogues by Chaucer and by Gower, in this version an elaborately worked cloth is featured. Thus in *Emaré* cloth and clothing take centre stage as the plot seems to be triggered, and the events throughout the poem influenced, by the seemingly enchanted and certainly ambiguous robe given to Emaré by her father. In a poem that consists of only 1035 lines, 98 (lines 82–180) are given to a description of the robe. The text is that of Laskaya and Salisbury (1995). The translation is by Louise Sylvester.

> She thawghth hyt curtesye and thewe,
> Golde and sylke for to sewe, (58–9)
>
> The ryche Kynge of Cesyle
>   To the Emperour gan wende;
> A ryche present wyth hym he browght,
> A cloth that was wordylye wroght. (80–3)
>
> He presented the Emperour ryght,
>   And sette hym on hys kne,
> Wyth that cloth rychyly dyght,
> Full of stones ther hyt was pyght,
>   As thykke as hyt myght be:
> Off topaze and rubyes
> And othur stones of myche prys,
>   That semely wer to se;
> Of crapowtes and nakette,
> As thykke ar they sette,
>   For sothe, as y say the.
>   The cloth was dysplayed sone;
> The Emperour lokede therupone
>   And myght hyt not se,
> For glysteryng of the ryche ston;
> Redy syght had he non,
>   And sayde, 'How may thys be?'
> The Emperour sayde on hygh,
> 'Sertes, thys ys a fayry,
>   Or ellys a vanyté!'
> The Kyng of Cysyle answered than,
> 'So ryche a jwell ys ther non
>   In all Crystyanté.'

She thought it courtesy and good manners to sew cloth of gold […]

The wealthy king of Sicily went to visit the emperor. He brought a rich gift with him, a cloth that was exquisitely made […].

He presented himself to the emperor and put on his lap that splendidly adorned cloth, it was studded with gemstones as thickly as could be: topazes and rubies and other jewels of great price that were beautiful to look at; it was thickly set with toadstones and agates, as I tell you truly.
   The cloth was quickly unfurled. The emperor looked at it and could not see it for the glittering of the rich jewels. He had no clear sight, and said 'How can this be?' The emperor said in a loud voice 'Certainly this is a magic thing, or else it is an illusion.' The king of Sicily answered, 'There is not as rich a jewel in the whole of Christendom.'

The Emerayle dowghter of hethenes
Made thys cloth wythouten lees,
    And wrowghte hyt all wyth pryde;
And purtreyed hyt wyth gret honour,
Wyth ryche golde and asowr
    And stones on ylke a syde.
And, as the story telles in honde,
The stones that yn thys cloth stonde,
    Sowghte they wer full wyde.
Seven wynter hyt was yn makynge,
Or hyt was browght to endynge,
    In herte ys not to hyde.
    In that on korner made was
Ydoyne and Amadas,
    Wyth love that was so trewe;
For they loveden hem wyth honour,
Portrayed they wer wyth trewe-love-flour,
    Of stones bryght of hewe:
Wyth carbunkull and safere,
Kassydonys and onyx so clere
    Sette in golde newe,
Deamondes and rubyes,
And othur stones of mychyll pryse,
    And menstrellys wyth her glewe.
    In that othur corner was dyght
Trystram and Isowde so bryght,
    That semely wer to se;
And for they loved hem ryght,
As full of stones ar they dyght,
    As thykke as they may be:
Of topase and of rubyes,
And othur stones of myche pryse,
    That semely wer to se;
Wyth crapawtes and nakette,
Thykke of stones ar they sette,
    For sothe, as y say the.
    In the thyrdde korner, wyth gret honour,
Was Florys and Dam Blawncheflour,
    As love was hem betwene;
For they loved wyth honour,
Purtrayed they wer wyth trewe-love-flour,
    Wyth stones bryght and shene:
Ther wer knyghtus and senatowres,
Emerawdes of gret vertues,
    To wyte wythouten wene;

The emir's daughter of heathendom made this cloth, without a word of a lie, and made it all with pride, and depicted on it brilliantly, with rich gold and azure and jewels on every part. And, as the story says, the stones that are set in this cloth were sought far and wide. It was seven winters in the making before it was completed: what is in the heart is not to be hidden.

In one corner the story of Ydoine and Amadas was depicted with love that was so true, for they loved each other honourably. They were portrayed with a true-love flower made of brightly coloured jewels: with carbuncles and sapphires and gems of Chalcedony and onyx so clear set in new gold, diamonds and rubies and other jewels of great price, and minstrels with their song.

In another corner was made, so brightly that it was lovely to look at, Tristram and Isolde. And because they loved each other truly, their depiction is as full of jewels, set as thickly as they can be: of topazes and rubies, and other jewels of great price, that were lovely to look at, with toadstones and agates they are thickly set, truly as I tell you.

In the third corner with great honour, because of the love between them, were Floris and Dame Blancheflower. Because they loved honourably, they are portrayed with a true-love flower, with bright and shining jewels. There were knights and senators, emeralds of great value, to know without doubt; diamonds and

>   Deamoundes and koralle,
>   Perydotes and crystall,
>   And gode garnettes bytwene.
>   In the fowrthe korner was oon,
>   Of Babylone the Sowdan sonne,
>   The Amerayles dowghtyr hym by.
>   For hys sake the cloth was wrowght;
>   She loved hym in hert and thowght,
>   As testymoyeth thys storye.
>   The fayr mayden her byforn
>   Was portrayed an unykorn,
>   Wyth hys horn so hye;
>   Flowres and bryddes on ylke a syde,
>   Wyth stones that wer sowght wyde,
>   Stuffed wyth ymagerye.
>   When the cloth to ende was wrowght,
>   To the Sowdan sone hyt was browght,
>   That semely was of syghte.
>   'My fadyr was a nobyll man;
>   Of the Sowdan he hyt wan
>   Wyth maystrye and wyth myghth.
>   For gret love he gaf hyt me;
>   I brynge hyt the in specyalté;
>   Thys cloth ys rychely dyght.'
>   He gaf hyt the emperour;
>   He receyved hyt wyth gret honour,
>   And thonkede hym fayr and ryght.   (86–180)

The emperor sends messengers to look for his daughter.

>   Forth gon they fare,
>   Both by stretes and by stye,
>   Aftur that fayr lady,
>   Was godely unthur gare.   (195–8)

The emperor wishes to marry his daughter and obtains papal permission for this.

>   Then was the Emperour gladde and blythe,
>   And lette shape a robe swythe
>   Of that cloth of golde;
>   And when hyt was don her upon,
>   She semed non erthely wommon,
>   That marked was of molde.   (241–6)

Emaré refuses and the angry emperor puts her to sea.

coral, peridots and crystal, and good garnets in between.

In the fourth corner was one of the Babylonian sultan's son with the emir's daughter beside him. The cloth was made for his sake: she loved him in her heart and mind, as this story testifies. A unicorn was depicted in front of the fair young woman, with his horn very high. Flowers and birds on every side, with jewels that were sought from afar, with a pattern crowded with images. When that cloth was finished, it was brought to the sultan's son who was very handsome. 'My father was a noble man, he won it from the sultan with force and with might. Because of his great love he gave it to me and I bring it to you as a rare gift; this cloth is splendidly made'. He gave it to the emperor who received it with great pride and thanked him properly and courteously [...].

Off they went through streets and paths, after that fair lady who was the best that ever wore clothes [...].

Then the emperor was gladdened and happy and quickly had a robe made of that cloth of gold; when it was put on her, she did not seem to be an earthly woman made out of clay [...].

> He lette make a nobull boot,
> And dede her theryn, God wote,
>   In the robe of nobull ble.
> She moste have wyth her no spendyng,
> Nothur mete ne drynke,
>   But shate her ynto the se.
> Now the lady dwelled thore,
> Wythowte anker or ore,
>   And that was gret pyté!   (268–76)
>
> her was nothur olde ny yynge
> That kowthe stynte of wepynge,
>   For that comely unthur kelle.   (301–3)

Emaré's boat lands in Wales where she is found by Sir Kador, the king's steward, and two knights.

> A boot he fond by the brym,
> And a glysteryng thyng theryn,   (349–50)
>
> When that lady, fayr of face,
> Wyth mete and drynke kevered was,
>   And had colour agayne,
> She tawghte hem to sewe and marke
> All maner of sylkyn werke;
>   Of her they wer full fayne.   (373–8)
>
> The lady that was gentyll and small
> In kurtull alone served yn hall,
>   Byfore that nobull kyng.
> The cloth upon her shone so bryghth
> When she was theryn ydyghth,
>   She semed non erthly thyng.   (391–6)
>
> Then spakke the ryche yn ray,
> To Syr Kadore gan he say
>   Wordes fayr and stylle:
> 'Syr, whenns ys that lovely may
> That yn the halle served thys day?
>   Tell my yyf hyt be thy wyll.'   (415–20)
>
> She ys the konnyngest wommon,
> I trowe, that be yn Crystendom,
>   Of werke that y have sene.'   (428–30)

The king wishes to marry Emaré.

He had a splendid boat made, and put her in it, God knows, wearing the brightly coloured robe. She was allowed no money nor food nor drink, rather he pushed her off into the sea. Now the lady sat there without an anchor or oar and that was a great pity [...]

There was neither an old nor a young person who could stop weeping for that woman the most beautiful that ever wore clothes [...]

He found a boat by the shore with a glittering thing inside it [...].

When that beautiful woman was restored to herself with food and drink, and her colour had returned, she taught them to sew and embroider and do all kinds of silk work. They were very pleased with her [...].

The lady, who was graceful and slender, served in hall before the king wearing just her kirtle. The cloth on her shone so brightly that she did not seem to be an earthly being when she was wearing it [...].

Then the one who was richly dressed began to speak. He said to Sir Kador in soft quiet words, 'Where does that lovely maid who served in hall today come from? Tell me, if you would not mind.' [...]

From the embroidery that I have seen, I believe she is the most skilful woman in Christendom. [...]

> The cloth on her shon so bryght
> When she was theryn dyght,
> > And herself a gentell may,
> The olde qwene sayde anon,
> 'I sawe never wommon
> > Halvendell so gay!'
> The olde qwene spakke wordus unhende
> And sayde, 'Sone, thys ys a fende,
> > In thys wordy wede! (439–47)

They marry and Emaré conceives but her husband is called upon by the king of France to help him fight the Saracens.

> The kyng of Galys, in that tyde,
> Gedered men on every syde,
> > In armour bryght and shene. (487–9)

The messenger with the letter from Sir Kador telling the king the news stops off at the king's mother's house to tell her.

> 'Madame, ther ys of her yborne
> A fayr man-chylde, y tell you beforne,
> > And she lyth in her bedde.'
> She gaf hym for that tydynge
> A robe and fowrty shylynge,
> > And rychely hym cladde. (520–5)

She forges the letter, saying that the baby is a monster. The queen intercepts the reply, forging a new letter ordering Emare's exile.

> And putte her ynto the see,
> In that robe of ryche ble (589–90)

> Ther was nothur olde ny yynge,
> That myghte forbere of wepynge
> > For that worthy unthur wede. (610–12)

> When she wente ynto the see
> In that robe of ryche ble,
> > Men sowened on the sonde. (643–5)

> Her surkote that was large and wyde,
> Therwyth her vysage she gan hyde,
> > Wyth the hynthur lappes (652–4)

The cloth shone so brightly on her when she was dressed in it, and she was such a noble looking maiden, that the old queen immediately said, 'I never saw a woman half so beautiful.' The old queen spoke discourteous words and said 'Son, it is a devil in this noble robe.' [...]

The king of Wales at that time gathered men on every side in bright and shining armour [...].

Madam, a beautiful boy-child has been born to her, I tell you now, and she is lying in her bed.' She gave him a robe and forty shillings for that news, and dressed him splendidly. [...]

And put her to sea in that richly coloured robe [...].

There was not an old person nor a young who could refrain from weeping for that well-dressed woman. [...]

When she went to sea in that richly coloured robe, men swooned on the beach.

She hid her face with the back folds of her surcoat that was large and wide [...]

A Roman merchant walking by the sea finds Emaré's boat.

> A bote he fonde by the brymme
> And a fayr lady therynne,
>   That was ryght wo-bygone.
>   The cloth on her shon so bryght,
> He was aferde of that syght,
>   For glysteryng of that wede;
> And yn hys herte he thowghth ryght
> That she was non erthyly wyght   (694–701)

He brings her and her child to his house.

> And she sewed sylke werk yn bour,
> And tawghte her sone nortowre,
>   But evyr she mornede stylle.
> When the chylde was seven yer olde,
> He was bothe wyse and bolde,
>   And wele made of flesh and bone;
> He was worthy unthur wede   (730–6)

The king returns and discovers the forgeries and who made them. He sets sail for Rome to see the pope and do penance.

> They drowgh up sayl and leyd out ore   (832)

The king's party lands up at the house where Emaré is staying and she instructs her son.

> Tomorowe thou shall serve yn halle,
> In a kurtyll of ryche palle,
>   Byfore thys nobull kyng   (847–9)

> The chylde wente ynto the hall,
> Among the lordes grete and small,
>   That lufsumme wer unthur lyne.   (862–4)

The king is taken with the boy and asks his name. This leads him to Emaré.

> Ayeyn hem come the lady gent,
>   In the robe bryght and shene.
> He toke her yn hys armes two,
> For joye they sowened, both to,
>   Such love was hem bytwene.
> A joyfull metyng was ther thore,
> Of that lady, goodly unthur gore,   (932–8)

The emperor (Emarés father) comes to Rome to do penance for what he did to his daughter. All are reunited.

He found a boat by the shore and in it a beautiful woman who was extremely unhappy. The cloth on her shone so brightly that he was afraid of that sight, because of the glittering of that garment and in his heart he believed that she was not an earthly creature [...].

And she sewed silk embroidery in a chamber and taught her son manners, but still she continued to mourn. When the child was seven years old he was both wise and bold and tall and well-built; he was the best that ever wore clothes [...].

And they hoisted the sail and laid out the oars [...].

Tomorrow you will serve in hall wearing a tunic of rich cloth before this noble king. [...]

The child went into the hall among the lords high and lowly who were the worthiest that ever wore linen.

The gracious lady came towards him in the bright and shining robe. He took her in his arms, the two of them both swooned such was the love they felt for each other. That was a joyful meeting for that lady, so good in her gown. [...]

> The chyld was worthy unthur wede,
> A satte upon a nobyll stede,
>> By hys fadyr syde;
> And when he mette the Emperour,
> He valed hys hode wyth gret honour
>> And kyssed hym yn that tyde ... (988–93)

7. John Gower's Tale of Constance

As the length of the extract below indicates, Gower appears to have little or no interest in cloth or clothing. The standard edition of Gower's *Confessio Amantis* is that of Macaulay (1901). The Tale of Constance appears in vol. 2, pp. 146–73. The Constance section of *Confessio Amantis* is reprinted in Correale (2005), 330–50. The translation is by Louise Sylvester.

> The dissh forwith the coppe and al
> Bebled thei weren oueral (699–700)

> And hath ordeined, as sche thoghte,
> A nakid schip withoute stiere (708–9)

> And whan it cam into the nyht,
> This wyf hire hath to bedde dyht
> Wher that this maiden with hire lay.
> This false knyht vpon delay
> Hath taried til thei were aslepe,
> As he that wolde his time kepe
> His dedly werkes to fulfille'
> And to the bed he stalketh stille,
> Wher that he wiste was the wif;
> And in his hond a rasour knif
> He bar, with which hire throte he cutte
> And priuely the knif he putte
> Vnder that other beddes side,
> Wher that Constance lai beside. (821–34)

8. Geoffrey Chaucer, *The Man of Law's Tale*

Chaucer's tale includes many of the same elements as *Emaré* but recognition is achieved through resemblance. When Alla travels to Rome near the end of the poem and encounters Constance's (and his) son at a feast, we learn that 'Now was this child as lyk unto Custance/ As possible is a creature to be./ This Alla hath the face in remembrance/ Of dame Custance, and ther on mused he/ If that the childes mooder were aught she/ That is his wyf' (1032–5). Thus human likeness obviates the need for items of clothing to function as tokens of recognition as they do in many romances and in versions of this one. It is still a matter of debate whether Chaucer drew on Gower's version to make his *Man of Law's Tale*. The tale appears in Benson (1987), the translation is a slightly adapted version of that of NeCastro (2007).

The child was the best that ever wore clothes and sat upon a splendid horse by his father's side; and when he met the emperor he lowered his hood with great courtesy and kissed him at the same time.

The dish with the tablecloth and everything else were covered with blood [...].

And [the mother of the Sultan] ordered, as she thought appropriate, a bare ship without a rudder [...].

And when it came to be night, this wife took herself to bed where the maiden lay with her. The false knight lingered, waiting until they were asleep, like someone who could take his time to fulfil his evil deeds. And he crept quietly to the bed where he knew the wife was. And in his hand he had a sharp knife, with which he cut her throat. And secretly he put the knife under the other side of the bed where Constance was lying beside her.

In Surrye whilom dwelte a compaignye
Of chapmen riche, and therto sadde and trewe,
That wyde-where senten hir spicerye,
Clothes of gold, and satyns riche of hewe.   (134–7)

And Custance han they take anon, foot-hoot,
And in a ship all steerelees, God woot,
They han hir set, and bidde hire lerne saille
Out of Surrye agaynward to Ytaille.
A certein tresor that she thider ladde,
And, sooth to seyn, vitaille greet plentee
They han hire yeven, and clothes eek she hadde   (438–44)

Wery, forwaked in hir orisouns,
Slepeth Custance, and Hermengyld also.
This knyght, thurgh Sathanas temptaciouns,
All softely is to the bed ygo,
And kitte the throte of Hermengyld atwo,
And leyde the blody knyf by dame Custance   (596–601)

This messager comth fro the kyng agayn,
And at the kynges moodres court he lighte,
And she was of this messager ful fayn,
And plesed hym in al that ever she myghte.
He drank, and wel his girdel underpighte   (785–9)

Hir litel child lay wepyng in hir arm,
And knelynge, pitously to hym she seyde,
'Pees, litel sone, I wol do thee noon harm.'
With that hir coverchief of hir heed she breyde,
And over his litel eyen she it leyde   (834–8)

THE LAUNFAL GROUP

The Launfal narrative can be found in several medieval versions, the earliest of which is Marie de France's twelfth-century *Lanval*. The Middle English Breton lay by Sir Thomas Chestre, *Sir Launfal*, can be traced directly back to Marie's collection. Marie claimed that her *lais* were translations of ancient Celtic tales of love and magic which she heard the Bretons sing. Her collection was written for an aristocratic audience and is preserved complete in one mid thirteenth-century manuscript, BL, MS Harley 978. The immediate and primary source for Chestre is the 538-line Middle English *Sir Landevale*, which is an adaptation from Marie's *Lanval*. All the narratives contain the elements of the supernatural mistress (Tryamour), the anger of Guinevere, the revelation of the secret and consequent loss of the lover, and the final rescue. The Anglo-French and the two Middle English versions all share detailed descriptions of the attire of Tryamour's handmaidens as first glimpsed by Launfal, the tent and Tryamour herself.

Once there dwelt in Syria a company of rich merchants, forthright and honest, who sent out far and wide their spices, their cloth of gold, and their richly hued satins. [...]

They took Constance instantly and set her on a ship, without a rudder, God knows, and told her to learn to sail from Syria back again to Italy. They put with her a certain treasure that she had brought, and, to tell the truth, they had given her a great store of food and she also had clothes [...]

Weary from being awake in prayer, Constance and Hermengild were sleeping. Tempted by Satan, this knight went very softly to the bed, cut Hermengild's throat in two, and laid the bloody knife beside Lady Constance [...]

The messenger returned from the king's court and again alighted at the court of the king's mother, and she was very glad about this and pleased him in all that she could. He drank and stuffed his girdle well. [...]

Her little child lay weeping upon her arm, and kneeling she said full of pity to him, 'Peace, little son, I will not harm you'. Having said that, she drew her kerchief from her head and laid it over his little eyes.

9. Marie de France, *Lanval*

This Anglo-French *lai* by Marie de France is believed to date from the 1160s. The shifts in the silhouette of fashionable women in this period are visible in the tight lacing and other details described in the poem. The standard edition is that of Rychner (1966), 72–92. The translation is slightly adapted from Burgess and Busby (1999), 73–81.

    Le pan de sun mantel plia,
    Desuz sun chief puis le cucha.
    Mut est pensis pur sa mesaise,
    Il ne veit chose ki li plaise.
    La u il gist en teu maniere,
    Garda aval lez la reiviere,
    Si vit venir deus dameiseles:
    Unkes n'en ot veü plus beles!
    Vestues furent richement,
    Laciees mut estreitement
    En deus bliauz de purpre bis;
    Mut par aveient bel le vis!
    L'eisnee portout uns bacins,
    D'or esmeré bien faiz e fins;
    Le veir vus en dirai sanz faile:
    L'autre portout une tüaile.   (49–64)

    Kar i venez ensemble od nus!
    Sauvement vus i cundurums:
    Vees, pres est li paveilluns.
    Li cheviers ode les vait,
    De sun cheval ne tient nul plait,
    Ki devant lui pesseit al pré.
    De si qu'al tref l'unt amené,
    Ki mut fu beaus e bien asis;
    La reïne Semiramis,
    Quant ele ot unkes plus aveir
    E plus pussaunce e plus saveir,
    Ne l'emperere Octovïan
    N'esligasent le destre pan.
    Un aigle d'or ot desus mis;
    De cel ne sai dire le pris,
    Ne des cordes ne des peissuns
    Ki del tref tienent les giruns:
    Suz ciel n'ad rei kis esligast
    Pur nul aveir k'il i donast!
    Dedenz cel tref fu la pucele;   (74–93)

He folded the skirt of his cloak, which he placed beneath his head very disconsolate because of his troubles and nothing could please him. Lying thus, he looked down-river and saw two damsels coming, more beautiful than any he had ever seen: they were richly dressed in tightly laced dresses of dark purple and their faces were very beautiful. The older one carried a gold basin, well and finely made – I will not fail to tell you the truth – and the other carried a towel. [...]

Come with us, for we will conduct you safely. Look, her tent is near. The knight went with them, disregarding his horse which was grazing before him in the meadow. They led him to the tent, which was so beautiful and well-appointed that neither Queen Semiramis at the height of her wealth, power and knowledge, nor the Emperor Octavian could have afforded even the right-hand flap. There was a golden eagle placed on the top, the value of which I cannot tell, nor of the ropes or the poles which supported the walls of the tent. There is no king under the sun who could afford it, however much he might give. Inside this tent was the maiden [...].

Ele jut sur un lit mut bel—
Li drap valeient un chastel—
En sa chemise senglement.
Mut ot le cors bien fait e gent!
Un chier mantel de blanc hermine,
Covert de purpre alexandrine,
Ot pur le chaut sur li geté;
Tut ot descovert le costé,
Le vis, le col e la peitrine;   (97–105)

Celes ki al tref l'amenerent
De riches dras le cunreerent;
Quant il fu vestuz de nuvel,
Suz ciel nen ot plus bel dancel!
N'esteit mie fous ne vileins!
L'ewe li donent a ses meins
E la tüaille a essuer;
Puis li aportent a mangier.   (173–80)

Quant del mangier furent levé,
Sun cheval li unt amené;
Bien li eurent la sele mise.   (189–91)

Il est a sun ostel venuz,
Ses hummes treve bien vestuz.   (201–2)

Lanval donout les riches duns,
Lanval aquitout les prisuns,
Lanval vesteit les jugleürs   (209–11)

Quant il deveient departir,
Deus puceles virent venir
Sur deus beaus palefreiz amblanz;
Mut par esteient avenanz!
De cendal purpre sunt vestues
Tut senglement a lur char nues.   (471–6)

'Reis, fai tes chambres delivrer
E de palies encurtiner,
U ma dame puisse descendre:
Ensemble od vus veut ostel prendre.'   (491–4)

Quant il ierent en cel esfrei,
Deus puceles de gent cunrei,
Vestues de deus palies freis—   (509–11)

She lay on a very beautiful bed – the bed-clothes were worth as much as a castle – clad only in her shift. Her body was well formed and handsome, and in order to protect herself from the heat, she had cast about her a costly robe of white ermine covered with purple Alexandrian silk. Her side, though, was uncovered, as well as her face, neck and breast. […]

Those who had led him to the tent dressed him in rich clothes; when he was newly dressed there was no handsomer man on earth. He was neither foolish nor ill-mannered. They gave him water to wash his hands and the towel to dry them and then brought him food. […]

When they had risen from the meal, his horse was brought to him, well saddled. […]

When he came to his lodgings, he found his men finely dressed. […]

Lanval gave costly gifts, Lanval fed prisoners, Lanval clothed the entertainers. […]

When they were about to leave, they saw two maidens approaching on two fine ambling horses. They were extremely comely and dressed only in purple sendal, next to their bare skin. […]

'King, make your chambers available and hang them with expensive cloth so that my lady may stay here, for she wishes to lodge with you.' […]

While they were in this troubled state they saw two finely accoutred maidens coming dressed in fresh expensive clothes […].

> Ele iert vestue en itel guise
> De chainse blanc e de chemise,
> Que tuit les costé li pareient,
> Ki de deus parz lacié esteient. (559–62)
>
> Sis manteus fu de purpre bis;
> Les pans en ot entur li mis. (571–2)
>
> Devant le rei est descendue,
> Si que de tuz iert bien veüe.
> Sun mantel ad laissié cheeir,
> Que mieuz la peüssent veeir. (603–6)

10. *Sir Landevale*

This Middle English poem is adapted from the *lai* of Marie de France. It is printed in Shepherd (1995), 352–64 from Oxford, Bodleian Library, MS Rawlinson C. 86, fols. 119v–128v, which is dated to the very late fifteenth or early sixteenth century by Shepherd (but here the u/v distinction elided by Shepherd is retained). Shepherd suggests a date of composition in the first half of the fourteenth century. There is an electronic edition in the Chadwyck-Healey English Poetry Full-Text Database (1992) based on an edition printed in *The American Journal of Philology* 10 (1899). The translation is by Louise Sylvester.

> For he was hote yn the weddir.
> Hys mantelle he toke and fold togeder (39–40)
>
> Than he sawe, comynge oute of holtys hore,
> Owte of the forest cam maydyns two,
> The fayrest on grounde that myght goo.
> Kyrtyls they had of purpyl sendell,
> Small i-lasid, syttyng welle;
> Mantels of grene veluet
> Frengide with gold were wele i-sette.
> They had on atyre therwithalle,
> And eache of them a joly cornall (52–60)
>
> That on bare a gold basyn,
> That othir a towail riche and fyn. (65–6)
>
> Anone he in that forest sy
> A pauylion, i-pight an hy,
> With treysour i-wrought on euery syde,
> Al of werke of the faryse.
> Eche pomell of that pavilione
> Was worth a citie, or a towne;
> Vpon the cupe an heron was —
> A richer nowher ne was;

The lady was dressed in a white gown and an undergown, laced left and right so as to reveal her sides. [...]

Her cloak was of dark purple cloth and she had wrapped its skirts around her. [...]

She dismounted before the king and in the sight of all, let her cloak fall so that they could see her better.

Because the weather was making him hot, he took off his cloak and folded it up. [...]

Then he saw something coming out of the dark woods: out of the forest came two beautiful maidens, the most beautiful that might walk this earth. They had gowns of purple sendal tightly laced and beautifully fitted. Their cloaks of green velvet fringed with gold sat well on them. They had on beautiful outfits altogether, and each had a pretty circlet. [...]

One carried a gold basin, the other a fine costly towel. [...]

Soon in that high forest he saw a tent pitched up high, made with treasures on every side. It was the work of the Persians and each ornamental knob was worth a city or a town. There was an eagle on the top: there was not a costlier one anywhere.

In his mouthe a carbuncle, bright
As the mone that shone light   (77–86)

There was a bede of mekyll price,
Couerid with purpill byse;
Thereon lay that maydyn bright,
Almost nakyd and vpright.
Al her clothes byside her lay;
Syngly was she wrappyd, parfay,
With a mauntell of hermyn,
Coveride was with alexanderyn.
The mantell for hete downe she dede
Right to hir gyrdillstede   (95–104)

And while they spake thus in-fere,
Other maidens ther commyn tho;
Well more fairer than the other two —
Riding vpon moilés of Spayne,
Bothe sadellys and bridels of Almayn —
They were i-clothed in atire   (384–9)

That on of them thise wordys spake:
'Sir, riche Kyng Arthure,
Lete dight thyn halle with honour,
Bothe rofe and grounde and wallys,
With clothys of gold and riche pallys;
Yet it is lithely, yef thou so doo
My lady for-to light therto'   (404–10)

A crowne was vpon her hede,
Al of precious stones and gold rede;
Clothid she was yn purpyll pall,
Her body gentill and medill smale;
The pane of hir mantell inwarde
On hir harmes she foldid owtewarde,
Whiche wel becam that lady   (439–45)

Her .iiii. maidens with gret honour
Agayne her came oute of the bowre,
And held her steroppys so   (465–7)

In its mouth was a bright carbuncle that radiated light like the moon. [...]

There was a very expensive bed covered with purple linen. On it lay that bright maiden almost naked and supine. All her clothes lay beside her; indeed, she was only wrapped in an ermine robe and covered with Alexandrian silk. Because of the heat, she had undone the robe as far as her waist. [...]

And while they were talking together, other maidens, more beautiful than the other two, arrived riding on Spanish mules with German saddles and bridles. They were dressed in fine clothes [...].

One of them said these words: 'Honourable sir King Arthur, let your hall be splendidly decorated, roof, floors and walls, with cloths of gold and costly curtains. If you do this, my lady will gladly stay there. [...]

There was a crown made entirely of jewels and red gold on her head and she was dressed in fine purple cloth. Her body was graceful and her waist slender. She had folded outwards the fur lining of her cloak on her arms which was very becoming to that lady. [...]

Her four maidens with great honour accompanied her out of the bower and held her stirrups in place.

11. Thomas Chestre, *Sir Launfal*

Thomas Chestre's *Sir Launfal*, written in the late fourteenth century, is preserved in only one early-fifteenth-century manuscript: BL, MS Cotton Caligula A ii. In this Middle English romance we see clothes as signifiers of poverty: difficulties include a lack of replacements when clothes become old and worn or damaged; and the impossibility of attending church because of a lack of appropriate clothing. The interaction between the weather and appropriate or adequate clothing is also brought vividly to life in the scenes in which Sir Launfal goes hunting and is caught in the rain and when he folds his cloak because of the heat (though the latter does not seem to affect the maidens he meets with whose garments include fur-trimmed velvet). The poet is careful to specify not only garments and other textiles, but the fabric from which they are made and the colours, and the richness (or otherwise) of the textiles. The text is that of Laskaya and Salisbury (1995). The translation is by Louise Sylvester.

> The Quene yaf yftes for the nones,
> Gold and selver and precyous stonys
>   Her curtasye to kythe.
> Everych knyght sche gaf broche other ryng
> But Syr Launfal sche yaf nothyng   (67–71)

> They seyd, 'Syr, our robes beth torent,
> And your tresour ys all yspent,
>   And we goth ewyll ydyght.'   (139–41)

> Noon other robes they ne hadde
> Than they owt wyth ham ladde,
>   And tho wer totore and thynne.   (154–6)

> But upon a rayny day hyt befel
> An huntynge wente Syr Launfel
>   To chasy yn holtes hore;
> In our old robes we yede that day,
> And thus we beth ywent away,
>   As we before hym wore.   (169–74)

> Today to cherche I wolde have gon,
> But me fawtede hosyn and schon,
>   Clenly brech and scherte;
> And for defawte of clothynge,
> Ne myghte y yn the peple thrynge.   (199–203)

> He rood toward the west.
> The wether was hot the underntyde;
> He lyghte adoun, and gan abyde
>   Under a fayr forest.
> And, for hete of the wedere,
> Hys mantell he feld togydere   (219–24)

The queen gave gifts for the occasion of gold, silver and jewels to display her courtesy; she gave a brooch or a ring to every knight. But she gave nothing to Sir Launfal [...].

They said, 'Sir, our clothes are in tatters, and your money is all spent, and we are badly dressed.' [...]

They had no other robes than those which they had taken with them and those were in tatters and threadbare. [...]

But one rainy day it happened that Sir Launfal went hunting game in the dark woods, and we wore our old robes that day, so that we went away dressed just as we were in his presence. [...]

'Today I wanted to go to church but I lacked stockings and shoes, clean underwear and an undershirt and so for lack of clothing I could not go among the press of people. [...]

He rode towards the west. The weather was hot that morning; he dismounted and lingered in a beautiful forest. And, because of the heat of the weather, he folded up his cloak. [...]

As he sat yn sorow and sore
He sawe come out of holtes hore
   Gentyll maydenes two:
Har kerteles wer of Indesandel,
Ylased smalle, jolif, and well —
   Ther myght noon gayer go.
Har manteles wer of grene felvet,
Ybordured wyth gold, ryght well ysette,
   Ypelured wyth grys and gro.
Har heddys wer dyght well wythalle:
Everych hadde oon a jolyf coronall
   Wyth syxty gemmys and mo.   (229–40)

That oon bar of gold a basyn,
That other a towayle, whyt and fyn,
   Of selk that was good and ryche.
Har kercheves wer well schyre,
Arayd wyth ryche gold wyre.   (244–8)

And when they come in the forest an hygh,
A pavyloun yteld he sygh,
   Wyth merthe and mochell honour.
The pavyloun was wrouth, forsothe, ywys,
All of werk of Sarsynys,
   The pomelles of crystall;
Upon the toppe an ern ther stod
Of bournede golde, ryche and good,
   Ylorysched wyth ryche amall.
Hys eyn wer carbonkeles bryght —
As the mone they schon anyght,
   That spreteth out ovyr all.
Alysaundre the conquerour,
Ne Kyng Artour yn hys most honour,
   Ne hadde noon scwych juell!   (262–76)

In the pavyloun he fond a bed of prys
Yheled wyth purpur bys,
   That semyle was of syghte.
Therinne lay that lady gent
That after Syr Launfal hedde ysent,
   That lefsom lemede bryght.
For hete her clothes down sche dede
Almest to her gerdylstede
   Than lay sche uncovert.   (283–91)

As he sat in sorrow and suffering, he saw two gracious maidens come out of the dark woods. Their gowns were made of indigo silk and were laced tightly and well. No one could have been more beautifully turned out. Their cloaks were made of green velvet bordered with gold beautifully adorned, and edged with grey and white fur. Their heads were beautifully coiffed and each wore a beautiful coronet set with more than sixty jewels. [...]

One carried a gold basin, the other a fine white towel made of good expensive silk. Their headcloths were very bright, they were decorated with rich gold wire. [...]

And when they were up high in the forest, he saw a tent pitched with joy and great honour. The tent was beautifully made, truly, indeed: it was all Saracen work, the ornamental knobs were crystal. An eagle stood on top made of expensive and good burnished gold embellished with costly enamel. His eyes were bright carbuncles which shone like the moon at night that spreads its beams over everyone. Neither Alexander the Great nor King Arthur in his greatest splendour had such a gem. [...]

In the tent he found a sumptuous bed covered with purple linen that was a beautiful sight. In it lay that gracious lady who had sent for Sir Launfal. The lovely one gleamed brightly. Because of the heat she had undone her clothes almost to the waist so she lay uncovered. [...]

I wyll the yeve an alner
Ymad of sylk and of gold cler,
    Wyth fayre ymages thre.   (319–21)

And of my armes oo pensel
Wyth thre ermyns ypeynted well,
    Also thou schalt have.   (328–30)

Than come ther, thorwgh the cité, ten
Well yharneysyth men
    Upon ten somers ryde;
Some wyth sylver, some wyth gold —
All to Syr Launfal hyt schold;
    To presente hym, wyth pryde,
Wyth ryche clothes and armure bryght,
They axede aftyr Launfal the knyght,
    Whar he gan abyde.
The yong men wer clothed yn ynde   (376–85)

The Meyr for schame away yede.
Launfal yn purpure gan hym schrede,
    Ypelured wyth whyt ermyne.   (415–17)

He yaf the messenger, for that tydyng,
A noble courser, and a ryng,
    And a robe of ray.   (544–6)

All that he hadde before ywonne,
Hyt malt as snow ayens the sunne,
    In romaunce as we rede;
Hys armur, that was whyt as flour,
Hyt becom of blak colour.   (739–43)

Tho saw they other ten maydenes bryght,
Fayryr than the other ten of syght,
    As they gone hym deme.
They ryd upon joly moyles of Spayne,
Wyth sadell and brydell of Champayne,
    Har lorayns lyght gonne leme.
They wer yclodeth yn samyt tyre;
Ech man hadde greet desyre
    To se har clothynge.   (883–91)

Sche hadde a crounne upon her molde
Of ryche stones, and of golde,
    That lofsom lemede lyght.

I will give you a purse made of silk and shining gold with three beautiful images. [...]

And you shall also have a pennon with my coat-of-arms with three ermines beautifully painted on it. [...]

Then ten armoured men came through the city riding on ten pack-horses; some had silver, some gold and all of it was to go to Sir Launfal, to be presented to him with pride. They wore costly clothes and shining armour and they asked for Sir Launfal and where he might be. The young men were clothed in indigo. [...]

The mayor went away ashamed. Launfal dressed himself in purple cloth trimmed with white ermine. [...]

For that news he gave the messenger a noble horse and a ring and a striped robe. [...]

All that he had gained melted like snow in the sun, as we read in romances. His armour, that had been as white as flour, turned black. [...]

Then they saw another ten shining maidens, more beautiful than the other ten to look at, as they were about to pass judgement. They rode on pretty Spanish mules with saddles and bridles from Champagne. Their harness gleamed brightly. They were dressed in clothes of samite: each man was filled with desire to see their clothing. [...]

She had a crown of rich jewels and gold on her head, that lovely one gleamed brightly. The lady was dressed in fine

> The lady was clad yn purpere palle,
> Wyth gentyll body and myddyll small,
>> That semely was of syght;
> Her mantyll was furryd wyth whyt ermyn,
> Yreversyd jolyf and fyn —
>> No rychere be ne myght.
> Her sadell was semyly set:
> The sambus wer grene felvet
>> Ypaynted wyth ymagerye.
> The bordure was of belles
> Of ryche gold, and nothyng elles
>> That any man myghte aspye.
> In the arsouns, before and behynde,
> Were twey stones of Ynde,
>> Gay for the maystrye.
> The paytrelle of her palfraye
> Was worth an erldome, stoute and gay,
>> The best yn Lumbardye.   (940–60)

THE FREINE GROUP

In the story told in this set of texts, a woman slanders her neighbour who has given birth to twin sons, claiming that for this to happen she must have sex with two men. Shortly afterwards, the slanderer herself gives birth to twin daughters. She is so mortified that she wraps one baby in a rich cloth, fastens a gold ring to her arm and leaves her in a 'fresne' (ash-tree) outside a religious foundation. As a young woman, Le Fresne becomes the lover of a wealthy nobleman. He is pressured to marry a legitimate wife (who is in fact Le Fresne's twin sister) and Le Fresne prepares the bridal chamber, covering the bed with the cloth in which she was found. In the final moments of the narrative her mother recognises the cloth, establishing Le Fresne's noble and legitimate birth, the lover's marriage is annulled and he marries Le Fresne. The cloth works to relocate the protagonist within the family unit and accomplish the triumph of the good.

12. Marie de France, *Lai Le Fresne*

This Anglo-French *lai* by Marie de France is believed to date from the 1160s. We may note the phrase 'le palie virent riche e bel': the costliness and beauty of Fresne's clothes suggest to those who find her that she is of noble lineage. Marie uses dress most often to suggest beauty and nobility (see Smith 2008: 100). The standard edition is that of Rychner (1966), 44–60. The translation is slightly adapted from that of Burgess and Busby (1999), 61–7.

> En un chief di mut bon chesil
> Envolupent l'enfant gentil
> E desus un paile roé;
> Ses sires li ot aporté

purple cloth. She had a graceful body and a slender waist that was lovely to look at. Her cloak was trimmed with white ermine with the edges turned back, prettily decorated. It was impossible that there could be a costlier one. Her saddle was beautifully adorned: the saddle-cloths were green velvet painted with images and fringed with rich gold bells and nothing else that could be seen. On the saddles-bows in front and behind were two most brilliant jewels from India. The ornamental collar worn by her palfrey was worth a noble and magnificent earldom. It was the best in Lombardy.

They wrapped the noble child in a large piece of fine linen and then placed over her the finest piece of striped brocade which her husband

de Costentinoble, u il fu:
unques si bon n'orent veü!
A une piece d'un suen laz
Un gros anel li lie al braz;
De fin or i aveit une unce,
El chestun out une jagunce,
La verge entur esteit lettree:
La u la meschine ert trovee,
Bien sachent tuit vereiement
Qu'ele est nee de bone gent.   (121–34)

Sur le freisne les dras choisi;
Quidat k'aukuns les eüst pris
En larecin e ileoc mis:
D'autre chose n'ot il regard.
Plus tost qu'il pot vint cele part,
Taste, si ad l'enfant trové.   (184–9)

Entur sun braz treve l'anel,
Le palie virent riche e bel:
Bien surent cil tut a escïent
Qu'ele est nee de haute gent.   (207–10)

A sun chastel l'en ad menee.
Son palie emporte e sun anel:
De ceo li poet estre mut bel.
L'abeesse li ot rendu
E dit coment ert avenu
Quant primes li fu enveiee.
Desus le freisne fu cuchiee;
Le palie e l'anel li bailla
Cil ki primes li enveia;
Plus d'aveir ne receut od li;
Come sa niece la nuri.
La meschine bien les gardat,
En un cofre les anfermat;
Le cofre fist od sei porter:
Nel volt lessier ne ublier.   (292–306)

La noit, al lit apareiller
U l'espuse deveit cuchier,
La damisele i est alee;
De sun mauntel est desfublee.
Les chamberleins i apela;
La maniere lur enseigna
Cument sis sires le voleit,

had brought from Constantinople, where he had been. A finer one was never seen. With a piece of her ribbon, the lady attached to the child's arm a large ring made from an ounce of pure gold, with a precious stone set in it and lettering on the band. Wherever she was found, people would then truly know that she was of noble birth. [...]

When he saw the cloths on the ash-tree his only thought was that someone had stolen them and put them there. He made his way over to the tree as soon as he could, felt with his hand and thus found the child. [...]

On its arm he found the ring, and when they saw the rich and beautiful cloth of silk, they were sure that she was born of high degree. [...]

He took her to his castle. She took her brocade and ring, for that might yet turn out to her advantage. The abbess had given them to her and told her what had happened when first she had been sent to her and placed in the ash-tree. Whoever had sent her in the first place had given her the brocade and the ring, but no other riches accompanied her; she had then raised her as her niece. The girl kept the brocade and the ring and put them in a casket which she carried with her, for she did not want to leave or forget it. [...]

That night, when the bed in which the wife was to lie was being prepared, the damsel went there and took off her cloak. She summoned

Kar meintefeiz veü l'aveit.
Quant le lit orent apresté,
Un covertur unt sus jeté;
Li dras esteit d'un viel bofu.
La dameisele l'ad veü:
N'ert mie bons, ceo li sembla;
En sun curage li pesa.
Un cofre ovri, sun palie prist,
Sur le lit sun seignur le mist.
Pur lui honurer le feseit   (389–405)

Quant la chambre fu delivree,
La dame ad sa fille amenee.
Ele la volt fere cuchier,
Si la cumande a despoilier.
La palie esgarde sur le lit,
Que unke mes si bon ne vit
Fors sul celui qu'ele dona
Od sa fille k'ele cela.
Idunc li remembra de li:
Tut li curages li fremi.
Le chamberlenc apele a sei:
'Di mei, fait ele, par ta fei,
U fu cist bons palies trovez?
—Dame, fait il, vus le savrez:
La dameisele l'aporta,
Sur le covertur le geta,
Kar ne li sembla mie boens.
Jeo qui que li palies est soens.'
La dame l'aveit apelee,
E ele est devant li alee.
De sun mauntel se desfubla,
E la mere l'areisuna:
'Bele amie, nel me celez,
U fu cist bons palies trovez?
Dunt vus vient il? Kil vus dona?
Kar me dites kil vus bailla!'
La meschine li respundi:
'Dame, m'aunte, ke me nuri,
L'abeesse kil me bailla,
A garder le me comanda.
Cest e un anel me baillerent
Cil ki a nurir m'enveierent.
—Bele, pois jeo veer l'anel?
—Oïl, dame, ceo m'est mut bel!'

the chamberlains and showed them how her lord wanted the bed made, for she had often seen it done. When they had made the bed ready, they covered it with a fabric coverlet. The damsel saw it and was dissatisfied, for it did not seem right to her. She opened the chest, took out her brocade and, to honour him, put it on her lord's bed. [...]

When the chamber was empty, the lady brought her daughter, whom she wanted to get ready for bed, and told her to undress. She saw the brocade on the bed, the like of which she had never seen, save for the one she had given away with the daughter she had concealed. Then she remembered her and trembled in her heart. She called the chamberlain to her. 'Tell me,' she said, 'on your faith, where was this fine brocade found?' 'Lady,' he said, 'I shall tell you: the damsel brought it and cast it over this coverlet which she did not like. I think that the brocade is hers.' The lady called her and she came. When she had taken off her cloak, her mother spoke to her: 'Fair friend, do not conceal it from me. Where was this good brocade found? How did you acquire it? Who gave it to you? Tell me from whom you received it!' The girl answered her: 'Lady my aunt, the abbess, who raised me, gave it to me and ordered me to keep it. Those who sent me to be brought up gave me that and a ring.' 'Fair one, may I see this ring?' 'Yes, my lady, with pleasure.' She brought her the ring and the lady looked

> L'anel li ad dunc aporté,
> E ele l'ad mut esgardé.
> El l'ad bien reconeü,
> E le palie k'ele ad veü.
> Ne dute mes, bien seit e creit,
> Qu'el meïmes sa fille esteit. (409–48)

> Deus filles oi, l'une celai;
> A un muster la fis geter
> E nostre palie od li porter
> E l'anel que vus me donastes
> Quant vus primes od mei parlastes.
> Ne vus peot mie estre celé:
> Le drap e l'anel ai trové.
> Nostre fille ai ci coneüe,
> Que par ma folie oi perdue. (472–80)

13. *Lay Le Freine*

This Middle English poem dates from the early fourteenth century and exists in only one manuscript copy: National Library of Scotland, Advocates 19.2.1, also called the Auchinleck manuscript. In this version the precious cloth is called by the name of a cloth that has become known in England since Marie de France's composition. The text is that of Laskaya and Salisbury (1995). The translation is by Louise Sylvester.

> Sche toke a riche baudekine
> That hir lord brought from Costentine
> And lapped the litel maiden therin,
> And toke a ring of gold fin,
> And on hir right arm it knitt,
> With a lace of silke therin plit;
> And whoso hir founde schuld have in mende
> That it were comen of riche kende. (137–44)

> An asche bi hir fair and heighe,
> Wele ybowed, of michel priis;
> The bodi was holow as mani on is.
> Therin sche leyd the child for cold,
> In the pel as it was bifold,
> And blisced it with al hir might. (174–9)

> And seighe anon in the stede
> The pel liggen in the tre,
> And thought wele that it might be
> That theves hadde yrobbed sumwhare,
> And gon ther forth and lete it thare.

at it carefully, easily recognising it and the brocade. She had no doubt, for she now knew for sure that this was indeed her daughter. [...]

'I had two daughters, one of whom I hid. I had her abandoned at a church and sent with her our brocade and the ring you gave me when you first spoke with me. It can be hidden from you no longer: I have found both the cloth and the ring, and have recognised here our daughter whom I lost by my folly.'

She took a cloth of rich baldachin that her husband had brought from Constantinople and wrapped the little girl in it, and took a ring of fine gold and fastened it onto her right arm with a cord of braided silk so that whoever found her would have it in their minds that she had come from a noble family. [...]

There was an ash by her with many branches and great excellence; the body was hollow, as many are. She laid the child, wrapped in the cloth, inside it because of the cold and blessed her with all her strength. [...]

And immediately saw there the cloth lying in the tree and thought that it must be that thieves had robbed somewhere and gone on their way and left it there. He went there and

Therto he yede and it unwond,
And the maidenchild therin he fond.   (190–6)

'A litel maidenchild ich founde
In the holwe assche ther out,
And a pel him about.
A ring of gold also was there.'   (214–17)

The porter anon it gan forth bring
With the pal and with the ring.   (225–6)

The abbesse hir in conseyl toke,
To tellen hir hye nought forsoke,
Hou hye was founden in al thing,
And tok hir the cloth and the ring,
And bad hir kepe it in that stede;
And ther whiles sche lived so sche dede.   (245–50)

The maiden grant, and to him trist,
And stale oway that no man wist.
With hir tok hye no thing
Bot hir pel and hir ring.   (297–300)

Than to the bour the damsel sped,
Whar graithed was the spousaile bed;
Sche demed it was ful foully dight,
And yll besemed a may so bright;
So to her coffer quick she cam,
And her riche baudekyn out nam,
Which from the abbesse sche had got;
Fayrer mantel nas ther not;
And deftly on the bed it layd;
Her lord would thus be well apayd.
Le Codre and her mother, thare,
Ynsame unto the bour gan fare,
But whan the levedi that mantyll seighe,
Sche wel neighe swoned oway.
The chamberleynt sche cleped tho,
But he wist of it no mo.
Then came that hendi maid Le Frain,
And the levedi gan to her sain,
And asked whose mantyll it ware.
Then answered that maiden fair:
'It is mine without lesing;
Y had it together with this ringe.
Myne aunte tolde me a ferli cas

unwound it and found the little girl inside it. [...]

'I found a little girl in the hollow ash out there with a cloth wrapped round her and there was a gold ring too.' [...]

The porter quickly fetched her out with the cloth and the ring. [...]

The abbess took her into her confidence to tell her she was not forsaken, she told her all the details of how she was found and gave her the cloth and the ring. She told her to keep them in that place and as long as she lived there she did so. [...]

The maiden acceded and trusted him and stole away so that no one knew. She took nothing with her except her cloth and her ring. [...]

Then the young woman sped to the chamber where the marriage bed was arrayed. She judged that it was poorly made and ill-befitting for such a beautiful maiden. She went quickly to her chest and took out her costly baldachin which she had been given by the abbess – there was no more beautiful covering – and gently laid it on the bed: her lord would be very pleased with it. Le Codre and her mother began to enter the bower together but when the lady saw that covering she almost fainted. Then she called the chamberlain but he knew nothing about it. Then that gentle maid Le Freine came in and the lady spoke to her and asked whose robe it was. Then the beautiful young woman answered, 'it is mine, without a word of a lie, I had it together with this ring. My aunt told me a wonderful thing, how I was wrapped in this robe and

> Hou in this mantyll yfold I was,
> And hadde upon mine arm this ring,
> Whanne I was ysent to norysching.'
>   Then was the levedi astonied sore:
> 'Fair child! My doughter, y the bore!'
> Sche swoned and was wel neighe ded,
> And lay sikeand on that bed.   (359–88)
>
> And this is sche, our doughter free;
> And this is the mantyll, and this the ring
> You gaf me of yore as a love-tokening.'   (396–8)

14. *Sir Degrevant*

This fifteenth-century Middle English romance is extant in two manuscripts: Lincoln Cathedral, MS A.5.2, the Thornton manuscript (L), and Cambridge University Library, MS Ff.i.6, the Findern anthology (C). The eponymous protagonist, who has been happy with his own company, is the object of a raid by a neighbouring earl. In the course of his retaliation, Degrevant meets the earl's daughter Melidor and they fall in love. The poet makes use of the alliterating tags relating to clothing that are common in tail-rhyme romance (and other poetic forms), for example 'Wys(e) under wede' (C lines 236, 408) with the variants 'Worthliest in wede' (L) and 'Vlonkest on wede' (C) (line 592); 'worthy in wedys' (L), 'worþely in wedus' (C) (line 1112) and Melidor is 'precyous in palle' (line 537). Elsewhere in the poem, the descriptions are filled with realistic detail, most strikingly in the long description of the interior and furnishings of Melidor's bedroom. The two manuscripts are edited in a facing page edition by Casson (1949). The C-text is chosen by Kooper for his (2006) edition, and selected here, because two hundred lines are missing from the Thornton manuscript. The translation is by Louise Sylvester.

> He lovede well almosdede,
> Powr men to cloth and fede   (81–2)
>
> And also gestes to call,
> And mensteralus her in halle.
> He gaff hem robes of palle   (85–7)
>
> And whan the batell enjoined
> With speres ferisly they foynede.
> Ther myght no sege be ensoynd
>   That faught in the feld.
> Wyth bryght swerdus on the bent
> Rych hawberkes they rent;
> Gleves gleteryng glent
>   Opon geldene scheldus.
> They styken stedus in stour,
> Knyghtus thorow her armere   (289–98)
>
> The doughty knyght Sur Degrevaunt
> Leys the lordes on the laund

had this ring on my arm when I was sent away to be brought up.'

Then the lady was utterly amazed: 'Beautiful child, my daughter, I bore you!' Then she fainted and was close to death and lay sighing on that bed. [...]

'And this is she, our noble daughter; and this is the robe and this the ring that you gave me long ago as a token of your love.'

He loved giving alms to feed and clothe poor people. [...]

And also to invite guests to hear minstrels in the hall to whom (i.e. to the minstrels) he gave robes of fine cloth [...].

And when they engaged in battle they thrust fiercely with spears. No warrior might be allowed to delay when they fought in the field. With bright swords turned on them they tore costly long coats of mail, glittering swords glanced on golden shields. They pierced horses in battle, knights through their armour [...].

The brave knight Sir Degrevant lays the lords on the ground through

Thorw jepun and jesseraund,
    And lames the ledes.
Schyr scheldus they schrede,
Many dowghty was dede,
Ryche maylus wexen rede,
    So manye bolde dedus.   (305–12)

Burnes he hadde yborn doun;
Gomes wyth gambisoun
Lyes opon bent broun,
    And sterff under stede.
Sir Degrevaunt the gode knyght
Bryttenes the basnettus bryght.   (317–22)

The Eorlus doughder beheld
    That borlich and bolde.
For he was armed so clen,
With gold and azour ful schen,
And with his troweloves bytwen,
    Was joy to behold.
She was comlech yclade   (467–73)

'I wolde nothing of their,
    Broche ne bye;
I wolde aske tham na mare
But hyr body all bare,
And we frendes for evermar,
    What doel that I drye.'   (571–6)

Sche come in a vyolet
With whyghth perl overfret,
And saphyrus therinne isett,
    On everyche a syde.
All of pallwork fyn,
With nuche and nevyn,
Anurled with ermyn,
    And overt for pryde.
To tell hur botenus was toor,
Anamelede with azour,
With topyes the trechour
    Overtrasyd that tyde.
Sche was recevyd aspanne
Of any lyvand manne;
Of rede golde the rybanne
    Glemyd hur gyde.
Hyr herre was hyghthtyd on hold

tunic and chain mail and maims the men. They cut the bright shields: many a brave man was dead. Rich coats of mail turned red. So many bold deeds [...].

He had borne down warriors, men with padded tunics lie on the brown battlefield and die under their horses. Sir Degrevant, the good knight, cuts through the bright helmets [...]

The earl's daughter saw that stately and bold one for he was so splendidly armed in shining gold and blue and with his true-love knots in between, he was a joy to see. She was beautifully dressed [...].

'I want nothing from them, not a brooch nor a ring. I would ask them for no more than her body all bare and that we become friends for evermore what distress that I suffer.' [...]

She came dressed in violet with white pearls embroidered on it and sapphires set in it in every part, all of fine pallwork with a brooch and a clasp, bordered with ermine and worn unfastened to show off. It would be hard to count her buttons, enamelled in blue; the head-dress was set with topazes for the occasion. She would be received with an embrace at the hands of any living man. The red-gold trimming made her dress shine. Her hair was pinned up with a circlet of gold. A

With a coronal of golde.
Was never made upon mold
   A worthelychere wyghth.
Sche was frely and fair,
And well hyr semed hyr geyr,
With ryche boses a payr,
   That derely were bydyghth,
With a front endent
With peyrl of Orient,
Out of Syprus was sent,
   To that burd bryghth.
Hur kerchevus was curyus,
Hyr vyssag ful gracious.   (641–70)

The knyght sat at hys avenaunt
In a gentyl jesseraunt   (813–14)

'He sendys thee syche a gretyng:
Lo, here ys a rede gold ryng
   With a ryche ston.'
The lady loked on that ryng,
Hyt was a gyfte for a kyng.
'This ys a merveylous thing!'   (990–5)

The Duk answerus on hyghth:
'Whereby knowus thou the knyghth?'
The Eorle taughth hym ful ryghth
   With wordys, I wene.
'He beres a cheef of azour
Engrelyd, with a satur,
With doubule tressour,
   And trewelovus bytwene.
Hys bagges is blake:
For he wol no man forsake
A lyoun tyed to an ake,
   Of gold and of grene.
An helme ryche to behold
He beres a dolfyn of gold,
With trewelovus in the mold,
   Compasyd ful clene.'   (1041–56)

And callyd to hym tow knyghthus,
   That pryvest were ay.
'Ha dyght yow on stedus
In two damysel wedus   (1187–90)

worthier being was never made on earth. She was lovely and beautiful and her clothes suited her well with a pair of rich ornaments that were expensively decorated, with a front inlaid with precious eastern pearls sent from Cyprus to that beautiful young woman. Her headcloth was finely made and her face was graceful. [...]

The knight sat comfortably in light armour of mail and padded cloth [...]

'He sends you a greeting. Look here is a red-gold ring with a precious stone.' The lady looked at that ring. It was a gift fit for a king. 'This is a wonderful thing' [...].

The duke answered aloud, 'How do you recognise the knight?' The earl informed him correctly with these words, I think. 'He carries a shield with a top third of azure engrailed with a saltire with a double band following the edge and true-love knots in between. His badge is white: because he would not abandon any man it has a lion tied to an oak in gold and green. On a helmet that is costly to see, he has a golden dolphin, with nicely devised true-love knots on top.' [...]

And called two knights to him who were always the most discreet. 'Get yourselves on horses in young men's clothes. [...]

Greyth myn hors on hor gere
    And lok that thei be gay,
That thai be trapped aget,
In topteler and in mauntolet,
In a fyn vyolet,
    And makes non delay.'   (1195–1200)

Sche sett a bourd of yvore,
Trestellus ordeyned therfor;
Clothus keverede that ovur –
    Swyche seye thei never are.
Towellus of Eylyssham,
Whyghth as the see ys fame,
Sanappus of the same   (1397–1403)

Hur bede was of aszure,
With testur and celure,
With a bryght bordure
    Compasyd ful clene.
And all a storye as hyt was
Of Ydoyne and Amadas,
Perreye in ylke a plas,
    And papageyes of grene.
The scochenus of many knyght
Of gold and cyprus was idyght,
Brode besauntus and bryght,
    And trewelovus bytwene.
Ther was at hur testere
The kyngus owun banere;
Was nevere bede rychere
    Of empryce ne qwene.
Fayr schetus of sylk,
Chalkwhyghth as the mylk,
Quyltus poyned of that ylk,
    Touseled they ware;
Coddys of sendal,
Knoppus of crystal
That was mad in Westfal
    With women of lare.
Hyt was a mervelous thing
To se the rydalus hyng
With mony a rede gold ryng,
    That home upbare.
The cordes that thei on ran
The Duk Betyse hom wan;
Mayd Medyore hom span
    Of meremaydenus hare.   (1489–1520)

Array my horses in harness, and make sure that it is smart, that they are dressed up in style, in fine violet ornamental coverings and caparisons. And don't delay.' [...]

She set a table of ivory and organised trestles for it; tablecloths covered that such as are never seen: towels from Aylsham white as seafoam and overcloths of the same fabric [...].

Her bed was blue, with a tester and canopy with a bright border neatly devised depicting the story of Ydoyne and Amadas. There were precious stones everywhere and green parrots and the coats of arms of many knights. It was adorned with gold and Cyprus gold, with bright bezants and true-love knots here and there. As a wall-hanging she had the king's own banner. There was never an empress nor a queen with a costlier bed. It had beautiful silk sheets, chalkwhite like milk, quilts embroidered in the same silk, that were tassled; pillows of fine silk; knobs of crystal that were made by skilled women in Westphalia. It was a wonderful thing to see the curtains hanging from the many gold rings that supported them. The duke of Betis brought back the cords that they ran on: the maid Melidor spun them from mermaid's hair. [...]

Thai lay doun in ther bede,
In ryche clothus was spred.
Wytte ye wel or thei wer wed
    Thei synnyd nat thare. (1557–60)

Syre Degrivaunt at evenelyghth
Armede hym and hys knyghth,
And toke on privayly for syghth
    Two gownes of grene.
Nothur schelde ne spere,
Ne no wepen of werre,
Bot twey swerdus thei berre
    Of Florence ful kene. (617–1624)

Whan thei Syr Degrivaunt mett
Sevene sperus on hym ysett,
Evene in hys bassonett,
    Brasten a two;
Some bare hym thorw the gown,
Some brast on hys haberjown.
Hys sqwyer was born down,
    Hys swerd cast hym fro. (1633–40)

She had wondur in hyr wyt
Why here clothus war toslyt,
As thei in holtus had byn hyt,
    With dyntus of spere.
Here gay gownus of grene
Were ful schamely besene.
'Leve syre, where have ye bene,
    Youre clothus to tere?'
The knyghth sat semely
And seide tyl hyr prively:
'We sey never selly
    That shold us aughth dere.
But as we passed by a thorn
Thus wer our gownus totorn.
We shalle have new tomorn;
    We cownte hyt not a payr.' (1697–1712)

Mynstrallus hade in halle
Grete gyftys withalle,
Ryche robus of palle
    With garnementus hale. (1877–80)

They lay down in their bed which was spread with rich bed-clothes. You must know that before they were married they committed no sin there. [...]

At nightfall Sir Degrevant armed himself and his knight, and under cover, against being seen, they put on two green gowns. They carried neither shield nor spear, nor any weapon of war except two very sharp Florentine swords. [...]

When they met Sir Degrevant they threw seven spears at him, straight into his helmet which burst in two. Some pierced him through his gown, some broke on his habergeon. His squire was brought down, his sword thrown from him. [...]

She wondered in her mind why their clothes were all torn, as if they had been in the woods, with strokes from a spear. Their bright green gowns were a shame to see. 'Dear sir, where have you been to tear your clothes?' The knight sat calmly and said to her quietly, 'We saw nothing unusual that would do us any harm but we passed by a thorn bush and that is how our clothes were torn to shreds. We shall have new ones tomorrow and we could not care less.' [...]

There were minstrels in the hall; great gifts indeed, costly robes of fine cloth with whole outfits.

15. *Sir Gawain and the Green Knight*

The poem is extant in only one manuscript, BL, MS Cotton Nero A x. From its linguistic forms scholars have mostly agreed that it must have come from the north-west, with a leaning towards Lancashire. It has been dated to the late fourteenth century (Tolkien *et al.* 1978: xiii). There are two elements to the plot: the arrival at Arthur's court and beheading challenge of the Green Knight, and the temptation of Gawain at the castle of Sir Bertilak on three successive days while the latter is out hunting. Gawain's final temptation, to which he succumbs, is the gift of a green girdle which renders the wearer immune to danger. Gawain and his host have agreed to play a game in which whatever each receives or wins during the day will be exchanged at night. Gawain breaks the agreement by accepting Lady Bertilak's terms for the gift of the girdle which include secrecy. The poem is steeped in realistic and precise details about aristocratic medieval daily life including the clothes and accoutrements worn by men and women. The text is edited by Tolkien and Gordon, revised by Davis (1967). The translation is by Louise Sylvester.

When the action of the poem opens it is Christmas at King Arthur's court at Camelot

> Whene Guenore, ful gay, grayþed in þe myddes,
> Dressed on þe dere des, dubbed al aboute,
> Smal sendal bisides, a selure hir ouer
> Of tryed tolouse, and tars tapites innoghe,
> Þat were enbrawded and beten wyth þe best gemmes
> Þat myȝt be preued of prys wyth penyes to bye,
>   in daye.   (74–80)

A strange and gigantic green knight rides in

> Ande al grayþed in grene þis gome and his wedes:
> A strayte cote ful streȝt, þat stek on his sides,
> A meré mantile abof, mensked withinne
> With pelure pured apert, þe pane ful clene
> With blyþe blaunner ful bryȝt, and his hod boþe,
> Þat watz laȝt fro his lokkez and layde on his schulderes;
> Heme wel-haled hose of þat same,
> Þat spenet on his sparlyr, and clene spures vnder
> Of bryȝt golde, vpon silk bordes barred ful ryche,
> And scholes vnder schankes þere þe schalk rides;
> And alle his vesture uerayly watz clene verdure,
> Boþe þe barres of his belt and oþer blyþe stones,
> Þat were richely rayled in his aray clene
> Aboutte hymself and his sadel, vpon silk werkez.
> Þat were to tor for to telle of tryfles þe halue
> Þat were enbrauded abof, wyth bryddes and flyȝes,
> With gay gaudi of grene, þe golde ay inmyddes.
> Þe pendauntes of his payttrure, þe proude cropure,
> His molaynes, and alle þe metail anamayld was þenne,
> Þe steropes þat he stod on stayned of þe same,

Guinevere, so elegantly dressed was in the middle, placed on a splendid platform decorated all around. There was fine silken cloth at her sides, above her a canopy made of Toulouse fabric, and many wall-hangings made of costly silk that was embroidered and decorated with the finest gemstones that money could ever buy. [...]

And all in green was this man and his clothes: a tight kirtle, fully fitted, that clung to his sides, with a fine mantle on top, adorned inside with a trimmed fur lining in full view, the elegant trimming with beautiful ermine, all white, and his hood too, that was pulled back from his hair and lay on his shoulders. Suitable, well-drawn up leggings of the same colour were fitted to his calves, and below bright spurs of shining gold on silk strips of embroidered fabric ornamented with stripes, and the man rode in there without shoes on his feet; and all his clothes, truly, were bright green, the ornamental bars on his belt as well as the beautiful jewels that were splendidly set on his bright clothing. About himself and his saddle was silk embroidery such that is difficult to describe half the ornamental details that were sewn on it with birds and butterflies and delightful green ornamentation with gold in between. The pendants hanging from his horse's breastplate, the splendid crupper, the studs on the bit of his bridle, and all the metal was enamelled, and the stirrups that he stood on were dyed the same colour, and his saddle-bows at

> And his arsounz al after and his aþel skyrtes,
> Þat euer glemered and glent al of grene stones;   (151–72)
>
> Þe mane of þat mayn hors much to hit lyke,
> Wel cresped and cemmed, wyth knottes ful mony
> Folden in wyth fildore aboute þe fayre grene,
> Ay a herle of þe here, an oþer of golde;
> Þe tayl and his toppyng twynnen of a sute,
> And bounden boþe wyth a bande of a bryȝt grene,
> Dubbed wyth ful dere stonez, as þe dok lasted   (187–93)
>
> Wheþer hade he no helme ne hawbergh nauþer,
> Ne no pysan ne no plate þat pented to armes,
> Ne no schafte ne no schelde to schwue ne to smyte   (203–5)

The Green Knight speaks

> 'For had I founded in fere in feȝtyng wyse,
> I haue a hauberghe at home and a helme boþe,
> A schelde and a scharp spere, schinande bryȝt,
> Ande oþer weppenes to welde, I wene wel, als;
> Bot for I wolde no were, my wedez ar softer'.   (267–71)

He challenges any one of them to strike him and then to allow him to do the same to them after one year has passed. Gawain accepts the challenge and beheads the Green Knight, but he survives. Now Gawain must go and find the Green Knight for the return bout.

> He dowellez þer al þat day, and dressez on þe morn,
> Askez erly hys armez, and alle were þay broȝt.
> Fyrst a tulé tapit tyȝt ouer þe flet,
> And miche watz þe gyld gere þat glent þeralofte;
> Þe stif mon steppez þeron, and þe stel hondelez,
> Dubbed in a dublet of a dere tars,
> And syþen a crafty capados, closed aloft,
> Þat wyth a bryȝt blaunner was bounden withinne.
> Þenne set þay þe sabatounz vpon þe segge fotez,
> His legez lapped in stel with luflych greuez,
> With polaynez piched þerto, policed ful clene,
> Aboute his knez knaged wyth knotez of golde;
> Queme quyssewes þen, þat coyntlych closed
> His thik þrawen þyȝez, with þwonges to tachched;
> And syþen þe brawden bryné of bryȝt stel ryngez
> Vmbeweued þat wyȝ vpon wlonk stuffe,
> And wel bornyst brace vpon his boþe armes,
> With gode cowters and gay, and glouez of plate,
> And alle þe godlych gere þat hym gayn schulde
>   þat tyde;

the back and his glorious skirts whose green gemstones constantly glimmered and glittered. [...]

The mane of the horse similarly, was well curled and combed, with a great many knots entwined with gold thread around the attractive green, always a strand of the hair with another of gold; his tail and forelock were plaited with the same and both bound with a bright green band adorned with very costly jewels, the whole length of the tail. [...]

Yet he had no helmet or any mail coat or a mail collar or plate armour or anything to do with weaponry, no lance or shield to thrust or strike. [...]

'For had I journeyed here in a company wishing for a fight, I have a mail coat at home and also a helmet, a shield and a sharp spear, shining bright, and other weapons to wield, as I know full well; but I wish for no war, my clothes are unthreatening'. [...]

He remains all that day and dresses in the morning. He asks for his weapons early and all were brought. First a richly coloured carpet was laid over the floor, and the amount of gilded armour that glittered upon it was huge. The bold man steps onto it and handles the armour, arrayed in a doublet of costly silk, and next a skilfully made cape closed at the top, that was lined inside with a pure white fur. Then they placed steel armour on the knight's feet and wrapped his legs in steel with beautifully made shin guards with separate pieces of armour protecting his knees attached to them and polished very bright, fastened about his knees with gold knots. Fine thigh pieces next, that closely encircled his thick muscular thighs attached with fastening cords. And next the coat of mail of linked bright steel rings enveloped that man over the lovely stuff, and well burnished pieces of armour were placed on both his arms with good and bright elbow pieces and iron gauntlets, and all the good accoutrements that would be of use to him at that time.

>   Wyth ryche cote-armure,
>   His gold sporez spend with pryde,
>   Gurde wyth a bront ful sure
>   With silk sayn vmbe his syde.
>   When he watz hasped in armes, his harnays watz ryche:
>   Þe lest lachet ouer loupe lemed of golde.   (566–91)
>
>   Bi þat watz Gryngolet grayth, and gurde with a sadel
>   Þat glemed ful gayly with mony golde frenges,
>   Ayquere naylet ful nwe, for þat note ryched;
>   Þe brydel barred aboute, with bryȝt golde bounden;
>   Þe apparayl of þe payttrure and of þe proude skyrtez,
>   Þe cropore and þe couertor, acorded wyth þe arsounez;
>   And al watz rayled on red ryche golde naylez,
>   Þat al glytered and glent as glem of þe sunne.
>   Þenne hentes he þe helme, and hastily hit kysses,
>   Þat watz stapled stifly, and stoffed wythinne.
>   Hit watz hyȝe on his hede, hasped bihynde,
>   Wyth a lyȝtly vrysoun ouer þe auentayle,
>   Enbrawden and bounden wyth þe best gemmez
>   On brode sylkyn borde, and bryddez on semez,
>   As papiayez paynted peruyng bitwene,
>   Tortors and trulofez entayled so þyk
>   As mony burde þeraboute had ben seuen wynter
>   in toune.
>   Þe cercle watz more o prys
>   Þat vmbeclypped hys croun,
>   Of diamauntez a deuys
>   Þat boþe were bryȝt and broun.
>
>   Then þay shewed hym þe schelde, þat was of schyr goulez
>   Wyth þe pentangle depaynt of pure gold hwez.
>   He braydez hit by þe bauderyk, aboute þe hals kestes,
>   Þat bisemed þe segge semyly fayre.   (597–622)

Gawain finally arrives at Hautdesert, the castle of Sir Bertilak who, unbeknown to Gawain or the readers, is also the Green Knight

>   And þere were boun at his [Bertilak's] bode burnez innoȝe,
>   Þat broȝt hym [Gawain] to a bryȝt boure, þer beddyng watz noble,
>   Of cortynes of clene sylk wyth cler golde hemmez,
>   And couertorez ful curious with comlych panez
>   Of bryȝt blaunner aboue, enbrawded bisydez,
>   Rudelez rennande on ropez, red golde ryngez,
>   Tapitez tyȝt to þe woȝe of tuly and tars,
>   And vnder fete, on þe flet, of folȝande sute.

With a costly garment depicting his coat-of-arms, his gold spurs fastened with pride, with a trusty sword hanging from a silk sash about his waist. When he was fastened in his armour, his gear was splendid: the least cord or loop shone golden. [...]

By that time Gringolet was prepared, and strapped on him was a saddle which shone very brightly with many ornamental borders, newly studded with nails especially. The bridle was ornamented with strips of bright gold. The trappings of the horse's breastplate and the splendid lower parts of the saddle, the crupper and the horse-cloth matched the saddlebows, and everything was set with costly gold studs that all glittered and glinted like the rays of the sun. Then he took up the helmet and kissed it quickly, it was strongly fastened together and its lining was filled with padding. It sat high on his head, fastened behind with a fine band of embroidered silk over the front piece of the helmet embroidered and twined about with the best jewels on a broad silk band, and birds of embroidered stitching about the seams such as parrots depicted with periwinkles between them, representations of turtle-doves and true-love flowers so thickly decorated with embroidery that it was as if many women thereabouts had spent seven winters at court. The coronet was more costly that encircled his head, of perfect diamonds, both clear and brown.

Then they showed him the shining red shield with the pentangle depicted on it in pure gold. He swung it by the baldrick, threw it about his neck, it suited the knight becomingly. [...]

And there were enough men ready at his [Bertilak's] command who brought him [Gawain] to a splendid chamber, there the furnishings for the bed were magnificent, of curtaining of elegant silk with bright gold borders and elaborately designed coverlets with beautiful fur edging of pure white ermine on it, embroidered at the sides. Curtains ran on cords through red-gold rings. Red Chinese silks hung on the walls, and underfoot on

> Þer he watz dispoyled, wyth spechez of myerþe,
> Þe burn of his bruny and of his bryȝt wedez.
> Ryche robes ful rad renkkez hym broȝten,
> For to charge, and to chaunge, and chose of þe best.
> Sone as he on hent, and happed þerinne,
> Þat sete on hym semly wyth saylande skyrtez
> Þe ver by his uisage verayly hit semed
> Welneȝ to vche haþel, alle on hwes
> Lowande and lufly alle his lymmez vnder   (852–68)
>
> A cheyer byfore þe chemné, þer charcole brenned,
> Watz grayþed for Sir Gawan grayþely with cloþez,
> Whyssynes vpon queldepoyntes þat koynt wer boþe;
> And þenne a meré mantyle watz on þat mon cast
> Of a broun bleeaunt, enbrauded ful ryche
> And fayre furred wythinne with fellez of þe best,
> Alle of ermyn in erde, his hode of þe same;
> And he sete in þat settel semlych ryche,
> And achaufed hym chefly, and þenne his cher mended.
> Sone watz telded vp a tabil on trestez ful fayre,
> Clad wyth a clene cloþe þat cler quyt schewed,
> Sanap, and salure, and syluerin sponez.   (875–86)

Gawain catches his first glimpse of the beautiful Lady Bertilak (see Plate 6).

> Bot vnlyke on to loke þo ladyes were,
> For if þe ȝonge watz ȝep, ȝolȝe watz þat oþer;
> Riche red on þat on rayled ayquere,
> Rugh ronkled chekez þat oþer on rolled;
> Kerchofes of þat on, wyth mony cler perlez,
> Hir brest and hir bryȝt þrote bare displayed,
> Schon schyrer þen snawe þat schedez on hillez;
> Þat oþer wyth a gorger watz gered ouer þe swyre,
> Chymbled ouer hir blake chyn with chalkquyte vayles,
> Hir frount folden in sylk, enfoubled ayquere,
> Toreted and treleted with tryflez aboute   (950–60)

Lord Bertilak and his court go out hunting. Gawain remains at the castle

> And Gawayn þe god mon in gay bed lygez,
> Lurkkez quyl þe daylyȝt lemed on þe wowes,
> Vnder couertour ful clere, cortyned aboute   (1179–81)

He hears a sound at his door

> And he heuez vp his hed out of þe cloþes,
> A corner of þe cortyn he caȝt vp a lyttel   (1184–5)

the floor were more of matching material. There, with humorous conversation, the knight was stripped of his mail coat and his fine clothes. Men promptly brought him costly robes to put on, change and choose the best. As soon as he had taken and fastened them on him, those that fitted him beautifully with flowing skirts, by his appearance it truly seemed to each person that spring had come with all its colours, so brilliant and beautiful all his limbs looked under the clothes. [...]

In front of the fireplace where charcoal was burning a chair with decorative cloths and cushions and quilted coverets both skilfully made, was set for Sir Gawain and then a fine mantle was thrown over him of a rich brown fabric, richly embroidered and beautifully lined with fur, with the best pelts, the best ermine in the world with a hood to match. And he sat in that fittingly noble seat, and quickly warmed up and his mood softened. Soon a table was set up on very beautiful trestles, dressed with a clean tablecloth that appeared to be bright white, and a table-runner and salt-cellar and silver spoons. [...]

But those women were not alike to look at, for if the young one was fresh, the other was withered; rich red was everywhere arrayed on the one, rough wrinkled cheeks hung on the other. The headcloth of the one, with many bright pearls, displayed her breast and her beautiful bare throat which shone whiter than snow that falls on the hills; the other was clothed with a gorget over her neck wrapped up over her black chin with chalk-white veils, her forehead was enfolded with silk, entirely veiled, edged and interlaced with decorative details. [...]

And Gawain, the good man, lies in his fine bed, lies snug while the daylight gleamed on the walls, under a bright bedspread, enclosed by curtains. [...]

And he lifts up his head out of the bedclothes, and raises the corner of the curtain a little. [...]

Lady Bertilak is visiting him

>And ho stepped stilly and stel to his bedde,
>Kest vp þe cortyn and creped withinne,
>And set hir ful softly on þe bed-syde   (1191–3)

>Whyle oure luflych lede lys in his bedde,
>Gawayn grayþely at home, in gerez ful ryche
>   Of hewe.   (1469–71)

It is the third day and the lady's third visit

>Whyle þe hende knyȝt at home holsumly slepes
>Withinne þe comly cortynes, on þe colde morne.
>Bot þe lady for luf let not to slepe,
>Ne þe purpose to payre þat pyȝt in hir hert,
>Bot ros hir vp radly, rayked hir þeder
>In a mery mantyle, mete to þe erþe,
>Þat watz furred ful fyne with fellez wel pured,
>No hwef goud on hir hede bot þe haȝer stones
>Trased aboute hir tressour be twenty in clusteres;
>Hir þryuen face and hir þrote þrowen al naked,
>Hir brest bare bifore, and bihinde eke.   (1731–41)

>'Nay, hende of hyȝe honours,'
>Quoþ þat lufsum vnder lyne,
>'Þaȝ I hade noȝt of yourez,
>ȝet schulde ȝe haue of myne.'
>Ho raȝt hym a riche rynk of red golde werkez,
>Wyth a starande ston stondande alofte
>Þat bere blusschande bemez as þe bryȝt sunne;
>Wyt ȝe wel, hit watz worth wele ful hoge.   (1813–20)

>'If ȝe renay my rynk, to ryche for hit semez,
>ȝe wolde not so hyȝly halden be to me,
>I schal gif yow my girdel, þat gaynes yow lasse.'
>Ho laȝt a lace lyȝtly þat leke vmbe hir sydez,
>Knit vpon hir kyrtel vnder þe clere mantyle,
>Gered hit watz with grene sylke and with golde schaped,
>Noȝt bot arounde brayden, beten with fyngrez   (1827–33)

>For quat gome so is gorde with þis grene lace,
>While he hit hade hemely halched aboute,
>Þer is no haþel vnder heuen tohewe hym þat myȝt,
>For he myȝt not be slayn for slyȝt vpon erþe.   (1851–4)

And she stepped softly and silently up to his bed, lifted up the curtain and crept inside, and sat herself very gently on the side of the bed. [...]

While our fair knight lies in his bed: Gawain stays pleasantly at home in gorgeously coloured bedclothes. [...]

The gracious knight sleeps healthfully at home inside the beautiful curtains, on the cold morning. But the lady could not sleep for love, nor could the intention fixed in her heart falter, so she got up quickly, took herself there in a fine mantle that reached the ground and was richly lined with trimmed pelts. She wore no head-dress on her head but finely wrought gemstones set about her hair net in clusters of twenty. Her fair face and well-formed throat were uncovered, her breast bared and her back too. [...]

'No, noble knight of high renown', said that lovely lady, 'Though I have had nothing of yours, yet you must have something of mine.'
 She offered him a precious ring worked of red gold with a sparkling stone set above that shone with beams like the bright sun. Know well, it was worth a great deal. [...]

'If you refuse my ring because it seems too costly and you do not wish to be so highly beholden to me I shall give you my belt that is of less profit to you.' She lightly took hold of a cord that was tied around her waist, looped about her kirtle under the fine mantle. It was fashioned of green silk and trimmed with gold, embroidered all round, decorated by hand. [...]

For whoever is encircled with this green braided cord, while he has it neatly fastened around him, there is no man under heaven who could cut him down, for he could not be slain through any cunning on earth. [...]

> When ho watz gon, Sir Gawayn gerez hym sone,
> Rises and riches hym in araye noble,
> Lays vp þe luf-lace þe lady hym raȝt,
> Hid hit ful holdely, þer he hit eft fonde. (1872–5)

In spite of their agreement, Gawain conceals the gift he has been given from Sir Bertilak (see Plate 7).

> He were a bleaunt of blwe þat bradde to þe erþe,
> His surkot semed hym wel þat softe watz forred,
> And his hode of þat ilke henged on his schulder,
> Blande al of blaunner were boþe al aboute. (1928–31)

> Deliuerly he dressed vp, er þe day sprenged,
> For þere watz lyȝt of a laumpe þat lemed in his chambre;
> He called to his chamberlayn, þat cofly hym swared,
> And bede hym bryng hym his bruny and his blonk sadel;
> Þat oþer ferkez hym vp and fechez hym his wedez,
> And grayþez me Sir Gawayn vpon a grett wyse.
> Fyrst he clad hym in his cloþez þe colde for to were,
> And syþen his oþer harnays, þat holdely watz keped,
> Boþe his paunce and his platez, piked ful clene,
> Þe ryngez rokked of þe roust of his riche bruny;
> And al watz fresch as vpon fyrst, and he watz fayn þenne
>   to þonk (2009–20)

> Whyle þe wlonkest wedes he warp on hymseluen --
> His cote wyth þe conysaunce of þe clere werkez
> Ennurned vpon veluet, vertuus stonez
> Aboute beten and bounden, enbrauded semez,
> And fayre furred withinne wyth fayre pelures --
> Ȝet laft he not þe lace, þe ladiez gifte,
> Þat forgat not Gawayn for gode of hymseluen.
> Bi he hade belted þe bronde vpon his balȝe haunchez,
> Þenn dressed he his drurye double hym aboute,
> Swyþe sweþled vmbe his swange swetely þat knyȝt
> Þe gordel of þe grene silke, þat gay wel bisemed,
> Vpon þat ryol red cloþe þat ryche watz to schewe.
> Bot wered not þis ilk wyȝe for wele þis gordel,
> For pryde of þe pendauntez, þaȝ polyst þay were,
> And þaȝ þe glyterande golde glent vpon endez
> Bot for to sauen hymself, when suffer hym byhoued,
> To byde bale withoute dabate of bronde hym to were
>   oþer knyffe. (2025–41)

When she was gone, Sir Gawain clothes himself immediately, gets up and dresses himself in noble apparel, puts safely away the love-lace the lady had given him. He hid it carefully where he would be able to find it again. [...]

He wore a long blue over-tunic that reached to the ground, his surcoat was softly furred and suited him well and his hood, made to match, hung on his shoulder. Both were trimmed with ermine. [...]

He was quickly dressed, before the day had dawned, for there was lamplight shining in his chamber. He called to his chamberlain who answered promptly, and asked him to bring him his mail coat and his white saddle. The other gets up and brings him his clothes, and dresses Sir Gawain up nobly. First he dressed him in his clothes that would keep out the cold, and then his other gear that had been kept carefully, both his belly protection and his plate-armour, very brightly polished, the rings of his rich mail coat burnished free of rust. All was as fresh as when he first put it on and he was keen to thank the servant. [...]

While he puts the loveliest clothes on – his tunic with the beautiful embroidered emblem, embellished on the velvet with jewels with special powers, set with gold and adorned with embroidery along the seams, and gorgeously lined inside with beautiful fur – but he did not leave off the girdle, the lady's gift, Gawain did not forget that, for his own good. When he had belted his sword on his muscular hips, he wrapped his love-token twice around him, quickly and sweetly the knight wrapped round his waist the green silk girdle, on the splendid red cloth that was magnificent to look at. But he did not wear this girdle for its value, for the splendour of the pendants, though they were polished, and though glittering gold glinted on the ends; but to save himself when he had to submit to face destruction without the resistance of a sword to defend him, or a knife. [...]

After the second part of the beheading challenge the Green Knight reveals his identity and his knowledge of the girdle which was given by his wife. He has been sending her to test Gawain who is covered in shame. He gives Gawain the girdle. Gawain refuses his hospitality.

> 'Bot your gordel', quoþ Gawayn, 'God yow forȝelde!
> Þat wyl I welde wyth guod wylle, not for þe wynne golde,
> Ne þe saynt, ne þe sylk, ne þe syde pendaundes,
> For wele ne for worchyp, ne for þe wlonk werkkez,
> Bot in syngne of my surfet I schal se hit ofte (2429–33)

Gawain returns to Camelot mortified

> Þe kyng comfortez þe knyȝt, and alle þe court als
> Laȝen loude þerat, and luflyly acorden
> Þat lordes and ladis þat longed to þe Table,
> Vche burne of þe broþerhede, a bauderyk schulde haue,
> A bende abelef hym aboute of a bryȝt grene,
> And þat, for sake of þat segge, in swete to were. (2513–18)

'But your girdle', said Gawain, 'God reward you! I will own it with a good heart, not to gain gold, not for the belt itself, nor the silk, nor the pendants at the side, not for wealth or for honour, nor for the glorious workmanship, but as a sign of my transgression I shall look at it often. [...]

The king comforts the knight, and all the court laughs loudly at this, and the lords and ladies amiably agree that whoever belonged to the Round Table, every knight of the brotherhood, should have a baldrick, a bright green sash tied slantwise round him, for the sake of that knight, to wear one to match his.

Glossary

The Glossary contains all of the terminology dealing with cloth, clothing, fashion and textiles from the various languages used in the textual extracts, including various parts of speech. Entries are arranged alphabetically. To assist navigation, an intuitive, rather than strict lexically systematic arrangement has been employed: variant forms of the same or similar term which appear across extracts are listed alphabetically at the beginning of each entry when they share a clear initial etymon ('**cendal, cendalle, cendallo**', etc., for example), whilst variants with significantly different spellings are often given their own entry but are crossed-referenced ('**cendato** cf. **sendato**', for example).

I	Wills
II	Accounts
III	Inventories and Rolls of Livery
IV	Moral and Satirical Works
V	Sumptuary Regulation, Statutes and the Rolls of Parliament
VI	Petitions
VII	Romances

abstersoria cloths used by the celebrant for wiping his fingers after handling the host. III.1*b*
aburioun variant of *harbergeon*, a coat or jacket of mail or scale armour. This form does not appear in *AND* or *MED*. I.23
acupicta embroidered. III.1*c*
ad aurum of gold, hence cloth-of-gold or gold thread. I.13
addubbata decorated, adorned. III.1*a*
afforc', afforciato strengthened, reinforced; backed or lined (*AND*2; *DMLBS*, s.v. 'afforciato'). II.3, III.1*b*, 2
aget fashion in dress (*MED* suggests the reading in IV.10 should be *aget*, s.v. 'aget, adv.'). IV.10
agnell, aignel lamb (i.e. lambswool). V.2, 9*g*
agrafenan engraved. I.2
agulettorum aglets, (metal) points or tags. II.4
aketouns quilted jackets, worn by men as padding underneath a breastplate or worn alone as protection (ultimately derived from the Arabic *al-qutūn* – lit. 'the cotton'); cf. *haketon*. VI.2
alba, albae, albam, albas, albe white, surplice-like tunic with close sleeves, for ceremonial or ecclesiastical use worn beneath the chasuble or cope (the name derives from the colour term *alba*). I.11, 12, II.5, III.1*b*, 1*c*

alba, albam, albarum, albi, albis, albo, album (of) white. I.10, 13, II.1*a*, 3, III.1*a*, 1*b*, 1*c*, 2
albæ et negræ (of) white and black. I.10
alexandrine 'alexandrian'; here, probably a reference to *soie alisandrin* 'Alexandrian silk'. VII.9, 10
Aleyn presumably Alain (Alanus) of Lille, *The Complaint of Nature*. IV.14
almandine garnets (s.v. 'alabandina' *DMLBS*). III.1*a*
almucium amice, scarf (usually linen), an ecclesiastical garment worn around the neck; cf. *amicta*. IV.7
alner alms-purse; a purse or small bag. VII.11
alyr of Lierre (Brabant; *MED*), describing cloth-of-gold. I.44
amall enamel. VII.11
anamelede, anamayld enamelled. VII.14, 15
amatistam, amatistis amethyst(s). III.1*a*, 1*b*
ameraudes emeralds; cf. *emerawdes, meraude*. I.15
amicta, amictae, amicti, amictibus, amicto, amictus, amyte, amytes ecclesiastical amice; a garment the shape and use of which developed over the medieval period: originally a scarf designed to protect the more precious vestments from sweat and hair grease, it became an ornamental garment. II.5, III.1*a*, 1*b*, 1*c*
anel ring, jewel; cf. *annulo*. I.15, V.2, VII.12
annuli capiantur signet rings. I.13
annulo, annulum, annulus, anulos, anul', anulis, anulum ring(s); cf. *anel*. I.13, 14, 19, 45, II.2, 4, III.1*b*, VI.7*b*
antiquarum of the old style/fashion. III.1*a*
anurled bordered. An orle, in heraldry, is a border following the outline of a shield, but within it. In VII.14 it probably denotes fur lining of Melidor's dress, which she wears turned back to show the fur (Kooper 2006). VII.14
aperturam opening, slit. IV.4
apparaile, apparaill, apparaille, l'apparaill (the) apparel, clothing; furnishings and fittings. V.2, 5, 8*p*, VI.6
apparaille de perre ornaments of precious stones. V.2
appelblome *MED* suggests cloth decorated with an apple-blossom design or else the colour of apple blossoms, citing a set of wills; here specifically the colour (pink). The term is a compound made up of an Old English term and a borrowing from Old Norse cited from *c.* 1200. I.18, 19
araide, arayd, arayit, arraied clothed, attired. I.47, IV.17, V.6, VII.5
araie pur son corps body apparel; in the sumptuary law, a specification implying that restrictions apply only to apparel worn on the body rather than on soft furnishings, etc. V.9*g*
araie, araies, aray, araye, arayes, arraie, arraies, array, arraye in its more general sense 'special preparation, order, arrangement'; also attested meaning 'outfit, attire, clothing' from a. 1400. IV.13, 14, 15, 17, V.4, 6, 8, 9, 10, VII.4, 15
arboreta decorated with figures of vines. III.1*a*
archam bed-frame or mattress-frame. I.18
arest', aresta, arista with *pannus* or similar, a rich fabric, possibly ribbed (Monnas 1989: 285). III.1*a*
argent, argent', argente, argentei, argenteis, argenteo, argenteus, argenti, argentis, argentums silver (often silver-gilt); of/with silver. II.2, III.1*a*, 1*b*, 1*c*, 2, V.2, 4, 5, 9*f*, 9*m*, VI.6, 7*a*, 7*b*, VII.3
argenter worker in silver-plate or gilt. V.5
armariolo wardrobe. III.1*c*
armere, armerur', armur, armure armour; cf. *armures*. I.32, VII.11, 14
armes, armez arms, the weapons of a warrior. VI.2, VII.15
armez armed; supplied with arms and armour. VI.2
armures arms, armour; cf. *armere*, etc. I.15, VI.2

arsouns the uptilted front and back of a saddle, saddlebows. VII.11, 15

asowr, azour, azure azure, blue enamel made of powdered lapis lazuli (the blue stone); a pigment or paint made of powdered lapis lazuli, ultramarine. VII.6, 14

assise official measure (of cloth). By the fourteenth century 'aulnagers' (cf. *aune* in Extract V.2) were responsible for the official *assize* or official measuring and sealing of cloth under licence (see Bridbury 1982: 106–7). VI.5

atertanum, ater-tan poison twig (= acid patterning on sword blade). VII.1

atiffai, atiffer (reflexive) to adorn, ornament, beautify (oneself). IV.2

atiffement adornment, ornamentation. IV.2

atiffur adornment, ornamentation. IV.2

atir, atire, atyre apparel; dress; fine clothing. IV.17, V.7, VII.3, 4

attaby a heavy, probably imported cloth; cf. the modern development *tabby*. II.5

attyres adornments. IV.14

atyre to attire, to dress (oneself). IV.3, V.7

aube, aubis alb; long, white, linen vestment with close sleeves, usually worn underneath the other vestments for mass (the name derives from the colour term *alba*; cf. *albe*). II.5

auentayle piece of mail neck armour (development of the helmet). VII.15

aune(s) ell(s) (from OF *aune*); the standard measure of length for cloth, one roughly equivalent to an arm's length, usually 45 inches in England though it varied from region to region. Different countries had different standard ells (Connor 1987: 91; *EMDT*, s.v. 'ell'); cf. *uln'*. V.2

aurat' (de) gilded. VI.7b

aurea, aurei, aureis, aureum, aureus, auri, auro (of) gold. I.12, 14, 45, III.1a, 1b, 1c, 2, VI.7b

auriculare pillow or cushion; from the Latin adjective (*auricularis*) meaning 'auricular; of the ear'. I.13

aurifabr' of gold; golden? II.4

aurifilo gold thread (also *filo auri*, etc.). III.1b

aurifrigia, aurifrigiis, aurifrigio orphrey(s) or orphrey-work, elaborate gold embroidery or bands on an item or garment. III.1a, 1b, 1c

aurifrigiata adorned or finished with orphreys or goldwork. III.1a

auripictae, auripicti painted in gold. III.1c

auterclothes altarcloths (with Middle English intrusion); including cloths such as the *frontal*, the *reredos* and altar curtains. II.5

aymelez enamelled. V.2

azureto (of) blue (colour). II.3

bacinetz, bacynetz, bassenet, bassnettus, bassonett, basynet referring to a type of helmet, item of armour for the head. This and many other (technical) terms for pieces of armour are borrowed from Anglo-French. I.23, 26, VI.2, VII.14

bægas, beagus ring(s). In the will of the Ealdorman Æthelmær this item appears in a list with weapons and horses as part of a formal repayment of an understood debt. I.3, 5

bænd, bænde(s), bende(s) band(s); a headband perhaps of metal; a band, fillet or wreath, worn as part of a headdress; also an embroidered band with goldwork; or the detachable decorative edge of a garment; see Crowfoot and Hawkes (1967); Rogers (2007: 212–13); Owen-Crocker (2004: 286; 2005: 41–52); Clegg Hyer (2012). Cf. *bende*, etc. I.2, 3, 4a, 6

bagges badges. VII.14

baldachin, baldekino, baudekin, baudekini, baudekinis, baudekino, baudekinum, baudekyn a rich textile of mixed silk and gold or silver thread (often made with gilded membrane *filé* thread) which could be embroidered or brocaded. I.13, III.1a, 1b, VII.13

baleys balas ruby or red spinel ruby. I.44

bancale cushion. I.4b

baneour banner, pennon. IV.2

bankers, bankerus, banquaria, banquario bench or chair cover(s), covering(s) of tapestry or similar, as covering for furniture, or occasionally as a wall-hanging. I.21, 28, 40, II.1*b*

banquaria, banquario see *bankers*.

barbet barbe, piece of head-dress, passing under the chin; frequently made of linen; the barbet was worn particularly by female religious and women in mourning. IV.9

barhides rawhide bags or trunks. A Middle English compound which (like many others) appears frequently in documents of various languages from the thirteenth to the fifteenth centuries (cf. Raine 1836: 'Cum quodam cloth sek et barehide' [1346], vol. 4, p. 29). VI.6

barred ornamented with stripes (of gold, etc.). VII.15

barres, barris ornamental bands or stripes; strips of gold, silver or precious stones on a garment, piece of armour or saddle. III.1*a*, 1*b*, VII.15

baseyne sheepskin leather (OF *basane, bazan*, originally from Arabic). III.2

baselard, baselardes, baselart, basilardes decorative or ornamental dagger(s) with an H-shaped hilt attached to a belt or girdle. I.24, 32, IV.10, V.4

bassenet, bassnettus, bassonett, basynet see *bacynetz, bacinetz*.

bauderyk baldric, sash worn diagonally from one shoulder across the body to the waist; leather strap or thong. VII.15

beadogriman, beado-grima battle mask (= face-guard of helmet). VII.1

beado-hrægl battle garment (mail coat). VII.1

beadomecas, beado-mece battle-sword(s). VII.1

beado-scrud, beaduscruda battle garment (mail coat). VII.1

beag, beages, beah, beg, beh, by ring(s). I.2, 5, 6, 7, VII.1, 14

beahðege, beah-ðegu receiving of a ring. VII.1

bed of Tapistree bed of tapestries. Tapestry is a technique in which patterns of contrasting colours are worked into a fabric while it is on the loom (cf 'bed of tapicers werk', I.21). I.32

bedbere bed-cover. I.27

bedd, beddum bedding. VII.1

bedde, bede bed. I.34, VII.7, 10, 15

beddreafes, bedreaf bed covering, bedding. I.2, 8, 9

beddyng bedclothes, furnishings or equipment for a bed. I.29, VII.15

bedes prayer beads, rosary. I.21, 30, 32, 40

bedis, bedys beads. IV.6, 15

bedwahrift bed-curtain. I.2

befongen, befon surrounded, encircled. VII.1

belt, beltis girdle(s), belt(s) or sash(es). V.6, VII.15

belted attached (a sword) to or with a belt, buckled on. V.6, VII.15

bendata bordered, edged; embroidered. III.1*b*

bende, bendes band(s), ornamental lace(s), ribbon(s), sash(es), etc., on a garment (usage in V.2 Ormrod 2005 glosses with 'bracelets'). See also *bænd*, etc. IV.11, V.2, VII.15

beorht, beorhtum bright. VII.1

besauntus, bisantii, bisantiis bezants, small plate- or coin-shaped ornaments. III.1*a*,

besettan, besette set round. VII.1

besshe, byce species of darker fur: Veale suggests 'made of the whole squirrel skin' (Veale 1966: 228), but it could equally represent 'tawny', 'brown' or a similar dark colour. I.30, V.4

beten embroidered; adorned, decorated; embroidered or painted with a design or figure. VII.15

betstow bedstead. I.4*a*

beuer beaver. I.25

bis dark grey. VII.9

bisantii, bisantiis see *besauntus*.
blæwenan blue. Whitelock *et al.* (1968: 83) suggest the colour was achieved by dyeing with woad. I.4*a*
blak, blake black; also, black cloth black. I.30, VII.11
blak lambe black lambswool. V.8*g*
blake in observance of the rule that metal shall never be placed on metal, nor colour on colour; in Extract VII.14 *blake* must mean either 'white' or 'yellow' and both senses are possible (Casson 1949: 134). In heraldry the term for 'black' appears to be *sable*. VII.14
blanc, blanke white. II.5, VII.9
blande interspersed, suffused. Tolkien *et al.* (1967) gloss the term 'adorned', and Andrew and Malcolm (1978) have 'trimmed'. *MED* derives the verb from OE *blendan* rather than Old Norse as Tolkien *et al.* (1978) suggest. VII.15
blanket powder used to whiten the face. IV.2
blanket, blancketes, blanketes, blankettes, blankettis earlier uses of the term signified a woollen cloth, usually white or left undyed, or a piece of such material (cf. *whythe blanket*); later uses specify a bedspread or covering (as in the will of Thomas Tvoky). I.21, 25, 32, 34, 36, 40, 47, V.2
blaunner kind of fur, possibly ermine. VII.15
blaveo, blavii, blaviis, blavij (of) blue (*blavus*, from OF *bleu, blou*); azure (heraldic)? III.1*c*
ble colour, hue. VII.6
bleaunt, bleeaunt a rich fabric; long over-tunic worn by men and women. We cannot tell how far the shape of the bleaunt in fourteenth century England preserved that of the 12th century French bliaut. There are archaisms in *Sir Gawain and the Green Knight* such as the trailing bliaut worn indoors with a surcoat and a hood hanging on the shoulder, though from his attitude to armour and architecture the poet seems unlikely to have intended archaism in dress (Nevinson 1958: 308; Tolkien *et al.* 1967: 101). See *bliauz* below. VII.15
blew, blewe, blu, blue, blwe blue. I.21, 27, 42, VI.7*a*, VII.15
bliauz garment, the exact nature of which is controversial. It is suggested that it was an ankle-length tunic with a skirt that flared out and long, hanging sleeves cinched at the natural waistline and worn over the *chemise* in 12th-century France and that variations included the one-piece *bliaut* and the two-piece *bliaut*, the *bliaut gironé* (Snyder 2009: 87). During the twelfth century the term *bliaut* signifies an elaborate dress and a costly fabric in texts from England and France; in texts from France the term was used so frequently with the meaning 'dress' that a description of the fabric was often added, while in German texts of the period there is no evidence of the meaning having extended from fabric to garment (see Chambers and Sylvester 2010: 67–8; Harris 1998: 101, note 4). Cf. *bleaunt, bleeaunt*. VII.9
blodii of blue. VI.7*b*
bloy, bloyeto, blueto (of) light blue cloth; 'bluet', a blue woollen cloth. Cf. *bluet'* etc. I.14, 18, 19
blu, blue see *blew*.
bluet', blueto, bluett' bluet; a fairly expensive blue woollen cloth. Cf. *bloy*, etc. Also, the colour blue (as in III.2). II.1*b*, 3
bocull buckle. I.28
bofet stool. I.36
bofu fabric, material. VII.12
boga, boge, bugee budge; lambskin, usually with the fur dressed outwards (and most often black or brown), increasingly popular during the fourteenth century. Variants of the term often refer to the dark, dressed lambskins imported from the Mediterranean region (Veale 1966: 134). II.1*a, b*, V.2
bokeled provided or fastened with a buckle. IV.17
bokeram buckram, a fine linen or cotton cloth used for lining (s.v. *EMDT*). III.2.

bokill buckler, small shield; cf. *buklar*. IV.17

bolster(s) padding, stuffing. The term seems to have been used with this particular sense only from the mid fifteenth century. The term is Germanic in origin and appears as a Middle English borrowing into Anglo-French (cf. Extract V.9), with its more common sense of a pillow or cushion, only as early as the 1420s. V.8*h*, 9*h*

bolstrum, bolster pillow, cushion. VII.1

bonetz head-coverings. At this time *bonnet* usually referred to a man's head-covering without a brim. VI.9

boorde cloþe, bord-cloth, bordcloth, bordclothe, bordeclothes table cloth(s), cloth(s) to cover a side-board or similar. I.23, 25, 27, 32, 36, 40

bordati, bordatus embroidered (with). III.1*a*

borde, bordes band, strip of embroidered material. VII.15

bordura, bordure, borduris border(s), edging (on a garment or textile); either structural or decorative. II.1*b*, III.1*a*, VII.11

boses bosses, frequently meaning 'buns' of hair on each cheek (called 'stylish' by *MED*); this kind of head-dress was popular with women in the later fourteenth and fifteenth centuries, and mocked by Lydgate in his poem *Horns Away* (Kooper 2006; IV.9). The use in VII.14 may refer to a medallion or a pendant, but as the text mentions 'a payr', it is possible that 'horns' are intended. The extravagances of contemporary headgear were repeatedly and ineffectually satirised by reforming writers, and this detail was singled out as the object of special attack. IV.9. VII.14

boteaux, boteux boots. In earlier Anglo-French usage the diminutive, plural ending was used for small boots or items of footwear, but 'boots' more generally is probably intended in V.8*k*. Variants are attested in Britain as early as the 1360s. V.8*l*, 8*k*, 9*k*

botenus buttons. VII.14

botonat', botonatarum, botonate, botoned, butonat', butonata provided or furnished with buttons or studs (rather than 'buttoned'). II.4, IV.17

botonibus, botons, botonum button(s) (frequently vernacular in Latin matrix). II.1*b*, 2, 5

bouclis buckles. III.2

bounden trimmed with ornaments, adorned. VII.15

bout part of woman's head-dress (probably the back), worn in association with a barbet. IV.9

bow bow (weapon for shooting arrows). V.6

bracal', bracalis breech-girdle or belt. II.1*b*

braccis breeches. II.4

brace pieces of armour covering the arm. VII.15

bradne broad. VII.1

braello cord or tie (for curtain); frequently a breech-girdle (s.v. 'braiellum, ~a', *DMLBS*: '[OF *braile* < *bracale*], belt, breech-girdle'). II.2

brayden embroidered. VII.15

brech, breche undergarment covering the lower part of the body. IV.10, 17, VII.11

breost-gewæde, breostgewædu breast garments (mail coats). VII.1

breost-net breast-net (mail coat). VII.1

brest plat breast plate; armour protection for the chest and torso. V.6

breudare, broudere to embroider (*breudare fecit* = to have embroidered, to cause to be emroidered). I.31, III.1

breudata, breudatae, breudatam, breudatas, breudati, breudatis, breudato, breudatus embroidered (with); cf. *breudatur, enbroudato*. III.1*a*, 1*b*

breudatur, breudantur embroidered with; cf. *breudata, enbroudato*. III.1*a*, 1*b*

bridels, brydel, brydell bridle(s). VII.10, 11, 15

broche brooch, decorative pin or fastener. I.32, VI.7a, VII.11, 14
brode yerde, brodeyerde broad yard, a measurement of width used in the cloth trade; a double yard; used in both Middle English and Anglo-French texts (cf. V.8m and 9m). Richard I issued an *Assize of Measure* in 1196 which required certain cloths to be sold at two yards in breadth. The size of 'broadcloth' was frequently regulated in the centuries that followed (see Connor 1987: 81 and following). V.8m, 9m
broden, bregdan woven. VII.1
brond, bronde, bront sword. VII.1, 15
brood clooth broadcloth; woollen cloth woven in strips of double width on the broad loom at which two weavers sat side by side; a piece of this cloth. IV.13
broudat', brudatis embroidered; cf. *browded, enbrawde*. I.10, 11, III.2
broudry embroidery. V.6
broun probably brown (in colour). In Extract VII.15, the diamonds are described as both clear and brown, i.e. they were of all tints (Andrew and Waldron 1978: 230). This may mean 'shining' as the term is used of metal but this would be redundant. Since medieval lapidaries regularly mention brown diamonds it seems more likely that these are what is meant (Tolkien *et al.* 1967: 92). VII.15
browded embroidered; cf. *brudatis, enbrawde*. I.33, III.2
brucel, brucell of Brussels; cloth of Brussels. II.4
bruddato integro fully embroidered, embroidered all over. I.13
brun' brown; brown cloth (cf. *broun*). II.4
brunfag bright. VII.1
bruny, bryné, byrne, byrnan, byrnum mail coat. VII.1, 15
bryddez birds. VII.15
bugee see *boga*.
buklar buckler, usually a small, round hand-held shield used to deflect blows; cf. *bokill*. V.6
bulʒeone metal ornament (in Old Scots). Whereas Middle English seems to have used the word to mean 'a bar or ingot of precious metal' from the fourteenth century (s.v. 'bullion *n*.', *MED*), it is not attested in English as being used to describe items of dress or jewellery until the 1460s (s.v. 'bullion, *n*.3', *OED*); the *DOST* cites the act of March 1429 but does not distinguish the sense (s.v. 'bulʒeon, bulʒeoun, *n.*'). V.6
burnet, burnett' fine, brown or dark woollen cloth (*EMDT* s.v. 'burnet'). II.1b
burra for *barris*, bars, stripes, bands? III.1b
burreafes hanging for a chamber. I.8
burrello burel, a coarse, woollen cloth. II.1b
bursam, bursas, burse, burses burse(s), purse(s); also bag(s) for ecclesiastical use. I.13, V.9p, VI.7a, 7b
bustian a type of cloth, probably of cotton and of foreign manufacture; frequently described as white. V.8g, 9g
butonede buttoned; done up with buttons (rather than having merely decorative buttons, as in other contexts). V.7
byrnan mail coats. I.5
bys, byse a precious kind of linen or cotton cloth. VII.10, 11
bywan burnish VII.1
cadac', cadas material used for padding or stuffing; either silk or cotton wool. The term is derived from AF *cadace*, from OF *cadaz, cadas*. II.1b, V.8h, 9h
calabre squirrel fur, originally from or associated with Calabria in Italy. See Veale (1966: 217–8). I.24
calciamentis, calciamenti footwear, shoes. IV.1
caleis [for *calceis*] shoes, footwear. IV.5

calig, caligae, caligarum, caligis (of) hose; (of) stockings; as a substantive, frequently refers to stockings or buskins worn under the *sandalia*. II.1*b*, 4, III.1*a*, 1*b*

caligas shoes (but cf. the previous entry). IV.11

calles head-dress. IV.17

cam', camalin', camelino, kamelyn rich fabric made from wool, silk or other fibres. *Cameline* is thought to have been used originally to describe camel's hair or fabric resembling camel's hair; it appears in various colours in medieval usage. I.14, 18, II.1*b*

camisiam, camisiis chemise(s), shift(s); in this period (typically sleeveless) undergarment worn by a woman; cf. *chemise*. IV.1, VI.7*b*

camoyseata chamois leather (s.v. '*camusiatus*', DMLBS – although the headword form does not really reflect the probable French influence on surviving forms). II.1*b*

canab', canabeorum, canabi, canabus (piece[s] of) canvas or similar; plain, hempen cloth; See *canevas*, etc. II.1*b*, 2, 3, 4

canape canopy. I.47

CandelWekstrete a reference to Candlewick Street in London, the area where cloth was produced from Edward IV's reign (and following). By 1330, the term *candlewickstreet* was being used as a toponym to refer to a kind of inexpensive cloth produced in Candlewick Street, but in Extract VI.2 it is used to refer to the area where the cloth was manufactured or purchased ('cloth . . . of Candlewick Street'). VI.2

canevac', canevas, canuas, canvas, canvase a sheet of cloth used for various purposes (as in II.4); also (as in III.1*c*), fabric or material made from flax and/or hemp; came to be associated with a sturdy, typically undyed fabric often used for bags or humble garments but could be decorated as furnishing fabric; See *canab'*, etc. I.21, 23, 32, II.4, 5, III.1*c*

cang', canguim a silk or cotton, striped fabric. II.1*b*

capa, capae, capam, caparum, capas, capis cloak(s), cape(s) or ecclesiastical cope(s): long outer garment or cape usually elaborately decorated. I.10, 11, 12, 13, II.3, III.1*a*, 1*b*, 1*c*, IV.7

capados garment covering the neck and shoulders, a cape. In the fourteenth century, instead of mantles, which, except for ceremonial occasions became quite rare, men wore short hooded cloaks in the open air. In VII.15, the Green Knight's *capados* was probably a hood with shoulder-pieces (Nevinson 1958: 305). The armour was put on over the knight's clothes (the doublet capados); cf. line 2015 (Andrew and Waldron 1978: 229), probably from OF *cap à dos* = 'cape for the back'). II.4, VII.15

capello ferri helmet (lit., 'iron hat/hood'). II.1*b*

capillorum of hair. IV.1

capitegia head-dress. IV.5

cappers makers and dealers of caps and other items of headgear; also members of the guild or company of Cappers. VI.9

cappes caps, close-fitting head coverings. V.7, 8*p*, 9*p*, VI.9

cappes of astate caps or head-dresses reserved for persons of higher rank or worn to display one's rank (estate). V.7

cappis head-dress, hat or small head covering worn under a hood. IV.12

capsa cover or case for the corporal or corporals (Eucharistic bread and wine). III.1*b*

capuc', capucia, capucii, capuciis, capucio, capucium, capucinum, caputium hood(s); hooded cape(s) covering the shoulders; (woman's) cowl; cf. *chaperon*. I.18, 19, II.1*a*, *b*, 3, 4, III.2, IV.7, VI.7*b*

carbuncle, carbunkull, carbonkeles, charbonclys precious stone(s), any of the gems called carbuncle. IV.14, VII.6, 10, 11

card', carde (var. *karde*) carde, a basic quality textile, usually of linen, typically used for curtains and linings. I.34, II.1*b*, 3, III.2

carpitura carding or teasing (of wool). II.1*b*
casula, casulae, casulam, casulas, casulis chasuble(s), the sleeveless ecclesiastical vestment in the form of a wide cloak that slips over the wearer's head and remains open at the sides; worn over an alb and stole during the celebration mass. I.10, 11, 12, 13, III.1*a*, 1*b*, 1*c*
cathenulæ small, ornamental chains. III.1*b*
cauda, caudas, caudis tail or train (of a garment). IV.4
ceincture, ceynture, ceyntures, seintures belt(s), straps(s); girdle(s), sash(es). V.2, 4, 9*f*, 9*m*
celure canopy over a bed; cf. *selour*. I.21, VII.14
cendal, cendalle, cendallo a costly, lightweight silk cloth which was sometimes confused with *sindon* (a linen, cotton or sometimes silken textile); see *EMDT* s.v. 'sindon' and Monnas (1989); cf. *sendal, sendel, sendre*. I.13, II.1*a*, VII.9
cendato cf. *sendato*. III.1*b*
cercle metal band, often set with gems, encircling the head. Here, such a band encircling the knight's helmet. VII.15
cerico silk; cf. *serico*. III.1*c*
Cesyle Sicily. The silks in VII.6 were imported from Sicily. VII.6
ceynture, ceyntures see *ceincture*. V.2
chainsil garment made from chaisel, linen (typically an overgarment); a cloak or robe. VII.9
chalkquyte white as chalk. VII.15
chalon' bedcover. I.18
chamelet a rich, silken textile; originally thought to mimic animal hair (particularly camel hair). Lisa Monnas notes that 'Chamelett [. . .] is often associated with woollen cloths, particularly those made from camel hair, or with cloths made from mixtures of wool and silk. But in the Wardrobe accounts, chamelett refers to a silk cloth' (Monnas 1989: 286). Cf *cam', camalin'*, etc. V.10
chape cloak; cf. *mantellus*. IV.7
chaperon hood, hooded cloak: various hooded garments worn by men or women and by both secular and religious (including the clerical cowl, a ubiquitous part of monastic dress in the period); cf. *capuc', capucia, capucinum*. II.5, VI.1, 3, 7*a*
chapes metal plates or mountings as heraldic charges (s.v. *MED* 'chape, n.', which cites the bequest in the late-fourteenth century will of Lady Alice West). I.21
charbonclys cf. *carbuncle*. IV.14
chat cat: refers to 'skins of the large wild mountain cat, the smaller wild cat, or the domestic cat' (Veale 1966: 218). V.2
chauceure shoes, footwear. V.2
change a change of clothing; clothes used for this purpose. IV.17
chauses hose; leggings or similar of two separate pieces; cf. next entry. V.9*m*
chausez closez 'close' or 'closed' hose; joined hose; hose that are attached as one piece. V.9*m*
chausons shoes. II.4
cheef the upper third of a shield. VII.14
cheisnes, chenʒeis chains, necklaces; cf. *cheyne*. V.2, 6
chemise shift, undergarment; cf. *camisiam, camisiis*. VII.9
chesible chasuble, the sleeveless ecclesiastical vestment in the form of a wide cloak that slips over the wearer's head and remains open at the sides; worn over an alb and stole during the celebration mass; cf. *casula*. II.5
chesil fine linen. VII.12
chete sheet; cf. *shete*. I.29
cheuerons, chevrons device(s) consisting of a bar bent like two meeting rafters: /\. I.21
cheyne chain; cf. *cheisnes, chenʒeis*. I.24, 28

cheyne of gold, cheyne of goold chain of gold, perhaps a chain of office. I.24, 42
chief bolt, large piece of cloth. VII.12
chymbled wrapped up. *Sir Gawain and the Green Knight* provides the only citation. VII.15
ciclatouni, ciglatoun, ciglatun fine silken fabric; type of cloth-of-gold. III.1*b*
cilicinus sack cloth or hair-cloth. III.1*c*, VII.2
cindone, cindonis a fine linen material; often used as a substitute for, or confused with the lightweight silk *cendal* (*EMDT* s.v. 'sendal'; Newton 1980: 135; cf. *sindon, sindone, sindonis*). II.1*b*, 3
Cipre (of) Cyprus cloth; usually referring to a fine cloth-of-gold; cf. *cyprus* (*EMDT*, s.v. 'cyprus'). III.2
circumferencia, circumferenciis border. III.1*c*
cirotecae, cirotecarum cyrotecarum glove(s); gauntlet(s). II.4, II.1*a*, 1*b*
cissor, cissore, cissorem, cissori, cissoris tailor(s). II.1*a*, 2, 3, 4
clad, cladde, cled clothed, provided with clothing, covered. IV.16, 17, VII.6, 15
clamidis cloak. III.2
clathes, clathis clothes, clothing (northern/Old Scots; see *cloth*, etc.). V.6
cleithinge clothing. IV.16
cloc, cloca, clocam, cloch, cloche, clochis, cloke, clokes cloak(s). I.25, 36, II.1*b*, 4, IV.10, V.2, 8*i*, 9*i*, 9*j*, III.2
clooth cloth. IV.13
clos buttoned, stitched or otherwise form-fitting; worn close against the body. It is likely the *surcot close* was a sleeved garment worn under the *surcot ouert* (see Chambers 2011). VI.3
close hoses joined hose; hose that are attached as one piece. The sumptuary act at V.8*m* specifies that *hose* be 'close', indicating that they were normally separate garments worn as a pair. Before the fifteenth century, hose had normally been worn separately, like modern stockings. V.8*m*
cloth-of-gold, cloth of gold, cloth off gold, clothes of gold, clothis of gold various fabrics (generally silken) woven or brocaded with gold thread, gold wire, strips of gold or similar. I.30, 31, 44, V.8*a*, VII.8
cloth of siluer cloth woven or shot through with silver thread. I.42
cloth to provide (someone) with clothing. I.30, VII.14
cloth, clothe, cloþes, clothes, clothis (Old Scots variants *clathes, clathis*) garment(s); clothing, dress. I.24, 32, IV.3, 17, V.6, VII.5, 8, 11
cloþ, cloþez decorative cloths, hangings, tapestries; bedclothes; tablecloth(s). Note the Middle English term *bordcloth*, a tablecloth. VII.10, 14, 15
clothsekkes bags for cloths, linens, etc. VI.6
cloþyng, clothyng clothing, dress. IV.3, V.8*m*
cnapp, knoppus (ornamental) knob, tassel, or similar. I.28, VII.14
coddys pillows, cushions. VII.14
cointer to adorn (oneself). IV.2
colerii, coleriis collars; chains of office (or representations thereof). III.1*c*
colers collars. IV.11, V.10
collobium sleeveless garment, shirt; this is sometimes an undergarment. I.18
color', colore, coloris (de) of a single/solid/uniform colour. II.1*b*, 3, III.2
coloris, colour 'colour'; 'coloured cloth'; used to describe cloth of a solid or single colour. VI.3, 4, 7*a*, 7*b*
combe of yverie comb of ivory. I.39
conil coney, rabbit (skin or fur). The more general term *rabbit* was used only for young coneys until the Early modernperiod (Veale 1966: 221; *OED*2; cf. *conyng*). V.2
consuebatur, consuendam, consuend', consuendum forms of *consuere*, to sew. II.1*b*, III.2

consuta, consuti, consutis, consutum, consutus sewn, stitched; sewn together, joined. III.1*a*, 1*b*, 1*c*

consutur', consutura sewing, stitching; tailoring. II.4

contextis, contexto, contextum woven (past participle of *contexere, contextere*). III.1*a*, 1*b*, 1*c*

contrefaitz counterfeit, imitate, in imitation of. II.5

conyng coney, rabbit; cf. *conil*. V.4

conysaunce device, emblem, or badge by which a knight's allegiance is made known. VII.15

coopertorii, coopertorium cover(s), covering(s). II.1*b*

cope cope; ecclesiastical garment, a semi-circular mantle often elaborately decorated. I.27

coppe for Extract VII.7, Correale suggests that it appears to mean cover or tablecloth rather than the usual sense of 'cup'. VII.7

cops copes; also synecdoche for the Augustinian brothers of a priory. I.21

corall, koralle red coral, an arborescent species, found in the Red Sea and Mediterranean, prized from times of antiquity for ornamental purposes, and often classed among precious stones, often used for rosary beads. I.30, VII.6

cordes rope(s), cord(s). VII.9, 14

Cordewaneres leueray Cordwainer's livery; official uniform of the London company. Described as 'of .ij. Coloures', it was pied or parti-coloured in design. I.22

cordon' a cordon; perhaps a decorative fillet or similar. The only attestation in *MED* comes from the *Promptorium Parvulorum* of *c.* 1440 ('Coordone [Win: Cooydone]: Nicetrium amteonites'; s.v. *MED*, 'cordon, n.'). The use in the Latin pardon of Alice Ball extracted at VI.7*b*, then, would appear to be the earliest in sense relating to items of dress. As the corresponding Anglo-French term has not survived in the petition on which the pardon is based, it is not possible to be certain what particular item was intended. VI.7*b*

coreo leather. III.1*a*

cornalle, coronal, coronall coronel, a precious circlet, often of gold and gems, worn about the head for ornament or to show rank. VII.10, 11, 14.

cornelinae, cornelinis, cornelinum, cornelinus cornelian(s), a reddish or reddish-white semi-transparent quartz. III.1*a*, 1*b*

cornua, cornues horns (of a decorative head-dress). IV.5, V.4

corounes pur cappes des enfaunts crowns or peaks of children's caps. V.9*p*

corouns crowns, chaplets, diadems. IV.3

corpertorio covering; perhaps a horse-blanket. I.14

corporalia communion cloth(s); usually of linen, where the consecrated elements (the body of Christ) are placed during the Eucharist. II.1*b*

corse, courses girdle(s), belt(s), sash(es); from the word for body, French *cors*, Latin *corpus*; cf. *course*). V.8*a*, 8*d*, 9*a*, 9*d*, 9*f*

corsettorum corsets; tight fitting undergarments. II.4

cortin', cortinarum, cortines, cortynes curtain(s). II.2, 5, III.1*a*, VII.15

corueser, corvyser cordwainer, leatherworker, shoemaker; originally from Anglo-French and OF *corvoiser* (in British texts from the 1130s). V.8*l*, 9*l*

corunez (of ladies) horned, wearing horn-shaped head-dressing or hairstyle. IV.2

costers, costures wall-hangings or side curtains (especially for a bed). I.21, 23, 32, 33, 47

cosyonys cushions; see *quisshens*, etc. I.36

cote, cotes coat(s), outer garment fitted to the upper body (worn by men or women, either alone or under a mantle or other overgarment); also, a kind of surcoat. I.36, IV.2, 17, VI.2, VII.15

cote-armure garment embroidered or painted with heraldic arms and often worn over armour. VII.15

coton, coton', cotona, cotoun cotton or cotton wool. In the later-medieval period variants of the word *cotton* could refer to various fibrous materials used for stuffing and padding (from Arabic *qutn, qutun*; s.v. *OED*2; cf. *aketouns*). I.18, II.1*b*, III.2, V.8*h*, 9*h*

coue train (of a gown or similar long garment); *tail, trail, train, trayn*. IV.2

couerled, couerlet, couerlete, couerlide, couerlit, coverlet, coverlyt coverlet, bedspread or bed cover. *MED* suggests that this is an Anglo-French term. It is said by *OED* to occur in the fourteenth century in Anglo-French but suggests that these usages may be from English. The attestations in *MED* are all in documents where the matrix language is either Anglo-French or Latin until *c.* 1380. I.18, 25, 29, 32, 40, 47

couertor, couertorez, couertour, covertur trapping(s) for a horse, caparison; coverlets, coverings for a bed. I.21, VII.12, 15

course, courses girdles (belts, sashes or the like; cf. *corse, corses*). V.8*d*, 8*f*

courtby short cloak or jacket. Cf. *courtepet*, etc. I.19

courtepet, courtepetum, courtepie(s) short cloak, jacket or tabard. Cf. *courtby*. II.4, III.2

couverchiefs, coverchief coverchief(s) in the fifteenth century, usually referred to a piece of cloth primarily used to cover the head (as a veil or similar) or worn in various other ways; often fine material and adorned with jewellery (hence the limit on expense in sumptuary law; in the Anglo-French law extracted at V.9*f*, note the corresponding use of *kerchef* in the Middle English Roll of Parliament at V.8*f*). V.9*f*, 9*m*, 9*n*

cowters piece of armour to protect the elbow, elbow-pieces. VII.15

crapowtes toadstones, a semi-precious stone. VII.6

cremosyn the term *crimson* and its variants referred to a dark red or purple cloth that was dyed with kermes. Its use here (with *velvet*) places the semantic emphasis on the style or quality of the cloth rather than its colour. V.4

crencestran 'woman weaver' is the suggestion of Whitelock (1930) but there is no certainly. The woman is named with another slave, who is a seamstress. The juxtaposition suggests the *crencestre* is also a textile worker. The term suggests cranking or turning, perhaps associated with winding woven cloth on to the cloth beam of the loom; or reeling or winding spun thread. I.2

crestes crests, possibly referring to helmets or else to peaks or decorative devices on the top of masks or helmets. III.2

crimiles open work or fringe or a piece of fabric with such work. The term *crimel* is frequently associated with borders or edging; there is some suggestion that the term could be used for a kind of fillet or headband (*AND*2). V.2

crines, crinium hair; decorative ornamentation resembling hair. II.1*b*, IV.1

cristallinum, cristallis, crystall crystal(s), a mineral, clear and transparent like ice; esp. a form of pure quartz having these qualities. III.1*a*, 1*b*, VII.6, 11

cristigray, cristy gray a type of grey squirrel fur. Veale suggests that the name may have been applied to early or late winter skins, and was possibly equivalent to browngrey (Veale 1966: 228). The *MED* derives the initial element of the term through OF *cresté*, suggesting the fur may have had 'tufts, or crests, of some kind' (s.v. 'cristi-grei', *MED*). I.30, V.4

croceali yellowish; cf. the colour term *croceo, crocei*, etc. Cf. the following. III.1*a*

crocei, croceis, croceo yellow or saffron. I.18, III.1*a*, 1*b*, 1*c*

croket 'crochet', ornamental head- or hairdressing (*LCCD*). In later uses this referred to an ornamental roll of hair or hairstyle (glossed in the text as 'chaplet'; Furnivall 1862: 112). IV.2, 3

cropore, cropure cover for the hindquarters of a horse, or a crupper (a leather strap attached to the back of the saddle and passed under the horse's tail to prevent the saddle from slipping forwards). VII.15

crosse werk a variety of patterned linen cloth; cf. *werk*. I.40

croun, crounne, crowne crown of the head. VII.15. Also, crown; crown-like head-dress or ornamental tiara. I.44, VII.11
crounes of cappes for children crowns or peaks of children's caps. V.8p
crucyfixes crucifixes (often worn as jewellery). V.7
cuffian head-dress, presumably held on with the *bindan* (as in the will of Wynflæd); see Chambers and Owen-Crocker (2008). I.2
culcitra, culcitræ, culcitras, culcitre, culcitris quilt(s); cushion(s), often used as church ornaments (as in St Paul's Cathedral Inventory of 1295); cf. *quissini*. II.1a, 1b, III.1a
cuniculis rabbit. VI.7b
cunreerent dressed. VII.9
curches kerchiefs; cf. *kerchef*. V.6
cursu coarse. II.1b
curteynis, curteyns curtains; cf. *quirtayns*. I.28, 34
custura stiching; sewing. II.1b
custurariis seamsters, tailors. II.1b
cuttyng cutting up. IV.17
cyprus costly fabric, the earliest or only *MED/OED* citation is provided by *Sir Degrevant* (Davenport 2000: 117, cf. *Cipre*). VII.14
cyrtel tunic; the term derives from Latin *curtus* 'short'. It sometimes means a man's short tunic, but it is also used for a woman's garment (and there is no evidence that this garment was short). In the will of Wynflæd extracted at I.2 it seems to signify the woman's main, visible garment; see Bulotta (2007) who suggests that in OE texts the *cyrtel* is decorated and the *tunece* plain; also cf. the form *kyrtyll*. I.2, 4a
d'aignel, dagnell of lamb (i.e. lambswool; cf. *agnell, aignel*). V.2, 9g
d'argent, dargent of silver; cf. *argent*. II.5, V.2, 4, 9m, VI.6, 7a, VII.3
d'ermyne, dermyne of ermine (see *ermyn, ermyne*, etc.); made of ermine fur. V.9
d'essex 'of Essex', cloth produced or sold in Essex; cf. *essex*. VI.8
d'or, d'ore of gold; also, of gold thread; cf. *or, ore*. II.5, V.2, 3, VII.3, 9
daggers daggers. V.4
dalmatica, dalmaticis long, tunic-like ecclesiastical overgarment(s), often with wide sleeves; worn over the alb and beneath the chasuble or cope; originally believed to be in the fashion of Dalmatia and introduced by Pope Sylvester I in the fourth century. I.11, 13, III.1a, 1b
damasceno, damaske damask, a silken fabric of various colours; originally associated with Damascus; usually woven with elaborate pattern. I.42, III.1c, V.8e, 9e
damasksengill a textile of black-coloured damask of single thickness (a fine silken fabric). I.42
damysel wedus young men's clothes. The word usually denotes a young lady (OF *damoiselle*), but in Extract VII.14 it is obvious from the context that the masculine sense is required (as in OF *damoisel*; Kooper 2006). VII.14
dancel young gentleman. VII.9
deamondes, deamoundes, diamauntez diamonds. VII.6, 15
dearacione gilding; the act of gilding (verbal noun). II.4
deaurati, deauratis, deauratum, deauratus gilded. III.1b, 1c, 2
deauratis adorned/decked/ornamented (with). III.1a
decisos cut or slashed in an ornamental fashion. V.1
decore uenustissimam beautifully adorned. Appearing in extract VII.2, the corresponding passage in BL, MS Cotton Vitellius A xx has *uestitam* 'clothed'. VII.2
del suite ové of the same suit (as). II.5
demy drap cloth of half a length; a half-cloth (as opposed to a whole cloth of standard measure). VI.3

depeyntez painted. II.5
depictae, depicte, depingend' painted. III.1c, 2
desfublee cloakless. VII.12
destrallyng see *strallyng, strandling*. II.3
deuestuz naked. VII.3
diasperato, diaspero, diaspro, dyaspero (of) diasper; fabric of silk or similar material, often decorated with a repeated pattern or texture; a textile with all-over pattern of embroidery or ornament, or in the form of a lattice which is formed by contrasting the weave's warp and weft faces. III.1a, b
disgysed disguised. With regard to Extract IV.17, two senses listed in *MED* for 'disguise', *adj.*) seem pertinent: 'altered from the conventional or simple style'; or 'strange in fashion, newfangled, showy, ostentatious'. III.1a, 1b, IV.17
doblet see *doubeled, doublet*, etc. I.27
docere, dosur curtain, hanging, a decorative textile hung behind a bed, seat or altar; cf. *dorsalia*. I.21, 28
dorez gilded. VI.7a
dorré of gold, gilded; AF *de* + *orré*. IV.2
dorsalia dorsal, a decorative textile hung behind a bed or altar; cf. *docere, dosur*. I.11
doubeled, doublat, doublet, doublett', doublettes, dublet (var. *doblet*) a man's tight-fitting garment, covering the body from the neck to the hips or thighs: it was double thickness and had padding between layers; its use in Extract VII.15 refers to a similar garment reinforced with metal rings or plates (see also *doublet of fence, doubeled of defence*). I.25, 27, III.2, IV.12, 14, 17, V.6, 8h, 8j, VII.15
doublat of fence, doubeled of defence 'defensive', or reinforced doublet; a close fitting upper garment worn by men, often for combat. A 'doublet of fence' was probably reinforced with padding but may suggest an upper-body garment reinforced with mail and/or worn under armour (similar to *pourpoint*; also cf. *doublet*). I.25, V.6
doublet stuffed a doublet which has been stuffed or padded to give parts of the torso a 'puffed out' effect; cf. *doublet*, etc. V.8j
doublettys imitation jewels made of enamel and glass. IV.14
doubule tressour a double band following the edge of the shield; *tressour* is a heraldic term for a narrow band of one-quarter the width of the bordure. The earliest or only *MED/OED* citation of the term *tressour(e)* in its heraldic sense comes from *Sir Degrevant*. VII.14
doun goose or duck down. I.25
drap d'or, drape d'or, draps d'or, draps dor cloth(s)-of-gold; generally a fabric made with gold thread interwoven with silk or wool. II.5, V.2, 3, 4, 9a
drap de soye silk cloth. V.3
drap de velewet sur velewet a cloth of patterned velvet. Compare the elaborate patterned velvet called *riccio sopra riccio* ('loop over loop'), produced in Italy from about the 1430s and apparently referred to as 'tissue' in some English texts (Scott 2007: 125). V.9b
drap, drape, draps cloth(s); length(s) or measure(s) of cloth; garment(s); bed-clothe(s). II.5, IV.7, V.2, 3, 4, 9b, 9c, 9d, VI.2, 4, 5, VII.9, 12
drapers drapers, those who buy, sell or otherwise deal in cloth fabric. V.2
dras cloths. IV.7
dressez dresses. VII.15
dubbed attired, arrayed. VII.15
dunnan dun-coloured. Whitelock *et al.* (1968: 82) suggest that the dun-coloured kirtles appearing in I.4a were almost certainly woollen kirtles made from undyed 'self-coloured' fleeces of the sheep. I.4a

duoden', duod dozens (from Latin *duodenus*); measures of cloth woven to lengths of no less than 12 yards. VI.8

dupplicato lined; doubled (of cloth). II.1*b*

dusseyns 'dozens', measures of cloth woven to lengths of not less than 12 yards (the *MED* incorrectly says 'feet'). It is interesting that in Extract IV.8 the vernacular is used at the while abbreviated Latin forms (*duoden'*, *doud*, lines 3 and 6) are used below it in the same document. VI.8

dyght adorned. VII.6

dyademata crowns, diadems. III.2

eafor-heafod-segn boar's-head standard or banner. VII.1

ealdgestreon, ealdgestreona ancient treasure (= heirloom weapon, specifically sword). VII.1

earm-beag, earmbeaga arm-ring. VII.1

earm-read, earmreade bracelet. VII.1

ecg, ecge (sword) edge, synecdoche for sword. VII.1

embroidez, embroydez embroidered. II.5, V.2

emerawdes emeralds; cf. *ameraudes, meraude*. VII.6

enarmyt armed, wearing arms and armour. V.6

enbrauded, enbrawde, enbrawded decorated with needlework or with ornaments, especially precious stones, sewn on; embroidered. I.23, VII.15

enbroudato embroidered; cf. *breudata, breudatur*. III.1*c*

endent inlaid. VII.14

endorrez gilded. V.4

enfoubled covered or veiled. *Sir Gawain and the Green Knight* provides the only citation. Notice the verb forms found in Anglo-French: *afubler, afublier, afublir; afebler; enfubler; fubler* (to don, to dress, etc.; also as ppl.). VII.15

engrelyd a heraldic term meaning having a series of curvilinear indentations in the edge. VII.14.

ennurned decorated, ornamented, embellished. VII.15

enorre, enorree, enorrez covered or decorated with metal (usually silver). V.5

enorrour metalsmith (such as a silversmith or goldsmith). The statute that resulted from the parliamentary act of 1420 in which this occupation title appears (Extract V.5) mentions neither the *enorrour* nor the *argenter*. Unlike the act, the statute does not specify that *l'enorrour* is responsible for forfeiting a penalty, nor that the accuser is to gain a third of any fine, although the other details are the same (cf. Luders *et al*. 1816: II.203). V.5

entayled decorated with embroidery. VII.15

entired d'Evelyn (1935) tentatively suggests 'attired' and notes that the term is not recorded in *OED*. *OED*2 online includes 'entire *v.*', but the senses are 'to make whole of; to unite' and 'to attach exclusively; also in weaker sense, to attach closely or intimately', and the earliest citation is 1624. *MED* offers the sense 'Dressed, attired, decked out; esp., provided with an ornamental head-dress' with two citations, both from Idley *Instructions to his Son* (lines II.A.1039–42 and II.B.335; s.v. 'entired, *ppl.*'). IV.17

entiscne, eotonisc, etonisc giant-made. VII.1

eorclan-stan precious stone. VII.1

eorfor-lic boar image (on helmet). VII.1

eorl-gewæde, eorlgewædum noble clothing (armour). VII.1

ereminis (representations of) ermines/ermine fur? III.1*b*

ermyn, ermyne, ermyns, ermyns, hermine, hermyn ermine (fur or the furs of). The white winter fur of the European ermine (*Mustela erminea*, a member of the stoat family) was used for costly garments or trimmings and was a highly valued fashion commodity, although its popularity diminished by the Early Modern period. V.2, 4, 8*d*, 8*e*, 9*d*, 9*e*, VII.9, 10, 11, 14, 15

ersgerdyll 'arse-girdle', probably a low slung belt. I.42

esclaires *AND* 2 suggests 'a kind of fur'. This is possible in Extract V.2, but seems unlikely given the other items in the list. The PROME translation suggests 'adornments'. V.2

esmallis enamel plaques or emblems. III.1a

espeie sword. I.15

esperons spurs. V.5

essex referring to cloth produced or sold in Essex. VI.8

estaple the staple; the authority of a town or region in charge of weighing, measuring, buying and selling particular goods (such as cloth or wool). II.5

estraites, estreites, estroites 'narrows', cloth of a single width (as opposed to broadcloth). VI.5

estreitement tightly. Harris (1998: 90) comments on the increasing importance attached to the proper fit of garments in the twelfth century, noting that *estroit vestu* (in a close-fitting robe) or *menu cosu* (stitched up tightly) are terms frequently used to describe the dress of heroines in romances, lays and *chansons de geste*. VII.9

extencellato spangled (past participle of *extencellare, estencellare*, from OF *estenceler*, ultimately from Classical Latin *scintillare*; s.v. 'estencellare', DMLBS). III.2

faccion fashion. IV.11

fæted-hleore, fæted-hleor with (gold-)plated cheeks (bridle pieces). VII.1

fætum, fæt (gold) plate. VII.1

fah decorated. VII.1

fanone, fanones, fanonis maniple(s) in the contexts here. Originally the term was used of a circular cape worn about the neck, similar to an aumice, but use of this was confined to the pope from the twelfth century, predating the texts here; the term is sometimes employed today by textiles specialists for the lappets of a mitre, but this usage is not recorded in *OED*. II.5, III.1c

fardés adorned, ornamented. IV.2

feld folded. VII.11

fellez skin of animals stripped from the bodies and left with or without the hair attached; skins, hides, pelts, or fleeces; also, such skin, or a piece of such skin, treated and used for clothing. VII.15

felvet see *veluet*.

feor-mynd polisher (from the present participle of *feormian*, to polish). VII.1

feretria shrine(s). III.1b

fermaill, fermeil brooch, clasp or buckle; cf. *firmaculum*. I.15, V.2

fete the lower ends or sides of a strip of cloth, a hanging, etc. (s.v. *MED*, citing the will of Sir William Langeford). I.23

fetels belt or sheath including sword belt. I.7

fetherbed feather-bed. I.32, 40

ffurrereur, ffurrurs fur lining or trim; furs or fur garments; cf. *furrour, furrura*. I.31, 44

ficheux, fycheux fitchew, fur of the polecat. I.24, 42

fildore gold thread. VII.15

filet narrow flat band often worn round the head, stiffened or made of metal, often ornamented with pearls or gems; a frontal; a ribbon, string of pearls. IV.9

fili, filis, filo, filum thread; cf. *filo auri, filo aureo*. II.2, III.1b, 1c, 2, IV.7

fili de lyno, fili lini, fili lyni, filo lyni, Filo lini linen thread. III.2

filo auri, filo aureo gold thread (also *aurifilo*). III.1a; III.1b

firmaculum brooch, clasp or buckle; cf. *fermaill, fermeil*. I.13

flet-ræste, flet-ræst floor-bed (a bed in the communal hall). VII.1

florigeratum 'flowered (with)', decorated or ornamented (with). III.1a

foill leaf (in the will of Thomas Tvoky, an ornamental pattern of three leaves). I.25

fol3ande sute matching material, colour, shade, etc. VII.15
foldid folded. VII.10
forratae variant of *furrata(e)*, lined or trimmed. III.1*a*
forre, fure, furre, furres (also *ffure, ffures*) fur(s). I.24, 25, 31, 40, 43
forred furred (s.v.). VII.15
foteclothes some sort of cloths used with a bed; valences? floor-cloths placed beneath the bed? II.4
foynes fur of foins, stone martens, members of the weasel family; cf. *funes, fun3eis*; see Veale 1966: 219. I.42
fracta (of cloth) frayed (s.v. 'frangere' 4a, *DMLBS*). III.1*b*
frætwe ornaments. VII.1
freawrasnum, frea-wrasn lordly band. VII.1
frees, frys' frieze, a coarse woollen cloth with a thick nap, usually on one side (*EMDT* s.v. 'frieze'. I.25, II.4
frenge, frenges ornamental borders of cloth or thread (on a garment, saddle, etc.); fringe. II.5, VII.15
fret ornamental design or border or decorative work consisting of an interlaced pattern or net, or an ornament of jewels, flowers, etc. in an interlaced pattern. I.25
frisiati fringed. III.1*c*
front frontal; an altar frontal, a decorative altar-hanging. II.5
frontale, frontello decorative cloth used to cover the front of an altar; cf. *frontalia* and *frontel(s)*; also, an ornamental border for an altar-cloth. I.13, III.1*c*
frontalia frontal, frontlet; usually a kind of headband; cf. *frountel*. IV.5
frontel(s) veil or curtain for an altar; cf. *frontale*. I.21
frontlettes headbands or chest-bands (in V.10 made of fabric). V.10
frounciand' pleating or gathering; cf. *frounciat', frounciata*. II.4
frounciat', frounciata, frounciate, frounciatarum 'frounced', pleated or gathered (often as a past participle). Stella Mary Newton believed that the term first appears in English in Thomas de Crosse's Wardrobe accounts for 1342–3, originally stemming from OF *froncie, froncir* (Anglo-Norman *fruncir*), suggesting that 'The actual term, if not the fashion, may have been picked up during the king's residence in Antwerp, where the great wardrobe had been temporarily situated between 1338 and 1340' (Newton 1980:16). However, there is some linguistic evidence that the term (if not the fashion) was in use in England as early as 1331 (in National Archives E 101/385/4; s.v. 'frunciare' in *DMLBS*). II.4
frounciat', frouciata the act or product of pleating or gathering; the providing of pleats or gathering; cf. *frounciand'*. II.4
frountel a headband or frontlet; an ornament worn on the forehead (usually described as being worn by women; cf. *frontalia*). IV.9
frys' see *frees*.
fugeree covered with figures, images or patterns, or containing satin brocade; cf. Anglo-French *figuré*, ME *figure*. V.8*d*
funes, fun3eis furs of the European beech marten or stone marten (*mustela foina*). Veale suggests the term is an 'imported French word for the fur of the stone marten', an animal with a 'white throat and breast' (Veale 1966: 23; cf. *foynes*). I.31, V.6, 8*f*, 9*f*
fur', furre, furres fur(s). II.4, IV.17, V.4, 8*a*, 8*d*, 9*f*
furrand', furrurand' lining or trimming (with fur). II.3
furrata, furratam furred, lined or trimmed; cf. *furred*, etc. III.1*a*, VI.7*b*
furre d'ermyn fur of ermine; cf. *ermyn, ermyne*, etc. The ermine is a member of the stoat family; its white winter fur was also a highly valued fashion commodity. V.4

furred, furrez, furrit, furryd 'furred', trimmed or lined with fur; cf. *forred, y-furred*. I.25, 36, 42, VI.7a, VII.11

furring(is) fur lining or trim. V.6

furrour, furrura, furruris, furur', furura, fururie, fururis fur trimming or lining for a garment; also, a measure, group or pane of furs. II.1a, 1b, 3, 4, IV.13

furur' agni lambswool. I.19, II.1b, 3

fururac' (the act of) lining with fur; providing a trimming or lining (of). II.4

fururand' see *furrurand'*. II.3

fururez furred. V.2

fusca dark. III.1a

fustian, fustien, fustyans a type of cloth described as being made of cotton, flax or wool, or most often a mixture of these in weft and warp. Whilst not the cheapest of fabrics, it was relatively durable and used for everyday wear. Modern *fustian* usually implies a 'hard-wearing, heavily wefted fabric' (*EMDT* s.v. 'fustian'). I.32, III.2, V.8g, 9g

fyrd-hom war-garment. VII.1

fyrd-searo, fyrd-searu armour. VII.1

galea helmet. IV.5

gambisoun military tunic made of leather or thick cloth, sometimes padded; it covered the trunk and thighs and was originally worn under the habergeon to prevent chafing or bruises, but was sometimes used as a defence without other body-armour. VII.14

gardecors', gardecorsatorum padded garment such as a gambeson or similarly padded tunic; also, a breech-girdle; a belt or band worn across the belly. II.1b

garderoba, garderobe (*magne*) wardrobe; also used for the 'Great Wardrobe' or royal office charged with provisioning and making purchases on behalf of the royal household (as in II.4). I.14, II.4

garminum garment(s). II.1b

garnementes, garnementus, garniament', garniamentis garments, articles of clothing; especially outer garments, coats, cloaks, gowns. II.4, III.2, IV.13, VII.14

garnettes garnets. VII.6

garnia[...]s garments? cf. *garnementes*, etc. VI.2

garnissand' ornamenting, adorning, embroidering; arranging; garnishing. II.4

garnisse trimmed or ornamented. V.9f, 9m

garnit' 'garnished', trimmed or ornamented. III.2

garnyr to provide; to equip. VI.2

garter, garteriis garter(s). III.2, V.2, 8b

gaudi ornamentation. VII.15

gaudys large, ornamental beads in a rosary. I.40

gauntz de plate, gauntz de plates au meyns gauntlets of plate or armoured gloves; protective garments for the hands. VI.2

gebroden, gebregdan woven. VII.1

gelocen woven (from past participle of *lucan* to weave). VII.1

gemellis stripes. III.1a

gemmes, gemmys precious stones, gems. VII.11, 15

gerdylstede 'the girdle place'; since a girdle was worn around the waist or hips, presumably this compound in Extract VII.11 suggests that Tryamour is undressed almost to the waist. VII.11

gere, gerez, geyr clothes; harness; bedclothes. VII.14, 15

gertiers garters. I.42

gesæled, sælan twisted. VII.1

gesseran see *jesseraund*. I.31

ge[t]elde tent. Also *teld*. I.2

geweorðad, weorðian honoured, adorned. VII.1

gewiredan preon wired brooch or pin, described as being old (*ealdan*) in the will of Wynflæd, perhaps referring to an heirloom and therefore precious. Whitelock suggests filigree for *gewiredan*. I.2

geynes sheaths/scabbards. Appearing in a parliamentary act of 1420, the resulting statute has *geines* (Luders *et al.* 1816: II.203, n2). V.5

Gildeford cloth produced or sold in Guildford in Surrey. VI.8

gilt gilded. V.8f

ginillato striped (for *gemellato* or similar; s.v. 'gemellatus', *DMLBS*). III.1a

girdeles, girdell, girdill, girdle, gordel, gordell, gurdil, gurdill, gurdyll, gyrdille, gyrdils, gyrdles, gyrdyll girdle(s), belt(s), strap(s), sash(es); in later uses, often an embroidered band or textile girdle; belt worn around the waist or hips and hanging down at the front, used for fastening clothes or for carrying a sword, purse, etc.; a fashionable accessory especially in the fourteenth century. In some instances girdles were perhaps adorned with studs or metal ornaments or else woven or shot through with silver thread (cf. the *girdill of siluer* in the will of John Chelmyswyk and the *siluere girdeles* in the will of Roger Flore). I.24, 27, 28, 32, IV.15, V.7, 8f, 8m, VII.10, 15

giruns tent-flaps; in VII.9 perhaps the sides or walls of the tent. VII.9

giselie elegantly, foppishly (*MED*). IV.17

gisie elegant, foppish. IV.17

gladeolata ornamented, 'flowered' (with fleur-de-lis). III.1a

gladeoli, gladeolis fleur(s)-de-lis (figures of). For the 1295 St Paul's inventory (extracted at III.1a), Simpson suggests 'swords' (an emblem of St Paul's; Simpson 1887: 448), but this seems unlikely given the context. III.1a

gleves swords. VII.14

glouez of plate, glovis of plate, gluffis of plate iron gauntlets. I.23, V.6, VII.15

godely unthur gare 'goodly under gown'; the expression is derived from ME *gor(e), gar(e),* used to refer to a woman's garment or dress, from OE *gára*. This jingle runs through the poem extracted at VII.6, and variants of the tag appear throughout the corpus of Middle English lyrics and romances. VII.6

godwebbenan a fine, especially silk cloth or, specifically, purple cloth of the same (cf. Whitelock *et al.* 1968: 83). I.4a

gold, golde, goolde gold; also, implying gold thread or cloth-of-gold (as in IV.14, V.8a, VII.6, 8, 10, 11, 14, 15); specifying *cloth-of-gold* (I.31, 44, etc.). I.2, 24, 31, 32, 34, 39, 42, 44, IV.14, 17, V.7, 8a, 8f, 14, VII.1, 4, 6, 8, 10, 11, 13, 14, 15

gold-fag gold decorated. VII.1

gold wyre gold wire. VII.11

golde, goldes of gold, golden. I.5, 6, 7, 8, 26, 28

Goldsmythes werk decorated with gold or gold ornaments. I.42

gopil fox; cf. *gupille*. V.2

gorde with the waist encircled (with a belt or girdle). VII.15

gordoll see *girdell*. IV.15

gorgeat a mail collar or armour for the throat; metal protection for the chin and neck. V.6

gorger article of female dress covering the neck and bosom. VII.15

gossamer gossamer, a filmy substance consisting of fine webs; also, something light, trivial, or worthless. IV.14

gote leþer leather made from goatskin. I.25

goulez red. VII.15

goune, gounne, govne, govnes, govnys, gowen, gowne, gownes, gownus, gownys gown(s); long outer garment(s). I.22, 26, 27, 30, 36, 37, 38, 39, 40, 42, 43, 44, 47, IV.12, 17, V.2, 4, 8*i*, 8*j*, 9*i*, 9*j*, 10, VII.14

graithed, grayþed prepared; dressed; ornamented. Andrew and Waldron (1978) suggest 'seated', but this sense does not appear in *MED*. VII.13, 15

grana, grano, grayn, (in) (*en*) fast-dyed 'in grain', the expensive insect dye kermes (*Kermes vermilio*) producing a dark red or scarlet, or used in association with other dyes to make other colours. II.3, 4, 5

granis literally 'grains' or 'seeds', used to refer to small jewel or gemstone (cf. 'granum' 7a, *DMLBS*). III.1*b*

gravatum engraved. III.1*b*

gray, grey standard species of squirrel fur, in particular the grey fur from the backs of the north European red squirrel in winter (also 'gris'; see Veale 1966: 228); but it could also simply mean 'grey' or a similar dark colour. I.25, V.4, 8*f*

grene green; (of) green cloth. I.27, 39, 42, VII.10, 15

gret menyvere untrimmed fur or fur of the whole animal (squirrel), equivalent to OF *gros vair*, fur from the back of the squirrel, also called *gris*. It was rated lower than *miniver*, the white belly fur (Newton 1980: 68). I.30

greuez greaves, armour for the lower leg, shin guards. VII.15

grifonibus griffons, embroidered motif of a mythical winged beast, half lion, half eagle. I.11

grisio, grisis, grys (var. *gro*) grey fur, typically from the backs of northern European squirrels; an expensive fur, it was often used for lining (Veale 1966: 228). I.21, II.3, 4, V.1, VII.11

gro see *grisio, grisis, grys*. VII.11

grosses chaparons long hoods, hooded cloaks or cowls. Such garments were a ubiquitous part of clerical dress in the period. V.4

grosso vario equivalent to OF *gros vair*, fur from the back of the squirrel, also called gris (see *grisio, grisis, grys*). It was rated lower than *miniver*, the white belly fur (Newton 1980: 68). II.3

gryre-geatwum terrible armour. VII.1

guð-byrne battle garment. VII.1

guð-gewæde, guðgewædu battle garment. VII.1

guð-searo battle armour. VII.1

guð-sweord battle sword. VII.1

gupille fox; cf. *gopil*. V.4

gurde encircled with a belt or girdle. IV.17

guttate spotted (past participle of *guttare* = 'to drip, drop'; s.v. *DMLBS*). III.2

guyse, gyse fashion, manner of dress. Often collocates with *new*, as in *newe gyse, newe guyse*. IV.3, 13, 17

gyde, gydes a kind of long gown (from OF *guite*). IV.10, VII.14

gyld overlaid wholly or in parts with a thin coating of gold. VII.15

gyldenne, gylden golden. VII.1

gympeu, gympeus wimple(s), a woman's head-dress or head veil. There were many varieties, but the wimple typically covered the top, back, and sides of the head, including the cheeks and chin, and was wrapped so as to cover the neck (see *winpil*). IV.2

gyrede, gyrwan dressed, prepared. VII.1

haberdasshers members of the guild or company of Haberdashers; sellers of haberdashery (various items of mercery or small wares: specifically hats, caps, etc.). VI.9

habergeon, habergeone, haberjown, habirgoun, habirion (var. *aburioun*) mail jacket, often sleeveless, typically worn under plate armour or similar; similar to a hauberk (if not the same)

– although the *habergeon* is a fourteenth-century derivative that was often shorter and tighter than the traditional hauberk (*EMDT*, s.v. 'mail'); cf. *aburioun, hauberghe, hawbergh*, etc. I.31, 34, V.6, VII.14

hæft-mece hilted sword. VII.1

haȝer of jewels: seemly, tasteful. *Sir Gawain and the Green Knight* provides the only citation for this sense in *MED*. Tolkien *et al.* (1967) glosses the term 'skilful, well-wrought', whilst Andrew and Waldron (1978) have 'goodly, noble'. VII.15

haketon aketon, padded defensive jacket or similar worn by men, sometimes embroidered; cf. *aketouns*. II.4

halched fastened round, looped. *MED* lists senses (a), (b) and (c) for this headword supported by six citations all of which are from *Sir Gawain and the Green Knight*. VII.15

haliryft holy veil. I.2

hallyng, hallyng' wall-hangings, room hangings or tapestries. I.24, 47

hare grey. VII.1

harnesed, harneised, harneysed, herneysed adorned, decorated; trimmed/ornamented (often with gold or with silver). I.34, V.7, 8f, 8m

harnesse, harneys, herneis, herneises, hernes', hernies, hernois, hernoys in early uses: clothing, attire, bedding, etc.; more generally, accessories, trappings, 'accoutrement' (in the will of Richard Dixton extracted at I.42, for example, accessories are presumably intended); also trappings for a horse (as in the *herneis dorré* of William of Wadington's *Manuel* – Extract IV.2). I.25, 26, 34, 42, III.2, IV.2, V.4

hasped fastened (of a helmet, buckle or lace). VII.15

hatters hat makers; also members of the guild or company of Hatters. VI.9

hauberghe, hawbergh, hawberkes long coat of mail, or military tunic, usually of ring or chain mail (cf. *habergeon*, etc.). VII.14, 15

heaðo-byrne battle garment, mail coat. VII.1

heafod-beorg, heafodbeorge head protection (= helmet). VII.1

heafodgewædo head-dress, possibly a veil. I.4*a*

heallwahriftes, healwahrift hall tapestry or hangings. I.2, 8

heals-beag, healsbeaga, heals-beah neck-ring, torque. VII.1

heaþo-steap, heaþosteapa, heaðosteapne battle-high, tall (of a helmet). VII.1

helid covered. I.30

helm, helmas, helme, helmes, helmum helmet(s). I.5, VII.1, 14, 15

helm-berend helmet-bearing (warrior). VII.1

hemmez edges or borders of a cloth or garment. VII.15

here-byrne battle mail coat. VII.1

here-net war-net (mail coat). VII.1

here-pad battle garment (mail coat). VII.1

heresyrcan, here-syrce battle-shirt (mail coat). VII.1

hermine, hermyn see *ermyn, ermyne*, etc. VII.9, 10

hernes', herneis, herneises see *harnesse*. III.2, IV.2, V.4

hernois, hernoys see *harnesse*. V.4

heuedshite headsheet, a sheet put at the head of a bed. It is not always clear whether it covers the pillows. I.21

hewe hue, colour. IV.17

hewk huke, a hooded cloak or shoulder cape; cf. *hukes*. I.25

hewyt hued, coloured. V.6

hilde-bil(l), hildebille battle-sword. VII.1

hilde-cumbor battle-banner. VII.1

hildegeatwa, hilde-geatwe battle gear. VII.1
hilde-sceorp battle-garment (mail coat). VII.1
hilde-setl battle saddle. VII.1
hiltan hilt. I.7
hilted hilted. VII.1
hleorberan, hleor-berg cheek-protector (on helmet). VII.1
hleor-bolster cheek-pillow, cushion. VII.1
hod, hode, hodes, hoode, houd, hoyd, hudis hood(s); worn by men or women and often attached to an outer garment or worn as a separate head-covering with or without attached shoulder cape. In the fourteenth century the hood was fashionable and was worn in various ways – not always on the head (*EMDT*, Figs 29–38). I.22, 26, 27, 39, 40, 47, IV.10, 17, V.6, VII.6, 15
hole be fore whole in front; without a (front) opening, a garment that slips over the head. V.7
honge hang. IV.15
honourement adornment; cf. *ornament*. V.8p
hoode see *hod*. IV.17
hoose see *hose*. IV.17
hoppscytan bed-curtains or hangings (although Bosworth and Tollers' *An Anglo-Saxon dictionary* suggests 'A coverlet [?]', *s.v.* 'hopp-scýte, an; f.'). I.8
hornes, horns horns or rolls of hair worn on the sides of the face by women during the fourteenth and fifteenth centuries or the head-dress covering such a hair style. IV.10, 14, 17
hose, hosen', hoses, hoose, hossyn, hosyn leggings, stockings; often described as being a 'pair', typically of woven cloth or leather, with or without feet (often pl.). I.22, 27, IV.11, 15, 17, V.8m, VII.11, 15
hrægl, hrægla, hrægles garment(s). VII.1
hricghrægles ornamental cloth, usually embroidered, hung at the back of the altar or at the sides of the chancel or at the back of a seat; see Coatsworth (2007). I.8
hring, hringa, hringas ring(s) (as jewellery); ring(s) (as mail). VII.1
hringde, hringed ringed (made of mail). VII.1
hring-iren ring-iron (mail). VII.1
hring-net ring-net (mail coat). VII.1
hroden decorated (past participle of *hreodan*, to decorate). VII.1
hrof roof, crown (of helmet). VII.1
hudis hoods; see *hod*, etc. V.6
hukes probably hooded robes; long, lined outer garments usually described as being worn by women; cf. *hewk*. V.10
hure, hures covering(s) for the head, a cap(s), hat(s), or similar items of headwear. IV.17, VI.9
hurers cappers, makers and dealers of *hures*; also members of the guild or company of Hurers. VI.9
hustilmentis items, furnishings. I.24
hwef Andrew and Waldron (1978: 271) translate this term as 'coif' following Gollancz's suggestion that the manuscript *hwez* (BL, MS Cotton Nero A x) is a form of OE *hūfe* 'head-covering' and suggest that the implication of its use in *Sir Gawain and the Green Knight* is that it would have been a more seemly head-dress for a married woman. Tolkien *et al.* (1967: 120) find that Gollancz's (1940) suggestion would involve a greater change of form than he allows and argue that it is not supported by the passage in *Purity* which he adduces. VII.15
hwit, hwita shining. VII.1
hyrst, hyrsta ornament. VII.1
hyrst, hyrste armour. VII.1
hyrsted (from verb *hyrstan* to ornament) decorated. VII.1
iaggyng slashing (of clothes, for decorative effect). IV.17
ibrideled with headgear put on. IV.17

i-laside, ylased laced. In the text extracted at VII.11 (as in all of the versions of the *Launfal* story), the women's garments are tightly laced; this detail almost certainly survives from Marie de France's narrative, though lacing had gone out of fashion by the late fourteenth century when this version of the story was written – a period which saw laces give way to buttons and to looser, more flowing shapes. VII.10, 11

imperiali imperial, a fine, silk cloth. In later accounts (fifteenth century) it referred to a lampas silk manufactured in Italy (King 1988: 68; Monnas 1989: 285, 290). III.1a

inciso cut (describing cloth)?; perforated? III.1b

Indesandel a thin, rich, silken material; indigo silk. VII.11

indici, indico indigo (colour), dark-blue or purple. III.1a, 1b

interlaqueata, interlaqueatis interlaced (design or pattern). II.1b, III.1b

interularum undergarments, chemises. IV.1

ionetis genets, the fur of the genet or civet cat (as in the will of Thomas Tvoky). I.25

iren, irena iron (= sword). VII.1

iren-byrn, iren-byrnan iron mail coat. VII.1

isernbyrnan, isern-byrne iron mail coat. VII.1

jagunce jacinth (a precious stone). VII.12

jaket jacket. V.8i, 8j, 9i, 9j

jaune yellow (or similar); yellow- or brownish-yellow-coloured cloth. II.1b

jelu yellow or yellowish; coloured with a yellow dye. IV.8

jepun jupon, tunic. VII.14

jesseraund (variant *gesseran*) jesserant, a coat of light armour made up of padded cloth and mail or of riveted metal pieces, such as scale armour. I.31, VII.14

jocalia jewels. I.13

juell, juellis jewel(s). VI.6, VII.11

juncturarum (of the) seams, joints. IV.7

kamahutis cameos (engraved gemstones; an Anglo-Latin form of OF *camaieu*). III.1b

kamelyn see *camalin', camelino*. I.18

kanabo canopy. III.1a

karde see *card'*. II.3

karolis jewelled rings or circlets (s.v. *DMLBS* 'carola'). III.1b

kassydonys the gem chalcedony (pl.). VII.6

kelle head-dress, cloak, garment or shroud from OE/ME *caul/calle*; compare Modern English *caul*; *comely unthur kelle* is a tag similar to *godely unthur gare*. VII.6

kenchia apparently 'of Kenzig', cloth made in the Kinzig river region of Germany (s.v. *DMLBS*, following Guiseppi). II.1b

kerche, kerchef, kercheiffes, kercheves, kerchevus, kerchiefs, kerchofes, kovercheef kerchief(s), piece(s) of cloth primarily used to cover the head (as a veil or similar) or worn in various other ways; often of fine material and adorned with jewellery (hence the limit on expense in the sumptuary legislation). IV.14, 17, V.8f, 8m, 8n, VI.7a, VII.8, 11, 14, 15

kerseys coarse narrow-cloths woven from long wool, usually ribbed; first appearing in thirteenth-century texts, cloth originally made in or associated with Kersey, in Suffolk. VI.5

kerteles, kertill, kurtull, kurtyll, kyrtel, kyrtell, kyrtels, kyrtyll, kyrtyls woman's gown(s) or man's short tunic(s); from being the outer garment in Anglo-Saxon times (see *cyrtel* in the wills of Wynflæd and of Æthelgifu), by the end of the Middle English period the term referred to a garment worn under a woman's gown (see the wills of Isabel Gregory and of Margarete Asshcombe), when it was on its way to becoming the petticoat of early modern times. I.36, 39, IV.6, V.7, VI.7a, 7b, VII.6, 10, 11, 15

ketil hatte round, iron helmet (literally a cooking-pot-shaped hat). I.23

knit formed a noose or loop in (a cord, etc.), looped, tied (a cord, etc.) in a loop; *absol.* formed a ligature with a thread. VII.15

knoppus see *cnapp*. VII.14

knot knot. Note that *MED* includes a sense 'knitten ~' under *girdel* meaning 'tie a knot in one's girdle' (s.v. *MED* 'girdel'). IV.15

knotez ornamental knobs on armour or garments; a button; perhaps tassels or tufts. VII.15

koralle see *corall*. VII.6

kyngle girdle or brooch; Middle English term, borrowed from Old Norse. It is cited only from a fourteenth-century set of wills in the *MED*. I.18

kyrtel, kyrtell, kyrtels, kyrtyll see *kertill*, etc. I.39, IV.6, VII.15

labellis lappets (such as those hanging from a mitre) or similar ribbons or dangling strips of cloth. III.1c

lace, lases, laz cord(s), string(s), ribbon(s) made of braided or interwoven strands of silk, threads of gold, etc. V.7, VII.12, 13, 15

laceatos trimmed with lace, fringe or similar. V.1

lachet loop of cord, leather, etc., used as a fastening for armour. VII.15

laciees (of a garment) laced on, fastened; dressed, laced into (a garment). In the twelfth century belts and laces tightened loose fabrics closely around the upper body (see Harris 1998: 89; Smith 2008: 96). VII.9

laine, lana, lane wool. II.1b, 4, III.2, V.9h

lambe lambswool. I.39, V.8g

lana, lane see *laine*. II.1b, II.4, III.2

lapid, lapides, lapidibus gemstone(s). I.19, III.1a, 1b, 1c

lapis gemstone. III.1a, 1b

lapped wrapped. VII.13

lappes parts of a garment loose enough to admit of being raised, folded or seized; the lower part of a shirt, skirt, etc. VII.6

laqueis, laqueos lace(s), band(s), ribbon(s), tie(s), draw string(s). I.13, II.1b, 4

lased laced; decorated with laces. See *i-laside, ylased*, etc. (and cf. *laciees*). V.7

lases see *lace*. V.7

lavne, lawn, lawne lawn, a fine linen; originally, linen associated with the Laon region of France. V.6, 8n, 9n

lecto, lectum bed. II.1b, 4

legge harneys metal armour for the leg. I.23

legsplentis leg-splints, armour protecting the leg. This usage seems to have been particular to fifteenth-century Old Scots (s.v. 'leg-splent, n.', *DOST*; and 'leg, n.', *OED*). V.6

leme glitter. VII.11

leoðosyrcan, leoðo-syrce mail shirt. VII.1

leþer, lethyr leather, skin (insultingly, of a woman; Furnivall 1862). IV.3, 17

letuce, letueses, letuse, letuses, letyce fur or furs of the European snow weasel; usually the white winter fur. Such furs were 'more valuable fur than *minever* [*sic*], less expensive than ermine, for which it was often used as a substitute' (Veale 1966: 220). V.2, 4, 8f, 9f

lic-syrce body shirt (= mail coat). VII.1

lienge tele linen cloth. V.2

limbati, limbatur fringed (with); provided with a hem or fringe. III.1a

limbis border, hem; fringe. III.1a

lin' linen? II.4

linchiamentis, linteamen, linthiaminum, lyntheux, lynthiamina sheets or cloths of linen used for various purposes: as bedsheets, table cloths, towels; as linings, etc. I.18, II.1b, 2, VI.6

linea, lineae, lineis (of) linen (*pannae lineae*, of linen cloth). II.1*b*, III.1*c*, 2
lineatas thread; cf. *lineis*. I.12
lineate, lineato lined. III.1*b*, 2
lineatorum, lineis (of) linen. II.1*b*
lineis thread; cf. *lineatas*. I.12
lini, lyni, lyno (of) linen; cf. *lineae*. III.2
liniand', liniande lining (as a verbal noun), often with fur; or lined (with fur). II.4
linnenne linen. I.2
linnenweb linen cloth. I.2
linure in texts from the thirteenth to the fifteenth centuries, *linure* and *linura* are used to refer to a lining of lawn or fine linen. In the sumptary law extracted at V.2, however, the textile itself is probably intended (i.e. 'they may wear fur in winter, and fine linen/lawn in summer'). V.2, 9*h*
lit, litz bed(s); bedding; hangings, covers and other soft furnishings for a bed. IV.2, VI.6, VII.3, 9, 12
liuerey, liveree, livery, lyuere, lyveree, lyverree livery, official recognisance, garment or uniform; also, an allowance or provision (for clothing, food, income, etc.). I.26, 31, 43, VI.1, 3
longure length. VI.2
lorayns harness. VII.11
lorier pillow; vernacular forms include *oreillier, oreiller; orailler, oriler, oreiler, oriller*, indicating the connection to the Latin *auriculare* (pillow) from the adjective meaning 'auricular, of the ear'; cf. *oraillers*. VII.3
loupe loop of cloth, rope, leather, etc. VII.15
Lucis in this context evidently some kind of ornament attached to a tapestry (perhaps to do with St Luke?) although the word itself suggests a fine cloth originally associated with or manufactured in Lucca in Italy, or Liège in Belgium (*Luyck* in e. Middle Dutch) is also possible (but cf. *Leg'* above). II.1*b*
lufsum vnder lyne, þat lit. 'that lovely one under linen', a conventional formula for 'that lovely lady'. These kinds of formulae are not uncommon, for example *godely unthur gare* in *Emaré* and *wys under wede, vlonkest on wede, worthely in wedus* etc. in *Sir Degrevant*. VII.15
lyne linen; occurs in tag of approval involving clothing: *lufsumme [. . .] unthur lyne*. IV.9, VII.6
lure a cloth originally produced in Lierre, in Brabant, very often black. I.39
lyned, lynyt lined. I.36, 42
lynges linens, napery. II.5
lynne bed linen bed. I.25
lynyng lining. V.8*h*
lynyt see *lyned*. I.36
lytere bedding. VI.1
maðþum-sweord treasure-sword (a sword made with precious materials). VII.1
mæssereafes mass garment, the term refers to a garment which could be worn by any ecclesiastic for religious services. I.8
mancesum, mancosan, mancussum, mancysan a mancus is recorded as both a weight of gold and a gold coin. I.2, 3, 5, 6, 7, 8
manches, maunches sleeves (cf. *manicis*). V.2, 4
manicis sleeves (cf. *manches*, etc.). IV.1
manipula, manipulam, manipuli, manipulis, manipulo, manipulus maniple, a narrow cloth, shorter than the stole, worn over the left forearm by the celebrant at mass; originally a napkin or cloth used for wiping the vessels used in the performance of mass, but came to signify an ornamental band used as a vestment; sometimes in a matching set with the stole; cf. *fanon*. I.11, 12, III.1*a*, 1*b*

mantel, mantell, mantelle, mantellum, mantellus, mantile, mantyle, mantyll, mauntel, mauntelle cloak, outer garment worn by men and women; robe. I.14, 18, 32, II.4, IV.7, V.2, VII.10, 11, 12, 13, 15

mantellatur made into a mantle (see *mantullus* in previous entry); this is a unique attestation in British texts from a presumed infinitive *mantellare* (s.v. *DMLBS*). IV.7

mantica travel bag or portmanteau; wallet. II.4

manutergiis napkins or hand towels (either as household napery or as ecclesiastical altar cloths). II.1b

manutheca, manuthecæ glove(s). IV.7

mappa, mappis general term for napery: table, bed or altar linens. II.1b, 3

marbryn kind of cloth with a marbled, mottled or parti-coloured pattern. II.4

margarita, margaritarum, margaritis pearl(s). III.1a, 1b, 1c

marmorea, marmoreo (of) marble, a cloth that is marbled or resembling marble. III.1a

marterount, martir, martirs, martirons, martrens, martrons, martrouns, mattrones marten(s) or their furs; marten fur. The European marten (*mustelid genus Martes*) was a long, bushy mammal resembling a large weasel; cf. *mertrikis*. I.25, 30, 31, 41, 42, V.4, 8f, 9f

massehakele, messehaclen mass garment; in Extract I.1 – given the ornamentation – evidently a chasuble or cope. I.1

materacio, materacium, materacii mattress(es); cf. *materas*, etc. II.1b

materas, matras mattress. According to *OED* this is an Anglo-French term. It appears in *MED* which suggests that it is an Middle English term borrowed from Old French. I.18, 32, 36

mauntolet woollen covering for a horse. This is among a number of terms for which the romance of *Sir Degrevant* provides the earliest or only *MED/OED* citations (Davenport 2000: 117). VII.14

maylus mail coats. VII.14

mece sword. VII.1

medled of alternating colours or furs (as with the beaver and otter fur in the will of Thomas Tvoky). I.25

medley medley cloth of a single color (*MED* cites the will of Richard Dixton to illustrate this sense [b]. Sense [a] is 'cloth made of wools dyed and mingled before being spun, and either of one color or of different shades or colours'). I.42

melle, melly medley. I.19, 25

menevoir, menuueyr, menyuer, menyver, menyvere, miniver (vars. *menevera, meneverus*) fur of the white belly of the Northern European squirrel. The white, winter belly fur of the European miniver was highly prised in medieval fashion. The term is formed from OF *menu* ('small') and *vair*, a term which originally referred to the skin of the whole animal. *Miniver* generally refers to the white belly fur without the backs. A more valuable variety could be specified as 'pured' meaning that any remaining grey fur had been trimmed from the edges (see Veale 1966: 228–9). I.21, II.3, V.2, 4, 8f, VI.3

mensked adorned. VII.15

mentelpreon a brooch or pin for fastening the cloak. The compound appears only once, in the will of Wynflæd (I.2), though the term *preon* is attested in this will and others of women. I.2

meraude emerald; cf. AF *ameraude, emerawdes*. I.19

mercerye the Worshipful Company of Mercers of London – those trading in textiles and fabrics, usually considered exotic or of fine quality, etc. II.5

mere-hrægl, merehrægla sea-cloth (= sail). VII.1

mertrikis martens, furs of marten. *Mertrik* (likely from Latin *martix*, with the same meaning) seems to have been a form particular to texts from Scotland; cf. *marterount, martir*, etc. V.6

metail, metaille metal. V.5, VII.15

miniver see *menevoir*, etc. II.3, III.2
mitra, mitrae mitre(s), ecclesiastical head-dress(es) for the ranks of bishop and archbishop. III.1*a*, 1*b*
mixt', mixte, mixti, mixto, mixtorum (of) mixed (cloth); patterned or variegated cloth; motley. II.1*b*, 3, 4
moillez fulled; processed by a fulling mill. VI.2
molaynes stud on the bit of a horse's bridle; a bridle-rein. VII.15
monile brooch; necklace (*CPR Hen. IV* suggests 'a necklace': 4 Henry IV, 2.265). VI.7*b*
morsellis trimmings; the remainder of cloth that has been trimmed. IV.7
morsum, morsus clasp(s), fastener(s), especially the elaborate centrally worn brooch for an ecclesiastical cope. III.1*a*, 1*b*, 1*c*
mos, modo style. I.12, IV.1, 5
musterdevylers a grey-coloured textile of late-medieval manufacture, originally from Montivilliers in Normandy. I.39
mylyngis stripes. I.40
naapri, naperie, napery linen for household purposes; sheets, tablecloths. I.24, 32, 35, VI.6
nakette a precious stone – probably an agate. VII.6
nakid made bare. VII.5
naylet studded with nails. VII.15
naylez metal nails; ornamental studs on armour. VII.15
neaþene at the bottom (a hem). I.4*a*
nettes thin sheets of a fine, silken fabric (for curtains). I.25
nevyn precious stone or ornament; in Extract VII.14, referring to some sort of ornament or clasp (Casson 1949: 129). The earliest recorded romance/poetic occurrence of this term which is otherwise found only in wills, inventories, etc. is in the romance of *Sir Degrevant* (Davenport 2000: 117). VII.14
niger, nigra, nigram, nigri, nigro black. I.12, 13, II.1*a*, III.1*a*, 2
nodato 'with knots', knotted; either an embroidery technique, such as French knots, or an interlaced design. III.1*b*
nodis knots. III.1*a*, 1*b*
nodulis small button(s) or knot(s). III.1*b*
noych, nuche see *oyche*, etc. I.44, VII.14
nun's'crude nun's clothing. It was a common practice among Anglo-Saxon widows to take a vow not to remarry and live a religious life at home without entering a nunnery. The term used in Ethelred's reign to distinguish a woman living outside a nunnery under religious vows from a cloistered nun was *nunne*. I.2
nyfels kerchiefs of some sort of fine cloth. In early uses, 'nifle' was used to refer to a trick or jest and to a trifle, a thing of little value. V.8*n*, 9*n*
oblaunchre or *blaunchre* powder used to whiten the face (LCCD; AND2). IV.3
ocriarum (of) boots or leggings. IV.11
oeverunt working; (in specific instances) weaving. VI.4
omig rusty. VII.1
onichinis onyx(es). III.1*a*
onyx onyx, a form of chalcedony consisting of plane layers of different colours, much used in jewellery. VII.6
opera, opere 'work', workmanship; (specifically) embroidery. III.1*a*, 1*b*, 1*c*
opera pectineo, opere pectineo 'comb work': an embroidery stitch probably with a woven effect (see Christie 1938: 22). III.1*b*
opera pulvinario 'cushion work': an embroidery stitch, perhaps cross or tent stitch. III.1*b*

opera saracenico, opere Saracenis, opere sartacinito (of) 'Saracen work', embroidery work imported from or originally associated with the Near East. III.1*a*, 1*b*

operarariis workers; (specifically) seamsters, tailors, embroiderers. II.2

operata, operatis, operatum 'worked', embroidered. III.1*a*, 1*c*

opere Parisiensi 'Paris work', embroidery made in or associated with Paris. III.1*c*

opere plumario stitching; embroidery (in general). Christie (1938: 22) suggests a 'feather or plumage stitch' (also s.v. 'opus plumarium', *DMLBS*). III.1*b*

opyn be-for open at the front; not buttoned or fastened. I.31

or, ore gold; also, gold thread. I.15, II.5, V.2, 3, 9*f*, VII.3, 9, 12

oraillers pillows; cushions. Cf. *lorier*. VI.6

orbiculari opera (or *opus orbiculari*) embroidery work with a circular pattern (cf. *orbiculariter operata* at III.1*a*). III.1*a*

orbicularibus in the phrase *in orbicularibus* meaning '(woven) in small circles or circular patterns'. III.1*a*

ord point (of a weapon). VII.1

ordre of the garter (ordre del Jartier) the Most Noble Order of the Garter, the select society of knights founded by Edward III *c.* 1348. Some of the earliest references to the Order are found in the Great Wardrobe accounts (see III.2), where its newly coined motto – 'Honi soit qui mal y pense' (Shame on him who thinks this evil) – is found embroidered or depicted on garments made for the order. III.2, V.8*b*, 9*b*

orfrays, orfreys decorated bands on vestments, often embroidered, often with gold or silver thread. I.11, II.5

ornament, ornamenta, ornamentes, ornaments adornment(s); accessories. In some instances (such as V.5), the term could refer to fabrics, hangings, ornaments of precious metal, etc. I.24, III.1*a*, V.5, 9*p*

ornata, ornate ornamented; finished. III.1*a*, 1*b*, 1*c*

ornatur, ornatus ornamented, adorned. III.1*b*

ornatus ornaments, adornments; jewels; finery. IV.4

ornyd horned, having horns; (of a woman) wearing 'horns', either a horn-shaped hair style or head-dress. IV.6

oter, oterre otter. I.25, V.4

ouches, oyche, uches (vars. *noych, nuche*) clasp(s), buckle(s) or brooch(es); mounted gem or cluster of gems; earring(s) ornamented with gems; necklace. I.44, V.2, 6, VII.14

ouer-gilt, ouerguld, overgilt gilded; in the will of Thomas Bathe (I.28), used to indicate that a girdle is covered with gilded silver metal studs or possibly that the girdle is heavily embroidered with gold thread. I.28, 32, V.8*f*

overfret embroidered. VII.14

overt open; of clothing, unfastened. VII.14

paile, pailes, pal, pall, pel fine or rich cloth, especially as used for the robes of persons of high rank; purple cloth for such robes; also, decorative cloth hangings, curtains. VII.6, 9, 10, 11, 12, 13, 14

pair' of bedys, pare bedes, payre off bedes, peire bedes, peyr' of bedys, peyre off bedes set of prayer beads, a rosary. Cf. *bedes*. I.21, 30, 32, 40

pal see *paile*. VII.13

pala vertical stripe. III.2

paled, palid striped (past participle of *palen, pale*). I.21, 32, 47

pallarum copes. III.1*c*

pallia in this context, possibly referring to rich cloths, such as those hung over coffins in procession. I.11

palliorum robes. IV.1

pan, pane tail (of shirt); skirt; flap; (more broadly) garment. Also, a section of the fur lining or trimming of a robe or mantle; cf. *pane*. VII.9, 10, 15

pane pane (of furs); a certain quantity of furs sewn together for use as a lining. II.3

pann', panni, pannis, panno, pannos, pannorum, pannum, pannus (of) cloth; cloths; clothing. I.10, 13, 14, II.1*a*, 1*b*, 3, 4, III.1*a*, 1*b*, 1*c*, 2, IV.7, V.1, VI.8

panni aurei, panno aureo, panno auri (var. *panno ad aurum*) (of) cloth-of-gold; fabric made of gold brocade, gold thread, gold wire, strips of gold or similar, generally interwoven with silk or wool; also applied to gilded cloth. It is documented in various colours including red, blue and white. From the fourteenth century, the designations *imperial*, *nak* and *racamaz* were used for various types of cloth-of-gold (Monnas 2001). I.13, II.1*b*, III.1*b*, 1*c*

panno Antiocheno cloth of Antioch; cloth made or purchased in, or originally associated with Antioch (s.v. LCCD). III.1*b*

panno Damasceno aureo damask, a silken cloth originally associated with Damascus, often woven with elaborate patterns; here specifically a cloth-of-gold. III.1*c*

panno de Reynys a fine linen cloth made in or associated with Rheims in Champagne-Ardenne (France; previously – erroneously – associated with Rennes in Brittany). III.1*c*

panno Tarsico cloth of Tars, silk cloth originally from or associated with the Mongol Empire in Asia (Tharsia?). Cloths of Tars could refer to figured silks, probably woven in twill damask; some were all silk, some cloth-of-gold, often described as powdered with decorative designs (i.e. with embroidered motifs distributed on the textile; see Monnas 2001: 4–5). See *tars*. III.1*b*, 1*c*, V.6

panno Yspaniæ ad aurum Spanish cloth-of-gold. I.13

pans, paunce a piece of armour covering the belly or lower abdomen (from AF *pance*, 'belly'; cf. Modern English *paunch*). I.23, V.6, VII.15

papageyes, papiayez 'popinjays', representations of parrots (embroidered motif). VII.14, 15

par, paria pair or set (of garments, vestments, etc.). III.1*b*, 2

parted divided, mi-parti; a garment made of two contrasting cloths, divided down the middle. I.25

parura, paruram, paruras, parures, paruris an apparel, ornamental part of an alb or other ecclesiastical garment (including altar curtains); decorative band, trimming or embroidery. II.5, III.1*a*, 1*b*, 1*c*

parys werk embroidery made in, or associated with Paris; cf. *werk*. I.40

pat' not', pater noster, paternosters paternoster beads, a rosary. I.16, 17, 32

pauillion' 'part of or covering for a helmet' (s.v. '*papilio, pavilio*', 3, DMLBS; cf. *paveilluns*, etc.). III.2

paunce see *pans*. I.23, VII.15

pauteners, pawteners purses or wallets. Cf. British Latin *pautonera* (s.v. DMLBS, attested c. 1290), a beggar's bag. V.8*p*, 9*p*

paveilluns, pavyloun (var. *pauylione*) pavilion(s), tent(s). VII.9, 10, 11

pavonibus peacocks (embroidered motif). I.11

paynted depicted. VII.15

paytrel, payttrure poitrel, a protective breastplate or pectoral armour for a horse; also, ornamental trappings or caparison for the front of a horse. VII.11, 15

pec', pecie, peciis piece(s); localised, standard measure for cloth. II.1*a*, 1*b*, III.2, VI.8

peerless, pearls (var.) – see *perl*, etc. I.30

peked of a shoe or boot: provided with a long, pointed toe; cf. *piked*. IV.12

pelic' pelisse or pilch; an outer garment made of animal skin (with fur on). Cf. *pell'*, etc. II.3

pell', pelle, pelles, pellis, (la/the) (the) pelt(s), hide(s) or skin(s) (of animals). However, note similar variants under *paile*, etc. Also cf. *pelic'*. III.2, IV.7

pelleure, pellure, pelure, pelures fur(s), as trimming, lining, etc. (as in V.8g); occasionally used to refer to apparel or clothing more generally. I.32, V.2, 3, 8g, 9d, 9g, VI.3, 6, VII.15

pellicula hide, skin or pelt ; cf. *pel, pelle, pellis*. IV.7

pelowe, pilwes, pylowe pillow(s.) I.21, 40, IV.17, VII.4

pendaundes, pendaunt, pendauntes, pendauntez pendant(s), referring to (an) ornament(s) attached to or suspended from the hanging end of a girdle. I.28, VII.15

pendaunt hanging down. IV.13

pendulis, pendulum, pendulorum pendule(s); a hanging ornament or similar object, specifically the lappet on an ecclesiastical mitre. III.1*b*

pene fur, skin. IV.7

pensel, penuncell small pennon or streamer; token worn or carried by a knight. III.2, VII.11

penyworth a pennyworth (a measure, worth one penny). I.22

perecé adorned (with); variegated with or shot through (with). *AND*1 suggests 'tattered, torn', but this seems unlikely given the context. IV.2

peres preciousez precious stones. VII.3

peridotis, perydotes peridot, a green gemstone; may refer specifically to chrysolite. III.1*a*, VII.6

perl, perlae, perle, perlez, perlis, peyrl (plural var. *peerless*) pearl(s). I.11, 30, III.1*a*, 1*b*, V.6, VII.14, 15

perpoint pourpoint, a tight-fitting, padded and quilted jacket, often of expensive material; male civil costume; particularly popular in the fourteenth and fifteenth centuries; equivalent to ME *doublet*. V.9h, 9j

perre, perree, perreye precious stones or jewels. IV.14, V.2, 3, VI.6, VII.14

pers', pers, perse, persico, perso blue or dark bluish cloth of some quality. I.14, II.1*b*, 3

pertica, perticae, perticis rod(s), pole(s); wooden rod used in a cupboard or wardrobe to hold clerical vestments. III.1*c*

peruyng periwinkle. The periwinkle is a common feature of medieval manuscript illustration and was equally appropriate for embroidery. It is recognisable by its opposed leaves and five-petalled blue flowers (Tolkien *et al.* 1967: 91). Appearing in *Sir Gawain and the Green Knight* (VII.15), the term may be read *pernyng* as a present participle meaning 'preening themselves', but the sense is inappropriate and the syntax and form abnormal as the present participle usually ends in *–ande* in this poem (Andrew and Waldron 1978: 230; Tolkien *et al.* 1967: 92). VII.15

pesane, pisanibus, pysan 'pisane(s)', mail collar(s), worn with armour, usually attached to the helmet and covering the neck, breast and shoulders. III.2, V.6, VII.15

philetris (for *phylacteris*), phylactery, ornamental reliquary or receptacle for a relic. III.1*b*

pieces measures of fabric, variously standardised for different kinds of cloth at different periods. VI.5

pigacias, pigatiarum long points or spikes on the toes of shoes; shoes with long, pointed toes (*pigatiarum* is the genitive form). Chibnall notes that in France in the seventeenth century similar shoes were known as 'souliers à la poulaine' (Chibnall 1973: 187); cf. *pikes, poyntes*. IV.1

piked pointed; cf. *peked*. IV.17

pikes, pykes elongated points on shoes. The term 'pikes' used to name these points appears as early as the Wardrobe accounts of Richard II in 1394; an adjectival form (*pyked* or *pikede*) appears as early as *Piers Plowman*, *c.* 1380 (Passus 20, line 318). Elongated points on shoes, boots and armoured feet came in and out of fashion in the late fourteenth and early fifteenth centuries. Various names for similar fashions are used in various British texts from the period, including *crakow, poulaine*, and *rostrum* (see Chambers and Sylvester 2010: 72–6); cf. *pigacias, poyntes*. V.8k, 9k

pilis, pilo skin. IV.7

pilleo cap. IV.1
pilosa hairy. IV.7
pisanibus see *pesane*, etc. III.2
plana, planae, plano, playn plain, unadorned or unembroidered; flat? I.32, III.1a
plate, platez plate armour worn by a knight or by a foot soldier; especially in the early period: an iron or a steel plate used to reinforce chain mail; later, a breastplate and backplate combination, a cuirass; also, a piece of armour; also, armour composed of overlapping plates. VI.2, VII.15
pleytid pleated, folded. IV.12
plia folded. VII.9
plite, plyght a unit measure for cloth. English use of this term with this sense is first attested in 1394 (cf. 'plight', LCCD); it is most often used to measure fine cloths such as crimel and lawn). V.8f, 8n, 9f, 9n
plusculis buckles. II.4
poisies heraldic emblems. IV.17
poke, pokis small puffed-out shape(s) on the sleeves (referred to in fashion histories as a 'poky', 'bagpipe' or 'bombard' sleeve). Such sleeves were popular in the middle decades of the fourteenth century. V.6
polaynez separate pieces of armour protecting the knee and fastened to the thigh piece. VII.15
polles heads, fur taken from the heads of the animal. I.25
pomelle(s) ornamental knob(s) or decorative boss(es). VII.10, 11
popre fur of the European squirrel taken in summer, or a piece of this fur. II.3
poudr', pouderat' 'powdered', decorated all over (cf. *pulverisatis*, etc.). III.2
pounac', pounacium a purplish-blue-coloured cloth (cf. Anglo-French *poun, pon, paon, pown*; Latin *pavo* = 'peacock'). II.1b
poyned embroidered. VII.14
poyntes in this context, points on shoes; cf. *pigacias, pikes*. IV.11
preon, preonas brooch(es). I.4a, 8
presme inferior kind of emerald. III.1a
pulverisatis, pulverisato, pulverizata, pulverizatur 'powdered', decorated all over, with ornaments, decoration (usually embroidered motifs). III.1a
pulvinar, pulvinaria, pulvinaribus cushion(s); cf. *culcitra, quissini*. III.1a, 1b, 1c
puratis, puray 'pured'; (of fur), trimmed; often used for miniver, where the squirrel's white belly fur has had the surrounding grey fur trimmed off; cf. *pure, pured* and *puree, purez*. II.3, V.6.
purces, purse purse(s), pouch(es) or bag(s). I.27, V.8p
pure, pured trimmed; used attributively for fur that has been trimmed so that only one colour is visible, raising its value; cf. *puree, puratis*. IV.17, V.2, 4, 8f, 9f, VII.15
pure grey, pured grey trimmed fur of the grey squirrel; both the Middle English act at V.8f and the Anglo-French statute at V.9f use the pre-modifying adjective. Cf. *puree de gray ne de byce* and *pured de gray* in the petiton of Sept. 1402 (V.4). V.8f, 9f
pure meniver the white belly fur of the European miniver, trimmed of any surrounding grey fur. With regard to the sumptuary legislation at V.9f, the corresponding Middle English Roll of Parliament (8f) does not specify that the *menyver* is pure. V.9f
pured de gray trimmed fur of the grey squirrel. V.4
puree, purez used attributively for fur that has been trimmed so that only one colour is visible, raising its value; cf. *pure, pured* and *puray*. V.4
purfil, purfile a decorative border or trimming of fur. V.2, 4
purfilac' the providing of trim; the trimming (of), the adorning (of). II.4
purfiland', purfiliand' trimming, adorning (usually with fur), trimmed, adorned. II.3, 4
purfilat', purfilata trimmed or adorned. II.4

puri, puro pure, unadulterated. III.1*a*, 1*b*

purpre, purpull, purpur, purpurea, purpureae, purpurei, purpureis, purpureo, purpyl, purpylle purple. Adjectival forms such as *purpul*, *purpel*, *purple*, etc. stem from the Old English (Northumbrian) adjective *purpul*, etc., and appear to be alterations of *purpure*, Latin *purpura*, etc. These latter forms were in common use as both nouns and adjectives in pre-Modern texts. III.1*a*, 1*c*, 2, V.8*c*, 9*c*, VII.9, 10, 11

purpura rich, silken cloth; later identified with shot-silk taffeta (cf. Crowfoot *et al.*, 2000: 90; Dodwell 1982: 147). III.1*a*

purse see *purces*. I.27

pylowe pillow; see *pelewes*, etc. VII.4

pyne de Euere ivory pin. I.16

pynnes pins, brooches. V.7

pysan see *pesane*, etc. VII.15

pytrelled d'Evelyn (1935) suggests wearing a peitrel or poitrel, the breast-armour for a horse. IV.17

queldepoyntes quilted coverlets (Andrew and Waldron 1978) gloss this term as 'quilted seats' but Tolkien *et al.* (1967) note that the term's etymology is OF *coiltepointe*. AND1 offers 'counterpane' with a citation reading: 'un lit [...] une keulte ou une keutepoynt, deux oraillers'(a bed [...] a quilt or a counterpane, two pillows). VII.15

quirtayns curtains; cf. *curteynis*. I.25

quisseux, quyssewes cuisses, pieces of armour for the thighs. III.2, VII.15

quisshens, quysshonus, quysshons, quyssonus (other vernacular variants include *cosyonys*, *whyssynes*; also see the entry following) cushions. I.25, 28, 36, 40, VII.15

quissini cushions; bolsters; cf. *culcitra*, *pulvinar*. III.1*c*

quyltus quilts, covers stuffed with wool, down, hair, etc., used as a mattress, cushion, or coverlet for a bed. VII.14

quyt white. VII.15

rad' ray; a striped or variegated cloth; cf. *raié*, *ray*. II.1*b*

radiato striped, of striped cloth; cf. *rad'*, *raié*, *ray*. I.13

ragyt ragged, tattered. V.6

raié striped ('rayed'); cf. *rad'*, *radiato*, *ray*. II.5

Rakemask', Racamaz originally a type of silk cloth of gold (or silver), which was heavy and expensive. III.1*c*

ray array (Laskaya and Salisbury 1995). VII.6

ray striped cloth (French and Hale 1930, who derive the term from *ray*, Latin *radius*, a stripe or striped cloth). This was typically a tabby-woven wool cloth; cf. *radiato*, *raié*. I.27, II.5, VII.11

rayes striped or panelled. VI.4

rayman the ray (striped cloth) merchant; a Middle English compound. II.5

re\a/de, reed red, applied to various shades of purple, crimson, scarlet, pink, etc.; coloured with red dye. I.2, 23

rede golde pure or reddish gold. VII.14

rerebrace, rerebrasaris pieces of armour, originally protecting the back; subsequently (as in V.6) pieces of armour protecting the upper arm and shoulder, worn in conjunction with the *vambrasaris*. I.23, V.6

retonsura re-shearing; re-fulling or finishing a cloth. II.1*b*, 3

revers revers, the border or edge of a garment which has been turned back so that it is visible (as a turn up or collar). Usually the *revers* is furred, trimmed, ornamented, embroidered, or similar (hence its prohibition in the sumptary law alongside *purfil*). V.2

reuersat', reversate, reversed of garments: trimmed, with edges turned back and decorated. Cf. *yreversyd*. III.2, IV.10

reynes, reyns, ryns (also *panno de Reynys*) a fine linen cloth made in or associated with Rheims in Champagne-Ardenne (France; previously – erroneously – associated with Rennes in Brittany; cf. *ryns*). I.21, II.4, III.1c

ribane, rubans, rybanne ribbon(s), ornamental band or border, trimming; an ornament, a necklace; a bracelet, an anklet. V.2, 3, VII.14

riches prepares (himself), dresses. VII.15

ridelli curtains (often altar curtains). Cf. *rudelez, rydalus*. III.1c

riding gowne gown worn whilst riding horseback. I.47

roan leather; probably made from soft, pliable goatskin. III.2

rob', roba, robam, robarum, robas, robe, robes, robis (of) robe(s); a set or suit of matching garments. I.13, 14, II.1b, 3, 4

robe, robes garment(s); also clothing (in general). IV.2, VII.6, 11

roé striped. VII.12

ropez slender ropes, cords, strings. VII.15

rostra point(s) (on boots) spurs? IV.11

rotostan Whitelock *et al.* (1968) translate as 'brightest' (OE *rot* elsewhere appears to mean 'cheerful' or 'excellent', not 'red'.) Here the *cyrtel* described seems to be the woman's main, visible garment (cf. *kirtle* in the later will of Isabel Gregory de Hakeney). I.4a

rotundi rounded (describing the toes of shoes). IV.1

rouencel rouge, red face make-up. IV.2

rub', rubea, rubeae, rubei, rubeis, rubeo, rubeus red (colour); red cloth. I.13, II.1b, 4, III.1a, 1b, 1c

rubetum ruby. I.13

rubyes rubies. IV.14, VII.6

rudelez, rydalus curtains, curtains for a bed. Cf. Latin *ridelli*. VII.14, 15

russet, russeto inexpensive woollen cloth; often of a dull brown or brown-red, but is variously specified as 'grey' and also as 'black' (as in the will of Thomas Tvoky). It is also used to describe the colour russet, a neutral colour of grey or (more often) reddish-brown (as in the will of the countess of Warwick). I.25, 26, 36, 39, 42, 44, V.2, VI.7a, 7b

ryng, rynge, rynges, ryngis, rynk ring(s) (as worn on the hand or body). I.32, IV.6, V.7, VII.11, 14, 15

ryngez metal rings attached to an object for fastening, lifting, etc.; curtain rings. Tolkien *et al.* (1967) gloss the usage in *Sir Gawain in the Green Knight* (VII.15) with 'rings of mail-shirt', but although that sense is given in *MED* specifically in the phrase 'in ringes', the usage in line 857 from the poem is cited in illustration of the sense given here. This sense seems to be a better fit for the context. VII.15

ryns see *reynes*, etc. III.1c

sabatounz pieces of protective armour for the upper side of the foot, held in place by laces or straps. VII.15

sabelo, sables sable, fur of the European sable, a northern variety of the marten (a long, bushy mammal, larger than a weasel). Its fur was typically dark brown to black and was quite valuable (Veale 1966: 22). V.1, V.8a, 8e, 9a, 9e

sacca cilicino sackcloth; from Latin *cilicinus*, derived from the noun *cilicium* (goats' hair or similar). The term is often used to describe penitential garments or bedding. VII.2

sadel, sadell, sadelles, sadol saddle(s). VII.1, 10, 11, 15

sadol-beorht 'bright of saddle'. VII.1

sælan twisted. VII.1

safere, saphyrus sapphire(s). VII.6, 14

saffroned, safronez dyed a saffron colour (*AND*1 'safroné'). IV.2

sal rope. VII.1

sambus elegant saddlecloths. VII.11

sameto, samit, samito, samuti, samyt samite, a plain silk cloth in weft-faced compound twill. Its appearance has the diagonal lines of a twill weave and a lustrous quality produced by the long weft floats. It was made in various weights, but was usually quite heavy and suitable as background for embroidery in gold thread. Monnas notes that though samites were sometimes woven competely in silk, they could also be half-silks, with linen main warps (Monnas 1989: 284–5). I.13, II.1*b*, III.1*a*, 1*b*, VII.11

sanap, sanapes, sanappus cloth(s) serving as table-runner(s); also, overcloth to protect the tablecloth. I.32, 40, VII.14, 15

sandalia, sandalium ecclesiastical footwear, a slipper or half-shoe of very fine quality. III.1*a*, 1*c*

sanguineo, sangvyn red; blood red colour. I.37, II.3, III.1*a*

saphiris, saphiro, saphyr, saphyrum sapphire(s). I.13, 14, 45, III.1*a*

sarcenet a fine silken textile, made both plain and twilled. The word is derived from Anglo-French *sarzinett*, a variant of OF *sarrasinat*. V.10

satain fugeree, sateyn fugery ornamented – probably embroidered – satin. Extracts V.8–9 contain some of the earliest appearances of this form in British texts (cf. the ME *fugery*). V.8*d*, 9*d*

satain, sateyn, satyn satin, a plain, twill, closely woven silk fabric, often with a lustrous or shiny surface produced by long floats of closely woven warp threads which conceal the weft; originated in China. V.8*e*, 9*d*, 9*e*, 10, VII.8

sayl sail; cf. *segl, sigle*. VII.6

saylande flowing. This seems to be a figurative extension of the verb *seilen* 'to travel on water in a ship', and *Sir Gawain and the Green Knight* provides the only usage in *MED* in this sense. Tolkien *et al.* (1967) suggest that this passage is difficult, perhaps slightly corrupt, and much disputed. VII.15

sayn, saynt, saynte belt, girdle, sash; cf. *ceincture*, etc. VII.15

scarl', scarlet', scarlet, scarleto, scarlett, scarletto scarlet, a rich, highly shorn cloth. Scarlet cloth was of various colours in the period, although it could be dyed scarlet-colour with expensive kermes dye. In most cases, *scarlet* probably refers to a kind of fulled woollen broadcloth of fine weave and quality wool (Munro 1983, 2012). The *OED* suggests that the term is an aphetic of OF *escarlate*, the later, related textile term *ciclaton* thought to derive from a common Persian ancestor (s.v. 'scarlet, *n*.', *OED*). Munro suggests an alternative etymology through Old High German (Munro 2012: 477–81). I.25, 42, II.1*b*, 3, 4, IV.13, V.1, 8*g*, 9*g*

schafte spear, lance. VII.15

schaped mounted, trimmed. Tolkien *et al.* (1967) note that *schaped* may be derived from *chape*, a metal mount or trimming. VII.15

schefe bundle of arrows; quiver. V.6

schelde, scyldas shield(s). I.5, VII.15

schete, schetes, schetis, schetus, schetys, shete, shetis, shetys *MED* indicates a wide range of meanings for this term including any length of cloth, especially linen; a linen garment of some sort; a cloak or robe; an infant's swaddling clothes; a bed sheet; a towel; a napkin. Many of these senses seem possible, for example, in the scant context provided in the will of John Pyncheon (I.20), though bed clothes seem most likely; cf. *chete* (I.29). I.20, 21, 24, 27, 32, 34, 36, 39, 40, 47, VII.14

scochenus, scochôns coats of arms. I.21, VII.14

schon see *shoen, shone* (not to be confused with 'schon' in VII.15, meaning 'shown'). VII.11

scurtes, skyrtez skirts, lower parts of a saddle or garment. VII.15

searo-fah cunningly decorated. VII.1

searo-hæbbend, searohæbbendra armour-bearing (man). VII.1

searwum, searo devices (armour). VII.1

secta suit (of matching garments). II.4

segen, segn, segne standard. VII.1
segl sail (OE); cf. *sayl, sigle*. VII.1
seintures see *ceincture*. V.4
sele saddle. VII.9
sele-rest, selereste bed in the hall. VII.1
selk, selke see *silk*.
selour, selure, silour celure, a canopy; cf. *celure*. I.25, 34, VII.15
semellis soles. III.1a
semez embroidery or ornamental work along the seams of a garment. VII.15
seminatis 'seeded'? from Classical Latin *seminare* (to sow), probably the equivalent to 'powdered' with embroidered motifs. The *DMLBS* reports that by 1368 the past participle was used by transference to mean 'to decorate by sprinkling' but does not cite the usage from Bogo de Clare's account of 1284–5. II.1b
sendal, sendel, sendelle fine costly fabric (silk or lawn, cotton or linen); most frequently a tabby-woven silk cloth, usually light, but available in heavier weights. It was the least expensive and most common silk cloth of the Middle Ages (King 1963; cf. *cendal*). I.21, VII.10, 14, 15
sendato sendal, a tabby-woven silk cloth; cf. *sendal*, etc. III.1a, 1b
sendre fine costly fabric, probably silk (form in *MED* but not *AND*; cf. *cendal, sendal*, etc.). I.18
sengill of single thickness (cloth). I.42
serenarum, sereni (of) Sirens; embroidered figures of the Sirens (*Sirena*), the mythical creatures, part woman, part bird, supposed to lure sailors to destruction by enchanted singing. II.1b
serici, sericis, serico, sericum, sericus (of) silk; cf. *cerico*. I.13, II.1b, 2, 4, III.1a, 1b, 1c, 2
serpe, serpis ornamental chain, collar or necklace. I.42, V.6
sethrægl, sethregl seat cover. I.2, 4a
sewe sew. VII.6
sharpe gold or silver baldric. I.44
shete(s), shetis, shetys see *schete*.
shethes sheaths. V.5
shoen, shone, shoon (var. *schon*) shoes. IV.12, 17, V.8k, VII.11
shrude outfit. IV.9
sid wide. VII.1
sigle sail (AF); cf. *sayl, segl*. VII.3
silk, silke, sylk, sylke silk, silk cloth. I.25, 28, 31, 42, II.5 IV.17, V.6, 7, 8d, 8f, 10, VII.6, 11, 13, 14, 15
siluere girdeles belt(s) possibly lustrous in colour or woven or shot through with silver thread, but more likely with silver matal attachments such as studs and bars; cf. *girdill*. I.32
siluere, silver, syluere silver. IV.17, V.7, 8m
sinc, since, sing treasure, variously an item of jewellery or armour. VII.1
sindon, sindone, sindonis, syndon' a fine linen material; often used as a substitute for, or confused with the lightweight silk *cendal/sendal* (*EMDT* s.v. 'sendal'; Newton 1980: 135; cf. *cindone*). II.1b, III.2
singulo single; unlined (of cloth). II.1b
skinner, skynner, skynners skinner(s), one/those who deals in furs, hides and skins; also the London company of the same (as in I.43). I.31, 34, 43, IV.13
slefes, slefis, sleues, sleves, slewis sleeves. I.25, 39, 42, 44, V.6, 10
sleveles sleeveless. IV.6
smið smith. VII.1
smok, smoke chemise, shift; (typically sleeveless) undergarment worn by a woman. IV.9, VI.7a, VII.5
soie, soy, soye silk. II.5, V.2, 3, 9c, 9d, 9f

solers shoes (ME *shoen*); from OF *souler*; cf. Modern French *soulier*. V.9k
sortes lengths or measures of cloth. V.2
sotulares shoes. III.1*a*, 1*b*
spere, speru spear(s), thrusting weapon(s). I.5, VII.15
spissam heavy. I.12
sporez, sporis, sporres, spures spurs. IV.11, VII.5
spousaile bed marriage bed. VII.13
squirello squirrel. II.1*b*
stanford high-quality woollen cloth originally produced in or associated with Stamford, Lincolnshire. II.3
stapled fastened together or attached with clasps or similar devices, i.e. at the joints (Andrew and Waldron 1978: 230). VII.15
stayned coloured. Although staining was technically different from painting, the former using water-soluble dyes, the latter oil-based, staining is unlikely in this context (colouring of stirrups) and the demands of 's' alliteration may explain the choice of terminology VII.15
stel weapon or part of a weapon made of steel; a blade, sword, etc.; collectively, weaponry, arms. VII.15
steropes, steroppys stirrups. VII.10, 15
stirap representation of a stirrup used as a heraldic device. IV.10
stodys studs, decorative metal ornaments. I.28
stoffed see *stuffe, stuffed*. VII.15
stola, stolae, stolam, stoles ecclesiastical stole(s), long narrow cloth, often expensively embroidered, worn over the shoulder or neck, worn in different ways by ecclesiastics of the rank of deacon and above. I.10, 11, 12, II.5, III.1*a*, 1*b*
ston, stones, stonys jewel(s), gemstone(s). I.44, IV.14, VII.6, 11, 15
stragulato, stragulatum striped or panelled. III.1*b*, 1*c*
strallyng, strell probably *strandling* (or *stralling, strenling*; Latin *stranlingum*); kind of squirrel fur, usually from the thicker (and therefore more expensive) autumn coat. II.1*b*, 3
strell see *strallyng*. II.1*b*
strict' used to describe narrow cloth; cloth of a single width (opposed to broadcloth). VI.8
strictis, strictissimis (var. *strecte*) tight-fitting or constricting. IV.1, 11
stuffe (n.) padding, stuffing. V.8*h*, 9*h*
stuffe, stuffed (var. *stuffat', stoffed*; p.ppl.) padded, stuffed; in V.8*j* and 9*j* referring to a garment which has been stuffed or padded with material, originally as protection, but also as a fashion item, to give the torso a 'puffed out' effect. Also cf. the preceding and following entries. III.2, V.8*j*, 9*j*; VII.15
stuffed in this context 'crowded'; an expensive cloth is packed with decoration (see *MED*). VII.6
stuffer material used for padding or stuffing; cf. *stuffure*. V.8*h*
stuffure material used for padding or stuffing. The Middle English Roll of Parliament of 1463 has *stuffer*. V.9*h*
subtolares shoes. IV.1
sudaria sudary or sudaries, humeral veil; an oblong cloth worn over the shoulders and used to handle sacred objects; by extension, a cloth or veil used to drape over the chalice. III.1*c*
suerde, suerd, sweord, swurdes, swyrd sword(s). I.7, V.6, VII.1
suisorre gilt; gilding (*en ascun part dicell suisorre* = 'in any part of the same gilt'). This Anglo-French term is found in the Rolls of Parliament with this sense as early as the 1363. V.9*f*
suisorrez gilded; the form represents the Anglo-French plural past participle of *suisorre*, q.v. The Roll of Parliament (V.8*f*) corresponding to the Anglo-French statute (V.9*f*) has *overgilt*. V.9*f*
supermappis surnaps; table cloths or napkins on top of the table linen for wiping the hands. II.1*b*

supertunica, supertunicam, supertunicarum, supertunicas, supertunice surcoat(s); long, usually sleeveless overgarment(s) (note also the form *supertunicale*). I.18, 19, II.1*a*, 3, 4, III.2

supertunicale surcoat or similar long overgarment; cf. *supertunica*, etc. I.14

surcot, surkot, surkote surcoat or similar long overgarment. Discussing the appearance in *Emaré* (VII.6) Hopkins (2000: 80) notes that *wede*, line 699, can only mean the embroidered robe, but Iurdan should not be able to see it as the heroine is wrapped in a 'surkote that was large and wyde' (line 652). VI.3, VII.6, 15

surcote de este a 'summer surcoat'; a (light) overgarment worn during the summer months. Cf. the ME *somersercotes* listed in the accounts of the Abbey of Durham for 1363–64 (Fowler 1899: 566). VI.1

sutores leatherworker, cordwain; (specifically) a shoemaker. IV.1

sweorbeah, swyrbeages neck ring. This term provides important Anglo-Saxon evidence for the existence of neck rings for which there is little evidence in art and archaeology. I.3, 6

sweþled tied, wrapped, bound. VII.15

swin-lic, swinlicum boar-figures. VII.1

swynes mawe belly of a pig, perhaps used as a purse or pouch (cf. *MED* 'maue, n.', although only anatomical senses are given). IV.10

syde nekit hudis 'side necked hoods', hoods which were worn off the head, over the shoulders with the fabric collecting or folded around the neck. V.6

sylk, sylke see *silk*. I.28, 31, 42, II.5, V.7, 10, VII.6, 14, 15

Sylkwommannes craft the work, trade or mistery of making silk; a company (of women) who specialise in making silk. II.5

sylvryn' lustrous, resembling silver. I.27

syndon' see *sindon*, etc. III.2

syrce shirt (probably = mail coat). VII.1

tabar, tabardo tabard; sleeveless or short-sleeved overgarment. II.1*a*, VI.1

taffata taffeta, a firm, tabby-woven silk textile. II.4, III.2

tail tail, train; cf. *coue, tayles, trail, trayn*. V.6

taillour, taillours tailor(s). I.31, IV.13, V.8*j*, 9*j*

talaris probably an ankle-length garment. In earlier (OE) uses could refer to footware such as sandals, but by the thirteenth century seems to have been used to refer to a clerical garment. III.1*b*

tamsery werke specific kind of embroidery; possibly derived from OF *tamis* or *tamise* (sieve, screen), used to describe the embroidery on a dorser in the will of Thomas Bathe. I.28

tapecery tapestry work. I.34

tapeta, tapetiis, tapetis, tapeto, tapite, tapites (of) piece(es) of decorative fabric bearing a painted, embroidered, or woven pattern or figures and used variously as carpets, coverlets, bed or wall-hangings; where the product of the tapicer, probably tapestries rather than painted cloth. I.21, 32, II.1*b*, III.1*a*, 1*c*, VII.15

tapicers weavers of tapestries, also of striped and plain fabrics that could be embroidered or painted. I.21

targe a buckler, targe, light shield; cf. *bokill*. IV.17

tars a costly fabric, perhaps a kind of silk, made (or originally made) in Tharsia, a kingdom said to border China on the west or Tartary (denoting China); cf. the following entry. Cf. *panno Tarsico*. VII.15

tartaryn, tarteron, tartyn' tartarin, a silk, tabby-woven textile; originally imported from or associated with Tartary but manufactured in Europe by the later-medieval period. I.47, II.4, 5, V.10

tassellis, tassello, tassellos, tassellus tassel(s); pendent decorations on copes and occasionally on chasubles, often consisting of metal plates, often jewelled and with religious images. III.1*a*

taune, tawne, tawny orange-brown colour, presumably *tauni*, a Middle English term adopted from Anglo-French. I.18, 21, IV.17

taylis trains, trailing parts of long garments; cf. *coue, tail, trail, trayn*. IV.12

taylour tailor, maker of clothes. I.22

teille, tel', tela, tele fabric; linen. II.1b, 5, III.2

tela lin' linen cloth? II.4

tela parys' cloth of Paris? II.4

teld tent. Also *ge[t]elde*. I.9

tele de Leg', tele de Leges linen cloth of Liège, in modern Belgium. II.1b, 3

temply pair of ornamental bosses, often bejeweled, used to enclose hair coiled at the temple (*MED*). I.44

testour, testur bench or chair cover, a covering of tapestry or similar, covering for furniture, or occasionally a wall-hanging; for its uses in VII.14, Kooper (2006) suggests 'headboard'. I.47, VII.14

thalones (probably *chalons*) lengths of a kind of woollen cloth or frieze originally associated with or produced in Châlons-sur-Marne in France, used as hangings or coverings. III.1a

þeod-gestreon, þeodgestreona people's treasures. VII.1

threde thread; a fine threadlike filament of a material other than a textile, such as gold; a fibrous material from which cloth is made, yarn; sometimes distinguished from silk; the fabric made from flaxen or woollen thread. IV.17

þrotes throats, fur taken from the throats of the animals. I.25

þwonges thongsor cords used as fastenings for shoes, clothing, or armour. VII.15

tir' decorative row or strip of fur(s) (see Veale 1966: 28). II.3

tire, tires, tyre attire, apparel, clothing; an outfit; a woman's fine head-dress; an ornament of woman's dress. IV.17, VII.10, 11

tirreten' cloth of wool mixed with linen or cotton. II.1b

Tistours Weavers; members of the Weavers' Guild (of York: *d'Everwick*). VI.4

toga, togæ, toge cloak(s), mantle or gown; often an overgarment of some quality. IV.4, VI.7a, 7b

tolouse high quality fabric from Toulouse, France. VII.15

topacio, topatii, topaze, topaziis, topyes topaz(es); gemston(es) III.1a, 1b, VII.6, 14

topteler ornamental covering for a horse. *Sir Degrevant* provides the earliest or only *MED/OED* citation for this term (Davenport 2000: 117). VII.14

torent 'torn'. VII.11

toreted edged, ornamented; perhaps veiled. *Sir Gawain and the Green Knight* provides the only citation. Gollancz (1940) reads the term as *toret*. VII.15

tortors turtledoves. Here, representations on textile of turtledoves, birds associated with love and fidelity. VII.15

toslyt cut, slitted. VII.14

totore, totorn torn, frayed, tattered. VII.11, 14

tounduz sheared, clipped, trimmed, finished; of cloth, to have the nap removed by clipping or shearing. VI.2

touseled tasselled. VII.14

towail, towailes, towaille, towayl, towayle, towayls, towell, towellus, tüaile, tuall', tuallium towel(s); hand-towels; usually referring to a piece of cloth of linen or hemp, for wiping something dry; also, altar cloths or towels for the altar (I.21). I.13, 16, 21, 25, 27, 40, II.3, 4, VII.9, 10, 11, 14

towellus of Eylyssham towels from Aylsham. Aylsham in Norfolk was famous for its linen in the late-medieval period (Casson 1949: 139). VII.14

tracto drawn (of gold thread). III.1a
trail train (of a gown or similar long garment); cf. *coue, tail, train, trayn*. IV.8
trailende trailing (of trains or tails on ladies' robes or dresses). IV.8
trainant trailing (of trains or tails on ladies' robes or dresses). IV.2
trapped elaborately dressed (*MED*). IV.17
trayn trail, train. IV.4
trechour, tressour net, arrangement of ties, bands, ribbons etc. for the hair, a head-dress; an ornamented arrangement of the hair into plaits, coils, etc.; netting or decorative cord, probably of gold, used to adorn a woman's attire. VII.14, 15
tref beam; tent. VII.9
treleted latticed, interlaced, meshed. *Sir Gawain and the Green Knight* provides the only citation. VII.15
Treselencellis, Trieslincellis d'Evelyn notes that in William of Wadington's *Manuel des Pechiers* and Robert of Brunne's *Handlyng Synne*, the name of the fiend is Tyre-lincele, Terlyncel(s). His name and function are explained in a passage from Bromyard's *Summa Predicantium* quoted by Owst (1961: 412): 'God [...] made the night for rest and the day for waking, and these infernal owls turn night into day and vice versa. Such are of the household of "Draw sheet", who is the chief Chamberlain of Hell and is said to have told someone that his job was to make men lie for a long while under the sheets'. Owst adds (note 5): 'Bromyard also gives the demon's name in French – "Tyrelincel". Idley, who does not understand his name, makes Terlyncel also responsible for inattention during service' (d'Evelyn 1935: 233) – a role more often attributed to the devil Titivillus. IV.17
trewe-love-flour, trowelovesflour 'true-love's flower', an ornament or figure symbolic of true love; kind of knot, of a complicated and ornamental form (usually either a double-looped bow, or a knot formed of two loops intertwined), used as a symbol of true love; a figure of this. VII.6, 14
trifoliis trefoils, three-leafed ornaments. III.1a
triforiatus, triphoriatus, triphuriati ornamented; probably ornamented with trefoil(s), three-leafed ornament(s); cf. *trifoliis*. III.1a, 1b
Tripl', Triple of Tripoli?; usually referring to a type of sindon cloth (originally associated with Middle Eastern manufacture)? II.1b, III.2
troefles trifles; in clothing contexts, probably showy ornaments or decorative devices; 'knick-knack[s]' (*AND2*); cf. *tryflez*. V.2
trulofez usually 'true lover's knots' but such devices are rare except in tapestries and the references is probably rather to the flower *Paris quadrifolia* or Herb Paris. Cf. *Emaré* and *Sir Degrevant* (Tolkien *et al.* 1967: 92; cf. *trewe-love-flour*, etc.). VII.15
trussyngbedes trussing-beds; trundle- or portable beds. Whilst the term intrudes into non-English texts, there are no recorded medieval uses of the compound *trussyngbed* in English-language texts; its appearance in the petition extracted at VI.6 appears to be the earliest. VI.6
trussynge cofres trunk(s), packing chest(s); the word can mean small packing case, jewellery box, a money box divided into compartments. I.21, 32
tryflez trifles; ornaments, decorative details, decorations, etc. applied to a costume or used as accessories; cf. *troefles*. VII.15
tüaile see *towail*, etc. VII.9
tualliam see *towail*, etc. I.13
tulé, tuly an attribute of silk, tapestry, etc. of a rich red colour; perhaps originally applied to such fabrics imported from Toulouse. VII.15
tunecena tunic (see following entries). I.2

tunic', tunica, tunicam, tunicarum, tunicas, tunice, tunicis, tunicum, tunic(s); sleeved overgarment; ecclesiastical garment worn under the dalmatic (and cf. the following entry). I.11, 14, 19, II.1*b*, 4, III.1*a*, 1*b*, 2

tunicis tunics, here referring specifically to a short coat or similar fitted outer garment. IV.1

tuniculae, tuniculis ecclesiastical garment worn under the dalmatic. Cf. *tunic'*, etc. III.1*c*

twilibrocenan a very contentious word. Whitelock 1930 suggests double badger skin; Owen 1979 discusses it at length and suggests broken twill. I.2

tyffe, tyffest to adorn (v.), to ornament, decorate, beautify. IV.3

tyffed adorned, decorated. IV.3

tyffure ornamentation; decorative head- or hairdressing. IV.3

tyffyng adornment. IV.3

typet tippet, ornamental piece of cloth, usually long and narrow, worn separately over the shoulders or as part of a hood, the sleeves, etc. IV.13

uches see *ouches*, etc. V.6

uestiebantur dressed, clothed in (third person plural). IV.1

uln', ulne, vlnis unit of measurement usually translated as ell(s) though R. D. Connor argues that medieval Latin *ulna* usually referred to, in fact, a yard of approximately 36 inches (Connor 1987: 83). The cloth ell was usually 45 inches in English measure, though it varied according to region. Different countries had different standard ells. II.1*b*, 4, III.2

ulratur bordered, edged (with). III.1*a*, 1*b*

umple fine cloth, possibly linen, mentioned in fifteenth century texts, appears frequently alongside fine cloth such as lawn and Reims, often describing kerchiefs. V.8*n*, 9*n*

ungerenad unornamented, untrimmed. I.1, 4*a*

unstopped of a cushion: without stuffing. I.40

unwond unfolded. VII.13

urner to ornament, adorn (*AND*1). IV.2

user specifically: to wear. V.2

valence thin, woven fabric, perhaps openwork, associated with Valence or Valenciennes. IV.14

vambrace, vambrasaris vambrace, set of armour plates for the front of the upper arm. I.23, V.6

vario squirrel fur, typically of the northern European variety, which had a greyish back and a white belly and was used to line or trim garments. V.1

vayles, voile(s) fabric head-dress(es), usually covering the forehead and the sides and back of the head and hanging down to the shoulders or below, worn chiefly by women; also, cloth(s) worn to conceal the face or head. V.2, 7, VII.15

vela, velis, velum curtain(s); cloth divider(s). III.1*a*

velamina veils, kerchieves or similar (*kercheves* in the Anglo-French petition at 7*a*). VI.7*b*

velewet, vellewet, veluet, veluett', velvet, velvett, velvetto, velwet, velwette velvet; silken textile with a soft, short pile which is raised in loops above the ground by the introduction of rods during weaving; luxury imported fabric; velvet cloth. I.23, 44, II.1*b*, 5, III.1*b*, 2, V.4, 8*b*, 8*d*, 9*d*, 10, VII.10, 11, 15

velewet uppon velewet (*cloth of*) apparently cloth of some sort of patterned velvet. Compare the elaborate patterned velvet called *riccio sopra riccio* ('loop over loop'), produced in Italy from about the 1430s and apparently referred to as 'tissue' in some English texts (Scott 2007: 125). V.8*b*

veluto (of) velvet. III.1*c*

velwetmotley parti-coloured or variegated velvet cloth; in the parliamentary petition of 1402 (V.4) probably a fine fabric woven from threads of two or more colours. V.4

ventaile probably the piece of the helmet covering the front of the neck and/or chin. I.23

ventes vents, slits or openings in a garment, especially popular from the later fifteenth century. Such openings were trimmed with fur or fine fabric. If they ran the length of a garment, they would be held closed with a brooch or similar ornament. V.10

verdure green. VII.15

veste, vestem, vestes, vestis, vestium garment(s), clothing; vestments. I.14, IV.1, 4, 7

vestement, vestimento, vestment, westment, vestimentis, vestmentes, vestmentʒ vestment(s). I.13, 24, 30, 32, 34, 42, II.5

vestiendos from the verb meaning to clothe. I.14

vestimenta, vestimentis, vestimentorum, vestimentum garments; ecclesiastical vestment or suit of ecclesiastical vestments. III.1*a*, 1*b*, 1*c*, IV.7

vestment entier whole suit of robes or vestments. VI.6

vestu, vestues dressed, dressed in. VII.9

vesture, vestures clothing, attire; garment; vestment. IV.17, V.2, 4, 8*p*, 9*m*, 9*p*, VI.2, 6, VII.15

vestez, vestuz clothed. VI.2

vexillum banner. III.1*c*, VII.14

vineata decorated with figures of vines. III.1*a*

vir', viridem, viridi, viridibus, viridis (of) green; (of) green cloth. I.11, 13, 18, II.1*b*, 4, III.1*a*, 1*b*, 2

virg' units of linear measure (Latin *virga*); a yard or ell. Lisa Monnas notes that 'The ell was used interchangeably with the yard from the twelfth to the fourteenth century [...]. Another measure, the verge (*virga*) was identical to the yard' (Monnas 1989: 304–5, note 4). Legend had it that the yard equalled the length of the arm of Henry I from tip of the nose to tips of the fingers. In the thirteenth century the 'Statute for Measuring Land' established definite legal measures: 3 barleycorns to the inch, 12 inches to the foot, 3 feet to the yard, 5½ yards to the perch (Luders *et al*.1810: I.206–7). However, by the later period there was substantial local variation, particularly in the cloth trade (Connor 1987: 81). VI.8

viridenti greenish. III.1*a*

vitere de ornamented with; decorated with (slashes, tags, fringe, etc.). IV.10

vitta fillet. IV.1

vlnis usually translated as ell(s) (the cloth ell, usually 45 inches in English measure), but Connor argues that medieval Latin *ulna* usually referred to, in fact, a yard of approximately 36 inches (1987: 83). II.1*b*

voile(s) see *vayles*. V.2

voluper' headscarves. II.4

vrysoun ornamental band or piece of silk attached to or covering a helmet. The *vrysoun* was a band of embroidered silk which attached the *auentayle* (or *camail*), a piece of chain mail for the protection of the neck, to the bottom of the helmet (Andrew and Waldron 1978: 230). VII.15

vyolet cloth of violet colour. VII.14

wæll-seax, wællseaxe battle-knife. VII.1

wæpen, wæpna weapon. VII.1

wahrift, wahryfte wall-hanging. I.4*a*, 8

walu crest. VII.1

wapynis of fens weapons used to defend oneself. V.6

warniamente garment or suit of garments. I.19

warp put (clothing) on. VII.15

wasshyngtowels towels for cleaning and drying. I.32

web woven textile. VII.1

webbe linen weaver. II.5

weddynggown wedding gown. I.44

weddys, wede, wedes, wedez dress, apparel, attire. I.41, VII.6, 15

wer, were to wear (v.). This English verb (ME *weren, were*), which is common in Germanic languages, is borrowed directly into the Anglo-French statute of 1463. IV.15, V.6, 8*e*, 9*e*, 10

werede, werian protected. VII.1

werk embroidery ('of werk', covered with embroidered figures or decoration). I.25, 28, 32

weryng wearing. In the Anglo-French statute of 1463 (Extract 9), the word seems to be a borrowing from Middle English in the form of a verbal noun. V.8p, 9p

white white cloth; white garments (as in the will of Sir Thomas Brook, I.46). I.27, 46

whyssynes cushions; see *quisshens*, etc. VII.15

whyghth, whyt, whyte, whythe white (adj.); perhaps 'undyed'. I.28, 36, VII.11, 14

wifscrudes a woman's outfit. I.8

winpil, wympill, wymples wimple(s); a woman's head-dress or head veil. There were many varieties, but the later-medieval wimple was typically quite voluminous, covering the top, back, and sides of the head, including the cheeks and chin, and was wrapped so as to cover the neck; cf. *gympeu, gympeus*. IV.3, 8, VII.5

wires wires, as used to hold up or stiffen the 'horns' of a woman's head-dress. With regard to IV.17, d'Evelyn notes that although Idley's text takes its cue from Lydgate's *Fall of Princes*, this detail does not appear in that work: the horned head-dress is one of the most frequent objects of satire in the late fourteenth and early fifteenth centuries; see Lydgate's *Horns Away* and discussion in Owst (1961: 229). IV.17

wode woad, indigo or bluish dye made from the leaves of the woad plant (*Isatis tinctoria*). I.36

wolle wool. I.28, V.8h

wollen woollen. V.10

worcested worsted; cf. *worsted*, etc. (following). II.1b

worsted, worsteyd, wursted, wurstede (var. *worcested*) worsted; a cloth made of wool, but distinguished commercially from the more expensive 'woollens'. Worsted was typically characterised by its smooth yarn produced from fibres of long-stapled wool that have been laid parallel by combing, giving it a visible weave. The name derived from Worstead, a village in Norfolk, but production was not confined to that place. I.23, 24, 25, 32, 47, II.1b, III.2

wroght worked, embroidered. I.25

wunden twisted (from verb *windan*, to twist). VII.1

wylde catis wild cats, the fur of wild cats (as distinct from *genets* in the will of Thomas Tvoky). I.25

wympill see *winpil*, etc. IV.3, VII.5

wytele probably a blanket; from Old English *hwitel* which could mean a cloak or a blanket, originally undyed (*hwit*). It means bedding in *Piers Plowman*. The term survives in modern dialectical usage, mostly southern, as a woman's shawl. I.29

ybordured bordered. VII.11

yclade clothed. VII.14

yclodeth clothed. VII.11

ydyght dressed. VII.11

yelow yellow dye or pigment. IV.17

yerdes, ȝerdes, ȝerdys yards (measure of 3 feet). I.36, 40, 42

y-furred furred; lined, cf. *furred*. I.42

yheled covered. VII.11

ylased see *i-laside*. VII.11

ylorysched embellished. VII.11

ymagine, ymagines, ymaginibus image(s), representation(s). III.1a, 1b, 1c

ynde indigo (-coloured). II.5, VII.11

ypelured trimmed with fur. VII.11

ypouthered powdered, with a design scattered across it; usually embroidered but occasionally painted or appliquéd. I.21

ypoynet embroidered; decorated with embroidery work (s.v. 'poinen', *MED*). I.21

yreversyd trimmed, with edges turned back to reveal the rich lining. Cf. *reuersat'*, etc. VII.11
yrn hat iron hat, helmet. V.6
zieren shearing(s), the product of shearing sheep. I.28
zonam girdle. I.13

Bibliography

DICTIONARY RESOURCES

An Anglo-Saxon Dictionary, Based on the Manuscript Collections of the Late Joseph Bosworth 1898–1972, ed. J. Bosworth, T. Northcote Toller *et al.* London: Oxford University Press

Anglo-Norman Dictionary 1977–92, 1st edn, ed. W. Rothwell, L. W. Stone *et al.*, MHRA 8–. London: MHRA and Anglo-Norman Text Society

Anglo-Norman Dictionary 2002–, 2nd edn, ed. D. Trotter *et al.* Anglo-Norman On-line Hub. Online at http://www.anglo-norman.net

Dictionnaire de l'ancienne Langue Française 1888 ed. F. Godefroy. 10 vols. Paris: F. Vieweg and E. Bouillon

Dictionnaire du Moyen Français, version 2010 ATILF CNRS – Nancy Université. Online edition at http://www.atilf.fr/dmf

Dictionary of Medieval Latin from British Sources 1975–, ed. R. E. Latham, D. R. Howlett *et al.* British Academy Series, 12 fascicles to date. Oxford: Oxford University Press

Dictionary of the Older Scottish Tongue 1931–, ed. W. A. Craigie *et al.* Chicago; London: University of Chicago Press; Oxford University Press

Encyclopedia of Medieval Dress and Textiles of the British Isles, c. 450–1540 2012, ed. Gale R. Owen-Crocker, Elizabeth Coatsworth and Maria Hayward. Leiden and Boston: Brill

Lexis of Cloth and Clothing in Britain, c. 700–c. 1450 Project Database 2006–, ed. Gale R. Owen-Crocker, Louise Sylvester *et al.* London and Manchester: Universities of Manchester and Westminster. Online at http://lexisproject.arts.manchester.ac.uk/

Middle English Dictionary 1952–, ed. S. Kuhn, H. Kurath and S. McAllister. Ann Arbor, MI: University of Michigan Press

Oxford English Dictionary Online at http://www.oed.com

Revised Medieval Latin Word-List from British and Irish Sources with Supplement 1965, ed. R. E. Latham. London: British Academy

PRIMARY SOURCES

Manuscript sources

Manuscripts of the National Archives (Kew) including accounts and inventories related to the Royal Wardrobe and subsidiary documents are found in manuscripts filed under 'King's Remembrancer: Accounts Various' (MSS E 101); the petitions are filed under 'Special Collections: Ancient Petitions' (MSS SC 8). Specific manuscripts consulted are as follows:

C 66/369	SC 8/221/11037
E 101/91/6	SC 8/238/11890A
E 101/91/7	SC 8/238/11890B
E 101/354/21	SC 8/255/12724
E 101/364/29	SC 8/29/1410
E 101/389/14	SC 8/29/1411
E 101/391/15	SC 8/302/15058
E 101/393/15	SC 8/302/15059
E 101/405/14	SC 8/307/15336
SC 8/125/6225	SC 8/33/1604
SC 8/196/9797	SC 8/4/193

In addition, the extract from the will of Martin St Cross (I.13) was transcribed from Durham County Record Office MS D/Sh/H/1030.

Print and online sources

Andrew, Malcolm, and Ronald Waldron, eds. 1978 *The Poems of the Pearl Manuscript: Pearl, Cleanness, Patience, Sir Gawain and the Green Knight*. London: Edward Arnold

Anon., ed. 1889 'Sir Landevale', *The American Journal of Philology* 10. Reproduced in Chadwyck-Healey English Poetry Full-Text Database (1992) at http://xtf.lib.virginia.edu/xtf/view?docId=chadwyck_ep/uvaGenText/tei/chep_1.2027.xmlandchunk.id=d3andtoc.id=d3andbrand=default, accessed 29.12.2010

Benson, Larry D., ed. 1987 *The Riverside Chaucer*, 3rd edn. Oxford: Oxford University Press

Birch, Walter de Grey 1885 [1883]–99. *Cartularium Saxonicum: A Collection of Charters relating to Anglo-Saxon History. (Index Saxonicus: An Index to All the Names of Persons in Cartularium Saxonicum, etc.* London: Whiting & Co.

Blake, E. O. 1962 *Liber Eliensis*. London: The Royal Historical Society

Block, K. S., ed. 1922 'Passion Play I', in *Ludus Coventriæ or The Plaie Called Corpus Christi (Cotton MS. Vespasian D. VIII)*, EETS, ES 120. London: Oxford University Press

Blyth, Charles R., ed. 1999 *Thomas Hoccleve: The Regiment of Princes*. Kalamazoo, MI: Medieval Institute Publications. Electronic edition available at http://d.lib.rochester.edu/teams/text/blyth-hoccleve-regiment-of-princes, accessed 18.7.2014

Brand, Paul, with Shelagh Sneddon, eds. 2012 *The Parliament Rolls of Medieval England*. 16 vols. Woodbridge: The Boydell Press

Brock, Edmund, ed. 1872 'The Life of Constance from the Anglo-Norman Chronicle of Nicholas Trevet', in *Originals and Analogues of Some of Chaucer's Canterbury Tales*, ed. F. J. Furnivall, Edmund Brock and W. A. Clouston, Part I. The Chaucer Society. London: Trübner, 1–53

Brock, Edmund, ed. 1876 'The Story of Constance', in *Originals and Analogues of Some of Chaucer's Canterbury Tales*, ed. F. J. Furnivall, Edmund Brock and W. A. Clouston, Part III. The Chaucer Society. London: Trübner, 221–50

Bromyard, John 1586 *Summa Prædicantium, omne ervditione revertissima, explicans præcipuos catholicæ disciplinæ sensus, ad locos; . . . apud Dominicum Nicolinum*. 2 parts. Venice

Burgess, Glyn S., and Keith Busby, trans. 1999 *The Lais of Marie de France*, 2nd edn. Harmondsworth: Penguin

Calendar of the Patent Rolls: Preserved in the Public Record Office: Edward II [*CPR Ed. II*] 1894–1904, 5 vols. London: HMSO

Calendar of the Patent Rolls: Preserved in the Public Record Office: Henry IV [*CPR Hen. IV*] 1903–9, 4 vols. London: HMSO

Casson, L. F., ed. 1949 *The Romance of Sir Degrevant: A Parallel Text-Edition from MSS Lincoln Cathedral A.5.2 and Cambridge University Ff.1.6*. EETS, os 221. Oxford: Oxford University Press

Chibnall, Marjorie, ed. and trans. 1969–80 *The Ecclesiastical History of Orderic Vitalis*. 6 vols., vol. 4 (Books VII and VIII) 1973. Oxford: Clarendon

Correale, Robert M., ed. 2005 'The Man of Law's Prologue and Tale', in *Sources and Analogues of the Canterbury Tales*, ed. Robert M. Correale and Mary Hamel, 2202–5. 2 vols. Cambridge: D. S. Brewer, II, 277–350

Crick, Julia, ed. 2007. *Charters of St Albans*. Anglo-Saxon Charters 12. Oxford: Oxford University Press for the British Academy.

Dean, James M., ed. 1996 'On the Times', in *Medieval English Political Writings*. Kalamazoo, MI: Medieval Institute Publications. Online at http://www.lib.rochester.edu/camelot/times.htm, accessed 18.7.2014

D'Evelyn, Charlotte, ed. 1935 *Peter Idley's Instructions to his Son*. Boston: D. C. Heath; London: Oxford University Press

Devon, Frederick 1835 *Issue Roll of Thomas de Brantingham, Bishop of Exeter, Lord High Treasurer: Containing Payments Made out of His Majesty's Revenue in the 44th Year of King Edward III. A.D. 1370*. London: John Rodwell

Dugdale, William 1818 *The History of St. Paul's Cathedral in London . . . with Continuations by Henry Ellis*, 3rd edn. London

Eccles, Mark, ed. 1969 *The Castle of Perseverance*, in *The Macro Plays*, EETS, os 262. London: Oxford University Press, 1–111

Eccles, Mark, ed. 1969 *Mankind*, in *The Macro Plays*, EETS, os 262. London: Oxford University Press, 153–84

Fairholt, Frederick William, ed. 1849 *Satirical Songs and Poems on Costume: From the 13th to the 19th Century*, in *Early English Poetry, Ballads, and Popular Literature of the Middle Ages: Edited from Original Manuscripts and Source Publications XXVII*, Percy Society. London: Richards St Martin's Lane

Fowler, J. T., ed. 1899 *Extracts from the Account Rolls of the Abbey of Durham, From the Original Manuscripts*, vol. 2, Surtees Society 100. Durham: Andrews, 1899

French, Walter Hoyt, and Charles Brockway Hale, eds. 1930 *Middle English Metrical Romances*. New York: Prentice Hall

Furnivall, F. J., ed. 1862 *Roberd of Brunnè's Handlyng Synne… With the French Treatise on which it is founded, Le Manuel des Pechiez of William of Wadington*. London: Roxburghe Club

Furnivall, F. J., ed. 1866 *Political, Religious and Love Poems from the Archbishop of Canterbury's Lambeth MS. No. 366, and Other Sources*. London: N. Trübner and Co.

Furnivall, F. J., ed. 1872 'King Offa's Intercepted Letters and Banisht Queen', in *Originals and Analogues of Some of Chaucer's Canterbury Tales*, ed. F. J. Furnivall, Edmund Brock and W. A. Clouston, Part I. The Chaucer Society. London: Trübner, 71–84

Furnivall, F. J., ed. 1872 'Merelaus the Emperour', in *Originals and Analogues of Some of Chaucer's Canterbury Tales*, ed. F. J. Furnivall, Edmund Brock and W. A. Clouston, Part I. The Chaucer Society. London: Trübner, 55–70

Furnivall, F. J., ed. 1964 [1882] *The Fifty Earliest Wills in the Court of Probate, London AD 1387–1439*, EETS, OS 78. London: Early English Text Society

Furnivall, F. J., ed. 1901 *Robert of Brunne's 'Handlyng Synne', A.D. 1303, With those parts of the Anglo-French Treatise on which it was founded, William of Wadington's 'Manuel des Pechiez'*, 2 Parts, EETS, OS 119, 123 (London: Kegan Paul, Trench, Trübner and Co.). Available online through the Corpus of Middle English Prose and Verse, University of Michigan 2006, at http://name.umdl.umich.edu/AHA2735.0001.001, accessed 18.7.2014

Furnivall, F. J., Edmund Brock and W. A. Clouston, eds. 1872–6 *Originals and Analogues of Some of Chaucer's Canterbury Tales*. The Chaucer Society. London: Trübner

Gibbons, Alfred, ed. 1888 *An Abstract of All the Wills and Administrations Recorded in the Episcopal Registers of the Old Diocese of Lincoln Comprising the Counties of Lincoln, Rutland, Buckingham, Oxford, Leicester, and Hertford, 1280–1547*. Lincoln: printed for subscribers by James Williamson

Given-Wilson, Chris, ed. 2005a 'Henry IV, Parliament of September 1402, Text and Translation', in *Parliament Rolls of Medieval England, 1275–1504*, ed. Chris Given-Wilson et al. Scholarly Digital Editions. Internet version at http://www.sd-editions.com/PROME, accessed 18.7.2014

Given-Wilson, Chris, ed. 2005b 'Henry V, Parliament of December 1420, Text and Translation', in *Parliament Rolls of Medieval England, 1275–1504*, ed. Chris Given-Wilson et al. Scholarly Digital Editions. Internet version at http://www.sd-editions.com/PROME, accessed 18.7.2014

Given-Wilson, Chris, ed. 2005c 'Richard II: Parliament of November 1391, Text and Translation', in *The Parliament Rolls of Medieval England*, ed. Chris Given-Wilson et al. Scholarly Digital Editions. Internet version at http://www.sd-editions.com/PROME, accessed 18.7.2014

Gollancz, Israel, ed. 1940 *Sir Gawain and the Green Knight*. EETS, OS 210. Oxford: Oxford University Press

Guiseppi, M. S. 1899 'On the Testament of Sir Hugh de Nevill', *Archaeologia, or, Miscellaneous Tracts Relating to Antiquity* 56: 351–70

Guiseppi, M. S., ed. 1918 'The Wardrobe and Household Accounts of Bogo de Clare, A.D. 1284–6', *Archaeologia, or, Miscellaneous Tracts Relating to Antiquity* 70: 1–56

Hale, W. H., and Rev. H. T. Ellacombe, eds. 1874 *Account of the Executors of Richard, Bishop of London, 1303, and of the Executors of Thomas Bishop of Exeter, 1310*. Camden Society,

NS X. London

Halliwell, James Orchard, ed. 1840 *A Selection from the Minor Poems of Dan John Lydgate*. London: The Percy Society

Horrox, Rosemary, ed. 2005 'Edward IV, Parliament of April 1463, Text and Translation', in *Parliament Rolls of Medieval England, 1275–1504*, ed. Chris Given-Wilson *et al*. Scholarly Digital Editions. Internet version at http://www.sd-editions.com/PROME, accessed 18.7.2014

Horrox, Rosemary, ed. 2005 'Edward IV, Parliament of January 1478', in *Parliament Rolls of Medieval England, 1275–1504*, ed. Chris Given-Wilson *et al*. Scholarly Digital Editions. Internet version at http://www.sd-editions.com/PROME, accessed 18.7.2014

Horrox, Rosemary, ed. 2005 'Edward IV, Parliament of January 1483, Text and Translation', in *Parliament Rolls of Medieval England, 1275–1504*, ed. Chris Given-Wilson *et al*. Scholarly Digital Editions. Internet version at http://www.sd-editions.com/PROME, accessed 18.7.2014

Horrox, Rosemary, ed. 2005 'Edward IV, Parliament of November 1461, Text and Translation', in *Parliament Rolls of Medieval England, 1275–1504*, ed. Chris Given-Wilson *et al*. Scholarly Digital Editions. Internet version at http://www.sd-editions.com/PROME, accessed 18.7.2014

Horstmann, Carl, ed. 1892 *The Minor Poems of the Vernon Manuscript*, EETS, os 98. London: Kegan Paul, Trench, Trübner and Co.

Hoskin, Philippa M., ed. 2005 *English Episcopal Acta 29, Durham 1241–1283*. Oxford: published for the British Academy by Oxford University Press

Jefferson, Lisa 2009 *The Medieval Account Books of the Mercers of London: An Edition and Translation*, 2 vols. Farnham, Surrey, and Burlington, VT: Ashgate

Kemble, John Mitchell 1839–48 *Codex Diplomaticus Aevi Saxonici*. London: English Historical Society

Kooper, Erik, ed. 2006 *Sentimental and Humorous Romances*. Kalamazoo, MI: Medieval Institute Publications

Laskaya, Anne and Eve Salisbury, eds. 1995 *The Middle English Breton Lays*. TEAMS edition. Kalamazoo, MI: Medieval Institute Publications

Luard, Henry Richards 1872–83 *Matthaei Parisiensis, Monachi Sancti Albani Chronica Majora*. London; Longman

Luders, A., *et al*., eds. 1810–28 *Statutes of the Realm: Printed by Command of His Majesty King George the Third, in Pursuance of an Address of the House of Commons of Great Britain: from Original Records and Authentic Manuscripts* [*Statutes*]. London: Eyre and Strahan

Macaulay, G. C., ed. 1899–1902 *The Complete Works of John Gower*, 5 vols. Oxford: Clarendon

MacIntosh, Gillian H., Alastair J. Mann and Roland J. Tanner, eds. 2007–13 *The Records of the Parliaments of Scotland to 1707*. St Andrews. Online at http://www.rps.ac.uk, accessed 18.7.2014

Martin, Geoffrey, ed. 2005 'Richard II, Parliament of April 1379, Text and Translation', in *Parliament Rolls of Medieval England, 1275–1504*, ed. Chris Given-Wilson *et al*. Scholarly Digital Editions. Internet version at http://www.sd-editions.com/PROME, accessed 18.7.2014

Matthews, William, 1972 'Thomas Hoccleve', in *Manual of the Writings in Middle English*, ed. A. E. Hartung, 9 vols. (1919–93). New Haven, CT: Connecticut Academy of Arts and Sciences, vol. 3

McCracken, Henry Noble, ed. 1961 [1934] *The Minor Poems of John Lydgate*. EETS, os 192 London: Oxford University Press

Mustanoja, Tauno F., ed. 1948 *The Good Wife Taught her Daughter; The Good Wyfe Wold a Pylgremage; The Thewis of Gud Women*. Annales Academiæ Scientiarum Fennicæ, series B vol. 61 no. 2. Helsinki

National Library of Wales, *A Middle English Miscellany* Online at http://www.llgc.org.uk/index.php?id=amiddleenglishmiscellanybro

NeCastro, Gerard, ed. and trans. 2007 *eChaucer: Chaucer in the Twenty-First century*. Mathias, ME: University of Maine

Nicolas, Nicholas Harris, ed. 1826 *Testamenta Vetusta: Being Illustrations from Wills of Manners, Customs, etc. as well as the Descents and Possessions of Many Distinguished Families from the Reign of Henry the Second to the Accession of Queen Elizabeth*. Vol. 1. London: Nichols and Son

Nicolas, Nicholas Harris, ed. 1846 *Archaeologia, or, Miscellaneous Tracts Relating to Antiquity* 31: 5–103, 109–63, 373, 376–9, and 384

Ormrod, W. M., ed. 2005 'Edward III: Parliament of October 1363, Text and Translation', in *Parliament Rolls of Medieval England, 1275–1504*, ed. Chris Given-Wilson et al. Scholarly Digital Editions. Internet version at http://www.sd-editions.com/PROME, accessed 18.7.2014

Phillips, Seymour, ed. 2005 'Appendix of Unedited Petitions, 1307–1337', *Parliament Rolls of Medieval England*, ed. Chris Given-Wilson et al. Scholarly Digital Editions. Internet version at http://www.sd-editions.com/PROME, accessed 18.7.2014

Raine, James, ed. 1835 *Wills and Inventories Illustrative of the History, Manners, Language, Statistics, etc. of the Northern Counties of England from the Eleventh Century Downwards*. Publications of the Surtees Society 2, part 1. London: J. B. Nichols and Son and William Pickering

Raine, James, ed. 1836 *Testamenta Eboracensia or Wills Registered at York, Illustrative of the History, Manners, Language, Statistics, etc., of the Province of York, from the Year MCCC Downwards*. Publications of the Surtees Society 4 (6 vols. in total, 1836–1902) Part I, Vol. 4. London: J. B. Nichols and Son

Robbins, Rossell Hope 1975 'Poems Dealing with Contemporary Conditions', in *Manual of the Writings in Middle English*, ed. A. E. Hartung, 9 vols. (1919–93). Vol. 5. New Haven, CT: Connecticut Academy of Arts and Sciences

Rogers, James E. Thorold, ed. 1881 *Loci e Libro Veritatum: Passages Selected from Gascoigne's Theological Dictionary Illustrating the Condition of Church and State 1403–1458*. Oxford: Clarendon

Rychner, Jean, ed. 1966 *Les Lais de Marie de France*. Paris: Librarie Honoré Champion

Schlauch, Margaret, ed. 1941 'The Man of Law's Tale', in *Sources and Analogues of Chaucer's Canterbury Tales*, ed. W. F. Bryan and Germaine Dempster. London: Routledge and Kegan Paul, 155–206

Shepherd, Stephen H. A., ed. 1995 *Middle English Romances*. New York and London: Norton

Simpson, W. Sparrow, ed. 1887 'Two Inventories of the Cathedral Church of St. Paul, London, Dated Respectively 1245 and 1402; now, for the first time, printed, with an Introduction',

Archaeologia, or Miscellaneous Tracts Related to Antiquity 50: 439–524. Internet version at http://www.archive.org/stream/archaeologiaormo2unkngoog#page/n4/mode/2up, accessed 18.7.2014

Strachey, John, ed. 1783 *Rotuli Parliamentorum: ut et petitiones, et placita in Parliamento* [*Rotuli Parliamentorum*], 6 vols. London

Stubbs, William, ed. 1879 *The Historical Works of Gervase of Canterbury*, 2 vols. London: Longman/Trübner

Sullens, Idelle, ed. 1983 *Robert Mannyng of Brunne: Handlyng Synne*. Binghamton, NY: Center for Medieval and Early Renaissance Studies, State University of New York

Swanton, Michael, ed. and trans. 2010 *The Lives of Two Offas: Vitae Offarum Duorum*. Devon: The Medieval Press

Tanner, Norman P., ed. 1990 *Decrees of the Ecumenical Councils*, vol. 1, *Nicaea I to Lateran V*. London: Sheed and Ward

Thompson, A. Hamilton, ed. 1918 *Visitations of Religious Houses in the Diocese of Lincoln, Vol. 2: Records of Visitation Held by William Alnwick, Bishop of Lincoln, A.D. 1436 to A.D. 1449*. Part 1. Horncastle, Lincs.: W. K. Morton and Sons for the Lincoln Record Society

Thompson, A. Hamilton, ed. 1929 *Visitations of Religious Houses in the Diocese of Lincoln, Vol. 3: Records of Visitations Held by William Alnwick, Bishop of Lincoln, A.D. 1436 to A.D. 1449*. Part 2. Lincoln: J. W. Ruddock and Sons for the Lincoln Record Society

Thomson, Thomas, Cosmo Innes and Archibald Anderson, eds. 1814–75 *The Acts of the Parliaments of Scotland, 1124–1707*, 12 vols. London: The Record Commission

Thorpe, Benjamin 1865 *Diplomatarium Anglicum Ævi Saxonici. A Collection of English Charters, from the Reign of King Æthelberht of Kent A.D. DCV. to that of William the Conqueror. Containing I. Miscellaneous Charters. II. Wills. III. Guilds. IV. Manumissions and Acquittances. With a Translation of the Anglo-Saxon*. London, 1865

Tolkien, J. R. R., and E. V. Gordon, eds., rev. Norman Davis 1967, *Sir Gawain and the Green Knight*. Oxford: Clarendon (republ. 1978)

Watts, William, ed. 1684 *Matthæi Paris Historia Major. Juxta exemplar Londinense 1640 verbatim recusa; et cum Rogeri Wendoveri, Willielmi Rishangeri authorisque majori minorique historiis, chronicisque MSS... collata. Huic editioni accesserunt, duorum Offarum Merciorum regum; et viginti trium abbatum S. Albani vitæ. Una cum libro additamentorum*. London: A. Mearne

Whitehead, William V., ed.1960 'Nicholas Trevet's Chronicle: An Early Fifteenth-Century English Translation'. Harvard University Ph.D. thesis

Whitelock, Dorothy, ed. and trans. 1930 *Anglo-Saxon Wills* with a General Preface by H. D. Hazeltine. Cambridge: Cambridge University Press

Whitelock, Dorothy, ed. 1968 'The Latin Abstract of the Will and the Attached Witness List', in *The Will of Æthelgifu*, ed. Dorothy Whitelock, Neil Ker and Lord Rennell. Oxford: The Roxburgh Club, 38–48

Whitelock, Dorothy, ed. 1968 'The Text and Translation of the Will', in *The Will of Æthelgifu*, ed. Dorothy Whitelock, Neil Ker and Lord Rennell. Oxford: The Roxburgh Club, 5–17

Whitelock, Dorothy, Neil Ker and Lord Rennell, eds. 1968 *The Will of Æthelgifu* Oxford: The Roxburgh Club

Woodruff, C. Eveleigh, ed. 1926 *Camden Miscellany* vol. 14, part 2, Camden 3rd Series vol. 37. London

Wright, Thomas, and James Orchard Halliwell, eds. 1841, 1843 *Reliquiæ Antiquæ. Scraps from Ancient Manuscripts Illustrating Chiefly Early English Literature and the English Language*. London: William Pickering

Wright, Thomas, ed. 1839 *The Political Songs of England, from the Reign of John to that of Edward II*. London: Camden Society

SECONDARY SOURCES

Altschul, Michael 1965 *A Baronial Family in Medieval England: The Clares, 1217–1314*. Baltimore: Johns Hopkins University Press

Baldwin, Francis 1926 *Sumptuary Legislation and Personal Regulation in England*. Baltimore: Johns Hopkins University Press

Bell, Clifford, and Evelyn Ruse 1972 'Sumptuary Legislation and English Costume: An Attempt to Assess the Effect of an Act of 1337', in *Costume: Journal of the Costume Society* 6: 22–31

Biggam, C. P. 2006 'Old English Colour Lexemes used of Textiles in Anglo-Saxon England', in *The Power of Words: Essays in Lexicography, Lexicology and Semantics, in Honour of Christian J. Kay*, ed. Graham D. Caie, Carole Hough and Irené Wotherspoon. Amsterdam and New York: Rodopi, 1–21

Blanc, Odile 2002 'From Battlefield to Court: The Invention of Fashion in the Fourteenth Century', in *Encountering Medieval Textiles and Dress: Objects, Texts, Images*, ed. Désirée Koslin and Janet E. Snyder. Basingstoke, Palgrave Macmillan

Blomfield, Francis 1806 'Hundred of Humble-Yard: Keswick', in *An Essay towards a Topographical History of the County of Norfolk*, vol. 5, 43–6. Online at http://www.british-history.ac.uk/report.aspx?compid=78150, accessed 18.7.2014

Bradley, Helen 1994 'The Datini Factors in London, 1380–1410', in *Trade, Devotion and Governance: Papers in Later Medieval History*, ed. Dorothy Clayton, Richard Davies and Peter McNiven. Stroud, Gloucestershire: Alan Sutton, 55–79

Bridbury, A. R. 1982 *Medieval English Clothmaking: An Economic Survey*, Pasold Studies in Textile History. London: Heinemann

Bulotta, Donata 2007 'Anglo-Saxon Female Clothing: Old English *cyrtel* and *tunece*', in *Rivista di cultura classica e medievale*, Nuova Serie 49: 307–25

Burke, John 1831 *A General and Heraldic Dictionary of the Peerages of England, Ireland, and Scotland, Extinct, Dormant and in Abeyance*. London: Henry Colburn and Richard Bentley

Burkholder, Kristen M. 2005 'Threads Bared: Dress and Textiles in Late Medieval English Wills', *Medieval Clothing and Textiles* 1: 133–53

Chambers, Mark C. 2009 '"What is this, a betell, or a batowe, or a buskyn lacyd?": Lexicological Confusion in Medieval Clothing Culture', in *Textual Healing: Studies in Medieval English Medical, Scientific and Technical Texts*, ed. Javier E. Díaz Vera and Rosario Caballero Rodríguez. Bern and New York: Peter Lang, 55–74

Chambers, Mark C. 2011 '"Surcot overt" and "surcot clos": The Specifics of Clothing Names in Some Late Medieval Petitions', *Medieval Clothing and Textiles* 7: 82–104

Chambers, Mark C., and Gale R. Owen-Crocker 2008 'From Head to Hand to Arm: The Lexicological History of "Cuff"', *Medieval Clothing and Textiles* 4: 55–68

Chambers, Mark C., and Louise Sylvester 2010 'Redressing Medieval Dress with the *Lexis of Cloth and Clothing in Britain* Project', *Everyday Objects: Medieval and Early Modern Material Culture and its Meanings*, ed. Tara Hamling and Catherine Richardson. Farnham, Surrey: Ashgate, 71–82

Christie, A. G. I. 1938 *English Medieval Embroidery*. Oxford: Clarendon

Clegg Hyer, Maren 2012 'Recycle, Reduce, Reuse: Imagined and Re-imagined Textiles in Anglo-Saxon England', *Medieval Clothing and Textiles* 8: 48–62

Coatsworth, Elizabeth 2007 'Cushioning Medieval Life: Domestic Textiles in Anglo-Saxon England', *Medieval Clothing and Textiles* 3: 1–12

Connor, R. D. 1987 *The Weights and Measures of England*, for the Trustees of the Science Museum. London: HMSO

Crowfoot, Elisabeth 1969 'Early Anglo-Saxon Gold Braids: Addenda and Corrigenda', *Medieval Archaeology* 13: 209–10

Crowfoot, Elisabeth, and Sonia Chadwick Hawkes 1967 'Early Anglo-Saxon Gold Braids', *Medieval Archaeology* 11: 42–86

Crowfoot, Elizabeth, Frances Pritchard and K. Staniland 2000 *Textiles and Clothing, 1150–1450*. London: Boydell Press (for the Museum of London)

Davenport, W. A. 2000 '*Sir Degrevant* and Composite Romance', in *Medieval Insular Romance: Translation and Innovation*, ed. Judith Weiss, Jennifer Fellows and Morgan Dickson. Cambridge: D. S. Brewer, 111–31

Dodd, Gwilym 2007 *Justice and Grace: Private Petitioning and the English Parliament in the Late Middle Ages*. Oxford: Oxford University Press

Dodwell, C. R. 1982 *Anglo-Saxon Art: A New Perspective*. Manchester: Manchester University Press

Fletcher, Alan J. 1998 'Performing the Seven Deadly Sins: How One Late-Medieval English Preacher Did It', *Leeds Studies in English* 29: 89–108

Fryde, E. B. *et al.* 1996 *Handbook of British Chronology*, 3rd revised edn. Cambridge: Cambridge University Press

Given-Wilson, Chris 2005 'General Introduction', in *The Parliament Rolls of Medieval England*, ed. Chris Given-Wilson *et al.* Scholarly Digital Editions. Internet version at http://www.sd-editions.com/PROME, accessed 18.7.2014

Green, Mary Anne Everett 1857 *Lives of the Princesses of England, from the Norman Conquest*, vol. 3. London

Harris, Jennifer 1998 '"Estroit vestu et menu cosu": Evidence for the Construction of Twelfth-Century Dress', in *Medieval Art: Recent Perspectives: A Memorial Tribute to C. R. Dodwell*, ed. Gale R. Owen-Crocker and Timothy Graham. Manchester: Manchester University Press, 89–103

Harte, N. B. 1976 'State Control of Dress and Social Change in Pre-Industrial England', in *Trade, Government and Economy in Pre-Industrial England*, ed. D. C. Coleman and A. H. John. Weidenfield and Nicolson, London, 132–65

Heller, Sarah-Grace 2004 'Anxiety, Hierarchy, and Appearance in the Thirteenth-Century Sumptuary Laws and the *Roman de la Rose*', *French Historical Studies* 27 (2): 311–48

Heller, Sarah-Grace 2007 *Fashion in Medieval France* 2007. Cambridge: D. S. Brewer

Hopkins, Amanda 2000 'Veiling the Text: The True Role of the Cloth in *Emaré*', *Medieval Insular Romance: Translation and Innovation*, ed. Judith Weiss, Jennifer Fellows and

Morgan Dickson. Cambridge: D. S. Brewer, 71–82

Horrox, Rosemary, ed. 2005 'Edward IV, Parliament of April 1463, Text and Translation', in *Parliament Rolls of Medieval England, 1275–1504*, ed. Chris Given-Wilson et al. Scholarly Digital Editions. Internet version at http://www.sd-editions.com/PROME, accessed 18.7.2014

Hudson, John 1994 'Anglo-Norman Land Law and the Origins of Property', in *Law and Government in Mediaeval England and Normandy: Essays in Honour of Sir James Holt*, ed. George Garnett and John Hudson. Cambridge: Cambridge University Press, 198–222

Hunt, Alan 1996 *Governance of the Consuming Passions: A History of Sumptuary Law*. Macmillan: Basingstoke and London

Jaster, Margaret Rose 2006 'Clothing themselves in Acres: Apparel and Impoverishment in Medieval and Early Modern England', *Medieval Clothing and Textiles* 1: 90–9

King, Donald 1963 *Opus Anglicanum: English Medieval Embroidery*. London: Arts Council, Victoria and Albert Museum

King, Donald 1988 'Silk Weaves of Lucca in 1376', *Opera Textilia Variorum Temporum: To honour Agnes Geijer on her Ninetieth Birthday*, ed. Inger Estham and Margareta Nockert. Stockholm: Statens Historiska Museum

Lachaud, Frédérique 1992 'Textiles, Furs and Liveries: A Study of the Material Culture of the Court of Edward I (1272–1307)'. D.Phil thesis, University of Oxford

Lachaud, Frédérique 1996 'Liveries of Robes in England, c. 1200–c. 1330', *English Historical Review* 111: 279–98

Lloyd, Simon 2002 'The Crusading Movement, 1096–1274', in *The Oxford History of the Crusades*, ed. Jonathan Riley-Smith. Oxford: Oxford University Press, 35–67

Lyon, Mary et al., ed. 1983 *The Wardrobe Book of William de Norwell: 12 July 1338 to 27 May 1340*. Brussels: Académie royale de Belgique, Commision royale d'histoire

Monnas, Lisa 1989 'Silk Cloths Purchased for the Great Wardrobe of the Kings of England, 1325–1462', *Textile History* 20 (2): 283–307

Monnas, Lisa 2001 'Textiles for the Coronation of Edward III', *Textile History*, 32 (1): 2–35

Moules, A. C. 1946 'Cloth of Reynes', *Notes and Queries* 191.4 (August 1946): 83–5

Munro, John H. 1983 'The Medieval *Scarlet* and the Economics of Sartorial Splendour', in *Cloth and Clothing in Medieval Europe: Essays in Memory of Professor E. M. Carus-Wilson*, ed. Negley B. Harte and Kenneth G. Ponting. London: Heinemann Educational Books, 13–70

Munro, John H. 'Scarlet', *Encyclopedia of Medieval Dress and Textiles of the British Isles, c. 450–1540* 2012, ed. Gale R. Owen-Crocker, Elizabeth Coatsworth and Maria Hayward. Leiden and Boston: Brill, 477–81

Nelson, Alan H., ed. 1980 *The Plays of Henry Medwall*, Tudor Interludes. Cambridge: D. S. Brewer; Totowa, NJ: Rowman and Littlefield

Nevinson, J. L. 1958 'Civil Costume', in *Medieval England*, ed. Austin Lane Poole, 2 vols. Oxford: Clarendon, 300–13

Newton, Stella Mary 1980 *Fashion in the Age of the Black Prince, A Study of the Years 1340–1365*. Woodbridge, Suffolk and Rochester, NY: Boydell Press

Nicolas, N. H. 1846 'Observations on the Institution of the Most Noble Order of the Garter', *Archaeologia, or, Miscellaneous Tracts Relating to Antiquity* 31: 5–103, 109–63

Ormrod, Mark 2008 'The Road To Boroughbridge: The Civil War of 1321–2 in the Ancient Petitions', in *Foundations of Medieval Scholarship: Records Edited in Honour of David Crook*, ed. Paul Brand and Sean Cunningham. York: Borthwick, 77–88

Ormrod, Mark 2009 'The Language of Complaint: Multilingualism and Petitioning in Later Medieval England', in *Language and Culture in Medieval Britain: The French of England c. 1100–c. 1500*, ed. Jocelyn Wogan-Browne. Woodbridge, Suffolk, and Rochester, NY: York Medieval Press, 31–43

Owen, Gale R. 1979 'Wynflæd's Wardrobe', *Anglo-Saxon England* 8: 195–222

Owen-Crocker, Gale R. 2004 *Dress in Anglo-Saxon England, Revised and Enlarged Edition*. Woodbridge: Boydell

Owen-Crocker, Gale R. 2005 'Pomp, Piety and Keeping the Woman in her Place: The Dress of Cnut and Ælfgifu-Emma', *Medieval Clothing and Textiles* 1: 41–52

Owst, G. R. 1961 *Literature and Pulpit in Medieval England: A Neglected Chapter in the History of English Letters and of the English People*. Oxford: Blackwell

Pearsall, Derek 1970 *John Lydgate*. London: Routledge and Kegan Paul

Phillips, Seymour 2005 'Edward II: 1307–1327, Introduction', in *The Parliament Rolls of Medieval England*, ed. Chris Given-Wilson et al. Scholarly Digital Editions. Internet version at http://www.sd-editions.com/PROME, accessed 18.7.2014

Post, Paul 1955 'La naissance du costume masculin moderne au XIVe siècle', *Actes du Ier congrès international d'histoire du costume, Venise, 31 août–7 septembre 1952*. Venice: Centro internazionale delle arti e del costume

Power, Eileen 1922 *Medieval English Nunneries, c. 1275 to 1535*. Cambridge: Cambridge University Press

Prosopography of Anglo-Saxon England, online at http://www.pase.ac.uk/index.html, accessed 18.7.2014

Richardson, Henry Gerald, and George Osborne Sayles 1981 *The English Parliament in the Middle Ages*. Manchester: Manchester University Press/London: Hambeldon

Riddy, Felicity 1996 'Mother Knows Best: Reading Social Change in a Courtesy Text' *Speculum* 71: 66–86

Rogers, Penelope Walton 2007 *Cloth and Clothing in Early Anglo-Saxon England, AD 450–700*. York: Council for British Archaeology

Rose, Christine M. 1992–3 'The Provenance of the Trevet Chronicle (fMS Eng 938)', *Harvard Library Bulletin* 3 (4): 38–55. Online at http://nrs.harvard.edu/urn-3:FHCL:139076?n=18701, accessed 18.7.2014

Sayles, George Osborne 1975 *The King's Parliament of England*. London: Edward Arnold, 75–84

Schendl, Herbert 2013 'Multilingualism and Code-Switching as Mechanisms of Contact-Induced Lexical Change in Late Middle English', *English as a Contact Language*, ed. Daniel Schreier and Marianne Hundt. Cambridge: Cambridge University Press, 41–57

Schlauch, Margaret 1927 *Chaucer's Constance and Accused Queens*. New York: New York University Press

Scott, Margaret 2007 *Medieval Dress and Fashion*. London: British Library

Sheehan, Michael M. 1988 'English Wills and Records of the Ecclesiastical and Civil Jurisdictions', *Journal of Medieval History* 14: 3–12

Smith, Nicole D. 2008 'Estreitement bendé: Marie de France's *Guigemar* and the Erotics of Tight Dress', *Medium Aevum* 67: 96–117

Smith, Nicole D. 2012 *Sartorial Strategies: Outfitting Aristocrats and Fashioning Conduct in Late-Medieval Literature*. Notre Dame, IN: University of Notre Dame Press

Snyder, Janet 2009 'From Content to Form: Court Clothing in Mid-Twelfth-Century Northern French Sculpture', in *Encountering Medieval Textiles and Dress: Objects, Texts, Images*, ed. Désirée Koslin and Janet Snyder. Basingstoke: Palgrave Macmillan, 85–101

Sponsler, Clare 1992 'Narrating the Social Order: Medieval Clothing Laws', *CLIO: A Journal of Literature, History, and the Philosophy of History* 21(3): 265–83

Staples, Kate Kelsey 2010 'Fripperers and the Used Clothing Trade in Late Medieval London', *Medieval Clothing and Textiles* 6: 151–71

Summerson, Henry 2004 'Clare, Bogo de (1248–1294)', *Oxford Dictionary of National Biography*. Oxford University Press. Online edition (Jan 2008) available at http://www.oxforddnb.com/view/article/50346, accessed 18.7.2014

Summerwill, K. 2010 'Advice on Behaviour and Dress', The University of Nottingham. Online at http://www.nottingham.ac.uk/manuscriptsandspecialcollections/learning/medievalwomen/theme8/adviceonbehaviouranddress.aspx/, accessed 18.7.2014

Sutton, Anne 2005 *The Mercery of London: Trade, Goods and People, 1130–1578*. Aldershot and Burlington, VT: Ashgate

Tout, T. F. 1920–33 *Chapters in the Administrative History of Mediaeval England*, 6 vols. Manchester: Manchester University Press

Twycross, Meg 1983 '"Apparell comlye"', in *Aspects of Early English Drama*, ed. Paula Neuss. Cambridge: D. S. Brewer, 30–49

Twycross, Meg, and Sarah Carpenter 2002 *Masks and Masking in Medieval and Early Tudor England*. Studies in Performance and Early Modern Drama. Aldershot and Burlington, VT: Ashgate

Vale, Malcolm 2001 *The Princely Court: Medieval Courts and Culture in North-West Europe, 1270–1380*. Oxford: Oxford University Press

Veale, Elspeth 1966 *English Fur Trade in the Later Middle Ages*. Oxford: Clarendon

Wright, Laura 2000 'Bills, Accounts, Inventories: Everyday Trilingual Activities in the Business World of Medieval England', *Multilingualism in Medieval Britain*, ed. David Trotter. Woodbridge: Boydell and Brewer, 149–56